The Equitable

1859–1964

Henry Baldwin Hyde, Founder

Now that we are serving an institution one hundred years old—we have come of age. We are, indeed, required to think beyond ourselves, if we are to think effectively of ourselves. . . . Mankind is at the crossroads of civilization. The people must choose between the "road to serfdom" and the "road to freedom." *The time for decision is upon us.* . . . Our Society recognizes man as an end in himself and not as a mere instrument in an economic-political complex. Totalitarianism degrades man; we, on the other hand, believe that man is a sacred personality, that he, the individual, is the important unit in life and that the real aim and end of all government and of all business is to develop and serve the dignity, welfare and vital importance of the individual human being.

JAMES F. OATES, JR. 1959

The Equitable Life Assurance Society of the United States 1859–1964

Aeque Pauperibus Prodest Locupletibus Aeque

R. CARLYLE BULEY

VOLUME TWO

Appleton-Century-Crofts
Division of Meredith Publishing Company, New York

657-1

Library of Congress Catalog Card Number: 67-12656

PRINTED IN THE UNITED STATES OF AMERICA
R-15180

Contents

Parkinson elected President of Equitable—Personnel changes—The Russian cases: the Sliosberg case; *Perry* v. *Equitable Life Assurance Society; Dougherty* v. *Equitable Life Assurance Society;* Equitable upheld by New York Court of Appeals and Supreme Court of the United States

11 *Depression Decade* 983

Stock market crash—Decline in Equitable's business—The election of 1932—Bank crisis of 1933 and run on the life insurance companies—Emergency legislation on withdrawals—Closing of the banks—The gold standard abandoned by the United States government—Inflation—Conserving Equitable's assets; residential and farm mortgages; railroad and utility bonds—The "gold clause" question and the gold cases—Life insurance and the TNEC—Home Office and field: Equitable Diamond Jubilee, 1934; personnel changes; policy changes; annuities; the general agency versus the manager system—Social Security legislation—Equitable re-enters Texas—Equitable's Eightieth Anniversary—The World's Fair of 1939

12 *At the End of a Century* 1108

World War II: wartime personnel policies; death claims; wartime investments—Assured Home Ownership (AHO) and Insured Residential Mortgage (IRM)—Housing projects: Clinton Hill and Fordham Hill—Arkansas Valley Sugar Beet and Irrigated Land Company—Government and life insurance: wartime regulations; Social Security legislation—Life insurance companies and inflation—The South-Eastern Underwriters Association case and the McCarran Act—Federal income taxation, 1921–58—1959 tax law—New fields for investment: Gateway Center; purchase and leaseback; oil and gas investments; the Glenn McCarthy loans; tree farms—Personnel changes in the Home Office—Ray D. Murphy elected President of Equitable—Controversial events of 1953 and the reorganization of Equitable—Charles W. Dow elected President, 1956—James F. Oates, Jr., elected President, 1957—Equitable reorganized under four main divisions, 1958—Equitable in operation: Board of Directors; "Series 95" and "Series 100" programs; Assured Life Income Policy; the agency force; Cashiers Administrative Training Course; Sales Promotion Division and Equitable advertising—Equitable buildings—Methods and Production Analysis Program—Electronic data processing machines and Methods Research Department—Equitable publications: *Agency Items;*

Leadership News; *Equinews*; *Farm Loan News*—The Society's Hundredth Anniversary celebration—The death of James Hazen Hyde—A century of security

13 *Equitable Embarks Upon Its Second Century, 1960–1964* 1293

The Harvard committee report—Cost Analysis and Planning Unit—The Long-Range Plan Book—The big move to 1285 Avenue of the Americas—Changes in administrative personnel—Electronic data processing and Cashiers' Automatic Processing System—Further innovations and modifications: Disability Income Policy; Lifetime Major Medical Expense Policy; "Series 104" policies; Circle E and Diamond E group policies; "New York 65"—The investment year method—The Superior Sales Force: "manpower format" established and Career Advancement Division created—Personnel: Manpower Development Unit and graded system for jobs; "A Code to Work By" and "A Plan for Progress"—Management Training Program—Public relations and public affairs: Equitable as a corporate citizen; Office of Community Services and Health Education established; youth fitness film—Equitable at the New York World's Fair, 1964—A new symbol for the Society—Representative speeches made by President Oates—Grant Keehn elected President of Equitable, February 1964—Other management changes—At the end of 105 years: statistical summary; common stock program; real estate investments; Equitable Chicago building—The fundamental purpose, business objectives and implicit goals of the Society—Annual report to the Board of Directors, February 1965—Conclusion

Appendices

The Charter 1353
Equitable Directors, 1859–1966 1360
Chairmen of the Board, Vice Chairmen of the Board, Presidents, and Secretaries since 1859 1365
Officers, December 31, 1964 1367
One Hundred and Five Years of Growth and Progress 1370
A Code to Work By 1372

Bibliographical Note 1373

Index 1381

ILLUSTRATIONS

The Equitable

1859–1964

8

A New Era—A New Regime

Thus it happens that the mass of the plain and common people of the land who have life insurance in mind, or at least those who think at all well of it, love to dwell upon it as a strong defender against the havoc of death and a compassionate benefactor against the deprivations of pitiless want. Whether you will or not, these are the relationships in which your companies stand to your fellow countrymen; and these relationships, closely interwoven, constitute a powerful cable binding life insurance to the immovable rock of popular confidence. You who manage life insurance companies cannot afford to risk weakness in a single one of its threads. Their disintegration through breaches of good faith, through broken promises or through delusive misrepresentation, means a loss of strength which no actuarial mystery or managerial calculation can repair. Nor can you, with any pretense of conscientious susceptibility, overlook the fact that, as a direct consequence of this popular conception of life insurance and of your responsible connection with its management, your fellow citizens, whose confidence you have invited, have put upon you a trust, made sacred by the pathos of its purposes, and more unescapable in morals and good conscience than any that the law can create.—Grover Cleveland, December 1907.

After the disturbing events of 1905, Equitable needed not so much the brilliant and daring navigation of another Henry B. Hyde as the steady, if less spectacular, leadership of men of the Cleveland type—men in whom both policyholders and public had confidence because of their fundamental integrity. The Society was fortunate, for to direct its destinies for more than two decades were Presidents Paul Morton and William A. Day.

The Report of the Armstrong Committee, a document of almost 450 pages, was submitted to the Senate and Assembly of the State of New York February 22, 1906. The bulk of the report consisted of an analysis of the affairs of seventeen of the leading life insurance companies as revealed in the hearings. The remainder of the report dealt with possible remedial legislation. It recommended encouragement of the formation of mutual companies; prohibition of investment in stocks or participation in syndicate operations; limitation of new business to $150,000,000 a year for the largest companies; standard policy forms for all companies; prohibition of incorporation of assessment or cooperative insurance companies; amendment of the rebate law to make the receiver equally guilty with the giver; annual distribution of dividends; and limited commissions for agents.[1]

When hearings on the report were held March 9, President Morton, although admitting that serious evils had crept into the life insurance business, warned that some of the recommended legislation might have the opposite effect of what was intended. He opposed the recommended standard policy forms and too rigid investment controls. When some of the newspapers criticized him for registering his objections, President Morton said: "In justice to the policy-holders, to the Committee, and to myself, no other course was open to me." He believed that the rigid investment requirements "would operate to the disadvantage of present policy-holders by decreasing the return of the unused portion of their premiums, thereby increasing the cost of their insurance, and to those who should be insured in justice to their families. Should this fear be realized, the policy-holders would be in a position to justly criticize us in a few years, had we remained silent, for neglecting to protect their interests."[2] Actuary Joel G. Van Cise defended deferred dividend policies as being no more of a gamble than annual dividend contracts, and held that the policyholders should be allowed to make such contracts as they desired. He did not believe that surpluses built up as a result of deferred dividend policies had been any cause of mismanagement. Officers of other companies also registered protests against various recommendations of the report.

The recommendations of the Armstrong Committee eventually took form in eight bills which became law in April 1906. As finally amended, the laws filled more than a hundred printed pages. They limited expenses to the total loadings and expected mortality margins

[1] *Report of The Joint Committee of The Senate and Assembly of The State of New York Appointed to Investigate the Affairs of Life Insurance Companies*, Assembly Document No. 41, and printed as Volume X of the complete Armstrong Committee Record.

[2] In a long letter to *The Literary Digest* published in Volume XXXII (1906), June 2.

and limited new business to the scale outlined in the Report of the Committee, that is, $150,000,000 per year for the larger companies and according to a sliding scale for the smaller ones.[3] All policies issued after January 1, 1907, were to provide for automatic extended insurance in event of lapse. The companies were permitted to make a surrender charge equal to one-fifth of the policy's reserve, "or the sum of $25 for each $1000 of the face of the policy if said sum shall be more than said one-fifth." All policies issued by New York companies and by other companies in New York should, after that date, carry provisions for annual distribution of dividends. The laws provided directly for standard policy forms (by New York companies on New York business) for ordinary life, limited-payment life, endowment, and term policies, and authorized the Superintendent of Insurance to standardize other forms. (Companies of other states, however, did not have to issue the New York standard forms either in New York or elsewhere.) New York companies were prohibited from investing in corporation stocks—except municipal—and forbidden to underwrite syndicates and joint account transactions; they were given five years in which to dispose of their common stocks.

The laws made it possible to organize mutual life insurance companies in New York under the general laws. They stipulated that the insurance policy must contain the entire contract and prohibited estimates of dividends and misrepresentation. Other provisions applied to fixing the salaries of officers, pensions to officers, and the administration of expense accounts. The information to be furnished the New York Insurance Department was expanded and specifically listed.[4] Any company not organized under the law of New York was required to conduct its business within the expense limits of the New York law if it did business in New York. Such a company could issue only annual dividend policies in New York.

Meanwhile, even before the Armstrong Committee Report was pub-

[3] There was no limit on companies with less than $50,000,000 of insurance in force; from $50,000,000 to $100,000,000, the limit was 30 per cent of the insurance in force; from $100,000,000 to $300,000,000, 25 per cent; from $300,-000,000 to $600,000,000, 20 per cent; from $600,000,000 to $1,000,000,000, 15 per cent; in excess of $1,000,000,000, the amount was $150,000,000 annually.

[4] Among other items: securities—date of acquisition, book value, market value, gross and net income; investment commissions, legal expenses, legislative payments, with names of payees, etc.; all salaries more than $5,000; maximum bank balance for each month; all death claims resisted or compromised; gain and loss exhibit; rates of annual dividends for all plans of insurance and for various entry ages; statement on surplus funds, etc.

lished, about 100 governors, attorneys general, and insurance commissioners assembled in Chicago (February 1, 1906) to consider the problems which confronted the states and the life insurance companies.[5] The state delegations by vote of 22 to 7 adopted resolutions which outlined the platform of the conference. The resolutions declared the deferred dividend plan unsound in principle, unjust in operation, and recommended legislation to remove the evil. It was suggested that a plan be considered to give policyholders better control of mutual companies. Publicity was held to be an effective control on life insurance practices, though it was recognized that many states already had adequate laws for that purpose. The delegates recommended that investments be conservative and not speculative, but uniform requirements for all states were not considered practicable. The last recommendation was that earnest efforts should be made for standard policy forms. A Committee of Fifteen, headed by Commissioner Thomas D. O'Brien of Minnesota, was appointed to consider and recommend uniform legislation to carry out this platform.

The Committee of Fifteen held hearings, discussed the Armstrong legislation, and made its recommendations. It approved of the New York bills relating to political contributions, distribution of surplus, election of directors, and annual reports. It tentatively agreed upon a representative form of government for mutual companies, annual accounting for dividends, investment restrictions, complete publicity, and standard policy forms as essentials for adequate state legislation. Unlike the Armstrong Committee, however, it gave its approval to preliminary term valuation of policies.[6] Of the proposed legislation, that on standard policy forms met with the most opposition.

[5] This meeting had been suggested to President Theodore Roosevelt by Governor John A. Johnson of Minnesota and was formally called by Thomas E. Drake, Superintendent of Insurance for the District of Columbia.

[6] The preliminary term idea, which probably derived from the mind of the German actuary Dr. August Zilmer in 1863, was devised to modify the system of full net premium reserves so as to relieve the company of the necessity of establishing the reserve against the policy for the first year, when expenses were highest, and thus release all of the first year premiums not needed for death claims of that year for expenses incidental to the acquisition of new business. Under preliminary term, the reserve for the first year is borrowed, to be repaid in time from increased net premiums spread over the remaining life of the policy. The policy, so far as reserves are concerned, becomes term insurance for one year and permanent insurance beginning at the end of the first year, at which date the net premium becomes the net premium for "a policy issued at an age one year higher, at a date one year later, and for a term one year shorter."

Preliminary term valuation was strongly advocated by the newer and smaller

In its final report to the Governor of Minnesota, the Committee of Fifteen endorsed sixteen model measures for the consideration of the state legislatures. One of the model bills provided for limitation of the salaries of life insurance company officers to $50,000 per year. Although the recommendations of the Committee of Fifteen did not receive the publicity which the New York legislation received, nevertheless they were of considerable influence in molding the legislative programs of many of the western and southern states. Two of the midwestern states attempted a thorough overhauling of their insurance laws in 1907. In Indiana, Governor J. Frank Handly sought to create a much stronger State Insurance Department and recommended more stringent laws for the regulation of life insurance companies. The small companies of the state, however, charged that Governor Handly was influenced by President Paul Morton of the Equitable and The Association of Life Insurance Presidents and that his program would be detrimental to the Indiana companies. Most of Governor Handly's legislation was blocked and the state's insurance laws left practically unchanged.

Wisconsin on the other hand, already impregnated with the La-Follette version of the "Progressive" idea, sought to outdo New York in its insurance legislation. Some two dozen bills were introduced which defined and regulated life insurance in all of its details—elementary principles, definitions, actuarial technicalities, and "climaxing with drastic impracticabilities." Although opposed by the companies, eight of the bills became law. Among other things, the laws placed a limit on premiums, first year expenses, and salaries of company officers (maximum $25,000). The life companies said that their actuaries did not understand the bills, neither did the legislature; the Governor admitted that he did not. Several of the companies said that they

---

companies which found it very difficult to set up reserves on the net level premium basis, and in general was opposed by the older and larger companies as not safe or scientific. The smaller companies, mostly in the South and West, argued that the older companies were in effect achieving the same ends by borrowing from their surplus for first year expenses and repaying the sum borrowed from future net premiums. Preliminary term valuation, which had first been used by an American company in the late 1880's, had by 1900 become a basic issue between the older companies and the newer companies, and between the western and southern states and the eastern states in which the larger companies were domiciled. The controversy was not to be resolved until the 1920's. For the origins of preliminary term valuation, see R. Carlyle Buley, *The American Life Convention, 1906–1952*, Vol. I, pp. 169–179.

were willing to comply with the laws if they only knew what they meant. A number gave up, however, and by the end of the year eight companies, among them the Equitable, announced their intention of withdrawing from the state.[7]

The Armstrong and other state legislation constituted something of a revolution in the field of life insurance in the United States. What had started as a reform to correct home office evils had ended by making great changes which basically affected the whole business of life insurance. Opinion was divided in regard to what the results would be. Some thought that the remedies would prove to be worse than the disease. Commissioner Theron Upson of Connecticut thought the laws more drastic than any similar body of law in any country, and experimental in nature: "The abuses exposed were bad enough—let us see what the abuses invited will amount to." The consensus, however, seemed to be that the new rules, with all their defects, would have a salutary effect and do much good for the business. Life insurance men were counseled to remember the order of the famous German marshal who in the smoke of battle took a pinch of snuff and said, "Patience, gentlemen, and forward," or as the editor of the *Life Insurance Courant* said: "If there were no rain, there would be no grass with which to make hay when the sun shines." [8] Despite the grave doubts—even bitter feelings—held by many life insurance men at the time, their views mellowed with the years, and Charles Evans Hughes came to be thought of, together with Grover Cleveland, as one who had helped materially to put life insurance in the high position which it deserved.

Naturally the events of 1905, in addition to their effects upon the business of life insurance, profoundly affected the personal lives of several men who had headed the great companies. John A. McCall, who had repaid $235,000 to his company for funds advanced to Andrew Hamilton and unaccounted for by that agent, resigned the presidency of the New York Life in December. He died a broken man, February 18, 1906, just a few days before the official report of

[7] Equitable withdrew in December 1907.

Missouri had fixed a salary limit of $50,000 in 1906. March 3, President Morton wrote his daughter Caroline: "Missouri has passed a law that no insurance company can do business in the State which pays any officer more than Fifty-thousand per year—other states have similar laws pending and it may be your poor old father may be reduced to poverty." Morton family letters. Copy in Equitable Archives.

[8] *Life Insurance Courant*, XII (1906), June 7.

the Armstrong Committee was released. Coming as it did close on the heels of the investigation, his death attracted nationwide attention. Few papers wholly condemned the man in whose career was to be found both inspiration and pathos. His deathbed statement that he had "never deliberately done anything harmful to man, woman or child" was used as a basis for measuring the man in relation to his times. Few questioned that McCall at any time had any doubts regarding the rightfulness of his acts. It appeared rather that his standards were the standards of "a large part of the world of 'high finance' around him; and no inconsiderable part of the world of finance without the 'high,' and of the business world generally." He dealt with conditions as he found them and did not benefit personally from his acts. Some of these acts, whether regarded as criminal or not, were, in the light of the investigation at any rate, mistakes, but they resulted from the practical conditions of his time which he did not make and above which he did not rise. Many regarded him as the first victim of a system that had been challenged by public opinion. "He was a great man in practical things; not a precisian, not a dreamer, not an idealist in the sense of purism; but over his grave men can take off their hats in respect to him as one who accomplished great deeds in a vigorous and indomitable way." [9] He left a great company which he had trebled in size during the 14 years of his presidency and an estate which was appraised at $40,385. Vice President George W. Perkins also left the New York Life, but he still had the interests of J. P. Morgan and Company and other businesses, as well as politics, to consume his tremendous energies.

President Richard A. McCurdy of Mutual resigned late in November 1905, giving ill health as the reason, and retired to private life. Several actions were brought against McCurdy and other former officials of Mutual, and in 1909 a settlement of $750,000 was arrived at. Of this amount, $250,000 was assessed against McCurdy and paid by him. Total claims of the plaintiffs had been $6,000,000. McCurdy died in 1916.

James W. Alexander, after recovering his health in 1906, announced his retirement from active business and resigned a number of directorships in various corporations. In 1909 he embarked upon a trip around the world. Upon his return he avoided appearing at any of his clubs for a period of time, still uncertain as to what his reception might be.

[9] *The Insurance Field,* XII (1906), February 22.

When he finally appeared and was warmly received by his fellow club members, he renewed his contacts. He remained an enthusiastic and active alumnus of his alma mater, Princeton University, of which he had been a trustee. After his resignation from Equitable, Alexander scrupulously refrained "from even the slightest interference by word or act in the affairs of Equitable." He made this clear to his successor, President Paul Morton. In January 1912, at the time of the Equitable fire, he explained this policy to President William A. Day, but could not refrain from congratulating President Day on the way he had handled the situation and offering his services and support under the trying circumstances.[10] Alexander died in 1915. His will disposed of property valued at $232,042, of which life insurance provided $121,370.

Probably least affected of all was James Hazen Hyde, who, after leaving Equitable, was able to spend the remaining 54 years of his life —35 of them in France—pursuing interests nearer to his heart than life insurance. (See Chapter XII for a summary of these years.)

* * *

President Morton believed that candid publicity was the best remedy for the difficulties in which Equitable found itself as a result of the "recent agitation." In his letter to the policyholders, December 14, 1905, he had stated that one of his first acts as President had been to employ the firm of Price, Waterhouse and Company, chartered accountants of Great Britain and New York, and Haskins and Sells, certified public accountants of New York, to make a thorough examination and render exhaustive reports on eight points. The report was ready January 30, 1906; together with the exhibits it comprised more than 400 pages. The accountants found that the Society's published statement, sworn to by the Comptroller and the Secretary, on the remuneration paid to officers and others, seemed to have been made "for the purpose of not disclosing the true amount of expenses under this head . . . and, incidentally, it might be mentioned that it did deceive the Frick committee. . . ." They reported that in many instances payments of more or less extraordinary character had been made on the authority of one of the senior officers without subsequent approval of the Executive Committee. They called attention to the inadequacy of the form of statement required by the various state insurance departments for showing the actual amount of business done

[10] Alexander to Day, January 10, 1912. University Club stationery was used for this handwritten letter. Equitable Archives.

by the Society during the period covered by the statement. In regard to the statement in the Frick Committee report that James H. Hyde had involved the Society in various transactions and been guilty of various acts which were not in compliance with the Society's By-Laws or with sound business practices, the accountants said: "This is a general statement and requires no comment from us, as the facts in relation thereto may be obtained from our report. It is, however, questionable whether this criticism should fairly be applied to James H. Hyde in particular, rather than to the officers of the Society in general."

A supplementary report made March 15 dealt mainly with "certain matters of a peculiarly confidential character relating to individuals and transactions which took place many years ago"—the Turner Loans and special accounts kept with The Mercantile Trust Company—which had no particular relation to the current condition of the Society. The "Audit Report" for the year ending December 31, 1905, was submitted March 31. It was in this report that the accountants listed Equitable's surplus as $12,237,079 less than it had previously been listed. They found, however, that the Society's financial condition remained sound.[11]

As President Morton said in his December letter to the policyholders, it was doubtful if any American insurance company ever before had such an exhaustive examination.

Then in May 1906 he sent a circular letter to the leading newspapers and periodicals throughout the country so that they might "have a definite and authoritative statement as to the exact condition of the affairs in Equitable, and the policy which will be pursued by the new management." He stated that the Society would stand firmly against contributions for political campaigns or any other purpose; against lobbying or the payment of anything remotely suggesting blackmail; against securing new business on terms unprofitable to old policyholders; and against the conduct of the Society as an adjunct to any bank or trust company. He summarized the Society's report for 1905. New business for the year had totaled $141,695,255 and outstanding assurance amounted to $1,465,123,436; assets were $420,973,757.[12] The

11 The reports of the two accounting firms are contained in three bound pamphlets of 198, 205, and 108 pages. The audit report for 1905 consists of 30 pages. Copies are in Equitable Archives.

12 These figures are taken from Equitable's annual report and do not wholly coincide with those later issued by the Insurance Department, which, for instance, listed new business—not including revivals and increases—at $212,883,812. This figure included policies "written" but "not taken out."

Society had paid to beneficiaries and policyholders $41,159,574, and dividends to policyholders had totaled $6,709,003, which was a larger amount than had ever been distributed in dividends in any year by any life insurance company in the world. He made no effort to minimize the fact that as a result of the detailed examination by the two independent firms of public accountants the Society's surplus, reported a year earlier at $80,794,269, had been reduced to $68,557,190: "Nothing has disappeared since then, except over-valuation of securities and real estate. . . ." He said that the shrinkage in surplus had more than been offset by economies amounting to $1,000,000 per year, which at 4 per cent would be equivalent to an additional investment of $25,000,000.

Despite this good showing, more than 27,000 policies for $1,000 or less had been allowed to lapse, while only one policy for $250,000 had been surrendered. This large policy was later restored, but many of the holders of the small policies were not now insurable and many had died leaving their families without insurance. "This condition resulted from misapprehension, and with some newspapers, from misrepresentation of the real facts. This is a point which should be seriously considered by those who in any way shape public opinion and sentiment. I feel very strongly that the good newspapers of the country owe it to themselves and to their readers to reassure the public, and to point out the benefits of life insurance whenever the subject presents itself."

Although President Morton did not mention it in this letter, Equitable had in March announced that these lapsed policies would be reinstated on the old terms provided the policyholders could meet the physical requirements, and many of these policies were restored.[13] President Morton announced that it would be the Society's practice to make the examination by the accounting firms an annual affair.

This circular letter was well received and many favorable editorial comments were made. It was generally agreed that such frank publicity was both refreshing and enlightening. Equitable's type of publicity was recommended to other corporations.

Early in May, the Board of Directors adopted new By-Laws for the Society. Under these laws the financial administration was transferred from the Executive Committee to the Finance Committee, which was to consist of the President, Vice President, and four directors not officers of the Society. The President and Vice President only were to

[13] *The Spectator*, LXXVI (1906), March 29 and April 26.

be elected by the Board, but the Board would also appoint the Comptroller, Actuary, Treasurer, and Secretary.[14] The second and third vice presidents were to be appointed by the President, subject to confirmation by the Board, but might be removed at the President's discretion. Although all officers were elected and appointed for one year only, they might be removed or suspended by the Board at any time.

At the May 31 meeting, the Board re-elected Paul Morton President and elevated Comptroller William A. Day to the vice presidency; William Alexander remained as Secretary, Joel G. Van Cise as Actuary, and Henry Rogers Winthrop as Treasurer. Although there were rumors that Gage E. Tarbell would resign as Second Vice President, they proved premature, and he remained in that position. George T. Wilson remained as Third Vice President. In June Leon O. Fisher, formerly with the accounting firm of Haskins and Sells, was appointed General Auditor of the Society, and in December Winthrop resigned his position as Treasurer.

In May 1906, Grover Cleveland, trustee of the Ryan stock, pointed out that the Armstrong laws (Chapter 326, Section 13) had made it possible for Equitable to amend its Charter so as to provide for partial mutualization of the Society. The Charter was amended to permit the policyholders, at the annual December meeting, directly to elect 28 of the 52 directors under the same rules provided by the new law for the election of directors of strictly mutual life insurance companies. The trustees of the Ryan stock were heartily in favor of this change, but Cleveland suggested that the names of the policyholders' directors selected by the trustees since the reorganization of 1905 be placed upon the "Administration Ticket" to be presented at the December meeting. The amended Charter was unanimously adopted by the Board June 20, filed, and approved by Superintendent Otto Kelsey of the New York Insurance Department.[15]

[14] Although Equitable's Charter of 1859 provided for the election of the Society's Secretary, the By-Laws from time to time ignored this provision. It appears, however, that in practice the Secretary, as well as the President, has always been elected by the Board.

[15] After adoption by the Board, the amended Charter was submitted to the stockholders in July, but this was largely a matter of form since the trustees of the Ryan stock held a majority of the stock. Two-thirds of the stock, however, was voted for the partial mutualization, and some of the stockholders who voted against the plan did so in order to protect any legal rights which they might have under the Charter. Some of the minority stockholders were represented by counsel who registered a protest against the amendment. It may be recalled that an in-

In regard to the Charter change, *The Insurance Monitor* said: "The action taken certainly ought to free the company from much of the unfavorable criticism that has been directed toward the Ryan control. The policyholders may now enter upon their own if they elect, while the important stock interests will remain a guarantee for a conservative and intelligent direction of its affairs." [16] On the other hand, *The Spectator* pointed out that the stockholders' directors would still remain in control for at least four years and, since Thomas Fortune Ryan was the majority stockholder, the company would continue to be conducted in accordance with his ideas:

> All the talk about this being a step toward mutualization of the company is far outside of the facts, for mutualization of a stock company can only be effected by an arrangement between the stockholders and the policyholders. It has not yet been satisfactorily shown how the policyholders would be benefited if the company should, in fact, be mutualized, for it has always been conducted successfully as a stock company and placed in the front rank of life insurance companies of the world, and has acquired a deserved reputation for treating its policyholders with fairness, and even liberality, in the adjustment of claims under its policies. More could not be expected of it if the mutualization plan prevailed.[17]

Under the amended Charter, various classes of directors were made to retire automatically regardless of their elected terms, but the new men who had been added by the trustees of the Ryan stock since the reorganization of June 1905 were included in the "Administration Ticket." No opposition ticket was nominated. At the December election about one hundred policyholders cast their ballots in person and approximately 30,000 votes were cast, of which some 10,000 were proxies sent in to the trustees.[18] In ensuing annual elections the policyholders would elect seven out of thirteen directors.

---

junction had been secured against a very similar amendment in regard to the election of directors under the Alexander regime, which was sustained on the ground that the existing New York laws did not permit such a change. This objection had been obviated by the Armstrong legislation.

[16] *The Insurance Monitor*, LIV (1906), June.

[17] *The Spectator*, LXXVI (1906), June 28.

[18] The newly elected directors were John N. Beach, Emanuel W. Bloomingdale, Abraham Brittin, Joseph Bryan, James B. Forgan, Thomas A. Gillespie, Alexander C. Humphreys, John D. Kernan, Charles E. Littlefield, John T. Manson, Willis F. McCook, James McMahon, Eugenius H. Outerbridge, William E. Paine, Wallace L. Pierce, Tom Randolph, William C. Redfield, Edwin W. Robertson, Ferdinand W. Roebling, Jacob G. Schmidlapp, Thomas Spratt, J. Edward

But these first steps toward mutualization of Equitable were to run into trouble. After the law of 1906 permitted mutualization of a life company, Franklin B. Lord, who had sought to block mutualization of Equitable in 1905, attacked the constitutionality of the law and the legality of the steps taken by the Society's Board of Directors. (For the earlier Lord cases, see this history, p. 626.) The New York Supreme Court in Nassau County, in January 1908, held the law to be constitutional and the steps toward mutualization to have been carried out in accordance with its provisions; the Appellate Division affirmed this judgment in May. The whole mutualization procedure was thrown into confusion, however, in February 1909, when the Court of Appeals, though it upheld the constitutionality of the law and confirmed the right of the Board of Directors to give the policyholders the right to vote for 28 directors, ruled that the Board had exceeded its authority in depriving the stockholders of the right to vote for all directors. In reversing the decision of the lower courts on this point, the Court of Appeals said it did so "because we feel that the law calls upon us to maintain the rights of stockholders, even if they stand in their own light." The defendant might plead over upon payment of costs.

The question of whether the amended Charter was valid or not remained unsettled until 1911 when the Superintendent of Insurance refused to accept it and the second stage of mutualization was worked out. (See the following chapter.)

"THE OLD GUARD" STANDS BY

In 1890 the three leading New York companies held almost half of the legal reserve life insurance of the United States. During the next

---

Swanstrom, Eben B. Thomas, Daniel A. Tompkins, George F. Vietor, William Whitman, Frank S. Witherbee, and Charles H. Zehnder.

Of these directors, James B. Forgan was the only one who had served on the Board during President Alexander's administration. William E. Paine, Abraham Brittin, John T. Manson, Thomas A. Gillespie, and Eugenius H. Outerbridge had never served on the Board but were, like those who had served under the new management, nominated by the trustees of the Ryan stock after consultation with the policyholders.

The hold-over directors who represented the stock were: H. R. Winthrop, Levi P. Morton, Charles B. Alexander, Bradish Johnson, Alvin W. Krech, David H. Moffat, Valentine P. Snyder, Gage E. Tarbell, Sir William C. Van Horne, H. C. Haarstick, James Hazen Hyde, John J. McCook, William H. McIntyre, Paul Morton, Jose F. de Navarro, and George T. Wilson. The terms of the last seven named were to expire December 31, 1907. The terms of the others, with the exception of Winthrop, who had resigned as Treasurer and Director effective December 31, 1906, were to expire at the end of 1908.

decade and a half, however, some fifty new legal reserve life companies were organized. Then, as a result of the embarrassment of the large eastern companies by the Armstrong investigation, scores of new companies were organized, many of them in the South and Midwest. Some of these companies were converted assessment associations or fraternals, and most of them used special plans such as board contracts, stock options, and the like with which to secure business.[19] The majority were stock companies and they advocated preliminary term valuation as necessary to their getting a start. Late in 1905 fourteen of these small companies sent representatives to a meeting in Chicago which launched the American Life Convention, original membership of which consisted of 25 companies. The purposes of the organization were announced as follows:

> The American Life Convention is organized for the purpose of encouraging, upholding and maintaining the business of life insurance; the dissemination of information regarding the science of life insurance; the securing of the enactment of uniform laws governing life insurance; the upholding of correct principles in the conduct of the business of life insurance; the establishment and maintenance of confidence between the management of the companies composing the organization and their policyholders; the correction of any abuses which may arise in the methods of transacting the business of life insurance; the promotion of co-operation, acquaintance and exchange of ideas among the executive officers of its membership and any and all other things incident to the welfare of insurers, insured and the public in relation to the business.[20]

The American Life Convention early went on record in favor of state rather than Federal regulation of life insurance and in favor of preliminary term valuation.

Perhaps it was the organization of the southern and western companies which stimulated President Morton to write the following

[19] There were various kinds of board contracts, but one of the commonly used plans was to select a group of several hundred "leading citizens" to constitute an "advisory board" for the company which was being organized. Members of this board were given special privileges with their policies such as a small stipend—25 cents to $1 per thousand—for insurance to be written by the company. Since the places of members who might die or let their policies lapse would not be filled, the possible remuneration at the end of a ten-year period appeared to be very attractive to those who held on. The board contract was a different application of the tontine idea.

[20] Article II of the Constitution adopted at St. Louis, January 30, 1906.

letter to the executive heads of a majority of the life insurance companies which were operating in New York:

New York, December 3, 1906

I am impressed with the lack of co-operation among the large life insurance companies, and respectfully urge that we meet and discuss a plan of an organization the objects of which shall be:

1. To promote the welfare of policyholders.
2. To advance the interests of life insurance companies in the United States by the intelligent co-operation of officers in charge.
3. To prevent extravagance and reduce expenses by encouraging uniformity of practice among life insurance companies in matters of general administration.
4. To consider carefully measures that may be introduced from time to time in legislative bodies, with a view of ascertaining and publicly presenting the grounds that may exist for opposing or advocating the proposed legislation according as the welfare of the companies and their policyholders shall point to the one course or the other.
5. To consider anything that may be suitably a matter of general concern to the life insurance business.
6. If you agree with me that such an organization is necessary and are willing your company should become a member, I will be glad to call a meeting as early as possible to further consider the matter.

Personally, it seems to me that much good can be accomplished by more co-operation between insurance companies. Copies of this letter have been sent to the presidents of the principal life insurance companies.

Very truly yours,
PAUL MORTON, President [21]

In an interview President Morton said that the letter was not intended for publication at the time and regretted that someone who received it saw fit to give it out prematurely. He made it clear that he believed in a maximum amount of publicity and, as President of one of the large companies, was not going to enter into any agreement or combination that would not promote the public welfare. He thought it just as essential, however, for the executives of the life insurance companies of the United States to have a national association as it was for the fire underwriters, life insurance actuaries, national bankers, and physicians of the country, or any other body of intelligent men, to

[21] *The Weekly Underwriter*, LXXV (1906), December 15.

have similar associations. He believed that much good could be accomplished by mutual acquaintance, cooperation, and uniform practice and said that he would be much disappointed if great improvements could not be made in the administration of the business, and the cost of life insurance to the public be reduced.[22]

In commenting upon President Morton's letter, *The Spectator* said that while the idea was not a new one, the suggestion was most timely. It continued:

> Years ago there existed a so-called congress of life insurance companies, but its existence was brief and the circumstances leading to its disruption not particularly savory. The rock upon which it split was an attempt to control all companies virtually by one management in matters of too much detail. It is impossible to place them all upon one plane, or to measure plans and methods by the same yardstick. The outline of Mr. Morton's proposition avoids this mistake, and would have the proposed new organization assume jurisdiction only over such matters as are common to all alike. . . . A better understanding among the companies will also tend to reduce the cost of conducting the business, by eliminating many of the evils that owe their origin to high pressure competition. But no organization as outlined in Mr. Morton's letter can be made if the element of good faith is lacking. It is a notorious fact that, in their eagerness for volume of business, the leading companies have at times broken their agreements with each other, and were better pleased to steal business that one or the other had secured than to work in fresh and uncultivated fields. It will be a great boon to everyone interested in life insurance if an association of managers of companies can be formed that will place the business upon a legitimate business basis and root out the evils that have grown up in it, to the detriment of policyholders and the development of scandals that have brought the blush of shame to every honest citizen.[23]

On December 21, the presidents or other officers of 24 companies met at the Waldorf-Astoria and after an exchange of views appointed a committee of seven to formulate a plan of organization.[24] All of the

[22] Interview in *ibid.*

[23] *The Spectator*, LXXVII (1906), December 20.

[24] The committee was composed of Paul Morton, Chairman; John P. Munn, President of the Washington Life; Haley Fiske, Vice President of the Metropolitan; L. G. Fouse, President of the Fidelity Mutual; J. A. DeBoer, President of National Life of Vermont; Leslie D. Ward, Vice President of the Prudential; and J. R. Clark, President of the Union Central Life.

The companies represented at this meeting were Aetna Life, Berkshire Life, Connecticut General Life, Equitable, The Fidelity Mutual Life, Germania Life,

companies represented except two were eastern companies. Despite some criticism to the effect that the proposed organization was for the benefit of the New York companies, it was decided at a second meeting, December 28, to proceed with the formation of The Association of Life Insurance Presidents. A constitution was drawn up and the association invited Grover Cleveland to become chairman of the executive committee at a salary of $25,000. Cleveland continued to serve as trustee of the Ryan Equitable stock and as rebate referee for the Mutual, New York Life, and Equitable, but accepted no salary for this work. After James Victor Barry, popular Insurance Commissioner of Michigan, declined the position, Robert Lynn Cox, who had been a member of the Armstrong Committee, became secretary of the Association. President Morton was a member of the executive committee.

Thus came to fruition an idea which had been close to the heart of Henry B. Hyde forty years earlier, but for the carrying out of which he had never been able to get adequate cooperation. But as *The Weekly Underwriter* said: "*Tempora mutantur, et nos mutamur in illis.* There has been a life insurance cyclone." [25]

At the first annual meeting of the Association in December 1907, President Morton read a paper on the "Valuation of Assets." He could not understand why the basis for valuation of mortgage loans should differ from that of investments in bonds. Why should bonds be marked down to current market quotations and mortgages not? In view of the financial recession of 1907, this was a good question. But it was Grover Cleveland's address which was the highlight of this meeting—without doubt one of the most perceptive and statesmanlike addresses in the history of American life insurance. He spoke of the "powerful cable binding life insurance to the immovable rock of popular confidence," and advised the life company officers as follows:

Home Life, The Manhattan Life, Maryland Life, Massachusetts Mutual Life, Metropolitan Life, Michigan Mutual Life, The Mutual Life, National Life of Vermont, New England Mutual Life, New York Life, Provident Life and Trust, Provident Savings Life, The Prudential, Security Mutual Life, State Mutual Life, The Travelers, The Union Central Life, and the United States Life. The Washington Life, Equitable Life of Iowa, and Pacific Mutual Life were not represented but had expressed themselves in favor of the organization movement. A number of important companies were not represented, among them the Connecticut Mutual, The Mutual Benefit Life, The Northwestern Mutual, The Penn Mutual, and The John Hancock Mutual.

25 *The Weekly Underwriter*, LXXV (1906), December 15. For Henry B. Hyde's activities in connection with the Chamber of Life Insurance, see this history, p. 145–150.

You who manage life insurance companies cannot afford to risk weakness in a single one of its threads. Their disintegration through breaches of good faith, through broken promises or through delusive misrepresentation, means a loss of strength which no actuarial mystery or managerial calculation can repair. Nor can you, with any pretense of conscientious susceptibility, overlook the fact that, as a direct consequence of this popular conception of life insurance and of your responsible connection with its management, your fellow citizens, whose confidence you have invited, have put upon you a trust, made sacred by the pathos of its purposes, and more unescapable in morals and good conscience than any that the law can create.

Cleveland then pointed out that it was unfortunate that the business aspects of life insurance management were not as universally understood as its more sentimental value. He called attention to the "avalanche of legislation" which followed the "upheaval of investigation":

Must we shut our eyes to the fact that by playing upon the desire of honest men for reform, vicious and unreasonable laws have been passed, or are threatened in certain States, actually originating in nothing better than the mean political ambition of petty demagogues? Are we to disregard the proof we have that certain State Legislatures, taking advantage of the condition of life insurance companies struggling and staggering under continuous and fierce attack, have passed statutes with little pretense of reformatory legislation, but with inordinate requirement of contribution to State and local taxation, and embodying other exactions having sole reference to policyholders in the State, to the exclusion of the great body of the assured, whose interests cannot, with justice or honor, be subordinated or put at risk?

He did not think so. He believed that a well-managed company would much better accept exclusion from a state rather than "suffer the least loss of honor or diminution of the fidelity to trust obligations which constitute the life-blood of every dutiful and deserving life insurance enterprise." Such action would be upheld in "the tribunal of right, conscience and good faith, where life insurance policyholders look for scrupulous fairness and exact justice at the hands of the companies they have trusted." He concluded by saying that the management of the life companies was in strong and dutiful hands and that "American life insurance will live to bless our people as long as American civiliza-

The Three Trustees: Grover Cleveland, Morgan J. O'Brien, and George Westinghouse

tion lasts, and will endure and grow as long as civilized man, while living, takes forethought of the event of death." [26]

Although Equitable had suffered some loss of agents as a result of the internal difficulties in 1905, it did not begin fully to feel the effects of the distressing events of that year on its business until 1906. In April the largest of the general agencies in the Metropolitan district went bankrupt; a member of the agency said that one reason for its failure had been the endeavor to enforce the Society's rule against rebating upon the subagents. The same month circulars were sent out to the agency force announcing that all advances to agents would be discontinued after June 1, even though Section 97 of the Armstrong laws was not to take effect until the end of the year. The executive committee of the General Managers' Association met with the officers of the Society and agreed on a new commission scale which would meet the requirements of the law. The new scale provided for a maximum of 50 per cent on first year premiums with renewals of 7½ per cent for nine years. This limitation gave some of the more aggressive new companies of the South and West their innings, since, under preliminary term valuation, they could use practically all of the first year premiums for expenses. As a result, Equitable, as well as the other big New York companies, continued to lose agents.

It was at this time that the Managers' Association—"The Old Guard"— organized in 1905, proved its true worth. Veterans such as Edward A. Woods, Charles E. Townsend, Thomas B. Sweeney, Frank L. Levy, Charles Jerome Edwards, Henry J. Powell, William J. Roddey, Frederick W. Fuller, Herman Moss, and others had been through the wars before, and they had a deep sense of loyalty to Equitable; they might be threatened with severely curtailed incomes, but they would not transfer their allegiance. They held the demoralized agency forces together and served as a sound core around which to rebuild. Only the executive committee of the Association met in 1906, but in March 1907 the Association met at the Home Office. The executive committee's report included a memorial to Second Vice President Tarbell, which pointed out that many of the Society's competitors were paying much higher commissions than Equitable and prayed that the Society allow as first year commissions the bulk of the first year loadings and mortality savings as permitted by the law. Actuary Van Cise said that

[26] *Proceedings of the First Annual Meeting of The Association of Life Insurance Presidents*, held at New York, December 6 and 7, 1907, pp. 9 ff.

he was in favor of paying the agents every dollar that could be afforded under the new law. He did not, however, favor either reducing premium rates or increasing guarantees because, he said, there was an agreement among the three large companies in regard to rates and guarantees which was of advantage to Equitable even though the guarantees had been somewhat reduced as a result. Grover Cleveland spoke to the members and told them that it was their duty to satisfy the people in regard to the beneficence of life insurance but not to mislead them. He said the administration of Equitable was of good faith and honest purpose, and "it is a source of constant appreciation that we are so ably seconded by the agents of the Society, and they are entitled to a very great share of what has been accomplished in the reorganization of this immense organization." It was at this meeting that the Managers' Association voted the first of three changes in its official name; it became "The General Agency Association."

The Society's annual report for 1906 revealed a serious shrinkage in the year's new business; insurance written (not including revivals, increases or dividend additions) totaled $82,167,395 as contrasted with $221,729,570 for 1904 and $137,893,363 for 1905. Thus had proud Equitable, which a few years earlier had occupied first position among the life insurance companies, fallen to fifth or sixth place (depending upon how measured)—even below some of the companies which it had passed a generation before.[27]

In October 1906, Second Vice President Gage E. Tarbell went to Chicago to reorganize the agency forces; most of the general agents had resigned and the number of agents had dwindled to about a dozen. The reorganization of the agency forces, however, was not accomplished by Tarbell, for he resigned in February 1907, the resignation to take effect March 1. In his letter of acceptance, President Morton said:

> You have been identified with the society for more than twenty-five years, and much of its success has been due to your energy and effort.

[27] The total insurance in force for 1905 was on a "written" instead of a "paid-for" basis. On a "paid-for" basis, the total for 1905 was $1,449,440,390. The figures are taken from the *Forty-Seventh Annual Report of the Superintendent of Insurance of the State of New York* (Albany, 1906), Part II, Life Insurance, p. xlix, and the *Forty-Eighth Annual Report* . . . (1907), Part II, Life Insurance, p. 28.

It is difficult to quote new business figures on a consistent basis for the years 1904, 1905, and 1906. The 1906 figure reflects only business on which the initial premium was collected during the year, the pre-1906 figures reflect the net of new business released to the field during the year and of business returned during the

There is not the slightest doubt in my own mind that your services to the society have been as potential in results as the services of any other man who was ever connected with it. When I was elected president you came to me at once and volunteered your loyal support, and I thank you now for having given it to me since I have been here. It is a pleasure to me to heartily congratulate you upon the fact that, after all the examinations the Equitable has passed through during the trying period of the last two years, not the slightest suspicion has been found to indicate any wrong-doing on your part. I can also congratulate you upon having found a more profitable field of labor, and I have no doubt that your great energy, wonderful pluck and keen knowledge of human nature will prove of great value to your new business associates. With my best wishes for the greatest success in your new work, I remain . . .

There had been newspaper talk of Tarbell's resignation; it was even rumored that he was going over to Mutual. It was generally understood that the relations between Thomas F. Ryan and Tarbell had not been "so intimately cordial as to preclude the possibility of their severance," and that President Morton had not expected permanently to retain the man to whom many attributed the troubles of 1905. Then there was the possibility that Tarbell did not believe that he could adequately exercise his special talents under the restrictions of the new insurance laws. In commenting upon Tarbell's resignation, *The Weekly Underwriter* said that the beginning of Equitable's troubles of 1905 had generally been attributed to Tarbell, whose ambition to become President of Equitable had led to the effort to oust James H. Hyde. It was understood that Tarbell intended to go into the real

---

year as not wanted, some of which had been released to the field in the preceding year. The following table contains the essential figures from the official policy exhibits for the years 1904, 1905, and 1906:

	1904	1905	1906
New Business Written, other than Dividend Additions	$303,378,884	$211,735,698	$ —*
Dividend Additions	1,190,467	1,148,114	1,175,732
Subtotal	304,569,351	212,883,812	
Reported as Not Taken	81,649,314	73,842,335	—*
Net Total	222,920,037	139,041,477	83,343,127
Revivals	2,217,323	2,401,192	4,398,570
Increases	—	252,586	336,980
Total	$225,137,360	$141,695,255	$88,078,677

*Figures not available.

estate business and form a corporation to take over the holdings of the Garden City Estates Company of Long Island. He remained, however, a member of the Board of Directors of the Society and maintained his insurance policy of $500,000.[28]

At the annual meeting of the Board late in February 1907, George T. Wilson was made Second Vice President to take Tarbell's place. Charles E. Phelps was elected Treasurer, to fill the vacancy created by Henry Rogers Winthrop's resignation at the end of 1906.[29] As of January 1, Leon O. Fisher's title was changed from General Auditor to Auditor, and F. W. Jackson and A. W. Maine were appointed consulting auditors. On the same date, Dr. John Warren became Chief Medical Director of the Society.

About a month after the annual meeting, President Morton announced that he intended "to take a greater interest in agency affairs and devote more time to the production of business"; that he would take over the supervision of the western part of the United States and Canada, and that Second Vice President George T. Wilson would be director in charge of the eastern parts of these two countries. Henry L. Rosenfeld, who had been an Equitable agent in Atlanta, General Agent in Cincinnati, and since 1903 supervisor of agencies in the Home Office, became Insurance Assistant to the President, and William E. Taylor, who had been Agency Supervisor under Wilson, was appointed superintendent for the eastern states.

In May 1907 newspaper reports were revived to the effect that Equitable was planning to sell its Home Office building and build a new one. Some months earlier, President Morton had told the reporters that plans were "still in the future." He said that they were partly dependent upon satisfactory disposal of the leases on the safety deposit vaults in the basement, which were still held by the Hyde estate, and that it might take three or four years to work out this problem. He said: "The plans submitted to us have not been accepted, and may not be. We might not build here at all. We might sell this property and go somewhere else." [30] Some months later it was reported that the new office building would be located on Church Street, near Fulton, but this report was semi-officially denied. Since 1904 the Society had found itself quite overcrowded at 120 Broadway and construction of a supplementary building had been authorized. The Hazen Building,

28 *The Weekly Underwriter*, LXXVI (1907), February 16.

29 Winthrop entered the New York office of J. F. Harrison Company of Chicago, which was engaged in the general brokerage business.

30 *The Weekly Underwriter*, LXXV (1906), December 15.

on the west side of Greenwich Street, between Albany and Carlisle Streets, was constructed in two installments 1904–07. This twelve-story building was only about a three-minute walk from 120 Broadway. The Supply Department took over the lower floors and Auditor Fisher's department moved most of its records, including duplicates of some of the policy records, to the third floor. This move was to prove very fortunate for Equitable a few years later. Other floors were used for the storage of documents of the different departments, for the storage of furniture, and for meeting rooms for agents and the Collegiate School of Life Insurance. While this move was taking place, Home Office record-keeping and other office procedure was being modernized by Auditor Fisher. The great bound tomes in which the policy records had been kept gave way to card file systems, and typewriters and hand-operated calculating machines took over much of the work formerly done by hand.

In January 1906 the Society had purchased the small building at Nos. 23 and 25 Nassau Street which had been occupied by the banking house of August Belmont and Company; also the seven-story building and lot at 17 Nassau Street owned by John E. Schermerhorn. This acquisition rounded out the block bounded by Broadway, Pine, Nassau, and Cedar Streets, which was valued at $20,000,000. Despite further denials in April 1908 that Equitable intended to build a new Home Office building, plans were filed with Building Superintendent Edward S. Murphy of New York City June 29. The plans, prepared by Daniel H. Burnham and Company, Chicago architects, called for a building 34 stories high, with a square tower of 28 additional stories, which would result in a building 909 feet in height.[31] A flagpole 150 feet high was to surmount the tower. There were to be 38 passenger elevators. The general design was of the Renaissance type, and cost was estimated at $10,000,000. This building, which would have been 297 feet taller than the Singer Building, and 212 feet taller than Metropolitan Life's famed tower, would have delighted Henry B. Hyde. After the plans had been referred to engineers in both the Building Department and the Department of Sanitation, they were approved by Superintendent Murphy early in July. President Morton said the Equitable had not yet definitely decided when work on the new building would begin, but it was expected that it would be at least May

[31] According to the minutes of the Equitable Board, July 23, 1908, the Building Department had approved plans for a building of "maximum height."

1910 before tenants of the old building could be relocated and the building razed.

Bids for the construction of the 62-story structure were received from the Thompson-Starrett Company and George A. Fuller Company early in December. The bids were considered by the Equitable Board at their meeting December 17, but no action was taken. Plans seemed to be as much "up in the air" as the topmost story of the projected building. Again President Morton said that nothing definite had been decided though the project was being considered from every standpoint. One difficulty lay in the fact that The Mercantile Safe Deposit Company had leases on space in 120 Broadway which ran to January 1, 1951. Equitable was still debating whether to remodel or build anew when the problem was solved by events beyond the Society's control.[32] Not until the early 1920's did Equitable build a new Home Office building, and 50 years were to elapse before it undertook the building of a new "skyscraper."

As a result of the revaluation of Equitable's surplus at the end of 1906, the dividends on the tontine policies which came due in 1907 were cut about 13 per cent below those of the preceding year. Although the Society explained the reasons for this reduction, considerable dissatisfaction resulted. Thomas Watts, a New York policyholder, refused to accept his dividends and brought suit in equity for an accounting—an action which was permissible under the Armstrong legislation without the consent of the Attorney General. The Society demurred on the ground that the plaintiff failed to state a cause of action in equity. In July 1907 Justice Arthur S. Tompkins of the New York Supreme Court, Ninth Judicial District, sustained the demurrer and held that the plaintiff could not maintain his suit in equity because no trust relations existed between the insurance companies and the policyholders.[33] In Wisconsin, however, the Supreme Court in 1907 granted the petition of Albert Ellinger, a tontine policyholder of Racine, that he be allowed to examine the Society's books and accounts, but when the same policyholder sought to question the Society's Actuary, the Supreme Court (March 1909) held that his petition was unreasonable and the case was dropped.[34]

[32] For articles on the proposed building see *The Weekly Underwriter,* LXXIX (1908), July 4, August 8, December 12 and 19; and *The Spectator,* LXXXI (1908), July 2 and December 17.

[33] 55 Misc. 454. See also *The Spectator,* LXXIX (1907), July 4.

[34] 111 N.W. 567; 120 N.W. 235. For revival of the Ellinger actions see this history, p. 838, note 127.

There were also some expressions of dissatisfaction with regard to the tontine dividends from policyholders in Tennessee, and Insurance Commissioner Reau E. Folk of that state came to the Home Office and made a personal investigation. Afterwards, Commissioner Folk issued the following statement:

Some policyholders in this State have submitted to the Department the matter of settlements made with them by the Equitable Life, especially on twenty-year tontine policies maturing this year. Upon a comparison of the settlement of these policies with data in this office, I found that the dividend accumulations on policies maturing this year were considerably less than the dividends on the same class of policies maturing last year. I took the matter up with the society in person. The cause given by the society for this reduction was the depreciation in the surplus of the society by reason of . . . a revaluation of its real estate holdings, a reduction of something like $17,000,000 in the surplus of the company being made on account of this revaluation.

The society cheerfully and promptly complied with my request for information and exhibited to me the records, showing the accounting in bulk on all policies in the free tontine class. I found that the same settlements as to the Tennessee policyholders were made with all policyholders of the society of that class. So if there be any inequity, all are bearing it alike. I made particular inquiry from the time of issuance down to maturity, so that it might be ascertained whether the holders had received their equitable shares of the surplus.

The actuary of the society furnished me with a part of this accounting, giving the amount of the free tontine fund at the beginning of 1906, and the different items of accretions thereto and the different items charged against it, the net result being the total amount to the credit of this fund at the beginning of 1907, the time when the contracts maturing in 1907 would be entitled to have calculations as to their shares. . . .

When asked what he would do if he decided that Tennessee policyholders were not receiving the full amounts due them, he replied:

When that conclusion is reached it will be time enough to determine what action should be taken. My functions as Insurance Commissioner will always be employed to secure justice to Tennessee policyholders. If the settlements proposed by the society are in accord with what they ought to receive, they will be satisfied.[35]

[35] *The Spectator*, LXXIX (1907), August 8.

In 1907 Texas passed the famous Robertson law, which provided that 75 per cent of the reserves on Texas policies should be invested in Texas securities, and that the securities be kept on deposit in Texas, where they would be subject to state or local ad valorem taxes. This requirement, together with existing tax laws, resulted in the equivalent of about a 4 per cent tax on all premiums collected in Texas, or an amount equal to the rate of interest which Texas law required to be credited to reserves. As a result, Equitable and 18 other companies announced their withdrawal from that state.

To conform to the usage of the New York law, Equitable agreed in May 1907 to use "insurance" rather than "assurance" in all of its literature and reports to be issued in the future. Thus the Society, which had been something of a stickler for the English form, abandoned the tradition which had existed since its organization. The word "assurance" was retained, however, in the corporate title.

UNTANGLING EQUITABLE'S HOLDINGS

Several years were required to disentangle Equitable's affairs as revealed by the report of the Frick Committee, the investigation of the New York Insurance Department, and the Armstrong investigation. Only a few of the more important legal cases and settlements can be noted.

In March 1905, Mary S. Young, a Saratoga policyholder and the owner of one share of Equitable stock, brought suit against the Society and the directors thereof for an accounting for all sums alleged to have been wasted during the three preceding years and asking that these funds be restored to the Society's treasury; Senator Edgar T. Brackett served as counsel for the plaintiff. James H. Hyde, through his attorneys, interposed a demurrer as did other directors of the Society, and his demurrer was by agreement chosen for trial. Hyde's demurrer averred that the Young complaint did not constitute a cause of action, that causes of action were improperly united, and that the plaintiff was barred by Section 56 of the Insurance Law from bringing suit without the consent of the Attorney General. In February 1906, Justice John M. Kellogg, of the New York Supreme Court at Saratoga, overruled the Hyde demurrer, found that the causes of action were properly united and that "the commission of actual wrong by some of the defendant directors, with resulting damage to the society, has been stated in such unmistakable terms that no doubt remains of their liability to the society conceding the facts alleged to be true, and also that the other directors were guilty through negligence." In November the Appellate Division, Third Department, of the New York Supreme Court handed down two decisions against Equitable and its directors individually. The court affirmed the interlocutory judgment granted Mrs. Young by the lower court and certified three questions to the highest court for decision: 1) Does the complaint in each case state facts sufficient to constitute a cause of action? 2) Are the causes of action improperly joined in the complaint? and 3) Is there a misjoinder of parties plaintiff? The last question referred to Mrs. Young's having made herself plaintiff in her own behalf and in behalf of "all others similarly situated." The effect of these decisions was to allow the appeal of the defendants to go to the Court of Appeals on questions of law. In January 1907, the Court of Appeals affirmed the judgment of the lower courts, but a few weeks later the plaintiff, without having attempted to prove her charges, withdrew the suit because she thought the relief sought would be taken care of in a suit to be brought against the directors by the Attorney General under the new insurance laws.

The suit filed against the directors of the Society in July 1905 by Attorney General Julius M. Mayer was tried before the Supreme Court, New York Special Term, in August 1906. It may be recalled that Mayer had asked "that the defendants account for their official conduct in the management and disposition of funds and property committed to their charge," and that they be compelled to pay the Society any money they may have appropriated or lost or wasted in violation of their duties.[36] This action, in equity, was brought in behalf of the people under Sections 1781 and 1782 of the Code of Civil Procedure.[37] The defendants were asked to account not for what they had received but for what the Society had lost, that is for the damages which had resulted to the corporation from their negligence; any damages which

[36] For the beginnings of *Mayer* v. *Equitable*, see this history, p. 672.

Among the items mentioned in the complaint were the sale of stock of the Missouri Safe Deposit Company to the Society by some of the defendants; excessive commissions and loans to agents which resulted in a loss to the Society; the transaction whereby the Western National Bank was consolidated with the National Bank of the United States; the payment of excessive salaries to officers; the payment of salaries to officers of Equitable by companies in which Equitable owned stock; the payment of excessive attorneys' fees; the Society's loss on the loan made to the Depew Improvement Company on land in Erie County; etc., etc.

[37] Counsel for the defense were Samuel Untermeyer, George H. Wickersham, John G. Milburn, Abraham Benedict, Howard Mansfield, Edward M. Shepard, George Wellwood Murray, Charles P. Howland, Thomas Thacher, Graham Sumner, Lawrence Greer, and F. C. Nicodemus, Jr.

might be assessed would go not to the plaintiff but to the corporation. The defendants contended that an action for this purpose was not within the scope of the statute, which alone afforded authority to the Attorney General to bring them into court. Judge Henry Bischoff sustained the demurrers of the defendants based upon the improper joinder of causes of action and upon a defect of parties in the non-joinder of necessary parties for the purposes of the judgment sought for the distribution of the surplus of the Society. In other respects, however, the demurrers were overruled with leave to the defendants to answer within twenty days.[38]

In March 1908, the case of *Mayer* v. *Equitable* came before the Appellate Division of the Supreme Court of the State of New York, First Department. Judge Frank C. Laughlin held that the rule still existed that each director was liable only for his own acts or omissions and that no director was liable for the acts or omissions of another unless he participated therein to the injury of the corporation; nor were directors liable for mere errors of judgment where they were fairly competent to discharge their duties and acted without corrupt intent and in good faith. Since the general allegations of negligence were all to the effect that something was done or omitted, the facts had not been submitted. He said that the complaint appeared to have been framed upon the theory that it was intended by the legislature to require directors, when sued under Sections 1781 and 1782 of the Code, to account, as in the cases of trustees of express trusts, and that it was unnecessary to specify anything more than the fact that the defendant was a director. Judge Laughlin said that manifestly this was not the intention of the legislature. He held that it was incumbent upon the plaintiff, in accordance with the requirements of Section 481 of the Code, to allege the facts which constituted the negligence or misconduct, the acts of misfeasance or malfeasance. Hence the interlocutory judgment was reversed with separate bills of costs to each defendant and with leave to plaintiff to amend or apply for a severance of the actions.[39] In view of the settlements described below, both the Attorney General and the New York Insurance Department recommended, in March 1910, discontinuance of the suit of the people of the State of New York against Equitable *et al.*, and in June the

[38] 51 Misc. 339.

[39] Justices Edward Patterson, Francis M. Scott, and George L. Ingraham all concurred in the decision. 124 App. Div. 714.

Supreme Court in the county of New York (Special Term, Part II) ordered the action be discontinued "without costs to any party as against any other."

Most important of all was the series of suits brought in the endeavor to separate the holdings of Equitable and those of the estate of Henry B. Hyde, and to settle the liability in the Turner Loans and Amity Land deals. (See this history, Index.) In November 1905, The Mercantile Trust Company had brought suit against Equitable to establish the Society's liability in the Turner Loans and sued James Hazen Hyde to enforce the liability of the guarantors (or their descendants and representatives) on these loans. In December 1907, it was reported that James H. Hyde had offered to pay over to the Society certain sums and to readjust certain leases in consideration of withdrawal of the suits against him by the Attorney General. In March 1908, however, Hyde, Annie F. Hyde, and the representatives of the guarantors of the Turner Loans brought suit against Equitable for a temporary injunction to restrain the Society, the Mercantile Trust, and George V. Turner from bringing individual suits against the plaintiffs until the suit of the Mercantile Trust against the Society for the recovery of some $2,000,000 was decided. The injunction was granted by the Supreme Court in December.

A special committee of the Board of Directors made a study of the Turner Loans and the leases made by Equitable to the Mercantile Safe Deposit Company, the Security Safe Deposit Company of Boston, and the purchase of James H. Hyde's stock in the Missouri Safe Deposit Company. It reported in April 1907 and made supplementary reports in July 1908 and May 1910.[40] As a result of the labors of this committee, a settlement was arrived at in April 1909 between Equitable and the Hyde estate by which the Society agreed to pay $1,275,000 for cancellation of the leases of the two safe deposit companies, and $2,750,000 to The Mercantile Trust Company for Arkansas Valley Land Company bonds and thereby release all liability of the guarantors on the Turner Loans. A year later, the committee increased Equitable's payment in settlement of the Turner Loans to $2,911,000, in exchange for which the Society would receive $2,200,000 in 5 per cent

[40] Members of the committee in 1907 were Thomas Spratt, J. Edward Swanstrom, and C. H. Zehnder; William A. Day joined the committee in 1908. The reports of the committee as well as the settlement agreements and papers may be found in *Equitable-Hyde Settlement. Reports and Settlement Papers* (New York, May 2, 1910). This document comprises 402 pages and weighs about three pounds.

Land Gold Bonds of the Amity Company and $550,000 deferred certificates of interest. (By this time it had become fairly clear that the Society was liable as guarantor of the Turner Loans and that its liabilities in connection with the Amity Land projects totaled some $3,592,000. The Amity interests owned the Arkansas Valley Sugar Beet and Irrigated Land Company, which controlled about 60,000 acres of irrigated land in Colorado.) [41] The Society also agreed to call off all actions in which James H. Hyde was defendant and have The

[41] It may be recalled that the stock of the Amity Land and Irrigating Company (incorporated in 1893) was the main collateral for the Young loan made by the Western National Bank in 1894 and taken over by The Mercantile Trust Company by way of the George V. Turner loan in 1895. (See this history, p. 499.) Chief assets of the Amity Company at that time were an irrigation canal and a small tract of land in Prowers County, Colorado. A minority interest in the stock of the Amity Company was owned by English investors who were represented by Close Bros. and Company of Chicago. This English group also held about 40,000 acres of land in Hamilton County, Kansas, just across the Colorado line. It was planned to unite these two holdings, build extensive reservoirs, and enlarge the irrigation canal. Though engineers thought the project feasible it was found that it was impossible to irrigate the land and to sell it. After relations with the English interests were terminated, Amity decided to buy lands in Colorado near the source of water supply, to irrigate and then sell the land at a profit. In 1899 the advances on account of the Colorado property by The Mercantile Trust Company amounted to about $2,000,000. On the death of Henry B. Hyde, who had taken a keen interest in the Amity project, President James W. Alexander informed The Mercantile Trust Company that Equitable would hold Marcellus Hartley, Henry B. Hyde, and Louis Fitzgerald, guarantors of the Turner Loan, "harmless from any loss that may be incurred by reason of said purchase, loan, or advances, and from any future loans and advances that may be made for the care and protection of the property." (Alexander to Mercantile Trust, May 11, 1899.) After the American Beet Sugar Company erected a plant at Rocky Ford some miles up the Arkansas River from the Amity property, Amity contracted in 1900 to turn the management of its property over to Henry T. Oxnard and his associates in the American Beet Sugar Company. It was hoped that successful operation of the sugar beet business would warrant the construction of another factory at Holly, on the lands of the Amity Company. When the Oxnards failed in their efforts to sell the Amity lands to the American Beet Sugar Company, relations with them were terminated by the Amity people in December 1904.

The following year, the Amity interests—which had incorporated in New Jersey in 1901 as The Arkansas Valley Sugar Beet and Irrigated Land Company, a combination of The Amity Land Company of Colorado and The Great Plains Water Company—made an agreement with Grant B. Schley of New York City by which Schley was given 80 acres of land on which to erect a sugar plant at Holly; also water rights. The Amity interests, after receiving from the proceeds of sales of lands and water rights the sum of $1,575,000, plus moneys expended on the property for construction, maintenance, and improvement, and after receiving interest at the rate of 5 per cent per annum on the above advances, would divide the proceeds of the sale of lands in excess of the foregoing equally between the two interests. At this time, Arkansas Valley controlled about 60,000 acres in Colorado, of which

Mercantile Trust Company discontinue its action against the guarantors of the Turner Loans. Hyde agreed to release to the Society the $63,233 ($61,446 as reported by Hyde in 1905) syndicate profits which he had deposited with the Cashier in 1905, and Annie F. Hyde agreed to cancel all claims to a pension.

Unfortunately, former Comptroller Thomas D. Jordan did not live to learn of these settlements or the fact that the Attorney General's actions against Equitable had been discontinued. When he returned to the state in May 1907, he voluntarily went before the grand jury and pleaded not guilty to eighteen indictments for forgery in the third degree and one for perjury. Most of the forgery indictments grew out of the so-called loans which Jordan, as Comptroller of the Society, had made to various employees of Kuhn, Loeb and Company. He was released on $1,000 bail and died suddenly in July 1908, before trial took place. While there was little doubt that he had been guilty of some irregularity in handling the Society's funds, he was, to a large degree, merely carrying out orders of his superiors in approving vouchers and the like, the nature of which he did not know and could not question. He was a proud man and his dismissal by President Morton and the indictments which followed hastened his end.

EQUITABLE WINS ITS APPEAL IN FRANCE

The stirring events of 1905 had numerous repercussions in foreign countries. In England and Russia, as well as elsewhere, the newspapers played up the troubles of the American companies; in France, policyholders' protective committees were formed.[42] President Morton sought to apply to the European situation the same frank publicity

---

about 40,000 were first class, irrigable land. In addition, it held land contracts on about 11,000 acres on which about $350,000 was still unpaid.

In the autumn of 1906, a committee of the Board of Directors, together with President Paul Morton and his brother, Joy Morton, both of whom were well acquainted with the Colorado lands held by Amity, examined the properties and reported that they were valuable. As of January 1, 1907, $2,892,146 remained unpaid on account of the original indebtedness and advances later made; in addition, Equitable had paid $700,000 to Mercantile Trust to be applied on the Turner Loan. For the later history of the Arkansas Valley holding, see this history, pp. 937 and 1120.

[42] One of these committees, the Union of French Policyholders, was headed by Eloi Duboin, who had previously sued Peixotto and Equitable (see this history, p. 565). Duboin had a number of "scandal papers" translated into French and distributed them to French policyholders. Peixotto replied in "strong language." Paris Office files, Equitable Archives.

which he had used so successfully at home. In July 1906 he and Emory McClintock, Vice President and Actuary of the Mutual Life, appeared before a select committee of the House of Lords on life insurance companies. He explained the methods by which Equitable was conducted and called attention to the special provision made for the security of British policyholders by the $500,000 deposit in the Bank of England. He stated that the various investigations had clearly established the sound financial condition of the Society but admitted that confidence in it had been restored more completely in the United States than in Europe.[43]

President Morton then went on to Paris to study the situation which would exist when the deposit requirements of the French law of March 17, 1905, went into effect, that is, on August 27, 1906. (For the law of 1905, see this history, p. 559.) Though Equitable had been reluctant to accept the various deposit and investment requirements, which were obviously intended to be retroactive, President Morton finally decided, on the basis of assurance given in December 1905, that the provisions relative to annual notices to policyholders of dividends accumulated on tontine policies (Article 7) would not be retroactive, to have Equitable apply for registration and remain in business in France. "After the most deliberate consideration," he reasoned that the new French laws were no more stringent than the new American statutes, and that although Equitable did not like the retroactive features, it would comply with them. Since the Society already owned valuable real estate in Paris, complying with the requirement to invest in French securities would constitute no additional hardship. He believed that it was the intention of the French Government to treat the American companies fairly and that withdrawal would result in loss of business already held. Since Equitable was well within the annual limit of new business established by the Armstrong laws, and France was a good market for life insurance, he hoped that, with the hallmark of government behind it, Equitable would fare even better in France than before. He added that the scandals concerning American life insurance companies, par-

[43] *The Spectator*, LXXVII (1906), July 12.

McClintock gave the committee reports on Mutual's business and stated that the documents showed a satisfactory condition of Mutual's investments. He did not think it was desirable for his company to make a special provision for its British policyholders; since Mutual was a mutual company and both the British and American policyholders shared in all of the advantages of mutuality, he was opposed to the creation of any special reserve for British policyholders.

ticularly the Equitable, had been grossly exaggerated and pointed out that in view of the cordial feeling which existed between the French and American peoples, and the rapid business development in the United States, French investors would have exceptional opportunities to invest in sound American securities which yielded larger returns than investments anywhere else in the world.[44]

President Morton's decision to remain in France caught Actuary Van Cise by surprise and, in the absence of Assistant Actuary Robert G. Hann, who regularly handled the foreign business, he was hard put to get together the necessary records. They were finally provided, however, the Society made the necessary deposits of some 70,000,000 francs, and applied for registration under the new law.

In his letter to the French policyholders, President Morton called attention to the fact that Equitable had not waited for the new law to establish substantial guarantees for the benefit of French policyholders, but already held much French real estate and many French securities; also that under the new law Equitable would be subject to two governmental supervisions—"a double pledge which will command the most absolute confidence of the public." He spoke of the law of 1905 as having been passed in a "spirit of impartiality and justice," and felt sure that Equitable's friends in France would congratulate themselves on hearing that the Society claimed the right of citizenship among them. He said that one of Equitable's motives was a "desire to contribute to the maintenance and development, so desirable, of the ever-improving relations between France and the United States, united by so many ties of esteem and solidarity." [45] This was a diplomatic and effective letter, which stood out in strong contrast to the pamphlet just previously published by one of the other New York companies referring to the decrees and administrative regulations as having been made "to the utter disregard of all promises made and the law itself as obviously intended to run out the American companies."

In March 1907, a ministerial decree was published in the *Journal Officiel* which stated that Equitable had given full satisfaction under the requirements of the law and was duly registered to carry on business in France.

[44] President Morton's statement is quoted and summarized in *ibid.* See also September 6 issue of *The Spectator*.

[45] A copy of this letter is in the Paris Office files, French Insurance Law of 1905 (1904–07 folder), Equitable Archives.

Having made the decision to stay in France, the Society decided to embark upon a project which James H. Hyde had hoped to achieve, that is, to build a new building for Equitable's Paris offices. Since both Mutual and New York Life had fine buildings in Paris, Equitable, in 1901, had authorized Mark Percy Peixotto to purchase properties at Nos. 23–25 Rue de la Paix and Nos. 17–21 Boulevard des Capucines; three years later he purchased 21 Rue de la Paix. The building which Equitable occupied at 36 and 36 bis Avenue de l'Opéra, had been yielding only about 2.6 per cent on the investment, or about 1 per cent less than the average on the Society's foreign buildings. It was thought a new building would yield 4 per cent and also serve to meet the deposit requirements of the French law.

Equitable proposed to build a twenty-story building on the new site, but Paris did not intend to be Americanized with skyscrapers and the city authorities refused to allow it. The lots constituted an irregular plot, with a short frontage on the Place de l'Opéra and longer frontage on the two other streets. The building, as eventually completed in 1910, was six stories high facing the Place de l'Opéra and eight stories on the sides. The exterior was faced with stone, with square Corinthian half-columns to decorate the façade; there were stone balconies with metal balustrades at the third, fifth, and sixth floors. Inside were a large rotunda and a grand staircase. The detached building at 21 Rue de la Paix was left standing but four stories were added to it. The new Equitable building was a beautiful and well-situated structure and contributed greatly to the Society's prestige. It was described as "a palace, with severe and solemn lines, a large mass, with a solid base, and harmonious, as if it intended to take possession of the ground. It is a ground-squeezer. Here, for us Frenchmen, is the architecture of a great artist: elegant and symbolic, displaying at the same time simplicity, solidity and duration." Like the company which it represented, it had indestructible foundations. "One may say of the Equitable, as of the vessel of the city of Paris: *Fluctuat nec mergitur.*" [46]

Much to Equitable's astonishment, the French Government in May and June 1908—after Equitable's new Paris building was well on its way to completion—decided that Article 7 of the French law of 1905, calling for annual reports on their policies to tontine policyholders,

[46] As described by Dr. Alexandre Lacassagne, Director of the Medical Department for France, at the meeting of French agents and guests, June 22, 1910. See this history, pp. 752–753.

affected all policy contracts whatever their date. James C. Rocquet, Equitable's Secretary General for Europe, reported that A. Millerand, one of Equitable's French counsel, was of the opinion that even if new business were discontinued the French Government would probably apply the penalties as per Article 15 of the law of 1905 each succeeding year until individual accounts were furnished to the policyholders. Vice President William A. Day cabled the Paris office that it was impossible to give any reliable approximate estimates on deferred dividend policies: "If the government of France insists upon such an unjust, useless and misleading statement, we cannot comply, and being helpless, must submit to whatever the superior power of France may inflict and rely upon the future to redress what we feel would be a great wrong to the Society and its policyholders throughout the world." [47]

In August Equitable commissioned Maurice Léon, New York lawyer, as special counsel to go to France and endeavor to find a satisfactory solution to the problem. Léon interviewed Edmond Bruwaert, Minister of Finance and President of the Franco-American Tariff Commission, who understood and sympathized with the position of the American life companies.[48] Peixotto conferred with Georges Paulet, Director of Insurance in the Ministry of Labor, which was headed by René Viviani. According to Peixotto, Paulet seemed to be convinced of the sincerity of Equitable's efforts to satisfy the requirements of the law, as well as the justice of the Society's position; although embarrassed, he felt that he must maintain his stand.[49] Léon was not so sure about Paulet, who, he said, had a "pet notion of how the law should be applied retroactively to the Equitable's contracts," but who might change his mind if ordered to do so by his superiors.[50]

André Ulrich, who, together with Pierre Waldeck-Rousseau, A. Millerand, and Raymond Poincaré, had served as Equitable's French counsel at the time the law of 1905 was passed, recommended that Equitable comply with the law by furnishing individual statements to the policyholders which would make it clear that the figures mentioned were merely approximations of the present status of their particular

47 Day to Peixotto, August 28, 1908. Paris Office files, French Insurance Law of 1905 (1907–10 folder), Equitable Archives.

48 Bruwaert had formerly been French Consul-General in New York.

49 Peixotto to Rocquet (in Madrid), September 22, 1908. Paris Office files, French Insurance Law of 1905 (1907–10 folder), Equitable Archives.

50 Léon to Day, September 15, 1908. *Ibid.*

class of tontines, and that exact calculations could be had only at the end of the period of that class. But in a long and able memorandum, Actuary Joel Van Cise explained the nature of the tontine contracts and stated that Equitable had no policies in force such as would fall under the requirements of Article 7; since no laws existed in any country at the time these policies were first issued, the Society had adopted its own method of keeping accounts on them, and never in forty years had it kept any individual accounts nor had it ever promised to do so. Distribution of the surplus was promised only at the end of the tontine periods, and it would be impossible to change the accounting system at this late date. In its annual reports to the various states, the Society had always answered "none" for "amounts set apart, apportioned, etc., upon deferred dividend policies," and these reports had been acceptable to the state insurance departments. Under New York law, Van Cise did not think it would be possible for Equitable to furnish French policyholders something not furnished to domestic policyholders. Even if it were possible, the expense of endeavoring to calculate the amounts accumulated to more than 300,000 deferred dividend policyholders, sending out the notices and handling the ensuing correspondence, would be terrific. Besides, a great number of policyholders, noting the unfavorable comparisons with the original estimates, would be disappointed and let their policies lapse. Rival companies would seize upon these figures for competitive purposes and if the figures were not accurate the Society would be in trouble, for, under New York law, misrepresentation incurred a penalty of fine and imprisonment.[51]

Vice President Day agreed with Van Cise's reasoning and said that if Equitable made any statements to the deferred dividend policyholders, it "could only truthfully state that in accord with the contractual conditions the amount due was Fcs. O. . . . "

Léon did not think that Viviani would be much help; he said that Viviani was "a politician not overly endowed with character and interested only in the questions which furnish topics for speeches in the House of Representatives and before great public gatherings."[52] Consequently, he would not be interested in Equitable's trouble with Article 7. Léon thought that Paulet, Director of Insurance under

[51] Van Cise's memorandum was received in Equitable's Paris office September 7, 1908. Copy in *ibid.*

[52] Léon to Day, September 14, 1908. *Ibid.*

Viviani, could be reached by way of Foreign Minister Stephen Pichon. André Tardieu, foreign editor of *Le Temps,* gave the impression that the proper approach to the French Government would be by way of United States Ambassador Henry White to Prime Minister Georges Clemenceau, but White was not certain that that was the proper procedure; he assured Equitable, however, that he would render whatever help he could. Léon conferred with Jean Jules Jusserand, French Ambassador to the United States, who realized that injustice was being done Equitable but explained it to be the result of the feeling of impatience with the United States caused by the "hard, tricky, and altogether unfair interpretation which the American customs authorities gave the Customs Act as applied to French importations into the United States." He said that he was swamped with complaints from French exporters in regard to what they considered unfair treatment. Consequently, it was hard to arouse the French officials when the shoe was on the other foot. He thought the animosity would continue until Washington did something about the tariff situation. Léon told Jusserand that Equitable had always been friendly to the French, and if France wanted to retaliate as a result of the tariff problem it should do so against American importers and not against Equitable.

A day or two later Léon told Ambassador White that an officer in the French Foreign Office had reported that, at lunch, Jusserand had said that Equitable's cause was perfectly legitimate ("la cause de l'Équitable est parfaitement légitime, on ne l'a pas exagérée.") [53]

After Tardieu and Jusserand had prepared the way, the documents pertaining to Equitable's case were sent to Foreign Minister Pichon; he would thus be prepared for any conversation which he might have with Clemenceau. When Ambassador White approached Clemenceau on September 15, the Prime Minister promised to take up the matter with the ministry in charge, and requested White to deliver to Pichon a memorandum on Equitable's case. Clemenceau said such a memorandum would strengthen his hand. Léon had pointed out to Ambassador White that Section 60 of the New York Insurance Law prohibited what the French decree called for. One stumbling block in Equitable's way was the fact that the New York Life in its statement had reported $37,000,000 as "set aside" for deferred dividends, whereas Equitable had not reported any such item.

By this time Léon had become thoroughly suspicious of William

[53] Léon to White, September 18, 1908. *Ibid.*

I. Buchanan, who was counsel for the New York Life and presumably working for the same cause as Equitable. Buchanan had tried to get Peixotto not to raise the question of Section 60 of the New York law. Léon said that Buchanan had not had an interview with Vice President Day as he had claimed. He wrote Peixotto:

> We are all convinced that Mr. Buchanan has been scheming to thwart us in our recent endeavors.
>
> I BEG YOU TO BE MORE SUSPICIOUS THAN EVER BEFORE OF THE NEW YORK LIFE AND ALL CONNECTED WITH IT.
>
> Buchanan sought by deliberate lies to get you to divulge to him confidential information in order that he might use it against the Society. By his act, which must have the approval of the New York Life for the reason that Mr. Buckner, vice-president of the New York Life, took a hand personally in the attempt to draw out Judge Day, the New York Life and all those connected with it have forfeited all right to even common respect from the Equitable and its representatives and they should be treated as dangerous enemies.[54]

By November it appeared that Paulet's office was ready to present a report in Equitable's favor but wished to have its case so well in hand that criticism could be avoided when the favorable decision was given. Peixotto thought that if President Morton got President Theodore Roosevelt to give things a final push, everything would be fine.

Despite the excellent outlook at this point, the French Ministry of Labor on December 14 issued a *lettre ministérielle* which stated that Equitable must furnish individual accounts to the policyholders; these statements, however, would not be binding on Equitable or taken as an admission that the sum mentioned therein would become legally due to the policyholders, but would be merely an indication or conjecture of what the Society thought the policy would be entitled to if the divisions should be made at the stated annual periods during the life of the policy.[55] "In other words," as Vice President Day later put it, referring to René Viviani, who had signed the letter, "he says that he simply requires that we shall make a guess at what sum would under such circumstances be attributable to the policy; and that this 'guess'

[54] Léon to Peixotto, September 28, 1908. *Ibid.*

[55] Viviani's letter stated that the purpose of an annual and individual accounting to policyholders was to give "a simple indication to the insureds of the progressive formation of the eventual part of the dividend which will be attributed at the end of the accumulation period, if the conditions contained in the policy are fulfilled."

or 'conjecture' shall be sent in writing, signed by our officers to each policyholder." [56] Equitable was given one month in which to comply.

On December 19, President Morton received a cable from Peixotto, Rocquet, and Millerand to the effect that the government's letter of December 14 required Equitable to furnish individual accounts but that such accounts would create no obligation whatever. Millerand and Ulrich gave their opinion that such individual accounts would make no change in the Society's contracts or bookkeeping and would create no new rights for policyholders. President Morton was advised to withhold any decision until he received the full opinion of counsel by letter. Without waiting for receipt of the letter, President Morton on December 22 cabled Peixotto as follows: "Reaffirm W. A. Day's cable August 28th. Action French Government will force cessation new business." [57] Meanwhile, Rocquet had written Second Vice President George T. Wilson on December 18 and informed him that Viviani's letter stated "that our form of so-called account to the policyholders may be drawn up with the reservations that may be deemed necessary or advisable, that it is essentially a provisional and contingent account, which does not create an immediate right for the policyholder but which permits him to follow the oscillations of the share of profits which will eventually come to him when the conditions stipulated in the policy shall have been fulfilled." Rocquet reported that Ulrich and an official in the Ministry of Labor who was friendly to Equitable had assured him that a letter such as Viviani's would bind not only the existing government but all succeeding governments and dispose of the question so long as the law remained unchanged. Rocquet also presumed that a Home Office decision would be deferred until he was able to send a report of further consultations with counsel. The opinion of Millerand and Ulrich was forwarded the same day to the effect that Viviani's letter required from Equitable "a simple formality which brings no change to the contracts . . . which creates no new rights for the insureds and imposes no new obligation upon the Company. . . ." Also on December 18, Peixotto wrote the Home Office that if Equitable did not comply with the requirements of Viviani's letter, the

[56] William A. Day to Secretary of State Philander C. Knox, April 23, 1909. Copy in Paris Office files, French Insurance Law of 1905 (1907–10 folder), Equitable Archives.

[57] The Day cable referred to (see this history, p. 735) was the one which stated: "If the Government of France insists upon such an unjust, useless and misleading statement, we cannot comply."

Conseil d'État would not recognize an appeal but would throw out the Society's objection because, in complying with the terms of Viviani's letter, the Society would be creating no new right or privilege for its policyholders and undertaking no new liability towards them.

When Peixotto received President Morton's cable of December 22, he cabled Morton to defer action on new business until he could come to the Home Office for consultation. Peixotto sailed for New York December 30, but, knowing that he would still be in New York when the month's deadline arrived, he dictated and signed two letters to Viviani and dated them January 14, 1909. One, a very short letter, promised full compliance with Viviani's terms; the other, a four-page letter, set forth the reasons why Equitable could not possibly comply. Peixotto intended to cable Rocquet from New York which letter to send to Viviani on January 14.[58] After Peixotto succeeded in convincing President Morton and Vice President Day that Equitable could comply with the formalities laid down in Viviani's letter of December 14, Day cabled to Rocquet January 14 to deliver to the Administration the letter of acceptance and accompany it with a personal letter to Paulet as follows: "M. Peixotto, absent from Paris, asks me to inform you that on his return from the Home Office he will hasten to let you know personally the form and manner in which he is authorized to comply with the ministerial letter of last December 14. As soon as he arrives he will ask to see you for this purpose. Meanwhile, he will confirm the present communication directly by letter to you next week." Rocquet delivered the two letters to Paulet in person.

Upon his return to Paris, Peixotto presented Equitable's proposed form for meeting Viviani's requirements. Presumably, the form was as follows:

The Equitable Life Assurance Society of the United States has deposited with the French Government, securities to the amount of Fcs. ______, on account of surplus derived from payments made on policies of accumulation.

If policy # ______ shall be in force at the end of its accumulation period, it will be apportioned its full share of the accumulated surplus of the Society, as shown by the experience of the class to which this policy belongs.

58 The longer letter, which was never sent, carries the date January 14, 1908—obviously the typist's error. Original letter and carbon copy in Paris Office files, French Insurance Law of 1905 (1907–10 folder), Equitable Archives.

> Under the terms of the contract, no apportionment of surplus can be made previous to the end of the accumulation period, when alone the amount of the apportionable surplus can be ascertained, and before which time it cannot be known what policies will be in force, and, therefore, entitled to participate in the division of surplus.[59]

Peixotto also conferred with Ambassador Henry White, who said that he wanted instructions from the State Department to intercede on Equitable's behalf.[60] Washington cabled the proper instructions on February 22, and two days later Peixotto delivered to White a memorandum which contained the following paragraph:

> The Society's opinion was that one of the prescriptions of the law of 1905, viz., that which is specified in the Article 7, and which concerns the keeping of individual accounts of profits, could not refer retroactively to the contracts issued prior to the said law. The Minister gave it the opposite interpretation which the Society accepted although it still has the conviction that in Justice, if the Council of State had to decide upon an appeal its thesis of non-retroactivity would prevail.[61]

When Ambassador White called upon Prime Minister Clemenceau, he emphasized the fact that if Equitable's form of compliance were not accepted by the French Government, it would mean that Equitable would have to leave France. Clemenceau then said to White: "That cannot be, that must not be, that is out of the question." [62] Peixotto reported that White "has been a splendid support, adviser, and wheelhorse to us" in this affair. He also reported that Director of Insurance Paulet wished to be "technically" covered by his own experts if anyone tried to raise trouble later, that is, after the existing government went out of office.

On March 21, 1909, *L'Argus* (*Journal International des Assurances*) published a front-page story on the law of 1905, referring to a certain insurance company which was "well embarrassed" by the provisions of Article 7. The writer wanted to know whether this article was to be

[59] The one-page translation is undated and unheaded, but is filed among the papers in the 1907–10 folder just after Peixotto's letter to Morton and Day dated February 26, 1909, in which Peixotto reported that he had presented Equitable's form to Paulet. *Ibid.*

[60] Peixotto cable to Morton and Day, February 18, 1909. Copy in *ibid.*

[61] Day to Peixotto, June 7, 1910. Copy in *ibid.*

[62] Peixotto to Morton and Day, February 26, 1909. Copy in *ibid.*

a "dead letter." Whether or not this story was of influence, the Ministry of Labor warned Peixotto March 25 and on March 31 issued a decree (dated March 25 and signed by President Armand Fallières and Viviani) which ruled that since Equitable was no longer operating in conformity to the law of 1905, its registration in France was no longer valid. Equitable was given eight days in which to register an appeal with the *Conseil d'État.*

When President Morton received news of this decree by cable on March 26, immediate steps were taken to appeal. Peixotto secured the services of Maître Jean Labbé as special counsel and the appeal was filed.[63] André Ulrich also helped prepare the appeal.

Peixotto thought that Equitable should furnish the *Conseil d'État* every means possible to enable it to recognize that fair, honorable and scientific methods alone determined the actual results on its deferred dividend policies; failure to give complete information would, in the opinion of counsel, be fatal. The French companies had exploited the fact, in a "prejudicious" manner, that Equitable's directors might dispose of this surplus in any way they saw fit:

A danger, not only far greater but more real and made of more stubborn stuff exists and has existed throughout the entire history of this long and exhaustive fight,—long before the preparation of the French Law—all through the parliamentary debates in the Chamber and the Senate—, in 1904 & 1905,—and which the events of 1905 did not little to spread and increase.

It is the odious and despicable legend that our Surplus is nothing but a "Caisse noire"—(a corruption fund) with which the Board of Directors can do as they please, from which is withdrawn such part or portion—as may suit their convenience—tempered with such practical and prudent facts and circumstances as may obtain—when dealing shrewdly with a policyholder of high standing and influence—in such communities where results on policies may be bluffed on the public as a means of commercial publicity and used by the Equitable as an element of self glorification and agency propaganda. It is this infamous legend, this venomous defamation, which should and must be eradicated for all time, and with which it is—above all at present—necessary that the members of the Council of State should not be contaminated. All our Counsel agree that *this* is the "danger" which we cannot do too much to overcome and avoid, and to overcome and avoid which—nothing in their judgment and in mine—could be more

[63] It appears that none of Equitable's previously retained counsel was eligible to plead before the *Conseil d'État.*

forceful, more effective, healthier and more irrefutable, than the complete, fair and clear analysis of what we have, and what we do, in our loyal, fair and legal respect and execution of our policy contracts.[64]

On April 23, Vice President Day wrote Secretary of State Philander C. Knox and requested the State Department's good offices to aid Equitable in its argument with the French Government. Day said that President Morton was leaving for France later in the month and "if Ambassador White could be instructed to lend him such support and assistance as the rules and customs of diplomacy permit of, it would be a great help." Day's personal letter to Knox was accompanied by a formal letter which reviewed the history of the case. He pointed out that if the penalties for non-conformity to the French Government's interpretation of the law were merely to exclude Equitable from France, the Society might view them with equanimity even though it would be required to leave behind the $12,000,000 deposit. But this would not be all, since the law imposed heavy penalties which were "not only cumulative but go on perpetually until the last policy in France has been closed." If the law were enforced, these penalties would "assume in the final aggregate a stupendous sum." Such a result would do violence to the plainest principle of natural justice and do irreparable injury to every one of our half million policyholders: "In this situation and under these circumstances it is the belief of this Society that we are warranted in asking our own Government to use

[64] Peixotto to Day, May 31, 1909. Copy in Paris Office files, French Insurance Law of 1905 (1907–10 folder), Equitable Archives. The portion of the above quotation in regard to Equitable's surplus in Peixotto's letter was copied with some change in the wording from a letter written by Ulrich May 29, 1909, to Peixotto.

Peixotto's letter to Day was written in connection with the Vasselot case—a suit for accounting of dividends by a policyholder which had been decided against Equitable in the lower court and was being appealed to the Court of Appeals. It seems that in a similar suit in Hungary Equitable had won on the strength of Actuary Van Cise's thorough account of how the dividends on the policy were figured. Labbé and Ulrich wanted the same kind of affidavit or exhibit for the Vasselot case when it came to appeal, and in addition wanted the affidavit presented to the *Conseil d'État* to support Equitable's appeal then pending; such an exhibit would be an example of the fairness and mathematical soundness of Equitable's methods of calculating dividends at the time of maturity of a policy. The Home Office, however, was dubious, since it thought that furnishing such information might indicate that Equitable could easily produce such an exhibit annually, during the life of a policy—in other words, just what the Ministry of Labor said Equitable could do and Equitable said it could not. Peixotto's letter of May 31, 1909, was an attempt to dissuade the Home Office from this idea, and to convince it that the *Conseil* would react very favorably to such a presentation on the part of Equitable.

its good offices to prevent, if possible, the threatened injury to such a large number of our people." He then explained why Equitable had refused to make "idle guesses" in annual statements to policyholders. He concluded as follows:

> From the foregoing you may perceive that the matter at stake is but a tempest in a teapot on the one side, and a desperate tragedy on the other side; and it all results from a bureau of the Government of France giving to the law of 1905 a retrospective application to contracts, many of which we made years prior to the enactment of such law, and this in the face of the expressed provisions in the policy that no accounting of profits, i.e. "dividends," should be made or required until the maturity of the policy.
>
> If any ground for diplomacy can be found for doing so the Management of this Society earnestly requests the assistance of their Government in preventing this most serious injustice at the hands of another Government.[65]

The appeal to the *Conseil d'État* presented serious difficulties, and it appeared that the odds against Equitable's winning it were overwhelming. First, this was not an ordinary case in litigation brought before courts of ordinary jurisdiction such as the Tribunal of First Instance, the Court of Appeal, or the Court of Cassation; it was an appeal to a special jurisdiction. The *Conseil d'État* was less a court than an administrative body, the function of which was to give the government opinions and advice. The council was subdivided into various sections, such as the Section of Public Works, Commerce and Labor, the Section of Finances, and the like, each of which worked with the related ministry or ministries in connection with the decrees which concerned them. Then there had developed a Section of Litigation which had the function of passing upon the measures taken by the ministries and against which private parties or corporations had raised objections by means of an "appeal for excess of power." Although this section had some of the characteristics of a court, it did not, when it adjudicated upon appeals, make pure law; it was not called upon to apply the Civil Code or the Penal Code or to determine the validity or nonvalidity of contracts between private parties—a role performed by the courts of ordinary jurisdiction. When it decided whether or not measures taken by an administration were justified and did not exceed the bounds, it was guided not by any principle of private law

[65] Day to Knox, April 23, 1909. Copy in *ibid.*

but by public law, and public law rather than being a set of concrete principles was "the notion of general welfare such as it is understood, such as it is interpreted; it is the impression which each one has of what must be the public interest." Guided from this viewpoint, the *Conseil d'État* was inclined to decide that measures taken by the administration expressed this general welfare and were inspired by it. It was likely to approve the decisions of the ministries, since these ministries were never supposed to be guided by motives of private interest; their role was to concern themselves with *res publica,* as did the Council itself. Hence an appeal before such a body, which was less a neutral court than an associate of the ministries in the work of public interest, had few chances of being entertained.

Second, there was between the two parties involved, the Equitable on one side and the Ministry of Labor on the other, a deep inequality. Equitable was one of that group of American companies against which public opinion had been hostile for a number of years. The French Government had reflected that hostility in the debates in the legislature in 1904 and 1905 when these companies, because of their scheme of accumulation of profits, were called corruptionists and deceitful and nefarious institutions. This attitude had not been mitigated by the revelations of 1905 which involved the Equitable. Now the Society was, through its appeal, complaining of the treatment which the Ministry of Labor was giving to the supervision of its deferred dividend policies. In view of the fact that deferred dividend policies had been so severely judged by the French legislature, it might appear that an appeal against the decisions of the Ministry of Labor in regard to these policies would be based on the least favorable ground.

On the other hand, the defendant, the Ministry of Labor, would seem only to be fulfilling the mission of supervision entrusted to it by the law of 1905 and limiting itself to regulations in the interest of the general welfare. No one could suppose that the ministry was inspired by interested motives, whereas Equitable might be. Further, Equitable's stand appeared the more inexplicable since three other companies —New York Life, Norwich, and Gresham—which had deferred dividend policies had submitted to the requirements of Article 7 and prepared annual individual statements.

Nor was the complaint against any individual for malfeasance or incompetency. Director of Insurance Paulet, who had had much to do with the measures taken against Equitable, not only possessed considerable authority but his competence and professional probity were above suspicion. His administrative position and title of Councilor of State practically made him a member of the household of the *Conseil d'État.* Then the Ministry of Labor was represented in this case by the consulting committee on life insurance composed of senators, deputies, government officers, actuaries, lawyers, and other specialists. It was thought that this body had been unanimous in approving the withdrawal of Equitable's registration. In addition, the decrees of the ministry had been signed by the President of the French Republic.

Third, the precedents seemed to run against Equitable. The Society's contention that the provisions of the law of 1905 must not be retroactive seemed condemned in advance by solutions already given to that question. The Senate in a discussion on March 2, 1905, had voted that Article 21 of the law of 1905 on the subject of the computation of reserves was retroactive. Then the *Conseil d'État* had worked with the Ministry of Labor in establishing by the decree of June 9, 1906, that Article 8 on the subject of investment of reserves should be retroactive and affect contracts entered into prior to the law. To be consistent with these decisions, the *Conseil* would have to decide that the provisions of Article 7 were also retroactive.

The counsel for the Mutual Life, impressed by these precedents, had repeatedly warned Equitable that it could not win its case unless by its arguments it could also cause the decree of June 9, 1906, which provided for retroactivity in matters of investment, to be nullified. It was possible that when Equitable, in its two briefs, asked the *Conseil d'État* to go back to the sources, the parliamentary debates, it was jeopardizing its own case. While Equitable maintained that no proof would there be found which would condemn its system of deferred dividends, the *Conseil* would actually find many statements which condemned the American companies and their system of accumulated profits.

There was one other obstacle to a favorable decision. Preliminary examination of appeals was handled by a master of the rolls (*Maître des Requêtes*), a reporter who did not enjoy absolute tenure of office but was always subject to dismissal. The incumbent reporter was an official in the midst of his career who would soon be a candidate for the post of Councilor of State. Would it be likely that he would place himself in opposition to the opinion of the legislature, the Ministry of Labor, and previous decrees of the *Conseil*, and thus risk his career?[66]

Despite the fact that Peixotto thought that Equitable could win only by claiming that all of the retroactive provisions of the law of 1905 should be nullified, Maître Labbé in his briefs stuck to the major argument that making Article 7 retroactive would impair the Society's rights under the policy contract and create a new contract, thereby doing violence to the plain principles of justice.

Labbé's summary (*plaidoirie*) before the *Conseil*—a document of some 27 pages—was clear, logical, and effective. He came to the main point at once, that is whether Article 7, Section 1 of the Law of 1905 was applicable to all contracts whether written before or after its enactment. He then explained the difference between nonparticipating and participating policies and pointed out that, under the latter, the insured had a right not only to the face value of the policy, but at the same time, under his contract, a right to a part of the "profits" on the policy ("*il a droit à une part des bénéfices que la Société aura réalisés dans sa gestion*"); the policyholder became a partner (*associé*) in the company. He distinguished three types of participating policies —those under which the "dividends" (*bénéfices*) were distributed at regular intervals; those under which the "dividends" were calculated and credited to the policyholder at the end of stipulated periods but not paid to him; and those under which the terms of the contracts provided that the policyholder had no rights to the "dividends" up to the moment that the policy arrived at maturity, for only at that time did the quality of partnership or mutuality become apparent. It was this last kind of policy—a "deferred participation policy" (*police à participation différée*)—which Equitable had been issuing before passage of the law of 1905.

Labbé quoted from the debates on the Law of 1905 to show that various senators and members of the House of Deputies well understood the nature of these deferred dividend policies and that under the system practiced by "the great American mutuals" the policy contract was so devised that the companies assumed no obligations or promises in regard to "dividends" until the final accounting at maturity

[66] The above summary is taken largely from an 11-page typescript entitled "Difficulties of the Appeal." The document is unsigned and undated, but the author's guess is that it was prepared by Labbé or Ulrich and sent to the Home Office sometime in 1910. *Ibid.*

of the policy. He asked how the Ministry of Labor could defend its view that the requirement for annual individual accounts did not modify the contractual situation between the company and the policyholder. He did not believe it could. He cited the opinion of M. Lyon-Caën, Dean of the Faculty of Law of Paris, given Equitable in 1905 in answer to two questions: first, was it possible to apply the prescriptions of Article 7 to deferred dividend policies; his answer was no. Second, if there existed absolute incompatibility between the requirements of the law and the system of deferred dividend policies, was it necessary to conclude that the system could no longer be used without the company's exposing itself to severe penalties or, on the contrary, that the system could continue to be freely used as in the past. In answer to the second question, Lyon-Caën had replied that he doubted whether the legislator had intended to apply this clause to deferred dividend policies.[67]

Labbé then considered what would have been the situation if Equitable had complied with the government's demand for individual annual accounts. Suppose the company had declared a *bénéfice* of 150 francs to the policyholder in 1907 on a policy at the end of its thirteenth year:

> Now this sum is not what the policyholder is entitled to, it represents nothing, absolutely nothing for him, since the total profits due him, under the law, are not only the total profits produced by 1907 business, but the total profits produced by all business transacted while the policy was in force.
>
> The Company has said: "We cannot send this account under the terms of the law, which only obliges us to send an account referring to 1907, because we would be deceiving our insureds. Yes, we are declaring a dividend of 150 francs, but this will not at all represent the actual situation of the insured in regard to the Company; this will be a false situation and not the one the legislator had in mind. This is another proof that Article 7 cannot apply to contracts written prior to the law."
>
> That is the main reason why the Company did not send individual accounts when it undertook to conform to this same law.[68]

[67] "*. . . M. Lyon-Caën avait répondu qu'il était douteux que le législateur eût entendu viser cette clause (des polices comportant répartition différée) dans l'article 7, § 1 du projet de loi et, par conséquent, l'ait prohibée.*" Pamphlet, *L'Équitable des États-Unis devant le Conseil d'État—Conclusions, Plaidoirie* (L. Denis, Paris, n.d.), p. 37. Copy in *ibid.*

[68] *Ibid.*, p. 44.

Although the desire not to appear to be misinforming its policyholders was the main reason Equitable had not sent the individual annual accounts, there was another reason. These statements for very inadequate sums, if sent, would have resulted in numerous suits on the part of the policyholders and if, as Labbé had pointed out earlier in the pleading, Equitable appeared in court and told the judges, "These accounts mean nothing," the judges would have replied, "They must mean something, because one cannot suppose that the legislator would have imposed an obligation upon the companies if that obligation relates to nothing." Labbé reminded the *Conseil* that Equitable had always fully covered its reserves on French policies by deposits in France, and that at the time it had some six million francs on deposit with the *Caisse des Dépôts et Consignations* to cover dividends not yet distributed.

M. Pichat, Maître des Requêtes, in presenting his conclusions to the *Conseil,* first took up "matters of substance" (*moyens du fond*), and concluded that "the individual account is irreconcilable with the contracts written by the Society before the enactment of the law; to require this individual account is to give a retroactive effect to the law, which is impossible; consequently, the prescriptions of Article 7 cannot be applied to the Society's contracts written prior to the enactment of the law." Pichat then discussed two "matters of form" (*moyens de forme*). The first concerned the abrupt withdrawal of Equitable's license by the Ministry of Labor without any intervening penalties. He concluded that the Ministry was within its rights in so doing, since a provision to the effect that withdrawing a company's license should be done only as an extreme measure, although proposed, was not included in the Law of 1905 and the law in its final form did allow the government full option between the penalties provided in the law and the withdrawal of registration.

The second "matter of form" which Pichat presented was the question of whether Equitable's license should have been withdrawn before the Society had had a chance to present its case both in writing and at a hearing:

> There was indeed, on December 14, 1908, an official order, in response to the requirements of Article 7, but, in consequence of this order, by a letter of January 14, 1909, the Company wrote the Minister that it would conform to the injunction in the manner authorized by the home office; then it advised the Minister that it would establish individual accounts

totaling O franc. And, gentlemen, the decree [of March 25, 1909] was handed down without a new official order.

The Company's response certainly was not consonant with the law, but it was serious, it could have been discussed. We believe that following that offer, the Administration, finding it unacceptable, should have sent a new official order to the Company. The Company could well have believed that its offer had been accepted and that it did not have to furnish the means of defense prescribed by the law of 1905. We believe that in this regard there was an irregularity of procedure.

But we have dealt very quickly with matters of form, and it is solely on matters of substance that we very definitely request that you revoke the decree of March 25, 1909.[69]

It appears that Peixotto knew that Equitable's appeal was going to receive a favorable decision even before the *Conseil* acted formally, for in a letter of May 24, 1910, to Vice President Day, he spoke of "our success" and the arguments of French counsel "which have won the battle." Already he and Vice President Day were arguing over whose strategy had won the appeal.

On Saturday, May 28, 1910, the *Conseil d'État, "réuni en Assemblée Générale,"* sat on Equitable's appeal. After a number of "whereases" (*considérant que*), the *Conseil* declared that the purpose of Article 7 of the Law of 1905 was not merely to enact a regulatory measure, but also to impose on all companies a method of distribution of dividends absolutely different from the one provided in deferred dividend contracts such as Equitable had previously issued. These contracts, however, when issued, had violated no existing law, and the only condition under which the government could interfere with their operation would be if the new law, by a formal provision for retroactivity, in effect declared them null. Article 7, the *Conseil* decided, was not such a provision. It had no retroactive quality at all and could be applied to contracts already in effect only in so far as it created no change in contract provisions. The decree of March 25, 1909, which canceled Equitable's registration in France, was declared to be "in excess of power" and annulled.

The decision was not to be announced until the following Monday, but Maître Labbé telephoned Peixotto, who had worked long and hard on the case and had probably been more excited about it than anyone. Peixotto immediately took a piece of note paper and wrote in

[69] *Ibid.*, p. 19.

William Alexander
Secretary, 1880–1937

James C. Rocquet
Secretary General for Europe, 1904–1941

longhand to Rocquet, who was then away from Paris: "Most exceptional and satisfactory event . . . we have won. GOD BLESS THE EQUITABLE."[70] He said that he was going to Italy for a rest. To Peixotto, like the battle of Blenheim—" 'twas a famous victory."

Peixotto did not leave, however, until he took care of one more thing. Although the announcement of the annulment of the decree by the *Conseil d'État* did not appear in *Le Temps* and *Le Figaro* until June 4, Peixotto had a four-page pamphlet ready for distribution on June 1.[71]

The reasons for the success of Equitable's appeal can only be surmised. The State Department in Washington twice instructed our ambassadors in France to do everything possible to aid the Society, and Ambassador Henry White and his successor Robert Bacon had given the case their best attention and done effective work. Maître Labbé had presented the case well; his arguments were precise, clear, and logical. Then Vice President Day, who had handled the purchase of the interests of the French Panama Canal Company for the United States, was well versed in public law and helped direct the legal steps. Perhaps it was a matter of simple justice. After all, establishing retroactive requirements in regard to deposit of reserves on policies already written was one thing; making retroactive requirements which affected policy contracts previously made was another.[72]

On June 22, 1910, Equitable's French agents, the Directors General for Russia, Germany, and Holland, as well as government officials and other prominent guests, met at the Élysée Palace Hôtel to celebrate three important events: 1) the Society's fiftieth anniversary (which

[70] *Ibid.*

[71] Copy in *ibid.*

[72] The argument between Peixotto and Vice President Day in regard to whose strategy won the appeal was summarized in a long letter, Day to Peixotto, June 7 1910. In this letter Vice President Day cited Peixotto's letter of May 24, in which Peixotto had maintained that the Home Office argument was based on the fact that Article 7 of the Law of 1905 could not be applied to Equitable because the Society's deferred dividend plan did not provide for individual annual accounting; and that the argument used by Labbé had been based upon the fact that the law stated nowhere that it was to apply to policy contracts already written. Said Peixotto: "We confined our defense to that principle. . . . There is therefore a profound difference between our legal system and line of defense and those of our Home Headquarters including the one formulated in your cable of August 24th, 1908."

Day proceeded to set Peixotto right by summarizing the whole affair step-by-step and explaining that the basic "Home Headquarters" argument had never been other than that used by Labbé in presenting the appeal.

had not yet been celebrated in France); 2) the dedication of Equitable's new Paris building; and 3) "the memorable victory gained by the Company before the Council of State." Director General Peixotto reviewed the accomplishments of Equitable and introduced President Paul Morton: "Joy was in all the hearts and beamed on all faces." President Morton wondered whether France's influence on the world came most from its art, its literature, its pleasures, or its savings: "Its art is unique, its literature without equal, its temptations delicious, even when one resists them, and its sense of saving is too well known to make it necessary to insist upon it." How would one measure the wealth of the people of France, if to their sense of saving there was to be added the habit of life insurance? He made it clear that Equitable's policy in any country was to operate in absolute conformity to the laws and regulations of that country; if it did not think it was possible to do so it believed that it was more dignified to withdraw loyally from that country. He thanked especially Secretary General for Europe Rocquet, Director General Peixotto and Equitable's counsel, Ulrich and Labbé; also Messrs. Bouvard and Lalous, architects for Equitable's new Paris building.

Second Vice President George T. Wilson, who followed, as usual established immediate and intimate rapport between himself and his audience: "Knowing how to diversify his manner, going from 'the grave to the sweet, from the pleasant to the severe,' pleasantly mixing humor with serious matter, he succeeds by his facial expression and by all the outward manifestations of an art wherein he excels, to communicate to his attentive listeners, his intense love for the Equitable, his ardent desire to see it always greater and more prosperous." As Peixotto said, one saw manifested while listening to Wilson, that mysterious strength which passed from the chiefs to the soldiers and gave to the Equitable army its conquering power.

Maître Jean Labbé spoke briefly of the things he had learned about Equitable in handling the appeal of the *Conseil d'État,* and Dr. Alexandre Lacassagne, Professor of the Faculty of Medicine of Lyon and a Director of Equitable's Medical Department for France, spoke of Equitable's work in removing barriers between two great nations. He compared Equitable to the Gulf Stream, "an immense sea river" which brought with the waters of the Equator warmth and life to the coasts of France and England: "I see such a salutary and social influence in the advantages that our great Company pours out upon these two countries, bringing to them, as does the Gulf-Stream, the results of long experience, of formidable reserves and the demonstrated and unassailable strength of the largest life insurance company." The last toast at this dinner meeting posed by Peixotto was to the health of Equitable's policyholders. Everyone approved, and the dinner ended with a vibrant "Long live Morton." The following day, June 23, the agents held a business meeting in Equitable's new building on the Place de l'Opéra. Despite the fact that it was a year late, the Paris celebration of Equitable's fiftieth anniversary was one of the most interesting and stimulating.[73]

RECOVERY

Equitable's report for 1907 showed new business of only $69,491,044 (not including revivals, etc.), or about $13,000,000 less than for 1906, and the lowest for any year since 1883. As a result of the financial recession of 1907, the Society had had to write down some of its collateral loans. Even so, assets of the Society as of December 31, 1907, were $427,271,408 and the surplus was $48,176,790.[74] Much more encouraging was the fact that average interest realized on investments was 4.39 per cent as compared with 4.03 in 1905 and 3.90 in 1904; on securities alone the yield was 5.44. Many policyholders were helped to tide over the financial stringency by way of policy loans—about $9,000,000 in the last quarter alone. In 1908 the Society marketed $87,721,480 of new insurance, and assets rose to $472,339,509. During the year, the New York Insurance Department had examined the Equitable—the first examination since 1905. It noted that lapses were but one-third of what they had been in 1905, which seemed to indicate that "this company has recovered from the effects of the investigation and that it no longer indulges in high pressure methods"; also, that the Society

[73] The proceedings of this meeting were published in pamphlet form under the title *Réunion à Paris des Agents Français de l'Équitable.* The pamphlet carried the motto *"Pas pour un jour, mais pour toujours."*

[74] The figures are taken from the Society's Annual Statement. The surplus shown included unassigned surplus and dividend funds, but did not include capital stock. Dividend funds were not shown separately from unassigned surplus until 1909. Based on market value of securities held, assets were $432,647,703.

Governor Charles Evans Hughes, in his annual message to the legislature, January 6, 1909, thought it advisable that provision be made for the valuation of securities held by insurance companies upon a fairer basis, that is, with due regard to their investment value, so that the companies might be saved an apparent impairment owing to temporary fluctuations which did not represent actual losses. He thought that the plan adopted in 1908 for savings banks might be safely applied to insurance companies. Under this plan, securities not in default were valued at their investment value by amortization. He also recommended that the cost of examining insurance companies should be borne by the state rather than by the companies.

was well within the expense limitation established by the law of 1906. Attention was called, however, to the fact that there had been some inequality in the granting of surrender values to certain classes of free tontine policyholders, but this situation had been corrected. The Society was also criticized for permitting the President to make collateral loans under authority granted by the Board instead of making these loans through the Board or the Finance Committee: "The less such companies attempt to perform the functions of discount banks the less likely a recurrence of conditions developed in recent years." The report also called attention to the section of the law which required life companies "to fix the salaries of their officers at least every twelve months."

Grover Cleveland, trustee of the Ryan stock and chairman of the executive committee of The Association of Life Insurance Presidents, died in June 1908. His work during the last three years of his life had done much to restore the confidence of the people in life insurance; it constituted a most distinguished final chapter in a distinguished career. At the second annual meeting in December 1908, President Morton, who was still President of the Association, said:

> Mr. Cleveland came into the life insurance situation late in life—some years after he had twice been the victorious leader of his party and the Chief Executive of this great nation. At the time he was easily the first citizen of the country.
>
> His advent first as a Trustee of the Equitable and afterwards as Chairman and General Counsel of this Association met with the emphatic approbation of the American public because every one knew that in no way would Grover Cleveland wink at any wrong-doing, or in any way be connected with mal-administration.
>
> He was a grand old pilot taken on board a very important ship that was in danger among the rocks, and at once all on board were pacified and confidence fully restored.
>
> As Chairman of this Association he added character, dignity and probity to our cause, and he accepted the position more on account of its being a great public duty than for any other reason. He became intensely interested in the study of life insurance and its benefits, and was greatly impressed with the fact that it is one of the best institutions of civilization. . . .
>
> Grover Cleveland was a most conscientious man. He never for one moment hesitated as to what was right and what was wrong. His courage in doing right was no less than his courage in denouncing wrong.
>
> Mr. Cleveland was a patriot—not a partisan. His love of country was greater than his love of party. He frequently did things which he knew

would benefit the nation, and which he knew would not meet the approval of his party. If his own conscience told him a thing was right he acted and took the consequences. He never did things because they were expedient. His creed was that honesty was the best expediency in the long run. He never did things for temporary effect. He always had his eye on what was the best thing to do in the long run, and when once that conclusion was reached he followed his conviction.[75]

And the many obituaries in the press of the country paid sincere tribute to both the man and the statesman.

Robert Lynn Cox became executive officer of the Association to succeed Cleveland, but no replacement was made for Cleveland as trustee of the Ryan stock. Starting in 1908, the Association began electing its presidents annually.

More than 800 agents, officers, Home Office personnel, and guests assembled at the Waldorf-Astoria July 26–28, 1909, for Equitable's fiftieth anniversary celebration. After the usual welcomes, most of those participating enjoyed a steamboat excursion up the Hudson to West Point. On the second day, President Morton presided over a meeting of the agents at which Joseph Bowes of Baltimore and Charles Jerome Edwards, one of the Society's New York General Agents and president of the National Association of Life Underwriters, spoke. Bowes, speaking on "The Old Guard," paid a glowing tribute to the founders and builders of Equitable, and emphasized character as the most important asset held by these men: "Character is the only enduring thing in the world, and that is what the Old Guard stands for. The only permanent thing in the universe that will survive the wreck of matter and the crash of worlds is character." Edwards urged the elimination of the undesirable agent and unfair methods such as twisting. Second Vice President George T. Wilson presided over the afternoon session during which several speeches were made. On Wednesday, July 28, Henry L. Rosenfeld, Insurance Assistant to the President, presided over the meeting of agents while Edward A. Woods of Pittsburgh presided over the meeting of general agents and managers.

The semi-centennial jubilee culminated in a dinner in the great dining room of the Waldorf-Astoria on Wednesday evening, July 28; President Morton served as toastmaster. In his address, he made an

[75] *Proceedings of the Second Annual Meeting of The Association of Life Insurance Presidents,* held at New York, December 4 and 5, 1908, pp. 10–11.

important announcement to the effect that Equitable was working on a plan by which men and women in moderate circumstances might, by the means of life insurance, be enabled to purchase their own homes, and to provide against the loss of their homes in the event of early death. The plan had evolved as a result of Henry L. Rosenfeld's trip to England in 1908. While studying the insurance of British railway employees by a system of payroll deductions—which stimulated Equitable's interest in the development of group insurance—Rosenfeld also found that some of the British life companies had a system of "home purchase insurance," which they called a "plan to abolish rents." After reviewing Equitable's accomplishments during its first fifty years, President Morton said:

> There is a much greater sphere of usefulness in which I hope to see the Equitable do its full share. That sphere is to give protection to the people who cannot afford to carry a big line of life insurance. I refer to the artisan, to the man behind the plow, to those engaged in the humbler walks of life, to clerks who get their pay every month, to men and women who need protection against the contingencies to which they are subject, and by means of which protection they can be guarded against the disastrous results of illness or accident or improvident old age, or death.
>
> It is our intention, if it can be worked out (and we have no doubt that it can be), to so arrange that these men and women of moderate means, with only their daily or monthly wage—which in the majority of cases is so small as to preclude their accumulating a great competence—may by the means of life insurance as practiced by the Equitable purchase their own homes, and by a series of small monthly payments provide their own roofs for their families, while at the same time they provide against the loss of their homes in the event of early death.
>
> Insurance by the State is neither desirable nor necessary in this land of the greatest life insurance corporations the world has ever known. There is no work of more importance, no service of higher merit to be performed than that in which it is proposed that this company shall take the lead. In no other way can it so justify its mission and render a better account of itself than by pioneering in this field. Therefore, I am prepared to announce to you that we are carefully considering, and, unless prevented by the powers that be or obstacles not now seen, the future of the Equitable will embrace this very important work.[76]

Although President Morton was not to live to see the first Equitable policies to protect mortgages on homes, this announcement was the

[76] As reported in *The Weekly Underwriter*, LXXXI (1909), July 31.

beginning of the Home Purchase plan—later to be known as Assured Home Ownership.[77]

As a memento of the occasion, the little history entitled *The First Fifty Years of the Equitable Life Assurance Society of the United States* was distributed to agents and guests. Although this book bore the name of Paul Morton as author, it, as well as the other anniversary histories, was written by Secretary William Alexander.

On December 2, 1909, it was announced that J. P. Morgan had purchased Thomas F. Ryan's Equitable stock, "subject to the trust under which Grover Cleveland, Morgan J. O'Brien and George Westinghouse were made voting trustees for the benefit of the policy-holders." The reason for the sale was not stated, though it was known for some time that Ryan had been reducing and consolidating his varied interests.[78] During the four and a half years in which he had held the stock, Ryan had given the trustees a free hand. In March 1908 Cleveland, after admitting that he had originally been doubtful of Ryan's motives, said:

> You know that I became a trustee of the Equitable and that I am still one and I can say to you that from that day to this Thomas F. Ryan has not offered a suggestion nor has he approached the trustees directly or in-

[77] See this history, pp. 770–771, 1111.

[78] The number of shares purchased by Morgan was not mentioned in the press, nor was there any mention of Ryan's having earlier sold half of his Equitable stock to E. H. Harriman. Yet Harriman's biographer states that probably two or three years before Harriman's death (in 1909) he had succeeded "after persistent and long-continued negotiations" in buying one-half of Ryan's stock. George Kennan, *E. H. Harriman* (Cambridge, 1922), I, p. 421. No source is indicated for this statement. In his testimony before the Pujo Committee, J. P. Morgan said that he had paid Ryan about $3,000,000 for 510 shares of the stock. When asked why, he said: "I thought it was best to have that stock where there was no danger of its being divided up into small lots. Mr. Ryan had already sold half of it, and you could not tell. Mr. Harriman died a few months afterwards, and if that had gone into his estate you could not tell how it would have been divided." In regard to Ryan's ownership, Morgan said: "I only know that he owned it at one time." *Investigation of Financial and Monetary Conditions in the United States before a Subcommittee of the Committee on Banking and Currency* (Washington, 1913), Part 15, pp. 1070 ff.

If the trustees of the stock knew of Ryan's sale to Harriman they gave no evidence of that fact. Nor is there any mention in Equitable's corporate records of the transfer of any stock to Harriman. Whether Ryan repurchased the shares from Harriman before the latter's death or Morgan purchased them from the Harriman estate it is impossible to determine at this late date. The Harriman papers were burned in the Equitable fire of 1912 and Ryan's papers, if preserved, are not available.

directly. He is a man with ideas; nobody can gainsay that. I have asked him many times to give his opinion on various subjects, but he has never responded. . . . If he had not done what he did in Equitable nobody can tell what would have happened.[79]

And the same month President Morton said to the Society's Pittsburgh agents:

We have passed through so much grief the last three years, and have become so calloused to it, that I really believe six months of uninterrupted tranquillity would unfit your managing officers to conduct the society's affairs. If certain of the prominent yellow journals of this country would omit mentioning us unfavorably even for a few days I would feel much like apologizing to our friends, because censure from such a source can really be considered the highest praise. Under the head of troubles I take it that the principal item that you have now to contend with is the fact that one man owns the majority shares of our society; that he is being savagely attacked by the muckrakers as being a very bold and dangerous man. As you already know, the stock owned by him is in the hands of distinguished trustees. It is charged that the entire assets of the society are at the disposal of one man; that he dictates the investments that shall be made; that he dominates the management; that vast sums of money are already invested in the securities of companies in which he is interested, etc. The assets of the society are no more at the disposal of any one man than they are at the disposal of the editors of the newspapers making the attacks. The assets of the society are looked after by the finance committee; it takes a unanimous vote of that committee to buy or sell the society's assets, and never since the committee has been in existence has there been a transaction except by unanimous consent. The committee is not even in touch with the owner of the majority of the shares, and, to my knowledge, he has never made a suggestion to it. In fact, in no sense that I can behold is he in any way, shape or manner entitled to anything but commendation for his attitude toward the society. His position toward the society has been like the Monroe Doctrine—one of non-interference.[80]

Cleveland too seemed to have been happy with the Ryan-Equitable relationship, for he said to George F. Parker, secretary to the trustees:

On the whole, I have never been so well satisfied with any public service that it has fallen to my lot to render as with what I have been able

[79] In an interview with *The World*, quoted in *The Weekly Underwriter*, LXXVIII (1908), March 28.
[80] *The Weekly Underwriter*, LXXVIII (1908), March 14.

to do as trustee of the Equitable. Its results have more than repaid me for the labor and anxieties. I can now see that the scandals growing out of the insurance irregularities were really a manifestation of popular hysteria. Nothing could have been more fortunate than to have the situation met in the courageous way taken by Mr. Ryan. Looking back it is next to impossible to imagine what harm might have been done to confidence and credit had not some such action been taken in the nick of time.[81]

Although Ryan had promised Morton in 1905 not to sell his stock "except to the Society or under some plan for the benefit of the Society and its policyholders," he apparently did not consult either President Morton or the two other trustees before selling his stock.[82] On learning of the sale, President Morton said that "under Mr. Morgan's ownership of the majority stock of the society its affairs will be conducted as heretofore by its board of directors with an eye single to the interest of its policyholders. More than this there is nothing to be said." And Trustee Morgan J. O'Brien said that he did not know what Morgan's idea was in purchasing the stock but was quite positive that the transaction would result to the benefit of the policyholders:

I do not know what he intends to do, but I am of the opinion that either a stock or a policyholders' control would be better than the present system of joint control. Under the present system responsibility cannot be fixed. While I do not know just what is going to be done, it would not surprise me if the society would be made a mutual one and the affairs put in the hands of the policyholders. At the present time I do not know that any such step is contemplated. By making this society a mutual one it would be considerably benefited. I think that under that system the business would increase.[83]

Some of the more sensational newspapers made editorial inferences in regard to Morgan's motives. *The World,* of course, was thoroughly suspicious and said that what Morgan bought from Thomas F. Ryan "was not a majority of the stock of the Equitable Life Assurance Society but the privilege of controlling over $460,000,000 of other

[81] George F. Parker, "Cleveland and the Insurance Crisis," *McClure's Magazine,* XXXIII (1909), June.

[82] For Ryan's letter to Morton, June 26, 1905, see this history, p. 654.

[83] *The Weekly Underwriter,* LXXXI (1909), December 4.

people's money." It stated that the Morgan interests had long dominated the New York Life and now with the assets of Equitable in their possession they would wield what was probably the most tremendous financial power concentrated in the hands of any set of private individuals in the world: "Wall Street exists, not by reason of its own money, but by reason of other people's money." [84] There were rumors to the effect that Morgan was planning a merger of the banks and trust companies under his control with the National Bank of Commerce, Equitable Trust Company, and The Mercantile Trust Company, in which Equitable had had heavy interests, but Henry P. Davison of the firm of J. P. Morgan and Company said that there was absolutely no foundation to these rumors.[85] According to *The Wall Street Journal,* Morgan's purchase of control of Equitable brought two insurance companies, four national banks, seven trust companies, twelve railroads, and five industrial "trusts," with capital resources of $6,278,000,000 under control of a single private banking institution. This paper summarized the views on this development as falling into three types: 1) it would be a positive advantage to the financial and business world; 2) it was bound to be taken as a danger signal and such "colossal consolidations" were likely to stimulate agitation for limiting the power of financial institutions; and 3) the transfer of control of Equitable did not make much difference, except that Morgan control was better than Ryan control.[86] The most striking feature of the whole thing was that the transfer of stock was "received with almost unanimous expression of high approval." [87] *The New York Times* said that despite the fact that the world was inclined to look with apprehension upon the centering of so great a financial might in the hands of one man, nevertheless it was safe to say that no other man in the country, in acquiring a majority of the shares of Equitable, would have provoked so little criticism as J. P. Morgan:

He has all his life been acting in a trust relation to a multitude of individuals and interests. His pre-eminent fitness and worthiness for such service have been established so conclusively that it can readily be understood that any policyholder of the Equitable might prefer to trust Mr. Morgan's judgment rather than the collective judgment of his fellow policy-

84 In editorials in issues of December 3 and 5, 1909.
85 *The Wall Street Journal,* December 4, 1909.
86 *Ibid.,* December 6, 1909.
87 "Holland's Letter," in *ibid.,* December 8, 1909.

holders in choosing the persons immediately in control of the administration of the Society.[88]

The consensus was that the transfer of the Ryan stock to Morgan had been a voluntary and harmonious transaction, quite in contrast to the circumstances which led to James H. Hyde's sale of the stock to Ryan in 1905.

News of the stock transfer led to rumors that President Morton might be replaced by George W. Perkins, Morgan's right-hand man and Vice President of the New York Life, but Henry P. Davison, one of the partners in J. P. Morgan and Company, said that he knew nothing of such plans nor did Perkins.[89] Another story had it that Morgan proposed to have George B. Cortelyou, President of the Consolidated Gas Company and former Secretary of the Treasury of the United States, made President of Equitable at the Board meeting March 1, 1910.[90] In regard to a possible change in the presidency, President Morton said: "That is a matter entirely for the directors, and on which up to the present time I am not informed." [91]

When Superintendent of Insurance William H. Hotchkiss called upon Morgan in the endeavor to find out the latter's plans, Morgan said that he had purchased the stock to prevent its being sold to different individuals and thus being used to the detriment of the policyholders. He expressed the hope that the control of Equitable stock could be put outside any existing or future financial situation and thus end for all time the danger which lurked in an individual holding. Two years later, when testifying before a Congressional committee (the Pujo Committee) which was investigating the "money trust," he said merely that he thought the Equitable stock would be better taken care of in his hands than in the hands of others.

The trust deed drawn up by Ryan in 1905 expired June 15, 1910. In March it was reported that Morgan, who then held about 60 per cent of Equitable's stock, was considering a plan to mutualize the Society; it was understood that Governor Hughes, as well as the Insurance Department, had been consulted. The big question was: "How can the Equitable be mutualized so as to have the mutualization equitable." December 31, 1910, a new trust agreement was drawn up

88 *The New York Times*, December 4, 1909.
89 *The Wall Street Journal*, December 4, 1909.
90 *Ibid.*, December 6, 1909 (editorial).
91 *Ibid.*, December 4, 1909.

for five years; it was identical with the Ryan trust except that the agreement might be canceled at any time by Morgan to permit him to carry out a permanent plan of mutualization. The trustees were Morgan J. O'Brien, George W. Perkins, and Lewis Cass Ledyard.

Once again, in 1909, a troublesome suit against the Society for control of its surplus was settled. J. Wilcox Brown had sued in 1905 on behalf of himself and 560,000 policyholders for a general accounting and the appointment of a receiver for the Society. He claimed that the Society had been extravagantly managed and that the policyholders were entitled to more of the surplus. In January 1906 the United States Circuit Court for the Southern District of New York had dismissed the case on a demurrer, but in February 1907 the United States Court of Appeals for the Second Circuit held that the Society should be required to answer the charges. When the United States Supreme Court reviewed the case in March 1909, it held that the relation between the insurer and the insured was that of conditional debtor and creditor, and not of trustee and *cestui que* trust. Even though a policy provided that the insurer would pay at the end of a tontine period not only the face value but such equitable share of the surplus as might be apportioned to such policy, the general rule was that the insured was not entitled to an accounting in equity unless he could show fraud or mistake. The court reversed the decision of the lower court and ruled that Brown had failed to allege a cause of action and that he was entitled to neither an accounting nor the appointment of a receiver.[92]

The recovery in the Society's business which became evident in 1908 continued in 1909 and 1910. Second Vice President George T. Wilson had been busy on both sides of the Atlantic and added many agents. Though it was possible to sell increasing amounts of life insurance, the old problem of lapses still remained. In the autumn of 1910, President Morton emphasized to the agents the importance of "conservation of insurance" and asked them to unite in a campaign of education. He told them that the most important thing to the company was a loyal army of policyholders; not only should the agents look after their own clients but after the interests of all policyholders. "The man who has been insured by some other agent and then surrenders his policy can do you as much harm as a deserter from your own ranks." At the same time President Morton had directed his assistant, Henry L.

[92] *Equitable Life Assurance Society* v. *Brown,* 213 U.S. 25.

Rosenfeld, to make an exhaustive study of a type of insurance especially designed "for industrial institutions and pension funds"—which would soon lead Equitable into the field of group insurance.

The Society's report for 1910 showed new business of $111,381,126 and total insurance in force of $1,347,158,692; assets were $494,715,923 and the total surplus had risen to $85,095,459. The policy of broadening the geographic distribution of the Society's investments had continued and the percentage of mortgage loans in the southern and western states had increased perceptibly; investments in first class railroads had passed a quarter of a billion dollars. Gross yield on investments for 1910 was 4.48 per cent, an increase of almost one-half of 1 per cent since 1905. During the year, the Board had authorized the Society to introduce the Home Purchase Plan of insurance, which had been mentioned by President Morton at the fiftieth anniversary dinner. Loans were to be restricted to buildings ready for occupancy, and two forms of policies were issued for the Plan: 1) an Endowment Policy which would provide for cancellation of the mortgage at the end of ten, fifteen, or twenty years or in the event of the prior death of the insured; and 2) an Ordinary Life Policy with sinking fund features which provided for repayment of the loan at the end of ten, fifteen, or twenty years, and in the event of the death of the insured, for cancellation of the mortgage. Any excess of insurance over the unpaid amount of the mortgage was to be paid to the beneficiary. These policies carried monthly premium payments if desired. The amount of Home Purchase loans was not large in the early years but was to grow in importance with time.

A number of persons who had been connected with Equitable's history left the scene in 1909 and 1910. Jose Francisco de Navarro, the last surviving original director of the Society, died early in 1909. Actuary Joel G. Van Cise, who had joined Equitable as a bookkeeper in 1865 and became Actuary of the Society in 1898, resigned early in 1910 owing to ill health; he was appointed Consulting Actuary. Dr. William R. Bross, chief Medical Director, who had succeeded Dr. Edward W. Lambert in February 1904, died in November 1910. His successor was Dr. Franklin C. Wells.

January 19, 1911, President Morton died suddenly of a heart attack; he had presided that day at a meeting of the Board of Directors. Though to outward appearances a large and strong man, Morton had known for some time that he had heart trouble. He had sought to increase his policy with Equitable so as to arrange for a $50 Christmas gift each year to his four grandchildren, but had been refused additional insurance. An arrangement was made, however, by which the gifts were provided for out of the existing policy. Though to some persons Paul Morton appeared to be a rather formidable personality, he was, in intimate circles, a charming and affectionate man. Less than a year before his death, he had written his wife on his fifty-third birthday: "This is the day I was born fifty three years removed. When a man reaches the beginning of the sere yellow period he begins to wonder why—He was born at all? What he has accomplished? and How much longer he is going to be here?" He said he had accomplished little compared to what he should have accomplished, that as a boy he was mentally lazy and did not study or realize the value of study; only after he understood the responsibilities of life did he make much effort. And whatever he had accomplished had been owing in large part to his wife's affection and interest. He concluded: "My expectancy of life by mortality tables is about 19 years longer. I wonder what our lot will be during this period. Only time can tell." [93]

Paul Morton had assumed the grave and difficult responsibilities of chief executive officer of the Equitable at a critical time in its history. He had performed a valuable service. In five and a half years not only had the Society been reorganized and put on a sound business basis but the confidence of its policyholders and the public throughout the world had been firmly and permanently established. Thomas Fortune Ryan's comments on Morton are worth noting. Once, when asked how he came to "choose" Morton for the presidency of Equitable, he said:

> I never did that. It may interest you to know that when I took Mr. Morton into my business affairs I neither knew him nor was I certain just what place he could or would fill. I was engaged in large ventures and needed somebody to take off my hands many details. I had known Mr. Morton's father, and his own work had attracted my attention. From the first day I placed the utmost confidence in his competence and honesty, and I now tell you that during all my manifold activities I have not come into contact with a man who at every turn gave me such a feeling of satisfaction as did Paul Morton. . . .[94]

Said *The New York Times:*

[93] Letter to "My dear Charlotte," May 22, [1910]. Morton family letters, Equitable Archives.

[94] George F. Parker, "Grover Cleveland's One Business Venture," *The Saturday Evening Post*, CXCVI (1924), March 29.

Paul Morton, President of the Equitable Life Assurance Society, brought with him when he was called to New York to head that institution and still the strife which had rent it in twain, the reputation of an administrator, competent at once to plan the broad policy of a great concern and at the same time to enter into the details which make so much for efficient management. . . .

From the day Mr. Morton arrived in New York the troubles of the Equitable began to fade into the background. Though it had suffered more severely than any of the insurance companies it has now for two or three years been completely rehabilitated. . . .

Personally he was a man who charmed all who came near him. Well over six feet in height and well proportioned, there was business-like directness about him that inspired trust in all his doings and sayings.

To his subordinates and those who came in contact with him he was considerate in every way, but as he worked hard himself and went straight to the point so he expected his visitors and associates to treat him with the same outspoken directness and honesty of word and purpose.[95]

[95] *The New York Times,* January 20, 1911.

9

Fire, War, Pestilence

> *It is a common saying that corporations have no souls to save nor bodies to kick, but we of the Equitable believe that it is possible at least for a life insurance company to have both a heart and a soul, and to show it in its relations with the policy-holders and the public.*—William A. Day, 1912
>
> *A life insurance policy is the insured's covenant with society that he will contribute to higher standards of life by increasing the future opportunities of his own dependents.*—*William A.* Day, 1927
>
> *For a thousand years the world will marvel as it reads the story of the days we are seeing one by one go by.*—Charles F. Nesbit, 1917

Since under the By-Laws of the Society Vice President William A. Day had assumed the duties of the President after the death of President Morton, the Board of Directors at its annual meeting, February 16, 1911, decided to defer the election of a President and Vice President "for the reason that the period which has elapsed since the death of the late President has not been sufficient to give the matter proper consideration." Other officers, however, were reappointed, and Robert Henderson, Assistant Actuary, was made Actuary to fill the vacancy caused by the resignation, on account of ill health, of Actuary Joel G. Van Cise in February 1910.

During the next month various persons were mentioned in the press as possible successors to President Morton, but many in the financial community surmised that George W. Perkins, no longer a Morgan partner or Vice President of New York Life, would be the man chosen. When the directors met on April 20, it was thought that they would again decline to take action since J. P. Morgan, who was in Europe, advised delay, and Superintendent of Insurance William H. Hotchkiss, who at his request had been invited to attend the meeting, suggested postponing the election of the President pending the consummation of a plan to mutualize the Society. On the recommendation of "Judge" Thomas Spratt and the Nominating Committee, however, the Board elected William Alonzo Day to the presidency of Equitable. After the election, the Board issued the following statement:

At their meeting to-day the board of directors, after careful consideration, decided that it was against the interests of the policyholders that the position of president should longer remain vacant. They accordingly proceeded to an election, with the result that Vice-President William A. Day was unanimously elected to the office.

The directors also voted to continue the Special Committee on Mutualization, appointed pursuant to a resolution adopted at the January meeting, consisting of Messrs. Spratt, Witherbee, Kernan, Mather, and Joy Morton, and also unanimously adopted the following resolution on the subject of mutualization:

'Resolved, that it is the sense of this Board that mutualization, as suggested by Superintendent Hotchkiss in his letter of January 18 to Mr. Morgan, is desirable; viz: in a manner that will avoid protracted litigation or substantial reduction of the free surplus of the Society, and that the Committee on Mutualization continue to co-operate with the Superintendent of Insurance, the trustees and Mr. Morgan to that end.'

This committee, in consultation with Superintendent of Insurance Hotchkiss, have had several meetings with Mr. Morgan's trustees, at which various suggestions looking toward the complete mutualization of the Society have been discussed. Notwithstanding the disposition of all concerned to favor mutualization, it has been found impracticable to carry the negotiations to a definite conclusion in view of Mr. Morgan's absence in Europe, to say nothing of the grave and difficult questions involved. A majority of the present directors are policyholders, who were elected by the votes of the policyholders, and the Board and President Day, who joins his associates in favoring mutualization, may be counted upon to earnestly co-operate in an effort to bring about some plan of mutualization which will be fair and just to the policyholders and to all of the interests concerned.

The reforms in the interest of the policyholder which signalized the administration of Paul Morton will be perpetuated. The Society is and will be conducted in the spirit of the laws which have been placed on the statute books to secure justice to every member. The aim will be to make the administration more efficient and economical. The policy of investing the Society's funds in the territories where the premiums come from will be maintained. To furnish the best insurance at the lowest cost epitomizes the purpose of the management. Policyholders will be faithfully and frankly advised of all features of the Society's business by the largest measure of publicity attainable. The practice of having unbiased and independent audit of accounts by public accountants will be continued. The highest rates of interest on investments consistent with absolute safety will be sought, which, with the policy of retrenchment, should increase the dividends on policies.[1]

"Judge" Day was born in Wilmington, Delaware, on June 11, 1850, the son of Isaac and Mary Lowe Day. Little is known about his early education, but he did attend the Harvard Law School for one year (September 1871 to June 1872). He began the practice of law at Champaign, Illinois, and served two terms in the Illinois house of representatives. In 1883 he was elected Mayor of Champaign and the following year served as a delegate to the Democratic National Convention. It is probable that his work for the nomination of Cleveland in that convention led to his appointment by the President as Second Auditor of the United States Treasury Department in charge of Army, Navy, and Indian affairs; he served in this office from 1885 to 1889.[2] In 1900 Day became Special Assistant to the Attorney General of the United States to aid in the preparation of civil and criminal cases which arose under the Interstate Commerce Act. He helped prepare the case against the Northern Securities Company, which was decided in favor of the Government in 1904 and which at the time was regarded as a great victory for President Theodore Roosevelt, then at the height of his trust-busting career. In this case Day participated in the examination of James J. Hill, J. P. Morgan, and E. H. Harriman. In 1903 President Roosevelt asked Congress to create the position of Assistant to the Attorney General and it was reported that he had Day in mind for this position. As Assistant to the Attorney General, Day worked on the title problems in connection with the Panama Canal project and in 1904 went to Paris as head of the mission to arrange transfer of title and payment of $40,000,000 to the new Panama Company for its rights and work done on the canal. To enhance the prestige of J. P. Morgan and Company in Europe, he had Morgan appointed as Commissioner to make the payment. The same

[1] *The Eastern Underwriter*, XII (1911), April 27.

[2] Thomas I. Parkinson, later President of Equitable, was positive in his statement that as Second Auditor Day possessed judicial authority and that it was from this office that the title of "Judge" derived. Various interviews with the author, 1955–57. Parkinson was former Dean of the Columbia University Law School and had served in various capacities in Washington as well.

year he was sent to Alaska by President Roosevelt to investigate complaints of oppression of the people by government officials, particularly the judiciary. Thus, when he was brought to Equitable by President Morton in 1905 as Comptroller of the Society, William A. Day had handled problems which involved railroads, finance, the antitrust laws, and international public law.

President Day was a quiet and modest man; he did not think his services had been important enough to warrant publication of articles about him, nor did he have a recent photograph to supply either the press or Equitable agents. He had a gentle sense of humor but could on occasion be firm almost to the point of stubbornness. He wrote the agents: "The reforms which signalized the administration of the last five years will be perpetuated. The ground gained in this respect will be steadfastly maintained. There will be no backward steps." And about a year later: "In whatever degree my administration merits approbation, it is because I and my fellow officers and directors have wholeheartedly devoted ourselves to the task of bringing the policyholder into his own. That work will go on untiringly."

Early in 1912 President Day brought in John B. Lunger, who was Vice President of Travelers, as Vice President of the Society in charge of agency affairs; Auditor Leon O. Fisher was made Third Vice President in charge of Home Office administration; and Henry L. Rosenfeld became Assistant to the President. George T. Wilson remained as Second Vice President and devoted most of his time to foreign business. The following year Alfred R. Horr, former Vice President of the Cleveland Trust Company, was appointed Treasurer of the Society to succeed C. E. Phelps, who had resigned. In 1914 Rosenfeld was made Fourth Vice President and given charge of the foreign agencies as well as supervision of the Group, Home Purchase, and Monthly Premium Departments. John Van Etten Westfall, who had been in the Auditor's Department since 1907, became Assistant Third Vice President in 1913 and Assistant to the President in 1916. Westfall was a graduate of Cornell and held a Ph.D. degree in mathematics from the University of Leipzig. He was teaching mathematics in the University of Iowa when his friend Leon O. Fisher persuaded him to join Haskins and Sells and later Equitable. President Day was proud of his official staff; in 1917 he said: "Each has performed the task assigned to him and has co-operated with the other officers to put the Equitable upon its present plane. I presume that it is true a hypercritical person must find something to criticize in each, but taking them by and large I would not exchange them for the staff of any other company, life insurance or otherwise."

EQUITABLE PIONEERS IN GROUP INSURANCE

Although President Morton had announced in July 1909 that Equitable was considering a plan by which people would be protected by life insurance in the purchase of their homes, the Home Purchase Plan did not go into effect until July 1911. After consideration by the Committee on Insurance and a Special Committee of the Board of Directors a plan was submitted October 18, 1910. It provided for loans which should normally be limited to 50 per cent of the Society's appraisal of the property—but in no event to exceed 66⅔ per cent—at an interest rate of 6 per cent. Loans were to be restricted to those made on properties completed and ready for occupancy, and preferences should be given to applicants who lived in, or carried on business in, the property to be mortgaged. Home Purchase loans were to be placed through building and loan associations, trust companies, title guaranty companies, savings banks, responsible brokers, real estate agents, or attorneys; these agencies might charge the usual fee for placing a loan. The mortgage would be covered by either an endowment policy or an ordinary life policy with sinking fund features; in either instance the mortgage would be limited to a maximum of twenty years. If the borrower died before the mortgage matured, any excess of the insurance over the unpaid amount of the mortgage would be paid in cash. In the early years at least, the Home Purchase Plan would be limited to such cities or towns in the United States and Canada as the President might designate. The real estate transactions and appraisals would be put under the direction of the Comptroller and the insurance part in charge of an officer to be selected by the President. The Board of Directors, after specifying that the interest rate should be "not less than 6 per cent," adopted the report October 20, 1910.[3]

Though the idea of protecting home loans with life insurance was not strictly new, Equitable's Home Purchase Plan was new.[4] The

[3] Corporate Records, Equitable Archives.

[4] For Henry B. Hyde's plan for protecting home mortgages, see this history, p. 377.

The Insurance Monitor for February 1893 stated that "The Prudential's New Feature" for 1893 was a combination of life and building-loan policy which would be a special boon to the Industrial classes with which Prudential did much of its business. The policy was labeled "Yearly Renewable Reducing Term Policy or Building Loan Policy." This policy was not exactly comparable to those used under the Equitable Home Purchase Plan. It provided only term insurance, the face

Home Purchase business was relatively small in the early years, but later as Assured Home Ownership (A.H.O.) was to become an important part of Equitable's business.

With the "Progressive Movement" and its "quest for social justice" in the early 1900's, came ideas of government-sponsored social reform and government responsibility for the amelioration of the conditions under which people live and work; individualism and *laissez faire* were to be replaced by paternalism and governmental promotion of the general well-being. Laws for workmen's compensation, unemployment compensation, and even state life insurance were being enacted by the states; some states were even considering public pension systems. But there were those who did not agree that the only limitation upon the powers of government should be its ability to do good. As Henry L. Rosenfeld said: "State solution of the social and economic problems of society is impossible in this country." [5] Hence it was incumbent upon life insurance, which had shown its ability to serve the individual and the family, to show its ability to serve the group.

---

amount decreasing annually to correspond with the decreasing balance of the loan which was secured, on a mortgage, from a building and loan association. Under the Equitable plan the insured received both the mortgage loan and the life insurance from the Equitable, and the insurance was on a permanent level amount plan for the original face of the loan.

When Henry L. Rosenfeld went to England in December 1908, he found a number of companies in London which were called "House Purchase Companies." These were life companies which specialized in the house purchase plan of insurance and Rosenfeld said that they were the ones "from which our 'Home Purchase Plan' is the direct outcome." Rosenfeld also knew about the plan which had been in use by the United Security Life Insurance and Trust Company of Philadelphia for a number of years. He never claimed to be the "father" of the Home Purchase idea. Rosenfeld to Alfred R. Horr, February 17, 1921. Copy in Controllers files, Equitable Archives.

In 1923, one Richard Alfred Uhalt of New Orleans filed suit in Federal district court against Equitable for $5,000,000. He claimed that in 1909 he had had his "homestead plan" copyrighted and that Equitable had distributed more than a million copies of his plan and lent $46,000,000 on it after changing the name to "Home Purchase Plan." *The New Orleans Item,* May 21, 1923, and *The Times-Picayune,* May 22, 1923. Uhalt died September 22, 1924, and his heirs, through their lawyers, offered to settle for $10,000. The case was argued twice on preliminary matters and the attempt to force Equitable to produce all its records on all Home Purchase policies issued to date and its advertising literature was successfully resisted. The case was finally settled in June 1927 for $1,000. The fee of Equitable's local counsel in New Orleans was $2,500. Correspondence on this case may be found in the closed legal files of the Law Department, Equitable Archives.

5 "Life Insurance as a Factor in the Solution of Sociological Problems," a lecture delivered at Adelbert College, March 14, 1912. Pamphlet copy in Equitable Archives.

Group insurance, like many other important ideas, did not spring into being spontaneously and fully developed at any given instant. In fact, the idea had a considerable background history prior to 1911. In 1823 the Louisiana Insurance Company insured the safe delivery of 72 slaves from Norfolk to New Orleans in the amount of $25,200. In 1854 five life insurance companies insured the safe delivery of 720 Chinese coolies from China to Panama for construction work on the Panama Railway.[6] Since fourteen of the coolies died or jumped overboard, the five underwriting companies paid a total of $1,633. Though the policies which covered these coolies were written as life insurance policies, they were insuring property rather than lives since the indemnity went to the owners or shippers. In 1861 one of the German life insurance companies issued instructions to its agents in regard to insuring societies, clubs, and other types of organizations without medical examinations, premiums to be collected by the head of the group. In 1872 an Ohio agent of the Metropolitan Life suggested that his company issue blanket coverage, without physical examinations, for the workers in a mill or factory: "Make the bookkeeper or foreman or paymaster . . . the agent. Let him retain from the pay or collect from each insured, at the end of each month, the premium due."[7] Though President Joseph Fairchild Knapp of Metropolitan was much interested in "insurance for the masses" and had several "thinkers" at work on the subject, nothing came of the agent's brilliant idea.

Some writers have classified certain of the accident policies written in the 1890's as group insurance but the premiums on these policies were paid entirely by the employees.[8] Then in the same period the

[6] The companies were the New England Mutual and The Manhattan Life Insurance Company, which underwrote one-fourth of the total risk of $84,000; the Howard Life (one-fourth); Aetna of Hartford (one-fourth); the Knickerbocker Life (one-eighth); and the New England Life (one-eighth). The premium on Manhattan Life's $21,000 risk was $840. For a reproduction of the original policy, which Manhattan Life's historian calls "the first group policy ever written by an American company," see Wendell Buck, *The Manhattan Life Insurance Company of New York, 1850–1950* (New York, 1950).

[7] Quoted in Marquis James, *The Metropolitan Life*, p. 53.

[8] For the court cases involving these policies, see Earl T. Crawford and Samuel P. Harlan, *The Law of Group Insurance* (Rochester, New York, 1936), and Louise Wolters Ilse, *Group Insurance and Employee Retirement Plans* (New York, 1953), p. 35.

The chief sources for the study of the early years of Equitable group insurance are the papers of Henry L. Rosenfeld; the compilation of data on group insurance in Equitable by Alexis R. Wiren made during 1958–59; and the "Reminiscences of William J. Graham" recorded in 1960. All of these documents are in the Equitable

Provident Clerks Life Insurance Company of England inaugurated a plan for insuring the employees of the British railways through a system of payroll deductions. President James W. Alexander of Equitable was acquainted with this insurance plan in the early 1900's, for he discussed it by letter with Vice President James H. Hyde in 1903. He said that he had never been willing to insure a lot of people without reference to physical condition, but since Equitable had "crossed the Rubicon" in insuring impaired risks, he thought the plan might be looked into and the idea kept alive. He suggested that the arguments pro and con might be lined up and studied, but advised Hyde to approve nothing if any doubts existed; it would be fatal to make a mistake and Equitable would do much better doing a sound small business than a risky large one. He concluded: "If this thing does materialize it will be the first time I have ever seen a proposition to do life insurance business by wholesale turn out to be practicable. I rather feel in my bones that the thing will not prove feasible, but this is not an opinion on the merits of it. It would be well for us to imagine another company doing it and how their action would strike us as competitors." [9]

President Alexander did not mention the fact that already Equitable had insured a group of persons with only superficial medical examinations, for in November 1902 some 600 of the Society's Home Office employees had been given $1,000 policies, the premiums to be paid by the Society as long as the employee remained in its employ.[10] In

---

Archives. The Rosenfeld papers, though not extensive, are very important for the early years of group insurance. Alexis R. Wiren, for many years Director of Methods and Planning in Equitable's Group Department, in 1958 at the suggestion of Secretary Gordon K. Smith began to assemble and collate materials available in Equitable's various archives which dealt with group insurance. The more than 400 typescript pages constitute not only an inventory of the materials but a chronological account of Equitable's group insurance from 1908 to 1959. It was also at the suggestion of Secretary Smith that William J. Graham, who had more to do than any other individual with the actuarial processes and early sales of group insurance, dictated his memoir in 1960. This memoir of some 370 typed pages, despite a certain amount of repetition and a lack of organization, contains information on the early years of group insurance not available elsewhere. The subject of group insurance in general is well covered in Louise Wolters Ilse, *Group Insurance and Employee Retirement Plans* (New York, 1953).

9 James W. Alexander (in Venice) to James H. Hyde, April 2, 1903. Hyde papers, case P 12.

10 Henry L. Rosenfeld later spoke of the medical examinations of the employees as being "lenient." Memorandum to President Day, April 17, 1912. Rosenfeld papers, Equitable Archives. The employee insurance plan is described in *The Equitable News*, No. 36 (December 1902).

the event of death one half of the amount of insurance became payable to any designated beneficiary, and the other half went into a fund to be used by the officers for pensions or in other ways to provide for living employees who had grown old or infirm in the service of the Society. Vice President James H. Hyde had been especially interested in this employee insurance project as a means of recognition of faithful and efficient service. Then in 1905 Equitable, under three separate contracts, insured 315 employees of the United Cigar Stores Company. This was individual insurance and the premiums were paid entirely by the company.[11]

President Morton had learned of the Provident Clerks arrangement with the leading British railway companies by way of a prospectus in the autumn of 1908. Under this plan the premiums on the insurance, which was voluntary, were paid entirely by the employees; the railroad company merely gave its approval and collected the monthly premiums by payroll deductions. Since he had been a railroad executive, President Morton thought the plan might be applicable to American railroads, so he sent Henry L. Rosenfeld, his Insurance Assistant, to England to observe its operation.[12] Rosenfeld's report was favorable

[11] The three policies covered 35 employees of the United Cigar Stores Company of Rhode Island for $35,750; 45 employees of the United Cigar Stores Company of Illinois for $47,000; and 235 employees of the United Cigar Stores Company of New Jersey for $259,750. The individual employees made application for the term insurance on a special form and furnished medical examinations. The insurance coverage would terminate when the individuals left the employ of the company or reached the age of sixty-five. New lives were added from time to time until July 1923 when the United Cigar Stores Company adopted an Aetna contributory group life program on 5,000 lives. By that time, it appears that Equitable had insured some 788 lives of employees of the United Cigar Stores Company. Rosenfeld memorandum to Graham, October 10, 1927. Rosenfeld papers, Equitable Archives. When United Cigar Stores adopted the group plan in 1923, it was arranged that the employees insured under the Equitable contract had the privilege of continuing their insurance if they assumed the individual premiums required. Of the original 315 lives, 196 were still covered in 1910; 99 in 1920, and 10 in 1930.

[12] Dr. Lee K. Frankel, scientist turned sociologist, and Miles M. Dawson, consulting actuary, had also been sent to Europe in 1908—by the Russell Sage Foundation—to study working men's insurance. Frankel doubted whether the industrial insurance companies in the United States were doing all they could in taking care of the needs of the working man, and thought that some broader insurance plans might be pioneered by a philanthropic organization such as the Russell Sage Foundation. As a result of a talk made before the National Civic Federation in New York December 15, 1908, Frankel was invited to join the Metropolitan Life, where he set up the welfare department—and later became a Vice President. About the same time, Robert W. de Forest, corporation lawyer, railroad President, and head of the Russell Sage Foundation, was elected a Director of Metropolitan. President Haley Fiske had convinced both Frankel and de Forest that any new and broader in-

and the Insurance Committee of the Board approved (April 19, 1909) the creation of a new department to be called "The Equitable Industrial Branch." The department was established by executive order of President Morton April 26, and Rosenfeld was appointed head; it was to include Monthly Premium and Home Purchase plans and to continue investigation of the subject of group insurance.

The following year Rosenfeld suggested the possibility of Equitable's rounding out its insurance coverage so as to include old age pensions, employers' liability insurance, and disability and sickness insurance, "which would enable . . . corporations desiring to make any or all of the above provisions [as well as life insurance] for its employees, to do so under one blanket form of policy with the company." [13] At this time, Rosenfeld was cooperating with the National Association of Manufacturers in the study of employers' liability insurance and spoke on this subject at the annual meeting of the Association in May 1910.[14]

---

surance coverage for the "poor man in this country was better served by an insurance company of this type than any other new form of organization." The results of the 1908 European visit of Frankel and Dawson were published by the Sage Foundation in 1910 under the title *Working Men's Insurance in Europe*. *The Insurance Record* (March 30, 1927) in commenting upon this work stated that in 1911 Metropolitan had "brought out a group insurance plan on the lines of that now in familiar use." Metropolitan's first group policy—on some 17,500 of its own employees—was issued in 1914, but no outside group business was done until 1917. See Marquis James, *The Metropolitan Life*, p. 201.

13 Memorandum to President Morton, May 18, 1910. Rosenfeld papers, Equitable Archives.

14 Rosenfeld's paper was titled, "Co-operation and Compensation versus Compulsion and Compromise in Employers' Liability." After pointing out the difficulties of the employer's handling his own liability insurance, Rosenfeld concluded that such insurance could best be handled by a stock company operated upon the mutual principle. He said that President Paul Morton of Equitable had a keen desire "to place the services of his company at the disposal of the manufacturers and others, in performing this important public function, feeling that by so doing one of the great American life insurance companies can in largest measure fulfill its usefulness and render the greatest service."

As a result of this address, William J. Graham, Vice President and Actuary of the Northwestern National Life (Minneapolis) and soon to play a very important part in the history of group insurance, wrote Rosenfeld: "Permit me to offer congratulations on your recent treatment of 'Employers' Liability' . . . I have heard this proposition tackled vaguely by actuaries and thinking men galore, without apparent hope for a solution, which leads me to rejoice that through the initiative of yourself and the Equitable the problem is undergoing a critical analysis and is in prospect for vigorous treatment." Graham to Rosenfeld, May 26, 1910. *Ibid.*

Rosenfeld made another trip to Europe, later in 1910, to study the operation of employers' liability insurance in England, Germany, etc.

In October 1910, Equitable—as well as several other companies—received an inquiry from Montgomery Ward and Company of Chicago as to whether the Society could offer an insurance plan for employees which would provide death benefits, disability benefits, and annuities at a cost of 4 per cent of the payroll. This plan was intended to replace the modest protection offered by the Clerks Benefit Society which was managed by the employees. Owing to the composite nature of the requirements, Equitable decided that such a plan was not feasible, and Rosenfeld so notified Montgomery Ward by letter February 1, 1911.[15]

Meanwhile, November 29, 1910, the Society's Assistant Secretary, S. S. McCurdy, wrote Superintendent William H. Hotchkiss of the New York Insurance Department as follows:

> The Society has been approached by a large mercantile house of this city [it is probable that this referred to Montgomery Ward] which desires to place insurance upon the lives of all of its employees, the premiums on the insurance to be paid by the corporation but the insurance to be for the benefit of the family of the employee. In order to handle this business with the utmost simplicity, the Society has devised the enclosed form of employee's policy, which we desire to submit to the Department for its consideration and approval. We enclose with the policy a copy of the application to be used in connection therewith (individual applications will be taken from each employee insured), together with a copy of a form of certificate to be given by the Society to each employee. The object of a blanket policy is to save expense and labor in the handling of the business. We also enclose a blank page of the register referred to in the contract, which can be attached to the policy in order that the requirements of Section 58 of the Insurance Law may be met.
>
> We may add that this business will be written at the Society's regular premium rates for whatever form of policy is selected.
>
> The proof certificates enclosed are simply the draft forms. We enclose samples of a certificate at present in connection with a similar policy which has been outstanding upon the Society's books for many years, to show the general scheme proposed.

[15] George R. Durgan, attorney in charge of Montgomery Ward's welfare program, who later claimed much credit for originating group insurance, wrote in 1955 that he had tried to get Rosenfeld to "get action over my ideas of the possibility of insuring the lives of the employees of Montgomery Ward and Company as a group: Mr. Rosenfeld told me I was *chasing an ephemeris; that I had not proposed an insurable idea.*" Durgan to President Ray D. Murphy, July 14, 1955, Equitable Archives. Durgan did not mention the fact that the original proposals included much more than "insuring the lives" of the employees.

If this form meets with your approval, we shall appreciate the courtesy if you can advise us promptly, in order that we may proceed with the negotiations with the corporation in question. Several out-of-state companies are in competition for this business, and we are anxious, of course, to land it if we can.

The Department requested some minor changes, which were made and filed December 13 and approved by the Department February 15, 1911.[16]

In his report to the Equitable Board at the annual meeting February 16, 1911, President Morton referred to the possibility of insurance for working men, and the Board resolved that the question of insurance for industrial institutions, pension funds for employees, and accident and sickness insurance be referred to the standing Committee on Insurance for consideration, the fact to be noted, however, that the writing of accident and sickness insurance was not contemplated under the existing Charter of the Society.

The Insurance Committee at its first meeting to consider this subject resolved against the Society's "engaging in employee liability insurance" (accident and sickness insurance). At the second meeting, which was attended by William J. Graham, the principle of group insurance without medical examination was approved; one hundred lives was established as the minimum group, premiums were to be paid entirely by the employer, and no age limit of sixty-five was to be required. Policies would be issued to "members of labor organizations, lodges, beneficial societies or similar organizations, or employees of one em-

16 The policy form 1127 submitted to the Insurance Department was entitled "Yearly Renewable Term Employees' Policy." It stated that "all individual insurances accepted by the Society hereunder shall appear in the aforesaid register to be kept by the Society and a duplicate thereof to be furnished to the employer." The register was to be corrected yearly. Individual employees were eligible for conversion of policies after five years of continuous insurance under the group. A seven by eight inch form entitled "Notice to the Employees of the ——— Company" served as the employee's certificate. In 1911 two more group policy forms, Nos. 1127A and 1258, were also approved by the Department. The first of these contained no conversion privileges, and the second provided for monthly premium payments instead of annual, semi-annual, or quarterly. In August 1912, a variation of policy No. 1258 (No. 1400) was approved; it was entitled "Group Policy Employees' Yearly Renewable Term." Subsequently, revisions were made in the "Notice to the Employee" certificate so as to obviate issuance of a new certificate with each pay raise of the employee. In 1914 the Policy Forms Division filed a new form of register which provided more space for changes. The grace clause in these early group policies provided for an extra charge of 5 per cent for late payment of premiums; this charge was eliminated in 1916.

ployer." At a later meeting Rosenfeld laid down a number of considerations which should be kept in mind in regard to group insurance: the Society's rules governing hazardous occupations should apply, the conditions under which the employees worked should be carefully examined, and groups with "too large a proportion of female employees of tender ages," or too high a proportion of older persons, or of foreign-born persons, should be closely scrutinized. Territorial conditions should also be taken into consideration. Rosenfeld made it clear that no group should be accepted without approval of the Medical Department and that the Actuarial Department's approval be secured when any question arose concerning proper application of the authorized premium rates. As soon as possible special rates should be worked out for the group business "predicated upon a reduction in the scale of commissions to be paid in connection therewith." He thought that group business would require the services of "specialized experts" and recommended that it be established as a separate department of the Society under its own officer for administrative purposes.[17]

The Insurance Committee approved these recommendations April 20 and the Board gave its approval May 18. On May 26 the Insurance Committee fixed commissions on group insurance at 10 per cent for the first year with renewals of 2½ per cent not to exceed 25 years.

Equitable's first group insurance policy was issued June 1, 1911—to the Pantasote Leather Company. Eugenius H. Outerbridge, Treasurer of that company, was a Director of Equitable and a member of the Insurance Committee, and he was quick to take advantage of the new contract. The policy covered 121 employees.

The report on the triennial examination of the Equitable as of December 31, 1911, by the Insurance Department of the State of New York, contained the following paragraphs on Equitable's group activities:

> Group insurance comprehends the covering of the risks on a group of employees or all employees in certain lines of business, the premiums being collected monthly from the employer. No medical examination is required on groups of one hundred or more employees, although a rigid inspection of the premises and surroundings of the employees is made. Policies are issued in blanket form in the name of the employer and

[17] Memorandum to the Insurance Committee, April 18, 1911. Equitable Archives. The meetings of the Insurance Committee were held March 11, April 3, 12, 19, and 20.

cover the risks enumerated in an insurance register. Policies are upon the yearly renewable term plan at the regular rates of the society for such plan; the amount of premiums due each month are calculated by the society and billed to the employer in bulk, such computation taking into consideration all decreases and increases and changes in the number of employees insured.

Applications are signed by each employee and provide for the nomination of a beneficiary by the employee, who is to receive all benefits in case of death of such employee.

Dividends, however, are payable to the employer, the application bearing an assignment of same from the employee to the employer.

Group Insurance is not a new feature with the Equitable Life, as some years ago they insured all their home office employees in this manner. An examination was, however, required at that time and a separate policy issued on each life. The premiums are paid by the society and benefits payable to a beneficiary nominated by the insured. When an employee leaves, he is given certain options to continue or change the policy.

On the same day (February 1, 1911) that Equitable informed Montgomery Ward that it would not be able to supply that company's insurance needs, William Joseph Graham became associated with the Society as Superintendent of Western Agencies with headquarters in Chicago. Graham, a native of Louisville, Kentucky (born September 23, 1877), was graduated from St. Xavier College (Louisville) and received his Master of Arts degree from St. Francis Xavier College (New York). Mathematics was his favorite study and he qualified as an associate member of the Actuarial Society of America at the age of twenty-one. In 1898 he was appointed Actuary for the Sun Life Insurance Company of America (Louisville). His actuarial duties were concerned largely with industrial insurance although the company also marketed ordinary life. During Louisville days Graham became acquainted with Henry Powell and other well-known Equitable general agents, and with Young E. Allison, famous editor of *The Insurance Field*, one of the outstanding insurance journals of the country.[18]

18 Allison, a reporter on the *Louisville Courier-Journal*, had founded *The Insurance Herald* in 1888, but when that publication changed hands and moved to Atlanta, he and others of the *Courier-Journal* staff began publication of *The Insurance Field*, in 1899. Allison was reporter, editor, musician, historian, philosopher, and, to use one of his own favorite words, a person of "anagosity" and influence. His "Insurance at Piney Woods"—reprinted in the *Select Works of Young E. Allison* (Filson Club, Louisville, 1935)—is an insurance classic. He is best known outside insurance circles for his poem, "A Piratical Ballad" or "Derelict," which built

Allison was also a director of the Sun Life, edited that company's paper, the *Sunbeam*, and Graham wrote a series of unsigned editorial articles for *The Insurance Field*. No doubt the association with Allison helped develop in the young actuary the ability to express himself both orally and in writing.[19] When in 1902 the Sun Life was bought by the Metropolitan Life, Graham joined the actuarial department of the Metropolitan, where he remained until 1905.

In 1905, when the Insurance Commissioners of Tennessee, Kentucky, Wisconsin, and Minnesota decided to conduct their own examination of the New York life insurance companies, Graham was nominated to serve as consulting actuary for the group. Eventually, both Graham and S. Herbert Wolfe were appointed joint consulting actuaries.[20] Only the New York Life was examined in detail, but Graham received additional experience when he was sent to England for several weeks to look into the foreign records of that company. Then when he accompanied Commissioner Thomas D. O'Brien of Minnesota and other commissioners to Washington to interview President Theodore Roosevelt, he learned something of the technique by which a great executive disposed of visitors.[21] Soon afterward, Graham and Wolfe were consulted by the "Committee of Fifteen" which suggested insurance legislation for the western and southern states. In 1905 Graham

---

Robert Louis Stevenson's famous four lines starting "Fifteen men on the Dead Man's Chest . . ." into a "masterly and exquisite ballad of horrificness" in six stanzas.

19 Said Graham of Allison: "Young E. Allison was a terrific figure in my mind, a most gifted man. He was hard of hearing . . . and he took advantage of it. That taught me something too." Graham Memoir, p. 7.

20 For this examination, see this history, p. 673. Henry R. Prewitt, Kentucky's Insurance Commissioner, was vice chairman of the committee and it was he who recommended Graham as consulting actuary for the committee. Others recommended S. Herbert Wolfe, nationally known consulting actuary. When Commissioner Thomas D. O'Brien of Minnesota questioned the wisdom of appointing such a young actuary, Graham graciously withdrew his name. Then it was that Wolfe strongly endorsed Graham and offered to withdraw his own name. The Commissioners finally went into executive session and appointed the two men joint consulting actuaries for the committee. Graham Memoir, pp. 23 ff.

21 O'Brien was seeking to get some cooperative effort on the part of a number of the western and southern states in enacting sound legislation following the Armstrong investigation. His efforts culminated in the creation of the "Committee of Fifteen," for which see this history, p. 704. Roosevelt did most of the talking and practically prevented the delegation from stating the purpose of its visit. He was, however, "all for it." His private secretary, William Loeb, later proved of assistance, and eventually the meeting of governors, attorneys general, and insurance commissioners was called which led to the creation of the "Committee of Fifteen."

became Actuary and Vice President of the Northwestern National Life Insurance Company (Minneapolis)—which had formerly operated as an assessment-fraternal company, but at the time was operating under the Minnesota "stipulated premium" law—and completed the reorganization of the company into a legal reserve "old-line" life insurance company. He also found time to write a series of articles for *The World Today*. The second of these articles, "The Aftermath of the Investigation," although intended to undo some of the damage done by the muckraking writers, pulled no punches; it cleared the way for a constructive story of life insurance. Advance copies of this article were sent to the companies, so they could register any protests in advance of publication. Both the New York Life and Mutual accepted the story essentially as written, but Henry L. Rosenfeld tried to get Graham to come to New York and confer about the treatment of Equitable. Rosenfeld finally met Graham in Minneapolis, and the article was revised to meet his approval.[22] Other articles followed during the ensuing months and then were published in book form in 1909 under the title *The Romance of Life Insurance—Its Past, Present and Future, with Particular Reference to the Epochal Investigation Era of 1905–1908*.[23] Among the endorsements of the book, which proved highly successful, was that of Paul Morton, President of Equitable.

While in Minneapolis, Graham had become well acquainted with William J. Keating, Equitable's General Agent in that city, and with John A. Hartigan, Minnesota's Insurance Commissioner and President of the National Convention of Insurance Commissioners in 1910.[24] It was Hartigan who informed President Morton and Rosenfeld that

22 This article appeared in *The World Today*, XV (1908), July. The first article, which appeared in the June number, was entitled "Life Insurance—Everybody's Problem." Succeeding articles, published from August 1908 to May 1909, were entitled: "The Evolution of the Policy"; "You: How Life Insurance Can Serve You"; "The Three Systems of Life Insurance"; "Science and Human Life"; "Life Insurance Supervision"; "Life Insurance Legislation"; "Taxing a Tax"; "The Stewardship of Three Billions"; "Insuring the Masses"; and "The Life Insurance Ambassador."

23 The World Today Company, Chicago, 1909. In the book, the second article (Chapter I) was toned down somewhat.

24 Hartigan, a former Professor of Mathematics at the College of St. Thomas in St. Paul, had served as Actuary for the Minnesota Insurance Department; as Actuary and Commissioner, he had worked closely with Graham in the reorganization of the Northwestern National. After retirement from public office, he became Equitable's Northwestern Superintendent of the Department of Western Agencies at St. Paul.

Graham might be available for work with Equitable. Consequently, President Morton called Graham to New York and recommended his appointment to Rosenfeld's staff to head Equitable's western agencies. When Graham got back to Chicago, he heard the newsboys announcing that Paul Morton was dead. Acting President William A. Day carried through with the appointment, however, and Graham officially took over his work with Equitable February 1, 1911.

Thus when Graham joined Equitable at the age of thirty-four, he had had experience in ordinary life insurance, industrial insurance, and fraternal and assessment insurance and was familiar with state regulation of life insurance; he was also nationally known as an author. In addition, he had one qualification rather rare in an actuary—he was a salesman.

Before Graham left the Home Office for Chicago, Rosenfeld, as a sort of afterthought, gave him some papers which he thought Graham might be interested in looking into. These were the papers concerning the Montgomery Ward insurance proposals which Equitable had turned down by Rosenfeld's letter of February 1, 1911.[25] Effective January 1, 1912, Graham was appointed Superintendent of the Group Department of Equitable and brought into the Home Office. On January 17 in a talk to the General Agency Association of the Society he outlined his plans for establishing the new department. He said:

> Group insurance propositions must be approached through the employer; therefore it is essential to attain and preserve the employer's viewpoint. . . .
>
> The trend of the times is to take care of the workman, to give ear to his necessities and to direct expenditures to conserve the necessities of the employe rather than to use the same in fighting him or his heirs. In a word, to apply the doctrine of contentment for the doctrine of discontent.
>
> Socialism as we have come to know it in America seems almost entirely a protest against conditions as they are, just another expression of this same doctrine of discontent. The remedy must go to the root of the evil. Employers anxious to conserve their employes within the limits of sound business principles and economic *quid pro quo* are realizing the advantages of supplying workmen's compensation benefits and adding to the employe that feeling of security that his employment is guaranteeing him against those great necessities of his family that can only be covered through life insurance.
>
> Mutual benefit associations and associations born within large corpora-

[25] "The Equitable had definitely turned it down." Graham Memoir, p. 45.

Underwood & Underwood

William A. Day
President, 1911–1927

tions for taking care of their employes' insurance necessities are recognized more and more as not giving adequate protection to the employes. Lacking the surety of properly constituted life insurance the whole protection is hazarded upon the success of the corporation to meet unusual demands. In other words, it is recognized by corporations that they cannot afford to go into the life insurance business and the accident and health insurance business, which is entirely foreign to their particular fields, any more than they could afford to go into any other business that they know nothing about.

Although at the time the Equitable did not want to go into the group accident and sickness and group pension business, Graham explained that the Equitable would be glad to assist in establishing these plans:

Where it is desired to add accident or health features or where it is desired to cover liability placed by the Workmen's Compensation Laws the Society is in position to tender its good offices to work out these additional features to be carried by the best casualty companies, but assumes no responsibility for these features. Model plans and forms will be discussed and outlined by the best experts of this line of business.

Likewise pension plans will be devised for employers desirous of adding sound workable pension features to general protection plans for the benefit of employes. Casualty and pension benefits will be found to take varied form according to the ideas of the employers, and can only be intelligently treated by individual formulation of each proposition.

Despite Rosenfeld's letter of February 1, 1911, Montgomery Ward and Company had continued its efforts to secure a comprehensive insurance plan for its employees. Most interested of the officers of the company were Vice President and Treasurer Charles Hallett Thorne, nephew of the founder, and George R. Durgan, attorney for the company, who was in charge of its welfare program. Durgan, in his search for broader coverage than provided by the Clerks Benefit Society, had worked with consulting actuary Miles M. Dawson of New York in gathering and studying data in support of the idea of group insurance; he had also consulted John Führer, Actuary of The Germania. Particularly interested in the accident and health coverage were The Travelers, Aetna, and the Continental Casualty Company of Chicago. Continental Casualty had been a leader in franchise (accident) insurance, which, since it operated by way of the employer, might offer an approach to group life insurance.

While still in Chicago as Superintendent of Western Agencies, Graham had made contact with Durgan and reopened the Montgomery Ward case. In addition to the competition offered by several life insurance companies, numerous insurance brokers were soliciting the business. Durgan finally arranged a weekend trip to Mackinac Island on Thorne's yacht, and it was on this trip that he discussed more fully with Graham his ideas on group insurance and presented the statistical data which he had accumulated.[26]

The biggest obstacle in the way of the Montgomery Ward case was overcome when the program was split into two major parts—life insurance, and accident and health insurance. Graham played an important part in bringing about this division of the program. Two officers of the Continental Casualty Company, Manton Maverick, the Actuary, and Secretary William Betts, "the business getter," cooperated well and worked tirelessly to develop the plan for the accident and health insurance, which, however, was finally awarded to the London Guarantee and Accident Company of England. When it came to devising an application for the group life policy, Graham ran into trouble with Allan McCulloh of the firm of Alexander and Green, Equitable's legal counsel, who said that "it was a lot of nothing" and had no legal status. It satisfied the Montgomery Ward officers, however, and with the help of Robert Grass in the Actuary's Department a policy form was worked out.[27]

Under the policy, all employees who had been with Montgomery Ward for at least six months were insured without medical examination. Two master policies covered 2,054 employees at Chicago and 858 at Kansas City—a total of 2,912 for a total amount of $5,946,564. In the event of death, the policy provided immediate payment of $100

[26] Graham remembers that Thorne was rather surprised that no effort was made on this occasion to sell him additional personal life insurance. Later, however, Graham convinced Thorne that life insurance could "do something for him" by selling him a policy which provided a life income for his wife and heirs. In doing this, Graham emphasized the importance of the services which could be rendered by a mutual company—or one operated on the mutual basis. Graham even left the excitement of the Republican National Convention of 1912, in which "Standpatters" and "Progressives" were slugging it out, to get Thorne's signature on the dotted line. Graham Memoir, pp. 247 ff.

[27] Grass was of German descent and training and an expert policy creator; he was an enthusiastic supporter of the idea of insuring working people.

for burial purposes, and for those who had no dependents a lump sum payment of one year's salary but not to exceed $3,000. If the deceased had dependents, a weekly payment of 25 per cent of wages was guaranteed for four years certain, and until death of the beneficiary provided the beneficiary remained unmarried. Additional annuities were provided for children under sixteen years of age. Premiums, which were payable monthly, were based upon Equitable's published rates for one year term insurance; 5 per cent was deducted from these rates for group purposes.[28] All premiums were paid by the company. The policy was in effect a collection of individual insurances; each person insured had an individual policy.[29] The Montgomery Ward insurance went into effect July 1, 1912.

The Montgomery Ward group insurance attracted national—even international—attention in the insurance press, though it was crowded out in the general press by more spectacular events such as the sinking of the *Titanic* and the national political conventions.[30] During the remainder of the year, some twenty additional group policies were sold, among them those on the employees of the Commercial Trust Company of Philadelphia, the Northern Trust Company, the Pennsylvania Company for Insurance on Lives and Granting Annuities, the New York and Queens Electric Light and Power Company, and W. Atlee Burpee Company. The total amount of group insurance issued during the year was $12,948,755.

For a brief time, group insurance was a controversial issue. Since

28 The term rate was published for the purpose of settling questions involving life contingency where someone had some rights within a year; the rate could be used to calculate the actuarial costs. Graham recalls that the one year term rate was "the then American experience table at 3 per cent loaded 50 per cent." Since there was no valid experience on group insurance, Actuary Robert Henderson, who had no great faith in the idea anyway, determined to play it safe on his premium calculation; "he left it at the ridiculously high position of being 150 per cent of the American 3 per cent mortality table, reduced 5 per cent." Graham Memoir, p. 74.

29 Although the documents given to the employees were called "certificates," they were formally designated as "policies under a master policy of the employer." An individual application was required of each person insured and the premiums were calculated for each individual in the group. The sum total of the individual premiums constituted the group premium.

30 The first news story on the Montgomery Ward case was published in *The National Underwriter* (Chicago), April 18, 1912. In an editorial on May 16 the same journal said: "The old-timers shake their heads when the new 'schemes' of the Equitable are mentioned, say something about 'good advertising,' 'impracticable,' and other things: but others are wondering whether President Day has not 'started something' which will give a new and larger conception of the functions and duties of life insurance."

there were no laws on the subject, the state insurance commissioners were uncertain as to its legal status; agents feared it would cut into their sales. Many actuaries were skeptical of its mathematical soundness and believed it would discriminate against medically examined policyholders. Medical departments were reluctant to accept risks without medical examinations, and the national associations of the fraternals and the smaller life insurance companies resolved against it as discriminatory and a menace to legal reserve life insurance. Even some of the larger companies of the East, if not directly opposed, at least were not adverse to seeing Equitable burn its fingers on one of its own innovations.

Opposition to group was led by the politically powerful fraternal societies, many of which were facing loss of membership as a result of rigorous upward revision of premium rates and reserves; they feared that group insurance might obviate one of their chief reasons for being.[31] In August 1913, the Associated Fraternities of America, meeting in Chicago, unanimously approved a bill to prohibit the writing of group insurance on members of fraternal organizations and which would require medical examinations for all persons to be covered by a group policy; this bill was to be submitted to the state legislatures. At the same time, the American Life Convention, the organization of the western and southern life insurance companies, most of them stock companies, was meeting in St. Paul. On the same day that the Associated Fraternities prepared their bill, the Executive Committee

[31] In 1913, when a Michigan agent of the Metropolitan offered to insure local membership of any lodge consisting of not less than 100 members under a group policy for $1,000 each, such a protest arose that the Insurance Commissioner of the state disapproved of the group policy form of that company. Although the agent's activities were repudiated by his company, the incident was used by the fraternals in support of their arguments. *The Fraternal Monitor*, XXIII (1913), July 1. Ironically enough, in 1912 the Equitable insured the members of the Moses Montefiore Mutual Relief Society, Inc., under a group policy. This Society was formerly a Lodge of the Independent Order of the Sons of Benjamin. To meet the requirements of the Equitable, new-coming members of the Lodge organized into the Mutual Relief Society and seceded from the parent organization. Membership was limited to those under forty-five years of age. Said *The Eastern Underwriter*: "The Moses Montefiore Lodge has been newly incorporated under the title of 'The Moses Montefiore Mutual Relief Society,' and the insurance obligation will be assumed by the Equitable Life Assurance Society of this city, one of the strongest life insurance companies in the world, whose permanent solvency is a matter of public knowledge. The Montefiore Society will continue in operation all the good work it has heretofore carried on, and on the death of a member the insurance company will pay the beneficiary $500. In this way absolute protection is obtained." *The Eastern Underwriter*, XIII (1912), June 13.

of the American Life Convention drafted the following resolution, which was adopted the next day:

> Resolved, that the issuance of group insurance by a legal reserve life insurance company without individual medical examinations is a menace to legal reserve life insurance, a discrimination against regularly examined policyholders, is unfair in principle and dangerous in practice.[32]

When the Convention adopted this resolution, the secretary sent a telegram reporting the action to both the Associated Fraternities and the National Fraternal Congress which was also in session in Chicago. The news was received "with a demonstration of enthusiasm not even surpassed by that obtained upon the final vote to consolidate the National Fraternal Congress and the Associated Fraternities of America." The two fraternal organizations merged at this time, and President W. H. Powers of the new organization—The National Fraternal Congress of America—wired back immediately and endorsed the action of the Convention. This telegram was received and read at the last session of the Convention.[33]

When President Day learned of the action taken by the fraternals, he said: "The criticism of the fraternals when analyzed is not at group insurance at all, but at re-insurance, or as they call it, 'twisting' of fraternal business. . . . The Equitable has no desire to reinsure fraternal lodges or societies on any plan and I deplore the mistaken use of the words 'group insurance' in the discussion of the possible re-insurance of such societies." In regard to the action of the American Life Convention, he said:

> It is true that the American Life Convention, made up . . . for the most part of the newer and smaller companies, has not the same equality of opportunity in negotiating large insurance of the group variety. None the less I am sure that the action was taken hastily and misunderstandingly. I do not believe that the rank and file of that convention would de-

[32] *Proceedings of the American Life Convention* (1913), p. 77.

[33] John A. Sullivan of the Associated Fraternities to Thomas W. Blackburn, Secretary of the American Life Convention, August 29, 1913. Convention correspondence. See also *The Western Underwriter*, XVII (1913), August 14. The Convention *Proceedings* for 1913 do not mention the telegram. Officers of the American Life Convention many years later spoke of this resolution against group insurance as the one mistake of importance in the history of the organization. Since many of the member companies soon become interested in group insurance, the resolution was repealed in 1917.

liberately adopt a resolution condemning what was good and sound for a large company even though the same might not be advisable for the smaller institution. The statements made are without justification and are not supported by the facts.

President Day reasoned that group insurance was quite different from individual insurance without examinations, that it offered better selection of risks and a continuance of that selection, eliminated the moral hazard, centralized premium collections, made for administrative economy, reduced waste from lapses, and resulted in low writing and renewal expense.

Unlike the fraternal organizations and the American Life Convention, The Association of Life Insurance Presidents, in which Equitable had played an important part from the beginning, was favorable to group insurance and was promoting state legislation to give it legal status. After Day's defense of group insurance appeared in the insurance journals and newspapers, Sullivan, who headed the legislative committee of the National Fraternal Congress, sent out a bulletin to all fraternal societies, "hoping a bombardment on their part on insurance departments to stop them approving Group contracts" would bring results. He also hoped that Thomas W. Blackburn, Secretary of the American Life Convention, would get like action from the companies of that organization: "*Get your companies busy with the insurance departments*. The states in which the companies have sneaked through Group insurance statutory recognition are New Jersey, Pennsylvania, Minnesota, and Arizona. We must fight hard up to the December meeting of the National Convention of Insurance Commissioners among departments so as to get in our finishing work there." [34] Sullivan also wrote a long letter to Commissioner J. A. O. Preus of Minnesota, President of the National Convention of Insurance Commissioners, praying that the commissioners at their next meeting would give their best thought and action to this subject. A few days later he reported to Blackburn that the Mutual Life Underwriters in their meeting at Buffalo had also taken action against group insurance and that their President had made a reply to Day on group insurance "using adjectives in the superlative and adverbs in the imperative. Why can-

[34] Sullivan to Blackburn (from Kansas City), September 4, 1913. Convention correspondence. Blackburn had told Sullivan to regard their correspondence relating to group insurance "as of a confidential nature." Blackburn to Sullivan, September 2, 1913. Convention correspondence.

not you get President Abels going and you supplement such with one of your characteristic strong pronouncements. . . . Get busy." [35]

Blackburn acted almost immediately and early in September sent a long article in answer to President Day on group insurance. He stated that no company had carried group insurance long enough to establish any of Day's seven points, which he said fell of their own weight. He held that taking over fraternals was group insurance and not reinsurance; wherever the law included "lodges" and the like, it was group insurance. If there was no efficacy in medical examinations, why should the companies maintain expensive medical departments? As for reducing expenses, he said that a company might hire a Chautauqua lecturer "and bunch his audiences into groups of 5,000 men, women and children and issue a blanket policy, taking up a collection for the first premium and assuring every person present that if he will come the next year in time for the collection, his insurance will be maintained." He declared group insurance to be discriminatory: "I submit that group insurance without individual medical examination on groups of 50 to 100 members of 'labor organizations, lodges, benefit societies, or similar organizations, or employees of any employer' is exactly what the American Life Convention says it is—'a menace to legal reserve life insurance, a discrimination against regularly examined policyholders, is unfair in principle and dangerous in practice.' " [36]

At the annual meeting of the National Convention of Insurance Commissioners July 29–August 1, Sullivan and other representatives of the fraternals had accused the companies which were writing group insurance of "twisting" the business of the fraternals. E. E. Rittenhouse, former Colorado Insurance Commissioner who had joined Equitable as Conservation Commissioner in January 1911, and officers of the Association of Life Insurance Presidents denied these charges.[37] The subject was referred to the Committee on Laws and Legislation for consideration at the December meeting.[38] Attacks on group insur-

[35] Sullivan to Blackburn, September 8, 1913. *Ibid.*

[36] *The Western Underwriter*, XVII (1913), September 11; *The Insurance Field*, XXVIII (1913), September 12.

[37] July 29 President Day wrote Rittenhouse at Burlington, Vermont, attending the Commissioner's meeting: "Please state emphatically that Equitable has no desire and no intention to apply Group Insurance to insuring fraternal orders." Day letters, Equitable Archives.

[38] On September 24 President Day wrote W. B. Howard, Nebraska auditor, a long letter with the hope that it might help "prevent erroneous conclusions which

ance were renewed at the midwinter meeting of the commissioners and at this time Henry L. Rosenfeld, William J. Graham, as well as Rittenhouse, replied in defense; they were supported by James L. Howard, Secretary of The Travelers Insurance Company. The former Superintendent of Insurance in Illinois, Fred W. Potter, and R. L. Cox, President of the Association, also defended group insurance.[39] The Convention then adopted a resolution which disapproved of any attempt to apply group insurance to fraternal societies and recommended that other aspects of the question be recommitted to the Committee on Laws and Legislation for further study. A year later, the Committee presented its final report and the Convention, after reiterating its previous action, resolved that no further action on group insurance was desirable.

The labor unions, in general, also opposed group insurance and worked cooperatively with the fraternals. Their argument was that if the employer wanted to do anything for his employees he could do it by way of the pay check. Also, they were afraid that group insurance might serve as a club in the hands of the employers and prevent workmen from changing jobs or going on strikes. Opposition on the part of union leaders, however, was not always convincing to the rank and file membership who frequently became aware of the advantages of group insurance through personal experience. As a matter of policy, William J. Graham never replied in public to the speeches of union leaders.

Despite the continuing attacks of the fraternals—some of their publications compared group insurance to Asiatic cholera and the bubonic plague—the states had already begun to recognize group insurance by legislation. Arizona and Idaho exempted groups from individual medical examinations in 1913, and the same year Maine, Minnesota, and Nebraska permitted group insurance to be issued at rates lower than those charged for individual insurance; Florida did likewise in 1915.

---

might come from those who lack correct understanding of it [group insurance]." Since Equitable had established group insurance and had the most experience with it, he explained the fundamental principles and emphasized that reinsurance or the insurance of increasing-risk groups was not part of the Equitable plan. Equitable's group insurance was *new* insurance. It would be impossible for Equitable, under its plan, to reinsure the whole or part of the membership of legal reserve life insurance companies or of fraternals. *Ibid.*

39 Among the commissioners, a few such as Herman L. Ekern of Wisconsin and T. M. Henry of Mississippi took the side of the fraternals. The Wisconsin Insurance Department disapproved of group policy forms. On the other hand, commissioners such as Burton Mansfield of Connecticut and Saul Epsteen of Colorado defended the writing of group insurance.

In Texas, group insurance without individual medical examination was recognized by ruling of the Attorney General in 1915, and in Ohio by ruling of the Insurance Department in 1917.[40]

Although several of the larger eastern companies began writing group insurance soon after Equitable blazed the trail, the New York Life in 1913 was notifying its agents not to "waste much time on this class of business." Its instructions were as follows:

> Don't confuse Commercial or Partnership insurance, where members of a firm are carrying insurance for mutual protection, or for the protection of stockholders, with group insurance. Group insurance may be a good thing theoretically, but from a practical point of view the Bulletin would not advise wide-awake New York Life men to waste much time on this class of business. Group insurance is the kind of star that it does not pay to shoot at. Furthermore, the Company now, on account of the limitation of business, is in no position to consider insurance on groups of lives.[41]

And Arthur Hunter, Actuary of the New York Life and very prominent in the Actuarial Society of America, told William J. Graham that group insurance would be of great damage to President Day, to the Equitable, and to life insurance. He suggested that Graham try to persuade Day to drop this plan because it wouldn't work.[42]

Another company which was not at all enthusiastic about group insurance was the Metropolitan Life. According to Graham, two officers of this company visited Superintendent Fred W. Potter of Illinois and proposed that if he would withdraw his department's approval of group insurance, they could guarantee that the New York department would promptly withdraw its approval "and thus stop group insurance aborning." [43]

Nor was there any unanimity of opinion on group insurance even in the Equitable family. Graham thought that Actuary Robert Hender-

40 For early state legislation, see the article by Sterling Pierson, Legal Assistant, "The Legislatures Expand the Group Insurance Field," in the *American Bar Association Journal*, XV (1929), July.

41 *The Eastern Underwriter*, XIV (1913), August 14. At this time group insurance was included along with individual life insurance in the Company's total business for the year.

42 Graham Memoir, pp. 110 ff. Hunter paid his respects to President Day as a man but did not think that he was a life insurance man, whereas he considered Graham to be such a man, one who had his own reputation at stake as well as that of his company.

43 *Ibid.*, p. 116.

son never really approved of group insurance and even tried in various ways to undermine it. There were basic differences of opinion in regard to methods of calculating rates and dividends; internal politics and personal jealousies were also involved.[44]

Interestingly enough, the Society's Medical Department cooperated fully in the inauguration of group insurance. To comply with the law in some states which required medical examination for any life insurance, the group inspection would be made by Dr. Franklin C. Wells, Medical Director of the Society. After the employees were called together, they were questioned and the conditions under which they worked surveyed. The general assumption was that group insurance could be as safely issued to carefully inspected, active, and self-renewing groups without medical examinations, as to a similar number of individuals with medical examinations. Since the insurance covered only the period of employment, the death rate would remain virtually uniform; such a group would provide a natural and permanent selection whereas medical selection was only temporary in value. Graham did not consider medical selection so important as did many actuaries and medical directors. In fact, he believed that life insurance risks "were never selected by the doctors. They were self-selected, usually strongly urged by the agent." About all the medical men could do was eliminate those applicants who in their judgment were not good risks.[45] Early in 1914, Graham wrote:

> In such states as do not require [medical examination] by statute, I think we could make our article more serviceable and more economical by suspending our present requirement as to medical inspection of the new

[44] Graham believed that the group insurance rate ought to be considered as a unit of a complete one-month term and not as a fraction of a yearly premium. So calculated it would be possible greatly to reduce the amount of reserve required for the group. When Henderson suddenly adopted this plan without informing Graham, the actuaries reduced the reserve liability but did not remove the credit which had previously been taken when the figures were reported on the one-year term basis. When this mistake was corrected, the Society's surplus was reduced sufficiently to spoil a nice round figure which everyone had been anticipating. For a while it looked as if Graham would be made the scapegoat, but President Day understood the situation and absolved him from any blame. Graham felt that he had not received proper support from Rosenfeld and frequently spoke of Henderson, Westfall, *et al.*, as "the clique."

[45] Graham Memoir, p. 63. One of Equitable's directors at first did not agree and said that insurance without medical examination would be undertaken by Equitable only "over his dead body." He later changed his mind and decided that group insurance was perfectly sound. *Ibid.*

lives. Our mortality is very low on our present business, and we could still retain the privilege of requiring evidence of insurability satisfactory to the Society in our present contracts without exercising the same. If we had reason, therefore, to later change our minds on this point we would be in position to do so, although in making this recommendation I am strongly of the opinion that we will not change our minds and that the form of medical inspection we are now exacting and receive is of no particular value and that it serves to put restrictions around our Group Insurance service that are objectionable to some employers.

Considering the meager amount of experience on which to judge the risks involved in group insurance, embarking upon it was a fairly bold step. The only direct experience which Equitable had was with the insurance of its own clerks in 1902 and the employees of the United Cigar Stores in 1905 and 1906. A study of the policies issued to Equitable's employees showed, eight years later, a 48 per cent ratio of actual to expected mortality in the age group below forty, and 88.5 per cent in the age group above forty, or a total ratio of 50.7 per cent.[46] The experience with the 788 policies issued to the employees of the United Cigar Stores in 1905 and 1906 was even more favorable.[47]

Despite the lack of data on which to base rates, Equitable did very well on the group policies issued during 1912 and 1913 (to November 19). Total income from the policies was $262,699 and claims and expenses—including dividends and estimated Home Office expenses totaled $135,868, thus leaving a surplus of $126,831.[48]

One question which had to be resolved was who should sell group insurance and, if handled by the Society's agents, what the commission should be. President Day at one time thought that perhaps group insurance should not be handled through the agents at all. Graham pointed out, however, that though Day's suggestion to handle group through a special organization might simplify matters in one way, it would complicate them in another. He believed that since the agent had built up insurance to its existing stature, he could continue to help do the same with group; that Equitable simply could not afford to ignore the agent. So, starting with small beginnings, Graham built

[46] The total number of policies issued was 1,166. On the anniversaries in 1910 there were 545 policies still in force with 631 having terminated. Memorandum of J. V. E. Westfall, Superintendent of the Bureau of Statistics, to Rosenfeld, March 29, 1912. Rosenfeld papers, Equitable Archives.

[47] *Ibid.*

[48] Financial Statement, Group Insurance Business, November 19, 1913. *Ibid.*

up a sales organization which specialized in group insurance.[49] In the early years, many of the larger policies were originated by officers of the Society, with Graham writing most of them.[50] For these he received no commissions, and there were no rebates paid; on those cases sold without commission the employer paid the same rates as on other policies. On early policies, commissions for the regular agents of the Society were fixed individually for each case and based not only upon the agent's lead but also upon how far and how intelligently he had followed through with the sale.[51] Soon, however, commissions were fixed at 10 per cent of first year premiums and 2½ per cent on renewals from the second to the tenth year inclusive. In 1914 a schedule of graded commissions was adopted which provided for 20 per cent first year commission on the first $5,000 of annual premium on any one group, 15 per cent of the second $5,000, and 10 per cent of the excess above $10,000; renewals remained 2½ per cent for nine years.[52] Group business handled by an agent was of "a special character not covered by your regular contract"; it did not count in any way toward allotment of premiums stipulated in the agent's regular contract nor did it count toward membership in the agency clubs. The Society did not recognize territorial rights of any general agent as

[49] Expense accounts for 1916 listed twelve persons in addition to Graham who had incurred traveling expenses, and two years later four field agents were on the salary list.

[50] For instance, in December 1915 President Day prepared Graham's way for a group policy for the Santa Fe Railway system by writing several of the directors and also Joy Morton, who was well acquainted with the officials of that road. And in May 1916 he wrote John D. Rockefeller, Jr.; Waldo H. Marshall, President of the American Locomotive Company; and Burns D. Caldwell, President of Wells Fargo and Company, trying to interest them in group policies and arranging calls by William J. Graham. Day letters, Equitable Archives.

A few years later more system developed in lining up prospects when Graham began having "charts" prepared on the most important group cases handled by Equitable. These charts listed the directors of the companies which had policies with Equitable, and noted their connections with other companies. Thus when Equitable prepared a "proposal" (often referred to in the early years as a "proposition") for a prospective purchaser, it was able to reach important executives by way of a company director who was already familiar with Equitable's group policy. Graham's secretary and office manager during the 1920's was Edith Belle Hampton (Mrs. John Welling) who was responsible, among other things, for the preparation of group proposals. Edith Belle Welling to Assistant Secretary Grace W. Jordis, May 20, 1963. Letter in Equitable Archives.

[51] Graham Memoir, p. 125.

[52] Memorandum, Graham to Vice President John B. Lunger, February 16, 1914. Rosenfeld papers, Equitable Archives. The Superintendent of Agencies and the Actuary joined in the recommending of the new commissions.

applying to any lives resident within his field which might be covered by a group policy issued to a group having members throughout the country, unless such group transaction was written by the general agent to whom such territory was assigned.

Agents were supplied with information on group insurance by way of *Agency Items*, reprints of articles or addresses made by President Day, Rosenfeld, Graham, or by prominent businessmen who were willing to endorse group insurance, and by booklets on the subject. One of these booklets, "Development of Group Insurance," was published in 1913 under Rosenfeld's name, and another entitled "Group Insurance—Its Aims and Its Field" reproduced an address delivered by President Day in December 1913 at the annual meeting of the Association of Life Insurance Presidents.[53] To allay agents' fears that group insurance might cut into the sales of ordinary insurance, President Day said: "This plan is not a substitute, but rather a supplement to all other forms of insurance. It operates not to replace, but to create a demand for individual insurance."

Although there was no formal advertising of group insurance by Equitable, the newspapers as well as the insurance press published items and articles and featured individual group policies of importance.[54] For instance, the *Philadelphia Public Ledger* carried a story on the policy of W. Atlee Burpee and Company, the seed firm which adopted a group plan as a Christmas gift to its employees, and *The New York Times' The Annalist* devoted a page and a half to "The Employers' Enlightened Selfishness." [55]

Among the large group plans sold during the prewar years were those which covered 10,000 employees of the Studebaker Company, and 18,000 employees of the B. F. Goodrich Company of Akron—both in 1915. One of the most dramatic of the early negotiations was that

[53] In 1917 an editorial from the *Grand Rapids News* was reprinted under the title "Nerve and Faith," and an article by an Equitable agent, Ralph B. Trousdale, which appeared in the *Annals of the American Academy of Political and Social Science* in March 1917 was reprinted under the title "Group Insurance." A "General Summary of Group Insurance Rules and Procedures" was published in 1919, as well as a booklet of 108 pages entitled "Notebook of Industrial Safety Standards."

[54] Graham said that at that time "advertising would be like using a shotgun where a rifle was indicated." It was not thought that there was enough general interest in group insurance to support an advertising program. Graham Memoir, p. 147.

[55] *Philadelphia Public Ledger*, December 23, 1912; *The Annalist*, February 3, 1913.

with the Union Pacific Railroad and its affiliates, The Oregon Short Line Railroad Company and the Oregon-Washington Railroad and Navigation Company. As finally worked out, the noncontributory group life insurance plan covered 35,000 employees for a total of $30,000,000 of insurance, the premium on which was approximately three-quarters of a million dollars per year. The policy went into effect January 1, 1917, on which day Union Pacific announced the fact to its employees over its own telegraph system.[56] After the United States Government took over the railroads in December 1917, the Union Pacific, unable to continue payments on the policy, issued a notice of termination of the group contract to take effect December 31, 1918. William G. McAdoo, Secretary of the Treasury of the United States and Director General of the Railroads, was put in an embarrassing situation, since only the Union Pacific system had the advantage of group insurance for its employees. He thought continuation of the policy might be considered discrimination in favor of that railroad. He was persuaded, however, by Graham and Vice President William Betts of the Continental Casualty Company, which carried the accident insurance, that cancellation of the contract might lead to much dissatisfaction on the part of the employees of the Union Pacific. As a result, McAdoo, on December 16, 1918, issued a memorandum which became a part of the policy renewing the insurance for one year with all obligations to be assumed by the Director General of the Railroads.[57] This may well have been the first venture of the United States Government into group insurance.

It was during the war years that William J. Graham succeeded in selling the idea of group insurance to several of the Standard Oil companies. Graham had approached Clarence J. Hicks, former prominent Y.M.C.A. worker and in 1917 executive assistant to the President of the Standard Oil Company of New Jersey, concerning group insurance. Hicks had previously been executive assistant to the President of the Colorado Fuel and Iron Company—a Rockefeller controlled property—which in 1914 had received much adverse publicity as a result of a violent strike. It occurred to Graham that John D.

[56] *The New York Times*, Sunday, December 31, 1916, carried the story "Biggest Life Policy in Effect Tomorrow." In this case, Graham dealt largely with Vice President Charles B. Seger of the Union Pacific. The details of the plan were not worked out until December 31, 1916, and when Graham suggested payment of $1,000 as a binder, Seger made a token payment of one cent. Graham Memoir, p. 164.

[57] A facsimile of the memorandum is reproduced in Ilse, *Group Insurance . . .*, p. 272.

Rockefeller, Jr., though not directly connected with the operation of the various Standard Oil companies, was the key man in the situation. Rockefeller's interest in welfare projects of all types was well known, and if he could be interested in the advantages of group insurance as a tool to better industrial relations, new prospects might be opened for it. Since President Day had, while director of a bank, called its attention to certain facts which would have done an injustice to the Rockefeller interests, Graham felt justified in asking him for a letter of introduction to Rockefeller. The ensuing interview resulted indirectly in what was probably one of Graham's most outstanding sales achievements. When Rockefeller made it clear that he had nothing to do with the management of the various Standard Oil companies and hence would not be interested in group insurance, Graham finally convinced him that whether he admitted it or not Rockefeller was, in the eye of the public, one of the big employers of the world and that he was interested in any project which would enhance the welfare of his fellow human beings. Graham made it clear that he was not endeavoring to sell group insurance to Rockefeller but to inform him. He well knew that it would not hurt, in conversations with officers of the companies, to mention the fact that he had conferred with Rockefeller; and that if decisions in regard to group policies eventually came to Rockefeller's attention, he would be inclined in the right direction. Rockefeller later thanked President Day for sending Graham over to see him.

Hicks and Graham then worked out the plan for insuring the employees of the Standard Oil Company of New Jersey; the contract went into effect April 1, 1918. Although Graham made no effort to get any introductions to the officers of the other Standard Oil companies, he did get a photograph which included several of them from Charles T. White, Secretary of the Standard Oil Company of New Jersey. During the months following, contracts were made with the Standard Oil Company of Louisiana, the Standard Oil Company of Kentucky, the Standard Oil Company of Nebraska, and the Standard Oil Company of Kansas.[58]

[58] March 14, 1921, President Day wrote John D. Rockefeller, Jr., and said that he understood that Standard Oil of New Jersey was considering carrying its own group insurance and canceling its contract with Equitable. He pointed out that the experience of other corporations in handling their own group insurance had not been wholly satisfactory, and felt certain that Standard Oil would not leave the Equitable, which founded group insurance in the United States, for some other company. Day letters, Equitable Archives. Standard Oil did cancel its contract with

Although all of the early group policies issued by Equitable were of the noncontributory type—that is, the employer paid all the premiums—contributory policies were also offered. Under the noncontributory plan, all of the employees could be insured for one year's wages at a cost of about 1 per cent of the payroll; under the contributory plan, at least 75 per cent of the employees would be required to join the group before the policy could be written, and solicitation of the individuals was left to the employer. A limit of $3,000 was fixed as the maximum per individual; in 1919 the limit was $5,000.

After other life insurance companies began writing group insurance in 1913, active competition developed and Equitable's share of the total began to decline. A comparison of rates showed that in general Equitable's rates were higher than those of the other leading companies. As a result, premium rates were reduced effective January 1, 1914.[59] New rates were based upon a uniform loading of 25 per cent of the net American Experience Table 3 per cent rates. Some of the companies added total and permanent disability to their policies, and though Graham was opposed to this kind of insurance, he recommended that Equitable add it to its policy for competitive purposes.[60] The total and permanent disability benefit was authorized by the Insurance Committee January 18, 1917, and further reduction of premium rates made. Later in the year, a new principle was worked out

---

Equitable, however, in 1921, but again placed its group insurance with Equitable in 1932.

59 The Insurance Committee of the Board at a special meeting December 1, 1913, received a recommendation from Vice President Lunger, Actuary Henderson, and Henry L. Rosenfeld, Assistant to the President, that the reduced rates became effective on new policies as of December 1, 1913. The Committee was unable to determine what was a safe rate and left that power to the President. President Day later decided that the new rates would become effective January 1, 1914. Day memorandum, December 23, 1913. Copy in Rosenfeld papers.

60 October 2, 1916, Graham sent the following memorandum to Vice President Lunger: "The disability clause is being used against us in group insurance by our leading competitors. We are on the defensive by having to prove that it is not a matter of importance. The retort frequently to this is the one that you referred to the other day in reference to another matter; namely, if it's not important then why not include it? I deplore, for one, the presence of the disability clause in life insurance contracts but the same reasons which have compelled us to include the disability clause now operate to urge including the disability clause in our group insurance contract. I held out against doing this as long as I felt that we could stand against the tide, but I am disposed to think that we are merely weakening our position as competitors and therefore for the first time would earnestly advocate that we include the disability clause in our group insurance policy that will be on a par with the clause now being used by the Aetna, Travelers and Prudential."

for calculating dividends for group insurance under which each group would be largely judged on its own experience.[61]

As a result of the lack of uniformity of legislation on group insurance, the National Convention of Insurance Commissioners at their annual meeting in August 1917 decided to have a committee investigate and report a code of standards for group life insurance. In December a committee composed of six commissioners and six actuaries recommended that the Convention adopt the following definition of group life insurance: [62]

> Group life insurance is that form of life insurance covering not less than fifty employees with or without medical examination, written under a policy issued to the employer, the premium on which is to be paid by the employer or by the employer and employees jointly, and insuring only all of his employees, or all of any class or classes thereof determined by conditions pertaining to the employment, for amounts of insurance based upon some plan which will preclude individual selection, for the benefit of persons other than the employer; provided, however, that when the premium is to be paid by the employer and employees jointly and the benefits of the policy are offered to all eligible employees not less than seventy-five per cent of such employees may be so insured.

Standard group policy provisions were prepared and adopted by most of the states. New York added a section to its insurance law effective April 13, 1918, which incorporated the recommendations of the N.C.I.C.[63]

61 In July 1918 an analysis was made of dividends paid to 179 groups which had anniversaries from January 1 to May 31 of that year. It showed that roughly one half of the groups received a dividend of between 15 and 20 per cent, one quarter received less than 15 per cent, and one quarter received more than 20 per cent—a general average of about 19.12 per cent. As a result of this study, it was recommended that no dividends be paid to a first year group in which mortality costs exceeded total premium receipts; nor to any group more than one year old in which mortality costs, plus former dividends, equaled or exceeded total premium receipts. It was also suggested that a merit rating dividend plan include consideration of the nature of the policyholder's business.

62 The commissioners were: Jesse S. Phillips of New York, chairman; Walter K. Chorn of Missouri; M. J. Cleary of Wisconsin; Frank H. Hardison of Massachusetts; Burton Mansfield of Connecticut; and J. B. Sanborn of Minnesota. The actuaries were: E. E. Cammack of Aetna; James Douglas Craig of the Metropolitan; John K. Gore of the Prudential; William J. Graham of the Equitable; R. J. Hunter of the Germania (now the Guardian Life); and E. B. Morris of the Travelers.

63 New York had earlier—beginning with 1916—excluded group insurance from the provisions of the law which limited the total amount of new business which the life companies could write annually.

Thus did Equitable, in the face of much criticism and numerous difficulties, launch group insurance on the first leg of its career. Throughout the period in which the foundations were being established, the new plan had the support not only of Henry L. Rosenfeld, who had by 1915 become Fourth Vice President, but of Secretary William Alexander—the "Secretary of State" of Equitable. Rosenfeld believed that the new types of insurance were "justified in fullest measure as public service propositions" and that they had "served as sociological factors as well as brought to the Equitable excellent and profitable business together with much favorable comment." [64] The need for such insurance was obvious. As President Day said: "Businesses which employ considerable numbers of people are communities in themselves and the distress of one is the distress of all, and conversely the good of any one member is the good of all; therefore, whatever promotes the general welfare is worthy of approbation. By throwing around your employees this blanket of protection, putting on the Equitable the risk and burden which the family itself cannot well bear, you fraternalize your organization in a manner which will redound through higher business efficiency to the good of the business and consequently the good of each one who has a part in it. Society is realizing that those agencies which relieve and reduce shock and strain as much as is humanly possible, are fundamental factors of high value which make for stability and progress." [65] Equitable had adopted the plan because it saw the need for it, and believed that it would be performing a valuable public service and that it would be advantageous to the Society and the policyholders.[66]

MUTUALIZATION ADVANCES ANOTHER STEP

In January 1911, Superintendent of Insurance William H. Hotchkiss made public the voting trust agreement between J. P. Morgan, owner of the controlling stock of Equitable, and Morgan J. O'Brien, George W. Perkins, and Lewis Cass Ledyard, trustees, together with copies of

[64] Secretary Alexander, who defended group insurance in 1913, later said: "I regard Group Insurance as one of the most beneficial features of the business, for it helps the helpless and has a potent influence in bridging the gap between capital and labor." *The Eastern Underwriter*, XIV (1913), August 14; *My Half-Century in Life Insurance*, p. 83.

[65] Day to Joseph T. Carew, of Mably and Carew Company, Cincinnati, Ohio, December 24, 1912. Day letters, Equitable Archives.

[66] For the Rosenfeld-Graham controversy over who should receive credit for Equitable's adopting group insurance, see this history, p. 912.

letters on the subject which passed between Morgan and the Insurance Department.[67] Hotchkiss approved of the arrangement for this stock "pending the ascertainment of a legal means whereby The Equitable Life Assurance Society could, without protracted litigation or a substantial reduction of its free surplus, be made a mutual company, in fact as well as by representations. . . ." The same month Vice President Day appointed a Committee on Mutualization from the Board of Directors.[68] The Committee held a number of conferences with the trustees of the Morgan stock as a result of which it appeared that, should the Society acquire this stock, not only should the owner receive $3,000,000 which he had paid for it, plus interest, but that the minority stockholders should be paid at the same rate.

On April 20 Superintendent Hotchkiss met with the Equitable Board and told the members that, in view of the decision by the Court of Appeals in the Lord case, decided in February 1909, it was doubtful whether Equitable's amended Charter (1906) could legally confer upon the policyholders the right to vote for 28 directors.[69] The Society had, however, in 1909 and 1910 at its December meetings, gone through the form of an election of directors by policyholders and then ratified such election by vote of the stockholders. This action Hotchkiss did not consider legal and said: "From the above, you will at once see that your Society is now, in effect, back where it was before the outbreak of the 1905 controversy—i.e., a stock life insurance company without any voting rights in its policyholders." [70] About a week later, when the Society forwarded to the Department for filing a certificate of nomination for seven directors to be voted for by policyholders only, Hotchkiss, fearing that complications might develop, asked for an opinion from the Attorney General.[71] On May 4, 1911, Attorney General Thomas Carmody held that the whole electoral scheme incorporated into the Charter by the amendment of 1906 was illegal and

67 For the agreement, which was dated December 31, 1910, see this history, pp. 761–762.

68 The members of the Committee were Thomas Spratt, Chairman, T. DeWitt Cuyler, Joy Morton, E. H. Outerbridge, Charles D. Norton, and John D. Kernan.

69 For the Lord case decision of 1909, see this history, p. 713. For the Lord case of 1905, see this history, p. 626.

70 Quoted in *The Eastern Underwriter*, XII (1911), May 25.

71 Hotchkiss thought that as the law stood approval of this action might lead to a controversy harmful to the Society; the stock control might refuse to ratify the action of the policyholders, or, in the event it did ratify, it would be making valid an invalid policyholders' election.

void and that, therefore, policyholders, who by such Charter had been enfranchised as to 28 directors had, under existing conditions, no right to participate in the election of directors. The Society was informed of this opinion May 8 and the so-called certificates of nomination were returned unfiled. Four days later, President Day wrote the Insurance Department that the Attorney General's opinion would be submitted to the Executive Committee of the Board at its next meeting, but that meanwhile, upon advice of counsel, he was returning the certificates of nomination, the filing of which had, under the Attorney General's opinion, been refused. Since the Attorney General had held that Superintendent Hotchkiss should not recognize any procedure looking to an election of directors by policyholders, the certificates were returned to President Day the same day.

As a possible way out of this impasse, Superintendent Hotchkiss, who was much interested in the possibility of the mutualization of Equitable, had a bill which would facilitate that action introduced in the legislature. The bill had the approval of the Committee on Mutualization of Equitable's Board and of the trustees of the Morgan stock. It amended Section 16 of the Insurance Law, which prohibited insurance corporations acquiring or investing in their own stock, by inserting an exception in case such acquisition was in furtherance of a plan toward mutualization; and Section 95 so as to provide that a stock life insurance corporation might become a mutual life insurance corporation by carrying out any plan for the acquisition of its stock which should be adopted by majority vote of its directors and approved by a majority vote of its stockholders and a majority vote of its policyholders. Such a plan would have to be submitted to the Superintendent of Insurance and be approved by him in writing.

Although there were reports about Albany that the bill was strenuously opposed by Kuhn, Loeb and Company, which was said to own a large block of Equitable's stock, it passed both the Senate and Assembly within a few days and was approved by Governor John Alden Dix on May 19, 1911.[72]

George Westinghouse, former trustee of the Ryan stock, had his own idea as to how Equitable might be mutualized. He suggested that Equitable put out a new issue of 5,000 shares of stock at $1,000 per share and that 5,000 "public-spirited policyholders" buy one share each; the money thus raised would be used to purchase the Morgan

[72] *Laws of New York*, 1911, Chapter 150.

stock. Under this plan, control of the Society would then be vested in the company itself and the 5,000 investing policyholders would unite in the selection of a Board of Directors which would give the company the highest possible degree of stability and inspire the utmost confidence on the part of the public. *The Eastern Underwriter* pointed out that under Westinghouse's plan control would merely be transferred from one man to 5,000 and that the company would still be a stock corporation. *The Eastern Underwriter* said it could suggest a better idea as regards Equitable; namely, to let it alone: "In our humble opinion, the present management of the Equitable Life is rendering a fairly good account of its stewardship." [73]

After the amendment of the New York insurance law, Superintendent Hotchkiss pointed out that several plans for mutualization of the Society were available: 1) The general corporation law might be amended so as to provide for a permanent voting trust for the Morgan stock. 2) The Charter might be amended by joint action of the directors and a majority of the stock so as to give all the policyholders equal voting rights with the stockholders. This second plan, though not pure mutualization, would be mutualization in effect and would not require any monetary outlay. 3) The second plan might be combined with retirement of the stock as provided for by the amended law of 1911.

No further steps were taken at this time. The trustees of the Morgan stock continued to vote in favor of the directors chosen by the policyholders, and the Board continued to direct the affairs of the Society without any interference whatever from J. P. Morgan or the trustees of his stock. This was the status of mutualization when more pressing matters had to be faced.

THE HOME OFFICE DESTROYED BY FIRE

Equitable, having been through compurgation by oath, now had to face the lesser ordeal of fire—and water.

About 5:30 A.M. on January 9, 1912, No. 120 Broadway was reported to be on fire. What at first appeared to be just an ordinary basement fire, which was thought to have started in the Café Savarin, soon got beyond control. Thousands of gallons of water were poured into the building with little effect. As the fire spread, the outside temperature

[73] *The Eastern Underwriter*, XII (1911), June 22, Westinghouse's suggestion appeared in *The Insurance World*, XXXVIII (1911), June 20.

fell to about 18 degrees and hundreds of tons of ice added to the weight of the disintegrating structure. For a while the whole financial district was threatened. There were many acts of heroism. Night custodian Arthur E. Davis, when he saw that the building was doomed, drew the fires from the great boilers and crawled to safety. Tom Longfield (champion skater and bowler) of the Loan Department, with the assistance of three firemen who provided him with a water screen, climbed into his office and saved valuable records. When President William Giblin of the Mercantile Safe Deposit Company became trapped in the vaults of his company, firemen worked for two hours to get him out. Dodging falling stone and burning timbers, fireman Seneca Larke, encouraged by the Fire Commissioner and Fire Chaplain, sawed through the steel bars of the heavy door. John Campion, watchman for the Deposit Company, stayed on duty despite warnings and lost his life as a result. All told, six men lost their lives, one fireman and five employees of tenants; several were injured.

President Day arrived upon the scene before eight o'clock, looked over the situation, and went immediately to the Hazen building at 2 Albany Street, where he established temporary executive offices on the fifth floor, which had been occupied by the Medical Director. The Metropolitan Cashier took up quarters in the Mortuary Claim Department and was ready for business by nine o'clock, the usual hour for opening; a half hour later, the Cashier paid a death benefit for a policyholder who had died twenty-four hours earlier.[74] At the same time, a special "scouting committee" headed by Comptroller Gerald R. Brown and Auditor Leon Fisher was dispatched with orders to rent a building or a part of a building for Equitable's offices. One requirement was that there should be facilities capable of handling, among other things, the business of the Cashier with his 50 clerks, and the approximately 700 persons who called daily at the Cashier's windows. This committee within a matter of hours signed a contract for three whole floors of the City Investing Building at 165 Broadway. A "furniture committee" rounded up ready-to-deliver furniture from the stores and reported that

[74] While firemen were still pouring water into the ruins, agent A. Hollander, whose office was in the Singer Building, wrote a $150,000 policy on a young businessman, and the Cashier received the first premium at 1:30 P.M., and agent Edward L. Hunt sold a policy to Dr. Lee K. Frankel, head of Metropolitan Life's Welfare Department. Rosenfeld thanked Frankel over the phone, but President Day did not think it appropriate to make any mention of Frankel's policy in *Agency Items* or elsewhere. Day to Hunt, January 30, 1912. Day letters, Equitable Archives.

the necessary pieces would be delivered by late afternoon. Another committee secured a large safe for the Cashier's office and it was in place by five o'clock. Messengers were sent out to inform every employee of the Home Office that regardless of the fire there would be no interruption in the company's business; all were to report to the Hazen building. Henry L. Rosenfeld was instructed to send out frequent telegrams to all of the Equitable agents so that "they would not get panic-stricken, and ease off in their work." Second Vice President George T. Wilson was directed to call a meeting of all the agents in Equitable's metropolitan district so that they could be briefed on the situation. President Day then sent out through Conservation Commissioner E. E. Rittenhouse, who had been a reporter and editor in his early career, the following bulletin to the policyholders:

> The burning of the home office will cause but temporary inconvenience. The securities and important records are protected by fireproof vaults which are intact. Most of the office force and records were removed some time ago to the Society's new building at 2 Albany Street. The executive offices have been established at 165 Broadway, which for the time being will be the home office of the Society, where all business with the public will be transacted, including the receipt of premium payments.

By afternoon, President Day was answering numerous letters of sympathy and offers of help. Among them were letters from President George E. Ide of the Home Life Insurance Company, President Darwin P. Kingsley of the New York Life, Vice President Haley Fiske of the Metropolitan, President George C. Markham of the Northwestern Mutual, and various bank presidents. The office was besieged by reporters—and some, unable to get interviews with Rittenhouse, manufactured their own stories.[75] Although President Day's bulletin to the policyholders had been given to the newspapers, he said that

[75] The fact that the New York Stock Exchange had temporarily suspended delivery of securities led to rumors regarding the destruction of Equitable's securities. This suspension had no relation to the Equitable securities but to the personal securities in the vaults of the various banking institutions and safe deposit companies which were tenants in the Equitable Building. Another rumor was to the effect that J. P. Morgan had cabled from Europe regarding the construction of a new Home Office building for the Society. When *The St. Louis Post-Dispatch*, in an editorial January 12, mentioned this subject, President Day stated that Equitable had received no such telegram from Morgan and that the assets of the Society were not going to be used either directly or indirectly for stock market "pawn broking." Day to the editor, January 16, 1912. *Ibid.*

"their columns continue to be filled with preposterous stories about imaginary losses supposed to run into millions." He appreciated very much the published interview of Superintendent Hotchkiss to the effect that Equitable's assets were entirely safe. He expressed his regrets on behalf of the Society to Mayor William J. Gaynor for the loss of life and wrote the Fire Commissioner that Equitable had purchased the mortgage on the home of Battalion Chief William J. Walsh, who was killed by a falling floor. The Society later granted cash relief to the families of the other men who had been killed and took care of the medical expenses of firemen and policemen who were injured.

Normal business operations were quickly restored and by the end of the day the medical staff had passed on some 260 cases, and 22 death claims were filed of which 19 were paid.

The Equitable Building, which had been Henry B. Hyde's great pride in 1870, and again after it was expanded and rebuilt in the 1880's, was a mass of ruins. The thick stone walls had crumbled and the iron pillars and beams of the patchwork structure lay piled and twisted. But ticking away in the office of Mercantile Trust, still showing the correct time, was a clock with its case badly burned. Also surviving the destruction was the stained glass window which contained a reproduction of Equitable's Statue Group.[76] And standing amidst the debris and tons of ice was the bronze statue of the founder and builder, unscathed, calm and serene, as a symbol that Equitable, phoenixlike, was to rise again, if not to immortality, at least to greater heights than ever before. It was a symbol not overlooked by those in whose hands the management of the Society rested.

Until the Society's great vault was opened some three weeks after the fire, it was not known whether or not the $282,000,000 of securities had been destroyed. But the vault, with its great double doors and air spaces between the walls and inner safes, had served its purpose

[76] According to photographs of this window taken at the time the Equitable building was rebuilt in the mid-1880's, it also contained the portrait of Henry B. Hyde's son, Henry B., Jr., who had died in 1880. In 1960 the window was in a crate in a driveway at Equitable's Home Office, 393 Seventh Avenue. It was intact except that the pane which had contained the likeness of young Hyde had been replaced by clear glass. The portion which contained the Statue Group was later placed in the Policyholders Service area of the Cashiers' Department on the ground floor of Equitable's new Home Office building at 1285 Avenue of the Americas.

The window was originally designed and executed by Nicolas Lorin about 1879. It is possible that it was not finished until after the death of Henry B. Hyde, Jr. Hyde wrote Lorin, September 9, 1879, that the window "should be finished by now." Hyde papers, letterpress volume, A 12.

well. None of the securities was destroyed, but some which were stored inside metal boxes had to be replaced because the heat had caused the metallic paint to become a gummy mass and thus disfigure the papers. (A western newspaper surmised that it was the water in the stocks and bonds which kept them from being consumed.) The securities were moved under the personal direction of President Day to the vaults of the Carnegie Safe Deposit Company. Fortunately, the Society was able to maintain almost uninterrupted business as a result of Auditor Leon Fisher's foresight in providing a system of duplicate records. The records of policies, medical records, records of the accounting department, and of the auditor's office had been moved to the Hazen building during the preceding five years. The actuaries' basic policy record cards, however, and the policy "history cards," which had been separated in 1911 and put in the auditor's department, were still in the Home Office building. The policy record cards, which were in steel files, were destroyed, but the history cards, which were in wooden boxes, were merely charred. From the history cards, the Cashier's record cards, and data from the State Insurance Department, the basic policy records were reconstructed. Also destroyed in the fire were the records and data accumulated by the State Insurance Department in its triennial examination of Equitable. Examiners from the Department had been at work for several months and their report, which was to have been ready by February 1, was somewhat delayed.[77]

Though the Equitable building had not been insured, the financial loss as a result of the fire was not great. Henry B. Hyde had decided that the Society was capable of carrying its own risk on its building, and it was estimated that over a period of a quarter of a century he had saved about $3,000,000 by so doing; and the old building was valued at considerably less than $3,000,000. In fact, the appraiser for the New York Insurance Department some years earlier had reported that the building added nothing to the value of the land. E. E. Rittenhouse said:

> The company hasn't carried the building as an asset for years. The fire has not reduced the company's assets. On the contrary, it saves some of the cost of tearing down the building to rebuild a more modern structure which would earn an adequate interest on the capital invested, as the burned building has not done for several years. The burned building for

[77] Among valuable historical records destroyed, besides those of Equitable, were the papers of E. H. Harriman, whose offices were in the building.

years has not been able to earn the interest on the value of the land on which it was built. The cost of tearing down the building, even, would have been more than the building was worth. The land it occupied, which has been freed for the possibilities of a new and more modern structure by the fire, is worth from $12,000,000 to $15,000,000.[78]

The contract for making the ruins safe was awarded to the Thompson-Starrett Company and for removing them to the George A. Fuller Company. A large liability policy was taken out with $50,000 and $100,000 limits to cover the contractors and the Society.

The Home Office force was stimulated to extraordinary efforts by the trying conditions which resulted from the fire, and the Board of Directors expressed its appreciation in a resolution. President Day said: "Permit me to add that I am more than proud to head so capable and loyal a body of workers who are animated by the real Equitable esprit de corps." And a week after the fire he was able to report that "the Equitable is going along as usual pursuing the even tenor of her beneficent way undisturbed and unperturbed."[79] The fire was not without certain compensations. It had brought the Society a lot of incidental publicity and the agents were notified to take advantage of that fact. Said President Day: "I am anxious that our people everywhere shall take full advantage of the incidental publicity which has resulted from the fire. The Society's strength and standing have been more effectively advertised by the fire than they had ever been before." [80] The General Agency Association at its meeting late in January resolved to sell $150,000,000 of life insurance during the year.

In February 1912, the Board of Directors of Equitable decided to sell the plot bounded by Broadway, Pine, Nassau, and Cedar Streets if a fair price could be had. When it was rumored that the Society might build elsewhere, President Day said: "It looks to me as if the Equitable would not leave the general locality for many years, if ever." [81] Some interested citizens thought the block should be left open for a park, something rare in New York's financial district. One report was to the effect that Vincent Astor might purchase the space for a memorial park in honor of his father, Colonel John Jacob Astor, who

[78] Quoted in *The Eastern Underwriter*, XIII (1912), January 11.

[79] Day to I. L. Register, Philadelphia, January 17, 1912. Day letters, Equitable Archives.

[80] Day to Edward A. Woods, February 13, 1912. *Ibid.*

[81] Day to Timothy L. Woodruff, President, Jamaica Estates, March 13, 1912. *Ibid.*

had gone down on the *Titanic.*[82] It occurred to General T. Coleman du Pont, President of E. I. du Pont de Nemours Powder Company of New Jersey, however, that it was feasible to build a new building on the site of the ruins of the old Equitable Building. General du Pont, who was one of the more interesting and wealthy members of the famous family, had not entered the powder business until mid-life and now, after having built his company into a position of preeminence, was diversifying his interests.

August 12, 1912, Equitable signed an agreement to sell to du Pont, "or to a corporation to be organized by him," a plot of land in consideration of the sum of $13,500,000. Du Pont agreed to cause the new corporation to be formed on or before December 16, 1912, and by that date to produce executed subscription or underwriting agreements to cover "the purchase of the New Corporation's obligations or stock or both in amounts that will produce, as required for the New Corporation, the sum of $7,500,000"; it was understood that prior to the delivery of the deed, du Pont would provide satisfactory evidence of the financial responsibility of the subscribers or underwriters of the stock of the new corporation, and that at the time of delivery the purchaser would present to Equitable a duly executed bond and mortgage accompanied by a certificate of consent of the holders of two thirds of the stock. The purchaser agreed that the new corporation would, by December 16, 1912, make a contract for the erection of a 36-story fireproof office building to be completed by May 1, 1914. The agreement also provided that Equitable (the obligee) would lend to du Pont (the obligor) $19,500,000, to be repaid, both principal and interest, in gold coin "of the present standard of weight and fineness" in 122 semi-annual installments; $13,500,000 of this sum was for the purchase price of the land and $6,000,000 would be for the erection of the building.[83]

Since it proved impossible to have the plans and specifications for the new building ready by December 16, a supplemental agreement was made December 12 which extended the date of taking title to the

82 *The Eastern Underwriter,* XIII (1912), December 5.

83 The installments were to begin November 1, 1913, and run to May 1, 1974, but each of the first twelve semi-annual installments was to comprise interest only and amount to $300,000, plus an additional sum equal to interest at 2 per cent on all moneys advanced on account of the loan of $6,000,000. Semi-annual installments maturing after May 1, 1919, would include payments on principal also and consequently would run for 55 years.

land to May 1, 1913, and the date for completion of the building to May 1, 1915.[84] In January 1913, General du Pont asked for an additional loan of $2,500,000, to be secured by stock of the E. I. du Pont de Nemours Powder Company, but the Finance Committee of the Equitable Board turned down this request on the grounds that the law did not permit such loans; had the security been bonds, it might have been willing to consider the request.[85] Equitable did, however, agree to make an additional loan of $1,000,000 for the building.[86]

The Equitable Office Building Corporation was incorporated April 22, 1913; it was authorized to issue 80,000 shares of capital stock of no par value, but the number of shares might be increased by law. The certificate of incorporation also stated that "the amount of capital with which the corporation will carry on business is $400,000." [87]

The final papers—deed of transfer, bond, mortgage, and all other agreements—were signed April 24, 1913. Interest on the original purchase money mortgage of $13,500,000 was fixed at 4.6 per cent from May 1, 1919, and interest on the building loan of $7,000,000 was fixed at 4 per cent from the same date; the average for the total loan of $20,500,000 was thus 4.4 per cent.[88] The mortgage was said to have

[84] Equitable also agreed to pay one half of the taxes on the land for one year and to waive a portion of the interest on the land mortgage during construction. For a memorandum on the supplemental agreement, see C. J. Martin files, Equitable Archives.

[85] President Day to du Pont, January 28 and February 20, 1913. Day letters, Equitable Archives. Day wrote du Pont that Equitable expected "performance of your contract of August 12, 1912, as modified by supplemental agreement of December 12, 1912."

[86] When Superintendent of Insurance William T. Emmet inquired about this additional loan, President Day said he had reason to believe that if this additional loan had not been made, General du Pont would have failed in his contract with the Society, paid his $500,000 forfeit, and withdrawn from any further effort to complete his undertaking. Day to Emmet, April 14, 1913. *Ibid.*

[87] General du Pont agreed to take 79,800 shares and Lewis L. Dunham and Ross A. Mackey 100 shares each. Directors for the first year were General du Pont, Lewis L. Dunham, Ross A. Mackey, Leland B. Duer, and Charles V. Graham. The papers of incorporation were drawn up by Dwight W. Morrow, then a junior member of the law firm of Simpson, Thacher and Bartlett. It appears that the corporation later issued $4,000,000 of preferred stock and $8,000,000 of common stock, all of which was underwritten by General du Pont, though the "Report of the Committee on Mutualization" of July 19, 1917, speaks of $2,600,000 of 6 per cent preferred stock being "ahead of the common stock."

[88] The "Agreement" of August 12, 1912, and the final papers were printed in booklet form. Copy in Corporate Records, Equitable Archives. The essentials of the agreements between du Pont and Equitable, plus the modifications made in 1917 when the Society purchased du Pont's Equitable stock (see this history,

been the largest ever placed on a single piece of New York real estate.[89] President Day considered the Society fortunate in being able to dispose of the property and thus convert it from a questionable asset and a heavy expense to a sound and productive investment.[90]

As planned by the architect, Ernest R. Graham, the new building would consist of two towers of 36 stories each with a total height of 486 feet above street level. The architectural design was in the Italian Renaissance style with the façades of brick, limestone, granite, and terra cotta. The building was constructed by the Thompson-Starrett Company. The inside corridors were finished in marble and the offices were trimmed in mahogany. There were to be 44 electric passenger elevators, 20 of which were to run to the twenty-second floor and 24 to the top floor. When the building was completed, however, there were 48 "high-rise" elevators, plus five private elevators. An arcade ran through the building from Broadway to Nassau Street; shops faced the arcade and the remainder of the first floor was designed primarily for banks. In the sub-basement were the safety deposit vaults of the banks, and in the basement were café, bar, and dining rooms.[91] Estimated cost of the building was $14,900,000; the total investment in land and building was listed at $29,000,000. Equitable agreed to lease three floors for a period of twenty years at $244,982.50 per year; in return, it was to receive in perpetuity a sum equal to 9 per cent of all dividends paid by the new corporation from time to time out of its surplus earnings upon its common stock.

The building was finished on time, and in April 1915 Equitable began moving one department at a time, with the Actuarial Department leading the move. The various departments took over the fifth and sixth floors and the front half of the seventh and eighth floors. There was no interruption of business, and on Monday, April 26, the Home Office was again located at 120 Broadway. When President Day arrived at his office, he was greeted with some 1,900 applications for

---

p. 821), are contained in a tabulation entitled "Loan on 120 Broadway and Modifications" prepared by Vice President J. V. E. Westfall, April 30, 1920. Copy in *ibid.*

[89] *The Eastern Underwriter*, XIV (1913), May 1.

[90] Day to George J. Roberts, July 6, 1916. Day letters, Equitable Archives. Income on the old building for several years had been about 2.6 per cent and this did not take into consideration the great appreciation in value of the land investment.

[91] For a description of the completed building, see *The Real Estate Magazine* (February 1915).

$4,500,000 of life insurance presented by the agents in honor of "Home-Coming Day." He wrote: "There is no place like home."

Within little more than a year all the space in this "the largest office building in the world" was rented. Among the tenants were some of the leading corporations of the country such as the Diamond Match Company, United States Steel Corporation, the Chesapeake and Ohio Railway Company, and the Southern Railroad. Revenues totaled almost $3,000,000 per year.

MUTUALIZATION PLANS COMPLETED

In addition to the great fire, Equitable had other troubles. February 10, 1912, Superintendent of Insurance William H. Hotchkiss presented one of the most critical reports ever made on the Society. Hotchkiss was due to retire from office in ten days, but felt duty bound to present the facts and his conclusions thereon; a duty all the more unpleasant in that it "must be performed at a time when your Company and yourselves have enlarged and wearying responsibilities, due to the recent conflagration." This report was the result of the examination of Equitable which had begun in June 1911 and had been interrupted and delayed by the fire. In 23 legal-size typed pages, Hotchkiss stated that Equitable's expenses were too high; its per capita share of life insurance was falling; its investment returns were next to the lowest among leading companies; and its mortality, cancellation, and expense ratios were the highest. Also, the Society was paying among the lowest dividends and adding least to its reserves. These facts constituted "a combination of danger signals which, in a smaller or younger company, would cause alarm." He quoted the Insurance Department's specialist on statistics as follows:

> Of all classes of life insurance statistics, figures relating to expenses are the most interesting to study, since the expense element of the business is more directly under the control of the management than any other and the figures are pretty apt to be an accurate index of relative efficiency. The ill effects of transgressing the rule of efficiency accumulate slowly in a life insurance company, but when their results are felt, they are like the Old Man of the Sea on the back of Sinbad the Sailor.

Hotchkiss admitted that some of Equitable's troubles were inherited from pre-Armstrong days but was convinced "that these inherited diseases do not by any means explain the condition and relative rank of the Company, either from the standpoint of economic statistics or from the popular standpoint of a producer of insurance." Other companies, such as the New York Life and the Mutual, had largely recovered from the Armstrong Committee disclosures, whereas Equitable had not.

Since President Day had seriously considered what practical measures could be taken to reduce Equitable's expenses, Superintendent Hotchkiss called attention to a number of specific items which had cost Equitable heavily. He said that the expenditure for legal services in recent years had been excessive. Whereas the New York Life and Mutual maintained legal departments with salaried counsel, Equitable still relied largely upon outside counsel who, in addition to a salary from the Society, engaged in general practice; also Equitable frequently engaged special counsel. He noted the fact that Equitable had spent $20,000 for counsel in Missouri to attack the constitutionality of the law which would have ousted from the state any life insurance company which had paid any salary in excess of $50,000; since President Day's salary had been fixed at $50,000, this expense seemed unnecessary. Hotchkiss considered the Home Office payroll "to be unwarrantably large, both in its total and in the gross amount paid in certain of its departments." Expenses in the Comptroller's Department and the Auditor's Department were particularly alarming. In regard to agents' expenses, Hotchkiss would not accept the explanation that Equitable was still carrying heavy renewal commissions incurred in an earlier period. Whether compared with companies such as New York Life or Mutual, which had converted to the less expensive salaried manager plan, or to Northwestern Mutual or Mutual Benefit, which still adhered to the general agency system, Equitable's agency expenses were still the highest. Hotchkiss concluded that Equitable greatly needed "a complete resystematization of its Home Office work." He expected "prompt and resultful action" as a result of his report.

Superintendent Hotchkiss' report was read to the Equitable Board of Directors at their meeting February 15, 1912, at which time the Board authorized the appointment of a committee of its members "to confer with the Executive Officers of the Society with reference to the two communications of February 10 from the Superintendent of Insurance, and with full power to examine into the suggestions and criticisms with the view of reporting as soon as possible to the Board of Directors." Chairman of the Committee was Director John D. Kernan.[92]

With his report on Equitable, Superintendent Hotchkiss had submitted a seven-page memorandum entitled "Thoughts Suggested by Two Memoranda entitled 'Memorandum Relating to the Question of Mutualization' and 'Why the Society Could Not Afford to Pay $6,000,000, or Any Approximate Amount, for the Retirement of Its Capital Stock.'" These two memoranda had been accompanied by a letter submitted to the Insurance Department by President Day on January 24. The second of these memoranda had been prepared by John Van Etten Westfall, Superintendent of the Bureau of Statistics; it presented the facts to show that Equitable could not afford to pay $6,000,000 for the retirement of its capital stock without jeopardizing the Society's competitive position.

In his "Thoughts" inspired by the two memoranda, Superintendent Hotchkiss made no effort to discuss the question "of the absolute value of mutualization"; since both parties assumed that mutualization was desirable, the question was how could it be done without adding to the difficulty of getting new business: "All roads lead to Rome and in this case Rome appears to consist of that knotty problem: By what feat of legerdemain can the Society pay out $6,000,000, or any other large amount, without imperiling its dividend scale?" He criticized Westfall's analysis of Equitable's affairs in 1912, and a projection of them as they would be in the year 1927, as furnishing a "static view," whereas what was needed was a "moving picture," which would take into account the dynamic forces at work. He thought that a more optimistic statistician might be able to show that Equitable's future was more hopeful than some would believe. For example, improving mortality experience, higher earnings on its assets, and savings from lower renewal commissions might change the picture perceptibly. He suggested that the Society might secure an option to purchase the majority of its capital stock by some designated date in the future, setting aside annually a certain sum for this purpose. This action would enable it to pay for the stock on an installment plan without placing itself in a position where a large sum of money would have either to be paid out in cash or charged up as a liability. Since the Society had no serious mortgages on its future, he did not see why such an idea

[92] Other members of the Committee were A. C. Humphreys, Charles D. Norton, Jacob G. Schmidlapp, and Richard H. Williams.

The Fire of January 9, 1912

President Day emerges from the vault
in which he found the securities safe

would not be feasible; other than the heavy commissions for renewals, it had no serious problems—no insurance at inadequate rates, no impairment of reserves, no bad assets, no contracts difficult or impossible of fulfillment, no badge of financial weakness of any sort whatever: "Such troubles as exist constitute merely a sort of corporate bilious attack due to the Society's having had all kinds of indigestible things in its stomach." As an afterthought, Hotchkiss asked why not submit the question of mutualization to the policyholders; give them the facts in impartial language, tell them that it would probably cost each one about $2 a year for six years, and let the policyholders vote "yes or no": "Would not this cultivate the right kind of feeling among the policyholders? Would it not be worth a few cents per policyholder as a psychological proposition, even if it failed in other ways?"

The Kernan Committee made a verbal report to the Board March 21. It called attention to numerous errors in facts and figures in Hotchkiss' report and to his "mistaken conclusions." It thought these errors might be explained by the fact that many of Hotchkiss' records on his examination of Equitable had been destroyed in the fire. It noted that as late as July 1909 Superintendent Hotchkiss had issued a report on the Society which had been generally commendatory, and that since that date the Society had shown improvement in the matters discussed in that report. The Board resolved that it was the purpose of the Committee "to go to the bottom of every allegation contained" in Hotchkiss' report, "to the end that the just expectations of the Insurance Department may be met." [93]

April 18 the Kernan Committee submitted its findings to the Board in a 17-page report; accompanying the report was an analysis of Equitable's organization and accounting methods by Gunn, Richards and Company, public accountants. This report took up each of the points covered by Superintendent Hotchkiss, and in several instances, using the same figures, showed that different conclusions might be arrived at. For instance, in connection with mortality ratios, it pointed out that comparison with Northwestern Mutual and Mutual Benefit was somewhat unfair since these two companies, which had grown rapidly in recent years, had a larger proportion of freshly selected business with low mortality which helped bring down their averages. The Committee recommended an intensive promotion of business in

[93] Corporate Records, 1912, Equitable Archives.

the healthier two-thirds of the United States and a more critical medical selection in the South; also that the Society cease writing new business in those foreign countries where it was not profitable or where investment restrictions were too onerous. It pointed out that Equitable's high cancellation rate was accounted for in part by the many terminations which resulted from the Armstrong investigation, and in part by the large number of deferred dividend policies which were reaching the end of their accumulation periods and being surrendered. As for the litigation in Missouri, it was thought necessary because the Missouri law could be applied to the income of any valuable General Agent of the Society whose earnings in gross commissions might exceed $50,000 per year. Not only was comparison of Home Office expenses with those of the New York Life difficult because of the dissimilarity of the organizations of the two Home Offices, but Hotchkiss' figures for 1911 showed an error of several hundred thousand dollars. The Committee agreed with the Superintendent that the recent destruction of the Home Office building offered an excellent opportunity for a reorganization of the Home Office and that the control of the Home Office organization should be placed under a Vice President. It recommended that a "Committee on Efficiency and Economy" should be created to study the whole problem. The Kernan Committee's analysis of expenses for legal services presented a picture quite different from that contained in Hotchkiss' report, but it did agree that a separate legal department within the Society would be better than employing outside counsel. While conceding that there was some justice in the criticism that Equitable combined "the expenses and disadvantages of the Branch Office and the General Agency Systems without securing the full advantage of either," the Committee explained that the transition could not be made all at once; but it recommended that only Branch Office managers be used in the future in all sections where a material volume of acceptable business could be written.

The accompanying report from Gunn, Richards and Company, after going into detail in regard to Home Office organization and practices, made the following general suggestions: (1) reduction to a more compact and efficient organization; (2) reduction of salary expense by readjustment and concentration of duties and by a scientific system of grading salaries; (3) reduction of clerical and other expense by the rearrangement and concentration of accounting and operating functions and methods; (4) reduction of expenses by the use of certain modern mechanical and labor-saving devices not yet adopted by the Society.

The report of the Kernan Committee was accepted by the Board, which approved of the recommendations made. A copy of the report and the Board's resolutions were forwarded to Superintendent William T. Emmett on April 19.

There is little doubt that Superintendent Hotchkiss' report and comments upon mutualization intensified and speeded up Equitable's efforts toward greater efficiency and economy as well as toward mutualization.

On June 12, 1915, President Day announced that T. Coleman du Pont had on June 11 purchased 564 shares of Equitable stock from the estate of J. P. Morgan.

General T. Coleman du Pont—the title of "General" was honorary—was born in Louisville, Kentucky, December 11, 1863. He attended college at Urbana University (Ohio) and the Massachusetts Institute of Technology. His first extensive business operations were in coal and iron mining in Kentucky and in the construction and management of street railways. He joined his relatives in the powder business in 1900 and two years later became President of the E. I. du Pont de Nemours Powder Company. In 1908, while a member of the Republican National Committee, he had offered to subscribe $20,000 to William Howard Taft's campaign fund, but Frank H. Hitchcock, chairman of the committee, declined the check because the United States Government was investigating the powder business under the antitrust laws. In 1911 he offered to build a great road through Delaware, more than one hundred miles long, and give it to the state; he did so at a cost of almost $4,000,000. He donated $500,000 to the Massachusetts Institute of Technology. In 1912 he organized the du Pont Coal Company and became interested in motor boat racing. Late in 1914 he underwent an operation for appendicitis at the Mayo Clinic and soon thereafter suddenly offered to sell his du Pont de Nemours stock to the company, but the company voted not to purchase it. Cousin Pierre and associates, however, decided to take advantage of the offer and on March 2, 1915, purchased 36,900 shares of common stock for about $14,000,000; Coleman du Pont then resigned from the presidency.[94] Just why, on the eve of the great wartime boom in munitions, General du Pont

[94] General du Pont did not receive all cash for his shares. In the Dwight Morrow papers, Amherst College, is a copy of an agreement dated March 2, 1915, by which the du Pont Securities Company agreed to pay T. C. du Pont a certain amount (left blank) seven years after date. The agreement further states that 36,900 shares of the common capital stock of E. I. du Pont de Nemours Powder Company were deposited as collateral security for this note and others of the same date totaling the principal amount of $5,900,000.

decided to sell his stock is not clear. He knew that it was destined to become much more valuable—some years later it was worth more than ten times the sale price—but Coleman du Pont was an unpredictable character.[95] He was a large man and liked to do things in a large way. Perhaps he was merely seeking new experiences by way of new ventures.[96] He had built the McAlpin Hotel and contemplated building a chain of hotels. It had been announced that after completion of the new Equitable building he proposed to retire from active work. Fast on the heels of this announcement, however, came the news of du Pont's purchase of Equitable stock for the price of $4,394,540.10. (Some said he did not purchase the stock but that it was "wished upon him." No doubt Dwight W. Morrow, now a partner in J. P. Morgan and Company, who negotiated the transfer, was influential in making the decision.)[97] As soon as the news was released, President Day made the following announcement:

The majority of the capital stock . . . has been sold . . . to General Coleman du Pont, the principal owner of the new Equitable Building. The trust under which the stock has been voted remains undisturbed. . . .

It is fitting in making this announcement to state that the directors and officers of the Equitable Society appreciate highly the public spirited at-

[95] It was said that du Pont, who was something of a sleight-of-hand artist, would embarrass the Treasurer of the company by asking the time. When the Treasurer could not find his watch, du Pont would hand it to him and express the hope that he took better care of the company's money than he did his watch. When one of du Pont's loaded cigars would explode in the mouth of some dignified Director, he would slap his thigh and say, "I never knew the powder business could be so much fun."

[96] In his own words: "The idea of erecting the largest office building in the world appealed to me. . . . Now that the building has been completed and its organization working smoothly, it does not call for my attention. I like conceiving, planning, organizing, systematizing, getting a project established successfully. Then I want to start something else." Quoted in B. C. Forbes, *Men Who Are Making America* (New York, 1917), p. 76.

[97] June 10, 1915, Morrow put in the form of a letter the substance of a previous conversation with du Pont. After reviewing the history of Equitable he wrote: "I want to say in closing that I have told Mr. Morgan that with the sale recently made by you of your stock in the E. I. du Pont de Nemours Powder Company, and your resignation of the Presidency of the Company, you have practically ceased active business connections; that you have a large investment in the Equitable Office Building Corporation, the building in which the Society has its main offices; that you are interested in the success of the Society, and that it is your purpose, if you buy the stock, to transfer it to the Equitable Office Building Corporation, provided such a course is deemed advisable by the Society and the Equitable Office Building Corporation, and furthermore to give an option on the stock for a period of three years to the Society, for the purpose of mutualization, at cost to you, plus interest." Morrow to du Pont, Dwight Morrow papers, du Pont folder.

titude of the late Mr. Morgan and of his son during the period that the technical ownership of the stock has rested in their hands. During this entire period the directors and officers of the Society have enjoyed the fullest freedom in the administration of its affairs, without so much as a suggestion from the owners of the stock or trustees with respect to the management or conduct of the Society. The three trustees, whose sole duty has been to elect the directors, have selected men of integrity and known standing for these high positions with a full sense of responsibility for the trust imposed upon them. The directors so selected have administered the affairs of the Society free from any influence or control of the beneficial owners of the stock.

It is eminently appropriate that in the change in the ownership of the stock the interest in the majority of the Society's capital has now been acquired by a staunch friend of the Equitable, who states that his sole object is to protect the interests of the policyholders of the Society. . . .

June 28 du Pont informed the Superintendent of Insurance of the State of New York that he desired to cooperate in every way possible in effecting the mutualization of Equitable; also that the voting trust which had been in effect would continue undisturbed. A new trust agreement for five years, similar to those previously made by Thomas Fortune Ryan and J. P. Morgan, was made, to date from May 4, 1916. The trustees were Morgan J. O'Brien, Lewis Cass Ledyard, and Joseph H. Choate.[98]

The Equitable Committee on Mutualization began negotiations with General du Pont late in June 1915, but made no definite progress. In November du Pont wrote that so far as he had been able to learn, the Committee "has done nothing for two or three years and really nobody else has done anything." He said that he had purchased the stock of Equitable with the idea of mutualizing the Society and was "anxious to see this accomplished." He was willing to employ an attorney, or have Equitable employ one, who would make it his work

[98] William H. A. Carr in his *The du Ponts of Delaware* (New York, 1964), p. 278, says in regard to du Pont's purchase of the stock: "The importance of this acquisition lay not in the actual earning power of the insurance company, but in the fact that Coly now controlled its assets, which at that time amounted to about $600,000,000. These funds had to be deposited in banks or invested in railroad and other stocks; the man who could decree how and where the funds would be used was a power to reckon with in Wall Street." It would appear that the author was either not aware of the facts of the case or that he chose to ignore them, namely, that the shares remained in the hands of trustees who had the right to vote them, and that du Pont had already announced his intention of giving Equitable a three-year option on the shares at cost to him.

to devise a plan which would be of advantage to the Society.[99] In August 1916 he still thought that this would be a good idea. The following month Louis J. Horowitz, President of Thompson-Starrett Company, outlined a plan for mutualization of Equitable which he submitted to du Pont. He said: "I am afraid we made a mistake in allowing $2,800,000 to become fixed in the minds of Judge Spratt and Mr. Norton [of Equitable's Committee on Mutualization] as the figure for the purchase price of your majority stock, leaving for future trading the purchasing power of this cash amount in connection with acquiring a junior interest in the first Equitable Building mortgage." He thought that du Pont should insist in so far as he had a right, upon securing this junior interest in the mortgage.[100]

Apparently some progress was being made, for in October 1916 Charles D. Norton wrote that "a really extraordinary opportunity to mutualize the Equitable has come about. . . ." He had his worries, however: since the Committee had approved an expenditure of $3,000,000 for all of Equitable's stock, if the Society paid du Pont $2,800,000 for his 564 shares, that would leave only $200,000 with which to purchase the remaining 436 shares. He thought that the Committee should frankly ask those stockholders who could afford it to donate their stock to the Society. He stated that he and several other directors had already done so and that someone ought to get in touch with James H. Hyde to see if he would like to donate his stock.[101] But things were still pending as late as May 1917 when du Pont wrote President Day as follows:

> Your letter of May 3 received. I thought that while waiting for legislative action the Society would have worked out its plan anticipating action on my offer of September 17, 1916.

99 Du Pont sent this "foundation of a letter to Judge Day" to Morrow for criticism, November 12, 1915. Dwight Morrow papers, du Pont folder.

100 Horowitz then went into considerable detail in regard to how this could be done to the satisfaction of both du Pont and the Society. Horowitz to du Pont, September 11, 1916. *Ibid.*, Equitable Life folder. It was Horowitz who had first made contact with Morrow in regard to drawing up the papers for the Equitable Office Building Corporation and he became chairman of the Executive Committee of that corporation.

101 Charles D. Norton at Hot Springs, Virginia, to Allan McCulloh of the law firm of Alexander and Green, October 15, 1916. *Ibid.* Norton asked McCulloh whether he would take this matter up with James H. Hyde either by a personal visit to Paris or by letter. It may be recalled that Hyde still had some shares of stock. See this history, p. 645. Early in 1918 Hyde sold his 35 shares to Equitable for $52,500. Mircrofilm of canceled check in Equitable Archives.

Do you not think I have the right now to insist that the offer be promptly accepted or rejected to the end that I may be free to take such steps as seem to me wise.

I do not care to be in the position of indefinitely extending to the Society an option to take my stock at a figure which represents a great loss to me, and which I was induced to name only on the understanding that I was helping the Society in a difficult situation.

Finally a plan of mutualization was agreed upon and approved by the Equitable Board July 19, 1917.[102] In brief, the plan was as follows: Equitable would purchase 501 of the shares (the controlling block) at $5,400 per share, and the remaining 63 shares at $1,500 per share; payment of purchase price and interest was to be made in 40 semi-annual installments of $111,537.46 each. It has been stated that under this agreement General du Pont would receive $2,799,900, or $1,594,-640 less than the cost of his stock, but this statement does not take into consideration the fact that du Pont would receive interest at 5 per cent on the unpaid balances, and the fact that the Society agreed to release its right to receive in perpetuity 9 per cent of the amount paid as dividends on the common stock of the Equitable Office Building Corporation. This right may have been worth $2,000,000 or more. The semi-annual installments were given to General du Pont in the form of junior participations in the interest due on the mortgage on the Equitable Building as received by Equitable from the Equitable Office Building Corporation. (Under the law, the Society could not give an equal participation.) As it was du Pont's own corporation which was to pay principal and interest on the mortgage, he could be assured that the installments due for his stock would be paid. An extension agreement relative to the mortgage was made which provided for postponement of amortization of $1,000,000 of the principal amount

102 Thirty-three members of the Equitable Board attended the meeting; 30 voted in favor of the resolution to mutualize the Society and three refrained from voting. Schedule A, with the listing of annual installments to be paid on the mortgage on the Equitable Building, was not agreed to until July 23. On August 21 stockholders voted in person or by proxy; 615 shares were voted in favor of the resolution and 248 against. On December 6 policyholders voted—in person or by proxy—and the vote was reported December 24: 84,364 votes were in favor of mutualization and 3,162 against.

December 11 du Pont had written Morrow that he understood the vote to be the largest "that ever came in on any other matter, or with any other insurance company." He said it would take two weeks to count the votes and that "a dinner has been bet that 5% of them will not be against 'Mutualization.'" Dwight Morrow papers, Equitable Life folder.

from November 1, 1919, to May 1, 1936; the effect of this extension was to increase interest and reduce principal payments during the first seventeen years.[103]

An effort was made by the Royal Trust Company of Montreal as executors and trustees under the will of Sir William C. Van Horne, a stockholder, to restrain the officers and directors of Equitable from proceeding with the mutualization plan. In September, Judge Charles M. Hough of the District Court of the United States for the Southern District of New York ordered Equitable to show cause why it should not be restrained from carrying out its mutualization plans. After the hearing, however, the Court refused to issue the restraining order and the plaintiffs appealed. The plaintiffs, who were represented by Henry de Forest Baldwin, argued that if the legislature could "arbitrarily divide the corporate assets unequally, giving to certain favorite stockholders the lion's share, and those who are not among the favored majority as much or as little as the majority may choose to give them, the whole body of law upon which rests the security of shareholders becomes unsettled." The United States Circuit Court of Appeals,

[103] Morrow's biographer, Sir Harold Nicolson, makes much ado about the expedition and skill with which Morrow prepared the papers for the organization of the Equitable Office Building Corporation. This task did not present any extraordinary difficulties for a reasonably astute lawyer. Then Nicolson tells the story of how "one day in the Spring of 1917" Morrow and Thomas Cochran, also of J. P. Morgan and Company, had lunch together at the Plaza Hotel. Morrow ordered lunch but did not notice the food when it was put before him; he seemed to be in a sort of trance. Finally he came to and said: "That's done it!" When Cochran asked what had done what Morrow replied: "I've mutualized the Equitable! Now, Tom, let's go out somewhere and get something to eat!" Nicolson, *Dwight Morrow* (New York, 1935) pp. 153–54.

Then after discussing the agreement between Equitable and du Pont in regard to purchase of his Equitable stock, the biography states that "there remained the problem of how to induce General du Pont to part with his holdings at what would certainly represent a heavy loss. To this day it remains a mystery how Morrow was able to secure his consent" (p. 155). If Morrow did the persuading it was done long before the agreement which was ratified July 19, 1917. General du Pont had made his offer to accept $2,800,000 September 17, 1916, and as for the "heavy loss," Nicolson, although he noted the surrender to du Pont of the 9 per cent of the dividends on the stock of the Equitable Office Building Corporation, did not recognize its significance.

That du Pont and Morrow became very close friends is evidenced by their correspondence in the next few years. Morrow was frequently invited to go duck hunting at du Pont's estate in Delaware and du Pont ended some of his letters with "Love and kisses." On one occasion he sent Morrow a telegram in which he asked: "Why is an aeroplane deadly poison?" The answer arrived in another telegram the following day: "One drop kills you." Dwight Morrow papers, du Pont folder.

Second Circuit, in November upheld the decision of the lower court and said in part: "We think there is nothing in the complainant's claim that they, as stockholders, are injured in connection with the appropriation out of the society's surplus to purchase du Pont's stock, because they had no interest in the surplus whatever. If anyone has a right to complain on this point it is the participating policyholders and annuitants." [104] In regard to this decision, President Day wrote: "The decision is a most satisfactory one to us on all points." And to the agents he wrote: "Nothing has been nearer to my heart since the chief responsibility for the administration of the Society's affairs devolved upon me, and nothing in which we have succeeded has given me more pleasure."

The mutualization plan was approved by the policyholders December 6, and by Superintendent of Insurance Jesse S. Phillips early in February 1918. Phillips said that the only criticism which could be presented against the plan was the seemingly large price paid for the majority shares, the par value of which was $50,100. He appreciated the difficulties of accurately measuring the value of the controlling shares and mentioned the prices paid for them by Ryan, Morgan, and du Pont: "These sales indicate that great financiers have recognized the enormous value in the majority stock solely because of its power to control nearly $600,000,000 of trust funds and the effect of such control upon other financial institutions. The removal of this power of control, which at present may be exercised by a single individual, is, to my mind, a sufficient justification for the payment of a higher price for the dominating stock interest than the holding of the minority, even if such payment were to be made directly from the present surplus of the Society."

The mutualization of Equitable met with favorable comment from the insurance press. Representative of this comment was the lead article which appeared in *The Weekly Underwriter* under the title, "The Goal Reached":

The Equitable Life has at last achieved mutualization, for which it has striven consistently for years. It is a result of which President Day and his associates may well be proud, although from the policyholders' viewpoint of dollars and cents the stockholders were never to get more than seven per cent on their investment. Some of the latter seem to find that hard

[104] The opinion was written by Judge Henry G. Ward, with Judges Rogers and Learned Hand concurring. 247 Fed. Rep. 437.

to understand when discussing the price they are now offered for their stock. General duPont is entitled to credit and commendation for sacrificing two millions of dollars in order to let the policyholders own their own company. He could have sold it elsewhere at a handsome profit. The legislature paved the way for the mutualization by providing a means whereby the company may acquire its own stock with its own funds and retain it until all the shares have been acquired. This fact the minority obstructors also overlooked, or they would not have come forward with the claim that upon the retirement of the majority stock, which under the previous law would have been automatically coincident with its purchase from company funds, they would acquire the control of the company. The Equitable control, thanks to the action of General duPont, will be forever removed from anyone other than the company's policyholders as soon as the necessary legal routine work has been completed. From a competitive standpoint, the mutualization will afford the company's agents additional selling arguments, notwithstanding the company has always been operated upon the mutual plan. Actual mutuality in life insurance is inevitably more appealing to the public than theoretical mutuality.[105]

All but 23 shares of the minority stock were turned in by May 14, 1918, the deadline fixed by the purchase agreement. The success of the mutualization plan met with general acceptance from the policyholders. President Day said that he received more letters of approval from the policyholders during the early months of 1918 than during any of the preceding seven years of his presidency. Though the last of the shares were not to be acquired until 1925, Equitable was to all intents and purposes now legally a mutual company as it had been, in operation, since the beginning.

OTHER DEVELOPMENTS OF THE PREWAR YEARS

The United States revenue bills of 1913—which became the Underwood-Simmons Tariff Act with its income tax provisions—gave the life insurance companies, and particularly Equitable, serious concern. The House bill, which was prepared without hearings, would, it was thought, tax not only "dividends" or refunds to the policyholders, but also matured policies and additions to reserves. In March President Day wrote Oscar Underwood (Alabama), chairman of the Committee on Ways and Means, and called attention to the unjust taxation of life insurance under the revenue act of 1909; he hoped that the same injustice would not be inflicted by the new law. He explained the

[105] *The Weekly Underwriter*, XCVII (1917), July 28.

nature of "dividends" to Underwood and offered to furnish his committee with additional information.[106] In April Vice President John B. Lunger went to Washington to interview Secretary of Commerce William C. Redfield and Senator Underwood. Day wired Lunger that as the bill then stood, matured policies as well as "dividends" and additions to reserves would be subject to taxation: "Under this interpretation our policyholders would be mulcted approximately $700,000 per annum." [107] Robert Lynn Cox, counsel and General Manager of The Association of Life Insurance Presidents, also went to Washington, and President Day warned him to remember that if the Senate accepted the House bill the subject of taxation of life insurance could not be brought up in the conference committee.

President Day urged Equitable's general agents to get in touch with their congressmen and senators and point out the discriminating nature of the proposed legislation, and to urge the policyholders to do likewise. Probably most active in this work were Edward A. and Lawrence C. Woods of the great Pittsburgh agency. Copies of *The Human Factor*, Equitable's little magazine which was distributed to policyholders, with its article on the tax bill, were widely circulated. In his appeal to the policyholders, President Day said:

> It is neither the duty, the desire nor the intention of the Equitable Society to oppose the taxing of incomes. It is, however, our duty and our purpose to urge the correction of the very serious mistake that has been made in that part of the proposed Income Tax law which requires policyholders to pay taxes more than once on the same money. The proposed law as it relates to life insurance companies is extremely vague and difficult to understand. Whatever the intent may have been, the language used is clearly open to the interpretation that policyholders will be required to

[106] Day to Underwood, March 28, 1913. Day letters, Equitable Archives.

[107] Telegram, Day to Lunger, April 8, 1913. Copy in *ibid.*

April 21 Day wrote Secretary Redfield that life insurance companies had been taxed on net incomes only. As the House bill stood, they would be taxed not only on net income, but on parts of their capital. He explained the meaning of "dividends" and pointed out that the bill included "or the return of premium payments," which would run contrary to the practice of the Internal Revenue Bureau under the 1909 corporation tax law and to the decision of the United States District Court in New Jersey which had held that "dividends" were in reality unused portions of the policyholders' premiums and not income. He said that it would appear that whoever drafted this section was attempting to nullify the decision of the courts and to "hit the policyholders as a class while exempting all others such as savings banks, building and loan associations, fraternal societies and the like." *Ibid.*

pay three taxes in addition to the tax already required on their premiums by the States, making four taxes in all.

In the first place, the money paid as premiums would be directly taxed as a part of the income of the insured if he was a "taxable person." Second, the bill specifically required the payment of a tax on the "proceeds of life insurance policies paid upon the death of the person insured," and in addition required the payment of a tax on "income derived from any source whatever," which might include the proceeds of endowment policies, cash surrender values, and annuities. Third, the bill also required the life insurance companies to pay a tax on the annual savings returned to policyholders as dividends or refunds, whether these refunds had been accumulated in one year or over a long period of years. It also required a tax on the sums set aside out of premiums for the reserve, "or the amount which is accumulated from year to year to pay the policy." The reserve had always been considered as a savings bank deposit, therefore free from taxation. Day concluded:

> That Congress is endeavoring to deal justly with all classes of our people in the difficult task of distributing the revenue taxes goes without saying. That Congress should give the representatives of the millions of policyholders, and their beneficiaries and dependents, who number many millions more, an opportunity to be heard on this bill is a matter of elementary justice. . . . The taxing of life insurance savings is fundamentally and morally wrong. During the Civil War, in the hour of our greatest need, Congress held sacred the life insurance savings of the people and refused to tax them.[108]

Then May 1 President Day sent Cordell Hull (Tennessee) an advance copy of an "open letter" which he hoped would influence his views upon points of interest. Hull was in charge of drafting the income tax sections for the Committee on Ways and Means. In this letter, President Day replied to a speech made by Hull on April 26. He noted that the tax bill had been amended so as to exempt from taxation the net addition to reserve funds and the proceeds of policies paid upon the death of the person insured; these amendments were altogether satisfactory. But he pointed out that many policies were payable during the lifetime of the persons insured, while there were

[108] *The Eastern Underwriter*, XVI (1913), April 17.

other policies which were payable in installments after death. He resented the implication that "one of the large mutual companies" had sent out a letter designed to frighten policyholders into "the fear or belief" that the proposed tax upon the net income of the mutual companies would do the policyholders undeserved injury and injustice. Once again he emphasized that taxing "return of premium payments" would be levying a tax not only upon whatever of profits the policyholder might receive but upon that part of his premium which might be returned to him; this would be taxing capital.[109]

But these efforts had little effect. The bill passed the House May 8 with its provisions for taxing life insurance unchanged, and went to the Senate where it was referred to the Committee on Finance, of which Senator Furnifold M. Simmons of North Carolina was chairman. President Day wrote the members of the Finance Committee a long letter in which he expressed the hope that the Committee would permit hearings on the tax bill. After presenting the same arguments as previously, he said that both Underwood and Hull had stated that the House bill would simply carry on the existing provisions of the corporation tax, but that in so doing they had apparently overlooked the decision of the United States District Court in New Jersey in regard to the "return of premiums" clause.[110] He also wrote President

[109] Day letters, Equitable Archives.

[110] *Mutual Benefit Life Insurance Company* v. *Herold*, 198 *Fed. Rep.* 199. Herman C. H. Herold was Collector of Internal Revenue. The main point in this case (decided July 1912) was whether certain so-called dividends were or were not "income . . . received" within the meaning of the act of Congress approved August 5, 1909. Judge Joseph Cross of the United States District Court, New Jersey, pointed out that dividends paid by life insurance companies to policyholders were not really dividends, but an overpayment which operated "merely to abate or reduce the stipulated premium called for by the contract of insurance." He ruled that the clause in the law exempted from taxation dividends of the character in controversy. The Mutual Benefit had paid the tax assessments on dividends for 1909 and 1910 under protest and afterwards recovered judgment against the collector for practically the whole amount levied. The Circuit Court of Appeals, Third District, upheld the decision of the District Court in January 1913. 201 *Fed. Rep.* 918. The Supreme Court of the United States, in October 1913, denied a petition for a writ of certiorari. 231 *United States Reports* 755.

In April 1912 Charles W. Anderson, Collector of Internal Revenue, Second District, New York, assessed Equitable for supplementary amounts totaling about $100,000 on net income for 1909 and 1910. These assessments included, among other items, a tax on "dividends applied to pay renewal premiums." Equitable paid and entered claims for refund, which were refused. Equitable then instituted two actions against Anderson in the United States District Court for the Southern District of New York. The actions were on and off the court calendar for several

Darwin P. Kingsley of the New York Life, who, next to Day, had been the most active of the life company presidents in working against the proposed legislation: "Looking at the matter disinterestedly, the situation is one of those which affords a demonstration as to whether the Senate of the United States has the capacity to deal equitably in a large matter affecting the interest of the people as a whole. Let us trust that it will live up to its best traditions and vindicate our hopes." [111]

Though no hearings were held by the Finance Committee, President Kingsley and Robert Lynn Cox succeeded in getting an amendment added to the bill which would exempt the "dividends" or refunds paid (but not those credited) to policyholders of mutual companies. This amendment, however, did not solve Equitable's problem, for it would not cover the Society's dividends not paid out but credited to its Semi-Tontine policies issued prior to 1906; furthermore, Equitable was legally still a stock company although it had always done a mutual business. Consequently, President Day wrote Senator Simmons and suggested a change in the amendment so as to exempt all dividends paid or credited except those paid to stockholders.[112] He followed his letter to Washington immediately where he had a cordial interview with Senator Simmons, who promised to bring Day's suggestions to the attention of the subcommittee. Day's recommendation was not adopted and he said that it appeared as if Equitable had been singled out and deliberately classed among the purely stock companies.[113]

On September 4, the Senate Democrats held a caucus on whether or not to eliminate the paragraph which exempted the "dividends" paid to policyholders by mutual companies. President Day sent several telegrams to the senators most concerned in which he stated he would like to see the word "mutual" eliminated, but that he would

---

years but never came to trial. In October 1926 Equitable counsel and government counsel arrived at a compromise to the effect that judgment be confessed in the Society's favor for $16,385 for 1909 and $2,086 for 1910. In April 1927 judgments were entered, signed by the clerk of the District Court, granting recovery of these sums, plus interest. In August Equitable received a check for $35,061 but had to pay tax on the interest. The papers in regard to Equitable's dividend tax problems may be found in the files of the Law Department and the Controller's Department, Equitable Archives.

[111] Day to Kingsley, June 3, 1913. Day letters, Equitable Archives.

Kingsley had been corresponding with, among others, Senator John Sharp Williams of Mississippi, who was chairman of the subcommittee of the Senate Finance Committee.

[112] Day to Simmons, June 12, 1913. *Ibid.*

[113] Day to E. A. Woods, June 27, 1913. *Ibid.*

rather have the paragraph retained with the word "mutual" in it than eliminated altogether. At this time, representatives of the stock companies—including Thomas W. Blackburn of the American Life Convention—registered their protests; rather than see the "dividends" of mutual companies exempted from the tax, they preferred to have all "dividends" taxed. So the Senate took out the amendment, which, despite the efforts of President Day, Darwin P. Kingsley, and others, was not restored.[114]

The only hope now lay with the conference committee. President Day sent out telegrams to Equitable general agents who were located in the states of the key senators, and both he and Vice President Lunger again went to Washington. At the request of Senator Underwood, Presidents Day and Kingsley submitted an amendment which, however, did not meet with the approval of Robert Lynn Cox, who submitted his own amendment on behalf of The Association of Life Insurance Presidents. Neither of these amendments was entirely acceptable to the conference committee. It was then that Thomas W. Blackburn submitted an amendment which, with a few minor changes, was accepted by the conference committee. Both houses accepted the amendment, and the revenue act was signed by the President on October 3. It provided for a tax of 1 per cent on net income of life insurance companies—that is, gross income from all sources, including premiums, minus required net additions to reserves, expenses, sums paid on policy contracts and dividends to policyholders. In effect, the tax remained—as it had since 1909—essentially a tax upon the increase in earned surplus, plus dividends to stockholders. It had been a long fight, and no one had worked harder to achieve the desired end than President Day, who had done so much to make the policyholders of all companies aware of the nature and effects of the tax on dividends.

In 1914 the war revenue bill provided for a stamp tax of eighty cents

[114] Since the American Life Convention at this time was composed largely of the smaller western and southern companies, most of them stock companies domiciled in thirty-odd states, they had the advantage of having the support of far more senators than the large eastern companies which were domiciled in only a few states.

September 15 Blackburn sent the following memorandum to the member companies of the American Life Convention: "Senate Committee amendment exempting dividends of mutual life insurance companies taken out of Income Tax Bill. Does not give companies the exemption of dividends on participating business desired but does avoid discrimination between stock and mutual companies of which 'just complaint was made by stock companies.' "

per one thousand dollars on new policies. In September President Day wrote Oscar Underwood that for the second time within a year the obligations of his post as chief trustee of more than a half million policyholders, most of whom were working people, required him "to ask you not to think of penalizing them further in their effort to protect their dependents from becoming public charges." He pointed out that such a levy was more than 2 per cent of first year premiums, and further, that if it applied to group insurance, which cost only about one-third as much as regular insurance, it would result in taxing group insurance about three times as heavily. He telegraphed the Senate Finance Committee that if this tax were assessed against the policyholders it would inflict a penalty on the old policyholders which, though it might be legal, would not be morally right. Though reluctant "to go again and buttonhole Senators," President Day went to Washington to present the case of life insurance. This time not only The Association of Life Insurance Presidents and the American Life Convention, but the National Association of Life Underwriters lodged protests. As a result, the proposed tax was stricken from the bill.

* * *

By 1912, Equitable's Home Office force had grown to several hundred employees and in December of that year the Board set up both a pension plan and group insurance for them; officers were not included. Prior to this time the Society had taken care of its "superannuated" employees informally by placing them upon its reserve force at a reduced salary. Under the pension plan, employees at the age of sixty-five received annually 2 per cent of their aggregate salaries, with a top limit of $300 per month. The pensions were provided not by way of a group annuity but paid out of general funds. Premiums on the group insurance, which at first was limited to $2,400—$5,000 in 1919—were paid by the Society. An Employees' Association was formed through which the officers of the Society were enabled to keep in better touch with Home Office personnel and the Association established a co-operative retail store which was put in charge of Assistant Treasurer W. B. Bremner. Occasional meetings were held to which the officers and all Home Office employees were invited for social entertainment. On one occasion when President Day was compelled to turn down a request for a talk to the Women's Club he said that perhaps it was just as well, since on a previous occasion he had met a cool reception when he referred to the women as "working girls" whereas they wished to be thought of as "business women." In September 1914 a committee of Home Office and agency representatives organized the Equitable Veteran Legion to which employees with five or more years of continuous service became eligible. This organization was probably inspired by and modeled after a similar organization which had been established in the Edward A. Woods general agency at Pittsburg in 1907.[115] In time, the EVL certificate and gold pin with their designation of years of service became cherished awards.

There was no Society publication for Home Office employees after the discontinuance of *The Equitable Record* in 1905 until publication for a few months in 1919 of *The Equitable Home Office News;* this magazine was followed by *The Equitable Inter-Office Chronicle,* which was published until 1922. The field forces continued to receive *Agency Items,* first published in 1907, and from 1911 to 1915 the policyholders received *The Human Factor,* a sixteen-page quarterly designed to keep them in touch with the Society and to inspire them to conserve their life insurance.[116]

President Day, like Grover Cleveland, found it difficult to delegate details to subordinates. He felt a great responsibility to the policyholders, and as a result answered personally requests for information, policyholders' complaints, and the like. At times he would devote several pages to a patient and detailed explanation of the principles of life insurance to a policyholder who held a small policy. Then, in addition to the many official duties, he frequently found himself almost overwhelmed with requests from influential friends to find positions for their friends and relatives, requests to serve on boards and committees of many welfare societies, to attend ceremonies held by other companies, to make contributions—either personally or on behalf of the

[115] The Pittsburg Veteran Legion divided the personnel of the agency into groups based upon years of service, such as five, ten, fifteen, etc. At an agency convention, October 1 and 2, 1907, members of the various "Corps" were presented with certificates of membership and gold pins. Pins for the Five-Year Corps had no stone setting; those for the Ten-Year Corps had a sapphire; the Fifteen-Year Corps an emerald; the Twenty-Year Corps a ruby; and the Twenty-Five-Year Corps a diamond. This was the agency's method of recognizing long and loyal service. *The Equitable News,* No. 87 (October 21, 1906). (It may be noted that the original spelling of "Pittsburgh" was not officially recognized by the Post Office Department until 1908.)

[116] *The Equitable News,* an agents' journal, had been published from January 1, 1900, to July 1909.

Society—to many causes, and to help finance various projects. Most of these requests, of course, had to be refused.

Business in the United States in 1913 showed many evidences of entering upon a major recession. Equitable's sales for the first ten months registered a decline of about $7,000,000 and a decline in the foreign business of even greater proportion. The Society sought to economize still further by cutting certain expense allowances which had been made to agents in addition to those paid by the General Agent. President Day said that the success of the agent in the future would depend not so much upon the rate at which he was paid as upon the character of the company which he represented and the ease with which he could extend its business. President Day was very close to the older general agents and carried on lengthy and intimate correspondence with them, yet in 1914 he was reluctant to see Edward A. Woods, head of the largest agency of all, accept the presidency of the National Association of Life Underwriters. Incidentally, over the years the Equitable agents succeeded in acquiring this honor more often than their proportion of members might have indicated; they were outstanding men and so recognized by the agents of the country.[117] Also, they were active in NALU politics.

Although the Society had established a few agency managers—James Rubens had become a "salaried general manager" in New York City in 1906 and "agency manager" in 1914—President Day had no special preference for the branch office system and told the general agents that he would put no pressure upon them to convert to managers.[118] Early in 1917 Equitable extended its group insurance and pension plan to cover its general agents and agency managers.

[117] Equitable representatives who served as NALU presidents were: 1892–93 C. E. Tillinghast, Cleveland, Ohio; 1900–01 I. Layton Register, Philadelphia, Pennsylvania; 1907–09 Charles J. Edwards, Brooklyn, New York; 1910–11 Henry J. Powell, Louisville, Kentucky; 1915–16 Edward A. Woods, Pittsburgh, Pennsylvania; 1925–26 Frank L. Jones, Indianapolis, Indiana; 1934–35 Theodore M. Riehle, CLU, New York City; 1937 Theodore M. Riehle, CLU, New York City (filled the unexpired term of Alexander E. Patterson); 1940–41 Harry T. Wright, Chicago, Illinois; 1946–47 Philip B. Hobbs, Chicago, Illinois.

[118] It thus appears that Rubens was in effect the first Agency Manager of the Society. He had entered the Society as an agent in 1902, had become a General Agent in 1904, "salaried General Agent" (usually accepted to mean Agency Manager) in 1906, and Agency Manager in 1914. A copy of his contract and record is in the Equitable Archives. In 1954, when another agent was credited by *Agency Items* as being "the oldest Equitable Agency Manager" in point of service, Rubens wrote Vice President Alvin B. Dalager and corrected the record. Rubens to Dalager, May 16, Dalager to Rubens, May 19, 1954. *Ibid.*

In 1914 the Society introduced a new policy which it called an "Income Bond." This was a "return premium" contract which guaranteed that if the purchaser died before the date at which monthly income payments would begin, all premiums paid in would be returned, but without interest. This policy was intended for those who did not want life insurance for the protection of others, but desired to provide for their own old age. It was supposed to be particularly attractive for bachelors, widowers, fathers whose children were self-supporting, and independent women who did not wish to run the risk of being dependent in later life on the charity of friends and relatives. The following year Equitable presented a new "Convertible Policy," which gave the insured considerable freedom of choice. During the first five years this policy was a limited payment life contract, but at the end of that period the insured had the choice of several options: he might continue the policy as ordinary life with a reduction of 40 per cent in the cash premium, or continue to pay the same premium and have the face value of the policy increased by 50 per cent, also on the ordinary life plan, or the policy would become a paid-up life contract by continuing (on a policy issued at age thirty-five) thirteen additional premiums, after which, by the payment of nine more premiums, the policy would become an endowment for the face value.[119]

President Darwin P. Kingsley protested this policy as being unfair competition, but President Day explained that the new policy was not a cut-rate policy because it contained no provision for extended term insurance and carried lower surrender values. He said the policy was merely a revival of one which Equitable had put out in 1905 and withdrew at the end of 1906 so as to conform to the standard policy provisions of the New York insurance laws of that year. He said it had never occurred to the officers of Equitable that the new policy would be construed as a competitive attack against New York Life and Mutual any more than Equitable had considered the introduction of a recent low-rate policy by the New York Life as an attack against itself. Had it been Equitable's purpose to start a rate war, it would have issued a policy with at least as low a rate as those on the two new policies issued by New York Life. It would be impossible for Equitable to with-

[119] This was an annual dividend policy on the 3½ per cent reserve basis; it included the new disability feature optionally. Commissions were the same as on the 30-year endowment policies; that is, 40 per cent and renewals. The rate at age thirty-five for $10,000 was $349.20.

draw its convertible policy or increase the premium rate and inform the Society's agents of the reason for such action:

> If we explained that the reason actuating us was to conform to a standard of rates agreed upon by the large companies, it would be highly prejudicial to the best interests of all concerned. As you may know there has always been considerable talk of a combination between the Mutual, the New York Life, and the Equitable with regard to premium rates. This was recently emphasized at Albany, and I have been led to believe was the inspiring cause of the proposed legislative committee to inquire into life insurance rates. Nothing would so surely strengthen such an opinion as for the Equitable now to withdraw this policy or raise the premium rates to a 3 per cent standard. Would it not be the better plan for the New York Life to adopt the Convertible Policy, using any premium rates which in your judgment might seem advisable.[120]

President Day, keeping in mind "the friendly relations which have always existed between us," did not want his stand to be taken as in any way hostile to the New York Life or any other company, and nothing would cause him keener regret than reprisals from other companies; should reprisals follow, however, from any quarter, Equitable would prove its "good faith by refraining from any action which would tend to the demoralization of life insurance." He made it clear that Equitable did not intend to be a participant "in any war of rates, or for agents, or of methods."

In 1912 Equitable had offered optionally a disability clause to its policies which provided that, should the insured become permanently disabled prior to age sixty, payment of premiums would be waived; this provision required a small additional payment. In March 1915 the disability clause was liberalized to include, in addition to the waiver of premiums, an annual income of one-tenth of the face of the policy; the face amount of the policy would be reduced by the payments so made. This optional provision was available for other than Life Income Policies. The following year this disability clause was extended to include Life Income Policies.

"Conservation" was the order of the day—of human life and of insurance policies as well as of natural resources—and Equitable was among the leaders in this movement. As early as 1900, it had estab-

[120] Day to Kingsley, April 27, 1915. Day letters, Equitable Archives. Day wrote a similar letter to President Charles A. Peabody of Mutual.

lished a medical laboratory which was said to be the first of its kind to be maintained by a life insurance company. One of the main purposes was to achieve more uniformity in analysis and microscopic work.[121] President Day established the "Department of Conservation" and in January 1911 put E. E. Rittenhouse, former Insurance Commissioner for the State of Colorado, in charge. As "Conservation Commissioner," in addition to his work within the Society, Rittenhouse made numerous talks to national organizations such as medical societies and scientific groups, and wrote articles for publication in medical and other journals.[122] *The Human Factor*, which was sent to policyholders quarterly, was his idea. Its purpose was "to serve the great Equitable family and humanity in general by stimulating interest and action in the conservation of life and of life insurance." Frequent articles were contributed by Senior Medical Director Dr. Franklin C. Wells on such subjects as "Take Care of Your Health"; "Don't Worry"; "Sanitation"; "The House-fly"; and "Colds." A Home Office Employees' Health Center was established in 1912; rest rooms with facilities for attending to temporary physical ills were provided in the Hazen building, and all employees were given the opportunity of having one free physical examination by a Home Office physician at least once per year.[123] All drugs for slight ailments, as well as medical advice, were furnished free at all times to the employees.

In January 1914 Rittenhouse resigned his position with Equitable to head the Life Extension Institute, which had been organized to disseminate knowledge and offer its services for examining the physical condition of policyholders to the life insurance companies and the

121 First director of the laboratory was August Stephen Wolf, a native New Yorker who had been graduated from the New York College of Pharmacy in 1888. After study at the Bellevue Hospital Medical School and graduate research work at the College of Physicians and Surgeons of Columbia University, Wolf had served for ten years in the laboratory of the Women's Hospital in New York. He remained with the Equitable laboratory for forty years, during which time he published numerous papers on chemistry, bacteriology, and pathology in scientific journals. See *The Equitable Spirit*, II (1935), May 15, No. 4. In the early days of the laboratory, one man handled the work and 2,000 analyses were a fair average for the year. Thirty years later, seven chemists were employed and 65,000 analyses were made annually.

122 For example, Rittenhouse talked on "Human Life as a National Asset" before the Fourth National Conservation Congress at Indianapolis in October 1912, and on "The Upward Trend of Mortality in Middle Life and Old Age" before the American Association for the Advancement of Science at Cleveland in January 1912.

123 Established by Executive Order No. 32, November 25, 1912. Corporate Records, Equitable Archives.

public.[124] The same year, the Conservation Department offered annual health examinations to policyholders without charge at certain central points where Equitable had salaried physicians, and free chemical tests at "all points in the United States and Canada." [125] For more than two years the Conservation Department was without a head, but in April 1916 President Day appointed Senior Medical Director Dr. Franklin C. Wells as chief of the Bureau of Conservation. Dr. Wells was an excellent speaker and stimulated many groups to greater interest in health and safety. He was aided in this work by Lew Russell Palmer, who, as Director of Safety and Personnel, Group Department, made surveys of working conditions in industrial establishments, offered consultant services to employers, and put out special bulletins, circulars and posters on the subject of safety. This work proved particularly valuable during the war years when it was important to have the employee care for himself physically as well as financially.

* * *

Although the bulk of the Society's investments remained in municipal, government, and railroad bonds, and mortgages on urban business properties, the investment portfolio was being extended to include farm mortgages. Equitable made its first investments in this field in 1912 but cautiously limited its mortgages to strictly farm land, largely in the Middle West. Within three years it had farm mortgage loans in eleven states, which totaled more than $8,000,000. By the Armstrong legislation of 1906, the life insurance companies had been given until December 31, 1911, to dispose of their common stock holdings. As the deadline approached, some of the New York companies spoke in favor of repeal of this provision of the insurance laws,

[124] The Life Extension Institute was incorporated in New York on December 29, 1913. Ex-President Taft was made chairman of the board; Colonel W. E. Gorgas, whose medical work in the Canal Zone had attracted international attention, was made consultant in sanitation and hygiene; and Frank A. Vanderlip, Irving Fisher, and other prominent citizens were also members of the organization. Rittenhouse returned to Equitable in 1916 as Commissioner of Public Service and Conservation, and for the next two years worked largely with the Group Department. He became Assistant Secretary of the Society in 1918 and died in 1920.

[125] Some of the results of these examinations were reported by Dr. Wells in *The Weekly Underwriter*, XCIV (1916), January 8; tables were presented which showed the percentage of those examined who suffered from various impairments, the nature of the impairments, etc. It was pointed out that a life company which paid $20,000,000 a year in death benefits would save $1,400,000 if each policyholder's life was prolonged one year beyond its present duration.

but Superintendent Hotchkiss advocated extension of the deadline for three years, or until December 31, 1914. President Day wrote the legislative committee that, though Equitable held only a relatively small amount of stock (par value $19,601,010, acquired at a cost of $38,805,237), this stock was largely high-priced shares of trust companies and banks for which there was no general market. In its endeavor to comply with the law of 1906, the Society in 1911 still held the major portion of this stock. President Day recommended repeal of this provision of the law. At the same time, however, Equitable disposed of its shares in the Equitable Trust Company and the Mercantile Safe Deposit Company.[126]

In 1912, United States railroad bonds constituted about one-fifth of the Society's investments, but since the outlook for the carriers was not considered good the proportion of railroad bonds was considerably reduced during the next two years. Mortgage loans upon apartment houses, hotels, and other single-purpose properties were regarded with disfavor. The Society scrupulously refrained from investing a single dollar in the war loans of the belligerent nations; it felt it should maintain a policy of absolute neutrality. Investments made in 1913 yielded a little more than 5 per cent, and the return on all funds had risen to about 4.6 per cent—an increase of more than one-half of 1 per cent since 1905. In view of the fact the Equitable's deferred dividend policies were falling due in an increasing ratio each year, it was necessary that the investment program be planned so that securities would mature as these contracts became due.

In 1915 Wisconsin enacted a number of amendments to its insurance law of 1907 which had resulted in the withdrawal of Equitable from the state. The amendments had to do largely with expense charges, the "mortality charge," and terminal reserve provisions. Since these changes removed the main cause of Equitable's withdrawal the Society requested a license to re-enter the state. After some correspondence with the New York Department of Insurance the Commissioner of Insurance of Wisconsin issued the license October 5, 1915, permitting the Society to do business in the state for the year ending February

126 President Alvin W. Krech and associates of the Equitable Trust Company purchased the 14,531 Equitable Trust shares held by Equitable for $500 per share. This stock (par value $1,453,100) had been carried on the Society's books at $6,538,950. Equitable received $7,265,500 for the stock. *The Eastern Underwriter*, XII (1911), April 6. See also *Annual Report of the Superintendent of Insurance* . . . , 1910.

29, 1916. One stumbling block was the fact that during the period in which it was not licensed to do business in the state Equitable had appealed some of its law cases to the Federal Courts. The license was issued with the understanding that the law would not apply to Equitable's action during that period.[127]

On the eve of the entry of the United States into World War I, the Society's finances were in excellent shape. The mortality experience had declined from 81 per cent in 1912 to 76 per cent for 1916, and investment earnings above the assumed interest rate (3 per cent on most contracts) had increased by about 45 per cent during that period; gains from excess of loadings averaged more than $2,500,000 per year. In 1916, $16,379,453 was transferred from earnings to surplus, but most of this was earmarked for deferred policy dividends due in 1917. The accumulated surplus, not including this sum, was $75,368,659.

WORLD WAR I

Though the European war came in the summer of 1914 as a great surprise to most of the American people, it was no surprise to President Day, who was well aware of the existing tensions. Equitable, because of its extensive European business, was immediately affected. Dr. Karl Gründler, who had been in charge of the German business, had died in May, and the Society had great difficulty getting power of

[127] See correspondence between Chief Actuary L. A. Anderson of the Wisconsin Department and Nelson B. Hadley, Chief Examiner Life Companies, of the New York Insurance Department, September 1915. Copies in Equitable Archives.

Still pending in the Federal Courts was the troublesome Ellinger suit. (For the earlier Ellinger suits see this history, p. 724). After the Wisconsin Supreme Court in 1909 denied Ellinger's motion to examine Equitable's Actuary, the suit was removed to the Federal Court but plaintiff indicated no desire to proceed with it. In July 1914 Ellinger instituted a suit for an accounting in the Illinois courts, but the court ordered a stay of all proceedings until December 1, pending disposition of the Wisconsin suit, and the Supreme Court upheld the order. Meanwhile Ellinger renewed his Wisconsin litigation in September 1914 and a date was fixed for taking the deposition of Equitable's actuary, Robert L. Henderson. Several weeks were devoted to getting Henderson's deposition. Then in December plaintiff moved for the appointment of an auditor to examine the Society's accounts regarding his policy, and for a postponement of the trial. When the motions were denied and the trial came up, December 15, plaintiff elected to discontinue the action. On the same day Ellinger served papers on the Insurance Commissioner of Wisconsin for a new action against Equitable. This action was removed to the United States District Court which in August 1915 denied the plaintiff's motion to remand the case to the state court. Ellinger died in 1918 and Equitable forwarded a check for $19,665.91 in full settlement of all claims against the Society under policy No. 274,493. See docket and accompanying papers in legal files, Equitable Archives.

attorney through to Dr. Anton Klostermann, his successor.[128] It was feared that heavy penalties might be imposed by the Imperial Supervisory Department for Private Insurance if these papers were not filed. The assistance of the State Department was requested. The Rosillos in Spain were cabling insistently for funds as was Reginald Naish in London. International exchange had practically broken down. Fortunately, Fourth Vice President Henry L. Rosenfeld was in Europe and he sought to get credit established in Berlin through Swiss banks. Morgan, Harjes and Company placed $200,000 to the Society's credit in Paris, and Reginald T. Naish, Equitable's General Manager for Great Britain, negotiated a loan from the London banks on British consols held by the Society. After Klostermann went to the fighting front, Hermann Lasker and Cashier William Schacht took charge of the Berlin office. The Imperial Department released M.1,665,710 of Equitable's surplus deposit funds in August 1914 and March 1915, but refused to order further releases as surplus deposits accumulated. The funds released were pledged by Equitable for a loan from the Reichsbank to take care of necessary payments. Fourth Vice President Henry L. Rosenfeld went to Berlin in November 1915 and sought the help of United States Ambassador James W. Gerard. The Imperial Department held that the agreement of December 10, 1905, in regard to release of surplus deposits did not apply because of general conditions resulting from the war. President Day took the matter up with Count Johan H. von Bernstorff, German Ambassador to the United States, who informed him that the Imperial Government could not exercise any influence upon the Private Insurance Office, but that the latter was taking up the subject with Equitable's representative in a favorable way. In July 1916 Equitable was advised by cable that the Imperial Department for Private Insurance had released $325,000 in

128 Several persons had been eager to succeed Gründler as General Attorney and Manager of the Equitable for the German Empire and as its representative for the other European countries—among them Gründler's son, and Cashier William Schacht and his son, Dr. Hjalmar Horace Greeley Schacht, who at the time was one of the directors of the Dresdner Bank. Cashier Schacht was regarded as too old and without the qualifications and Gründler's son as "entirely out of the question." So the position went to Klostermann, who had been acting as Manager for some weeks. Rocquet to President Day (in London) June 30, 1914. Secretary General for Europe files—Germany—Equitable Archives.

One cannot help but wonder whether the later history of Europe might have been different had the younger Schacht been appointed to the position; would he then have become head of the Reichsbank and been able to finance Hitler's wars with his financial magic.

bonds—a portion of the Society's excess deposit. President Day then presented a long memorandum to von Bernstorff in which he pointed out that Equitable had ceased to do business in the German Empire some twenty years earlier and that its deposits were $1,532,224 (M.6,435,340) in excess of the amount required by law to protect its German policyholders. Since the United States and Germany were rapidly approaching the breaking point, nothing further was accomplished in regard to the excess deposits.[129] Diplomatic relations between the United States and Germany were severed February 2, 1917, and von Bernstorff was recalled to Berlin. Before he left President Day sent him a telegram as follows: "Wishing you bon voyage and a speedy and happy return. On behalf of the Equitable Life Assurance Society I thank you for your patience and sympathetic consideration of our business problems in the German Empire and the just and fair treatment you and your government have always extended us." [130]

Equitable also had excess deposits in Italy and took up the problem with United States Ambassador Thomas Nelson Page, but nothing was accomplished before the United States entered the war.

After the outbreak of hostilities in 1914, Equitable instructed its European managers quietly to avoid issuing policies on military personnel and to grant periods of grace and other extensions such as seemed advisable in the emergency; in so far as funds were available, priority should be given to death claims. Fortunately, the bulk of Equitable's insurance in Europe was protected by war clauses which called for an extra premium of $100 per $1,000 of insurance for those in military service. Although about 5½ per cent of the Society's insurance was in belligerent countries, most of the policies were held by persons beyond the age of military service.[131]

[129] For recovery of the deposits, see this history, p. 868. The above account is based upon letters of President Day to Frank L. Polk, Counselor, State Department, April 11; to von Bernstorff, June 14 and July 11, 1916. Day letters, Equitable Archives.

[130] Day to von Bernstorff, telegram February 14, 1917. *Ibid.*

[131] When the *Springfield* [Massachusetts] *Republican*, October 8, 1914, published an editorial which stated that American life insurance companies had large interests in Germany and Austria and that all of their European insurance had been written without war clauses, President Day wrote Editor Samuel Bowles and said that he thought the editorial might create some apprehension. He gave Bowles some data for his own information, as follows: 2 per cent of Equitable's total insurance was in France; 2 per cent in Great Britain; 1 per cent in Russia; .30 of 1 per cent was in Germany; .15 of 1 per cent in Belgium; .07 of 1 per cent in Austria; and .02

After the United States entry into the war, President Day instructed Secretary General for Europe James C. Rocquet not to communicate with Equitable's representatives in central Europe until he received a copy of trading with the enemy licenses. These licenses, when issued, appeared broad enough to take care of Equitable's policyholders in the Central Powers but did forbid the transmission of funds. President Day assumed that the governments of the Central Powers had taken over Equitable's offices and that they would use Equitable's deposits in some way to meet policy claims; he advised that Equitable officers not attempt to interfere: "We are obliged to submit to force *majeur.*" Equitable should keep its hands off so that some day the governments of the Central Powers could be held responsible for assuming the position of trustee for their policyholders and Equitable be in a position to demand an accounting; "When that time comes it would be embarrassing to the Equitable to be met by the contention of the German or Austrian governments that in sacrificing our securities for cash they did not act on their own initiative but merely followed our advice to our agents." If these governments should sell securities on deposit at a loss Equitable wanted to be in a position to insist that such losses should fall upon the nationals of the enemy powers and not upon the policyholders of the Entente Allies or neutral countries. The same policies should be followed with reference to Russia: "Some day a responsible government must be established in Russia and if our interests have suffered in the interim we must look to that government for an accounting and bear this in mind in all of our present transactions." [132]

The subject of "war clauses" as applying to policies issued in the United States became important long before the entry of the United States into the war. An investigation by The Association of Life Insurance Presidents early in 1916 showed that more than three-fourths of the life insurance in force in the United States carried no restrictions in regard to military service. Equitable's policies issued to persons who had not yet been called to the colors carried no war clauses; the Society assumed that it was amply protected by the premium loadings

---

of 1 per cent in Serbia. The Society had withdrawn from Serbia, Germany, and Austria twenty years earlier, and most of the persons in those countries who still held Equitable policies were in the upper age brackets; the Society had done little business in Russia during the preceding ten years. The bulk of Equitable's policies in Europe were protected by war clauses. Day to Bowles, October 30, 1914. *Ibid.*

[132] Day to Rocquet, December 21, 1917. *Ibid.*

and believed that Equitable losses should be distributed among all policyholders. Policies issued to persons already called into service, however, were limited to $2,000 and carried an extra charge of 3 per cent of the face value. During the summer of 1916, the Presidents' Association recommended war clauses for new policies and Equitable inserted such provisions for service outside the United States to take effect April 9, 1917. Any policyholder who entered such service within the first five policy years would be charged an extra annual premium of 10 per cent of the face value of the policy. If he failed to give notice of such service within 60 days of entry and did not pay the extra premium, death benefits would be limited to return of premiums. Equitable had also inserted war clauses in policies for civilians (including nurses) who by reason of their occupation might have occasion to travel or reside in a war zone. The liability of the Society was limited to return of premiums if death occurred within the first two years of the policy. After entry of the United States into the war the civilian clauses were revised: for policies of $5,000 and less the liability was limited to return of premiums, unless the insured paid a single extra premium of $25 per thousand; policies of more than $5,000 merely excluded the risk with no provision for an extra premium. Some modification was made in the clauses in September 1918.

President Day, in 1917, believed that Equitable was well prepared for the incidence of war. He pointed out the rapid improvement in Equitable's mortality experience and the gains in earnings over the assumed interest rate during the preceding five years; also there was the gain from excess of loadings and a substantial surplus which could be drawn upon if necessary. He estimated that an army of 1,000,000 men would not include more than $20,000,000 of Equitable insurance, and even 10 per cent of death claims would constitute but a small per cent of the $1,600,000,000 of Equitable insurance in force.[133]

Government war risk insurance for individuals in the armed services, as provided by the United States in World War I, was not only a colossal undertaking, but an original one; no government in history had ever proposed or conducted such a service for its military personnel. War risk insurance was, in the words of Secretary of the Treasury William G. McAdoo, "an evolution." In September, 1914, an act was approved to establish a Bureau of War Risk Insurance in the Treasury

[133] Day to Reau E. Folk, Equitable agent at Nashville, August 21, 1917. *Ibid.*

Department; the primary purpose was to insure merchant ships against the extraordinary hazards of the sea during war, a risk which private insurers were reluctant to undertake. In June 1917, the War Risk Insurance Act was amended so as to extend insurance to the personal effects of masters, officers, and crews of ships, and permit, whenever it should appear to the Secretary of the Treasury to be "desirable in the national interest," the insurance of masters, officers, and crews against the loss of life by personal injuries and provide compensation in case of capture. After the United States became a belligerent, McAdoo suggested to President Wilson—"on my own motion and as a result of my own initiative"—that war risk insurance be extended to cover the lives of soldiers, sailors, and nurses, and provide indemnity for injuries suffered. He said the idea came to him one morning when he was driving from his summer residence near Gettysburg, Pennsylvania, to his office in Washington, and that upon his arrival there he went to the White House and submitted it to the President. President Wilson thought the scheme a good one, and suggested that McAdoo talk it over with Justice Brandeis, for whose knowledge of insurance Wilson had a very high regard. This McAdoo did.[134]

He then called a meeting of life insurance company officers for July 2 to discuss plans for insuring military personnel. Equitable was represented by E. E. Rittenhouse and Actuary Robert Henderson. The officers recommended by vote of 103 to 4 that insurance to cover both death and disability be provided directly by the government; they also suggested that an advisory committee of insurance officers be appointed to confer with the government officials on the proposed insurance legislation.[135] McAdoo appointed George E. Ide, President

[134] Credit for the idea of war risk insurance has been variously assigned to Edwin F. Sweet, Assistant Secretary of Commerce; Judge Julian W. Mack, of the United States Circuit Court (Chicago); Justice Louis D. Brandeis; and others—but insofar as the idea was that of any one man, it was that of William Gibbs McAdoo. McAdoo revealed his interest in such protection, which went back to the time of the Spanish-American War when he had helped provide for the relief of dependent families of enlisted men from New York, in a letter to Thomas B. Love, July 6, 1939. Love was Assistant Secretary of the Treasury in charge of war risk insurance under McAdoo. Copy of letter supplied to author by Love.

[135] Earlier in the year, President Clarence L. Ayres of the Northern Assurance Company of Detroit had written a letter to President Wilson in which he stated that he and Dr. James W. Glover of the Department of Mathematics and Insurance of the University of Michigan had talked over a plan by which men engaged in the defense of their country might have protection without paying the extra premiums which the companies found it necessary to charge. Under this plan, the

of the Home Life Insurance Company, as chairman of a committee of twelve for this purpose; Charles Jerome Edwards, Brooklyn General Agent with Equitable and ex-President of the National Association of Life Underwriters, was appointed as a member of this committee. The advisory committee later met with government officials and helped draft a bill to submit to Congress.

The bill was introduced in Congress early in August. It provided for addition of a division of marine and seamen's insurance and a division of military and naval insurance to the Bureau of War Risk Insurance. Article II provided for a system of allotments and family allowances from the serviceman's pay compulsory as to a wife or child and voluntary as to any other dependent person, these allotments to be matched by the government. Article III provided for compensation for death or disability. Article IV provided for insurance benefits for death or permanent disability to officers, enlisted men, and army and navy nurses in an amount not less than $1,000 nor more than $10,000. The premium rates for this term insurance were to be the net rates based upon the American Experience Table and interest of 3½ per cent per annum. It was further provided that not later than five years after the termination of the war the term insurance should be converted upon application and without medical examination into ordinary life, 20-payment life, endowment maturing at age sixty-two, and other usual forms of life insurance.

Though there was no concerted opposition to the bill on the basis of any selfish motives on the part of life insurance companies, nevertheless it was obvious that many insurance men were convinced that if the bill were enacted into law the Federal Government would be in the insurance business for many years. The impression was given in the insurance press, as well as many newspapers, that life insurance men presented a solid front against the war risk insurance. This was not true, for the life insurance men realized the popular appeal of

---

men would be insured in varying restricted degrees at the companies' regular rates, the government agreeing, however, to make an annual audit of deaths of these risks and compensate the companies for any deficiency in the mortality fund in excess of that provided for in the American Experience Table. This insurance could be supplemental to or in lieu of any pensions or bonuses that might be paid beneficiaries of deceased servicemen by the government. Ayres pointed out to the President that the companies could not long subject themselves to the hazard of getting outside the solvency standards set up by the laws under which they operated; his plan, if adopted, would provide government maintenance of the solvency of the company only insofar as it would be jeopardized by the war risk.

this war measure and were well aware of the fact that any who openly opposed it in principle would be labeled "reactionary." The restraint shown on the part of those who were somewhat doubtful of the long-term effects of the government's entering into the life insurance business was all the more commendable in view of the fact that the United Press and newspapers generally had misrepresented the facts in regard to the cost of government war risk insurance compared to that issued by private companies. They had announced that the government would issue $10,000 of insurance at a cost of $80 per year compared with $302 for the same amount of insurance issued by the legal reserve life insurance companies. Most newspaper readers certainly did not comprehend that renewable term insurance, such as the government was offering, could in time of peace be furnished by the insurance companies at the government rate or less.

When the bill reached the Senate, Article IV, which provided the insurance features, was criticized as violating the underlying principle of the bill, which was to tax the nation as a whole to pay its just debt to all fighting men: under the optional provisions of that article, military personnel who could afford to take the upper limit of insurance would become a special class subsidized as to the war risk several times as much as those who could afford only $1,000 of insurance. In the hearings before the Senate Finance Committee, most of the men who represented the life insurance business advocated elimination of Article IV because it contained "manifest discriminations" and would lead to "consequent injustices." They advocated substitution of a provision which would give every member of the armed forces life insurance without cost to the amount that Congress thought the nation could afford; this would be fair to all. These recommendations were not heeded, however, and the bill became law October 6, 1917. Charles F. Nesbit, former Superintendent of Insurance for the District of Columbia, was appointed head of the Division of Military and Naval Insurance, and Thomas B. Love, former Insurance Commissioner for the State of Texas, was appointed Assistant Secretary of the Treasury and put in charge of the War Risk Insurance Bureau.

Though some of the life insurance men were concerned in regard to the long-term effects of the government's entering into the field of life insurance, most of them cooperated conscientiously. A commission of life insurance specialists headed by Dr. James W. Glover, Professor of Insurance at the University of Michigan, was appointed to advise with the Division of Military and Naval Insurance; and many of the companies released key personnel to serve the government for the duration. Among those from Equitable was Third Vice President Leon O. Fisher, who, after serving as head of a branch of the General Administrative Bureau under General George W. Goethals in the War Department, in February 1919 became head of the Insurance Division of the War Risk Bureau; he was given leave with pay by Equitable until January 1, 1920. The War Risk Insurance did not prove as disastrous to the life insurance companies as many had anticipated, not even during the war; the war stimulated interest in and sales of life insurance, and most of the military personnel dropped their government insurance soon after the war ended.

Though Equitable had refused to purchase the bonds of any of the belligerent countries, it supported the Liberty Bond drives to the limit of its resources. It purchased $5,000,000 of the first Liberty Loan in June 1917 and distributed the subscription among the agencies of the country. Equitable cashiers were authorized to take subscriptions from individuals for Liberty Bonds, and the Society announced that it would invest its first year premiums in future war loans. The Society purchased $10,000,000 of the second Liberty Loan and then, early in 1918, issued a special policy to enable individuals to buy bonds of the third Liberty Loan. This policy, which was limited to $5,000, provided for payment on the bonds in installments over four and a half years and protected the loan by a Five Year Term Policy. Though this type of policy had been in use in England, and Thomas B. Love, Assistant Secretary of the Treasury, had applied for the first policy, the Treasury Department was reluctant to give its approval; it finally did so, however. Equitable subscribed $15,000,000 to the third Liberty Loan and then, after consultation with the Secretary of the Treasury, William G. McAdoo, borrowed $23,000,000 in order to subscribe to $40,000,000 of the fourth Liberty Loan. Though still owing a large sum on this debt, Equitable took $5,000,000 of the Victory Loan in 1919. Second Vice President George T. Wilson served as chairman of the great Victory Loan meeting at the Hippodrome where, assisted by Marie Dressler, the actress, and other celebrities, they sold more than $11,000,000 of the bonds. All told, Equitable acquired $65,000,000 of United States War Bonds as a result of its subscriptions, plus $25,000,000 of Canadian War Bonds.

Scores of Home Office personnel entered the service, as well as many agents. Second Vice President Henry L. Rosenfeld toured the country in company with a group of disabled veterans and helped sell millions of dollars of Liberty Bonds to the people. To coordinate

Equitable Home Offices

120 Broadway, 1915

393 Seventh Avenue, 1924

the numerous wartime activities of the Society, a committee headed by Treasurer Alfred R. Horr organized the War Service League.

Despite the wartime handicaps, Equitable business increased in 1917. New business totaled $251,344,652, of which $67,000,000 was in group insurance. (Included in the group insurance was the policy with the Union Pacific Railroad previously mentioned.) In January 1919 Equitable began issuing Accident and Health insurance. The new Accident and Health Department was placed under Second Vice President Henry L. Rosenfeld, with Harwood E. Ryan, former Joint Actuary of the New York Insurance Department, as Superintendent.[136] Later in the year the new department was transferred to the Actuary's Department under the name of the Accident and Health Bureau of the Actuary's Department. The Society discontinued the writing of Accident and Health Insurance—other than group insurance—in February 1922.

In August 1919 the Equitable Board authorized the refunding of all war extra premiums and civilian travel premiums collected under special war service or travel clauses in policies issued during the war period. These refunds applied to all extras except those collected under the Mexican war clause. The Society also paid in full the death claims arising under all policies upon which the insured failed to pay the required extra premiums, or which contained war service restrictions.

INFLUENZA EPIDEMIC

Although President Day had fairly well anticipated the effects of the war upon our economy and upon Equitable's business, and planned accordingly, suddenly in the autumn of 1918 came another visitation of one of nature's plagues which no one could have foreseen. By mid-October people were dying from the Spanish influenza at a rate not equaled since the Asiatic cholera had visited our country in the early 1830's and the late 1840's. The death rate increased two to seven fold; the mortality of those stricken with influenza was from 4 to 7 per cent in different areas and age groups as contrasted with about 1 per cent in earlier influenza epidemics. Up until September 1, 1918, Equitable had the best mortality experience for any similar period in its history.[137] Starting with the third week of that month, however,

136 Ryan had previously been with the Provident Savings Life and the Travelers; he had also served as Actuary for the Massachusetts Insurance Department.

137 Interestingly enough the mortality under group insurance had been lower than that of the general business of the Society. President Day said that this was astonishing "for, as among that class of people are many who know less about hygiene, less

the increase in percentage of death claims began to mount precipitately and by the last week in October reached 745 per cent.[138] The Society's losses for the three months of October, November, and December were about three times the normal losses. Whereas total death claims reported in 1917 were $23,062,302, in 1918 they were $30,054,052. Medical Director Dr. Thomas H. Rockwell estimated the Society's loss from the epidemic through January 1919 at more than $8,000,000; more than $1,000,000 of this loss was in group policies.[139] Since the

---

about sanitation, and who are, therefore, more susceptible to the common maladies, one might think that an increase rather than a lessened mortality would be experienced." Remarks made to the Board of Directors, January 16, 1919. Corporate Records, Equitable Archives.

138 The weekly increase in percentage of death claims over the corresponding weeks of the preceding year was as follows:

September 22......29 per cent	November 27.....425 per cent
October 6.........111 per cent	December 18.....329 per cent
October 16.......314 per cent	December 31.....269 per cent
October 30.......745 per cent	January 15.......314 per cent
November 13.....419 per cent	January 22.......371 per cent

These figures are taken from Medical Director Dr. Thomas H. Rockwell's discussion of the influenza epidemic read at the twenty-ninth annual meeting of the Association of Life Insurance Medical Directors. *An Abstract of the Proceedings of the Association of Life Insurance Medical Directors of America, Twenty-ninth Annual Meeting, 1919* (New York, 1919). Also reported in *The Eastern Underwriter*, XX (1919), February 7.

139 Reported death claims month by month for 1917 and 1918 were as follows:

Month	1918 No. of Cases	1918 Gross Loss	1917 No. of Cases	1917 Gross Loss
January	618	$1,608,154	746	$2,221,633
February	774	2,146,658	763	2,075,680
March	837	2,408,279	760	2,189,106
April	832	2,102,163	568	1,676,717
May	918	2,245,167	794	2,109,138
June	658	1,616,992	600	1,993,481
July	769	1,848,329	645	1,648,904
August	645	1,897,160	704	1,881,629
September	647	1,883,212	591	2,269,157
October	1,465	3,331,000	612	1,543,650
November	2,091	4,464,313	649	1,524,899
December	1,913	4,502,625	827	1,928,308
Total claims	12,167	$30,054,052	8,259	$23,062,302

By the third week of November 1918, the Bureau of the Census, basing its estimate upon 46 cities for the period September 8–November 9, estimated a total of more than 82,000 influenza deaths, a figure in excess of the number of American lives lost in action during the war; in January 1919 it reported 102,357 deaths in the 46 cities for the twelve weeks, September 21–December 14.

A table of company losses for the main period of the epidemic was published in

mortality incidence fell largely in the younger age groups, with 47.5 per cent of the deaths occurring between the ages of thirty and thirty-nine, the net losses to life insurance companies were high; the claims were largely on policies on which no sizable reserves had been accumulated.[140] It was estimated that five years would be required to restore the mortality averages to normal.

Despite the war and the influenza epidemic—which was to the life companies what the great San Francisco earthquake and fire had been to the fire insurance companies in 1906—the life insurance companies met their obligations to their policyholders without hesitation or delay, while at the same time they continued buying government bonds and otherwise contributing generously to the winning of the war. For this they received no special acclaim; it was expected of them. As Thomas W. Blackburn of the American Life Convention said:

> The great institution of Life Insurance met in the year 1918 the casualties of war and pestilence combined. The companies met every obligation to their policyholders without hesitance or suggestion of delay.

The National Underwriter, XXII (1918), November 21. Henry Moir's statistical calculations were published in *ibid.*, December 12. Arthur Hunter's report on the New York Life was published in *ibid.*, XXIII (1919), February 13, and the reports of J. D. Craig and Louis I. Dublin of the Metropolitan on the "Influenza Epidemic of 1918" made at the spring meeting of the Actuarial Society of America in *ibid.*, May 22. See also *ibid.*, January 23, for actuaries' estimates on total incidence of the epidemic through January 1, 1919. Thomas F. Tarbell, Actuary of the Connecticut Insurance Department, read a paper at the National Convention of Insurance Commissioners meeting at St. Louis, April 15–16, 1919, on "The Effect of Influenza on Insurance."

140 The distribution by sex and age was as follows:

	Standard		*Sub-standard*	
	Influenza per cent	Other Causes per cent	Influenza per cent	Other Causes per cent
Female.....	8.1	6.1	9.3	5.8
Male.......	91.9	93.9	90.7	94.2
Age Groups:				
–29......	23.8	7.2	20.5	13.4
30–39......	47.5	9.0	51.0	17.2
40–49......	16.2	16.3	19.2	24.4
50–	12.5	67.4	9.3	44.9

In the milder epidemic of a quarter of a century earlier, those who died were older, the insurance had been in force longer, larger reserves had been accumulated, and the net loss to the company was not so great; yet it took three years to again reach normal mortality experience.

Not only so, but they took their full share of all the issues of Government bonds and contributed generously to every war work and every organization devoting itself to the soldiers and sailors. I think these facts are neither widely known nor fully appreciated! . . . Onslaughts of demagogues, ill advised legislation, inexcusable slander, attempted assassination, undertaken by conscienceless and skilled manipulators, the excessive expenses of a most costly war, the tremendous financial calls of a Federal Government, not considerate, if even friendly, taxation without limit or consistency, demands for public service, involving great outlays of time and money, war itself, of the most destructive character, a pandemic in America more fatal than any pestilence of the past, an utter indifference on the part of the public to the fact that Life Insurance income cannot fluctuate with the changes of economic conditions, and a studied effort in the legislatures to legislate and the Courts to construe legislation most harshly against the business, have not shaken or even threatened Life Insurance.[141]

On the other hand, both the war and the influenza epidemic led to increased interest in life insurance on the part of the people. Though taxes were high, the war had led to full employment and wartime inflation made money relatively plentiful. Equitable's new business in 1918 was $273,223,559, and by March 1919 it appeared that the leading companies might reach their maximum legal limit under the New York law some months before the end of the year. Said Assistant Secretary E. E. Rittenhouse:

The companies hardly know how to account for this tremendous volume of new insurance. The influenza last year took away an enormous amount of insurable lives, between the ages of twenty-five and thirty-five, and the war took millions of the boys across the sea, but in spite of those cases the companies have been writing new insurance on an unprecedented scale, without making any drive to get it.

It is proper enough to limit our volume of expenses, but to limit our volume of business merely because of its bigness is, I am sure, an economic mistake. The aim of the law was to foster the starting of new companies. The companies went through the epidemic in such fine shape that men and women who never thought before much about insurance apparently have got the habit. The business is coming to the companies in spite of themselves.[142]

[141] Blackburn to Franklin Webster, May 8, 1919. American Life Convention correspondence, Insurance Journals folder. American Life Convention Archives.

[142] *The Eastern Underwriter*, XX (1919), March 21.

10

The Booming Twenties

It is a great thing to feel that one has performed well his task, and especially when that task embodies a trust which touches so nearly the material welfare and happiness of hundreds of thousands of men and women and children, one's gratification is well complete.—William A. Day, 1921

We are engaged in an enterprise, the very essence of which is cooperation, and which exists not for gain but for service. To us are entrusted the savings of countless individuals who look to us to fulfill their self-imposed obligation to provide for those who come after them. Our trust is a great and continuing one, and with your assistance we shall strive to administer it faithfully and in strict adherence to its obligations both express and implied, to the end that we may deserve the confidence of those whose interests we serve.—Thomas I. Parkinson to the Board, 1930

The great demobilization following World War I involved more than getting several million men out of the armed forces and into peaceful pursuits; it also meant demobilization of the extra-constitutional wartime government with its many boards and bureaus which exercised control over most aspects of American life, the reconversion of industry from war production to production of the essentials of peace, and readjustment from a war psychology on the part of the people. Most Americans felt that a necessary but disagreeable task had been accomplished, and were willing to forgive and forget. Though they refused to underwrite President Wilson's plans for the League of Nations for fear of embarking upon entangling alliances and sacrificing national sovereignty, nevertheless the United States found itself occupying a position of leadership in world affairs for which it was not prepared, and the responsibilities of which many were reluctant to accept. While the United States was becoming more involved in world affairs, Equitable was withdrawing from the various continents to confine its business to the territorial limits of the United States.

Equitable celebrated its sixtieth anniversary August 25–29, 1919, when some 1,500 members of the various agency clubs assembled at the Waldorf-Astoria. Proceedings began on Monday afternoon with the unveiling of the tablet in the Home Office dedicated to the employees of the Society who had died in the war. During the evening a reception was held at the Bankers Club. Tuesday morning, at the general session over which President Day presided, the different agents' honor clubs presented their banners, which were greeted with much enthusiasm. A dozen women from the Florence Shaal agency in Boston appeared in the center of the room, dressed in white and wearing large and identical leghorn hats. They were asked to rise and show themselves, which they did while the club members applauded. President Day announced that during the first seven months of the year Equitable's agents had surpassed the same period of 1918 by more than $100,000,000 of paid for business. He explained that when it became obvious that Equitable was going to pass the quota of $250,000,000 as established by the Armstrong legislation of 1906, he had sent Vice President J. V. E. Westfall to persuade Superintendent Jesse S. Phillips that it would be in the public interest to raise the limit, which the Superintendent was authorized to do at his discretion. Superintendent Phillips did so, but cautioned the Society that the business must be legitimate and not secured by high-pressure methods. President Day was certain that the agents would make good on his promise to the Superintendent that his advice would be followed. Vice President Westfall reminded the agents that during the three years since their last big meeting the assets of the Society had increased $60,000,000 and the insurance in force by half a billion.

The convention concluded with a luncheon on Friday at which Director John D. Kernan of Utica made the chief talk. "Senator Kernan kept the crowd in excellent humor by his odd slants on life insurance, agents and directors. A rugged individual, with prominent features and a roguish looking eye, he took the viewpoint that the officers and agents of a life company are all right in their way, but it's really the board of directors who are responsible for the Society's success." [1] After stating that the Equitable Board held President Day in the highest regard, he said that there was one point on which they did not agree: whereas the presidents of other leading life insurance companies were receiving salaries of $72,000 to $100,000 per year, the

[1] *The Eastern Underwriter*, XX (1919), September 5.

President of Equitable, who was just as big a man with just as big a responsibility, was receiving only $50,000. When Kernan asked the agents whether President Day should have an increase in salary, the affirmative response was unanimous. (In 1920 President Day's salary was raised to $75,000.)

HOME OFFICE REORGANIZATION

As a result of ill health, death, and resignations, Equitable officer personnel underwent numerous changes during the early postwar years. Assistant Secretary Samuel S. McCurdy, who had had broad responsibilities in the administration of the Home Office, died in April 1918.[2] With Second Vice Presidents Leon O. Fisher and Henry L. Rosenfeld spending most of their time in government work, the Society found itself short of officers. Consequently, in April 1918, President Day appointed J. V. E. Westfall, who had been Assistant to the President, Executive Vice President to plan the reorganization of the Home Office; he was given supervision over all the departments excepting Agency, Treasurer's, Comptroller's, and Secretary's.[3]

In February 1919 President Day appointed Treasurer Alfred R. Horr to be Financial Vice President with supervision over the Treasurer's and Comptroller's Departments; by executive order issued by Westfall,

[2] In 1930, Secretary William Alexander wrote of McCurdy as follows: "S. S. McCurdy, who was my assistant for a time, was not a highly accomplished stenographer or letter writer in the beginning, but he became one of our best correspondents; was placed at the head of the largest department at the home office; was skillful in dealing with the Insurance Commissioners of the different states, and on one occasion was sent to deal with a complicated situation in Chili, South America, where the exercise of grave responsibility was necessary, and where he was conspicuously successful. He became an expert in all matters relating to policy contracts, acquired a fund of useful knowledge about insurance law, and was the connecting link between the Society and its legal advisers. His death, hastened by his enthusiasm for hard work, was a very serious loss." *Agency Items* (September 1, 1930).

[3] Under the Society's Charter, the Board of Directors were required, after each annual election, to elect a President and appoint a Secretary and such other officers as they might deem necessary; they might, at their option, also elect a Vice President. The By-Laws of May 31, 1906, required the Board also to elect a Vice President and to appoint, in addition to the Secretary, an Actuary, a Comptroller, and a Treasurer. The President was authorized, subject to confirmation by the Board, to appoint a Second and Third Vice President and such other officers as he might see fit. In July 1916 the By-Laws gave the President additional authority to appoint a Fourth Vice President, an Assistant to the President and such other officers and assistants as might be needed. The By-Laws as amended September 1918 limited the Board to the election of a President and Vice President and the appointment of a Secretary; the President was given the authority to appoint "such other officers and assistants as may be deemed expedient," subject to confirmation by the Board.

the real estate investment operations of the Law Department were placed under Horr's supervision the following month. When Vice President John Lunger died in June, Westfall's plan of reorganization, which called for three coordinate divisions, each to be headed by a Vice President, was put into effect. The Board confirmed the appointments of Westfall as Vice President in charge of the Executive Department, Horr as Vice President in charge of the Financial Department, and William E. Taylor, who had been a Second Vice President, as Vice President in charge of the Agency Department. This action was confirmed by the By-Laws, which were again amended in November 1919 so as to permit the President to appoint one or more vice presidents and such other officers as he thought necessary, subject to confirmation by the Board.

President Day, in speaking of the new vice presidents, said that Dr. Westfall had more degrees than any man in the life insurance business; that Taylor was a "wheel horse for work" who had the affection and respect of all the agency force; and that Horr, who had a real regard for virtue, law, and order, had devised new methods of guarding the Society's funds not only from without and within but from himself—"barriers which he himself erected." President Day also admired Horr's independent spirit and ability to speak his mind, even if his judgment did not coincide with that of the President, any Vice President, or any committee man.[4]

Second Vice President George T. Wilson, who had been with Equitable for forty-four years, resigned in November 1919 because of ill health; a red-faced, red-headed Irishman and a *bon vivant*, he had not had the support of President Day.[5] Many of Wilson's duties in the foreign field had been taken over during the war period by Second Vice President Henry L. Rosenfeld. Rosenfeld resigned (effective February 1, 1920) to become United States Manager of a British reinsurance company; he had been a first class life insurance man and President Day was sorry to see Equitable lose his services.[6] E. E. Rittenhouse, who had taken McCurdy's place as Assistant Secretary in

[4] President Day in his address to the agents at the Sixtieth Anniversary Convention, August 26, 1919, as reported in *The Eastern Underwriter*, XX (1919), August 29.

[5] During the administration of Mayor John Purroy Mitchel, Wilson had served as vice chairman of the committee to welcome distinguished guests. Among others he escorted former Prime Minister René Viviani and the French mission which visited the United States soon after its entry into World War I.

[6] Thomas I. Parkinson later said that Rosenfeld was the "best insurance man" in Equitable at this time. Interview with author, April 2, 1958.

1918, died in January 1920. The following month, Third Vice President William J. Graham and Actuary Robert Henderson were promoted to second vice presidents. Henderson, a Canadian, and one of the leading actuaries of the United States, had joined Equitable in 1897 and had been Actuary since 1911. In 1918 Walter G. Schelker became an Assistant Secretary of the Society and the following year Andrew E. Tuck was also made an Assistant Secretary.

In June 1920, two more second vice presidents were appointed—Frank H. Davis and Thomas I. Parkinson. Davis, a former schoolteacher, had become agency supervisor at St. Paul in 1913 and later had been placed in charge of the Chicago office and adjacent territory.[7]

Parkinson, a native of Philadelphia (born November 27, 1881), had gone directly from high school to the University of Pennsylvania Law School, from which he was graduated *cum laude* in 1902. While practicing law in Philadelphia, he had at one time contemplated becoming a life insurance agent, but the General Agent with whom he discussed this possibility doubted that he had the qualifications to make a success in life insurance. In 1908 Parkinson came to New York to serve as counsel to the Bureau of Municipal Research for the City of New York. In 1911 he became Director of the Legislative Drafting Research Fund at Columbia University and in 1917 was appointed Professor of Legislation. While Director of the Fund, Parkinson served as counsel for committees of the New York and other state legislatures; he helped draft workmen's compensation and insurance bills and the revised factory laws which followed the recommendations of the Wagner Investigating Committee in 1913. In 1916 he served as Special Assistant to the Attorney General of the United States, in which capacity he worked with Solicitor General John W. Davis; in 1918–19 he served as Major Judge Advocate in the War Department, assisted in drafting the War Risk Insurance Act, and then became Special Counsel for the Bureau of War Risk Insurance. In 1919–20 Parkinson served as Legislative Counsel to the United States Senate committees and helped draft the Railroad Transportation Act (the Esch-Cummins Act) and other important legislation; for the preceding six years he had also been chairman of the Committee on Legislation of the American Bar Association.

Senator Philander C. Knox of Pennsylvania was chairman of the

[7] For a sketch of Davis' career, see this history, p. 916.

Rules Committee of the Senate, and President Day had worked under Knox when the latter was Attorney General; Knox's secretary had been in Parkinson's law class at the University of Pennsylvania. When President Day consulted Knox in regard to Parkinson's abilities, he naturally received a most favorable response. Soon thereafter, Parkinson was invited to come to Equitable as part-time adviser, and his election as Second Vice President followed a few months later. For some years he continued to lecture at Columbia and in 1923–24 served as Acting Dean of the Faculty of Law, Columbia University. The new Vice President was boyish-looking but he had a keen mind, was a thorough student of law and legislation, and had become well acquainted with the basic problems in transportation, agriculture, finance, and life insurance. His personality was "a magnificent vehicle for expressing his ideas—vigorous, clear, gracious—altogether charming." Thomas I. Parkinson was destined to play a very important part in the history of Equitable.

In August 1920 John A. Stevenson joined Equitable as Third Vice President. Stevenson held a Ph.D degree from the University of Illinois and had taught in the public schools and at the Universities of Wisconsin and Illinois. As a result of his interest in education in salesmanship, he had become the first Director of the School of Life Insurance Salesmanship at Carnegie Institute of Technology. At Equitable Stevenson, who possessed a warm personality and was a fluent and entertaining speaker, took charge of the educational program for agents and prepared new sales manuals and policyholders' service materials. Success in this work resulted in promotion to Second Vice President in 1921.

President Day was very proud of the reorganization as well as the progress made by Equitable during the first decade of his presidency. When numerous letters of congratulation arrived in 1921, he wrote: "She has been rebuilt from turret to foundation."

The division of the Home Office organization into three departments continued until February 1922 when the Board elected J. V. E. Westfall Vice President to fill the official position left vacant by the death of Vice President Lunger in 1919. The three departments were abolished and Horr's title was changed to "Financial Vice President and Treasurer" and Taylor's to "Agency Vice President." Horr resigned and left the Society later in the year. In 1923 Frank H. Davis became Agency Vice President, and Ray D. Murphy, who had been Associate Actuary and Executive Assistant to Vice President Westfall, was appointed Second Vice President and Associate Actuary. Taylor became Second Vice President.

LIQUIDATING THE FOREIGN BUSINESS

Henry B. Hyde spent forty years in the endeavor to make Equitable not only "The Strongest in the World" but also the company which most widely covered the world. That had been a long, hard struggle, but withdrawal from the many countries was also a difficult operation. Although the Society had discontinued issuing policies in Prussia, Austria, and many of the minor countries during President Hyde's day, and in Australia and other countries later, nevertheless it had, at the outbreak of World War I, about $92,000,000 of life insurance in force in foreign countries and deposits totaling more than $42,000,000. Discriminatory tax laws, investment requirements, strange legal systems, and complicated administrative decrees were troublesome enough; but the disarrangement of currencies which resulted from World War I was too much.[8] In France, even though Equitable won its appeal against retroactive taxation in 1910, other problems remained. There were several lawsuits pending which involved deferred dividend payments, the mutuality of the Society, and policy contracts which required payment of premiums and benefits in gold.

In 1907 a French policyholder (F. E. A. Vincent) brought suit against the Society because, when the 20-year dividend period on his policy ended, he received much less than the agent who sold him the policy had led him to believe he would receive. This suit was of particular interest to Equitable because it involved the question of mutuality. When the Tribunal of Commerce upheld Equitable, Vincent appealed the case, but in July 1915 the Court of Appeals upheld the decision of the lower court, which noted that the insurance contract between the parties involved was formed entirely by the policy and that agents were not qualified to modify or annul contracts. A similar suit was started in 1907 by Marquet de Vasselot. At the end of the 20-year accumulation period, Equitable offered a cash value of fr.128,358 on the policy, whereas the plaintiff demanded a cash value of fr.228,000 plus fr.80,000 damages. This claim was also based upon estimates alleged to have been made by the agent. In 1909 the Tribunal of Commerce ruled in favor of the insured and Equitable was required to repay the insured all premiums, with interest, plus damages of

[8] For withdrawal from Prussia, Austria, etc., see this history, p. 869.

fr.80,000 and costs. Much was made of this decision by the insurance journal *L'Argus*, which was pleased to see Equitable thus embarrassed.[9] Since the Tribunal of Commerce was not a regular court of justice, Equitable was not too seriously concerned over this decision and took the case to the Court of Appeals, which, in July 1912, decided in favor of the Society.[10]

The question of payments in gold during the war period came up in connection with one of Equitable's French policies (No. 1,307,200) in 1915; the policy contained the clause which required all payments to be made in gold coin. Equitable's Counsel André Ulrich stated that such contracts were perfectly legal in France, and gave both the Society and the insured, or beneficiary, the right to refuse payments other than in gold; but if gold was not procurable, neither party could be held liable since the debtor could not be held responsible for non-fulfillment of obligation to pay in gold owing to a cause beyond his control.[11] This opinion was modified some months later, however, when Ulrich stated that a French law of February 12, 1916, prohibited, in time of war, the buying or selling of moneys of France at a price

9 According to James C. Rocquet, Secretary General for Europe, *L'Argus* was the organ of the French companies and its confusing and distorted description of the policy involved was purely for purposes of competition. The article from *L'Argus* was reprinted in *Volkswirtschaftliche Rundschau* in Berlin and also in the *Verzekerings Bode*, one of the leading insurance papers of the Netherlands. Rocquet sent copies of an article from *La Lecture* of February 20, 1909, which gave the facts in regard to the case and also threw light on the aims and purposes of the misleading report in *L'Argus*, to Equitable's managers in Berlin, Amsterdam, and Madrid. Paris Office files, French lawsuits (Marquet de Vasselot, etc.) folder, Equitable Archives.

10 In this appeal, A. Millerand, Senior Counsel for the Society in France, chose his assistant, J. Sarraute, rather than André Ulrich to handle the case for Equitable. Percy Peixotto, Equitable's Manager for France, did not have too high an opinion of Ulrich, who had figured prominently in Equitable's appeal to the Council of State two years earlier. He said that it was a positive danger for Equitable to depend upon Ulrich for any further defense before any court, for he "NEVER—NEVER once has put his mind, heart and soul in OUR cases—on our side—but ALWAYS—to quote the expression used here—he has been and is still 'in the skin' of the adversary. . . . His scepticism is such as to constitute a premium on failure." Peixotto to President Day, April 2, 1912. This was written in regard to a similar suit (G. E. Vallée) which was pending at the same time, and Peixotto was afraid that Ulrich would be used in the Vasselot case, which was the much more important of the two. *Ibid.*

11 Opinion enclosed in letter, Rocquet to E. E. Scott, December 24, 1915. Paris Office files, Gold Payment folder, Equitable Archives.

In May 1916, when Peixotto sent application for two sizable annuity contracts, President Day cabled him that thence forward all such proposals must be approved by the Home Office and none would be approved unless premium payments were made in United States dollars at New York, or in Paris by three days' draft on New York. Day cable to Peixotto, May 2, 1916. Day letters, Equitable Archives.

exceeding their legal value, or at any premium; violation of the law was punishable by fine or imprisonment or both, and the moneys thus dealt in were to be confiscated. Despite this law, the *Tribunal Civil de la Seine,* in 1917, decided in the case of *Deschamps* v. *New York Life Insurance Company* that the company had to pay a matured endowment policy in gold. The New York Life appealed the decision, lost again in the Court of Appeals, and again in the *Cour de Cassation* in June 1920. This decision affected several Equitable annuity contracts, under one of which the annuitant, who had received previous installments in depreciated francs, sought to recover the difference, as well as have the future installments paid in gold. Equitable instructed the Cashier in the Paris office to honor the contract.[12]

Business in Russia (including Poland) had languished since Equitable's resumption of new business in that country in the latter part of 1907. The agency organization, which had been dissolved when Equitable withdrew in 1906, never became firmly re-established. In 1910 the St. Petersburg Agency was reorganized; in order to relieve Manager Herman Schoofs of detail work and give him more time for production of business, the custody of the Society's funds and property was assigned to the Cashier, and all reports and records to an accountant, both directly responsible to the Home Office. But results in the Russian agency remained disappointing. Schoofs was no longer his former aggressive self, and seemed to realize it.[13] In August 1911 Schoofs presented his resignation, to take effect January 1, 1912 (January 14 new style); he said that the events of the past five years had seriously affected his nervous system. He was persuaded, however, to remain

[12] Thomas I. Parkinson to J. C. Rocquet, December 7, 1926. Paris Office files, Gold Payment folder, Equitable Archives. This did not settle this case, however, because the franc continued to fluctuate. As late as 1948, when the franc was 214.39 (official rate) to the dollar, and the free market rate about 307 to the dollar, the question arose anew as to how many paper francs Equitable should pay the annuitant.

In 1926 the decision in the case of *Deschamps* v. *New York Life Insurance Company* was contradicted by two other court decisions (*Damon* v. *The Gresham Life Insurance Company* and *Valancogne* v. *La Companie d'Assurances La Trieste*). In June 1928 a new gold franc was established by law which was about one-fifth the value of the former gold franc.

[13] January 18, 1911, Secretary General for Europe J. C. Rocquet wrote Schoofs: "Now, my dear Mr. Schoofs, a General that goes into battle with the feeling that he is going to meet defeat stands very little chance, if any, of winning the battle; and I very much fear that your mental attitude . . . may as much perhaps as anything else be responsible for the absence of success to which I refer, as the mental attitude of the General of an army might be for his defeat in battle." Paris Office files, Russian folder, Equitable Archives.

with the Society as Salaried Representative for Russia, the new contract to be effective March 14, 1912.

The outlook in Russia was further obscured by the discussion in the President's cabinet late in December 1911 of the expiration of the existing treaty of commerce between Russia and the United States. It seemed probable that if a new treaty were not signed before the expiration of the old, Russia would apply measures of reprisal to American products, but United States Ambassador Curtis Guild doubted whether the Russian Government would interfere with the business of life insurance. Meanwhile, Schoofs had "nothing pleasant to report." After making a business trip to Moscow, Kiev, Odessa, and other cities in the endeavor to secure agents, he was very discouraged. He found much criticism of Equitable's business policy, and doubt as to whether the Society would long remain in Russia; other companies were offering 80 per cent first year commissions as against Equitable's 30 per cent, and it was easier to place risks with them. He said that it was an easy thing to annihilate the Russian agency organization, and that the mere decision again to accept new business in Russia was not enough to rebuild it.[14]

Early in 1912, the Equitable Board accepted the report of a special committee which recommended that the Society should not revive new business in any foreign country in which it had ceased to write new business. In 1914, Schoofs was ordered to cease accepting new business in Russia and he informed his agents of this fact July 25. After the outbreak of the war, it became very difficult to communicate between the Home Office and Schoofs; all letters were sent in duplicate, one by way of Tokyo and the other by way of London; correspondents were notified to be careful to note the change of name of the Russian capital from "St. Petersburg" to "Petrograd," and to make sure that any documents sent from the Home Office to Petrograd were written in English or Russian as the use of the German language might result in a heavy fine.

Since Equitable's Russian business for 1915 showed a net loss of Rbls.146,887.55, the Society was required to pay no tax on profits, but it did incur a tax of Rbls.375 on its capital stock. The following year a new income tax law was enacted which changed the rates all along the line; any increase in income was considered "profit" and rates up to 12 per cent would apply. There was also a tax on capital

[14] Schoofs to Rocquet, October 19, 1912. *Ibid.*

stock and an income tax on the Society's employees.[15] Just why these taxes gave Equitable considerable concern is not clear since, having ceased to write new business, there would likely be no increase in income. The employees in the Russian agencies also had their problems, among them the fact that in 1918 wartime inflation raised car fare from 20 kopeks to 40 kopeks (before the war it had been 5 kopeks), resulting in an additional expense of Rbls.10 per month; they begged for refund of this additional expense by the Society.[16]

In March 1917 the government of the Czars was overthrown and in November the Bolsheviks took over. On December 1, 1918, the Soviet Government decreed that all kinds of insurance be a state monopoly and that existing companies be liquidated within four months. But more of Russia later.

In 1913 Japan reversed its policy of long standing and enacted a law which required a deposit of 60 per cent of reserves on life insurance policies; it applied to existing policies as well as new. Since the law would have required a deposit of more than a million dollars, Equitable ceased writing further insurance in Japan on January 31. The Society's Tokyo office was closed November 1, 1917, and after that date its outstanding business in Japan was handled by the International Banking Corporation through its Yokohama office.

In May 1908 Spain enacted a new insurance law which required the deposit in Spain of the full reserves on Spanish policies; it was later modified to provide that only 50 per cent of the reserve be deposited in Madrid under the control of the government.[17] The com-

15 Under the former law, rates on profit ran from 3 per cent when the profit amounted to not more than 4 per cent of the foundation capital, up to 24 per cent—minus 2 per cent of the capital stock—when the profit amounted to more than 20 per cent of foundation capital. Thus the tax on a profit of Rbls.150,000, calculated on the basis of foundation capital of Rbls.500,000, would be as follows: profit amounts to 30 per cent of capital; 24 per cent of profit is Rbls.36,000, from which 2 per cent of capital, or Rbls.10,000, is deducted. Percentage tax, therefore, is Rbls.26,000. Under the new rates, the tax would be 5 per cent if the profit was 3 per cent of the capital and run up to 12 per cent if the profit was 20 per cent of the capital. Using the new rates, tax on a profit of Rbls.150,000 would be Rbls. 17,500. Schoofs to Home Office Auditor H. R. Coursen, August 29, 1916. *Ibid.*

16 The petition, signed by twelve employees, was sent by Schoofs to the Home Office, June 7, 1918.

17 Property and policy loans were not accepted under the law as a part of the 50 per cent to be deposited in Madrid, but might form part of the remaining 50 per cent. Only 25 per cent of the reserve was required to be invested in Spanish

panies were given four months within which to apply for registration. This law, since it applied to both domestic and foreign companies, was more reasonable than similar laws enacted by other countries. Equitable was at this time the leading life insurance company in Spain; outstanding business totaled about $25,000,000, on which the premium income was more than $1,000,000, and prospects for increased business were good. Although the expense ratio in the Spanish agency was about the same as that in the United States, the mortality experience had been bad. Equitable had never had any important law suits or trouble with its Spanish business. If for any reason the Society should decide not to comply with the provisions of the law and apply for registration, it would still have to invest the reserves on outstanding business. In the opinion of Juan Angel Rosillo, Equitable's Manager for Spain, not only would this business "be slaughtered," but it would be impossible to reduce the mortality average by addition of new business.[18]

While it was still uncertain as to whether the law would require deposit of the full reserves in Spain, the Home Office was of the opinion that Equitable should not apply for registration under the law, and Rosillo was ordered to cease all new business on the night of September 12 (three days before the four months' period expired).[19] This order upset Rosillo, who said that the decision spelled ruin for the Society's outstanding business, as well as to his personal interests; he wondered whether Equitable might not arrange for the sale of his renewal account or might even be willing to reinsure its Spanish business.

In October 1908, Rosillo and James C. Rocquet, Secretary General for Europe, met in the Home Office with officers of the Society. After eight lengthy conferences, it was decided that Equitable would continue in business in Spain and Rosillo was authorized to apply for registration under the law. While the Equitable was still trying to get

---

securities; the remainder might be in such other securities, domestic or foreign, as might be approved by the Minister of Finance.

[18] Rosillo thought that Equitable's unfavorable mortality experience was the result of general conditions rather than poor medical selection by the Society's examiners. He said that in recent years sanitary and hygienic conditions were very much improved, and that future business would show a much better mortality experience. Rosillo's explanation, however, did not account for the fact that the mortality experience of the New York Life was much better than Equitable's.

[19] President Paul Morton to Rosillo, September 4, and cable of September 11. Paris Office files, Spanish folder, Equitable Archives.

its Madrid building included as a part of the Spanish investments, and deciding what kind of Spanish securities would be best to buy, the New York Life advertised in *La Correspondencia de España* that it was depositing the full reserves on its policies. Rosillo considered this an example of "the bad faith and tricks" of his chief competition, but did not think that it would help that company for, though his company had deposited only half of its reserves, it had the building, policy loans, and "the general prestige of La Equitativa."

Then it was discovered that one article of the law authorized the insurance department to issue almost any regulations which it might see fit, and this power was exercised by a Royal Order, dated April 28, 1909, and published in *Gaceta de Madrid* April 29; it proposed to regulate the accumulation system on deferred dividend policies. Equitable was "surprised and dumbfounded" by this order, which "out-Frenches the French requirement." If the Order meant individual annual accounts on deferred dividend policies, Equitable would not comply; it had refused to comply with such requirements in France and in Japan, and President Morton said that it would not do so in Spain.[20]

Equitable's registration under the new law was granted July 8, but on the same day another Royal Order was promulgated which clearly required annual dividend accounts on deferred dividend policies. Equitable immediately filed a "contentious appeal." Since it appeared, however (as a result of a decision on appeal of Gresham and New York Life companies), that the Royal Order did not apply to business written before the law was passed, Equitable decided to continue business in Spain on the condition that premium rates in that country be increased as of January 1, 1910, so as to be the same as those used in Russia. Both Equitable and the New York Life agreed to this condition.[21]

In October, representatives of a number of foreign companies met in Rosillo's office and petitioned the Minister of Finance to explain the regulations. In November 1910, the Royal Orders of April 28 and July 8, 1909, were canceled, but the following month another Royal Order was issued which gave the foreign companies three months to comply with the deposit requirements; no excuses or pretexts whatso-

[20] Morton to Rosillo (cable) May 10, 1909, quoted in Rosillo's letter to Morton dated May 11, 1909. *Ibid.*

[21] Second Vice President George T. Wilson to Rosillo, July 26, 1909. *Ibid.*

ever would be accepted for noncompliance. Under this Order, it appeared that Equitable would not be permitted to make deposits in United States securities, but would be expected to deposit Spanish, English, and German government bonds.[22] In January 1911 a "Project of Definite Regulation" was issued by the Ministry of Finance. Since this was not a definite regulation but merely a proposed draft, further confusion resulted.[23] This time the representatives of a number of foreign companies called upon the Minister of Finance and asked for further time in which to present their comments and also for an extension of time on the deposit requirements. Rocquet thought that the "Project" was making law on the insurance contract, a legislative function not within the power of an administrative body. The whole "Project" was "involved, complicated and objectionable in many respects," but since it was issued to draw the criticism of the companies, he expected the final order to be much modified.

Without waiting for the final order, Equitable in March 1911 authorized Rosillo to make the requisite deposit in the Bank of Spain; the 50 per cent which was required under the law consisted of Spanish Exteriors (4 per cent) and United States railway bonds in equal portions.[24] Pending final decision as to whether the remaining 50 per cent of the reserves would have to be deposited with the government, securities for that amount were deposited with *Crédit Lyonnais* in Madrid under the control of Rocquet. Rocquet continued to oppose such a requirement with the approval of President Day. President Day said: "While we propose to comply with the law and live up to its spirit and letter, we do not intend to relinquish any of our rights." [25] In May the insurance department released the mortgage on Equitable's Madrid building, and the Minister of Finance suspended the earlier order of April 18, which required the deposit of the remainder of the Spanish reserve in Spain.

Meanwhile, Juan A. Rosillo, whose mental health had been failing, resigned as Equitable's Manager for Spain—effective March 1, 1911—and turned his agency over to his sons, Fermin, Miguel, and Fernando

[22] Rocquet thought the words "*Obligaciones hipotecarias*" used in the Minister's decree might mean railroad bonds. *Ibid.*

[23] A translation of the "Project" as published in *Gaceta de Madrid* January 20, 1911, is in *ibid.*

[24] The railroad bonds were Northern Pacific Railway Company Prior Lien Railway and Land Grant 4s (January 1, 1997) and Atchison, Topeka, and Santa Fe Railway Company General Mortgage gold 4s (October 1, 1995). *Ibid.*

[25] Day to Rocquet, April 18, 1911. *Ibid.*

Rosillo. The Society placed its own Cashier in the Madrid office and he was given control of all accounts, collections, and investments of funds. At the end of the year, as a result of the decline in the rate of exchange, Equitable had to do some close figuring to arrive at a valuation of its Spanish assets and a calculation of its reserve liabilities. After the outbreak of World War I, the Rosillos cabled the Home Office rather insistently for funds. Also they complained about the terms of their contract.

In 1916 the Executive Committee of the Equitable Board decided that the interests of the policyholders of the Society would best be conserved if the writing of new insurance was discontinued in all countries which required a specific deposit against policy reserves. As a result of this decision, Equitable officially ceased writing new business in Russia, France, and Spain as of December 31, 1916. When Equitable withdrew from Spain, the Rosillos organized their own company, La Equitativa, and for a time it appeared that the Society might reinsure its Spanish business—which by this time had fallen to about $19,000,000—with this company. But when the Rosillos presented a claim for Ptas.1,000,000 against the Society, Julio Wais was appointed its representative to handle existing insurance.[26] The beautiful Madrid building was sold to the Banco España de Credito in June 1920, and Equitable obtained offices across the street. (Activities in Spain were not finally terminated until 1947, when the 495 outstanding policies were liquidated by payment of their face value, which, in view of the favorable rate of exchange, cost the Society little.)

Second Vice President Henry L. Rosenfeld was sent to Europe early in 1919, and President Day wrote Henry White in Paris and Ambassador Thomas Nelson Page in Rome to give Rosenfeld what help they could; he said that Equitable's business had suffered greatly as a result of the war and fallen into confusion.[27] October 1, 1919, Wolfram Charles Franklin Day, President Day's grandson, assumed his duties as Assistant Secretary General for Europe, to work with Secretary

[26] The Rosillos in time developed the Equitativa Group, which included several insurance companies, among them La Equitativa Vida and La Equitativa Riesgos Diversos. The Rosillos' companies sell insurance in Spain, Morocco, Portugal, and Belgium. See *Equinews*, VI (1962), December, for photographs of Juan Angel Rosillo and his grandson, Juan Jose Rosillo.

[27] Day to White and Page, March 17, 1919. Day letters, Equitable Archives. Day addressed both White and Page as "Ambassador." White was not Ambassador to France, but a member of President Wilson's peace commission.

General for Europe James C. Rocquet. Young Day had been with the United States Legation at Berne and after the armistice became Secretary of the United States Mission at Berlin. He was familiar with the European situation and during the ensuing months kept his grandfather—"the Governor"—posted on European affairs by way of detailed letters.[28]

In 1919 Equitable added $454,839,437 of new insurance; of this amount about $446,000,000 was written in the United States and the remainder in Canada and the British Isles, the only two foreign countries in which the Society remained active. After careful study, the Insurance Committee of the Board decided that the Society should cease writing further new business outside the United States. There were numerous reasons for this decision: 1) high mortality and excessive expenses of the foreign business, 2) onerous and restrictive legislation, 3) excessive taxation, 4) difficulties of administration and litigation, and 5) the war and its resulting disruption of the economies and currencies of the European countries. With Equitable having to get permission to exceed the legal limit on new business in the United States alone, there seemed to be little sense in continuing its expensive and troublesome foreign business. As President Day said: "I would like to get rid of it all and concentrate our energies in the United States." He decided to release the Society from liability on foreign contracts with the least possible delay and the utmost economy. Whether this was to be done by purchase of the policies, by reinsurance, or by sale to another company would be determined by the facts pertaining to each situation.

In June 1920 President Day wrote Secretary General for Europe James C. Rocquet that, since it was almost impossible for the Home Office to make decisions upon the foreign business on the basis of letters and cables, he was sending recently appointed Second Vice President Thomas I. Parkinson to consult with Rocquet and Franklin Day upon the possibility of "converting our German deposits into mark securities, or the buying up of policies in any of the countries in Europe, or, indeed, any other question that may come up." He

[28] President Day's son, Charles, had married a German (or Polish?) woman who had lived in Berlin for some time. Relations between President Day and his son had been somewhat estranged for a number of years, but relations between grandfather and grandson were most cordial. In December 1917, President Day sent Franklin the new draft board questionnaire, four pounds of sugar, and cigarettes "by the pouch." Young Day was given deferred classification under the draft because of his diplomatic duties. Day to "Frank" at Berne, December 26, 1917. *Ibid.*

continued: "Of course, it is utterly out of the question that we could close up our affairs in Europe in my lifetime, or yours. We can hope, however, to determine whether in the existing situation it is safe for us to buy foreign securities and exchange them for our American securities, taking down the latter, and whether we can profitably anticipate the payment of some of our contracts." [29] President Day then wrote Franklin Day that when Parkinson and Rocquet arrived in Berlin, it would be a good chance for him to get better acquainted with German officialdom; he should, if opportunity offered, try to meet Count Johann von Bernstorff, German Ambassador to the United States in 1917, who had been quite helpful to Equitable prior to the United States' entry into the war.[30]

Parkinson sailed for Paris on the *Aquitania* July 31. Since his first important business was in Berlin rather than Paris, the immediate problem was to get transportation from Paris to Berlin. With the aid of Rocquet's male secretary, Maurice Baquiche, and by exercise of considerable ingenuity—and a *pourboire* or two—he succeeded in getting a compartment for Berlin.[31] Time was of the utmost importance, for the Imperial Director of Insurance was to be in the city for only a day or two. At the Hotel Esplanda in Berlin there were "no rooms available." This time luck and coincidence played a part, for Parkinson recognized the hotel manager as a onetime waiter in the Hotel Carlton in London; and the manager remembered Parkinson as the person who, some years earlier, had practically exhausted the hotel's supply of out-of-season strawberries. For Herr Parkinson a room was immediately available.

29 President Day told Rocquet, confidentially, that Equitable had learned that the Mutual Life had been taking down its United States securities deposited in Berlin and substituting German securities for them, "this to the tune of several million dollars' value of American securities, substituting mark securities for them, of course at a great saving. They are also purchasing their outstanding Austrian policies under a plan which looks attractive." Day to Rocquet, June 30, 1920. Parkinson files, Equitable Archives.

30 Day to Franklin Day, July 29, 1920. Parkinson files, Equitable Archives.

31 Baquiche was born in Turkey, where his father, a French national, was practicing medicine. He was educated at the École Normale in Paris and taught for two years in Casablanca. After returning to Constantinople, he worked for the Standard Oil Company, then during World War I as translator in the United States embassy. He served as one of Rocquet's secretaries 1920–23, then came to the Home Office where he served as stenographer and translator until retirement in 1955. In 1950, Baquiche's thirtieth anniversary with the Society, President Parkinson wrote: "You were a very great help to me at that time and I have always recognized and appreciated it." Personnel Department records, Equitable Archives.

The Imperial Director of Insurance was persuaded to release several million marks of Equitable premiums which his department had taken over during the war, and probably gave Parkinson encouragement for the success of his next mission. This was to persuade the Vereinsbank of Hamburg to release Equitable's deposit, which had originally been made under the agreement of 1871 to cover all policies written in Europe and had increased over the years.[32] Under the terms of the agreement, Equitable was to be permitted to withdraw all or part of the deposit upon proof that all or some of the policies, guaranteed by the deposit, had been settled. Equitable had ceased new business in Germany except for the Hanseatic District (Hamburg, Bremen, and Lübeck) in 1894. A new Imperial Insurance Law was adopted January 1, 1902, which required a deposit of the reserves on the business in the German Empire. Equitable then ceased writing new business in the Hanseatic District June 30, 1903. As of December 31, 1904, the total German deposit was $4,671,879.[33] Other deposits were added to the fund, which by 1919 had increased to $5,668,097.[34] Since the Society's liabilities had been reduced considerably since the last deposit was made, it sought to recover the excess deposit. The Bank, however, contended that the original trust should be kept intact until all German policies were liquidated. Dr. Karl Gründler, George T. Wilson, Rocquet, Rosenfeld, Franklin Day, and President Day had all tried, but without success, to recover the excess deposit. But Parkinson, accompanied by Franklin Day, succeeded in persuading the Vereinsbank that the excess deposits were no longer necessary.[35] In November 1920 the Bank

[32] For the original Vereinsbank agreement, see this history, p. 280.

[33] This deposit covered the full reserves in accordance with the Imperial Law for all the policies issued in Germany and certain other countries as follows: policies issued on the continent of Europe from June 27, 1871, to May 1, 1881, together with those issued subsequent to May 1, 1881, in Germany (except Bavaria and Württemberg); Russia, to December 29, 1889; Denmark, to November 26, 1888; Holland, Switzerland, Sweden, and Norway, to October 17, 1887; Austria, to May 16, 1883; and Belgium, to August 31, 1884. Memorandum, May 16, 1950, by Auditor C. B. Lunsford. Parkinson files, Equitable Archives.

[34] One of the larger deposits was made in December 1905 when the Society signed over $500,000 of Northern Pacific Railway Prior Lien Railway and Land Grant gold 4s (1997) to the Vereinsbank. *Ibid.*

[35] President Day had written Franklin Day that it would be better if Rocquet did not go along for the interview since the officers of the Vereinsbank might feel that they were "being ganged on." President Day said he felt that way when several people tried to get something out of him. Day to Franklin Day, July 29, 1920. *Ibid.*

released $650,000 of railroad bonds, and in January 1921 $1,550,000.[36] (Other bonds were released in 1924, but the remainder of the deposit was not recovered until 1950.)[37] Getting this concession from the Vereinsbank was quite an accomplishment. President Day, in Florida, wired his heartiest congratulations to Parkinson, and Vice President A. R. Horr of the Financial Department wired: "Snappy work Tommy you are a peach."

Not content with this triumph, Parkinson tackled the problem of liquidation of the Equitable policies in the countries of Central Europe. He started with Austria, where he consulted Josef Redlich, former Minister of Finance in Austria-Hungary, whom he had known as a professor at Columbia University; Redlich helped devise a formula, and in September 1920 offers were made to purchase the outstanding policies, numbering approximately 480, which represented about kr.4,000,000 of insurance. Within eighteen months all but 35 of these policies had been surrendered—a reduction of about 93 per cent in the number of policies and about 98 per cent in the amount of insurance. In November 1921 the Austrian Government released the guaranty mortgage on Equitable's Vienna building and the deposit of securities

36 The November release consisted of Lehigh Valley Terminal 5s of 1941, and the January release was in the form of $1,000,000 Chicago and Northwestern 5s of 1921 and $550,000 West Shore 4s of 2361. *Ibid.*

37 After the releases of 1920 and 1921, the deposit consisted of $500,000 Northern Pacific 4s of 1997 and $34,000 Union Pacific 4s of 1947; also $1,550,114 in German securities and real estate. In 1924 Equitable deposited $100,000 of West Shore 4s of 2361 and secured the return of the $534,000 of railway bonds. After Equitable liquidated almost all its German policies, Doctor Anton Klostermann tried unsuccessfully to recover the remainder of the deposit. After the United States entered World War II, Equitable's deposit was subjected to the control of the Enemy Property Custodian (Dr. Paul A. Haber), who took over the Berlin building, the bank accounts, and the remnant of the insurance business. The Vereinsbank deposit was turned over to the Land Central Bank in Hamburg, and the Reich Insurance Department took over responsibility for settling any further claims of the policyholders of the Society. When the Military Government in 1947 provided for the return of the property of allied nationals, Equitable made every effort to obtain possession of its property. After some correspondence, a claim for release was filed December 28, 1948, which requested the British officials, through the Vereinsbank in Hamburg, to release the bonds and return them to the Society. The formal request was filed with the Vereinsbank August 8, 1949, and Equitable agreed to indemnify the British Government for any claims against it, and the Vereinsbank certified that it had no further claims on the bonds. Equitable's claim was approved and Equitable was so informed March 11, 1950. The bonds were finally received May 9, 1950. The history of the Vereinsbank deposit is summarized in Auditor Lunsford's memorandum of May 16, 1950.

(4 per cent Austrian Gold Rentes) amounting to gold florins 1,550,000. The little remaining insurance in Austria, as well as the Vienna building, were administered by Doctor Anton Klostermann until 1932, when Mrs. Mary Hofegger was given the Society's power of attorney. The beautiful building, which was considerably damaged during World War II, was finally sold to Continental Immobilien Ansalt in 1957.

Liquidation of the Hungarian policies began in January 1921, when the Society made purchase offers on about 480 policies representing insurance of kr.2,650,000. By the end of the year only 100 policies remained in force; the reduction in number of policies was about 74 per cent and in the amount of insurance about 83 per cent.

In Germany, as inflation progressed, many policyholders surrendered their policies for cash or allowed them to lapse. In March 1921, Equitable made offers on the 1,560 policies outstanding (M.18,600,000 of insurance); as an inducement to surrender, the Society paid two and five-sixths times the surrender value in marks. In less than a year, only 150 policies remained in force and the amount of insurance had been reduced by approximately 90 per cent.[38]

In February 1922, Alexander McNeill, who was Superintendent of the Home Office Bureau of the Foreign Department, wrote: "Considering the present very low exchange value of the currencies of these Central European countries, the amount of insurance remaining in force is almost negligible when converted into United States Dollars."[39]

Liquidation in Italy began in May 1921 when purchase offers were made on 550 policies representing about 4,400,000 lire of insurance. Eight months later, the number of policies had been reduced to 90 and the amount of insurance by about 86 per cent. Liquidation of the 385 policies outstanding in Belgium (fr.6,600,000) was undertaken in September, and by February 1922 the amount of insurance in force

[38] In 1918, a life insurance policy of M.25,000, or about $6,000, would buy a house; in 1920, it would about buy the furniture; in 1922, it might buy a dinner, but by 1923 it would not buy the postage stamp to send out a premium notice. Since no paper money was issued in denominations of millions of marks, it was impossible to pay or collect premiums, and the whole business of life insurance was practically stopped. This state of affairs was finally recognized by a law of July 19, 1923, which stipulated that insurances based on the paper mark were not to be conducted further and that the collection of premiums should be discontinued. For a brief summary of the effects of inflation upon German life insurance policies, see "German Life Insurance During the Inflation Period," published in *Best's Insurance News* (Life Edition), XXIX (1929), September 3, and reprinted in *ibid.*, XXXIV (1934), January 2.

[39] McNeill memorandum to Second Vice President Parkinson, February 1, 1922. Parkinson files, Equitable Archives.

had been reduced by 86 per cent. There were some 480 policies outstanding in Turkey, Greece, Egypt, and Tunis (fr.4,100,000), and by the same date 267 of these policies had been closed out and the amount of insurance reduced by about 60 per cent. In Scandinavia, where liquidation was also started in September 1921, purchase offers were made on 883 policies (kr.3,050,000) and all but 300 of these policies were turned in during the next four months. The amount of insurance was reduced by about 65 per cent. In Portugal, offers were made on those policies written in depreciated currency and about 75 per cent of them were liquidated. In Finland and Servia, Equitable had only a few policies outstanding and most of them were purchased in 1922.

In none of these countries was the amount paid to purchase the policies greater than the amount in dollars at which the reserve liability under the policies had been carried on the Society's books. At the same time, the policyholders were given as liberal terms as Equitable thought could be offered under the circumstances. That the policyholders believed they had been fairly dealt with was indicated by the large percentage who accepted the Society's offers.

Although Great Britain had been the only country of importance which had never enacted deposit legislation, Equitable ceased to write new business there December 31, 1921; since the Society maintained a small voluntary deposit with the government, the trust established in 1872 was terminated and about $500,000 in securities were returned. Equitable maintained an office in London to service its outstanding policies until 1949, when this work was taken over by the Sun Life Assurance Company of Canada. Equitable ceased new business in Canada in July 1920, but maintained an office in Montreal from which to service old business. During the period 1944–57 the Society was again licensed to write new business in seven of the Canadian provinces. Solicitation of individual life and health insurance was not resumed in Canada, but group business was written for our United States group policyholders having Canadian subsidiaries and employees, and in other special situations.

The process of withdrawal from foreign fields was practically completed by a series of reinsurance agreements. The first of these had been made with "La Suisse" Compagnie d'Assurances sur la Vie et contre les Accidents, of Lausanne, December 30, 1919.[40] Equitable

[40] The contract was signed by Second Vice President Henry L. Rosenfeld in Paris December 30, and by Max de Cérenville in Lausanne January 6, 1920. The contract was approved by the Equitable Board March 18, 1920.

had written no new business in Switzerland since 1891, but it had been required to maintain administrative agencies to care for the old business.[41] The 153 remaining policies, which represented 1,347,864 Swiss francs of insurance and annual annuity payments of 3,851 Swiss francs, were transferred to "La Suisse," and Equitable paid that company the mathematical reserves and other items totaling 864,281 Swiss francs; securities deposited with the Swiss Government were accepted as part payment.[42]

In 1922 Equitable reinsured its outstanding business in the following countries with the Sun Life: Argentine Republic, Chile, Brazil, South Africa, Mexico, Cuba, China, Japan, Korea, Formosa, Uruguay, Paraguay, Bolivia, Venezuela, Colombia, Peru, Ecuador, British Guiana, Dutch Guiana, French Guiana, Guatemala, British Honduras, Honduras, Salvador, Nicaragua, Costa Rica, Panama (excluding Canal Zone), Bermuda, Bahamas, Porto Rico and other Islands of the West Indies (exclusive of Cuba), India, Ceylon, Siam, Malay Peninsula, Philippine Islands, Sumatra, Java and other Dutch East Indies, New Caledonia, Fiji Islands, Samoa, and Cook Island. The Society paid Sun Life the reserves on this business and by supplementary trust agreements provided for maintenance of a fund sufficient to meet the liability on the reinsured business.

As of January 1, 1923, Equitable's outstanding business in the Commonwealth of Australia, where it had ceased writing new business in 1906, was reinsured with the National Mutual Life Association of Australasia Limited. There were 4,503 policies (£1,352,318 of insurance), on which the net reserve liability was £820,545. After the various debits and credits were calculated, Equitable promised to pay to National Mutual, through a Trustee mutually agreed upon, £734,506. In partial payment of this sum, Equitable turned over £40,000 in cash and certain Australian and New Zealand securities amounting to £35,000, all of which had been part of its required government deposit. In addition, Equitable gave to National Mutual title to the freeholds and buildings erected thereon by Equitable in Sydney and Melbourne, valued at £525,000. The Commercial Bank of Australia Limited at Melbourne was appointed Trustee, and, by an indenture which formed a part of the agreement, National Mutual agreed to maintain in the

[41] Premium income on this business in 1919 was $4,071, while expenses of caring for it were approximately one-fourth of that amount.

[42] Corporate Records, Equitable Archives.

hands of the Trustee in cash and securities a sum equal to the net reserve liability on the business reinsured. The trust for the protection of the reinsured policyholders was to continue so long as any part of the business remained in force, and the Trustee was to be compensated for its services by National Mutual. National Mutual agreed, among other things, to give all the reinsured policyholders the same benefits and privileges they would have received had they remained with Equitable, to assume and relieve Equitable of all expenses and responsibility in connection with the management of the reinsured business, and to assume all liability in connection with any policy claims pending.[43]

Reinsurance of the Australasian business did not mean that Equitable was relieved entirely of work and obligations in connection with it. For instance, various complications arose in regard to resale of the Melbourne Equitable building (to the Colonial Mutual Life Assurance Society Limited), and legal opinion held that, notwithstanding the reinsurance agreement, Equitable must be regarded as continuing to carry on business in any state, and be registered in that state, so long as any policy remained outstanding in the name of Equitable. Therefore, Equitable would be required to have a representative with the power of attorney in each state.[44] Second Vice President Parkinson did not agree with this opinion, however, and stated that transfer of Equitable's business was "absolute and complete," and that it would be an anomalous situation if Equitable had to continue to comply with Australasian requirements in these matters. Equitable did send power of attorney to various persons to satisfy the Life Insurance Act of 1908 in the Dominion of New Zealand. Then in 1931, when income of the National Mutual was reduced considerably as a result of legislation and new taxes in the state of Victoria, C. A. Norris, General Secretary of that company, wrote that if Equitable had continued to carry on its Australian business it would have had to differentiate between dividends allowed on its United States policies and similar policies in Australia; he thought that his company should be permitted to do so. Actuary Robert Henderson of Equitable, however, after

[43] The agreement was a lengthy document of 35 articles plus the indenture. The original is in *ibid.* Correspondence and summaries in regard to the reinsurance up to 1941 are in the files of the Reinsurance Division, Actuary's Department, Equitable Archives.

[44] Blake and Riggall, Solicitors and Notaries, Melbourne, to David Fell and Company (Equitable's business agents), May 22, 1923. *Ibid.*

careful consideration of material submitted, decided that Equitable would not have paid dividends during the year 1932 on any different scale in Australia.[45] And as late as 1951, the question arose as to whether or not certain policies written in Australia, but not in Australian currency, were the liability of Equitable or of National Mutual.[46]

The 95 outstanding policies in Norway, where Equitable had discontinued new business in 1906, were reinsured in 1924 with the Norske Forenede Livsforsikringsaktieselskap of Christiania. A similar agreement was made for the 35 policies in Sweden with the Svenska Lifforsakringsbolaget of Stockholm; there were more articles in the agreement than policies to be reinsured. Only 45 policies were involved in the reinsurance agreement with Livsforsikringsselskabet Danebroge A/S of Copenhagen, Denmark, made in June 1925; consent to the transfer was required from four-fifths of the policyholders. The 725 policies outstanding in the Netherlands, where Equitable had discontinued new business August 31, 1918, were reinsured with the Nationale Levensverzekering-Bank of Rotterdam in 1925, and Equitable's deposit of $133,000 of American securities with the Rooterdamsche Bankvereeniging of Amsterdam was released. The 32 remaining Equitable policies in Italy were not reinsured until 1935. The reinsurance agreement with the Instituto Nazionale delle Assicurazioni of Rome took effect January 1 of that year.

As Second Vice President Parkinson later said, the various reinsurance contracts were numerous and complicated. In each instance, he and President Day drew upon their knowledge of both law and life insurance to make sure that Equitable would fare as well financially as if it had retained the business. All of the contracts had to be approved by the Society's Board of Directors, by the Insurance Department of the State of New York, and by the corresponding regulative agencies in the various countries involved.

Although most of the German policies had been liquidated by 1924,

45 Since taking over the business in 1923, National Mutual had allotted dividends in strict accordance with schedules and instructions sent each year by Equitable. Secretary Norris said that the New York Life, whose business had been reinsured with his company, had consented to an appropriate adjustment of their American scale of dividends for 1932. C. A. Norris to President Thomas I. Parkinson, December 22, 1931; Robert Henderson to the General Manager, National Mutual Life Association, February 15, 1932. *Ibid.*

46 Vice President Joseph R. Boldt to the National Mutual, January 3, 1951. Australian Reinsurance Folder, Corporate Records, Equitable Archives.

Equitable still had its Berlin building and held various German bonds. Rents in the building were complicated by the currency debacle. Franklin Day wrote that the new "gold marks" were merely paper marks stabilized at 4.2 trillions, "being thus the old dollar gold parity times 12 cyphers." A bill which was still pending would, if it passed, provide that mortgages reading in the old mark would be paid at the rate of ten gold marks for each 100 old marks. This provision would not apply to government obligations or life insurance policies, which would still be payable in paper marks at face value, which in most cases would be nothing. Also in circulation were the "rentenmark," supposedly the same value as the "gold mark," and the "bill mark" (one billion paper marks). Rocquet complained bitterly that he could not check up on the rental accounts in the Berlin building, where some of the rents were paid in paper marks (at one billion to one rentenmark), while the remainder were paid in gold marks. Day had a long talk with Hjalmar Schacht, who, in 1933, was Reich Currency Commissioner (and the following year became President of the Reichsbank); Schacht said that the same process which then applied to mortgages would probably some day be applied to government bonds.[47] So Day thought that Equitable would better hold its bonds

[47] Franklin Day (in Basle) to Parkinson, February 11, 1924. Parkinson files, Equitable Archives. Hjalmar Schacht was the son of William Schacht, who for many years was a Cashier in Equitable's Berlin office.

The elder Schacht, who had entered the service of the Society in the Berlin office in 1884, became Cashier there in 1910. Late in 1919, when he was getting ready to retire, he petitioned Equitable to pay his pension (2 per cent of his total salary annually) at the rate of M.4.20 to the dollar. This the Equitable Board agreed to do, October 1, 1919. The pension amounted to $1,467 per year. "To get better food and have our quiet which I am afraid shall not arrive to our Germany during the short rest of my lifetime," Schacht and his wife moved to Copenhagen. Schacht's pension payments then (1920) were converted into Danish kronen, but by 1924, when the kronen had depreciated relative to the new German marks, Schacht thought Equitable should, like Germany, have an "Aufwertung" or "raising" of his pension. Equitable finally decided to pay his pension of $1,467 per annum in United States dollars. Schacht had explained that he had worked for Equitable up to the age of seventy-five without ever receiving any money for sick leave, vacations, or life insurance: "I was never a flatterer and talker nor pushed myself in the foreground, but I know that I always have tried to do my duty toward the Society to my best ability. With this feeling I shall take leave from the Society." A. Klostermann to Rosenfeld, August 30, 1919; Schacht to Rosenfeld, September 2, 1919; Alexander McNeill to Rosenfeld, October 14, 1919; Rocquet to Privatbanken i Kjpbenhavn, Copenhagen, July 6, 1920; Schacht to Auditor E. E. Scott, February 28, 1921; Schacht to Home Office, January 1, 1924; and Thomas I. Parkinson to Schacht, then in Berlin, March 24, 1924. Correspondence in Records Section, Personnel Department, Equitable Archives.

until that mysterious day arrived. Some of the Society's Württemberg bonds came due in 1924, but Dr. Anton Klostermann refused payment in depreciated paper; he said that it was quite impossible to explain the various currency laws when nobody in Germany seemed to understand them.[48] As late as 1928 the German Government was pressing for settlement on Equitable's few remaining outstanding policies.[49] President Parkinson said that about $13,000 would close out Equitable's policies on the government's terms, but would embarrass the New York Life, which was striving for a settlement on a lower basis.[50]

Equitable was fortunate to have been so nearly retired from Germany before the great inflation. At the beginning of World War II there

[48] March 1, 1924, Klostermann wrote Rocquet a six-page single-spaced letter, in which he endeavored to explain the situation in Berlin: the government, by decree of October 15, 1923, had established the Rentenbank, which was privileged to issue notes labeled "Rentenmarks," covered by "Rentenbriefe" (rent letters). "Rentenbriefe" were not issued in "Rentenmarks" but in "Gold Marks." In order to enable the Rentenbank to guarantee its "Rentenbriefe" by real estate pledges, the Rentenbank was granted a "Grundschüld" on certain kinds of real estate, in amount equal to 4 per cent of "War Tax Value" of the property. As the "Rentenbriefe" was labeled "Goldmark," so also was the "Grundschüld," acquired by the Rentenbank under the provisions of the decree, labeled "Goldmark." The value of said "Goldmark" was not fixed according to international parity of the national Goldmark with respect to some other foreign currency. In the sense of the decree, it was equal to a fixed quantity of gold; *i.e.*, one Goldmark equaled in value 1/2790 kilogram of fine gold. Since the "Rentenmark" had been put in circulation, the long figures expressing billions in paper money had been gradually shortened until it became the practice to call one billion of marks a "bill-mark." The "bill-mark" was then dropped and the terms used were "Rentenmark" (which had the same value as a Goldmark), and "mark," the latter meaning one billion paper marks. The two notes were in circulation simultaneously and equally accepted for payment. For instance, for the purpose of a payment of 100 Goldmarks, 60 Rentenmarks and 40 billions of paper marks might be used. In consequence of the computation and accounting on the basis of reduced figures, as above explained, the November and December reports on the Berlin rents and expenses in 16 Kronenstrasse, and expenses in the main building, were reported in paper marks (billions), while the rents in the main building were reported in Goldmarks (*i.e.*, one billmark=one Rentenmark=one Goldmark). Whether this letter made the matter clear to Equitable's Home Office accountants is doubtful. Paris Office files, German folder, Equitable Archives.

[49] Parkinson to Day (in Florida), March 13, 1928. Parkinson files, *ibid.*

[50] The New York Life had not liquidated its German business but had reinsured it. However, the company which took over the insurance was unable to carry the burden and placed the liability back into the hands of the New York Life. Parkinson believed that Equitable should clean up its own business in Germany without too much concern for the effects it might have on the New York Life, but that, other things being equal, Equitable should not do anything to make the position of the New York Life more difficult. *Ibid.*

were fewer than a dozen Equitable policies in force in Germany. The famous Berlin Equitable Building which, with the land, had cost $1,813,079, was totally destroyed during World War II. The site, located in East Berlin, became a hole in the ground and for many years was carried on the Society's books at $1; in 1965 it was written off to the sundry losses account.

The last of the important European countries to have its Equitable business liquidated was France. In 1922 Rocquet had received inquiries from two French life insurance companies—l'Union and the Compagnie d'Assurances Générales—as to whether Equitable would be interested in reinsuring its French business. Equitable was not interested at the time, but in April 1923 the Board authorized the President to enter into negotiations for the transfer or reinsurance of the Society's French business. Second Vice President Parkinson then wrote Rocquet that he might let these companies know that Equitable would be willing to entertain their proposal.[51] By 1926, however, Equitable, "after long and careful consideration," decided that it would be to its best interest to liquidate the French business by purchase of the policies.[52] Franklin Day sailed for Paris and on June 15 offers on the more than 3,000 French policies were mailed; within two months, about 87 per cent of these policies were turned in. The policyholders received several times the value of their policies as measured in depreciated francs. Yet for a cash outlay of $2,069,245, reserves carried on the Society's books at $6,270,464 were released, as was the mortgage on the Paris building and $275,000 of French dollar bonds. Subsequent marking down of assets and liabilities pertaining to the remaining French business from book values to actual values reduced the net profit from the liquidation to approximately $2,000,000. Liquidation of the French business was effected largely through the efforts of Rocquet, Franklin Day, and Alexander McNeill, who became Assistant Secretary of the Society in 1928.

James C. Rocquet remained in charge of the Paris office to administer the remnant of French insurance until his death in 1941. His career with Equitable had been a distinguished one—fifty-eight years of loyal and faithful service.[53]

51 Parkinson to Rocquet, April 23, 1923. Paris Office files, French Liquidation folder, Equitable Archives.

52 President Day to Rocquet (Personal and Confidential), May 3, 1926. *Ibid.*

53 Rocquet came to the Home Office in 1933 for the celebration of his fiftieth anniversary with Equitable. Despite ill health—rheumatism and finally Parkinson's

Liquidating the foreign business added measurably to the work and worries of the Society's officers, and since it could not be handled entirely by remote control, necessitated numerous trips to Europe by President Day, Vice President Parkinson, Franklin Day, and others; not since James H. Hyde found reason for frequent visits to France had Equitable officers made so many trips to Europe. Home Office administration of the remaining foreign business was in charge of Thomas I. Parkinson, with Alexander McNeill as Superintendent of the Foreign Bureau until 1938 when he was elected Secretary of the Equitable. William H. Mathers, Jr., replaced McNeill as Superintendent of the Bureau, which operated until 1941 when it was abolished.

THE ELIZABETH ALEXANDER CASE

In addition to his work in connection with the foreign business, Second Vice President Thomas I. Parkinson was given another difficult assignment, and that was to see whether Equitable had any adequate defense in the suit brought against the Society by Elizabeth B. Alexander, widow of former President James W. Alexander. It may be recalled that in 1888 the Finance Committee of the Board of Directors had agreed to pay an annuity of $18,000 per year to the wife of James W. Alexander, then Vice President of Equitable, in the event that she should outlive her husband. In 1905, the Board of Directors had declined to recognize this agreement and the resolution was reaffirmed in 1918, whereupon Mrs. Alexander sought judgment against the Society for $77,448.[54] The Society employed special counsel and sought an opinion from Charles Evans Hughes. Since the records on the original agreement had been lost in the fire of 1912, some doubt existed as to whether evidence could be found to support the defense. President Day suggested that Parkinson get in touch with Thomas DeWitt Cuyler, who had been a member of the Board at the time

---

disease—Rocquet continued to go to his office until October 27, 1941. The war affected him. He often said that he had started life with a war (he was born in New Orleans in 1858) and that he would end it in a war. Severance of communication with the Home Office and the lack of milk, fresh meat, and vegetables, further increased his troubles. He died December 9, 1941, and was buried in the family vault at the Père Lachaise Cemetery in Paris. Rocquet's later years are described in a letter written by Miss Germaine Nortier, his secretary, to Rocquet's sister, Mrs. Noemie Mysing, January 8, 1945. Copy in Miscellaneous Foreign file, Corporate Records, Equitable Archives.

[54] Board Minutes, VIII, June 20, 1918, p. 18. Corporate Records, Equitable Archives. See also President Day to Judge William N. Cohen, June 6 and June 25, 1918, and to Wallace Macfarlane June 7, 1918. Day letters, Equitable Archives.

Underwood & Underwood

Thomas I. Parkinson
President, 1927–1953

the Finance Committee approved the annuity for Mrs. Alexander. He also thought it possible that Charles B. Alexander, who had aligned himself with James H. Hyde in the big fight of 1905, would be helpful.[55]

The case first came up in the Supreme Court, New York County, on March 11, 1921. The plaintiff put in evidence the contract, a resolution of the Finance Committee of Equitable, and an admission that at the date of the contract the plaintiff and James W. Alexander were husband and wife and continued to be until the husband's death. Counsel for the Society moved for a dismissal of the complaint on the ground that the plaintiff had failed to prove a cause of action. When the motion was denied, Equitable put in evidence its Charter and By-Laws and asked for a favorable verdict on the ground that the contract was unreasonable, unlawful, and unenforceable. This motion was denied and on March 14 judgment of $77,448 was entered in favor of the plaintiff. Equitable appealed, but in May the Appellate Division of the Supreme Court in the First Department affirmed the judgment of the lower court. At this point Equitable's counsel told President Day that Parkinson was wasting the Society's money and to pay the claim; the lawyers said that the case was hopeless and that they were going to retire from it. This statement antagonized Parkinson, who said that President Day, and not the lawyers, would decide in regard to disposal of the case. Parkinson then talked over with Secretary William Alexander and Dean Harlan F. Stone of Columbia University Law School the possibility of applying the doctrine of laches; his thought was that when officers of a corporation entered into a supplementary contract to receive remuneration for services "outside of and in addition to the services required of them as incumbents of those offices," they would have to give "adequate consideration and render these outside services."

The case was argued before the Court of Appeals for the State of New York on March 21, 1922. Although Parkinson prepared the argu-

[55] President Day, from Pine Forest Inn, Summerville, South Carolina, wrote Parkinson that there had been a time when Charles B. Alexander "would have cheerfully destroyed his cousin James W. Alexander," but Day doubted that he would now be willing to "help damn his father's memory." (Henry M. Alexander had been a member of the Finance Committee in 1888 when the secret agreement in regard to the pensions for Mrs. Henry B. Hyde and Mrs. James W. Alexander was made.) In this letter, Day spoke rather contemptuously of Mrs. Alexander and said that it was a "d——d shame that [she] should get this money out of the policyholders for whom you and I are trustees." The letter, probably written in 1921, is in the Parkinson files, Equitable Archives.

ments, Dean Stone appeared for Equitable. The validity of the judgment of the lower court was attacked mainly upon the ground that the contract on which it was predicated was invalid and not binding on the defendant. The Finance Committee resolution of February 2, 1888, read in part as follows: "That in consideration of the services rendered and to be rendered by him outside of and in addition to the services required of him as incumbent of his office and as full compensation to him for all such extra services, the Society agrees in addition to said salary to pay, and are hereby directed by said James W. Alexander to pay to Elizabeth B. Alexander, wife of said James W. Alexander, an annuity of eighteen thousand dollars during her natural life . . . ; said annuity, however, shall be paid only from the death of Mr. James W. Alexander, her husband." Dean Stone argued, and the court agreed, that the express and entire consideration was the payment and satisfaction of claims by James W. Alexander "for extra services theretofore rendered and for extra services thereafter to be rendered." While there was nothing in the contract by which Alexander specifically obligated himself to render services in the future, that fact was implied and should be read into it. The resolution as well as the contract indicated that Equitable, by payment of such a large sum of money, expected to secure the benefit of Alexander's services in the future as well as in the past, and that he had intended to render such services. The fact that he had resigned in 1905 and ceased to render such services was a bar to the plaintiff's recovery. Judge Chester B. McLaughlin, who read the opinion of the court April 25, stated that the general rule was that, in the absence of an express contract, an officer or director of a corporation could not recover for services rendered without proving they were outside of his duties as such officer or director, and in addition thereto that the same were rendered with the expectation by both parties that they would be paid for. Even though the contract bore the official seal of the Society, that did not necessarily make it valid: "I do not think the defendant, under its charter and by-laws, had power to make such a contract as now urged upon us for any such consideration. . . . This was a wagering contract and I think, as indicated, beyond the power of the corporation to make." The judgments of the Appellate Division and the trial court were reversed and the complaint dismissed.[56]

[56] Judge McLaughlin's opinion was concurred in by Chief Judge Frank H. Hiscock and Judges John W. Hogan, Benjamin N. Cardozo, Cuthbert W. Pound, Frederick E. Crane, and William S. Andrews. 233 N.Y. 300.

Thomas I. Parkinson later said that this was the most interesting and important case in which he had ever participated.[57]

GROUP INSURANCE ALMOST ABANDONED

While the foreign business was being liquidated, Equitable's growth in the United States was more than keeping pace with the postwar expansion of the country's economy. With sales of $454,839,437 of new business in 1919, Equitable's total insurance in force reached $2,270,903,931; only three years later, the total was $3,061,423,952. This tremendous increase stood the Society in good stead, for many millions of dollars of tontine policies issued prior to the Armstrong legislation of 1906 came due during the period 1921 to 1924, and these obligations were met out of incoming cash; to have had to sell railroad bonds, for instance, at existing market prices would have been a costly operation.[58] Whereas in 1910 almost $900,000,000 of the $1,347,158,692 of Equitable's insurance was in the deferred dividend policies, by the end of 1923 deferred dividend policies comprised only $100,000,000 out of a total of $3,446,574,467 in force.

In 1920 Equitable issued an endowment policy to provide for a college education, and an endowment annuity at age sixty-five. The following year a new policy rider was announced—"a salary continuance agreement"—which provided for settlement of death benefits in equal monthly installments over a five-year period.

In 1921 Equitable also introduced the Retirement Annuity Contract, a savings-pension contract for individuals, which produced a large volume of business during the next decade. This contract was written on the basis of premium units of $100 per year and provided optionally, subject to insurability at date of issue, disability income and waiver of premium benefits for an additional premium of $5 per year (later increased to $7); it was based on a 3½ per cent interest assumption and the American Annuitants' Mortality Table. This "savings-pension plan for employees"—which was devised largely by Associate Actuary Dwight A. Walker—would, if taken in addition to group life insurance, enable the employee to take care of his needs both during his working life and in retirement years. While the Retirement Annuity

[57] Interview with author, October 19, 1954.

[58] For example, in 1921 the market price of the railroad bonds held by Equitable was $44,434,844 below the cost of the bonds; and in 1922 $27,518,394 below cost.

contract proved popular it also proved to be rather costly to the Society. Said former President Ray D. Murphy in 1961:

> An experiment of unfortunate result was the introduction of so-called "Retirement Annuities" which were based on interest earnings of 3½ per cent, and mortality tables which proved deficient. This contract was very popular on the annual premium form and a large volume developed. While the interest rate of 3½ per cent appeared to be reasonably conservative when new investments had yielded 4½ to 5 per cent, the unforeseen but drastic downward turn in interest rates produced a different story. Instead of having an interest margin to offset the gradually lowering of mortality among annuitants, there appeared gradually an interest deficiency.[59]

Other factors which made the Retirement Annuity contract costly were the disability provisions and the liberal cash values allowed if the annuitant discontinued. Although the interest assumption for the Retirement Annuity was reduced to 3 per cent in 1935, the contract continued to lose money and was withdrawn in 1939 when extra reserves were established to take care of probable future deficiencies.

In 1921 Equitable raised its limit for insurance on an individual life from $200,000 to $300,000. Three years later the actuarial basis for nonparticipating immediate annuity rates for individuals was revised by increasing the interest assumption from 3 to 4 per cent and strengthening the mortality basis by using the American Annuitants' Mortality Table.[60]

At the end of 1929, Equitable carried on its books 67,822 individual immediate and deferred annuity contracts (including a large volume of participating Retirement Annuity contracts) which represented current and deferred annual payments to annuitants of $38,232,832, or more than any other life insurance company. The immediate annuity contracts were of the nonparticipating type, which Vice President William J. Graham thought was an anomalous situation for a mutual company to be in. The Society did not issue participating immediate annuities until 1934.[61]

[59] Ray D. Murphy "Recollections," February 1, 1961. Typescript copy in Equitable Archives.

[60] In 1933 the interest assumption for nonparticipating immediate annuities was reduced to 3¾ per cent and the loading for expenses was increased.

[61] For a number of years, David Parks Fackler, former Mutual Actuary and later Consulting Actuary, had contended that it was illogical for a life insurance company to operate life insurance on the participating plan and annuities on the

Group insurance, which under Equitable's sponsorship had made such an auspicious start in the prewar years, found itself in a precarious position in the early 1920's. Despite the fact that group mortality had been lower than that of the Society's other business, some of the actuaries had slight faith in group insurance; also there were those within the Equitable organization who thought that Second Vice President Graham and his Group Department had been given a position of too great importance, and who were laying their plans for its discontinuance or at least its relegation to the background. Then many of the general agents, agency managers, and agents opposed group insurance because they believed that it lessened the market for individual policies and, when Frank H. Davis became Agency Vice President in 1923, he threw his influence to the side of those who were opposed to group insurance.[62]

By the end of 1919, Equitable had $325,000,000 of group life insurance in force and total premiums collected to date had been $9,137,000. Excluding the more than a million dollar loss which resulted from the influenza epidemic, the claim rate had been slightly more than 55 per cent of the premiums. Personnel in the Group Department had expanded from a handful of clerks in 1912 to 186 in 1920.

In October 1920 the Insurance Committee of the Board held a special meeting to consider the full question of group insurance and to decide whether it should be continued or abandoned, and, if continued, what should be its place in the Society's organization. The five officers, in recommending that group insurance be continued, said: "If the question before us were as to whether the Society should now

---

nonparticipating plan. Graham had been one of the few actuaries in the country who had supported Fackler in this idea. When another company began featuring participating annuities, Equitable came around to Graham's way of thinking.

The Society resumed issuing individual nonparticipating immediate annuities in November 1960. Vice President and Associate Actuary Harry Walker said in April 1965: "The introduction of the investment-year method for allocating investment income has highlighted the desirability of mutual companies issuing their immediate annuities on a nonparticipating basis, and this was one of the considerations which led my company to switch from participating to nonparticipating immediate annuities." *Transactions, Society of Actuaries,* XVII, p. D31.

[62] An outstanding supporter of group insurance among the Agency Managers was Frank L. Jones of Indiana (Indianapolis), who at a meeting of the Agency Managers, General Agents, and District Managers in Chicago vigorously opposed any discontinuance of group insurance. His speech brought other managers to change their views.

enter the Group Insurance field, the expediency of so doing might be open to question. As a matter of fact the Equitable was the pioneer in this field and the writing of Group Insurance is now a public service which is widely recognized, and in which many prominent companies participate. Its discontinuance at this time, therefore, without an important and compelling reason, would result in loss of prestige to the Society." The report was signed by Vice Presidents Westfall, Horr, and Taylor and Second Vice Presidents Henderson and Graham; and soon after this meeting Vice President William E. Taylor informed the agents that, starting January 1, 1921, group insurance would be incorporated in the agents' contracts with renewal commissions for the same period of years as on the regular business, and that group policies would also participate in club qualifications on an equitable basis.

Meanwhile, a committee headed by Associate Actuary Ray D. Murphy and Comptroller E. E. Scott had recommended April 19, 1920, that it would be to the Society's best interests to distribute the work of the various sections of the Group Department to the regular departments—that is, to departments which handled similar functions for individual insurance. A long minority report, filed two days later, however, protested this approach and stated that all group operations, owing to their specialized nature, ought to remain under the Group Department, and thus be under the supervision of and benefit by the suggestions of specialists in group insurance.[63] The recommendations of the majority of the committee were carried out, and the following units of the Group Department were dispersed: the Accounting Division, the Correspondence Division, and the Issue Division. The Premium Collections Section of the Group Department and records of general accounting were transferred to the Auditor's Department, and part of the work in preparing data for payment of claims was taken over by the Society's Claims Department. About all that was left in the Group Department was Sales and Underwriting. These changes were taking place at the very time that Second Vice President William J. Graham was planning to expand his organization and place "high grade, special representatives" in Boston, Philadelphia, Chicago, Cleveland, Pittsburgh, Atlanta, and San Francisco, "to educate the agency force and close business, to work on salary and commission." For key posts in the new organization, Graham had in mind Frank

[63] The minority report was signed by H. W. Herrman and H. B. Steeg, both of the Group Department.

L. Jones as "Field Superintendent," T. S. Lowry as "Supervisor of Special Representatives," and Mervyn Davis as "Head of Underwriting." The only one of these appointments which materialized was that of Davis, who in May 1921 was placed in charge of statistical work in the Actuary's Department and of Group Insurance underwriting.[64] Ballard Dunn, former Assistant to the President of the Union Pacific Railroad, also joined the Group Department as Supervisor of Group Insurance Service and Graham's general assistant.

In 1921 the Group Department issued a 36-page booklet entitled "Suggestions for Selling Group Insurance," which was intended to aid the agents. It emphasized the fact that group insurance was an important factor in the humanizing of industry: it drew the laborer closer to the employer, lessened the employee's anxiety, and reduced labor turnover. The increased efficiency on the part of the employee might pay for the cost of the insurance. The booklet also emphasized that Equitable would, through its Medical Department, make a survey of the plant and outline a program for the installation of hospital services, nurse services, and the like; also, that the Group Department, through its Safety and Personnel Division, and the Bureau of Health and Conservation would be prepared to make surveys of working conditions and submit recommendations for increasing safety.[65]

The fourth edition of another booklet, "General Summary of Group Insurance Rules and Procedures," was also issued in 1921; it contained

[64] Mervyn Davis, a graduate of Cambridge University, had, after serving with three other companies, joined the Equitable in July 1918 as an assistant actuary. He was a brilliant mathematician who delighted in finding "elegant solutions" to problems; he was also a salesman who understood the realities of group competition and actively participated in placing some of the most important group cases. At times he was impatient with Actuary Henderson's rather rigid rules, which sometimes interfered with sales. Davis took great pride in tutoring some of his young assistants, among whom were Arthur M. Browning, Wendell A. Milliman, and J. Henry Smith. Smith eventually was to take the leadership in group actuarial work, and later still to be placed in charge of all functions connected with ordinary underwriting.

[65] Agents were warned to give their prospects a chance to talk: "This is the most difficult thing that a highly trained expert has to learn, because he may feel that the interview will be more valuable if it was uncovering expert knowledge on the subject. Not so. The executive knows best . . . the needs of his own organization."

In charge of Safety and Personnel was Lew R. Palmer, who became one of the organizers of the National Safety Council and for many years did valuable work on a nation-wide basis. Equitable later decided that such policyholder services as health and safety were not a proper function of the Group Department and they were discontinued.

sixteen pages on group life and six pages on group accident and health insurance. This publication made it clear that the agent should not confuse the total and permanent disability feature with group accident and health insurance, and stated that the permanent disability clause would be included in all group life insurance contracts without additional premium charge, except where extra hazards existed.

Although Equitable had issued some contributory group insurance contracts prior to 1920, it had generally discouraged this type of group insurance because it feared that the plan would result in selection against the insurer and also because of the greater cost of installation and servicing.[66] In December 1920, however, the Group Department decided to accept the contributory plans without prejudice, provided (1) that all eligible employees who did not subscribe within 60 days would be allowed to be insured only by their furnishing satisfactory evidence of insurability, (2) that employees pay at least 50 per cent of the premium except when legally prohibited from doing so as in groups of municipal employees, (3) that a provision be added to policies which would permit termination of the contract when fewer than 75 per cent of the employees were insured, and (4) that on group disability contracts no employees would be accepted after the age of sixty. Sometimes when the percentage of employees fell below the required 75 per cent, special "medical waiver campaigns" were conducted and uninsured employees were accepted without evidence of insurability, just as if they had been among the original subscribers.

Although 1921 was a recession year in industrial employment, Equitable wrote 193 new group policies, with more than $30,000,000 of insurance involved—more than any other group-writing company.[67] The loss incurred as a result of the influenza epidemic was wiped out and a surplus of $404,000 remained.

During this period the Group Department had some interesting

[66] In the earlier days of group insurance, there was some confusion in regard to the terms "contributory" and "noncontributory." Some contracts were termed "noncontributory" if the employees met the entire cost of the insurance and the employer did not contribute. Later, the terms came to mean the opposite; that is, "noncontributory" meant that the employes paid all, and "contributory" meant that both employer and employee shared the cost. Memorandum from Louise Ilse, April 19, 1963, to Secretary Gordon K. Smith.

[67] Equitable would have shown a gain of about $14,000,000 in group insurance in force had it not been for the termination of the group policy with Standard Oil Company of New Jersey ($36,000,000), which was replaced by a self-insured plan. Later, however, the Company returned to an insured plan with Equitable.

decisions to make in regard to "association groups," such as groups of doctors, lawyers, teachers, and ministers. The difficulty with insuring groups of this type was mainly the fact that there was no responsible head to bring in members, keep them in, and to collect the dues. Although Graham believed that schoolteachers, for example, deserved group life insurance, on at least one occasion he told a group of teachers of the weaknesses and difficulties involved in the proposal to insure them, but the more he talked the more insistent the teachers became that they were entitled to group insurance. As he said: "When you try to tell school teachers something, they naturally rebel at once, for you are stepping into their historic role of telling you!" Even more deserving of group insurance were the ministers, but most of them could not qualify under the definition of group insurance. As early as 1914 Equitable had issued a group policy to the Methodist Book Concern, a publishing company at Cincinnati.[68] But insuring the Methodist ministers was another thing. When the question came up in 1922, Equitable's counsel, Alexander and Green, were unable to convince themselves that the relation between the Annual Conference of the Methodist church and the ministers was that of employer and employee within the meaning of Section 101A of the New York Insurance Law. At first the New York Insurance Department was inclined to agree, but in 1924 Superintendent James A. Beha decided that ministers appointed by the Methodist Conference might be issued group policies provided the policies covered at least fifty ministers.

The movement to downgrade group insurance in Equitable was but one part of the plans of Vice Presidents J. V. E. Westfall and Alfred R. Horr, and it began shortly after the end of World War I. These two men were, next to President Day, the two most influential officers in the Society. Just what their overall plans were is not clear, but both men were ambitious and, for a while at least, they did work together. According to William J. Graham, they began by attempting to eliminate Vice President John B. Lunger, who was in charge of agencies, and Second Vice President Leon O. Fisher, even though Fisher had been instrumental in bringing these two men into the Equitable. Lunger died in June 1919, and his successor in charge of agencies, Vice President William E. Taylor, was added to the list of those to be eliminated,

[68] The Methodist Book Concern was originally established in 1789. The Western branch was established at Cincinnati in 1828 and became an independent concern in 1836.

Horr and Westfall intimating to Graham that he would be Taylor's successor if he would "play along." Graham made no promises, for he believed that if the situation got too bad he could always go to President Day.[69] Which of the two men was the leader in these plans is hard to determine; Graham always thought that Horr was the dominant figure, while Thomas I. Parkinson believed that Westfall was the leader and Horr the follower.[70] At any rate, the two officers agreed that Equitable had introduced enough "innovations"; that if any more were to be introduced, Equitable should let some other company do it; and that group insurance, Equitable's latest "innovation," should be abandoned or at least de-emphasized. Equitable should just go along, "not looking for trouble, and not looking for opportunities that would mean more work, more care, and more responsibility." [71] At the same time, Horr was spreading the idea that, though President Day was a fine old man, he was no executive. It was about this time, however, that President Day found out that Westfall and Horr were checking almost daily with Associate Medical Director Robert M. Daley on the condition of Day's health (he had had a heart attack in 1919). Day was furious and began watching the two officers carefully; he also replaced Daley with Assistant Medical Director Arthur Geiringer as his personal physician. Suddenly, Westfall complained to President Day that Horr was undermining him and pretended to switch to Day's side. Just what the cause of the split was is not known, but Horr, probably feeling that his future in Equitable was somewhat handicapped, resigned and left the Society in July 1922.

After William E. Taylor was relieved of his agency vice presidency and Frank Davis was promoted to that position (October 3, 1923), the destruction of the Group Department was completed.[72] On July 15, 1924, Davis issued the following order:

69 Graham Memoir, pp. 210, 215–16.

70 *Ibid.*, p. 215; Thomas I. Parkinson interview with the author, June 17, 1958. Graham said of Horr: "Horr was the dominant figure. He had an executive's capacity to size up organization and to use organization, which capacity he exercised for the benefit of A. R. Horr to the full." On the other hand, Edith Belle Welling, Graham's assistant, said that Horr "did not play as important a part in this 'stew' as Mr. Graham believed." Letter to Assistant Secretary Grace W. Jordis, May 20, 1963. Parkinson said that Westfall and Horr "started some kind of a game."

71 Graham Memoir, p. 217.

72 Said William J. Graham: "Taylor had the disadvantage in that outfit of being a gentleman. Taylor wasn't a strong man. He was a competent man, not a vigorous, powerful man, not one of the Gage Tarbell type." *Ibid.*, p. 214.

Both Davis and Leslie York, who had been Agency Superintendent of the South-

A complete consolidation of the agency end of Group insurance with the Agency Department proper has been brought about, and all matters pertaining to the agency phase of Group insurance should be taken up with this office.

All other phases of Group insurance, including underwriting, service, etc., have been transferred to departments having similar responsibilities in connection with our regular insurance.[73]

Graham had the heartbreaking task of announcing this order to the Group Department personnel. He introduced William M. Rothaermel, Davis' assistant, to them and explained that in the future they would report to him.

Most of the positions in the Group Department were simply abolished; some of the remaining clerks were transferred to other departments; those who were not retained were given terminal pay equal to one month's salary for each year of service. Eventually, of the personnel who had constituted the Group Department, all but three or four left the service of Equitable. During the ensuing year and a half, the Agency Department sought to let group insurance die of neglect. Shortly before his department was completely dismantled, Second Vice President William J. Graham went to Europe "and let events take their course." For the time being, at least, he was a Vice President with a job but practically no specifically assigned duties. He contemplated resigning from Equitable, but decided that that would look too much like resigning from group insurance, in which he had a deep-seated faith. In Europe he studied particularly the experience of the British companies in developing life insurance without medical examination, with the hope that ultimately group insurance could make life insurance as universal as the pay check.

As group sales began to decline, protests began to come in from the general agents, among them Edward A. and Lawrence C. Woods of the great Pittsburgh agency, and Herman Moss of Cleveland, who had been deeply interested in group insurance from the beginning. Into this situation, which was not a good one, President Day called Vice President Thomas I. Parkinson and asked him if he could work with

---

west with headquarters at Kansas City, had been brought to the Home Office under Taylor. According to Graham, York was, in the opinion of those having to do with the agencies, senior to Davis, but, "being a kind and considerate man," was not adept in the struggle for position and power; it was Davis who "played along with those in power, to his own considerable elevation, emerging as the one in command of the Agency Department." *Ibid.*, p. 218.

[73] Agency Department files, Equitable Archives.

Westfall. Parkinson said that it would be difficult but that he was willing to try.[74]

The new setup for group insurance failed to improve Equitable's competitive position. In August 1925 Vice President Parkinson asked Actuary Robert Henderson whether "your mathematical ingenuity cannot devise some changes in our formulas which will improve our position competitively"; he wanted the charges against group insurance for administrative expenses, taxes, surplus, and commissions cut to a minimum.[75] Henderson agreed to "some slight revision" of charges against group insurance for advertising, conventions, clubs, and premiums on fidelity bonds. But this did not solve the problem. The chief trouble lay in the fact that Equitable was charging uniform overhead to all groups, regardless of size, whereas some other companies were granting large groups substantially decreased expense ratios which resulted in larger dividends. Later in August, Vice President Parkinson expressed to Second Vice President and Associate Actuary Ray D. Murphy his general dissatisfaction with the Home Office organization for handling group insurance: "It seems to be agreed that there *is something* wrong with it," especially the handling of negotiations and solicitations of new groups. It was at this time that Equitable made its bid for the group business of the United States Rubber Company and Second Vice President Graham said that the terms proposed were not competitive with those submitted by Equitable's leading competitors: "I am in position to say to you confidentially that the overhead cost of the Equitable is nearly twice the overhead cost of the other two mutual companies for the five year period for which we are submitting quotations." He said that there was no reason for this fact except that the other companies assessed expenses equitably among

[74] Parkinson later said that though Westfall was a man of considerable ability, he was "mentally lazy"; he would work hard when in "hot water" but otherwise would spend much time in his office working with his cameras and other apparatus. Interview with author, June 17, 1958.

In a letter to Parkinson (July 22, 1925), President Day said that he was turning over various memoranda in regard to the important question of internal organization, with the desire that Parkinson handle it so as to reconcile all points of view to the best interests of the Society. A copy of this letter was sent to Westfall, Davis, Fisher, Taylor, Henderson, Graham, Stevenson, Murphy, and William Alexander. Day letters, Equitable Archives.

[75] Parkinson to Henderson, August 6, 1925. Parkinson also asked Vice President Frank H. Davis (August 26) if he would agree to discontinue renewal commissions on new group business. Memoranda in Sterling Pierson files, Equitable Archives.

groups of various sizes.[76] Vice President Parkinson continued to try to get Henderson to scale down expenses with the hope that they might be got down to 6.6 per cent exclusive of commissions.

President Day asked Westfall for a report on the conduct of group insurance, and Westfall asked Graham for his views. Graham, in a memorandum, again pointed out that canvassing for group business was a specialized service and that the development of group insurance by Equitable could not have been successfully accomplished except under a specialized department, "yet from the beginning there seemed to be a strong but uninformed sentiment in various departments of the Society for decentralization of the group work." Despite the fact that the Group Department had been one of the most efficient and economical departments of Equitable, sentiment for its decentralization had persisted. After reorganization was effected, costs increased and many serious errors were made. Neither managers, agents, nor patrons of the Society knew where to turn for group information. Graham recommended that Equitable re-establish group insurance "as an executive department to cooperate with and to be supported by all departments of the Society." He attached a chart which showed the organization of the department before decentralization and suggested that it be reconstituted in substantially the same way.[77]

Westfall submitted his report to President Day on June 18, 1925. In it he noted that Equitable had not kept pace in group insurance with Travelers, Aetna, Metropolitan, and Prudential. Not only did the industrial and multiple-line companies such as Travelers and Aetna

76 Graham to Parkinson, September 25, 1925. *Ibid.* In addition to the U.S. Rubber case, Graham was having trouble with three of Equitable's group patrons who maintained that the amount of overhead retained by Equitable as evidenced by dividends paid to them was, in their judgment, excessive. The patrons were Guggenheim Brothers (including American Smelting and Refining Company) and International Motor Company and Mack Truck Company. In addition E. I. du Pont de Nemours had informed Graham that if Equitable expected to continue their group insurance, the overhead charges against them would have to be reduced.

77 Memorandum, Graham to Westfall, June 10, 1925. J. V. E. Westfall files, Equitable Archives. Graham attached a copy of the minority report made by Herrman and Steeg to the committee headed by Ray D. Murphy in 1920. For this report, see this history, p. 884.

Graham's chart showed five divisions under a general supervisor who was directly responsible to the Second Vice President in charge of the Group Insurance Department. The five divisions were Sales, Service, Office Administration, Records and Accounts, and Underwriting. The organization under each of these divisions was outlined in some detail.

have certain advantages because of the intimate relations existing between those companies and employers, but "the Equitable's organization for handling Group Insurance has been lacking in the aggressiveness, harmony, and co-ordination necessary for the procurement of the volume of Group Insurance that we would have a right to expect." The report included statistics which showed that the Equitable had the most favorable ratio of claims to net costs and that there had been a steady decrease in the expense rate of conducting the group business.[78] Westfall concluded his report by recommending an aggressive campaign for group insurance so as to secure a satisfactory volume of business: "In my opinion, this result can be obtained only by placing at the head of the selling department of Group Insurance, under the general direction of the head of the agency department, a man who is able to command the confidence, co-operation, and sympathetic interest of those in the Society engaged in the conducting of the Group business. Such an organization does not exist at the present time and until it is remedied, I do not see how we can hope to get the result we ought to expect." [79]

About a month later, Westfall submitted a supplementary report in which he stated that the Society was confronted with a rate war in group insurance. He reviewed the steps by which he thought it would be possible to increase group dividends and recommended that the commission scale be cut and renewal commissions on future business eliminated. Again he recommended that an enthusiastic group insur-

[78] Equitable's ratios of actual to expected mortality, and of expenses paid to premiums received, were as follows:

	Ratio—Actual to Expected Mortality	Ratio—Expenses Paid to Premiums Received		Ratio—Actual to Expected Mortality	Ratio—Expenses Paid to Premiums Received
1911	——	17.4%	1918	115.7%	17.3%
1912	48.9%	40.9	1919	68.8	15.0
1913	43.6	21.8	1920	70.5	16.9
1914	55.9	20.3	1921	57.0	15.5
1915	62.5	25.7	1922	63.9	13.7
1916	61.3	19.0	1923	66.0	11.5
1917	64.8	18.6	1924	68.5	11.1

The group surplus at the end of 1924 was $1,378,112.74.

[79] Memorandum, Westfall to the President, June 18, 1925. J. V. E. Westfall files, Equitable Archives.

ance man should operate under the general direction of the head of the Agency Department: "If Second Vice-President Graham cannot function in this capacity, then there ought to be some one else, for without an enthusiastic head, we cannot hope for satisfactory results."

On November 20, 1925, President Day informed all heads of departments that, from that date, development of the group insurance business and all Home Office activities relating to solicitation of new groups and training of salesmen would be under the direction of William J. Graham. The next day Agency Vice President Frank H. Davis released the following announcement to the "Managerial Staff":

> For your information, you are advised that from and after November 20th, 1925, the development of the Group insurance business of the Society and all Home Office activities relating to the solicitation of new groups or the extension of old groups, including the supervision of special group salesmen and the preparation and rendering of group sales aid to the Agency forces of the Society will, by order of the President, be under the direction of William J. Graham, Second Vice President.
>
> You will, therefore, take up with Second Vice President Graham questions which refer specifically and particularly to the sale of Group insurance.[80]

Davis had received his orders. The operation was completed on December 31 when President Day issued his executive order which read: "The organization heretofore constituting the Group Issue Division of the Bureau of Issue is transferred out of the Bureau of Issue and will hereafter be under the supervision of Second Vice President Graham."

So the Group Department was reconstituted substantially along the lines which Graham had recommended; his "exile of 1924–25" was ended. Thomas I. Parkinson had done his work well, and William J. Graham got the credit, or blame, for the re-establishment of the Group Department under a separate head.[81]

80 Agency Department files, Equitable Archives.

81 Some years earlier, while Parkinson was still with the Legislative Drafting Research Fund at Columbia University, he had been called in by Vice President Westfall to help prepare a resolution for the legislature which would recognize group insurance; this memorandum included a definition of group insurance which was essentially the same as that later drafted by the Actuarial Group Insurance Committee and incorporated in the New York law. Thomas I. Parkinson, interview with the author, November 30, 1955.

In his very brief report to President Day, Parkinson had simply recommended

It is difficult to estimate how much of a setback Equitable's group insurance suffered as a result of the controversies of the early 1920's. Whereas in 1922–23 the Society had issued 11.8 per cent of the group insurance written by the five major group-writing companies, by 1924-25 the percentage had fallen to 7.4. After the Group Department was re-established, this percentage climbed to 18.8 for the years 1926–27. On the other hand, it is possible that without the disappointing experience of 1924–25 the Group Department might not have been reconstituted as a separate department with the ensuing long-term salutary results. Also, Graham had not been idle during the twenty months when he was not in charge of group sales, and the studies which he made in that period no doubt helped develop group insurance to its most important role. Well aware of the fact that much of the resistance to group insurance came from a fear that it would hurt the sale of ordinary life insurance, he had doubled his efforts to prove the contrary. For instance, in an article which appeared in the *Journal of Commerce* late in 1924, he stated that group insurance was promoting rather than curtailing the sale of ordinary insurance; it was to a large extent reaching the great mass of workers who had little or no other insurance; it was not complete insurance for any life, but rather a "shock absorber," and helped educate the worker to the value of adequate life insurance.[82] In another article in *The Insurance Press* early the following year, he said that one of the most pleasing developments was the fact that group insurance had been consistently accompanied by an extraordinary growth in the sale of the regular forms of life insurance.[83]

Graham lost no time in reorganizing his Group Department. His first step was to rebuild the sales organization and to furnish it with a new series of pamphlets, dividend illustrations, and other helps for the agents. Henry Kranz returned from the John M. Riehle agency, where he had been superintendent since 1922, to serve as sales supervisor in charge of sales and service personnel. He immediately began recruiting field staff and established offices in fifteen strategically

---

that a separate department be established to handle all phases of group insurance. Parkinson to author, April 2, 1958.

[82] *Journal of Commerce*, December 18, 1924.

[83] *The Insurance Press*, April 22, 1925. In still another article entitled "Eliminating Examinations," he related how the Sun Life in Great Britain had gradually come around to issuing ordinary life insurance up to $75,000 without medical examinations. *The Weekly Underwriter*, CXI (1924), November 8.

located cities of the United States.[84] Field salesmen were allowed drawing accounts and commissions, providing the commissions were greater than the drawing accounts; clerical personnel was provided in eight of the field offices. Several persons who had worked with group while it was under Rothaermel's direction asked to be reassigned after Graham again took charge of the department, and Graham believed that they were being influenced by advice which they received from Actuary Henderson.[85] Consequently Graham, himself an actuary, told the Society's actuaries that he would "resent to the full any endeavor of theirs to inject themselves in the affairs" of the Group Department from that point on. As far as he was concerned, they were completely out; but, since all were on the Equitable payroll, and serving the same company, he thought that it would be well for them to cooperate rather than serve as obstructionists. He made it plain that he was in charge and that he did not want their help except as they acted through and with him.[86] When he requested that Mervyn Davis be transferred to the Group Department from the Actuary's Department, Actuary Henderson opposed the move. Henderson did not believe that any underwriter should be responsible to an officer whose function it was to bring in new business and whose reputation depended upon volume. If Davis was transferred, Henderson wanted it understood that the Actuary's Department would not be responsible for his actions, and that the Actuary was to retain the functions assigned to him by the Code of Administration "even though such functions may relate to group insurance business." Davis was transferred nevertheless.[87]

To serve as Superintendent of the Group Department, Graham brought in Joseph Boldt from the Bureau of Policy Claims.[88] Although Boldt had little knowledge of group insurance, he learned rapidly and became a specialist in handling delicate and difficult situations; he

84 The cities were Chicago, Columbus, Detroit, Indianapolis, Kansas City, Milwaukee, New York, Philadelphia, San Francisco, Springfield (Massachusetts), St. Louis, St. Paul, Syracuse, Washington, D.C., and Wheeling (West Virginia).

85 Graham Memoir, p. 228.

86 *Ibid.*, p. 229.

87 Memorandum, Henderson to Parkinson, July 30, 1926. Sterling Pierson files, Equitable Archives.

88 Boldt had joined Equitable in 1895 as an office boy under Assistant Actuary Joel G. Van Cise. When Van Cise signed the numerous premium notices, Boldt blotted his signature. The headquarters of Van Cise's group at this time was known as "Castle God." Boldt to author, September 1, 1954.

became the diplomat of the Group Department. Herman Steeg returned from the Prosser and Homans agency and became Assistant Superintendent. Louise Wolters Ilse, who had joined Equitable in 1924, became Graham's secretary.[89] The clerical force of more than 100 persons in the Group Issue Division which had been with the Bureau of Issue in the Actuary's Department came back to the Group Department January 1, 1926.

While the Group Department was being rebuilt, several important problems arose, among them the rate war and the effort to develop some form of cooperation among the group-writing companies (the Group Association); the Employee Benefit Association plans written as union groups; the rebating problem; the dividend question; and competition in general and the use of gain and loss exhibits as a tool in competition.

Early efforts at cooperation among the group-writing companies began with the "Actuarial Group Insurance Committee," which first met in October 1917. The informal meetings of this committee dealt largely with group life insurance legislation and the maximum amounts of insurance which could be considered safe. The conferences resulted in a joint study of group mortality experience for the period 1913–20, which was presented in 1921. Equitable participated in these conferences until July 1924, when Actuary Robert Henderson wrote that his company would not take part in any future meetings but that it would still be governed by the spirit of the conference agreements. (This action was taken soon after Equitable's Group Department had been disassembled.)

As the competition among the group-writing companies became more vigorous, Superintendent of Insurance James A. Beha suggested to Graham that the establishment of a cooperative, self-governing body among these companies would serve the interests of group insurance as a whole. So, February 3, 1926, at a luncheon meeting of sixteen representatives—mostly actuaries—of Equitable, Prudential, Metropolitan, Travelers, Aetna, and possibly two or three other companies, it was agreed that the companies represented form an association to consider underwriting rules and other matters concerning Group Insurance, except premium rates.[90] An organization committee was

[89] With Graham's encouragement, Mrs. Ilse continued her college studies in night classes and in 1951 was granted the Ph.D. degree by Columbia University. Her doctoral dissertation, "Group Insurance and Employee Retirement Plans," was published in 1953.

[90] The meeting was probably called by William J. Graham. Present were William J. Graham, Mervyn Davis, and Andrew E. Tuck of Equitable; James D.

appointed which drew up a constitution, and the constitution was adopted at a meeting held at the Hotel Pennsylvania on March 5. According to the constitution, the purposes of the Association were "to promote the welfare of holders of Group policies; advance the interests of Group Insurance; promote economy and reduce expense in the matter of general administration by an interchange of views on practice among insurance companies which issue contracts of Group Insurance; represent the members of the Association in matters pertaining to, or which may affect, Group Insurance before the Insurance Departments and other public and quasi-public official bodies; and to collect and analyze the Group experience of the members of the Association." [91] The constitution provided for quarterly meetings of the Association, and member companies agreed to follow established rules of conduct once the rules were unanimously approved; no member was to change his practices except after sixty days' notice. William J. Graham was elected chairman of the Association and served until November 1927.

At a meeting held in August 1926, the Association adopted a set of rules in regard to rates and commissions. Some questioned the agreement in regard to rates as possibly being construed as an agreement "in restraint of trade," but it was believed that since these rates had been promulgated by the Superintendent of Insurance, the companies would be on the safe side.[92] Commissions on group insurance

---

Craig, James E. Kavanaugh, and Leroy A. Lincoln of Metropolitan; E. E. Cammack and Henry S. Beers of Aetna; James F. Little, Prudential; C. D. Rutherford, Sun Life; Benedict D. Flynn, Travelers; Walter I. King, Connecticut General; and Henry Reichgott, Missouri State Life. William A. P. Wood represented Canada Life, and London Life (Canada) also had a representative. E. M. Thomas of John Hancock was present as an observer only.

91 There were ten charter members: Aetna Life Insurance Company; The Canada Life Assurance Company (Toronto); Connecticut General Life Insurance Company; Equitable; The London Life Insurance Company (London, Ontario); Metropolitan Life Insurance Company; Missouri State Life Insurance Company (St. Louis); The Prudential Insurance Company of America; The Travelers Insurance Company; and Sun Life Assurance Company of Canada (Montreal).

In August 1926 Pan American and Minnesota Mutual became members. John Hancock, although invited to become a charter member, did not become a member until 1931.

92 Mervyn Davis had called attention to this danger in a letter to E. E. Cammack, Aetna's Vice President and Actuary, who was also Secretary of the Association, December 26, 1926. He said: "The particular part of the rule to which I refer is the clause 'issued in accordance with the rates promulgated by the Superintendent of Insurance of New York.' It seems to me that to agree on the terms of a contract to be issued at certain rates is equivalent to entering into

were a more complicated matter than on ordinary life; for instance, there was always the question as to whether first year commissions should be granted on extensions of existing groups.[93]

Some of the most difficult situations which the Association had to attempt to resolve concerned additional insurance and association policies which were to be replaced by employer-employee contracts. Naturally, each member company was desirous on the one hand of protecting its insurance when it represented only one unit or one plant of a large company and, on the other hand, of having a reasonable chance of competing for open business when another company held the insurance on only a portion of a large group. Equitable followed the general rule that when a large company bought a smaller company and the large company had group coverage and the small one did not, then extension of coverage of the original carrier should be considered as practically automatic; if, however, the small company had coverage and the large one did not, then competition would be allowed to enter. If both had coverage, the coverage of the original carrier should govern.[94] There was considerable difference of opinion as to what should be considered "new business" which required only the standard rates, and rules had to be devised in the endeavor to clarify this point.

---

agreement as to rates, or at least that it might be so construed, so that the inclusion of this clause in the rule is not without danger."

[93] Equitable, in 1927, had a rule that no first year commissions on group life would be paid if the increase in insurance was less than $25,000 in any one case. Auditor Walter H. Jones was for strict enforcement of this rule, but Mervyn Davis did not think that this was fair to the agent. An example was the case of the Bank of Italy (California), which had extended its Equitable group insurance to a number of smaller banks which it had acquired, where the total increase was large but in none of the banks amounted to $25,000. Davis believed that the agents should be allowed first year commissions on any number of extensions during a calendar year provided they totaled more than $25,000. He thought the same principle should apply to cases where a single group increased to a large extent—sometimes 25 times the original group. Memoranda from Walter H. Jones and Mervyn Davis, February 17 to April 23, 1927, to William J. Graham. Sterling Pierson files, Equitable Archives. Davis' views prevailed and the rule was established that several units brought in as of a common date, so long as the total of additional insurance equaled $25,000, was recognized as new business. The rule remained in force until January 1962. Memorandum from Group Department, May 22, 1963.

[94] For example, when Dodge Brothers bought Graham Brothers Truck Company, Equitable's insurance with the latter was terminated and transferred to Aetna. Memorandum, Mervyn Davis to William J. Graham, May 14, 1927. Sterling Pierson files, Equitable Archives.

In April 1925 the Insurance Law of the State of New York was amended to permit the issuance of group life insurance "covering the members of any labor union . . . and insuring only all of its members who are actively engaged in the same occupation. . . ." The prime prospect became U.S. Steel Corporation, and permission was secured from its headquarters for payroll deductions at the various operating plants. Members of associations who desired group insurance under the association plans could give payroll authorizations, which had not been permitted by the Corporation previously. Superintendents of the separate works of U.S. Steel were canvassed successfully, and in March 1926 the association of employees of the Carnegie Steel Works in New Castle, Pennsylvania, took out a policy with Equitable which covered 1,096 members. Numerous other plants of U.S. Steel and of other companies in the steel industry took similar action, and while other insurance companies secured some business, the Equitable had the major prize—a total of 39 group contracts which covered 58,000 members and represented almost $90,000,000 of life insurance.

Although these contracts were sound from the underwriting viewpoint, some of the agents in soliciting the business made promises of doubtful validity. A few, for instance, not being too familiar with group underwriting practice, told the associations that the insurance would continue after the employees' retirement. Irritated by Equitable's success in selling the prize prospect, agents of some of the competing companies tried to upset the Equitable coverage and protested to the Insurance Department of the State of New York. The Department had to decide not only whether this business represented sound underwriting but whether it complied with the insurance law. There was little question in regard to the first point, but there was a question as to whether an association of employees of one employer could be considered as a union, and whether insurance issued on a union basis could be continued on retired employees. After a conference with the Department, Graham wired Edward A. Woods: "Please be advised that in agreement with the Insurance Department, New York, our labor union insurance policy on groups written from now on is to be construed as not continuing coverage on members after they become pensioners." After further investigation, the Department instructed Equitable not to pay commissions on some of the association cases.

An interesting situation arose in Indiana, where the Insurance Commissioner informed the life insurance companies that group life insurance policies could be issued in Indiana only if they required premium payments by both the employer and the employee. To overcome this legal obstacle, the association group arranged to have the steel company turn over 10 per cent of the cost of the insurance as its contribution. This 10 per cent represented the company's estimate of the cost of handling the deductions for group insurance. The employee association then reimbursed U.S. Steel for the cost of collecting employee contributions, and the steel company contributed an identical amount to be used as a part of premium payments. The Insurance Commissioner did not definitely approve this arrangement, but, since it appeared that the steel company was making a 10 per cent contribution, he did not press the matter further.

Other embarrassing situations arose as a result of the association cases, and Graham wrote the "Managerial Force" June 16, 1926, as follows: "On and after July 1st next, the Society will not be prepared to consider the issuance of group life insurance on the Labor Union basis to Unions or Associations composed entirely of employees of one employer." He stated that this decision had been reached in agreement with the other companies; that is, the members of the Group Association.[95] This letter was followed by a memorandum which stated that his earlier instructions were "not subject to interpretation." Graham's handling of this problem dispelled any doubts that the Insurance Department may have had in regard to Equitable's intention of insuring only on a sound basis. As Alexis Wiren, in his account of the U.S. Steel association policies, said: "The important fact is that 58,000 employees of steel companies, not only had chosen to become insured, paying the full cost of this insurance, but kept it up. Even during the depression years, when some of the steel employees had to be on relief or receive handouts of food, most of them somehow scraped up enough money to bring to the company to pay their group insurance premium." Another fact is that July 1, 1935, United States Steel adopted a contributory group insurance plan which covered 220,000 employees; Equitable's share of this plan covered 70,000 lives and the remainder were covered by seven other companies. While most of the associations disbanded on the adoption of the U.S. Steel contributory plan, some of them were kept in force for many years, and one—The Clairton Works Association—still remains in force (1966).

[95] *Ibid.*

The problem of replacing association policies by employer-employee contracts came up in 1927 in connection with the American Sash and Door Company, the employees of which had an employee association policy issued by the Equitable. The question was, could other companies compete for the new employer-employee contract. When the Travelers asked Graham about this situation, he wrote:

> We are of the opinion that in the case of the American Sash and Door Company . . . the Travelers was free to make any quotation . . . inasmuch as this group is an additional group and not in competition to a group already written.
>
> We believe that where there is an Association Group outstanding, covering substantially all employees, that those employees be not disturbed by any other company, and that the company carrying this Association group should have the right to continue this group without it being jeopardized by canvass of employer to substitute contributory insurance which would practically mean a canvass to substitute for the group already in force.[96]

New questions came up at almost every meeting of the Association. By the November 1927 meeting, the Association had grown to a membership of twenty-one companies. It was at this meeting that Graham declined re-election to the chairmanship of the Association; James Douglas Craig, Actuary of the Metropolitan, became his successor. Although Graham did not attend all of the Association meetings after this time, he always kept in close touch with them through Mervyn Davis, Superintendent Joseph Boldt, or Nathaniel E. Horelick, Deputy Director of Pensions and Annuities.

The question of total and permanent disability clauses came to the front in 1932, and a committee of the Association recommended that no disability clause in a group contract should contain any provision for: 1) payment during lifetime of the employee, 2) waiver of premiums for a period longer than one year, or 3) any payment of benefit if death occurred after the lapse of the group policy. No general agreement was arrived at at this time, although it was understood that the companies would exert their best efforts to eliminate the disability feature on the policies on their books. On the question of waiver of premium provisions for extended protection of employees, Graham took a firm stand in opposition. Since Equitable was the only large

[96] Graham to Benedict D. Flynn, April 6, 1927. Group files, Equitable Archives.

group-writing company which took this position, it finally came over to the majority practice in 1943, and most of its group policies written after that date contained waiver of premium provisions.

The problem of rebating had existed in connection with life insurance almost from its beginning in the United States, and there was no reason to expect that the writing of group insurance would be immune. Rebating came to be prominently aired in connection with the General Motors case in 1926. In August of that year, Superintendent Beha of the New York Insurance Department had written Benedict D. Flynn, Secretary of the Travelers, that credit could be given on a large policy for commission savings. When General Motors went into the market for a group policy, it asked the various companies point-blank if they would give credit for the commission saved when it came to computation of dividends. Several of the companies, including Metropolitan, answered that they would. Equitable answered in the negative, and the business was awarded to Metropolitan.

The entire subject was discussed at a meeting of the group-writing companies with Superintendent Beha and Chief Examiner Nelson B. Hadley. Graham was quoted as saying at that meeting that when "the ruling in the Flynn letter had come up before the Group Association, there had been a recommendation that life insurance companies represented in the organization should not operate under the ruling"; he thought that all the companies except one had been in harmony with the spirit of this action. Superintendent Beha apparently took no decisive stand and said in effect that the companies would have to settle this matter among themselves.[97] The Group

[97] *The Eastern Underwriter,* XXVII (1926), December 31, gave a rather facetious account of this meeting: "The hearing in the Insurance Department was a little drama masterpiece. . . . The Metropolitan Life was represented by Leroy A. Lincoln, counsel, A. C. Campbell of the group division, and James D. Craig, actuary; and directly across from Mr. Campbell and with no gleam of affection flashing across the table either way, sat William J. Graham, chief officer of the new group association and second vice president of the Equitable." As for Beha's attitude, the *Underwriter* surmised it was this: " 'Here you are doing something which is now considered objectionable. . . . Decide among yourselves that you will behave in future. If you can't decide I'll have to come in, spank you, and make you behave. . . .' " The article continued: "The atmosphere during the hearing was surcharged with poignant feelings, suppressed indignations, and some resentments growing out of the experiences of a dozen or so companies with the most hotly contested business in insurance. There are more wires pulled, more influence exerted, more heartburns felt, more traveling required, more personality expended, more tempers lost, more friendships split in soliciting and selling group insurance than in any line of competitive effort in America."

Association finally agreed not to write any more policies on a non-commission basis, with the understanding that the savings on commissions would result in a direct saving to the group insurance account of the policy.

The subject of group rebating was well covered in an article written by Charles Dobbs, editor of *The Insurance Field.* The subheads were: "Peril to Agents' Commission Practice—Rebate Laws Powerless to Prevent Discrimination—Danger of Price Cutting and Resultant Demoralization of Group Insurance." The article read in part:

> Big problems of the utmost gravity are pressing for solution since the ruling of the New York Insurance Department regarding groups of ten thousand or more. . . . Neither company agreement nor statute law effectively controls the group insurance situation and fears are expressed that life insurance has entered a phase of price cutting and rebating which may easily entail demoralization and disaster. It has been the best of life insurance that prices were the same for rich and poor for large and small policies. The contract with the General Motors Corporation and other exceptionally large transactions suggest the possibility that a big corporation can secure from the insurance company preferential price privileges denied the small applicant for group insurance. . . . No charge has been made that the Metropolitan violated the anti-rebate laws . . . but the contention is advanced that under New York departmental ruling permitting single groups of ten thousand or more to be made into "special classes" the door is opened wide for substantial rebating and price cutting. . . . More than once situations have arisen in group insurance which recalled the old days in railroading when large shippers were favored with rebates, the resulting censure bringing on the vast fabric of regulatory law in that field. . . . Students of the situation contend that under the special ten thousand group practices, effective insurance department regulation is impossible.[98]

Early in 1927, in an endeavor to correct the trouble caused by his letter to Flynn, Superintendent Beha wrote E. E. Cammack, Secretary of the Group Association, as follows:

> After giving this matter careful consideration, it is the opinion of this department that where a group life policy is written without the payment of commissions, there should be charged against the class to which such group belongs, either in the computation of dividends or arriving at

[98] *The Insurance Field,* LIV (1926), December 17.

experience rating refunds and experience rating deductions, the regular commissions the company would have paid under its agency contracts if the business had been written through an agent. The amount so charged should be credited to the general overhead of the group business as a whole. This is based on the assumption that the commissions paid by the company on a risk of this kind would be reasonable and in no way excessive, considering the amount of premiums involved.

This department is willing at any time to consider the facts in any individual case which might justify the modification of this rule.[99]

In 1927 Mervyn Davis prepared a pamphlet for the agents entitled "Meeting Competition in Group Insurance." This pamphlet stated that solicitation of group insurance was much different from solicitation of ordinary insurance. The two biggest evils of competition were misrepresentation and rebating. Davis pointed out that it was now not possible to rebate to a corporation, ". . . and I want to add in this connection that, during the recent period, fortunately of short duration, when a ruling of the New York Insurance Department permitted the rebate of commissions to a large group closed without the assistance of agents, the Equitable was the only large group company which consistently refused to even consider offering any proposition which included such rebate." The size of group cases made competition keen, but it was more out in the open than with ordinary insurance. In the case of ordinary insurance, the competitor might win by offering "double-barrelled, reciprocating, non-skid, accelerating endowment options," but in group insurance there was only one product, and everyone was offering it; namely, yearly renewable term on a standardized form at the same gross premium rates. There was no question of cash surrender values, interest earnings, or options; competition narrowed down to two things—service and net cost. The two requirements of efficient group service were 1) prompt and efficient settlement of claims, and 2) efficient handling of the needs of the employer and employees from the installation of the policy on. The booklet reminded the agent that Equitable did not go in for services which were not of direct value to the employer, such as nursing, health investigations, wage studies, and the like, but that it conducted its group business at an expense rate far below that of any competitor.

In June 1927 Graham attended the Eighth International Congress

[99] Beha to E. E. Cammack, January 8, 1927. Sterling Pierson files, Equitable Archives.

of Actuaries, which was held in London. Here he presented his paper on "Development of Group Insurance," which was reviewed by, among other publications, *The Economist* and *The Insurance Record*. *The Economist* said: "It is not too much to say that no development in the entire history of life insurance is more dramatic and remarkable than the history of group life insurance in the United States." Copies of Graham's paper were sent to Equitable's agents; also articles on group insurance which appeared in *The New York Times* and *The Sun*. While Graham was away, Henry Kranz began issuing packets of group sales aids to the agents; these monthly releases continued until August 1934. In the summer of 1927, Isaac Baldwin, as field instructor, conducted a number of group training schools for agents.

In 1926 Equitable decided to extend its group coverage to coal mining companies. To spread the risk on these policies, the Group Department negotiated a reinsurance agreement with the General Reinsurance Corporation for excess losses on industries in which a large portion of the employees were engaged in hazardous occupations. Before all the details were worked out, however, the General Reinsurance Corporation was reorganized and became the International Reinsurance Corporation. In January 1929, Equitable signed a reinsurance treaty with this company which continued until 1933, when International went into bankruptcy. Equitable then (June 15, 1933) signed an agreement with Lloyds of London. This agreement, which was for one year only, provided that Equitable would pay all claims within the maximum limit agreed upon, and the reinsurer would pay the remainder of the losses. The agreement was renewed and continued until May 1942. It appears that Lloyds never had to pay Equitable any losses, but Vice President Graham thought the agreement was justified for its psychological and public-relations effect. By 1942 group insurance had grown to such an extent that Equitable believed it could absorb any extra hazardous risks without any form of reinsurance. Not only had the Society worked out a system for rating groups on the basis of the group's own experience, but with the sanction of the New York Insurance Department it and other group-writing companies had earlier adopted the practice of accumulating a catastrophe reserve by withholding 2 per cent of premiums, less dividends, until the amount withheld represented 50 per cent of a normal year's premium income for the given group.

Group insurance continued to present its problems throughout the 1920's. Chief of these was costs. For instance, in the first half of 1929, premiums exceeded claims and dividends by only $7,200, but if expenses were taken into account, the actual disbursements in the Group Department exceeded income by $454,900. Mervyn Davis believed that, from whatever angle the figures were examined, one was forced to conclude that Equitable had, for some time past, been paying too high dividends. He recommended a flat charge of at least $100 against each policy, and that total returns to any group in any policy year should be limited to some arbitrary percentage such as 96 per cent.[100] It was the smaller groups which were proving the most expensive. Not only did they require attention out of proportion to their size, but in some instances they fell below the requirement of 50 lives; in these cases Graham felt that Equitable would be justified in paying no dividends. In a talk before the Actuarial Society of America in October 1929, Actuary Robert Henderson pointed out that there were two important considerations in connection with dividends and group insurance. First, since small groups were more liable to fluctuations than large, it was necessary to have "some smoothing formula of some kind which will operate more intensely on small groups than on the large." Second, not only should actual claims and actual expenses (including initial expenses) be taken care of, but a surplus to cover contingencies should be built up and maintained. Equitable's dividend formula was so devised as ultimately to build up a surplus.[101] Since each new group started with a deficit, a rapid expansion of the volume of group insurance on the books of the company resulted in a slowing up, if not a decrease, in the accumulation of surplus for group insurance as a whole. Bad group mortality experience would also lead to the same result. Even though the average age of a group with small turnover might tend to increase, this increase in age would be counteracted to a large extent by the gradual increase of credit from surplus to the benefit of that particular group.

One factor which constituted a serious element in the cost of group insurance was the increased cost which resulted from converted group

[100] Davis memorandum to W. J. Graham, September 27, 1929. *Ibid.*

[101] This was accomplished by the expense charge in the formula being made somewhat higher than current renewal expenses and adding a charge, calculated as a percentage of the initial deficit of the year, which was much higher than the rate of interest. When a surplus had been accumulated, a corresponding credit was given, so graded as to result in the ultimate objective of a surplus at least equal to 50 per cent of one year's premiums on each individual group. *Transactions, The Actuarial Society of America*, XXX (1929), pp. 604–5.

policies. An Equitable study showed, that, after making full allowance for savings and expenses, the extra cost during the first ten policy years on converted group policies averaged about $75 per thousand of insurance converted; about $35 of this extra cost came from first year claims. To take care of this cost, Henderson recommended that all death claims during the first year on converted policies be added to the death claims in the group for that year, and "in addition 4% of the face of all converted policies less the death claims." [102]

The tentative report of the New York Insurance Department on its examination of Equitable for the years 1927–29 inclusive contained some statements in regard to group insurance which Vice President Graham and other officers thought most important to have corrected or revised before the final report was filed. One statement in particular which they did not like was to the effect that group expense was "inaccurately and unscientifically compared and therefore misleading"; they believed that this was exactly the sort of statement that Equitable's competitors had been trying to get into the records for years. Another statement which was questioned was the one to the effect that the Group Department, although taking account of all direct expenditures, had not given a fair allocation to indirect expenses both at the Home Office and in the field; included among the latter would be the proportionate part of the cost of managers' salaries. The final report of the Insurance Department, filed July 31, 1931, was modified somewhat, and on the subject of allocation of group expenses contained the following statement:

> The methods employed by the society in connection with the allocation of expenses to group business were investigated. It was found that in some instances an improvement might be made in the allocation of indirect expenses both at the home office and in the field. Differences of opinion arose between the examiners and the society's representatives over the distribution of field expenses, notably over the items of salaries of managers, assistant managers and supervisors and expenses of conventions and agency meetings. The desirability of adopting a more comprehensive and uniform system of expense assessment was recognized by the society and a thorough survey of the matter of allocating expenses as between different branches of its business was undertaken by the society. As a result new methods of assessing expenses have been arrived at and have now been

[102] Henderson memorandum to President Parkinson, December 22, 1931. Sterling Pierson files, Equitable Archives.

put into effect. It appears that the charges arrived at under the new methods will be adequate provided a periodic check-up is maintained and proper modifications of the bases of distribution are made from time to time.

The surplus in Equitable's group business built up slowly. In April 1932 Superintendent George S. Van Schaick of the New York Insurance Department wrote Equitable as follows: "According to your annual statement reports to this Department, the deficit in your Group Branch, which has accumulated during the past six years, is $1,959,232, whereas dividends paid to policyholders during this time aggregate $14,414,325." Van Schaick asked the Society to explain this situation.[103]

In 1927 Equitable took the next logical step in the rounding out of its group program; that is, the offering of group annuities. Back in 1916, when the question of employee pensions came up, Graham had written Vice President Lunger that pension funds under workaday conditions could better be handled by the employer than by a life insurance company, and that Equitable did not "attempt to insure superannuated pensioners." The Society would, however, supply actuarial advice to its group patrons for pension purposes as a sort of "social insurance service." And President Day, in an address December 7 of that year, said that "Group insurance has stimulated the study of the subject of old age pensions . . . and had strong influence in effecting improvements in existing pension systems. . . . The pension systems operated in this country are almost all actuarially insolvent. . . . Group insurance has done much to call attention to the pension subject as the related provision for protecting the employee, and has the equipment of experts at the disposal of those concerned."

In December 1919 Equitable submitted to the New York Insurance Department special group annuity forms for a plan "to provide old age pensions for employees covered under group life policies by a deferred annuity blanket policy." These forms were never followed through for final approval. Though Graham was very much interested in pensions, up until 1927 he believed that the life insurance company, and particularly Equitable, could best help by rendering only advisory service.[104]

[103] Van Schaick to Equitable, April 19, 1932. *Ibid.*

[104] Graham had served on the committee of the Industrial Welfare Department of the National Civic Federation, which had made a study of pensions, and in 1925 sent copies of the committee's report to Equitable's group patrons. Two years later, he sent them a more up-to-date booklet on the subject.

Early in 1927, the Edward A. Woods Company applied for a group pension coverage of its employees to be effective, if possible, by July 4, the date of the Company's annual educational conference. Associate Actuary Dwight A. Walker and Ray M. Peterson formulated a contract acceptable to the Society's general counsel and submitted it to the New York State Insurance Department.[105] Although the contract was not completed by July 4, it was announced at that time and employees were enrolled under it. On November 17, 1927, Equitable's Board of Directors authorized the issuance of group annuity contracts and the following day Superintendent of Insurance James A. Beha gave his department's approval of the contract and application forms. Edward A. Woods was so pleased with Walker's work on the pension plan that he suggested the contract prepared for his company be used as a standard form.[106]

In December 1929 Henry Kranz got the Chairman of the Board of General Cable Corporation, which had a group life insurance policy with Equitable, to sign a preliminary application for a group annuity contract; a similar application was sent to Metropolitan. About 4,000 lives were eligible to be included in the plan. After some delay, Equitable worked out an entirely new type of group annuity contract, called a Deposit Administration Contract, and was awarded the business. Under this plan, which was devised to fit General Cable's particular needs, the employees' contributions were applied from year to year to purchase deferred annuities, but the employer's payments were held in an unallocated fund to be applied at an employee's retirement date

105 Peterson, later to become Vice President and Associate Actuary, was then head of the Reinsurance Section of the Mathematical Bureau in the Actuary's Department.

106 Under the plan devised for the Woods agency, any person who had been a member of the agency staff for five years was permitted to deposit any amount from $3 to $10 per month while an employee of the Woods agency, to purchase deferred refund annuities beginning at age 65, and for every dollar of annuity so purchased, the Woods agency would purchase a matching amount of deferred annuity. Members also could make additional deposits to purchase deferred annuities that were not matched by the Woods agency. In the event of the member's death before the annuity began, the named beneficiary would receive the member's total deposits with 3½ per cent interest plus any extra interest apportioned. Optional retirement ages were available between 55 and 70. Total and permanent disability benefits of $25 per month for each year of service after entering the plan, up to a maximum of $100 for women and $170 for men, were provided by the agency. All members of the agency who attended the 1927 educational conference signed for the plan. The members of the agency were already covered by group and salary-savings policies. Edward A. Woods died during the preparation of the contract and probably was never included under it.

to purchase for him a benefit under the corporation's pension plan. This contract—which was not delivered until March 1932—was Equitable's first deposit administration group annuity contract and is generally conceded to have been the first of its kind to be offered by any insurance company; sometimes referred to as the "modernized group annuity," this plan resulted in some warm arguments in actuarial circles in the early 1930's.[107]

A Pensions and Annuities Division, Group Department, was established late in 1927 with G. Powell Hamilton as Director and Nathaniel E. Horelick as Deputy Director.[108] The first sales material furnished agents was a reprint of a newspaper article, but early in 1928 Graham put out a letter entitled "Guide for Agents—Group Annuity Proposals" and a twelve-page folder, "The Equitable's Basic Pension Plans." Another folder, "The Complete Protection Plan," described a combination of group life (with total and permanent disability), weekly indemnity, accidental death and dismemberment, and retirement benefit, with illustrations. The following year Hamilton sent out a booklet, "Essentials of a Pension Plan," which pointed out the weaknesses of many plans examined by the Equitable. Various departments in Equitable—Auditor's, Claims, and Actuary's—worked closely together to adapt the practices established in other group lines to the problems created by group annuities. Detailed records of group annuity contracts and equities held by individuals insured under these con-

107 See Dorrance C. Bronson, "Pensions—1949," *Transactions, Society of Actuaries*, I (1949), November. Ray M. Peterson was never happy with the term "Deposit Administration"; he believed a more accurate descriptive term would be "Collective Deferred Annuity." *Ibid.*

Many interesting complications arose during the development of this contract. Actuary Walker was concerned over the continuance of annuity payments to existing pensioners as the General Cable contract contained a "dishonesty" provision by which pensions could be terminated, and one for reduction of pension on account of Federal or state pension benefits that might thereafter become available. Also, the unallocated fund approach introduced a new concept into annuity contracts. The approval of the State Insurance Department for the contract was not received until January 1932.

108 Hamilton came to Equitable from Canada and had been working on group accident and health insurance. Horelick came to Equitable from Mutual; he had been trained as an engineer (Carnegie Institute of Technology) and later became interested in actuarial science; he was also interested in sales.

It will be noted that at this time there was a distinction between "annuities" and "pensions." In the early years, "annuities" meant that portion of the retirement plan benefits bought with the contributions made by the employees, while "pensions" referred to the arrangement by which the employer provided an income for retired employees. Eventually, "group annuities" came to be used to cover both.

AFTER THEM, MEN. THEY'RE DESPERATE CHARACTERS!

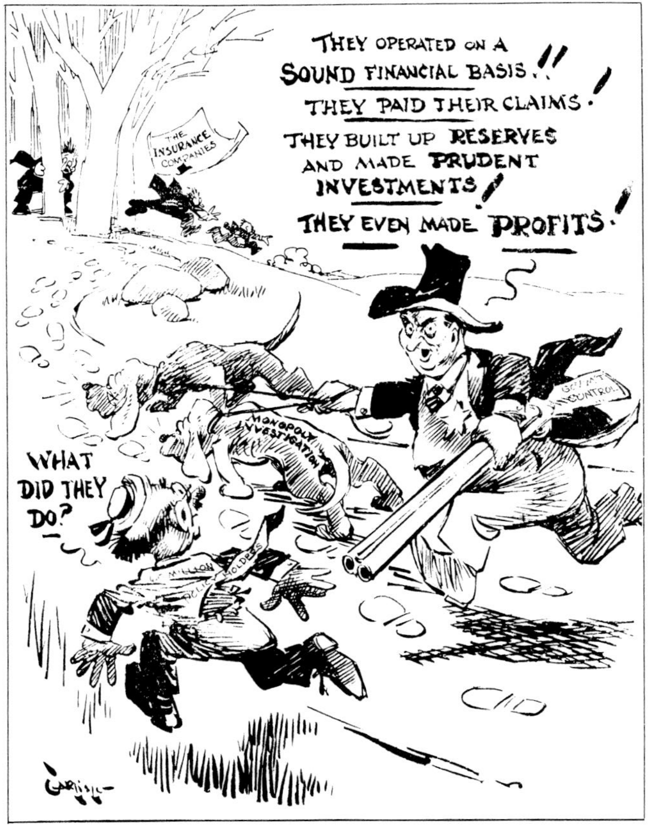

The New York Herald Tribune

THAT'S THE WAY THOSE THINGS GET STARTED

The Des Moines, Iowa, Register and Tribune

TNEC Cartoons

tracts were, from the beginning, handled by the Actuary's Department. When the volume of these problems warranted it, a Group Annuity Administration was set up under Ray M. Peterson which by 1936 became the Group Annuity Division in the Mathematical Bureau of the Actuary's Department.

In October 1929, Vice President Graham spoke before the National Association of Manufacturers on "Group Insurance and Pension Plans as a Cause of Old Age Hiring Limits." He maintained that very few firms established maximum hiring age limits because of their group insurance or pension plans: "Group insurance, including life, disability and pensions, are not the *cause* of the ills which beset the older worker—they are largely the *cure!*"

Although the Group Association had considered adopting rules for group annuities as early as 1928, not until 1934 were the rules prepared. They covered ten pages and were adopted the following year; the action of the Association served as a stabilizing influence in the field of group annuities as previous action had in group life insurance.

After the Group Department was reconstituted in 1925, William J. Graham threw himself into his work with renewed energy and increased confidence. He drove himself hard and also his subordinates. It was said that on occasion he made tasks more difficult by not letting others know, as soon as he realized it, that some special work would have to be done. Then at his "Monday morning meetings" the pressure would be put on. Though he did not readily accept contradictions or questioning of his opinion in public, he would, at times, reprimand a subordinate in the presence of the group; later, however, he would usually take the edge off the reprimand in a cordial private talk. To some it appeared that at times Graham operated on the principle that motivation of fear on the part of subordinates was helpful to good performance. At the same time, he admired anyone who "stood up to him" and convinced him that he knew what he was talking about. Graham's own ideas and decisions often seemed to be arrived at by brilliant intuition rather than logic, but he was not always able to convey his ideas to others. His knowledge of industrial conditions and processes was wide and his mastery of details phenomenal, and he expected those in his department to "know"—not merely to "think they know." At times he could be imperious.

On the other hand, Graham's personality was characterized by a polished courteousness which was the result of his early training as well as an expression of his personal philosophy. He would be courteous to a person for whom he may have had little use, and abhorred discourtesy in others. His personal correspondence was wide and friendly, and his consideration for others included children. He kept in his office a supply of toys—"gimcracks" or "un-birthday presents" —for small visitors. His wide range of friendship and contacts with the business world not only helped with the advertising and promotion of group insurance but of William J. Graham as well.[109] His acquaintance with the business world often enabled him to give news reporters items of value; appreciative of these favors, the newsmen were usually willing to print Graham's news releases. It was this flair for publicity that led to a rather warm controversy between Graham and former Vice President Henry L. Rosenfeld over who was the originator of group insurance.

In 1914, when Rosenfeld was appointed Fourth Vice President, various articles in the insurance press ascribed the origin of group insurance to him, and in 1918 Equitable's *Agency Items* stated that the group insurance branch had been under Rosenfeld's jurisdiction "since its conception about ten years ago." [110] In June 1927, however, when Graham was in Paris on his way to the Eighth International Congress of Actuaries, which he was to address in London, the Paris edition of the *New York Herald* carried a story on Graham and accompanied it with his photograph. Then a few days later, the *Herald* said: "Mr. Graham, sponsored by The Hon. William A. Day, President of the Equitable, is said to be the originator of the group insurance method in the United States in 1912." This was too much

[109] Graham during these years of the late 1920's and early 1930's participated in the meetings and work of the Chamber of Commerce, the National Industrial Conference Board, the Silver Bay Conference, the Princeton University Round Table, the Committee on Pensions for New York City Employees of the National Civic Federation, and other organizations. He was President of the American Management Association 1930–32 and was largely instrumental in raising funds to help carry that organization through a financial crisis during the depression.

Graham kept an extra dinner jacket in his office and often, following a busy day, would attend some official dinner. "He had a reputation as a 'table-hopper,' because frequently, in the middle of the dinner, he would start on a round of tables, stopping to speak to old friends and to make new ones. He liked people." Wiren manuscript, p. 78.

[110] It may be recalled (see this history, p. 775) that President Paul Morton in April 1909 had established "The Equitable Industrial Branch," which was to include Monthly Premium and Home Purchase plans as well as to continue investigation into the subject of group insurance. This branch was under the jurisdiction of Henry L. Rosenfeld, who was then Insurance Assistant to the President.

for Rosenfeld, who was in Paris, so he wrote Vice President Parkinson as follows:

Dear Parkinson:

Graham seems to run wild for publicity. He had a long article with his portrait in the Paris *New York Herald* a few days before the attached article appeared, in which Judge Day received minor and subordinate mention.

I wrote Graham a note in London when I saw this article asking him how long he intended to parade in borrowed plumage. I also let several prominent London actuaries know the correct facts in re Group Insurance in the ELAS.

Now if the Judge wants a public showdown on this question I am willing and am quite prepared to show the facts by documentary evidence. If not, please try and get this swollen headed Vice-President of yours to stick to the truth. There is enough credit for him as it is without this constant craving for a credit which is not his; I feel that my work in the Equitable fairly belongs to me and while the Judge has never seen fit to acknowledge it in re Group I do not intend to sit by and see another claim the fruits of my labor. . . .[111]

Various articles in the United States press also generally gave credit to Graham, with Rosenfeld's name seldom being mentioned.[112] Rosenfeld believed these articles to be inspired by Graham or his press bureau, and claimed "deliberate, and, in the light of my previous letters to you on the subject, apparently intentional misstatement of facts." In a long letter—his third—to Graham, October 10, 1927, Rosenfeld traced the history of group insurance from the time when President Paul Morton sent him to England in 1908 through to its adoption by the Society in 1911: "All this occurred before I had brought you to New York and named you for appointment as Superintendent in the Department of Group Insurance." He reminded Graham that he had started the Montgomery Ward negotiations before Graham was even connected with Equitable. He continued:

I challenge your claim to be the originator of Group Insurance in the Equitable—or any place else for that matter—because of the fact that it is

[111] Rosenfeld to Parkinson, June 28, 1927. Parkinson files, Equitable Archives.

[112] See, for instance, *The Journal of Commerce*, September 29, 1927; *The Sun*, June 26 and July 13, 1927; and *Agency Items*, August 8, 1927, which quoted from the English *Insurance Record*.

not true. . . . In the light of such documentary evidence, some of it over your own signature, how can you claim credit for the origin of these plans? What good can it do you to acclaim yourself as the originator of Group Insurance in the Equitable in 1912 when, as shown, Group Insurance was already an established department in the Society and in full operation when I first employed you. . . . I gave you your chance in the Equitable. I want no credit for anything which you may have done. I distinctly resent your claiming credit for what I did. You may take refuge in silence to this communication as you have to my letter recently addressed to you in London in June 1927 and my letter to you from Paris last year. In this event it would seem hopeless to further attempt to make you realize your position with reference to this subject.[113]

Rosenfeld returned the presentation copy of Graham's *The Romance of Life Insurance* and Graham's photograph, which had been inscribed "to my good friend, Henry L. Rosenfeld." Said Rosenfeld: "True, I proved to be 'your good friend' as is evident by your present position and in other ways. However, the friendship seems to have been an entirely one-sided one." Graham was somewhat upset because he could not make Rosenfeld understand that he never had inspired or released any publicity featuring himself as the originator of group insurance, and that he had no control over the press outside of Equitable.

Then in 1930, Rosenfeld, retired in Paris, wrote President Thomas I. Parkinson:

I thought that after my letter to Judge Day some two years ago Graham would abstain from making this absurd claim on his part. Evidently I overlooked the megalomania of the man. However he may rest assured that so long as I am alive he will find his statements refuted whenever his press agency gets busy along the same line. I have never minded the fact that after my leaving the Society no reference was ever made to whatever small part I may have played in the development of new ideas in the company. I do protest however the appropriation to himself, without regard to the truth, of a credit for the work I did in getting this idea across for the benefit of the Equitable. I wish that it were possible for you, whom I respect as a fair and just man, to put a stop once and for all to similar statements being made by my former subordinate. But for

[113] There are several drafts of this letter in the Rosenfeld papers, Equitable Archives. The last draft was dated October 10.

me he would have never been in the Equitable and sense of common decency should deter him. Evidently it does not.[114]

Rosenfeld also wrote his old friend, Louis M. Wiley, business manager of *The New York Times,* and called attention to a statement made in the *Times* August 24 which referred to Graham as "the man who originated the idea of group insurance." He said:

With all modesty I think I may lay claim to having been the originator of group insurance, certainly in the Equitable Life, and the "idea" was in actual effect under my charge, during the administration of the late Paul Morton as well as under his successor, the late Judge Day, long before Mr. Graham was associated with the Equitable. In fact Mr. Graham was employed by me to come into the Equitable as my assistant in the group department after the adoption of the plan and had absolutely nothing to do with the origin of the idea. Since my resignation as Vice-President of the Equitable and Mr. Graham's succession to my position as head of the group business of that company he has made repeated attempts to appropriate to himself the credit for the origin of group insurance and I have repeatedly brought definite proof to the contrary to the attention of the officers of the Equitable.[115]

It was unfortunate that reasons for Rosenfeld's bitter feeling should have existed. Allowing for the tendency of the press to personalize and misquote, one is forced to conclude that Graham, if not directly responsible for this publicity, at least did nothing to correct or minimize it. Rosenfeld, at President Morton's suggestion, inaugurated group insurance in the United States, but the original concept was quite elemental as compared to later developments; William J. Graham carried on from there and, more than any other individual, was instrumental in developing group insurance into the great aid to economic security which it became. There should have been ample credit for all.

AGENCY AFFAIRS

For more than half a century, Equitable had been known as "The Agents' Company." This did not mean that the agents ran the company—certainly not under Henry B. Hyde—but they were an impor-

[114] Rosenfeld to Parkinson, September 8, 1930. Parkinson files, Equitable Archives.
[115] Rosenfeld to Wiley, September 8, 1930. *Ibid.*

tant influence in the Society's affairs and one of its greatest assets; the practical experience of the agency force compensated for the sometimes impractical theories of the agency vice presidents. Neither President Morton nor President Day had had any experience in selling life insurance, and both had to rely heavily upon the agency vice presidents and leading general agents for guidance in handling agency problems.

John B. Lunger, despite his knowledge of agency affairs, had never been able to win the warmhearted support of the general agents; though intelligent and capable, he was regarded by many as a cold personality. Besides, he was an advocate of the Agency Manager system.[116] William E. Taylor was a Southern gentleman who could bear down on occasion, but Frank H. Davis, his successor as Agency Vice President in 1923, was a veritable powerhouse of energy—the agents' idea of an agency officer.

Davis was born in Hastings, Iowa, in 1880. After attending Western Normal School at Shenandoah for a year, he had tried farming, taught a country school, worked in a seed store, and finally served two terms as clerk of his county. In 1910 at the age of twenty-nine he studied his past, analyzed his abilities, and charted his future. He decided that his chief interest was in human beings and that he was best qualified to be a salesman. While still undecided as to what business would best suit his talents, he was approached by a life insurance agent, who had no difficulty in selling him a policy. Davis decided that life insurance was the business for him. He sold his home and moved to Omaha where several companies had offices.

Quite by accident, he met an agent of the Reliance Life Insurance Company of Pittsburgh, who signed him up and gave him a package of forms and literature. It was weeks before Davis sold his first policy, but once underway he accumulated momentum rapidly.[117]

[116] William J. Graham described Lunger as a "suave, gentlemanly man . . . Lunger had a way about him of instantly commending himself to people and then gradually working away from that favorable impression. He was successful in those attempts." Graham Memoir, p. 213.

One of the agency managers who knew Lunger well described him as "the coldest fish he ever looked at—but one who was probably burning up inside." He thought it probable that Lunger maintained a hard front in order to cover up inner sentiments, and would frequently do good things for people while not letting the fact be known.

[117] In 1958, William Washington Klingman—later to be one of Davis' successors as Equitable's agency Vice President—testified that when he signed his first agency contract with The Security Mutual Life Insurance Company of Lincoln, Nebraska, "Frank H. Davis was Agency Vice President of The Security

In 1911 the Reliance Life announced a contest and a trip to the Home Office for the agent—and his wife—who would write the greatest volume of business for the month of August, and for the agent who would write the greatest number of policies. Davis told his wife to get some new clothes and be prepared to make a trip. He knew he had no chance to win the greatest volume award but was confident he could place the greatest number of policies. During the four weeks he worked day and night and covered a number of counties. As a result of this whirlwind campaign, he broke all of his company's records.[118] He got both the trip and a bonus, and soon was training agents as well as engaging in personal production. When put in charge of the state of Ohio, he built up an effective and enthusiastic organization.

At this point, after only two years in the life insurance business, Davis decided that he needed larger fields in which to operate, and despite the fact that his company offered to give him the entire state of Texas, he refused to reconsider his resignation, and severed his connection with Reliance Life December 15, 1912.[119] Now "out of a job," Davis wrote letters to nine of the largest mutual life insurance companies in the country—and received nine replies, the least favora-

---

Mutual at that time." Lloyd Klingman to Secretary Gordon K. Smith, July 14, 1958; this letter was written in consultation with William Washington Klingman. Klingman's memory must have been in error, for there is no record of Davis' ever having been employed by the Security Mutual. T. A. Sick, Chairman of the Board of Security Mutual, to author, June 10, 1963. And C. C. James, who became Cashier of the Reliance Life of Omaha in the spring of 1910, states that Davis had already been an agent with that company for "some months." C. C. James, Equitable agent at Hagerstown, Maryland, to author, May 31, 1963. James has a photograph of the Omaha agency of the Reliance Life which was taken in 1910 or 1911; it included Davis. O. G. Wilson, who was in charge of the Omaha agency, told James that Davis, who had previously been in western Nebraska and Wyoming on a ranch, came into the office dressed in a ten-gallon hat, boots, and spurs; Wilson persuaded him to get a business suit before he started work.

In June 1923, *The American Magazine* published an article, "The World Makes Way for a Man Who Knows Where He's Going." This article, by Merle Crowell, was based upon an interview with Davis and, though it sketches his career and delineates his personality, does not mention by name the company for which he worked prior to the time he was employed by Equitable.

118 It developed later that in his eagerness to get applications, Davis had examined many of the applicants himself. When some of these failed to pass later medical examinations, Cashier James was assigned the task of returning the premiums paid. James to author, May 31, 1963.

119 According to records of Reliance Life now in possession of The Lincoln National Life Insurance Company. Secretary G. M. Bryce to author, July 19, 1963.

ble of which was from Equitable. When Davis reported to Equitable's Superintendent of Agencies, William E. Taylor, he was interviewed for three days, at the end of which time Taylor asked him what he wanted to do, where he wanted to go, and how soon he could leave. His answers to the three questions were, "anything," "anywhere," and "anytime." Further inquiry, however, brought out the fact that Davis would like to try his hand at organization work; he would like to tackle Equitable's most unproductive territory and be given a free hand to build up his own organization. So he was given (January 1, 1913) the northwest territory with headquarters at St. Paul. This had been one of Equitable's most unproductive agencies. His salary as agency supervisor was $3,600, or about half what he had received in his previous position.

Davis rebuilt the St. Paul agency from top to bottom. At least half of the agents were replaced by new men, most of whom had had no experience in selling life insurance. Davis never advertised for a salesman: "Wherever I went I kept my eyes 'peeled' for individuals who handled themselves in a manner that convinced me that they had the makings of real salesmen. I found them in the most unlikely places." Within a year sales had doubled, and by the end of two years they had almost doubled again.

January 1, 1915, Davis was put in charge of Equitable's Chicago agencies with the title of Inspector of Agencies. During the next five years sales in the Chicago district increased from $6,000,000 to $30,000,000 per year. Early in 1919 he was called to the Home Office as Superintendent of Agencies, and sixteen months later (June 1920) he was appointed Second Vice President; in 1923 he became Agency Vice President at a salary of $50,000.

From his first day in the life insurance business, Davis had read and reread all of the life insurance literature that he could get his hands on. Just how he acquired his ability as a speaker is not so clear, but he seldom failed to stimulate and thrill his audience. Wrote one of his associates:

> His second gift was that of natural oratory, never of the Ciceronian, full-flowing type, but of the man-to-man kind, with an appeal to various emotions, and always to that high moral sense which had instant acceptance by every such audience. And on his way through an address he lightened it with swift, sudden touches of humor, either an epigram of his own coining or an apt, brief story. In one moment the audience would

rock with laughter at such a sally, and the next moment their solemnity befitted them for judgment-day appearance. All of his public work brought to him reams and reams of publicity in the insurance and other journals, which carried his fame far and wide. And though that fame acclaimed him as one of the chief public speakers within life insurance ranks, it built up his surpassing reputation for fineness of principle, sound judgment in matters of policy, and passionate devotion to the men and women who, through their exacting work among the public, supply the life-blood without which no company can progress or even retain its health.[120]

Davis was of imposing physique, more than six feet tall, broad-shouldered and massively built—230 pounds of optimistic energy in action: "When he stood in your doorway, no doorway was left. When he stood upon a platform, he filled it." It was said that one could feel the impact of his personality even when first viewing the man from the rear. He was generous with his time and his money, and took a sincere personal interest in the agents; when an agent whom he had selected failed to succeed, he felt himself somehow to blame. He had a good sense of humor and always insisted that the agent needed not only a sense of humor but also a sense of proportion and a sense of direction. He was fond of expressing his philosophy in quaint and homespun phrases. When overwhelmed with problems or pressure of business he would say, "To hell with poverty, we'll kill a hen." His favorite song was "Billy McCoy was a Wonderful Boy." One

[120] *The Penn Mutual Newsletter*, XX (1936), June.

Though Davis had help from his secretary, R. Roy Hale, in the preparation of his scheduled speeches, much of the effect came from the impromptu and extemporaneous delivery. Many people testified as to Davis' oratorical ability. For example, Sara Frances Jones, Equitable agent in Chicago, in describing the effect that Davis had on an audience there of life underwriters from various companies (this was after Davis had left Equitable), said that although a half dozen speakers had preceded him, he climaxed the program: "But even I, who generally do not care for this sort of thing, because it's so boring to listen to many speakers, feel I have been repaid a hundredfold. As one after the other gave their message, it seemed impossible the high standard could be kept up. And then at the close of a long day, our beloved Frank Davis closed the meeting. He attended the full session. I think I have never seen him look so splendidly fit. . . . It was wonderful to see him in such fine health after all he has been through. He is alert, and *Oh* what a welcome they gave him. He was the only speaker for whom the crowd stood, and I have an idea, being as human as he is, it must have warmed his heart. And it was an Association crowd, not just an Equitable crowd." Miss Jones was so inspired that immediately upon reaching her home late in the evening, she sat down and wrote President Parkinson. The letter, which was undated (probably 1929), is in the Parkinson files, Equitable Archives.

Equitable agent who in his career worked under numerous agency vice presidents maintained that Frank H. Davis was the outstanding Agency Vice President in the history of Equitable and all other companies.[121]

* * *

The older general agents, such as Edward A. Woods, Henry J. Powell, Thomas B. Sweeney, and William J. Roddey, were very close to the President—ran the company, some said. Woods, of course, as head of the country's largest general agency, was perhaps the most influential of the group; he was a student of life insurance, a salesman, and an administrator. Powell, at Louisville, was the diplomat of the group; when things got critical he would tell a story and ease the tension; he had many friends both within and outside the business of life insurance. Sweeney, at Wheeling, got sales results by hard-driving tactics and supplemented his income with overriders on home loans and by selling fire insurance. He also wrote poetry. Roddey, at Rock Hill, South Carolina, was the father of the club idea in Equitable and became nationally known because of his frequently used expression, "punk agent." [122] Other outstanding general agents of this period were Charles Jerome Edwards and Jerome J. Wilson in New York, Courtenay Barber in Chicago, and Herman Moss in Cleveland.

While the general agents—the "Dodo Birds"—still played an important part in Equitable's organization, the new agency managers were beginning to wield more influence. A number of these managers were trained by a general agent who was no longer with Equitable in the 1920's. William E. Bilheimer, a former Y.M.C.A. physical training director, had received his early training under Thomas W. Vardell, Equitable's General Agent at Fort Worth.[123] In 1908 he became

[121] In addition to the material on Davis contained in the Crowell article previously mentioned and in *The Penn Mutual Newsletter*, the author has relied upon other material supplied by Davis' secretary, R. Roy Hale, A. M. Embry, and C. C. James.

[122] Roddey, whose nickname was "Rex," had been largely instrumental in the organization of the Southern Century Club in the latter part of 1908; this club held its first convention in New Orleans, February 1910. Equitable adopted the idea and in January 1912 organized two clubs—the Century Club and the Quarter-Million Club—with membership being based upon production of $100,000 and $250,000 of business paid for in a calendar year. The Million-Dollar Club was not organized until 1942.

[123] When Equitable withdrew from Texas as a result of the Robertson Law (see this history, p. 726), Vardell organized his own company, the Southwestern Life Insurance Company (Dallas), of which he later became President.

General Agent at Little Rock, his home town.[124] Within the next four years, he recruited and developed some of the men who were to become famous Equitable agents. Among them were "The Four Horsemen"—Forrest N. Croxson, Marion C. ("Mickey") Nelson, Marion A. Nelson, and Ayelette Moarning ("Pick") Embry. Croxson, the first to sign, had been operating a cigar stand in Little Rock; "Mickey" Nelson had been a salesman for a grain company; and M. A. Nelson had been the secretary of a lumber firm. "Mickey" Nelson and another agent recruited "Pick" Embry in his home town of Atkins, Arkansas; Embry had been a horsetrader and a salesman for a Memphis drug firm.

Bilheimer did much more than give his new agents a supply of applications and a pat on the back; he prepared a definite training routine. First of all came the "rate book drill." The agent then progressed through Secretary William Alexander's pamphlets and books on life insurance and was encouraged to take the correspondence course, prepared by William Alexander, which was handled through the Home Office. In addition, Bilheimer prepared a number of sales talks to fit various situations and gave them in pamphlet form to the agents. He demanded that the agent be meticulous in regard to his dress. The beginning agent always received firsthand instruction from Bilheimer or his field supervisor, and several times during the year the agents attended sales conferences at agency headquarters.

Selling life insurance in Arkansas in the early years of the twentieth century was not the easiest task in the world. There were relatively few well-to-do people and sales resistance was high. Many people still "did not believe in life insurance." Life insurance had to be sold largely on the basis of sentimental appeal, and premiums were frequently paid in notes due at harvest time or even in horses, mules or cows. Bilheimer was a tireless worker, full of energy and enthusiasm. Sometimes his high-pressure sales campaigns exhausted the energies of his staff. It was not without reason that he was frequently called the "Billy Sunday of life insurance." As a result, the Arkansas agency soon had twenty-three agents and rose rapidly on the Society's honor roll; in four years sales increased about sixfold. This record led Vice President Lunger and Agency Vice President William E. Taylor to

[124] Equitable's General Agent at Little Rock, Harry Ramey, had left the Society at the time of the Armstrong Committee investigation and taken his few agents with him to Chicago, where he became General Agent of another company.

persuade Bilheimer to try out the salaried-manager plan. In 1912 he moved to St. Louis as Inspector of Agencies (and Manager) to develop the territory in Missouri and surrounding states; with him went fourteen agents and his secretary, R. Roy Hale. St. Louis became the "Clearing Office" for the territory, which was developed by way of district managers.[125] M. A. Nelson went to Springfield, Missouri, and later to St. Louis, and M. C. Nelson, after working twenty counties in Iowa, was located in Springfield, Illinois. Both were very successful. Forrest Croxson remained in St. Louis in charge of the city organization and Hale served as secretary for the "Clearing Office." Embry went to Sedalia, Missouri, where he was given seven or eight counties.[126] With the aid of the Warsaw Bank, Embry secured agent prospects and the cooperation of some of the officers of the bank in securing sales prospects. A number of bank clerks and officers were signed up as part-time agents. After getting the Sedalia agency on its feet, Embry was sent to Creston, Iowa, then to Cape Girardeau, Missouri, where he established agencies. In 1914 he returned to Sedalia where, within a few years, the agency was producing more than $7,000,000 of life insurance annually.

The district managers used the St. Louis Cashier and conducted their sales campaigns from the St. Louis office even after some of them became agency managers. The St. Louis "Clearing Office" was dissolved in the early 1920's, and separate agency managers were set up for the territory. M. A. Nelson became Agency Manager in St. Louis, Forrest Croxson in Omaha, and M. C. Nelson in Des Moines. A. M. Embry became Agency Manager in Kansas City, Missouri, in 1924, where he built up one of Equitable's largest agencies. He was an outstanding example of a man who, largely self-trained, was also a very successful trainer of agents. Ultimately sixteen of his agents became agency managers for Equitable, a record not equaled to date by any other Equitable manager. In the earlier days many of Embry's agents had to rely largely upon native wit and horse-trading psychology; some no doubt operated with a "black jack in one hand and a bottle of chloroform in the other," but they did sell life insurance.[127] Some

[125] A. E. Lee was left in charge of the Arkansas agency, which, owing to the poor mortality record in that region, Equitable decided not to push too vigorously.

[126] His salary was $100 per month; in addition, he was given 10 per cent commissions and $75 per month travel allowance.

[127] Embry told the story of how an applicant for a large policy was firmly convinced by the simple strategem of sending for a second specimen of urine. Of course, he had not been told that the first specimen had passed the medical examination.

of the agents were diamonds-in-the-rough—"barefoot boys and a little hungry," who thought that they could bring the "blue-eyed, blister-blooded boys" in the Home Office up-to-date on how it should be done.

Embry's philosophy was simple but effective. He believed that in a successful agency, a man must either go up or out. If there was no opening farther up for him in Equitable, he might be helped to advancement with another company. Embry did not fear competition and did not want his agents to do so: "When you get scared of the other fellow, you are doing yourself more harm than he can do you." He wanted to have full confidence in each agent and each agent to have full confidence in the Manager; he kept informed on the agents' problems, personal as well as business; he frequently advanced money to agents, even after they had left his agency, and never lost a dime so doing.[128] Perhaps most important of all was his understanding of the human factor—how to exercise firm control without manifesting any of the elements of dictatorship. Embry's success had a direct bearing on Equitable's development of the manager and unit-manager system which was soon to replace the general agency system.

One of the rapidly developing agencies was that of William Washington ("Wash") Klingman at St. Paul. Klingman, one of seven children, had become an orphan while still a boy in drought-stricken Frontier County, Nebraska. At the age of fourteen, he was sent by neighbors over into Iowa to solicit relief; he brought back five carloads of food, clothing, implements, seed grain, and medicine. During the summers he farmed and in the winter months worked in the copper mines of Wyoming. After marketing a crop of wheat in 1901, Klingman moved into Eustis, Nebraska, where he established a livery business. Among his customers was a life insurance agent of whose methods Klingman did not approve; he did, however, interest Klingman in life insurance.[129] Klingman believed that life insurance could be sold without making too large promises, and, upon the recommendation of the President of the local bank, he became an agent for The Security Mutual Life Insurance Company (probably in 1906).[130] While

[128] Interview with author, June 15, 1955.

[129] It is possible that Klingman bought a policy from this agent. At any rate, in 1905 he purchased a policy from The Security Mutual Life Insurance Company of Lincoln, Nebraska. In his application he listed his occupation as "drayman." T. A. Sick, Chairman of the Board of Security Mutual to author, June 10, 1963.

[130] When Klingman became an agent for Security Mutual, he was running a pool hall in Farnam, Nebraska, a few miles west of Eustis. *Ibid.*

getting a start as an agent in and around Eustis, Klingman also worked at other jobs; he was a licensed veterinary, justice of the peace, and auctioneer. Then he sold his livery business and moved to Lincoln. But after a year or so in the state capital he signed a contract with Frank H. Davis and the Reliance Life Insurance Company of Pittsburgh and located at Cozad, Nebraska.[131]

While Klingman was at Cozad, two things happened. First, he served as a land agent for a group of promoters who were trying to interest Nebraska farmers in land in southeast Texas, made $20,000 in commissions, and sank his earnings in the project just in time to see the bubble burst.[132] Second, he suffered a stroke which left him entirely paralyzed on the left side. The old family doctor gave him but a year to live, and leading surgeons of the country were able to do little to help. Unable to meet the premiums on his $35,000 life insurance policy, which would lapse within a year, he was pretty well discouraged. While Klingman was sitting in the lobby of an Omaha hotel, an old friend came in, realized his condition, and gave him $500. The friend also told him that there was a doctor in Hastings who had just got back from Austria and that Klingman should consult him immediately. This he did. In a month he could walk without aid, and in five weeks he was walking back to Cozad, about one hundred miles away, writing life insurance as he walked. In Klingman's own words: "When I got home I had enough money owing to me to pay my debt to my friend and sufficient left over to buy a horse and buggy. One year from that time I was the biggest personal producer for the company I was then with." [133]

[131] According to a story in *The Eastern Underwriter*, November 9, 1923, Davis "arrived at a small Nebraska town at 1:00 in the morning" and found the hotel full. The clerk asked him whether he was willing to share a room over a pool hall in another building. The occupant of the room was Klingman: "Klingman and Davis were attracted to each other and talked most of the night. Klingman had sold lots of things but not insurance. Davis talked insurance so eloquently that Klingman became a convert." This story is obviously in error in regard to Klingman having to be converted to life insurance; what Davis was no doubt trying to do was convert Klingman to the Reliance Life.

[132] The promoters would charter a whole train and take prospective buyers to Texas to see the land. According to Klingman, William Jennings Bryan was given a piece of the property in return for lending his name to the promotion and making the train trip to Texas. The train was divided into two sections, the "wet section" and the "dry section." Bryan, of course, never set foot in the "wet section." Lloyd Klingman (in consultation with his father, William W. Klingman) to Secretary Gordon K. Smith, July 14, 1958.

[133] William S. Dutton, "You Can't Tell Where You're Going" (an interview with Klingman), *The American Magazine*, CVIII (1929), September.

When Frank H. Davis took over the Equitable managership at St. Paul, Minnesota, in 1913, he invited Klingman to join his agency force. Klingman did so, moved to Marshall, and during his first year wrote $1,135,000 in personal business. For a period of eighteen months, he had an applicant examined for insurance each day. His commissions during the first year were more than $20,000. In 1915, when Davis became Inspector of Agencies at Chicago, Klingman took over the St. Paul managership. He continued the development started by Davis and soon his agents were ranging the Northwest. By 1928, when the St. Paul agency placed $52,000,000 worth of new business, it ranked second only to the great Edward A. Woods agency of Pittsburgh. Some of Equitable's competitors said that "Wash" Klingman had so many agents that they had to wear badges to keep from trying to sell each other. Like some other successful agents, Klingman believed that the life insurance salesman was fulfilling a social and economic mission. He preached to his agents: "Forget policy terms; forget premiums; think only of protection! That's what you're selling these people—protection against want!" He started schools for his agents and the percentage of new men who succeeded rose from 4 out of 100 to 40 out of 100. Klingman also believed that the best men had to move upward and as a result many of his agents also became unit or agency managers. We shall hear more of Klingman later.

Whereas in 1912 Equitable had approximately 43 agency managers, by 1925 there were 72 managers and only 52 general agents. Ironically enough the man who had given considerable impetus to the development of the manager system did not remain with Equitable. William E. Bilheimer, despite his many fine qualities, had something of a temper and a mind of his own. In 1916 he became involved in a dispute with the Home Office, and particularly with Vice President Lunger, which led to his leaving the Society. He became Superintendent of Agencies for The Franklin Life Insurance Company of Springfield, Illinois. R. Roy Hale, after serving in the U.S. Marines in World War I, went to the Home Office to serve on the staff of Agency Vice President William E. Taylor. Soon thereafter he became secretary and assistant to Agency Vice President Frank H. Davis.[134]

The plan for compensation of agency managers adopted by the

[134] After Davis left the Society in 1928, Hale became Superintendent of Agencies for the Southern Department and then served for nineteen years as Agency Manager at Baltimore. The author is indebted to him for first-hand information in regard not only to the work of Bilheimer and the "Four Horsemen," but to agency affairs in general during the period 1910–30.

Society in 1919 provided for an annual salary based upon an assumed production of business by volume, and a further compensation based upon a percentage of 5 per cent or less of the first year premiums on new business in excess of the quota; in addition, the Manager was given a 1 per cent renewal commission to be paid in the fifth year of the policy. The purpose of this additional compensation was to interest the manager in the conservation of the business. This scale of compensation was based upon the average premium on Equitable policies of $38 per thousand. With the introduction of two- and five-year preliminary term policies, the average premium declined to about $32 per thousand. This fact resulted in an increase in the ratio of agency expense to premium income and also resulted in certain inequities of compensation. Since increases in quotas tended to reduce the gross compensation of agency managers with respect to first year compensation, there was considerable pressure from the managers to keep the quotas down. Consequently, in an endeavor to meet the objections to the existing plan, the Society adopted a new scale of compensation in 1929. The new scale was based upon both volume of insurance written and upon amount of premiums paid, with $32 per thousand as an average. Starting with an annual salary of $3,500 for $1,000,000 of insurance written with $32,000 of premiums, the scale advanced gradually to $18,000 for $50,000,000 of business with $1,600,000 of premiums. In addition to the salary compensation for supervising, the Agency Manager was given a sum equal to 3 per cent of the premiums paid through his agency during the year. As a reward for the conservation of business, the Manager was given one-half of 1 per cent upon second year premiums, payable at the beginning of the third year. Similar provisions, but on a lower scale, were made for assistant agency managers and unit managers.[135]

In 1922, upon recommendation of the agency officers, the Executive Committee of the Board adopted new regulations in regard to the outstanding contracts of general agents. The contracts were divided

[135] Sample salaries and commissions: for $1,000,000 of business, $3,500 and $960; for $10,000,000, $7,600 and $9,600; for $20,000,000, $10,600 and $19,200; for $30,000,000, $13,600 and $28,800; for $50,000,000, $18,000 and $48,000. Thus the percentage of salary to premiums declined with increased volume, but the percentage of salary and commissions to premiums remained fairly constant once the lower brackets were passed. Details of the plan were covered in Agency Vice President Frank L. Jones' memorandum to the Committee on Agencies of the Board of Directors, December 3, 1928. Copy in Sterling Pierson files, Equitable Archives.

into four groups. In Class I were those which were not producing an adequate amount of new business and were to be terminated. Class II consisted of those under which the production of new business during recent years had not been of sufficient amount to justify continuance on the existing basis; these were to have the terms of compensation reduced, and the subagents under contract were to be transferred to the more active agencies. The right of the general agent to produce new business through subagents was withdrawn, which automatically deprived him of the opportunity to earn extended renewal commissions of 5 per cent from the eleventh to the fifteenth year of the policy. In Class III were the general agents who were producing a satisfactory amount of new business, but running their agencies "to a certain degree in accordance with the individual wishes of each." These were to conform to certain general conditions; if they did so, "the collection fee which, under existing contracts, the Society now has a right to impose on business secured on and after July 1st, 1914, upon termination of the contract, shall be waived upon termination of the contract while in full force and effect by reason of the death of the General Agent." Among the conditions specified was one which required the General Agent not only to produce an adequate amount of new business, but to appoint and train assistants to aid in the management of the agency. Any General Agent who did not wish to comply with the conditions might surrender his general agency contract and accept a contract upon the Agency Manager basis. In Class IV were the general agents who, while producing a reasonable amount of business yearly, were not building up an organization of value to the Society. The contracts of these agents were to be continued upon the existing basis.[136]

In 1925 President Day, at "The Old Guard" meeting, announced another dividend increase on Equitable's policies. As a result he ran into opposition from Westfall and the actuaries, who did not think the increase justified. Actuary Robert Henderson, who confessed that he suffered from "foot and mouth disease," spoke of the "fictitious surplus." Some of the officers hesitated to take sides, but it was finally decided that what Henderson meant was a surplus which had been

[136] Minutes of meeting of the Committee on Agencies of the Board of Directors, May 1, 1922, at which the agency officers were present. The recommendations were adopted by the Executive Committee May 3, 1922. Corporate Records, Equitable Archives.

enlarged by nonrecurring increments—in this instance, the money recovered from the liquidation of the European business—or that he had in mind the excess of market values over book values of the Society's investments. The dividend increase was made and President Day's reputation with the agents was saved but later the dividends were reduced.

Although Equitable had introduced group insurance in 1911, almost eighteen years elapsed before the Society extended group coverage to its own agents. Meanwhile, Prudential had included agents in its group plan for employees in 1916.

In June 1918, Vice President John B. Lunger submitted a proposed plan to the New York Insurance Department which would provide insurance equal to the previous year's earnings to all Equitable agents who had been in the service of the Society for more than one year; maximum amount of insurance was to be $1,000 for the second year and $2,400 thereafter. Premiums were to be paid by Equitable. The Insurance Department raised several objections to the plan, most important of which had to do with the definition of "agent." The Department had a tentative ruling to the effect that a subagent who was not under direct contract with the company which he represented was an employee of the General Agent and not of the company. Thus the only way to insure these agents would be by way of a group policy taken by each General Agent on his subagents.[137] In addition to these difficulties, the plan suffered the handicap of open opposition from Vice Presidents Westfall and Horr. As a result, no further progress was made at this time.

By the mid-1920's, however, pressure from the agents revived interest in group coverage. The Prosser and Homans agency in New York City formed a special committee to promote the idea, and Pendleton A. Miller, district manager at Kansas City, prepared his own proposal in elaborate brochure form and sent it to the officers and directors of the Society. In June 1928, Thomas B. Sweeney (Wheeling) wrote President Parkinson and expressed the hope that Equitable could "see its way clear to include all its agents, or at least its Century Club mem-

[137] Lunger's letter and the ensuing discussion are summarized in a three-page memorandum by Assistant Actuary Mervyn Davis to Vice President William E. Taylor, July 22, 1919. Sterling Pierson files, Equitable Archives.

Some of Equitable's general agents had previously covered their employees by taking out group policies with Equitable. Memorandum from Assistant Secretary Andrew E. Tuck to Thomas I. Parkinson, May 22, 1926. *Ibid.*

bers, under a Group Insurance Policy, as so many other companies are doing." President Parkinson replied that the proposal had been under consideration before, but that there had been "a lack of enthusiasm for it on the part of the Agency Department" (now under Vice President Frank H. Davis). He went on to say, however, that Second Vice President William J. Graham had been urging it on him recently and that the matter would be given renewed and serious consideration. Consequently, on December 19, 1928, the Committee on Retirement and Employes' Insurance of the Board of Directors recommended the adoption of a contributory group plan for agents. Under this plan, agents who had been with the Society for at least one year were to be insured for a sum not to exceed $5,000; the agent's contribution was fixed at $3 per month, the Society to pay the remainder of the cost. Since the Society appeared on both sides of the account—that is, as the insurer and as the employer—the cost to it was roughly estimated at the amount of claims to be paid, plus a gross premiums tax, and less the agents' monthly contributions; it was thought that the agents' contributions would pay for most of the cost. Though there were some 10,564 agents under contract at this time, only about 6,000 were expected to qualify under the plan. One of the arguments advanced by the Committee was that the Society was in an anomalous position when it had its agents recommend group insurance to other organizations while not applying such coverage to its own agents.

The Board of Directors approved the plan the following day and President Parkinson wired the managerial staff that it would go into effect January 1, 1929.[138]

* * *

An important step in the training of agents had taken place in 1919 when the War Department organized an "Overseas Educational Corps." Among the courses offered was one in life insurance prepared by Frank L. Jones, head of Equitable's Indiana agency, Dr. Lee K. Frankel of the Metropolitan Life, and Secretary William Alexander of Equitable. Jones, who had been Superintendent of Public Instruction in Indiana, went to France in army uniform to supervise the teaching of this course, an important part of which dealt with the agent's calling. Textbooks used in the course were Solomon S. Huebner's *Life*

138 The important documents relating to group insurance for Equitable agents are in a folder in *ibid.*

Insurance and William Alexander's *What Life Insurance Is and Does.* Secretary Alexander, who had, over the years, prepared much of the Society's educational literature for agents and written several books on life insurance and how to sell it, believed that the only way to sell life insurance was through the agents. He did not favor advertising in the newspapers and magazines because he did not believe that such advertising interested people in life insurance. Arthur H. Reddall, Equitable's Advertising Manager, prepared many folders and fillers for the agents' use in reaching prospects. In 1927 he published a book entitled *Publicity Methods for Life Underwriters.*

Vice President J. V. E. Westfall agreed with Secretary Alexander. He said: "The agent is the backbone of life insurance, for it has been demonstrated time and time again that only through agents will the public be induced to carry anything approaching an adequate amount of protection." Then President Day—in view of the embarrassing events in 1905—had been reluctant to have Equitable too much in the public eye. Consequently, Equitable did little advertising—and no display advertising—in the newspapers and magazines in the early 1920's. It continued, however, to take space in the insurance periodicals. This policy stood in some contrast to an earlier period when Equitable advertisements, with pictures, appeared even in *The Theatre* and other specialized magazines, where the theme of "Living Insurance"—to be emphasized again in the 1950's—was presented. As Edward A. Woods said in 1924: "I know of nothing that can be advertised so well but is advertised so poorly as life insurance." [139]

For many years the life insurance business had been interested in developing a professional status for agents. Finally, after years of discussion, a big step in this direction was made with the creation of The American College of Life Underwriters in 1927. The College was not the product of the efforts of any one man, but two of the four men most responsible were Equitable men. As early as 1911, Edward A. Woods spoke before The Association of Life Insurance Presidents on the subject, "Life Insurance As a Life Work for College Men," and the talk was published in pamphlet form. The following year Woods published the talk which he made before the National Association of Life Underwriters; the title was "The Life Insurance

[139] In a talk made at the meeting of the Insurers Advertising Conference held at Pittsburgh October 27–28, 1924. Quoted in *The Weekly Underwriter*, CXI (1924), November 1.

Agent of the Future."[140] In 1913 Ernest J. Clark, General Agent for John Hancock Mutual and President of the National Association of Life Underwriters, discussed with Solomon S. Huebner, Professor of Insurance at the University of Pennsylvania, the need for preparation of literature in order to make feasible a professional movement in life insurance comparable to that already established in the field of accounting. The first step was the publication in 1915 of Dr. Huebner's *Life Insurance*, a textbook in fundamentals. Then Huebner became editor of a series of books on life insurance to be published by D. Appleton and Company.[141] By 1927 more than fifty colleges were using one or more of these books for the various courses on insurance.

From 1923 to 1925, a committee—the Committee on Nomenclature—of the National Association of Life Underwriters had been working on a plan to differentiate among the life insurance agents with reference to their length of service, amount of production, and skill in underwriting. This committee, of which Guy MacLaughlin of Houston, Texas, was chairman, filed its report with the Executive Committee. When it appeared that no action was going to be taken, Frank L. Jones, who was elected President of the National Association in 1925, stepped into the picture. Jones, who was very much interested in the education and training of agents, informed the Executive Committee of the Association that he intended to try to carry through with some of the recommendations presented by the Committee on Nomenclature. He believed that there were two more or less distinct goals to be achieved: 1) the certification of agents on some kind of graded basis, and 2) the establishment of a program of education and training that would encourage all agents to strive for a certification or

140 For Woods' work in connection with the early years of the National Association of Life Underwriters see "Across the Years with Equitable and the NALU," in *National Leaders*, III (1964), July–August.

141 All told, there were eight books in this series, which included Huebner's *Economics of Life Insurance* (1927) and Edward A. Woods' *Sociology of Life Insurance* (1928). Huebner also published in pamphlet form (The Convention Yearbook Company, 1924) his address made before the National Association in July 1924 entitled "The Human Value in Business Compared with the Property Value." Woods also wrote *Life Underwriting As A Career* (Harper and Brothers, 1923); with Alexander C. Robinson, *Creating and Conserving Estates* (F. S. Crofts and Company, 1926); and, with C. B. Metzger, *America's Human Wealth* (F. S. Crofts and Company). Second Vice President John A. Stevenson of Equitable wrote three books, which dealt primarily with salesmanship: *Meeting Objections* (1921); *Selling Life Insurance* (1922); and *Constructive Salesmanship* (1923). All three books were published by Harper and Brothers.

degree. MacLaughlin and Jones drafted the program, which was presented to the Executive Committee of the Association early in 1926. The report of the Committee was so complete that little remained to be done at the national convention of the Association later in the year. In January 1927 the Executive Committee formally approved the creation of the College, and Ernest J. Clark and Edward S. Brashears were appointed to attend to the legal phases of the incorporation. March 22, 1927, the College was incorporated as a legal entity in Washington, D.C.; all the incorporators were members of the National Association. A College Board was elected and Edward A. Woods became the first President of the College; Dr. Huebner was elected Dean.

Purposes of The American College of Life Underwriters were listed as follows: 1) to cooperate with the colleges and universities in the training of students for the career of professional life underwriting; 2) to cooperate with educational institutions in life insurance education; 3) to conduct if necessary its own institution for the training of resident students for the profession of life underwriting; and 4) to recognize properly qualified life underwriters with a professional designation. The "degree" to be awarded was that of Chartered Life Underwriter.

Dr. Huebner prepared the first curriculum for the course, and the first examinations—a series of five—were given in 1928. Of the first class of 22 students, 21 qualified for the designation. Five of these men had been students of Dr. Huebner's at the University of Pennsylvania; all except three of the group had attended college and sixteen were graduates. Although ten companies were represented, ten members of the class were Equitable agents and nine of the ten were associated with the Edward A. Woods Company.[142]

As planned originally, The American College of Life Underwriters was to be only an organization for setting up standards and carrying out its prescribed procedure; most of the work would be done by way of courses offered in the cooperating colleges and universities. Each applicant for a degree, upon completing the necessary studies, would

[142] William M. Duff, E. A. Woods' successor as President of the company, set his agents a good example by taking all five examinations himself. The other companies represented were the Berkshire Life and Equitable of Iowa with two men each and seven others with one man each. Of the fifteen men who were personal underwriters, all later became managers, general agents, or top-flight producers. S. S. Huebner, "The First Class of CLU's," *Life Association News* (September 1952).

submit his application to a committee of the College, which would pass upon his standing, ethical qualifications, and experience. If the application was passed upon favorably, the candidate was permitted to take the examinations which were to be conducted at colleges or universities easily accessible to the majority of applicants; the examinations were to be conducted and graded by the faculties of the colleges where they were held.

Naturally there were decided differences of opinion among the men most responsible for founding the College as to its nature and basic purposes. At times the differences were so sharp that two of the men were hardly on speaking terms. Dr. Huebner thought of the College as an institution at the collegiate level, the instructors of which would have Ph.D. degrees, if possible; its emphasis would be upon the whole field of life insurance. Edward A. Woods, on the other hand, believed that the emphasis should be upon salesmanship. Frank Jones thought rather in terms of a short course—a "package deal"—as far as the curriculum of the College was concerned, with the more advanced training to be left in the hands of the colleges and universities.

Basically important was the question of whether the College was to be merely an appendage of the National Association or an independent organization. If the College were to be a subsidiary of the National Association, a trade association of life insurance salesmen, it could not achieve status as a professional organization or receive the support of the colleges and universities. Then after the establishment of the College the question arose as to whether it should give honorary degrees to certain outstanding men. Woods stood firm in favor of giving the regular degree only to those who passed the examinations: "We may sometime wish to award some different degree to some notable man, woman, or underwriter, but the regular degree should not be given but won by everyone." [143] Dr. Huebner positively opposed honorary degrees. But after Woods' death later in 1927, and while Dr. Huebner was out of the country, the Board of the College decided to award a number of honorary degrees at $100 each. Despite the fact that Huebner was designated as one of the recipients, he threatened to resign as Dean if this action was taken. His view prevailed.

[143] Woods to Frank L. Jones, Chairman of the Executive Committee of the N.A.L.U., April 12, 1927. Copy in Equitable Archives. Woods thought that it ought to be made possible for some prominent life insurance men—company officers, for instance—who were not members of the National Association, to take the examinations and receive the regular diploma.

From the date of the chartering of the College there had been some doubt as to whether it would be permitted by the Educational Committee of the District of Columbia to issue the "degree" of Chartered Life Underwriter. In 1929, after an investigation, the Educational Committee failed to permit the granting of a "degree," so since that time the term "designation" has been used for the Chartered Life Underwriter diploma. The same year the American College became completely independent of the National Association of Life Underwriters, although that organization continued to give its strong moral support to the College. After the first diplomas were awarded, the recipients organized under the title National Chapter—Chartered Life Underwriters. In 1940 the organization adopted the name of The American Society of Chartered Life Underwriters and broadened its purposes and objectives. In 1946 the Society began publication of *The Journal.* This quarterly publication has maintained a high professional standard to date and despite its specialized nature has a wide circulation among the non-Chartered Life Underwriters, many of whom are members of other professions. In the early years, headquarters of the College were maintained in Dr. Huebner's office in Logan Hall at the University of Pennsylvania; but in 1948 a building at 3924 Walnut Street, Philadelphia, was purchased and remodeled to serve as headquarters for both the College and The American Society of Chartered Life Underwriters. In 1959 ground was broken for the College's new headquarters at Bryn Mawr, Pennsylvania, and both the College and the American Society moved to the new headquarters, Huebner Hall, in 1961.

Although Edward A. Woods very generously gave Frank L. Jones credit for being the "father" of the College, it is obvious that credit for its establishment should be shared by a number of men.[144] Both Clark and Woods had been leaders in the movement for the education of agents for a number of years; Jones got the National Association to act and played an important part in securing the cooperation of the colleges and universities; and Dr. Huebner was largely responsible for getting the College set up as a separate entity and for preparing its curriculum. These men had the help of many others.[145]

144 *Ibid.*

145 The above account of the founding of the American College of Life Underwriters was based largely upon information furnished by Dr. Solomon S. Huebner in an interview July 24, 1959. Also helpful were Ernest J. Clark, Sr., "The Founding of the American College of Life Underwriters," S. S. Huebner and

INVESTMENTS DURING THE 1920's

Although the great number of tontine policies falling due in the early 1920's did not leave the usual amount of funds for new investment, nevertheless Equitable did much to help relieve the postwar housing shortage by mortgage loans in the various states in which it did business. Under the Home Purchase Plan alone, more than $94,000,000 had been invested in the homes of some 30,000 families by 1925; a year later the figure had risen to more than $139,000,000 for 41,550 families.[146] President Day, however, did not favor a New York bill to enable life insurance companies to purchase land and erect tenement houses; he thought its enactment might result in competition among the life insurance companies for philanthropic opportunities to gain popular favor. The endeavor to cure a temporary evil might well result in creating a permanent danger by risking life insurance funds in real estate speculation.[147] Although Equitable had been giving preference in its new investments to residential and farm loans, it pursued a very conservative policy in regard to the latter. President Day believed that the existing condition of agriculture was owing in part to the overvaluation of the land; hence, Equitable expanded its loans very cautiously in this field and its experience was excellent.[148] All mortgage investments increased from 22 per cent of the Society's assets early in 1921 to 25 per cent a year later.[149]

Railroad stocks and bonds constituted the largest single group of Equitable's investments. President Day was much interested in the railroads, not only because of their importance to Equitable but also

David McCahan "Some Aspects of American College Operational History," both in *The Journal of the American Society of Chartered Life Underwriters*, March 1947, and a typescript memoir of Frank L. Jones entitled "The Founding of the American College of Life Underwriters." The main facts are also included in Mildred F. Stone *The Teacher Who Changed an Industry*, a biography of Dr. Solomon S. Huebner (Homewood, Illinois, 1960).

146 Day to the statistician of The Association of Life Insurance Presidents, December 17, 1926. Day letters, Equitable Archives.

147 Day to Thomas A. McWhinney, Assembly Chamber, Albany, February 18, 1922. *Ibid.*

148 Day to Seward Prosser, Bankers Trust Company, New York, May 23, 1924. *Ibid.*

149 Day to Samuel Untermyer, counsel for the Lockwood Legislative Committee, June 1, 1922. *Ibid.* The figures as of the end of May for the two years were: 1921, assets $628,478,934, real estate mortgages $139,464,174; 1922, assets $643,919,000, real estate mortgages $162,452,465.

because of their economic importance to the country. In 1920 the Society mailed to policyholders with their premium notices a leaflet entitled "Transportation, the Need of the Nation." Day believed that officers and directors of all financial institutions owed a duty to those whose funds they handled to spread the gospel in every proper way. At the end of 1923, railroad stocks and bonds, at book value, constituted 40.6 per cent of Equitable's investments (ledger assets, including cash but exclusive of policy loans), and 33.5 per cent of the Society's gross assets.[150] Consequently, President Day was particularly concerned about protecting the Society's interests in railroad and transit company reorganizations. Some years earlier he had had a warm argument with J. P. Morgan in regard to the purchase of $5,000,000 of Interboro Rapid Transit bonds which had just been brought out by J. P. Morgan and Company. In 1914, when President Day was on a trip to the West Coast, Vice President Lunger had persuaded the Finance Committee to purchase these bonds, but when President Day returned he refused to approve the purchase. Morgan came over to see him and reminded him that Equitable had entered into a legal obligation. But President Day said he would not go through with the purchase. The Insurance Department refused to help, and considerable heat was generated in the ensuing discussion. Equitable finally bought $3,500,000 of the bonds, which, by 1921, were giving trouble together with bonds of the Interboro Rapid Transit and Hyde's Brooklyn and Long Island bonds.[151] President Day thought that Morgan should have been more appreciative of the courtesy shown his father some years earlier, when Day had him appointed to handle the payments to the French Panama Canal Company.

In 1922 President Day was much concerned about protecting the Society's interests in Manhattan Elevated. When Manhattan's lease to the I.R.T. came up before the Equitable Board for readjustment, he wanted to make sure that the Manhattan stockholders were not sur-

[150] As of December 31, 1923, Equitable held $4,575,507 of railroad stocks and $225,825,612 of railroad bonds, for a total of $230,401,119. Some of Equitable's directors were in favor of Equitable's selling government bonds and purchasing rails, which would yield at least 1 per cent more. President Day was not sure that this was a wise policy and asked the advice of James B. Forgan, President of the First National Bank of Chicago. Day to Forgan, April 28, 1922. *Ibid.*

As of December 31, 1925, railroad stocks and bonds constituted 34.3 per cent of the Society's investments, and by December 31, 1930, the percentage had fallen to 24 per cent.

[151] Equitable took a loss on $1,120,000 B.R.T. secured notes when these were exchanged par for par for new securities with a market value of 74.

rendering their right to retake the property because of breach of lease. In 1924 Equitable had to take a loss on a block of 3½ per cent Chicago and Alton bonds. It sold $1,540,000 of the bonds at an average price of 47.7 just before the Alton went into receivership, but retained $955,000 so as to be represented on the bondholders' protective committee. When it appeared that the Society might get an offer from one of the investment banking houses for these bonds at 50, President Day was reluctant to sell them and thus lose Equitable's representation on the committee: "I would prefer not to add to the power of these reorganizing buccaneers. . . . The financial undertakers of this vicinity are hungry for the opportunity which they think the situation affords. Their procedure would probably be to get a majority of the 3½ per cent bonds under their control and use that control to force the Trustee to foreclose when it suits their purposes." He understood that the professional reorganizers would paint such a dismal picture of the condition of the Alton as would persuade the bondholders to sell their bonds on terms "which will provide both cream for the reorganizers themselves and molasses to attract new investors." [152]

Another investment which the Day administration inherited was the $2,361,000 in bonds of the Arkansas Valley Sugar Beet and Irrigated Land Company, which Equitable had accepted in the settlement of the Turner loans with The Mercantile Trust Company and the Hyde estate.[153] Second Vice President Leon O. Fisher was President of the Land Company and several of the members of Equitable's Board were directors.[154] The problem here was to liquidate the holdings of the Land Company gradually and with a minimum of loss. It was not to be solved for many years.

In the mid-1920's, the policy of the Finance Committee of the

[152] Day to Joy Morton, November 14 and 22, 1924. Day letters, Equitable Archives.

Vice President Horr advised Vice President Parkinson "not to fight the corner" (J. P. Morgan and Company). Thomas I. Parkinson, interview with author, November 30, 1955.

Equitable still held $955,000 of the 3½ per cent bonds, on which $270,185 interest was in default, in 1929. The question as to priority of the various bond issues of the road was not settled until that year, when a Federal court found in favor of the 3½ per cent bonds ahead of the 6 per cent and 3 per cent bonds.

[153] For the earlier history of the Turner loans and the Land Company, see this history, p. 499; for the later history, pp. 668, 729.

[154] Equitable directors who were also directors of the Land Company were Charles H. Zehnder, who was Vice President of the Company; Joy Morton; Thomas Spratt; and George S. Hovey. Charles J. Martin was Secretary of the Land Company and Franklin Day, Treasurer.

Board was in general to dispose of the Society's early maturing corporate bonds and reinvest in long-term issues which promised to become scarcer and higher as a result of the investment demand built up by the rapid growth of savings banks, life insurance companies, and other institutional investors.[155]

Although President Day had no great love for the investment bankers, he was largely dependent upon them for recommendations for investments since Equitable had no securities research department. To obviate this situation, he decided to bring in a specialist on securities. In 1919 Meredith C. Laffey, then with the Equitable Trust Company, was appointed an Assistant Treasurer of the Society. While the other assistant treasurers, Fred H. Richmond and Henry Greaves, handled the banking accounts and the bond trading, Laffey devoted most of his attention to security analysis and the recommendation of securities. He succeeded in interesting President Day and the Finance Committee in investments in the rapidly developing public utilities field. Many of the public utility bonds carried 5 per cent interest and were frequently brought out at substantial discounts. As Director Thomas DeWitt Cuyler of the Finance Committee said: "At times we have lost money on rails, we may as well lose some on utilities." Entry into the public utilities field was regarded as a daring move at the time, but results proved good. Upon the resignation of Financial Vice President and Treasurer Alfred R. Horr, Laffey became Treasurer of the Society in 1923. President Day continued, however, to consult on investments with Joy Morton, brother of former President Paul Morton, and James B. Forgan, President of the First National Bank of Chicago, both directors of the Society. Despite the plentiful supply of funds and the competition for good investments, Equitable was, in the mid-1920's, earning slightly more than 5 per cent on its assets.

In December 1925 President Day published his views on financial conditions and emphasized the signal service which life insurance was rendering in stabilizing the economy and social fabric of the country. He said:

> Its response to the manifold commercial and individual needs is an outstanding chapter in present day history. That service now reaches into factory, office, mine, railroad, school and university as effectively as does

[155] Day to Samuel M. Felton, President of the Chicago and Great Western Railroad Company, October 20, 1925. Day letters, Equitable Archives.

its service of the individual, home and fireside. And I believe we are on the threshold of significant changes and expansion of that service.

In 1925 by wise distribution of funds in careful investment in all sections of the country, the insurance companies contributed to stability and upbuilding of local communities. By extensive lending on mortgage on farm lands and on homes, through financing municipal improvements and public utilities, they constructively apportioned vast resources.[156]

The only "ominous" sign which he saw in the economy was the extreme speculation, especially in real estate, and the erection of buildings for which there was no economic demand: "This is born in a measure of inordinate desire to get rich quick and reckless indiscriminate lending on mortgage on such enterprises."

An amendment to the New York State Insurance Law which became effective early in 1928 enabled life insurance companies to invest in certain guaranteed and preferred stocks. Equitable immediately took advantage of this liberalization of the law and a year and a half later

[156] Day to W. S. Cousins, financial editor, International News Service, December 17, 1925. *Ibid.*

That this service did not please everybody was evidenced now and then by attacks, largely from the "Populist Belt," upon the big life insurance companies. For instance, in 1929 one John L. Powers published a little pamphlet at Indianola, Iowa, entitled "Do You Know Your Mules?" In it he said that "the greatest economic menace today is a very live hand—these great insurance companies which are controlling so large a part of our quick capital. . . . Who holds all this Power? It is common knowledge that Morgan and Company bought 51 per cent of the Equitable of New York for about $3,000,000. . . . What does Mr. Morgan do with all this insurance money? What is the present day policy in regard to reinvesting in farm loans for the benefit of the insured? The general policy is a liquidation or reduction of these loans in which case an increased interest rate is added. . . . Knowing what I know, do you think I would buy an eastern life insurance policy. No!" The author, a merchant, was equally vindictive against chain stores and other such "beasts" which drained good Midwestern capital to Wall Street. A copy of the pamphlet is preserved in the Sterling Pierson files, Equitable Archives. When the statements in the pamphlet were broadcast over two Minneapolis radio stations, Sterling Pierson wrote Stations WRHM and WDGY and said: "Under the circumstances a vicious libel has been published against the Equitable." He asked for a retraction which would be as prominently circulated as the original broadcast. The stations replied that the time on the air had been bought in the regular way by a man who was not an employee of the stations, and that they had prefaced and ended his talk with a statement that his views were his own. Equitable counsel at Des Moines got in touch with Powers, who revised his pamphlet and eliminated the portion concerning Equitable. Following this episode, Equitable published advertisements in the Midwest which showed, by a chart, the Society's mortgages on farms and homes, loans on policies, and holdings of railroad and other securities of companies domiciled in the area.

had invested more than $27,000,000 in railroad, utility, and industrial preferred stocks, on which the yield was slightly more than 5 per cent. As Treasurer Meredith C. Laffey pointed out in a talk to the agents, he could not go through a day without coming in constant contact with the products of the companies in which he had invested Equitable funds; these products included everything from his breakfast cereal, the cigarette he smoked, the shoes he wore, the car he rode in, to the carpet he walked on, and the plant food which went on his lawn.[157] As of December 31, 1929, Equitable had investments of $399,479,001 in bonds and $38,773,221 in stocks for a total of $438,252,222. These investments were widely distributed geographically, with bond holdings in all forty-eight states and the District of Columbia and preferred or guaranteed stocks in all of the states but three; also represented among the bond holdings were Canada, Chile, Cuba, and other countries.[158]

A NEW HOME OFFICE AND A NEW PRESIDENT

By 1921 Equitable had far outgrown the three floors which it had leased in the Equitable Building at 120 Broadway, and its two thousand Home Office employees were scattered among seven buildings in New York and Brooklyn. Early in the year the Board approved purchase of a plot of land on Seventh Avenue which had been assembled by the Pennsylvania Railroad Company. The lots occupied the block between Thirty-first and Thirty-second Streets and faced the Pennsylvania Railroad Station. President Day had no desire to emulate Henry B. Hyde in the building of a show place. He said: "What we need is a workshop that can be expanded to meet the Society's requirements over a long period of years." Plans for the new building were announced to the press in September. It was estimated that the Society would save several hundred thousand dollars annually as well as greatly increase its efficiency by once again having its own Home Office building. The new building was constructed of granite, Indiana limestone, and brick; there were twenty-two stories plus a four-story penthouse for tanks and machinery, and the basement extended three stories

[157] Meredith C. Laffey, "How the Financial Department of the Equitable Co-operates with the Field Force," a talk delivered at the 70th Anniversary Educational Conferences, September 1929. Pamphlet in Sterling Pierson files, Equitable Archives. See also Laffey, "The Equitable Policyholder, A Capitalist of Nation-Wide Interests." Copy in *ibid.*

[158] A tabulation of Equitable's bond and stock investments by states and foreign countries may be found in *ibid.*

underground. The great vault rested on bedrock. In the center of the building at ground level was a large vaulted rotunda from which arcades led to Seventh Avenue and the two other streets; a grand staircase led to the second story. There were twenty-four passenger elevators and a ventilating system for the first five stories—"the gasoline belt." [159]

During the weekend of October 10, 1924, Equitable moved from the historic site at 120 Broadway which it had occupied for more than a half-century. The 940 vanloads of office furnishings and records made their way to the new site without accident or incident; the hundreds of millions of dollars of securities were handled by the armored-car service of the Adams Express Company. The statue of Henry B. Hyde, however, did not take its place in the rotunda at the foot of the marble stairs which led to the second story until ten years later—at the time of the Society's seventy-fifth anniversary. While the moving was in process many office workers were housed in hotels. Though at the time "393 Seventh Avenue" was thought of as the "permanent home" of Equitable, there was to come a day. . . .

In 1925 President Day was seventy-five years old and his health had not been good since a heart attack in 1919. Naturally there was considerable rivalry—and some maneuvering—among the ranking officers for the succession to the presidency. As previously mentioned, two of the officers were discovered to be regularly checking on the President's health by way of Associate Medical Director Robert M. Daley, who was also his personal physician. Not only did these officers practically eliminate themselves from consideration, but President Day changed physicians and from that time on kept fairly close check on all of the officers. As the years went by, he spent more time away from the office—frequently in Florida—and early in 1926 he designated Thomas I. Parkinson, who had become Vice President in 1925, to be ranking Vice President with authority to act as President during these absences. October 20, 1927, President Day presented his resignation to the Board of Directors; he was made Chairman of the Board, an office previously held briefly by Paul Morton, and Thomas I. Parkinson was elected President of Equitable. After Parkinson's election, Judge Day said:

[159] A description of the new Home Office under the title "A Model Workshop for Life Insurance" appeared in *The Eastern Underwriter,* XXVI (1925), January 30. See also "The Home Office of The Equitable," an illustrated pamphlet published in 1934.

I have been able to carry the burden of the presidency as long as I have only because of the extraordinary help of our Vice President, of whose standing as a lawyer and of whose great executive ability I have no doubt you are aware. His selection as my successor insures the continuity of the policies under which the Society has prospered during my administration, for he will bring to it, besides his other qualities, not only youthful vigor, but also a firm determination to administer the Society's affairs in the interests of the policyholders only. . . . I bespeak your support of him in the office you once entrusted to me. . . . I may say that the Society has been in a very real sense my life, and I shall withdraw from its active control contentedly knowing that by his election you have insured its further disinterested management.

William A. Day believed that his most important accomplishment as President of Equitable had been completion of the mutualization of the Society. But perhaps there was a greater accomplishment—the example furnished, not only to the policyholders but to the world at large, of the immense competitive value of the union of ability and integrity. He expressed his ideals in a letter written to Edward A. Woods in April 1927 when he stated that he had "endeavored to adhere to certain fundamentals of conduct and policy. Not the least of these was a deep sense of obligation to the policyholder, who, by self-sacrifice and toil, had provided protection for those he loved. To merit that man's confidence and to discharge the trust which grew out of the relationship, in full faith, has always been my endeavor. Unless the officials of life insurance companies have that moral fibre, which at whatever personal cost will manfully resist predatory attempts, extravagance and injudicious handling of funds, they wantonly betray their sacred trust." Director John Bassett Moore agreed that these were basic principles. As he said to Day in 1927: "Humanity, with its strong emotional and variable tendencies, needs all the help it can get to be steadfast in doing that which is fair and honest and of good report."

The retired President died of pneumonia in Florida in April 1928. The memorial resolution of the Board—drafted by his old friend, the distinguished international lawyer and former Assistant Secretary of State, John Bassett Moore—read in part as follows:

Simple in his life and quiet in his manner, Judge Day performed his duties unostentatiously and without any effort at self-advertisement; but his love of justice and his stern and unyielding sense of right burned as a consuming flame, steady and unquenchable. He loved his country and revered its institutions. His loyalty was not of that calculated kind, which

Fabian Bachrach

Ray D. Murphy
President, 1953–1956

is gauged by the indulgence shown to particular classes or individuals. He not only obeyed the law but gave to it his full support. On the other hand, he knew his rights, and did not hesitate firmly to maintain them by all proper and lawful means. He regarded, and properly regarded, the great company which he served as a public institution, in the management of which the public and the private interest must be identical; and, with this ideal constantly before him, he gave himself without stint to the building up of the company and the enlargement of its sphere of usefulness. Not only did his example, supplemented on occasion by stirring appeals, encourage and strengthen the Society's personnel, to whom he was an ever-present, sympathetic and vital force, but it served to inspire in the public that confidence which today eloquently attests the general recognition of the sureness of his understanding, his rare capacity for business, and the high purpose, probity and fidelity that pervaded all his actions. As his services to the Society were of incalculable benefit, so will he stand in the first rank of those who have contributed most to its growth and prosperity, and have broadened and deepened the foundations on which that growth and prosperity rest.

Judge Day's philosophy was well expressed in a talk made to Equitable agents in Atlantic City in 1925. He agreed with Lord Moulton, British jurist and philosopher of the law, who had pointed out that in human action there is a domain which lies between that of positive law on the one side and free choice on the other; this was "the domain of Obedience to the Unenforceable" or "the domain of manners."[160]

* * *

Upon final mutualization of the Society in 1925 certain provisions of its Charter became obsolete. The amended Charter as approved by the Superintendent of Insurance in April 1927 provided for division of the Board into three classes, one class to be elected each year; also for gradual reduction of the Board so that by 1933 it would be composed of thirty-six instead of fifty-two members.

Additional important changes in Equitable officer personnel took

[160] When an Equitable agent asked for a copy of the speech, President Day said that he had spoken extemporaneously, but he did send the agent excerpts from Lord Moulton's article on "Law and Manners," which had appeared in *The Atlantic Monthly* for July 1924. Day to R. Henry Lake, Memphis, May 1925. Day letters, Equitable Archives. Lord Moulton's article was reprinted in *Atlantic Harvest*, edited by Ellery Sedgwick (Boston, 1947), pp. 398–403.

Equitable's Senior Vice President and Actuary Walter Klem called attention to Lord Moulton's philosophy in his presidential address on "Professional Ethics," delivered before the meeting of the Society of Actuaries, October 1955. The address may be found in the *Transactions of the Society of Actuaries*, Volume VII.

place in 1927–29.[161] Vice President J. V. E. Westfall had resigned in 1926 to head the European organization of the accounting firm of Haskins and Sells. This left Frank H. Davis, who had been appointed Vice President in February 1926, as the only Vice President. But the following year Davis' health became a problem; he had, or thought he had, cancer, and suffered, among other things, periods of extreme depression; his family insisted that in order to avoid a complete breakdown Davis curtail his activities. In the summer of 1927 he retired to his brother's ranch near Yoder, Wyoming. The general agents and agency managers were much "distressed and worried," but Vice President Parkinson wrote President Day: "I think that while we miss his driving force in the field we have absorbed the shock of his sudden collapse." [162] Davis returned to work in December, however, and Parkinson—now President—wrote: "Davis is again Vice-President." And the Executive Committee designated him to serve as acting President in the absence of President Parkinson.[163]

In the spring of 1928, however, Davis again went to the ranch, apparently on leave. In late May he wrote his close friend Henry J. Powell, Equitable's General Agent at Louisville, that his problem was a "difficult one," but that he was thinking of going East to have a talk with "Major Parkinson"; if he did so he would like to talk over with Powell some very confidential matters.[164] He wrote to President Parkinson the same day and said that he was thinking "of coming back for a few days for a talk." There is no evidence that Davis had a conference with President Parkinson, but on June 11 Davis was asked to meet in Chicago, June 13, with Henry Powell, William Washington Klingman, and Frank L. Jones, Equitable's managers at Louisville, St. Paul,

[161] Officers of the Society as of September 1926 were: President William A. Day; Vice Presidents Thomas I. Parkinson, J. V. E. Westfall, and Frank H. Davis; Secretary William Alexander; and Second Vice Presidents Leon O. Fisher, William E. Taylor, Robert Henderson (also Actuary), William J. Graham, Ray D. Murphy (also Assistant Actuary), and John A. Stevenson.

[162] Parkinson to President Day, August 19, 1927. Parkinson files, Equitable Archives. Assistant Medical Director Geiringer left the same day to visit Davis.

[163] Parkinson to Henry Powell, February 23, 1928. *Ibid.*

[164] Davis to Powell, May 24, 1928. Copy in Parkinson files, Equitable Archives. In this letter Davis said: "There is one phase of the matter which I have not discussed with anyone except my brother & I may decide to talk it over with you." Powell sent Davis' letter to President Parkinson and said: "My thought is that he intends to tell me just what is back of all of the trouble, and that it will be an admission of his weakness as I suggested to you over the phone this morning." Powell to Parkinson, May 28, 1928. *Ibid.*

and Indianapolis.[165] On the day of the meeting President Parkinson wired Davis as follows: "Have decided on Frank L. Jones. Hope you can arrange details with him." At the conclusion of the meeting, which Jones reported as "successful in every detail," Davis wrote President Parkinson, asked for further extension of his leave to October 1, and that on that date he be transferred from the Home Office to the field.[166] June 20 the Executive Committee of the Equitable Board granted the extension of Davis' leave and accepted his resignation as Vice President, to be effective October 1. The same day President Parkinson wrote Davis that though he was sorry to see him leave the Home Office he was delighted to know that he was to "continue as a field executive of the Society." At the same meeting the Executive Committee appointed Frank L. Jones to be Agency Vice President, effective immediately, but service not to begin until September 1.[167] Sometime early in August Davis decided to leave Equitable. He wrote President Parkinson from the Park Central Hotel, New York City: "I hereby tender my resignation as Vice President of the Society and as a member of the Board of Directors." [168] Davis' resignation was accepted by the Executive Committee August 15, to take effect immediately. Meanwhile, about a week earlier, the Penn Mutual Life Insurance Company announced that Davis had been appointed General Agent

[165] June 11, Davis wired Parkinson from Corry, Pennsylvania, and asked him what his plans were. Parkinson replied the same day and sent the message to Davis at the Secor Hotel, Toledo, Ohio. It was in this telegram that Davis was requested to meet with Powell, Klingman, and Jones at the Palmer House in Chicago. Copies of the telegrams are in *ibid.* Just what Davis was doing in Pennsylvania and Ohio is not known, since he was on leave at the time.

[166] Jones' telegram was sent from Culver, Indiana, at 11:29 P.M. It is interesting to note that he made no mention of Parkinson's telegram to Davis. Copies of telegrams in *ibid.*

[167] Executive Order No. 648, Corporate Records, Equitable Archives. Parkinson to Davis, June 20, 1928, Parkinson files, Equitable Archives.

In an interview with the author, June 17, 1958, Thomas I. Parkinson said that he had promised Davis a Manager's contract for the Rocky Mountain states with headquarters in Denver.

July 2, 1928, Parkinson wrote Henry Powell in regard to this understanding: "The readjustment seems to be well received with here and there an expression of surprise or skepticism. Fitting and Stevenson and possibly others show that they would have preferred to have been consulted. Both have expressed a suspicion that our announcement respecting Davis' taking a manager's contract is somebody's shock-absorber and will never become a fact." (William G. Fitting was Superintendent of Agencies for the New York Metropolitan Department.) Parkinson files, Equitable Archives.

[168] The brief handwritten note was undated but probably written about August 3. The letter is in the Corporate Records, Equitable Archives.

for that Company in Chicago, to become effective October 1.[169] On the same day that the Executive Committee accepted Davis' resignation it accepted that of Second Vice President John A. Stevenson. Stevenson had resigned to accept the Home Office agency of the Penn Mutual in Philadelphia.

News of Davis' resignation as Vice President was disturbing enough to the general agents and agency managers, but his defection to a competing company was a shocking event. Reactions from the general agents and agency managers were varied, but most of them soundly disapproved of Davis' action. Thomas B. Sweeney (Wheeling) first learned of Davis' defection in mid-August when the General Agent of Penn Mutual at Wheeling received a telegram announcing Davis' move and "held a celebration." Sweeney wrote that he had been shocked earlier when he learned that President Day had had to raise Davis' salary to keep him from going over to Metropolitan, but "I am doubly shocked now at his becoming a great Equitable competitor. In fact, it is the worst blow since 1905." Sweeney had always believed that a high degree of loyalty to Equitable was a virtue to be taken for granted among its head officers: "However, it has been my experience that when a man's loyalty is such that he will even entertain offers from other companies, his usefulness is badly impaired." Though Sweeney thought that Equitable's policy of replacing general agents with agency managers had been partly to blame for Davis' action, he wrote President Parkinson: "You now certainly have a free hand and clean deck and personally I am sure you can and will steer the Equitable ship out of the shoals." [170]

169 *The Spectator*, CXXI (1928), August 9.

170 Sweeney to President Parkinson, August 14 and 18, 1928. Parkinson files, Equitable Archives.

The exodus of Equitable agents and officers to Penn Mutual was led by Alexander E. Patterson, who had been with the Edward A. Woods agency in Pittsburgh since 1908. He had served as assistant to the President of the Edward A. Woods Company and in 1921 became Secretary of the Company. January 1, 1922, he became an Agency Manager of Equitable with his office at 120 Broadway, then in 1925 took charge of the Equitable agency in Chicago. February 1928, Hugh D. Hart, Vice President of the Penn Mutual, announced the appointment of Patterson as General Agent for his company in Chicago. In view of later developments, there is a touch of irony in the usual expressions of regret on the part of both Patterson and Equitable. Said *The Spectator*: "The Equitable parts with Mr. Patterson with extreme reluctance, but with that fine amity, both toward its retiring manager and his new employer, which nowadays characterizes relations between home offices, and of which both the Equitable and the Penn Mutual are exemplars." *The Spectator*, CXX (1928), February 23. Hart and Patterson made

Just what was Davis' position in regard to the question of general agents as versus agency managers is not clear. Many believed that he favored the Agency Manager system and that he relied upon the managers as being the chief strength of the agency organization. On the other hand Sweeney, a General Agent, believed that the trend toward the Agency Manager system was one of the chief reasons for Davis' discontent, and Powell, another General Agent, was apparently his most confidential adviser. And it was some of the older general agents who were trying to bring pressure to bear to bring Davis back to Equitable four years after he left.[171]

Frank H. Davis had, for almost a decade, been a power in Equitable's agency affairs. His one big mistake had been the failure to recognize group insurance as a vitally important part of life insurance. He became Agency Vice President for Penn Mutual in 1932, and died in 1936 at the age of fifty-six.

Westfall's resignation (1926), the election of Thomas I. Parkinson as President, and the departure of Frank H. Davis and John A. Stevenson all combined to make a number of Equitable's general agents and managers uneasy.[172] Frank L. Jones, whose appointment as Agency Vice President was confirmed by the Board June 21, 1928, received his Bachelor of Arts degree from Indiana University in 1898. He taught school for several years and served as State Superintendent of Public Instruction, the youngest man to fill that position. He became an Equitable agent in 1906 and Agency Manager at Indianapolis in 1914. In 1919 he directed the instruction in life insurance to the members of the American Expeditionary Forces in France, and in 1925 was elected

---

overtures to Frank Davis and promised him the Chicago agency with the understanding that Patterson was to have a more important position.

Former Vice President J. V. E. Westfall, who had resigned in 1926, joined the procession of Equitable men to Penn Mutual in 1930. Both he and Stevenson became Vice Presidents of that company in the early 1930's.

171 In November 1932, Courtenay Barber, General Agent at Chicago, wired William M. Duff (President Edward A. Woods Company) and probably other members of the General Agency Association that Frank Davis, then in Philadelphia, was "100 per cent physically and mentally okay" and suggested that these men wire Vice President W. W. Klingman and President Parkinson that if they wanted Davis back they would have to act immediately. Duff wrote President Parkinson on November 23 that the reaction to such a move would be bad; he also wired Barber that it "would be a bad mistake to reward disloyalty and reward a fellow that washed out when we needed him." Parkinson files, Equitable Archives.

172 President Parkinson told the Executive Committee of the Board that he believed that Equitable had grounds for legal action against both Penn Mutual and Frank H. Davis. Parkinson, interview with author, June 17, 1958.

President of the National Association of Life Underwriters. As President of the Association, he played a prominent part in the founding of The American College of Life Underwriters.

Although some of the western general agents and managers were skeptical in regard to Jones' appointment—they considered him to be somewhat intellectual and "standoffish"—W. W. Klingman had written President Parkinson that Jones "stands out alone" for the position, and would measure up 100 per cent.[173]

When Jones returned from Europe in late summer, however, Klingman persuaded him that he would need help to hold the western agents in line.[174] Jones agreed, and President Parkinson brought Klingman to the Home Office as a Second Vice President (August 30) under what was apparently intended to be a temporary arrangement. In addition to his salary as Second Vice President, Klingman was permitted to retain his salary and commissions as Agency Manager at St. Paul. At the same time, Albert G. Borden, Agency Instructor, was appointed Second Vice President, and both he and Klingman were assigned to the Agency Department under the direction of Jones.[175]

Soon, however, trouble arose; not only did some of the New York managers complain of Jones, but there developed a clash of personalities between Jones and his two subordinates. Jones, who blamed Klingman for the criticism which came from the general agents, finally said that either Klingman would go or he would go. Since Klingman, who by now was considering the arrangement by which he held two positions to be a permanent one, showed no signs of leaving, Jones re-

173 Klingman to Parkinson, June 15, 1928. Frank H. Davis wrote Jones July 12 congratulating him on his Vice Presidency and expressed the friendliest feelings. Jones wrote Parkinson from London August 4 and said that though he was sorry to learn that Davis was leaving, he anticipated no adverse effects on the agency forces. Letters in Parkinson files, Equitable Archives.

174 Jones' reputation with the western agents was no doubt enhanced somewhat about two years later when he was adopted as a member of the tribe of the Ponca Indians, who occupied a reservation in Northern Oklahoma. Chief Walkinghead delivered an address, presented Jones with an Indian pipe, pouch, and leather vest, and conferred upon him the name of Wahshe-Skar, which meant "the man of knowledge." The only other living white member of the tribe was John Philip Sousa, the composer and bandmaster. *The Eastern Underwriter*, XXXI (1930), October 31.

175 In the reorganization of the Agency Department, Jones in late October announced the appointment of six agency superintendents who would cooperate with the Home Office and the field in matters affecting organization and production. They were as follows: William G. Fitting, New York Metropolitan Department; Harold C. Nolting, Southern Department; Frank B. Runyon, Home Office Department; P. L. Girault, Jr., Central Department; John T. Haviland, Eastern Department; and William M. Rothaermel, Western Department.

signed. President Parkinson, realizing that Klingman would have to be "administered" back to St. Paul, accepted Jones' resignation.[176] Then Klingman, after taking leave of the key officers, left for St. Paul. At Chicago, however, he phoned the Home Office to the effect that if "the Chief" wanted him back he was willing to return, but that he could not work with Jones. At first President Parkinson refused to call Klingman back, but soon changed his mind and did so.[177] Klingman not only remained as Second Vice President but received a new Agency Manager contract as well (January 16, 1929). In February 1929 Jones' title was changed from Agency Vice President to Vice President, but he continued to head the Agency Department. In May 1931 Klingman was appointed Vice President; in December the same year he resigned as Agency Manager at St. Paul and in February 1933 was placed in charge of the Agency Department. When Klingman became head of the Agency Department Jones was given charge of Public Relations and Advertising.[178] The appointment of Klingman as head of the Agency Department did not eliminate or solve all problems. In 1934 Thomas B. Sweeney wrote to President Parkinson: "There seems to be such a vacillating policy existing at the Home Office at present that none of us know where we stand. We are told one thing one day and the opposite the next, and this condition is not confined to any one department. All the general agents and all the managers with whom I talked, have the same feeling of uncertainty and nobody knows just where he stands to-day or what may happen next." [179]

* * *

Franklin Day, who had been Assistant Secretary-General for Europe and Assistant Secretary of the Society since 1922, was also appointed

[176] Parkinson, interview with author, June 17, 1958.

[177] The above account is based upon interviews with Vice President Harold J. Rossman, August 27, 1963, and Peggy Bruce (Mrs. Augustus Berghane), July 30, 1963. Rossman was Klingman's assistant in the Home Office and handled the phone call to President Parkinson. Peggy Bruce, as a secretary in the Agency Department, worked for Davis, Jones, Klingman, and later William J. Graham. The exact date of Klingman's departure is not known but it was either in late 1928 or early 1929.

[178] Early in 1931 when it was rumored that Klingman was going to give up his position in the Home Office and return to his agency, President Parkinson received a number of telegrams from the agents on the West Coast to the effect that this move would be detrimental to the Society's best interests. Telegrams from Kellogg Van Winkle, San Francisco, C. J. Sauter, Seattle, etc. Copies in Parkinson files, Equitable Archives.

[179] Sweeney to Parkinson, February 22, 1934. *Ibid.*

Second Vice President in 1928 and devoted most of his attention to what remained of the foreign business. The following year, Second Vice Presidents William J. Graham, Leon O. Fisher, and Robert Henderson (also Actuary) were promoted to vice presidents, and Arthur H. Reddall to Assistant Secretary of the Society.

About a year after he was elected President of Equitable, Thomas I. Parkinson was offered the presidency of The Equitable Trust Company by John D. Rockefeller and associates; the salary offered was several times that paid to the President of Equitable and assurance was given that, should Equitable Trust merge with another institution, the new President would remain as head. President Parkinson consulted with several of the more active members of the Society's Board and told them that they now had an opportunity to select a President free from any influence from Judge Day. The Board made it clear that it was well satisfied with the President already selected and thought that Equitable should endeavor to match the offer salarywise. This was all that President Parkinson wanted to know. He remained as President of Equitable with no salary increase.

More than two thousand qualified agents attended Equitable's seventieth anniversary conferences in regional meetings held in October 1929 at Washington, D.C., Del Monte, California, and Toronto, Canada. Another thousand attended the meeting in New York where, at the concluding dinner, speeches were made by Alfred Irénée duPont and Charles Evans Hughes. Hughes found the human appeal of life insurance to be unfailing and endorsed it as a safeguard of imperative human needs—"the world's best bet"—and the skill with which the business was administered justified the public's great confidence in the institution which had "wrought the maximum certainty out of life's uncertainties." Coming as they did from the man who had helped give life insurance a hard time twenty-four years earlier, these words were duly appreciated.

In 1929 Equitable's total paid-for business, including group insurance and annuities figured on an agency production basis, amounted to $1,148,824,998, the greatest volume of new business ever written by the Society in a single year. This total exceeded the amount of insurance in force at the end of the Society's first forty years.[180] But, as

[180] Group life insurance amounting to $225,118,649 was paid for during the year and total group outstanding at the end of the year was $1,357,021,904. Group Accident and Health insurance premiums increased 171 per cent and

President Parkinson pointed out, lapses were heavy—more than $300,-000,000—and the mortality ratio (61 per cent) the highest since 1920. Whereas in 1859 Equitable had offered but one type of policy—ordinary life with a limit of $5,000—it now offered more than twenty individual insurance and annuity plans for its 10,465 agents to present to the people of the United States; in addition, it offered group insurance, salary savings, bequest, and home purchase plans. Equitable's traditional policy of liberalizing its coverage and adapting its practice to changing social and economic conditions had been carried on. Extended term insurance was added to the Convertible policies, and future premiums for double indemnity benefits under policies issued prior to 1918 were reduced; the Society also began writing individual policies and annuities on the monthly premium plan. In 1926, subject to a satisfactory nonmedical questionnaire completed by the agent, new insurance within specified limits was made available to Equitable policyholders who had qualified for standard insurance on the basis of a medical examination within the preceding ten years. Three years later general nonmedical life insurance was considered for issue on a similar questionnaire completed by the agent regardless of whether the applicant had been an Equitable policyholder or had been medically examined in the past.[181]

On Equitable's seventieth birthday (July 26, 1929) total life insurance in force in the United States had reached the $100,000,000,000 mark. In September President Parkinson spoke to The National Association of Life Underwriters; his subject was: "Conserving the First While Creating the Second Hundred Billion." Later, in summarizing the year's activities to the Board of Directors, he pointed out that the high mortality rate and unstable financial conditions had combined to furnish the most stringent test of financial stability that life insurance companies had had in recent years, but he was glad to be able to report that Equitable had met the test satisfactorily. In conclusion, he said:

---

during the year this type of coverage was extended to more than 40,000 new employees. The figures are taken from President Parkinson's annual report to the Board of Directors for 1929. Corporate Records, Equitable Archives.

[181] There were certain restrictions which applied to this insurance: the applicant's town of residence and business had to be smaller than 25,000 population, the insurable ages were twenty-one to forty-five, and the amount was limited to $2,500. Married women were not eligible. It lacked the approval of the Insurance Departments in Arizona, Massachusetts, and Nebraska, and in Iowa and Oklahoma the limit was $2,000. Bulletin to Cashiers, July 9, 1929. Copy in Sterling Pierson files, Equitable Archives.

We are engaged in an enterprise, the very essence of which is co-operation, and which exists not for gain but for service. To us are entrusted the savings of countless individuals who look to us to fulfill their self-imposed obligation to provide for those who come after them. Our trust is a great and continuing one, and with your assistance we shall strive to administer it faithfully and in strict adherence to its obligations both express and implied, to the end that we may deserve the confidence of those whose interests we serve.

THE RUSSIAN CASES

In all of Equitable's legal history, there is perhaps no more complex, interesting, and significant chapter than that which deals with the Russian Cases. The litigation began in 1925; all told there were some 863 actions involving 2,900 policies with face amount of insurance of Rbls.14,450,000 or about one-half of the total amount of Equitable's outstanding Russian business (6,452 policies for face amount of Rbls. 27,170,000).[182] The plaintiffs were represented by 42 attorneys, the printed legal documents ran into thousands of pages, and the litigation continued for 19 years. Though many millions of dollars were at stake, and involved were problems of Russian law, New York law, constitutional law, and international law, the cases carried a deeper significance, for they impinged upon matters of national policy. They might also be regarded as a portent of other things to come. At least a volume would be required to do justice to the Russian Cases.

The Bolsheviks took over the Russian Government in November 1917 and soon thereafter began, step by step, to put into effect their theories that banking, industry, and insurance were exclusively functions of the State. Banks were nationalized early the following year and industry in June, but not until December was action taken in regard to life insurance. December 1, 1918, the Central Executive Committee of all Russia promulgated a decree which declared that "All kinds of insurance, such as: fire insurance, transport insurance, life insurance, accident insurance, hail insurance, cattle insurance, crop insurance, etc., are declared to be a State monopoly." The decree further stated that the reorganization of the insurance companies already existing would have to be completed before April 1, 1919. The decree was signed by "The President of the Soviet and of The Commissaries of the People, by V. Ulyanov (Lenin); Secretary, L. Fotieva."

[182] As of December 31, 1918. Memoranda, February 2 and March 3, 1926, Assistant Secretary Alexander McNeill to Assistant Secretary Franklin Day. Law Department files, Equitable Archives.

Thus, without a word of warning, the foreign life insurance companies which had done business in Russia for forty years and complied with all its laws found that the business they had created had been seized and taken over by the Soviet Government as a government monopoly. When representatives of the companies protested, the Soviet Government reminded the representatives of the Equitable, New York Life, and Urbaine, a French company, that in accordance with the conditions of the concessions granted foreign insurance companies by the Russian Government in 1885 and 1889, such companies subjected themselves to the laws existing in Russia, and that the concessions granted them might at any time be rescinded; in this event, or in the event the companies should cease to do business for any other reason, they would be liquidated on a basis prescribed by the Russian Government. It was therefore decided that the agencies and branches of the foreign companies were to be liquidated in the regular way in compliance with the decree of December 1.[183]

The committee of official liquidators, headed by one Drujinin, ousted the managers of the foreign companies, took over their offices and employees, and took possession of all records, cash, and bank deposits, as well as the bonds deposited as security for the reserves under outstanding Russian contracts. The assets thus taken over were in excess of what would have been required to reinsure the existing business, and exceeded by many millions of rubles the liabilities which Russia assumed when it converted life insurance into a state monopoly.

News of the decree of December 1, 1918, did not reach Equitable until sometime in the summer of 1919.[184]

Since no official representative of any foreign company was permitted to remain in Russia and practically no correspondence was permitted to come out, information as to what happened during the next nine months is sketchy. From the few letters which reached the Home

183 A translation of this letter of February 8, 1919, may be found in "The Soviet and Its Attitude Toward American Life Insurance Companies," a pamphlet which carries the date November 25, 1925, but no other identification. Copy in Equitable Archives.

Immediately after the decree was promulgated, Hermann Ivanovitsch Schoofs, Equitable's Manager in Russia, wrote the Russian officials and requested them not to take any decisive steps with regard to the Society's Russian office until he could get in communication with the Home Office in New York. Later, he did not recall ever having received a reply to his letter. Memorandum, prepared by Schoofs, July 10, 1928. Parkinson files, Equitable Archives.

184 Undated, unsigned typed memorandum, "Russian Business of the Equitable." *Ibid.*

Offices of the American companies it is clear, however, that the Soviet Government continued to collect premiums from the policyholders.[185] But after collecting premiums for about nine months, the Soviet Government found that the taking over of assets was more profitable and agreeable than discharging the corresponding liabilities, for November 18, 1919, it issued another decree, which read as follows:

1. All kinds of life insurance (capitals and profits, in the R.F.S.S.R.) are canceled.
2. All the contracts with life insurance companies and savings banks for life insurance, capitals and profits, are canceled.
3. All insurance premiums (premium deposits of the insured) are transferred to the Treasury benefit.
4. All work-disabled persons and minors who have been deprived of the insurance benefit by the cancelation of the contracts, in execution of Paragraph 2 of the present Decree, are entited to social protection by means of the organizations of the Commissary of the People for Labor and Social Protection, on the same basis as the other citizens.
5. By the publication of the present Decree, all anterior decrees and decisions concerning all kinds of life insurance, are rendered null and void.
6. The Commissary of the People for Finances is charged with the application of the present Decree.[186]

Again developments of the next four years are obscured because of the secrecy and controls imposed by the Soviet Government. It appears, however, that it destroyed or dissipated all the records which it had confiscated, including thousands of life insurance contracts which had been pledged with the companies as security for loans, and that it turned over the securities and money which had been confiscated to the account of the government for purposes other than the payment of insurance. Even though it became a risk to life and liberty to have a policy in one's possession, some policyholders appear to have sought collection from, or at least made inquiry of, the Soviet Government. As late as October 1923 one such policyholder was informed by the State Insurance Department that "by Decree of November 18, 1919, of the Soviet of People's Commissars, all insurance contracts made in Russia are annulled." [187]

[185] The translation of a policyholder's premium receipt may be found in "The Soviet and Its Attitude Toward American Life Insurance Companies," p. 10.

[186] A translation of the decree as published in *Izvestia* November 20, 1919, may be found in *ibid.*, p. 11. The decree was signed by V. Ulyanov (Lenin), President of the Soviet and of The Commissaries of the People.

[187] *Ibid.*, p. 16.

Before the news of the decree of November 18, 1919, reached the United States, the National Convention of Insurance Commissioners at its meeting December 2–4, 1919, took action on the decree of December 1, 1918, which confiscated the assets of the United States life insurance companies. Some weeks earlier, when the N.C.I.C. Committee on Valuation of Securities met, representatives from the American companies which were affected by the Russian decrees appeared before the Committee and explained the situation in Russia. As a result, the Committee recommended that the N.C.I.C. at its December meeting authorize the companies to exclude from their annual statements for 1919 all items of assets and liabilities "in any way relating to their business in Russia." The report of the Committee on Valuation of Securities was adopted by the N.C.I.C. at its meeting December 3. The companies would thus be protected in their statements to the insurance departments of the various states.[188]

Following the action of the N.C.I.C., the Committee on Insurance of Equitable's Board, at a special meeting December 30, discussed the effects of the Russian decree of December 1, 1918, in all of its aspects.

188 The Committee on Valuation of Securities, which met at the Hotel Astor November 17, passed the following resolution:

Whereas, This Committee has been informed by representatives of American insurance companies, formerly doing business in Russia, that all private insurance companies including the American companies have been declared by the Soviet Government to be the property of the Russian Republic, and have been forced into liquidation by such government, and

Whereas, This Committee has been informed and believes that said government in taking over the property of said companies in Russia has also assumed the liabilities of said companies in Russia, and

Whereas, This Committee is informed and believes that the contract of said companies can be enforced only in Russia, and

Whereas, This Committee is informed by the representatives of said companies that the assets and liabilities of said companies in Russia are substantially equal in amount, and

Whereas, Said companies desire that their Russian business may be eliminated in their forthcoming annual statements to be made to the various insurance departments of this country; therefore be it

Resolved, That this Committee recommend to the National Convention of Insurance Commissioners to be held in New York in December, 1919, that the American insurance companies which have been doing insurance business in Russia be authorized and permitted to exclude from their annual statements covering the transactions of the year 1919 all and every item of assets and liabilities in any way relating to their business in Russia. . . .

Proceedings of the Fifty-First Session, National Convention of Insurance Commissioners (1920), p. 11.

Then, after incorporating the resolution passed by the insurance commissioners in their resolution, the Committee recommended that the Board of Directors authorize the officers of the Society to exclude items of Russian business from its annual statement. The next day (December 31) the Executive Committee of the Board, at its regular meeting, so resolved; the resolution was not confirmed by the Board of Directors until the regular meeting of January 15, 1920.[189]

Early in 1924 the Soviet Government changed its mind in regard to the policies which it had "canceled" by the decree of November 18, 1919. Official articles and notices began to appear in *Izvestia* and advertisements in various newspapers throughout Russia. These notices announced the creation of a "Credit Bureau" to which the holders of policies in foreign life insurance companies could turn over their policies for the collection of claims. Pertinent paragraphs from one of the advertisements were as follows:

> Many of you who have at one time entrusted your savings to the foreign insurance companies, the New York Life and Equitable, have in your possession policies which even now represent a real obligation of the said companies to you.
>
> However, the said insurance companies, have under various pretexts declined to pay the amounts due under the said policies to the citizens of the Soviet Socialistic Federative Republic.
>
> Having examined the question of your claims from a legal point of view, the Credit Bureau has as aim to bring suit against foreign insurance companies under such of your policies on which claims have already been made and the right to claim has not expired, and to do whatever is required in foreign law courts in your name as your Attorney on the following conditions. . . .

Though the next paragraph stated that "the holder of the policy will not bear any expenses for bringing and carrying on the lawsuit abroad," succeeding paragraphs announced fees to cover "organization expenses," and gave the percentages which the Credit Bureau would retain in the event the suit was won.[190] Policyholders were to give a notarial power of attorney to the Credit Bureau.

Thus the Russian Government was urging its policyholders in foreign

[189] Corporate Records, Equitable Archives.

[190] The percentages ran from 25 per cent on amounts to 999 rubles to 45 per cent on amounts of 10,000 rubles.

companies to cease acting individually and "organize into a collective organization." From various articles published in *Izvestia* it became obvious that the Soviet Government was using the life insurance issue as a part of its campaign for recognition by the United States. For instance:

> Leaving the matter of arriving at an understanding with Hughes & Co. in the domain of politics, concerning such claims as the payment of the debts contracted by the Czar's Government or disbursements incurred for the support of Koltchak, Yudenich, etc., we deem it to be our business to consider the matter of insurance operations, by means of which the American bourgeoisie succeeded, since the 70's of the last century, in pumping out of Russia, through a net of agencies of such companies as "Rossia," "Equitable," etc., immense amounts of gold.

These companies "In their attempt to evade payment . . . are stepping behind all kinds of subterfuges, the substance of which is nothing but open cynicism and mockery." It was time for the Russian policyholders to speak to the "American uncle" by way of the courts: "Thus, step by step, we must follow up our demands of judicial justice, and even reach the White House, so that we might hear from the American Senate a reply to our direct demand: 'Why do you not pay on your insurance obligation?' " (Naturally the Soviet Government made no mention of its repudiation of Russian debts of billions of rubles and of insurance assets confiscated.)

The Credit Bureau also advertised its activities in Canada and in Europe. The first action against Equitable in the United States was begun in May 1925, and before the end of the year suits on some 300 policies were instituted. When Equitable sought to get evidence, Hermann Ivanovitsch Schoofs, Equitable's Manager in Russia, who had taken refuge in Paris, found it impossible to get any testimony from Russian policyholders because of the government's regulations against "commercial spying"; he could not even get certified copies of the Russian decrees and did not think it would be possible to get a list of loans made upon the Russian policies. Schoofs said that it would be worth their lives for Russians to testify or send out papers.[191] Soon

[191] Franklin Day (in Paris) to Vice President Thomas I. Parkinson ("Strictly Personal"), October 1, 1925. Parkinson files, Equitable Archives. Schoofs said that a Miss Zamarina had a list of the policy loans but doubted whether she could get it out of Russia.

after the first action was brought, Equitable retained the law firm of Davis, Polk, Wardwell, Gardiner and Reed as counsel.[192]

In 1925, one Henry Sliosberg, a nonresident alien, brought suit against the New York Life on policies taken out in Russia. The defendant moved to dismiss the complaints for lack of jurisdiction of the subject matter. The Supreme Court (New York County, Special Term) ruled July 15 that the court had jurisdiction, and denied the defendant's motion to dismiss the complaint.[193] New York Life appealed the decision, but in July 1926 the Appellate Division, First Department, affirmed the decision of the lower court.[194]

While the appeal was pending in the Sliosberg case, the New York legislature, in April 1926, amended the Civil Practice Act so as to provide a stay of action on any case involving life insurance contracts in Russia until thirty days after the recognition of the Soviet Government by the United States.[195]

Acting on the Stay Law the New York Life made an original motion in the Appellate Division, First Department, to stay the further prosecution of the action. The Appellate Division held (May 27, 1926) that the Stay Law was unconstitutional on the grounds that it impaired the obligation of contracts, deprived plaintiff of property without due process of law and violated the equal protection clause of the Fourteenth Amendment; the Court denied the motion.[196] The New York Life appealed this decision to the Court of Appeals; Charles Evans Hughes

[192] Senior partner John W. Davis, a native of West Virginia, had served as a member of Congress and had been Solicitor General in the Department of Justice, Ambassador to Great Britain, and Democratic candidate for President in 1924. His firm was one of the outstanding law firms in New York.

[193] *Sliosberg* v. *New York Life Insurance Company*, 125 Misc. 417. The Court cited as authority the case of *Sokoloff* v. *National City Bank*, February 1924 (239 N.Y. 158), in which the plaintiff had obtained judgment.

[194] 217 App. Div. 685.

[195] Laws of 1926, Chapter 232.

While the Stay Law was pending before the legislature Equitable counsel John W. Davis, and John Foster Dulles of the firm of Sullivan and Cromwell, counsel for the New York Life, sent memoranda to Governor Alfred E. Smith in which they stated arguments in favor of its enactment. Superintendent of Insurance James A. Beha also favored enactment. On the other hand counsel for Polish, Austrian, and Russian policyholders argued against the law as being special, discriminatory and unconstitutional. The act was also disapproved by the Legislative Committee of the Bar Association of the City of New York. The memoranda and letters may be found in the Governor's Bill Jacket, 1926, Chapter 232. Legislative Reference Library, The New York State Library, Albany.

[196] 217 App. Div. 67.

argued the case before the Court and John W. Davis filed a brief as *amicus curiae*. March 1, 1927, the Court of Appeals affirmed and held that the Stay Law was unconstitutional and contravened section 10 of Article I of the Constitution of the United States, which prohibited any state from passing a law impairing the obligation of contracts.[197]

Vice President Parkinson believed that the Court's decision left a path open to the life insurance companies to apply to the United States Supreme Court for a writ of certiorari for a review of the case. He thought that not enough facts had been presented to the Court to enable it to realize the real nature of the Russian business of the American life insurance companies, its termination, and the status of claims arising with respect to it; that the opinion was largely an academic essay on a general question rather than a live issue: "There is too little of the real business situation and too much of academic generality in the case. . . . You know that we never did set our principal defense on this statute. It is merely a preliminary obstacle to the Russian suits in the New York Courts. If it is ultimately found unavailable, we shall proceed with the cases involving 1) the court's taking jurisdiction, and 2) the application for stays of trial." [198]

Meanwhile, litigation against the American companies had begun in England. In 1926, when suits were filed against the New York Life, President Day asked Hermann Schoofs to go over to London from the Paris office and cooperate with the New York Life as a witness.[199] Then in April 1928 suit was begun in London on one of Equitable's

[197] 244 N. Y. 482. The Court reasoned that the Stay Law provided for a stay of actions until a certain event—the recognition of the Russian Government by the United States—which might never occur; hence it was unreasonable. The essential part of the decision read: "For all these reasons we think that the contract of insurance in suit carried with its obligations resting in the laws of the State of New York; that chapter 232 of the Laws of 1926, if it withdrew, substantially, all remedies for the enforcement of the contract, impaired an obligation of the contract which had its source and sanction in the laws of the selfsame State."

[198] Parkinson to President Day, March 10, 1927. Parkinson files, Equitable Archives.

[199] President Day to Schoofs, September 16, 1926. Day letters, Equitable Archives. Schoofs was to charge his expenses to Equitable, but the New York Life had promised to refund them. Day to Rocquet, September 17, 1926. *Ibid.*

The New York Life had about five times as much business in Russia as Equitable had. As of December 31, 1918, the New York Life had approximately 28,900 policies in force, for approximately Rbls.134,900,000. Secretary Alexander McNeill to Assistant Secretary Franklin Day, Memoranda, February 2 and March 3, 1926. Law Department files, Equitable Archives.

Russian policies. Hearings in this case (*Perry* v. *Equitable Life Assurance Society of the United States of America*) began in March 1929, and thirty-five days later, April 29, the King's Bench Division in London rendered its decision. The Court held that the law of contract applying was Russian, and that the effect of the Soviet legislation was that the "contract between plaintiff and defendant was annulled by the cancellation decree if, indeed, there was any contractual nexus left in existence between them after the monopolization decree came into force." The Court went on to state that had the plaintiff been entitled to his Rbls. 10,000, he would have been paid in 1922-pattern paper rubles, the value of which, in any stable currency, was nominal.[200]

In 1929 two actions were brought against Equitable (Supreme Court, New York, First Judicial District) by one G. Frank Dougherty. The defendant interposed several affirmative defenses in which it contended: 1) the Russian decree had resulted in the substitution of the liquidating commission of the Soviet Government in place of the defendant in respect of its Russian policies; 2) plaintiff had failed to comply with certain provisions—that is, he had paid premiums not to the insurance company but to the Soviet Commission; 3) plaintiff could not maintain his action because his policies provided that all lawsuits were subject to the St. Petersburg courts of justice; 4) the contract was frustrated by superior force; and 5) the plaintiff was outside of Russia at the time the defendant's obligation under the policy arose and, by Russian decree, it was illegal to transfer moneys from Russia on account of any transaction made in Russia, without the consent of the government, and such consent had not been obtained. Plaintiff moved to strike out the defenses, and defendant challenged the sufficiency of the complaint.

The Court upheld Equitable in all sections of its defense and granted the motion to dismiss the complaint for failure to allege performance of conditions precedent. Judge Salvatore A. Cotillo said that the "plaintiff's motions to strike out as legally insufficient the affirmative defenses not only admit, for the purposes hereof, the truth of the allegations of such defenses, but also bring into question the sufficiency of the complaints which defendant now challenges." Judge Cotillo further stated that the plaintiff failed to aver that he was ready, willing, and able to perform the conditions which it was alleged the defendant by its act had prevented or waived; that the plaintiff should not be per-

[200] 45 *Times Law Reports* 368, King's Bench (1929).

mitted to enforce a Russian policy, written against Russian assets, at the expense of American policyholders, who had no recourse to that fund; and that the act of the Russian Government, in taking over the life insurance business of the defendant, was binding upon the plaintiff. He thought that the courts of New York might well decline to assume jurisdiction in cases of this kind, owing to the policy clause which provided that all disputes should be settled according to Russian laws and in Russian courts. In rendering his decision, Judge Cotillo denied the applicability of the decisions in the *Sliosberg* and *Sokoloff* cases to this case.[201]

On appeal (Appellate Division, First Department) the Court, in December 1929, reversed the orders of the lower court; plaintiff's motions to strike out Equitable's defenses were granted and defendant's motion to dismiss the complaint was denied on the ground that all the questions presented upon these appeals had been fully adjudicated and established favorably to the contention of the appellant by decisions of the Appellate Division and of the Court of Appeals in the *Sliosberg* and *Sokoloff* cases; consequently, none of the said questions could be regarded as being open.[202]

The following year (1930), it was agreed between Equitable and the firm of attorneys most active in promoting the suits against the Society that certain representative cases should be selected by each side and tried before a referee. A total of 26 cases, involving 27 Russian policies, were agreed upon (*Dougherty, and Others,* v. *Equitable Life Assurance Society*) and the referee selected was William S. Andrews, a former judge of the Court of Appeals.[203] Hearings began December 8 and continued for twenty days during December 1930 and January 1931, and eight days were spent in supplementary hearings in January 1932. Some idea of the work involved in preparation for the reference

[201] The decision was handed down October 8, 1929. *Dougherty* v. *Equitable Life Assurance Society,* 135 Misc. 103.

[202] 228 App. Div. 624.

[203] Judge Andrews' term as an Associate Judge of the Court of Appeals expired December 31, 1928, by force of a provision of the State Constitution (Article 6, Section 12) which prohibits a judge from holding office "longer than until and including the last day of December next after he shall be seventy years of age." It appears that Judge Andrews qualified as "Official Referee" pursuant to Section 115-a of the Judicial Law by reason of his former election to and service in the Court of Appeals and was assigned as "Official Referee" for service in the Supreme Court, New York County. An "Official Referee" has the same power and authority as a Justice of the Supreme Court, pursuant to Section 117 of the Judicial Law and Section 469 of the Civil Practice Act.

may be had from the size of the record and the number of citations and exhibits brought before the referee. The record contained 4,480 pages, and there were about 1,800 pages of the opinion, findings, and conclusions. Plaintiffs' citations numbered 777, of which 141 were Russian decisions and statutes; defendant's citations numbered 751, of which 105 were Russian decisions and statutes. Plaintiffs' general exhibits numbered 176, of which 136 were Russian, and defendant's exhibits numbered 227, of which 127 were Russian. Defendant retained Professor A. N. Sack, expert on Soviet and Russian law, to assist in preparation of the cases and to furnish testimony; Dr. S. Konkevitch, a former Russian lawyer, was engaged to assist Professor Sack. Boris Brasol, another former Russian lawyer, was engaged to collect and translate Russian documents, and Dr. H. Freund was employed as an expert on Soviet law.

The actions were brought for various purposes—for damages, for rescission and restitution, for specific performance, and for collection of amounts agreed on in the face of the policy. The great majority of the actions, however, were for rescission and recovery, with interest, of the premiums paid, and were predicated upon the defendant's repudiation of its obligations under the policies. This group was known as the restitution cases. The most important issue was whether Equitable was relieved of liability under the Russian policies by reason of the Soviet decrees, and if not, the measure of liability, the currency in which such liability should be determined, and the value of such currency in United States dollars. But involved were many subsidiary issues and points of law: were the plaintiffs in good standing when the actions were begun?; was action taken within the limits of the statutes of limitations (Russian and New York)?; was the policy contract ambulatory and unilateral or localized and reciprocal?; did it include the "rules" or "pravila"?; did the policy contracts bear Equitable's official seal?; which law applied, Russian or New York?; and so forth.

First, in regard to the statutes of limitations: the New York law for contracts not under seal specified six years and for those under seal twenty years. The Russian law provided ten years for both kinds of contracts. The New York limit began to run from the date when the cause of action accrued. If the cause of action was Equitable's writing off of its policies, then some of the actions would not fall within the six-year limit. Although ninety of the policies involved bore the wafer with the imprint of Equitable's Statue Group and the inscription "Equitable Life Assurance Society of the United States in New York.

Chief Management for the Russian Empire" defense counsel maintained that this was not the corporate seal of the Society. While counsel for the plaintiffs maintained that the Soviet laws of either liquidation or cancellation could not receive any recognition in the American courts since they were the acts of an unrecognized government, it argued, nevertheless, that so far as the Russian statute of limitations was concerned, this Imperial statute could no longer apply because it had been repealed by the Soviet Government.

Both plaintiffs and defendants agreed that the insurance contract was the important thing. Counsel for the plaintiffs maintained that Equitable, by writing off the Russian business, had repudiated upon the policy contract; this repudiation was "explicit," "wanton," "brutal," "deliberate," and "wholesale"; also "frivolous." Equitable counsel held that there never was a repudiation of the contract by Equitable, but that it came to an end "by causes over which we had no control; and we say there being no repudiation at all, necessarily the adjectives that accompanied the qualification of this repudiation fall with the noun to which they were attached."[204] Further, it denied that the contract was ambulatory and unilateral and firmly maintained that it was strictly localized (in Russia) and contained "reciprocal covenants necessary to keep it in force and mutual obligations on the part of the company and the assured. . . . The contract must stand as a whole, as it is written, or fall all together." It was not in the power of any court to write a new contract, and it was out of this contract and no other that the right of the plaintiffs to recover must arise.

According to the policy contract, all disputes which might arise were to be settled according to Russian law in Russian courts of justice. Plaintiffs' counsel emphasized, however, that the policy rules or "Pravila" also made the contract an ambulatory one—that is, one that could be enforced in New York or elsewhere—and cited the following: "That the exact fulfillment of the obligations entered into by the Society regarding the Russian assured shall be guaranteed, besides its sums and security found in Russia, by all the property belonging to the Society." [205] Defense insisted that there was nothing in that clause which

[204] John W. Davis' "Summation" before the Referee, January 1932, pp. 3147–48. Typed copy, Law Department files, Equitable Archives.

[205] Pursuant to the statute of July 7, 1890, which granted Equitable permission to enter Russia, the Minister of the Interior adopted and published certain policy rules which were to be inserted in and become a part of each policy. These rules were modified from time to time.

modified the strictly localized character of the mutual covenants of the contract. Equitable never denied that if its Russian assets were insufficient it would be bound by this rule, but since the Russian obligations were more than covered by the Society's Russian assets and these assets had been confiscated, it was impossible for Equitable to be guilty of nonperformance of its obligations in Russia.

Plaintiffs minimized the effect of the Russian decrees and seemed to argue as if nothing had happened in Russia to affect the terms of the contract. John W. Davis pointed out that things had happened in 1918–19 and were continuing to happen; these things were "real happenings" and not just "rumors of some unhappy far-off event." Not only had the contracts been overridden by superior force but were they still valid they would be payable in currency so depreciated that the average policy would not be worth a postage stamp.[206] And if plaintiffs had grounds for recovery, what were they entitled to receive?

> What could they possibly get except the premium reserve as it was when the contract came to an end? What more could they get without doing violence to the contract they made . . . with every other policyholder in this company, that they would be a mutual contributor to the expense and the risks of carrying on the business? Give them their premiums as if nothing had occurred here? Give them interest on their premiums from the time they were first returned? Permit them, having joined in this mutual enterprise, to march out of it as if they had never put their names to an application or become a policyholder?

In reply to the plaintiffs' argument that Equitable was not relieved from its obligations simply because the Soviet Government had seized its assets, Davis stated that defense had not claimed that it was. Many other conditions affected the contract: "If these conditions do not

[206] Davis said that every student of comparative law realized that certain great concepts of fundamental justice ran with practically no distinction through the laws of every people civilized and savage: "One of those concepts which I think you will find in the law of even the most unenlightened, is that when men have agreed to do something, and some superior force comes in and prevents it, the relationship between one another after that time is not of a contract breaker and contract demander, but that of people who have suffered by a common misfortune beyond the power of either one to relieve. That is basic in the law. You will find it in the civil law and in the Roman Law, and in the codes of every country, and you will find it in the Russian Law, and you will find it recognized in the State of New York and in every Anglo-Saxon jurisdiction." John W. Davis' "Summation," pp. 3216–17.

justify us in pleading impossibility of performing this contract which I have described and analyzed, in the name of high heaven, what conditions could?" As for the argument that since the United States had not recognized the Soviet Government the nationalization of insurance was not an act of government within the recognized principles of international law, and that the cancellation of the contract by the Soviet decree was not a release from the contract, Davis replied:

But as a matter of fact and of dominant force, can there be any doubt what its effect was? Was not that dominant force operating to expel us, not only from the contractual relationship but from the covenanted contact with the assured, expelling the assured from their covenant and contract with us, robbing us of the power to do the multiplied things which, by this contract we covenanted with the assured we would do, and robbing him of the power to do the things which he covenanted on his part he would do. Does it make any difference, so far as that particular defense is concerned, whether the Soviet Government is recognized or unrecognized? [207]

The Referee called attention to the fact that many of the plaintiffs were residents and citizens of Russia and apparently remained citizens even after they emigrated.[208] He then asked Davis whether the Russian decrees were effective regarding its own citizens, even though the United States sometimes did not recognize the decrees of the Soviet Government as affecting nonresidents. Davis replied that so far as he knew there was no binding law to guide a court in this matter; laws of a recognized government were honored as a matter of comity, but when it came to an unrecognized government, "We rely upon the political department for guidance." There was no reason why the courts should not recognize such laws:

I have no doubt that the courts have a perfect right in point of judicial power to accept the decrees of the Soviet Government as fact and to

[207] *Ibid.*, p. 3241.

[208] Some of the policyholders who had brought actions against Equitable were residents of Estonia, Courland, Livonia, and Lithuania, which had been established as separate sovereignties by the Treaty of Versailles and the governments of which had been recognized by the United States. Former Russian citizens residing in these countries became citizens thereof. Poland also became an independent nation whose government was recognized by the United States. By decree of the Soviet Government, Russian citizens who emigrated to another country lost their Russian citizenship.

regulate the rights of parties, so far as those decrees apply to them, by the language of the decrees themselves.

I do not think we can continue the ostrich policy, if I may call it that, of saying, here is a government which we know is in existence, and which we know is potentially a master of its territory, which we know is recognized by all the governments of the world, almost without exception, except ourselves, but we are absolutely ignorant of its existence. Although its codes of law are brought before us, although the decisions of the courts are here, we find them no more intelligible, no more cogent, than if it had been issued by the Grand Lama of Tibet. It is a position which seems to be intellectually impossible.[209]

Davis did not understand how a citizen of Russia, subject to its laws, could come to the United States and say: " 'Just forget all about what my government has done, and do not treat it as having any power over me, because you have not recognized it.' " He was not certain that the courts, in these Russian cases, would ever reach "a judicial status or a body of opinion which will stand, until we open our eyes to the facts and treat this government as what it is, the master of almost one-third of the inhabitable surface of the globe." [210]

One other point should be noted, and that is at what date were the policy contracts terminated by events beyond Equitable's control? [211] Although Davis thought that logically November 18, 1919 (the cancellation decree) would be the date to accept, he adopted December 31, 1919 (the date Equitable wrote off its Russian business) as the date to be considered. If plaintiffs were entitled to recovery, it would be from that date. Then, as mentioned previously, the question was, recovery in what? Much of the testimony, and a sizable part of the defendant's brief, dealt with the history and value of the Russian currency after 1917. In fact, Equitable counsel, William C. Cannon, in his summation before the Referee, went back to the first issue of paper money about 1768. After the devaluation of 1841—at a rate of 3½

[209] John W. Davis' "Summation," pp. 3245–46.

[210] *Ibid.*, pp. 3247–48.

[211] Chronology was further confused by the fact that Russia did not change from the Julian calendar to the Gregorian until January 1, 1918, by which time thirteen days were gained. Since Equitable had issued no new policies in Russia after the beginning of World War I in 1914, all the Russian policies were dated under the Julian calendar. Prior to January 1, 1918, all dates used in the hearings referred to the Julian calendar. All obligations maturing after July 1, 1918, under the Julian calendar, matured on the same date under the Gregorian calendar.

old rubles to one new ruble—the circulating currency consisted of "State Credit Notes," which were legal tender and continued to be used after the Soviet Government came to power. These legal tender notes were the money of Russia at the time when the Russian policies had been issued, and up to 1914 the ruble was valued at about 51 cents. But after it came into power, the Soviet Government began issuing printing press money in vast quantities, so that the ruble became worthless. Then in 1924 the government, in order to give its money an exchange value, created the chervonetz bank notes (one chervonetz was worth ten rubles) and a new issue of state treasury notes; only the latter were legal tender. The new treasury notes had a ratio of equivalence of one ruble to 50,000,000,000 rubles of pre-1922 pattern. All other currency was withdrawn and the new rubles, on a supposed gold basis, again became worth 51 cents in United States money. Plaintiffs claimed that all previous obligations, even those created in 1918 and previously, were payable "ruble for ruble" in the new gold currency—the chervonetz ruble. In other words, a policy which the day before the creation of the chervonetz bank notes was worthless, the next day was to be valued at rubles worth 51 cents each. Defense claimed that only the new treasury notes were legal tender and that by the law which created them the ratio was one to 50,000,000,000 of the pre-1922 notes, and that "the liability should be in what the person who is called upon to perform his contract by the payment of money, should pay to discharge liability, under the law of the land; and if there are two legal tender currencies, he ought to be able to present either legal tender currency, and there should not be any option about it. . . ."[212]

Referee Andrews rendered 69 "General Findings of Fact" and 23 "General Conclusions of Law." Among the former the following were most important: the words "Russian credit currency" used in the "Pravila" of 1890 and subsequent amendments thereto meant the bank notes circulating at the time and which were legal tender (No. 9); the seal used on the policies was not the corporate seal of the defendant (No. 12); during the two weeks in which Equitable's Manager, Hermann Schoofs, remained in the Society's office at St. Petersburg after December 1, 1918, he had been prevented "by superior force" from collecting

[212] John W. Davis' "Summation," p. 3274.
The currency situation in Russia 1917–24 was, if possible, more confusing than that in Germany during the same period. Despite the expert testimony of Professor A. N. Sack, the citation of various cases, and considerable mathematical calculation, it is not at all certain that the Court understood the situation.

any premiums or transacting any business (No. 20); an agent of the Soviet Government did, for a time, collect premiums but paid no claims (No. 25); after December 1, 1918, no claims of any of the plaintiffs against the defendant could be prosecuted in any Russian court (No. 30); transfer of money from Russia without the consent of the government had been prohibited by both the Kerensky and Soviet governments, and in none of the cases had such consent been obtained (No. 31); some of the plaintiffs had emigrated from Russia and thus, by decree of the Soviet Government, had lost their Russian citizenship (No. 32); in none of the cases, excepting one, had notice of rescission or cancellation of the policy been given by the defendant to any policyholder (No. 40); under the Russian law, if, because of superior force, a debtor was prevented from paying his debt in Russia, and a creditor was prevented from receiving the same, no cause of action arose in Russia because of the failure to make payment there (No. 61); under the Russian law, "where payment of a debt when due may be made there in currency which has become worthless, no action in Russia to recover that debt may be maintained" (No. 63); under the Russian law, in actions brought to recover the consideration paid on a contract illegally canceled, interest ran from the date when such consideration was paid (No. 64); no definite impossibility of performance existed with regard to these insurance contracts, nor was failure to perform them due to irresistible force or inavertible events, nor were they frustrated (No. 67). Conclusions Nos. 42 to 57 cited the depreciation of the ruble from the old Imperial ruble based upon gold or silver to the time when this ruble, as well as the rubles issued by the Soviet Government, became practically worthless both in St. Petersburg and New York.

It is likely that both plaintiffs and defendant would agree with Referee Andrews' general conclusion No. 68: "Each of the cases before me are difficult and extraordinary."

The most important "General Conclusions of Law" were: no decrees of the Russian Government, including those of December 1, 1918, and November 18, 1919, were a defense to any of the actions (Nos. 1–5); no rule as to superior force, frustration, etc., was a defense (No. 6); no action of the Soviet Government made the performance of these contracts by the defendant impossible (No. 7); the courts of New York had jurisdiction in all of these actions (No. 9); failure to give notices in regard to death or survivorship or to pay premiums after December 1, 1918, furnished no defense (No. 13); in each of the actions for insurance, stipulated ruble values were to be taken as of the date of the maturity of the policies, their value in St. Petersburg to be measured in dollars in New York (No. 14); in the actions for return of premiums with interest, the ruble values of these items were to be taken as of the date when the insured received notice of the rescission by the defendant of the various contracts (No. 15); "the rescission of these various contracts by the defendant was without just cause and was illegal" (No. 16); in each of the actions based on rescission, plaintiffs were entitled to 6 per cent interest from the date when the premiums were paid (Nos. 18 and 19).

The Supreme Court, New York County, in its opinion February 3, and supplemental opinion June 11, 1932, awarded judgment to the plaintiffs in nineteen of the restitution cases. The remaining cases of this group were dismissed together with some of the actions for recovery of the insurance stipulated, upon the ground of the Statute of Limitations or failure on the part of the plaintiffs to perform conditions precedent contained in the policies.[213] Judgment was entered in the office of the clerk of the County of New York July 26.

During the ensuing months, much discussion followed as to the status of the Russian Government. When Secretary of State Henry L. Stimson was asked if the United States had recognized the Soviet Government as "*de jure*," "*de facto*," or as a government "of paramount force," he replied that the United States had not recognized the Russian Government at all. Sterling Pierson, Equitable General Solicitor, consulted John Bassett Moore, Equitable Director and the United States' leading expert in international law. Moore's reply was of interest not only for its bearing upon the matter under discussion but for its reflections upon the policies of former President Woodrow Wilson. He wrote:

> I observe in the letter of Evarts, Choate, Sherman and Leon separate inquiries as to whether the Soviet regime has been recognized as a "government *de jure*," or as a "government *de facto*." This sorry lingo was introduced into our discussions in consequence of Wilson's unconscious revival of a distinction that naturally prevailed in the days when governments were classed as legitimate and illegitimate, and none were considered by *jure divino* rulers as legitimate except those that existed *jure divino*. In the old days when this theory prevailed the arbiter to whom the world deferred was God; but, under the dispensation introduced in 1913, the powers of

[213] 144 Misc. 363.

the Almighty were assumed by Woodrow Wilson; and his successors in the presidency, loth to relinquish this exalted function, have humbly but proudly followed him, although damning him, or at least intending to do so, on all other matters. It certainly is the extreme of absurdity even to intimate that only a government *de jure*, i.e., a government existing by the divine right of the Almighty at the head of the government of the United States, is capable of making laws or decrees, or of performing other acts which the courts in the United States may recognize and enforce.[214]

Equitable appealed from the judgment of the Supreme Court on the nineteen above-mentioned actions, and plaintiffs appealed from the judgment on the seven other actions. The Appellate Division, First Department, handed down its decision June 30, 1933. Judge James O'Malley, after agreeing in the main with the conclusions reached by Referee Andrews, stated that though some members of the Court as then constituted were not wholly in accord with the decision rendered by the Appellate Division in December 1929 (228 App. Div. 624), the Court was of the unanimous opinion that it must adhere to the view as then expressed, especially as that view had been adopted by the Referee and made the basis of an important part of his decision. The Court affirmed the judgments in favor of the plaintiffs and reversed those in favor of the defendant. Equitable was thus held liable on all of the policies at the rate of 51 cents to the ruble.[215] In October 1933 the Appellate Division granted motions for leave to appeal to the Court of Appeals.[216]

[214] John Bassett Moore to Sterling Pierson, October 13, 1932. Sterling Pierson files, Equitable Archives. See also John Bassett Moore, "The New Isolation," in the *American Journal of International Law*, XXVII (1933), October.

Moore had served as Assistant Secretary of State, Counselor of the Department of State, and Judge on the Permanent Court of International Justice, 1921–28; for many years he was a member of the Permanent Court of Arbitration, The Hague. Best known of his numerous scholarly works were *History and Digest of International Arbitration* (6 volumes, 1898) and *Digest of International Law* (8 volumes, 1906).

[215] 238 App. Div. 696.

June 9, 1933, John W. Davis wrote Presiding Justice Edward R. Finch and called the Court's attention to its unanimous decision rendered June 5 in the case of *Gilbert* v. *New York Life Insurance Company*. In this decision, the Court had held that even in a case of repudiation there could not be a recovery of the premiums paid. The letter apparently had no effect and the Court found the issue in the *Gilbert* case not to be the same as in the *Dougherty* case. Davis to Finch, June 9, 1933. Sterling Pierson files, Equitable Archives.

[216] 240 App. Div. 812.

The Roosevelt administration officially recognized the government of Russia November 16, 1933, and John W. Davis had his doubts as to whether Equitable could win its Russian Cases on appeal. At a conference in Davis' office, the New York Life, which had several times as much at stake as Equitable, declared its intention of compromising and urged Equitable to do likewise. But President Parkinson had decided that Equitable had a case and determined not to be sidetracked; he was supported in this stand by Allan McCulloch of Alexander and Green, and by James H. McIntosh (formerly legal counsel for the New York Life) of the same firm.[217]

Even before Russia was officially recognized, Equitable counsel was calling the attention of the State Department to the fact that, while New York courts were awarding Russian policyholders' claims in 51-cent rubles, the Equitable had claims against Russia which should, in justice, be paid in rubles of the same value. As Allen Wardwell, of the firm of Davis, Polk, Wardwell, Gardiner and Reed, wrote Assistant Secretary of State J. Walton Moore: "If this rate is to be exacted by Russian policy holders from an American insurer, it would seem only fair that the insurer itself should have recourse against the Soviet Government for the value of its securities and property confiscated in Russia at the same rate of 51 cents to the ruble." He agreed with the words of Judge Coleman in the recent case of *State of Russia* v. *Bankers Trust Company* when he said that to allow a sovereign to sue for its property and yet avoid a counterclaim for the defendant's property, was too much like tying the defendant's hands and letting the plaintiff go through his pockets.[218] And November 10 Sterling Pierson wrote Secretary of State Cordell Hull and submitted additional information in regard to Equitable's Russian business for consideration in connection with the negotiations then taking place between the Government of the United States and the Soviet Government. After reviewing the various decrees which confiscated Equitable's assets and canceled the policies, Pierson called attention to the fact that by reason of the decision of the Ap-

[217] As a result of opinion of counsel dated April 8, 1920, the New York Life had admitted liability on the former Russian policies held by persons in the new states carved out of Russia, but continued to deny liability on the "so-called Soviet Russian policies." The non-Soviet Russian cases were compromised in 1928. Vice President Walter Buckner of the New York Life to President Thomas I. Parkinson, October 24, 1930. Sterling Pierson files, Equitable Archives. This letter contained the counsel opinion of April 8, 1920.

[218] Allen Wardwell to J. Walton Moore, November 6, 1933. *Ibid.*

pellate Division of the New York Supreme Court, Equitable was now liable in 51-cent rubles on all the policies covered in the cases:

As will be seen from the foregoing statements the Society has sustained loss or damage attributable solely to the acts of the Soviet Government and its authorized representatives. We therefore respectfully request that in any action taken by the Government of the United States for the protection of the Society's interests due consideration be given not only to the taking over of the Society's property in Russia by the Soviet Government, but also to the liability which the Society has thus far been held by our courts to be under by reason of the legislative and administrative acts of the Soviet Government, and may hereafter be held to be under in other cases.[219]

When John Bassett Moore was again consulted, this time in regard to the defendant's brief before the Court of Appeals, he held that the fundamental question appeared to be that of the law by which the contract and its performance were governed. If the contracts had previously been legally annulled by the Russian Government, it seemed strange that the subsequent action of the Equitable Board should have furnished the basis for a recovery beyond the liability, if any, to which annulment of the contract by the Russian Government may have left the company subject. As to the effect of recognition of the Russian Government, he wrote:

If we were preparing an argument *de novo* I suppose that we should select the points decided against us on the ground that the Russian decrees were to be treated by us as invalid, or internationally invalid, because the United States had not "recognized" the Russian Government, and then treat these as having been determined in our favor by the recent formal act of recognition. If the case were put in this way I do not at the moment know just what the residuum would be. In this order of treatment I suppose the question of impossibility of performance would naturally precede the discussion of the effects of the formal recognition. Probably all the points are covered in one way or another in the present draft of the argument. It strikes me as important that no contention heretofore made that the Russian Government had been sufficiently recognized for all judicial purposes should be abandoned. Such an abandonment would imply that heretofore we had been wrong, or at any rate in doubt, as to the soundness of our contentions. . . .[220]

[219] Sterling Pierson to Cordell Hull, November 10, 1933. *Ibid.*
[220] John Bassett Moore to Sterling Pierson, February 16, 1934. *Ibid.*

A few weeks later, after the Court of Appeals in the case of *The Vladikavkazsky Railway Company* v. *The New York Trust Company* decided that recognition of a *de facto* government as a *de jure* government was retroactive in effect and validated all the acts of that government from its beginning, Moore was not certain that this opinion represented the views of Chief Judge Cuthbert W. Pound, who would likely be presiding when Equitable's appeal came up.[221] Then in April he wrote:

> As regards the Russian matter . . . the effect of the recent so-called recognition of the Soviet Government eliminates a question of controversy, and gives us the benefit of our contention that the Soviet Government should be treated by our courts as a government in the fullest sense. Whatever benefit could be derived from that contention we now undoubtedly have, and the benefit is very substantial in that the court cannot decide against us simply upon the ground that the Soviet Government is not to be treated as a government because it has not been formally recognized. But the way has already been opened for an adverse decision on two other grounds, the first being that the contract is a New York contract, and the second that the court will not give effect to Russian laws and decrees because they are contrary to our "policy." [222]

The case of G. Frank Dougherty and Others, Plaintiffs-Respondents, against The Equitable Life Assurance Society of the United States, Defendant-Appellant, was argued before the Court of Appeals on November 22, 1934. The record on appeal comprised 11 volumes (5,822 pages). The brief for the defendant-appellant ran to 323 printed pages, the appendix to the brief was 180 pages long, and the defendant's reply brief added 182 pages.[223] The opinion of the Court was read by Judge Frederick E. Crane (who had been elected Chief Judge November 6) on December 31, 1934.

Judge Crane stated that the first question in the case was the effect which recognition of the Soviet Republic by the United States had on the laws of the Soviet Republic passed in 1918 and 1919; the second question related to the valuation of the ruble after 1924, to

221 John Bassett Moore to Sterling Pierson, March 6, 1934. *Ibid.*
222 John Bassett Moore to Sterling Pierson, April 21, 1934. *Ibid.*
223 Equitable was still represented by Davis, Polk, Wardwell, Gardiner and Reed, with John W. Davis, William C. Cannon, and David E. Hudson serving as active counsel. Attorneys for the plaintiffs-respondents were Engelhard, Pollak, Pitcher and Stern.

be paid under contracts made prior to 1918. After emphasizing that the obligation of the insurance contracts was governed by Russian law, he said that the plaintiffs had read these contracts as if Equitable had said that if the Russian law would not give them relief, it would guarantee the continuance of the policy and of the Society's obligations in spite of Russian law; that is, as if the contract were to be governed by New York law: "There is no such contract." Judge Crane then reviewed the findings of the Referee in the lower court in regard to the Russian decrees. He said:

> In Russia, where all these insured were, with one or two exceptions, these decrees were laws to be obeyed. They were the laws of their government. As to them the Soviet Republic was no body of bandits, confiscating property, but an existing government, carrying out new theories of insurance. If the Russian people, under their Soviet form of government, determined to abolish all private insurance for their citizens and establish a system of social protection by the State, that was their affair, not ours, and however objectionable we may consider the monopolization of all business, including insurance and banking, and the conduct of it thereafter by the government, we at least must admit that other peoples can try the experiment if they desire.

The Referee's conclusions, having been made prior to recognition of the Soviet Government, would have to be modified, for recognition was retroactive in effect and validated all the actions of the government from its beginning. After citing numerous cases both English and American, Judge Crane stated that recognition did not compel American courts to give effect to foreign laws if they were contrary to our public policy, but it could not be against the public policy of New York to hold nationals to the contracts which they had made in their own country to be performed there according to the laws of that country: "Our conclusion, therefore, is that, since recognition, the Soviet decrees became the laws of Russia, governing the policies here in question, and that obligations thereunder were at an end."

There remained only the question of currency. Judge Crane failed to discover in the Referee's findings of fact any statement that pre-existing obligations in Russia were to be paid in 1924 in the chervonetz gold ruble note, ruble for ruble. He held that the plaintiffs could only recover when they showed that by the law of Soviet Russia pre-existing obligations were to be paid "ruble for ruble" in the new chervonetz

A CENTURY OF GROWTH

LIFE INSURANCE IN FORCE

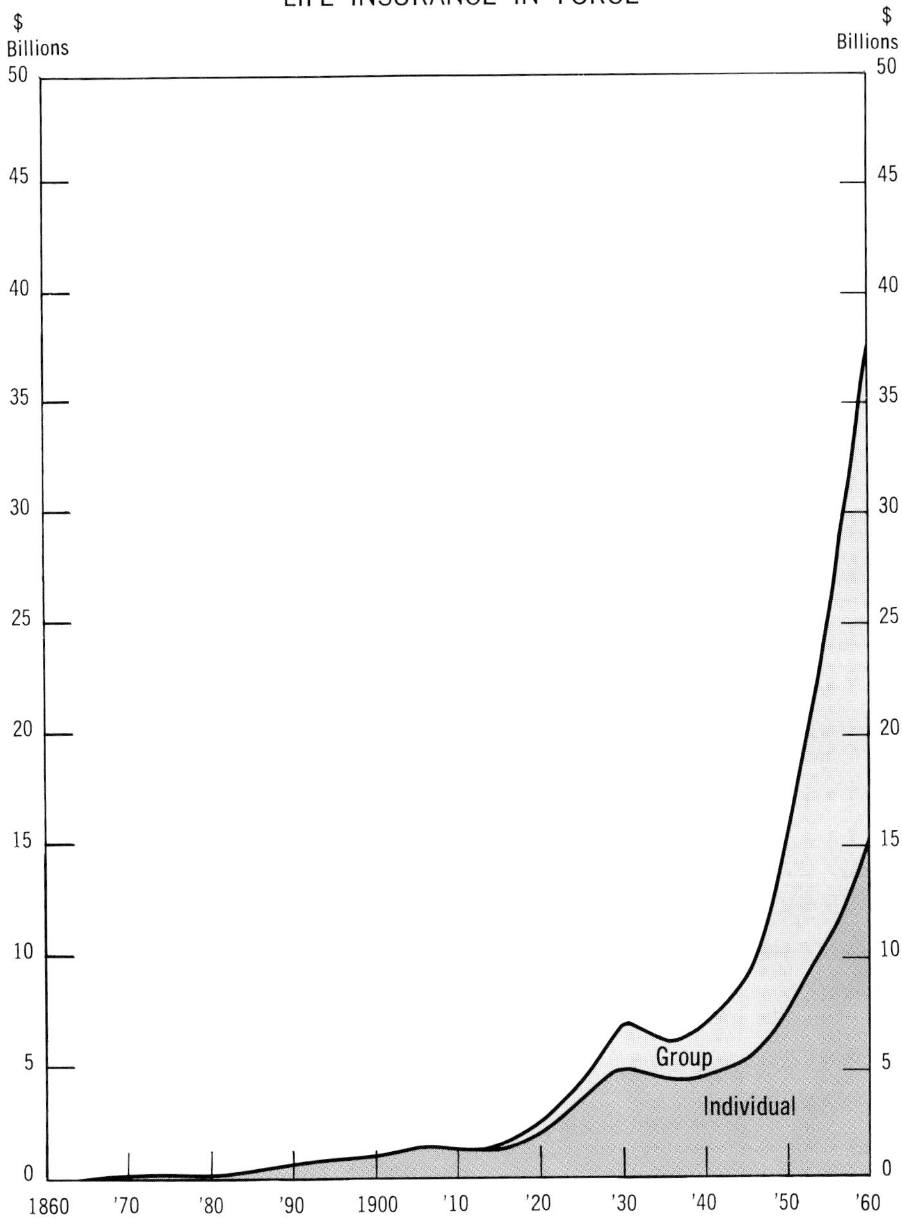

Individual life insurance in force more than trebled in the twenty years following the depression-ridden 1930's. But group insurance grew even faster, equaling the volume of individual life insurance in force in less than forty years from the date of its introduction by The Equitable in 1912.

A CENTURY OF GROWTH

ADMITTED ASSETS

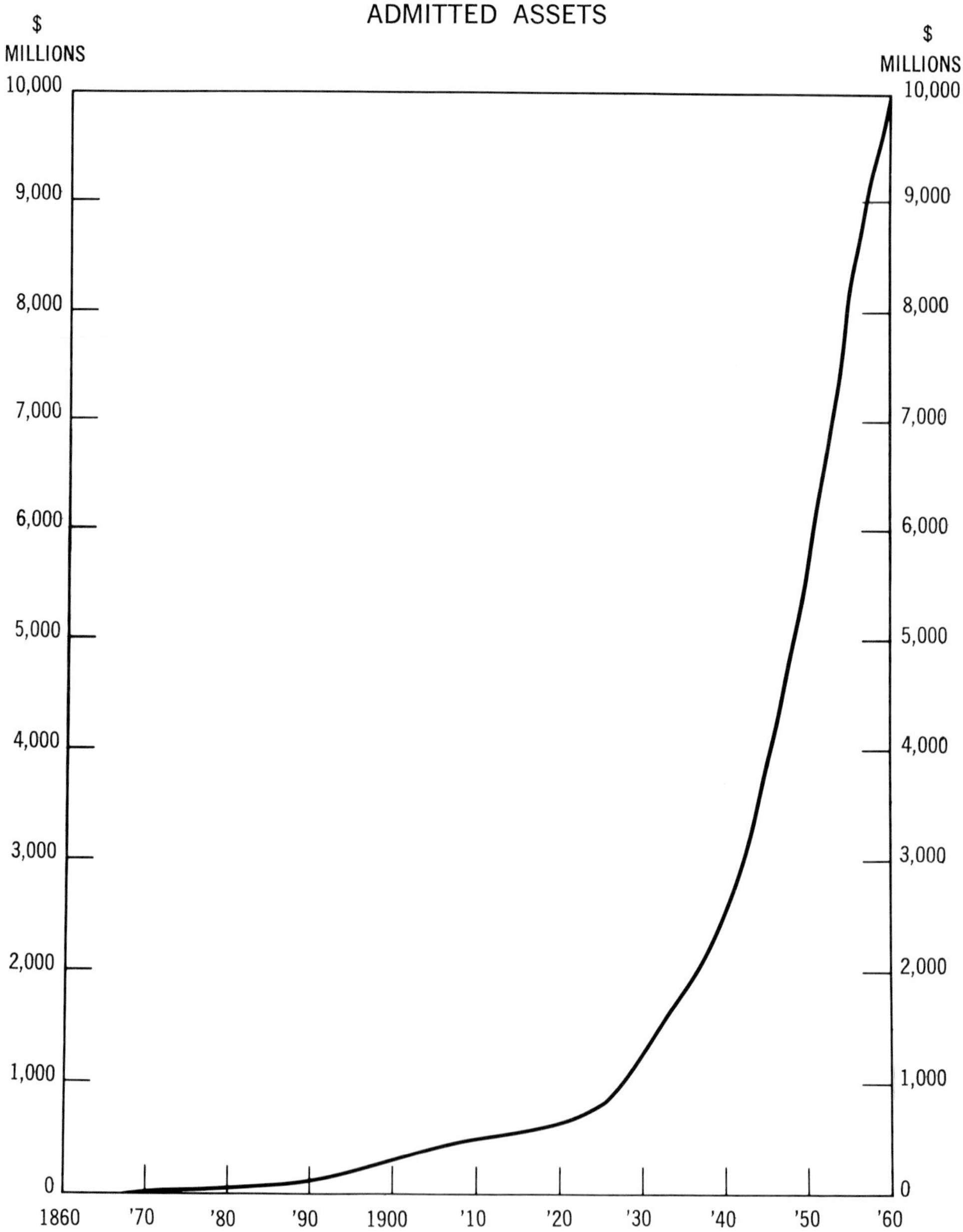

It took fifty years for The Equitable's Admitted Assets to reach $500 million and nearly seventy years to reach $1 billion, but only a little over thirty years more to reach $10 billion.

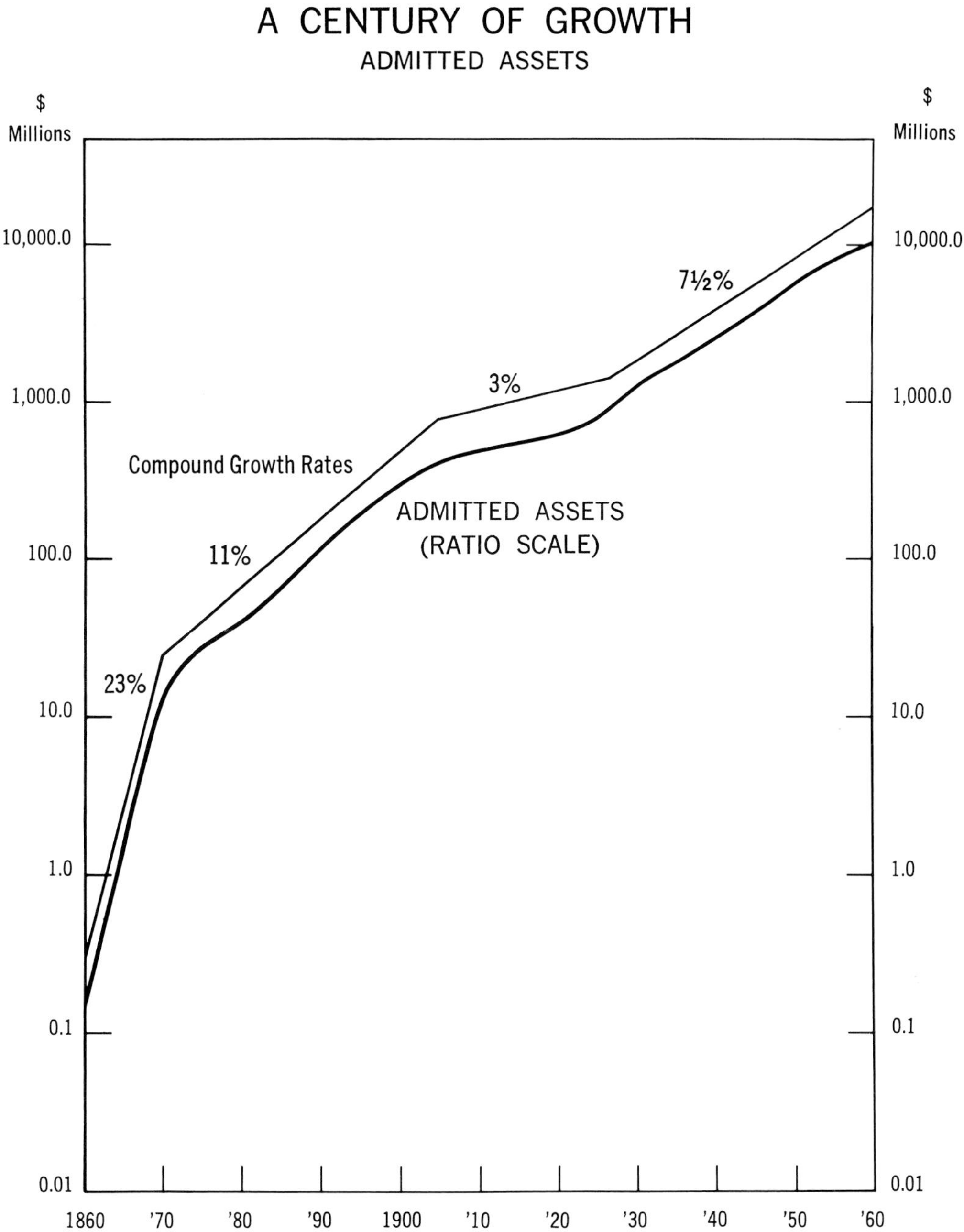

Growth rates are better observed on this chart of Admitted Assets plotted on a ratio scale. Four distinct periods are observed: Very rapid growth when the company was small; slower growth, but still extremely favorable by present standards, during the last quarter of the nineteenth century; much slower growth during and following the Armstrong investigation; and favorable growth during the second quarter of the twentieth century.

A CENTURY OF GROWTH

TOTAL RECEIPTS AND DISBURSEMENTS

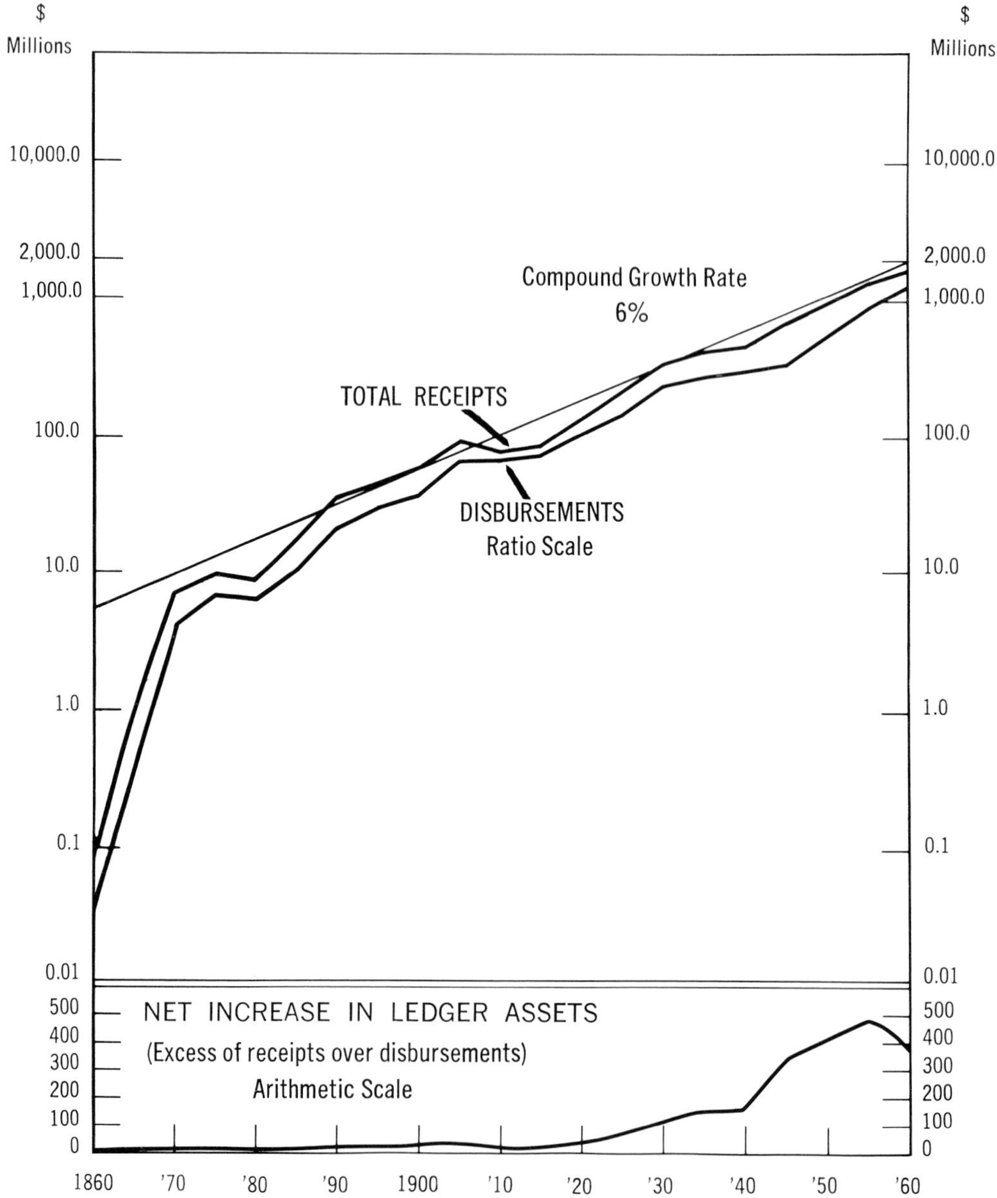

For most of the century Receipts and Disbursements, shown here on ratio scale, grew at a compound rate of about six percent. The spread between the two (which is equal to the net increase in Ledger Assets shown at the bottom of the chart) narrowed briefly following the Armstrong investigation and again in recent years because of heavy disbursements on Annuities.

gold note. Judge Crane concluded: "For the reasons here expressed we are of the opinion that, even taking the plaintiffs' view of these cases, they cannot recover. The ruble which they could recover is valueless; they at least have not proved its value in the present Russian currency. . . . The judgment of the lower courts should therefore be reversed, and the complaints dismissed, with costs in all courts." [224]

Judges Pound, O'Brien, Hobbs, and Crouch concurred in the opinion of Chief Judge Crane, and Judge Lehman submitted a separate concurring opinion with which Judge Loughran concurred.[225]

President Parkinson was well pleased with the decision. January 3 he wrote: "I read the opinions last night and I think they are clean-cut and complete." [226] Letters of congratulation began to come in. James H. McIntosh of the firm of Alexander and Green wrote:

> When I first heard of the decision of the Court of Appeals in the Russian Case I was so excited that I called you on the telephone because I wanted to congratulate you. Just now I have finished reading the Court's opinions. Of course I like Crane's opinion better than I do Lehman's but they both reach the same result, which is the thing we want. This is a victory, personal to you, which should give you joy and satisfaction for life. It took a lot of nerve to stand up as you did against influence the other way, and face the responsibility of a defeat when defeat was coming to you at every turn of the road, including the hearing before a referee who had been a Judge of the Court of Appeals. The Equitable owes you vastly more than it ever can pay, and those of us who like a man with a back bone owe you a lot too. Nothing that has happened in a long time has given me so much satisfaction, and I am only sorry that my old Company, which I shall of course have a life long interest in, made the mistake of settling the cases, thinking, of course, when they did so that they were doing the best for the policyholders.[227]

[224] Judge Crane agreed with the findings of the Referee in regard to the seven cases decided in favor of the defendant and added: "As there could be no recovery in any of these cases under our decision, we need not enter into a discussion of the individual facts." Literally speaking then, the judgment of the "lower courts," in this instance the Supreme Court, was not reversed as it applied to these seven cases.

[225] 266 N.Y. 71.

The opinion was separately published as a pamphlet, "Opinion, Court of Appeals of the State of New York, No. 582."

[226] Thomas I. Parkinson to David E. Hudson, Office of the Solicitor General, Washington, D.C., January 3, 1935. Parkinson files, Equitable Archives.

[227] James H. McIntosh to President Thomas I. Parkinson, January 16, 1935.

Thus once again Equitable fought through to a finish what it considered to be the right in the protection of its policyholders. In reply to McIntosh, President Parkinson wrote: "I realized the responsibility involved in pushing these cases to a final decision and there were times when that realization rested heavily on my nerves, but on the whole, it always seemed the best way to dispose of the issue which had arisen between our general policyholders and a special group claiming still to be policyholders and entitled to performance out of our general funds." [228]

Neither the newspapers nor the insurance journals paid much attention to the decision of the Court of Appeals. The *Novoye Russkoye Slovo* (New York), however, unburdened itself of a critical editorial. It said that New York's highest court had "suddenly and ruthlessly reversed itself" and that no one who had read the decision could accept the grounds on which it had done so. By way of explanation, the editor endeavored to show that only after recognition of the Soviet Government did American judiciary agencies learn of the role of the "double-faced Janus," the Credit Bureau, and its aim to make money out of the claims of the policyholders against the American companies. Thus the cases were decided upon psychological rather then judicial grounds. The editor blamed the Court for failing to distinguish between the majority of claimants, Russian residents who presented their claims through the Credit Bureau, and the minority policyholders, the Russian emigrés who had presented their claims independently: "The decision of the highest court of the State of New York has deprived thousands of Soviet citizens, as well as the Russian emigrés scattered all over the globe, of their hope to ever justly recover even a part of their hard-earned savings which in their time they had turned over to the American insurance companies. The lawyers who represented the interests of the policyholders in the cases have wasted ten years of labor, and the spending of great effort, time and money has turned out to be of no avail and useless." [229]

Reactions to the decision in the *Dougherty* case from the law

[228] Thomas I. Parkinson to James H. McIntosh, January 18, 1935. *Ibid.* President Parkinson in this letter recalled the support which McIntosh and Allan McCulloh had given him in that conference in John W. Davis' office, "in which our New York Life friends declared their intention to compromise and urged us to do likewise. I often feel and at moments like this I express concern over compromising and its effects on the mettle of the Bar."

[229] *Novoye Russkoye Slovo*, February 4, 1935. Copy, with translation, in Sterling Pierson files, Equitable Archives.

journals were not entirely favorable. The reviewer in the *Fordham Law Review* thought the decision rested upon unsatisfactory premises and added that it was all the more surprising when read in conjunction with that given in the *Sliosberg* case: "That case established the fact that independent of Soviet law, the law of New York had recognized the existence of these contracts and had given them the stamp of its approval and protection. Therefore it cannot be denied that the instant case made effective in New York the Soviet decrees which of their own vigor could have had no adequate jurisdiction or power to compel the cancellation of obligations enforceable by New York law." The reviewer said, however, that the decision was understandable since "the Equitable is a mutual company, and to have granted the plaintiffs' claims would have forced the American policyholders to make good the losses occasioned by a Russian revolution, for the sole benefit of former Russians." [230] The reviewer in the *Columbia Law Review* was mostly interested in the question of whether recognition of the Soviet Government gave retroactive effect to decrees made prior to recognition. He did not believe that such decrees should be treated differently before and after recognition. He believed, however, that "the exhaustive findings in the *Dougherty* case as to the worthlessness of the rubles in which the duty to pay could be discharged will probably be respected in future litigation. . . ." [231]

The writer in the *University of Pennsylvania Law Review* was even more critical. After noting that it was Russian law rather than American law which applied in the cases, he concluded that "the majority opinion is long and labored":

> The real significance of the decision can be appreciated only by noting the specific question involved, and how it had been answered by earlier cases. The debatable question was whether the usual conflict of law rules, turning on place of making, place of performance, or intent, should be applied where their application would require the court to give effect to a foreign decree confiscating or destroying a person's chose in action, without giving him any reasonable compensation therefor. After all, such a decree is not only shockingly different from the common law and statutory law of the United States, but even conflicts with its constitutional law. The real force of this "shock" to the judicial mind is revealed by the cases, for, in almost every case in which an American or English court was called upon to give effect to such a decree, but in which either the law of the place

[230] 4 *Fordham Law Review* 333 (May 1935).
[231] 35 *Columbia Law Review* 292 (February 1935).

of making or that of the place of performance would permit recovery, it was allowed. The instant case is the first involving a foreign decree of confiscation in which the law of neither place would permit recovery, so that its decision represents a significant contribution to the law of cases involving this type of decree. Of much deeper significance, however, is the fact that this decision represents a real triumph by a court over national provincialism. Such provincialism had manifested itself in other conflict of laws decisions, and might well have prevailed in so extreme a case as this one.[232]

Paralleling the *Dougherty* case to a certain extent was the case of *Nisel A. Goldberg-Rudkowsky* v. *The Equitable Life Assurance Society of the United States.*[233] Goldberg-Rudkowsky in 1932 sued to recover the surrender value on two endowment policies, one issued in 1902 and the other in 1905. At the trial before the Supreme Court, New York County, in November 1932, the plaintiff's second cause of action was amended from a demand for the surrender value to a demand for the value of a reduced paid-up policy. The Court dismissed the first cause of action (on the 1902 policy) on the ground that it was barred by the New York six-year Statute of Limitations but ruled that by the terms of the policy contract the plaintiff was automatically entitled to the proceeds of a reduced paid-up policy on the 1905 policy.[234]

Cross-appeals were filed by both plaintiff and defendant and on June 30, 1933, the Appellate Division, First Department, affirmed the judgment of the trial court in all respects; this decision was predicated upon the law as applied by the Referee in *Dougherty* v. *Equitable.*[235]

When the case was appealed to the Court of Appeals, that Court, December 31, 1934—the same date as the decision in the *Dougherty* case—affirmed the judgment appealed from by the plaintiff and reversed the judgment appealed from by the defendant.[236] February 25,

[232] 83 *University of Pennsylvania Law Review* 917 (May 1935).

[233] The plaintiff, under questioning by his counsel, admitted that he was also known as "Nisson A. Goldberg-Rudkowsky," "Nisel Aizikovitch Goldberg-Rudkovski," and "Nikolai Issakovitch Goldberg-Rudkovski." Equitable's counsel stipulated that the two policies in question were issued to "Nisel Aizikovitch (Nikolai Issakovitch) Goldberg-Rudkovski." Questioned about his occupation in Petrograd, the plaintiff stated that he had been the proprietor of a spaghetti factory.

[234] 145 Misc. 765.

[235] 238 App. Div. 704.

[236] 266 N.Y. 451.

1935, both Dougherty and Goldberg-Rudkowsky petitioned the Court of Appeals for reargument of their cases, but the motion was denied March 5.[237] Goldberg-Rudkowsky petitioned the Supreme Court of the United States for a writ of certiorari to the Court of Appeals of New York. October 14, 1935, the Supreme Court denied the petition.[238]

Although the remnants of the Russian Cases dragged on for several more years, the rest of the story is anticlimax. As a result of the judgments of the two lower courts, 46 liens had been filed against real estate owned by Equitable; one of these liens was in the Goldberg-Rudkowsky case, 19 were in the test cases (judgment of the Supreme Court); and 26 were in the test cases for cost (judgments of the Appellate Division). After the judgment of the Court of Appeals was filed, these liens were removed.[239] There remained the expenses of the litigation, which were considerable. Printing costs were $22,028, court stenographer's fees $11,780, and miscellaneous disbursements amounted to $22,894. Fees to Professor Sack and the other Russian experts totaled $42,022.92, and the Referee's fee was $30,000.[240] From 1925 through March 1935, Equitable had paid $140,000 counsel fees and, after several months of negotiation, in December 1935 paid John W. Davis' firm an additional $500,000; further services in actions brought in the Municipal Court of the City of New York, City Court of the City of New York, Supreme Court of Queens County, Supreme Court of New York County, and the United States District Court for the Southern District of New York, from October 1935 to October 1944, added $125,174 to the bill.[241] Offsetting these expenses were judgments rendered in the lower courts to the amount of $245,000 and, had the decision gone against Equitable, liabilities on the Russian policies to the extent of a possible $28,000,000.[242]

As noted above, numerous actions continued to be brought in vari-

237 266 N.Y. 615.

238 296 U.S. 583.

239 Davis, Polk, Wardwell, Gardiner and Reed to Sterling Pierson, May 29, 1935. Sterling Pierson files, Equitable Archives.

240 Secretary Alexander McNeill, typescript memoranda dated March 27, 1935. Copy in *ibid.*

241 Minutes of the Executive Committee, Equitable Board of Directors, various dates from February 4, 1925, to November 15, 1944. Corporate Records, Equitable Archives.

242 The figure used is that named by President Thomas I. Parkinson in his unofficial remarks to the Board of Directors, July 20, 1944. Equitable Archives.

ous New York and United States courts. Neither Equitable nor John W. Davis' firm seemed to be certain as to the number of actions which were pending at any one time. August 5, 1937, William H. Mathers —who in March 1938 became Superintendent of the Foreign Bureau —estimated that 262 actions (1,121 policies) were being continued and that 266 actions (326 policies) were likely to be dropped. Yet four days later Davis' firm reported that there were 470 actions pending which involved 1,114 policies: "161 actions . . . will be disposed of between now and October 1st, leaving 310 actions pending. I believe that before January 1, 1938, we will be able to discontinue another 200 actions . . . , which will leave pending about 110 actions on January 1, 1938." But Mathers reported that 353 actions (906 policies) were still pending December 31 and that 235 actions (774 policies) were still pending January 11, 1938; he expected, however, that more than 100 of these would be discontinued within a few weeks.[243] Many of the discontinuances occurred when plaintiffs failed to file complaints, while others resulted from the inability of attorneys to get replies to letters written to their clients; then, since most of the plaintiffs were nonresidents of the United States, Equitable could demand security for costs from them while the suits were in process.

In September 1941 President Parkinson reported to the Executive Committee of the Board of Directors that only 89 actions remained out of a total of 850; these actions involved 467 policies. Getting dismissal of these remaining actions was difficult because "the attorneys were in most instances adventurers, to say the least. They held on with the hope that they might get something." One attorney, however, claimed that with the help of his father-in-law, a distinguished professor at Harvard Law School, he had developed a new theory of liability by which it would be possible to recover for the plaintiffs in 83 of the actions, despite the decision of the Court of Appeals.[244] "Only by gentle pressure—pressure enough to bring them to an issue but not enough to blow the lid off," could these cases be disposed of, and that pressure was continually being applied by John

[243] Two folders on the remaining Russian cases as of January 11, 1938, are in the Sterling Pierson files, and additional folders of correspondence and lists of actions discontinued, etc., during the period February 1937–May 1940 are in the Law Department files. Both in Equitable Archives.

[244] It was at this point in his informal remarks to the Executive Committee that President Parkinson said: "It is an interesting picture with these damn lawyers —excuse me! There are some lawyers around—I am still one myself!" Unofficial remarks to the Executive Committee, September 3, 1941. Equitable Archives.

W. Davis and Sterling Pierson. As late as 1944, however, some of the cases were kept alive by this new theory, and, rather than run the risk and expense of another trial, President Parkinson recommended that they be compromised for $15,000: "This will wind up the cases and bring down upon us the final bill of John W. Davis." [245] In summarizing the Russian Cases at this time, President Parkinson contrasted Equitable's experience with that of the New York Life, which he said had paid out $12,000,000 before the Court of Appeals decision was handed down. Though the decision saved that company several times as much money as it saved Equitable, Equitable received no thanks for the fight which it had made.[246]

In 1950 James Tillman, one of the attorneys involved in the cases years earlier, called at the Home Office with an idea which he thought might be mutually advantageous to himself and Equitable. He said that by a supplementary agreement to the treaty of recognition of Russia in 1933, the United States was authorized to utilize Russian funds impounded in the United States at the time of World War I, to satisfy the claims of the Government as well as of American citizens against the Imperial Russian Government. He thought that as an American citizen and as an assignee under Russian policies covering other than Russian nationals, the 1933 agreement ran to his benefit; also that Equitable had a justifiable claim in connection with loans which the Society had made to some of the insureds under the policies on which he held assignments. After talking the matter over with Secretary McNeill and William H. Mathers, Associate Counsel Leo D. Fitzgerald informed Tillman that no action along the lines suggested was indicated.[247]

Public Law 285, 84th Congress, approved August 5, 1955, authorized

[245] Thomas I. Parkinson, unofficial remarks to the Board of Directors, July 20, 1944. *Ibid.*

Involved in the compromise were 83 actions, representing 310 Russian policies. Equitable had moved to dismiss the complaints in one of these cases and the Supreme Court had granted the motion, but the Appellate Division, First Department, had reversed the judgment and ordered the case to trial. Both the Appellate Division and the Court of Appeals refused to grant Equitable leave to appeal, although the decision seemed to conflict with the law as laid down by the Court of Appeals in the earlier Russian cases. When counsel for the plaintiffs agreed to accept $15,000 in full settlement of the claims involved in these policies, the Board of Directors of Equitable, July 20, 1944, authorized the payment. Minutes of the Board of Directors, Corporate Records, Equitable Archives.

[246] Thomas I. Parkinson, unofficial remarks to the Board of Directors, July 20, 1944. Equitable Archives.

[247] Memorandum, Harry Pike to Fitzgerald, January 13, 1950, and letter, Fitzgerald to Tillman, January 16, 1950. Law Department files, Equitable Archives.

the Foreign Claims Settlement Commission of the United States to receive and determine the validity and amounts of claims of United States nationals against Russian nationals and the Soviet Government. The funds to be used to discharge these claims were those mentioned in the "Litvinov Assignment," negotiated at the time of the recognition of the Soviet Government. The deadline for presentation of such claims was March 31, 1956. The question arose whether it was advisable for Equitable to file a claim as a result of the confiscation of the Society's assets in Russia by the decrees of 1918 and 1919. Since, after relief from liability on the Russian policies, the Society's loss was a small one, it decided not to present a claim. If it had, and was successful in obtaining an award, it might have imposed an obligation on the Society to turn over the amount of the award to its former Russian policyholders, a task which would have been virtually impossible to accomplish.[248]

Letters and inquiries in regard to the Russian policies continued to come in for thirty years; they came from all over the world—from policyholders, friends, relatives, insurance companies, Equitable cashiers, and the Department of Justice. To all, Equitable replied somewhat as follows:

> All of the policies issued in Russia had to be issued under and subject to the laws and regulations of Russia. These laws required that the entire reserves on Russian policies be maintained there and that all premiums due thereon as well as all sums payable thereunder be made in rubles in Russia. The Russian government in 1918 issued a Decree in pursuance of which that government undertook the liquidation of the Society's entire business in Russia. As a result of this Decree, the Russian government took over all the reserves of these policies and, in addition, other assets which the Society was required to maintain there. By this action the Russian government assumed all obligations under these policies.
>
> Since that time, several suits were brought in this country against insurance companies on Russian policies. The Courts of the State of New York, after consideration of this matter, have absolved the Society of all liability in connection with its Russian policies.
>
> Our records also indicate that this policy was the subject of a suit against the Society, which suit was subsequently dismissed.
>
> In view of the foregoing there is no liability upon the Society in this matter and it is regretted that we cannot be of service.[249]

[248] Memorandum, Solomon Klinger, Assistant Counsel, to Vice President and Counsel Leo D. Fitzgerald, March 1, 1956. *Ibid.*

[249] Correspondence in *ibid.*

11

Depression Decade

A free country is as strong as its currency, and a people remain free only so long as their savings and capital are represented by a sound currency. . . . The first step to the disappearance of civil liberties and total regimentation is the dissolution of the national financial structure.—Thomas I. Parkinson, 1948

My life is a failure if the purchasing value of the dollar in which The Equitable policies are paid decreases to the point where the policyholder and his beneficiaries cannot possibly get the things for which he bought those policies.—Thomas I. Parkinson, 1946

In 1927 when Thomas I. Parkinson was elected President of Equitable, Director Joy Morton said to him: "You have a tough time ahead of you. Your problems will be as difficult to solve as any which a President of the Equitable has faced."[1] Perhaps no one realized at the time how true those words were to prove. Few could have anticipated the clash of ideas, of men, and of institutions, as well as the demands of political leaders for universal government-supported security under the guise of "social legislation." How the Equitable faced the challenges of the 1930's and 1940's, and how its solutions of such challenges would affect its competitive position in the late 1950's and 1960's when one-man leadership gave place to organized and skillful professional management will constitute the substance of the remaining chapters of this history.

The booming twenties came to an end with the great stock market crash of October 1929. Despite the prevailing "new era" economics which had discarded many of the old rules, these rules appeared still to be in effect. Speculation on thin margins, mortgaging the future too heavily and too far ahead, and the desire "to eat the cake and have it too" led to the usual consequences. Then there was the economic

[1] Joy Morton to President Thomas I. Parkinson, quoted in *The Eastern Underwriter*, XXXIX (1938), February 25.

incidence of World War I, the most destructive war which the world had yet known. Though government officials and many leaders in the industrial and financial world endeavored to minimize the seriousness of the situation, the fact was that the United States was entering upon one of the major depressions of its history. It was to be a trying time for life insurance—the most trying since the 1870's.

The stock market crash did not seriously affect life insurance sales for about six months, but it did affect the mortality ratio and the demand for policy loans, which had already begun to increase a year earlier. Equitable's ratio of actual to expected mortality increased from 58.36 per cent in 1928 to 61.02 per cent in 1929, the highest of any year since 1920; policy loans of the large Eastern companies increased some 60 per cent in 1929. Looming also was the problem of farm mortgages and loans on urban property. At the year's end, however, President Parkinson agreed with most life insurance company presidents that the stock market crash had emphasized the importance of life insurance and would have a constructive effect on life insurance sales; people who had suffered financial losses would begin to realize more than before that life insurance was the stabilizer, an important anchor to windward against a wide and disquieting hysteria.

Early in 1930, Secretary of Agriculture Arthur M. Hyde asked the life insurance companies not to stiffen their requirements on farm loans. The officers of life insurance companies believed that Washington officials were unduly exercised over the apparent scarcity of funds for agriculture. One life company Vice President, who was also Vice President of a Joint Stock Land Bank, said that the farmer had been well supplied with cheap money, which "in many instances had not gone to farm betterment but for purchasing luxuries which might have been left unpurchased." [2] And A. A. Zinn, President of the Mortgage Bankers Association of America, said that there was plenty of money to lend on properly valued, well-organized farms: "But the banker is not going to loan to speculative farmers, or to farmers who are not managing or developing their farms to the highest point of efficiency." [3]

[2] Charles W. Gold, Vice President of the Jefferson Standard Life Insurance Company and President of the American Life Convention 1929–30, to Manager Byron K. Elliott, February 13, 1930. Correspondence files, American Life Convention.

[3] In his address to the Mortgage Bankers Association of America in Chicago, February 7, 1930. Quoted in the *Chicago Journal of Commerce*, February 8, 1930.

One result of the depression was the large increase in disability claims; as unemployment increased, more and more people seemed to become permanently disabled and claimed the benefits provided for under the terms of their contracts, including not only the waiver of premiums, but monthly incomes as well.[4] During the period 1929 to 1933 the volume of disability claims doubled. Although Equitable increased disability premium rates on new policies about 50 per cent in July 1930, losses continued to accumulate and as a result the Society discontinued writing disability income as an appendage to life insurance policies in 1934, a move which had already been taken by a number of other life insurance companies. Another matter of some concern was the increased mortality among the larger risks as a result of post-crash suicides. As early as 1930 the Federal Government was being presented with pleas for unemployment insurance and old-age pension schemes.

In 1930, Equitable's ordinary life business declined about 1.4 per cent as compared with the preceding year, but the new individual annuity business showed an increase of 15.3 per cent. Though lapses and surrenders were heavy, funds left on deposit by policyholders to be administered in accordance with various contractual options increased. Total insurance in force reached a new high of $7,118,735,000. Great as had been the material contributions which life insurance made, President Parkinson thought that it had rendered an even more fundamental service:

> It has helped to preserve the faith of our people in individual thrift. In the days of widespread prosperity the funds of millions who for the first time found themselves the possessors of surplus earnings were attracted to new types of so-called thrift plans the promoters of which held out alluring prospects of high returns speedily to be realized. During the past year participants in many of these plans have seen the institutions to which they entrusted their funds weaken and in many instances go out of existence. Under such circumstances it was not unnatural that many of those who suffered losses should feel that they would have been better off had they

[4] To the unemployed the establishment of a disability income not only offered a partial solution to financial problems and prevented the lapse of insurance, but also provided the unemployed person with a psychological justification for his inability to secure employment. To the unemployed nearing retirement age a disability claim which could continue for life provided a convenient substitute for an old-age pension.

spent their money when they had it, and that in the future it would not be worth their while to undergo the self-denial connected with any plan for systematic saving. To such individuals life insurance has given a forceful illustration of the fact that there is one plan for orderly thrift which is worth while and can be depended upon in any emergency. To many who might otherwise have despaired of hereafter accomplishing any useful purpose by thrift, life insurance has been a sentinel which from place to place has given assurance that all is well with the proper type of thrift.[5]

In 1931 Equitable's business really began to show the effects of the depression. Sales of individual and group life insurance exclusive of annuities dropped to $767,466,695, or more than $274,000,000 less than in 1929; total insurance in force at the year-end was $7,090,962,853. Assets of the Society at the end of the year were $1,400,232,748 and the average net rate earned on total investments was 5.14 per cent. Taxes, however, had increased by nearly $200,000 during the year—about equally divided between Federal taxes and state taxes—and numerous proposals were pending in both Washington and the state capitals for additional taxes. This fact led President Parkinson to devote a portion of his annual report to a discussion of the taxation of mutual life insurance companies. He pointed out that while life insurance was making a substantial contribution to the realization of the fundamental purposes of government, government seemed to overlook this fact when it chose to levy upon the funds of life insurance policyholders. He said:

Perhaps they fail to appreciate the effect of their tax measures, and if this be so, it is possible that we who administer the funds of our policyholders are partly to blame. By this I mean, first, that we have failed to educate our policyholders and the public to an understanding of the effect of such taxes, and second, that by emphasizing the enormous size of our enterprises we have given the impression that they were a legitimate object of heavy taxation. In either case it behooves all of us to clarify the public's point of view with respect to this matter in order that it may be made clear that the volume of our business is no indication that there are profits accruing from it similar to the earnings of the ordinary corporation, and furthermore that a tax laid upon a mutual life insurance company is in reality a direct tax upon the policyholder and hence upon individual thrift. If we exert some effort in this direction perhaps it may come to pass that we will some

[5] Annual report to the Board, February 19, 1931. Corporate Records, Equitable Archives.

day be regarded as entitled to the same favorable treatment for tax purposes which other co-operative institutions of thrift such as savings banks and building and loan associations now enjoy.[6]

As the weeks and months went by, the hoped-for recovery in the nation's economy did not materialize. Time and again the stock market staged a false recovery, then sank still lower. Unemployment increased to some 14,000,000 persons and, though there was plenty of credit available for the use of productive enterprise, few desired to use it. The ebullient and rampant optimism of the late 1920's had gone into reverse and instead prevailed a Stygian gloom; people were now certain that what had gone down would never go back up; some even thought that the system of private enterprise—perhaps even the United States—was breathing its last. By midsummer 1932 the total value of all stocks listed on the New York Stock Exchange was less than one-fifth of the 1929 listed value. The Dow-Jones Averages on industrial shares had fallen from 381 to 41. Stocks of some sound companies were selling for less per share than the pro rata of cash and government bonds held by the companies. Bond prices also declined and many bonds, including municipals, were in default; the railroads were particularly hard hit. Many banks, including some of the Federal Land Banks, brought pressure to bear upon debtors to borrow on or surrender their life insurance policies in order to reduce their bank loans. As a result, some of the life insurance companies had to sell their highest quality bonds, and the bond market declined still further. The "Farmers' Holiday" movement in a few of the western states received widespread publicity, and the agitation for moratorium measures increased; even Federal Government agencies granted "moratoria" on certain types of loans and urged that financial institutions treat their debtors likewise. Individuals saw foreign governments forgiven their debts without apparent loss of self-respect and began to feel that they were entitled to similar leniency. The idea gained ground that, since the life insurance companies had assets of billions of dollars, they were in a position to sacrifice the income therefrom whenever it became inconvenient for the debtors to pay. Then some of the life insurance companies, in the endeavor to strengthen their records for new business or because of heavy policy loans and cash surrenders, announced that they would treat as new business, and pay commissions on, policies

[6] *Ibid.*, February 18, 1932.

issued by them to replace policies already on their books.[7] Such "self twisting" not only redounded to the policyholder's detriment, but encouraged a practice which the business of life insurance had long sought to discourage.

To make matters worse, 1932 was a national election year and, like the Presidential elections of 1840, 1876, and 1896, that of 1932 was devoted largely to the discussion of causes of and remedies for the depression. As was generally true throughout our history up to this time, the platforms of the two major parties contained no fundamental differences; both accepted the republican form of government, division of powers between states and central government, the bill of rights, and the institution of private property. The differences were largely in degree, not in kind. The Republican platform defended the tariff law of 1930 and promised to support any plan to raise agricultural prices which was "economically sound and workable"; it pledged continuance of the gold standard and the stabilization of commodity prices. The Democratic party, "believing that a party platform is a covenant with the people to be faithfully kept by the party when entrusted with power," advocated an immediate and drastic reduction in government expenditures by abolishing useless commissions and offices and eliminating extravagance to accomplish the saving of not less than 25 per cent in the cost of Federal government; maintaining the national credit by a Federal budget annually balanced; "a sound currency to be preserved at all hazards"; extension of Federal credit to the states for unemployment relief; unemployment and old-age insurance under state laws; handling of farm mortgages through a reorganized farm bank system; protection of the investing public through the regulation of interstate holding companies and the securities and commodities markets; the removal of government from all fields of private enterprise except where necessary; and repeal of the Eighteenth Amendment.

The Socialist party platform called for a Federal appropriation of

[7] Some companies, in the endeavor to help out hard-pressed policyholders, had been replacing policies which had loans on them with new policies for the face amount of the old policies less the loan, and had been paying first year and renewal commissions, at a somewhat reduced rate, to the agents on the rewritten business. Second Vice President Albert G. Borden prepared a pamphlet, "The Mortgaged Policy," which supplied agents with arguments to use against policyholders who wished to replace their policies for this purpose. Borden and Vice President Klingman were much opposed to "paying our agents commissions for 'twisting' our own business." Borden memorandum to President Parkinson, September 30, 1932. Sterling Pierson files, Equitable Archives.

$5,000,000,000 for immediate relief of unemployment, and another $5,000,000,000 for public works, slum clearances, and homes for workers, to be promoted by Federal, state, and municipal government; a minimum wage and a six-hour day and five-day week without reduction in pay; compulsory government unemployment insurance, old-age pensions, and health and maternity insurance; laws facilitating the organization of labor unions; steeply increased inheritance taxes and income taxes in the upper brackets; and a two-year moratorium on foreclosures or tax sales of homes and farms.

With two such excellent major party platforms and two candidates pledging themselves to economy, efficient administration, and sound money, it appeared that the country could not go far wrong with either. Two things discussed in the campaign, however, were of particular concern to the business of life insurance. First, considerable anxiety was created in the public mind in regard to the financial position of the life insurance companies. Statements were circulated to the effect that many of them would have been insolvent had they not been aided by loans from the Reconstruction Finance Corporation, the Federal agency created early in 1932 to make loans to hard-pressed financial institutions and industrial corporations. Even President Hoover had gone so far as to state that the RFC had saved some 70,000,000 policyholders. One of the difficulties in refuting such statements was the fact that the RFC in its announcements did not differentiate between loans to life insurance companies and to other types of insurance companies, and it was practically impossible to obtain any authoritative information. As a matter of fact, RFC loans involved only about one-tenth of 1 per cent of the life companies' assets, which, incidentally, had increased by more than $2,000,000,000 during the period in which listed stocks had declined by more than 80 per cent.[8]

And second, though the Democratic Presidential nominee, Franklin D. Roosevelt, had paid his respects to his party's platform declaration

[8] Total loans by the RFC at the end of July 1932 were $866,047,522 (plus $223,882,599 authorized but not disbursed). Of these loans $49,142,315 had been made to insurance companies of all kinds, most of which were not life insurance companies. Figures are given in *The National Underwriter*, XXXVI (1932), August 26. Up to November 20, 1933, only $52,824,845 (including some agreements to purchase preferred stock by the RFC) had been lent to the life insurance companies. Still owed at this time on these loans was $29,556,444; assets of the life companies were $21,135,000,000. Leroy A. Lincoln, President of the Metropolitan, to The Association of Life Insurance Presidents, *Proceedings of the Twenty-Seventh Annual Convention*, December 8, 1933, p. 91.

for "sound currency," there was considerable doubt regarding his candidness. Four days before the election, he deprecated the idea that any "responsible government would have sold to the country securities payable in gold if it knew that the promise—yes, the covenant—imbodied in the securities" was dubious. He said: "The Democratic platform specifically declares, 'We advocate a sound currency to be preserved at all hazards.' That, I take it, is plain English." [9] But it was still not clear what the candidate's idea of "a sound currency" was. One of his earliest and most favorable biographers said that Roosevelt "had at least a mental reservation as to the possibility or desirability of maintaining the gold standard. But he could not admit it or even hint at it except in the most intimate circle of tight-lipped friends." [10]

As a result of the rumors and uncertainty, many troubled policyholders wrote their companies seeking assurance that the companies were solvent and their policies still valid. In most instances they were. It is a fact that during the year the life insurance companies paid to policyholders and beneficiaries more than $3,000,000,000, or about $500,000,000 more than in 1931.

In his report to the Board for 1932, President Parkinson said that "the past year has been a difficult one"; despite the uncertainties mentioned above and the tremendously depreciated value of securities, greater demands had been made upon the life insurance companies than ever before. Equitable's new business for 1932 declined to $620,110,451 and insurance in force decreased $425,864,791—to $6,665,098,000—yet the Society had paid to policyholders and beneficiaries $222,036,000 (including 1,175 suicide claims), or $25,122,000 more than in the preceding year.[11] While death claim payments had decreased, disability payments had increased and surrender value disbursements had increased by almost 60 per cent compared with 1931. The total disbursements of more than $285,000,000 "had a stabilizing and sustaining effect which is not to be measured by the size of these figures, but rather by the extent to which the sums paid out contributed to the welfare of thousands of our people." But in this connection, President

[9] Address at Brooklyn Rally at Brooklyn Academy of Music, November 4, 1932. *The New York Times*, November 5, 1932.

[10] Ernest K. Lindley, *The Roosevelt Revolution, First Phase* (New York, 1933), p. 64. Lindley accompanied the Democratic nominee on many of his campaign tours.

[11] These payments brought the total made from the Society's founding to almost $3,000,000,000. For the 1931 figures, see this history, p. 986.

Parkinson emphasized once more the fact that seemed not to be sufficiently appreciated by the public, namely, that life insurance companies could not create wealth—the most they could do was to distribute it. In order for a company to operate successfully, it would have to continue to receive premium payments from the policyholders and income from its investments: "I would not place so much emphasis on this point were it not for the fact that it seems to have become a widely accepted point of view that because life insurance companies have assets running into billions of dollars, they are in a position to sacrifice the income therefrom when it becomes inconvenient for debtors to pay. During the past year we have had abundant evidence of the growth in popularity of this idea which carries with it the seeds of real danger for our business." He continued:

There also developed during the year another idea, the further extension of which will be harmful to our institution. An economist of international reputation recently said that "a contract has nothing to support it except the self-respect and self-interest of the debtor. A loan the claims of which are supported by neither will not be paid for long." Until recently the element of self-respect undoubtedly played an important part in stimulating debtors to pay their debts, but in 1932 it lost a good deal of its motivating power. Private debtors in this country witnessed the spectacle of foreign governments failing to respond to their obligations without suffering any apparent decrease of self-respect. They learned that American bankers viewed with evident self-satisfaction a standstill agreement which they had evolved for large private debts of foreign debtors. They thought that there was every reason why as much or greater generosity should be extended by American financial institutions to domestic debtors. They saw American governmental authorities granting moratoria on certain types of loans and actively soliciting the granting of moratoria by financial institutions to their debtors. Another move tending to lessen the effectiveness of self-respect as an inducement to perform private contracts was observed in proposed legislation designed to entice the reluctant debtor into the bankruptcy court by applying to him the more self-respecting name of "debtor" instead of "bankrupt." As for self-interest, it is never easy to persuade an individual that the maintenance of future credit facilities is as important as relieving himself of the pressing burden of an immediate payment. When, as in these times, the immediate payment means more than the usual sacrifice, the task becomes one of the greatest difficulty.[12]

[12] Annual report to the Board, February 16, 1933. Corporate Records, Equitable Archives.

In the light of prevailing conditions, delinquencies and defaults might well have been expected to be worse than they were: 79 per cent of the mortgage interest due Equitable in 1932 had been paid and 83 per cent of the principal payable; the Society had received almost 89 per cent of the rents to which it was entitled under outstanding leases on the foreclosed properties and almost 99 per cent of the interest payable on its bond investments. Bond maturities had been met 100 per cent. After deducting overdue mortgage interest (not required in 1931 statements), the Society earned 4.76 net interest on its ledger assets and its total assets increased by $71,464,000 to $1,471,-697,000. Compared to many financial institutions, Equitable occupied an enviable position.

In December the National Convention of Insurance Commissioners voted to retain the rule of the preceding year in regard to valuation of securities held by the life insurance companies, that is, to value securities as of June 30, 1931, for the year-end reports for 1932.

THE BANK CRISIS OF 1933 AND THE RUN ON THE LIFE INSURANCE COMPANIES

After the election, the uncertainty in regard to monetary policy increased. The President-elect was known to be in close association with economists and politicians who advocated inflation, and neither President Hoover, a group of leading economists, nor the Federal Reserve Advisory Council could get any assurance that there would be no tampering with or inflation of the currency. Alexander Dana Noyes, financial editor of *The New York Times,* wrote: "It is probable enough that the present spirit of hesitancy, not only in financial markets but in general trade, is more or less influenced by lack of such reassurance. . . ." [13] Three weeks later, he again wrote: "However ill-grounded may be the fear of dangerous experiment with the currency, the mere fact that such things are publicly talked about by their promoters has necessarily thrown a shadow over financial confidence at a time when mental influences are of paramount importance and when confidence is needed urgently. The Federal Reserve gold holdings . . . never [were] equaled in its history except one period of a few months." [14] At the same time, Bernard Baruch, internationally known financier and head of the War

[13] *The New York Times,* January 23, 1933.
[14] *Ibid.,* February 13, 1933.

Industries Board in World War I, testified before a Senate committee on possible methods of recovery: "I regard the condition of this country the most serious in its history . . . inflation . . . is the road to ruin. . . . The mere talk of inflation retards business. If you start talking about that [devaluation] you would not have a nickel's worth of gold in the Reserve System day after tomorrow."

In January, it became generally known that Senator Carter Glass of Virginia, a sound-money Democrat and one of the creators of the Federal Reserve System in 1914, was being considered for the position of Secretary of the Treasury, and the assumption was that he would not accept the post unless he received assurances that the incoming Administration would preserve a sound currency "at all hazards."[15] After weeks of uncertainty regarding the intentions of Senator Glass, it was announced February 21 that he had decided to remain in the Senate in order to fight "radical" proposals regarding the currency.[16] Franklin D. Roosevelt then offered the Secretaryship of the Treasury to President Thomas I. Parkinson. When, from the conversation, it became apparent that the President-elect was flirting with the idea of tinkering with the currency, President Parkinson told him that the result of such action would be: 1) confiscatory taxation, 2) inflation, or, 3) "a crooked combination of the two." He did not accept the offer.[17]

The fear that the new Administration would not maintain the gold standard led to increased hoarding "on the part of men who were distrustful, not of the banks in which they kept their deposits, but of the currency. Deposits were withdrawn from strong banks by men who knew that the banks would be able to pay out dollars, but who doubted

15 *New York Herald Tribune*, February 15, 1933.

16 *The New York Times*, February 21, 1933. In an article signed by Arthur Krock, dated Washington, February 20, the well-known Washington correspondent stated that it was not believed that Glass in his three conferences with Roosevelt had received the assurance he required on the controversial points of finance and economics. For other evidence of the uncertainty regarding currency inflation, see William Starr Myers and Walter H. Newton, *The Hoover Administration, A Documented Narrative* (New York, 1936), Chapter XVIII, "Fear of Currency Tinkering Stops Recovery," and Chapter XIX, "The Gold Panic."

17 According to President Parkinson, he went to Hot Springs, Georgia, the first week in February and talked to the President-elect for two hours. He understood that Senator Robert M. LaFollette had recommended him to the President-elect. At this conference he was told that Cordell Hull was to be Secretary of State under the new administration. The following day when he had lunch with James Farley and Edward Flynn he revealed this news to them. Parkinson interview with author, September 2, 1958.

that the dollars would be redeemable in gold." [18] By mid-February, withdrawals for hoarding reached about $15,000,000 per day. Though the banking system, which had suffered severely during the depression, was in a generally stronger position than it had been in the late spring of 1932—gold holdings of the Federal Reserve System were the highest since the depression had begun—it could not stand this mass vote of the people by way of their pocketbooks. The banks of Michigan, particularly vulnerable as a result of loans to the depressed automobile industry, were closed by the Governor February 14. Three days later, President Hoover wrote the President-elect and stated that it would "steady the country greatly" if the latter would give assurance that there would be no attempts at inflation of the currency. In his reply, which did not reach President Hoover until twelve days later, the President-elect stated that "the real trouble is that on present values very few financial institutions anywhere in the country are actually able to pay off their deposits in full, and the knowledge of this fact is widely held." (Of the banks closed by Presidential order in March, banks holding 92 per cent of the country's deposits were reopened after a few days and declared by him to be sound.) All efforts of President Hoover and Secretary of the Treasury Ogden Mills to reopen the banks of Michigan through cooperation of the state legislature, the banks, and the Reconstruction Finance Corporation failed. The panic spread rapidly; Maryland took action on February 25 and Arkansas on February 27. By March 5, thirty-eight states had at least some closed banks while Mississippi, Wyoming, Kentucky, Ohio, West Virginia, Kansas, Florida, and Indiana had restrictions on withdrawals in some banks, but the banks remained open. South Carolina and North Carolina had restrictions on only a few banks. (Indiana was not, as has been stated in several instances, the second state to close its banks; the banks of the state were never closed by official action.[19] Had the

[18] Benjamin M. Anderson, *Economics and the Public Welfare* (New York, 1939), p. 282.

[19] The author of this history has been guilty of this error. See R. Carlyle Buley, *The American Life Convention*, II, p. 739, and *The Equitable 1859–1959*, p. 208. See also Benjamin M. Anderson, *Economics and the Public Welfare*, p. 288.

Following Michigan's declaration of a banking holiday, there were rumors that Indiana would follow suit, but February 23 Governor Paul V. McNutt positively declared that there would be "no bank moratorium in Indiana." (See *The New York Times*, February 24, 1933.) February 24, Governor McNutt signed the Financial Institutions Act, six sections of which became effective immediately. These sections authorized individual banks to limit withdrawals and granted the Banking Depart-

situation been deliberately planned to throw the country into financial chaos while the Hoover administration was still in office, it could not have been more effective.[20]

Banks and other financial institutions frequently brought pressure to bear upon life insurance policyholders to liquidate their debts by drawing upon their policy reserves.[21] Equitable was not too hard pressed, for it had foreseen this contingency and set aside some $78,000,000 for this purpose.[22] But many life companies were not so fortunately situated; with withdrawals from banks being restricted and premium income and mortgage interest practically cut off, they faced a secondary run at the very time that they were losing a material part of their cash income. The executive committee of the American Life Convention met in Chicago March 1 to consider the situation and the executive committee of the National Convention of Insurance Commissioners met at the same place for the same purpose the following day.[23] Meanwhile, on March 1, an emergency bill to protect the life

---

ment of Indiana general supervisory powers concerning withdrawal restrictions. February 26, all Indianapolis banks limited withdrawals on all types of deposits to 5 per cent of the balances. Banks in other parts of the state did likewise, but Governor McNutt, February 28, again stated that there would be no general banking holiday as in Maryland and Michigan (*Muncie Morning Star*, February 28, 1933); he repeated the statement March 4 (*The Indianapolis News*, March 4, 1933). The author is indebted to Robert R. Neff, author of "The Governorship of Paul V. McNutt" (Ph.D. dissertation, Indiana University, 1964) for calling attention to the facts in regard to the banking situation in Indiana.

20 Equitable had relatively small losses as a result of bank failures. It was involved in three bank closings in 1931 with total claims of $79,371, and nine closings in 1933 with claims of $426,732. By 1952 the Society had recovered 87 per cent of these claims.

21 President Daniel Boone of the American Life Convention referred to such institutions as "financial vandals." *The National Underwriter*, XXXVII (1933), January 13.

22 Even so, President Parkinson had a check made on the extent of the Society's withdrawable funds. Associate Actuary D. A. Walker, in a memorandum March 8, 1933, reported on the various types of contracts outstanding and concluded that the maximum aggregate cash or loan values on all contracts and annuities, exclusive of supplementary contracts and dividend deposits, was $944,000,000; there were $262,000,000 of loans outstanding against this figure, which left a balance of $682,000,000, all protected by 90-day clauses. Sterling Pierson files, Equitable Archives.

23 The meeting of the commissioners had been suggested by Herbert M. Woollen, President of the American Central Life Insurance Company of Indianapolis, to Superintendent of Insurance John Kidd of Indiana; Woollen thought that the commissioners had the power to act, if someone would just take the lead. Superintendent Kidd got in touch with Superintendent Joseph B. Thompson of

companies—sponsored by the Indiana companies—had been drafted and introduced in the General Assembly of the State of Indiana. This bill, which was not approved until March 8, authorized the Insurance Commissioner to make such rules as he deemed necessary "for the transaction of the business of the life insurance companies and for the purpose of safeguarding the interests of policyholders, creditors and shareholders respecting the withdrawal for payment of funds in time of emergency." [24]

The Indiana law, however, was not the first to be enacted. Superintendent George S. Van Schaick of New York, who, at the commissioners' meeting March 2 had firmly opposed any "moratorium" for life insurance companies, suddenly changed his mind when he returned to New York from the Presidential inauguration and found the New York banks closed. Sunday, March 5, and Monday, March 6, he conferred with the Governor, members of the legislature, and life company executives. President Parkinson opposed any "moratorium" for the companies and questioned whether the Superintendent had legal authority to impose restrictions; he thought that it would be all right, however, if the fact could be established that a large number of companies could not meet the demands made upon them.[25] The consensus, however, was that such restrictions were needed; but to eliminate any doubt as to legality, it was agreed that emergency legislation should be enacted. A bill was drafted and sent to Albany by plane; the legislature passed it during the night of Monday, March 6, and the law was declared to be in immediate effect the following day. The law thus went into effect one day before the Indiana law.

The New York law gave the Superintendent of Insurance power to prescribe rules and regulations for the conduct of the business of all insurance and gave him authority to vary or suspend the provisions of the insurance laws in the general public interest; the Governor, by letter, placed full responsibility for administering the emergency law in the hands of Superintendent Van Schaick. The original regulations

---

Missouri, chairman of the executive committee of the N.C.I.C., who called the meeting.

[24] A copy of the bill was published in the American Life Convention Special Bulletin of February 28 and soon was in the hands of most of the state insurance departments.

[25] Thomas I. Parkinson, interview with author, June 17, 1958.

issued under the New York law prohibited payments of loans or surrenders in any state by any company operating in New York, unless such payments were to be used for payment of premium or other obligations to the life insurance companies; in cases of extreme need, a maximum of $100 might be paid out.[26]

By the end of the month, 21 states had adopted emergency legislation and bills were pending in 12 other states; most of these laws were modeled either upon the Indiana or the New York law. In other states, regulations were issued by the insurance departments without special legislation.[27]

The major purpose of these laws and restrictions was to protect the life insurance companies from circumstances over which they had no control. Said the President of the American Life Convention, Daniel Boone: "The purpose of these new restrictions is to quickly close another door to those panicky persons who are endeavoring to protect themselves to the disadvantage of other policyholders and beneficiaries. Generally speaking, life insurance could continue to meet all obligations to policyholders. But in this national crisis, individuals and single industries must bow to that superior law—the well-being of the entire people."[28] It was unfortunate that newspapers generally referred to the restrictions on policy loans and cash surrenders as "moratoria" or the "moratorium on life insurance payments." Even some life insurance men fell into that error. Others, however, emphasized the fact that at no time during the depression had there been a "moratorium" on payments by life insurance companies: "Although nothing has interfered with the daily fulfillment of the major obligations in the life contract, it is not likely that this fact has been brought clearly to

[26] A week or two after the restrictions went into effect, an officer of the Chase National Bank, of which President Parkinson was a director, phoned and asked whether Equitable was subject to the restrictions; he wanted to know whether an exception could be made in the case of Secretary of the Treasury William H. Woodin, who wanted the $68,000 surrender value on his policies. President Parkinson said there could be no exceptions. *Ibid.*

[27] The status of emergency life insurance control measures in 42 states was summarized in *The Insurance Field,* XLII (1933), March 31, and the text of emergency laws enacted in 24 states was published in American Life Convention Special Bulletin No. 262, May 10. The Bulletins Nos. 1802–2033 of The Association of Life Insurance Presidents also cover the special legislation from March 7 to September 28, 1933. This material, as well as additional material, is contained in folders in the Sterling Pierson files, Equitable Archives.

[28] As quoted in *The Insurance Field,* XLII (1933), March 31.

the attention of the public. Is it not important that both the companies and the field set out at once to drive from the public mind any misconception as to the extent of the restrictions?"[29] The life companies continued to pay promptly all death benefits and maturing policies; only their "banking" functions had been interfered with.

Monday, March 6, two days after the inauguration, President Franklin D. Roosevelt by proclamation ordered the closing of all banks in the United States; and on March 9 Congress, by law, gave the President wide powers in the field of money and banking, including the right to seize the gold and the gold certificates held by the people. The following day the President, by executive order, halted the export of gold without Treasury license; on April 5 he forbade the hoarding of gold and gold certificates and on April 19 he prohibited the free movement of gold both within the United States and to foreign countries. On April 19 Senator Elmer Thomas of Oklahoma introduced, with Administration support, an amendment to the pending agricultural bill which would authorize the President to issue $3,000,000,000 of United States notes, establish bimetallism at any ratio, and reduce the weight of the gold dollar by a maximum of 50 per cent. Senator Glass regarded this amendment, which would enable the Government to repudiate its promises to pay gold on Government bonds, as a dishonorable act, and Senator Thomas P. Gore of Oklahoma used even stronger language.

In October the President announced that the Treasury would purchase gold at a price to be fixed by itself, and in December he ordered the Treasury to buy domestically mined silver at 64.5 cents an ounce.[30] January 15, 1934, he asked Congress for legislation which would

[29] Manager Byron K. Elliott of the American Life Convention to Managing Director Roger B. Hull of the National Association of Life Underwriters, April 12, 1933. Correspondence files, American Life Convention.

[30] The Treasury raised its purchase price of gold gradually, and licensed private organizations to buy gold for it. In New York City (Empire State Building), the United States Gold Buying Service, a private organization, advertised and broadcast daily that it was buying gold "such as Gold teeth and bridgework, rings, watches," etc. at approximately $34 a fine ounce. When John Bassett Moore received a copy of one of the advertisements, he wrote Sterling Pierson as follows: "It shows . . . that the great song and dance men of today—such as Prof. Warren and Prof. Fisher—can be interpreted and forecasted only by those who have a sense of humor. I say *forecasted* deliberately, because they *broadcast* themselves. Moses, Elijah, and the rest would be out of the running today." January 24, 1934. Sterling Pierson files, Equitable Archives.

authorize the United States Treasury to take over the gold held by the Federal Reserve Banks, direct the President to reduce the weight of the gold dollar by not less than 40 per cent or more than 50 per cent, and set up a $2,000,000,000 Stabilization Fund out of the "profit" created by devaluation of the dollar. The bill was signed January 30 and the following day the President fixed the weight of the gold dollar at 59.06 per cent of the existing gold dollar (15 5⁄21 grains, nine-tenths fine, instead of 25.8 grains). This was achieved by fixing the price of gold at $35 per ounce, instead of the previous figure of $20.67 per ounce. Thus was the dollar devalued and, since there were now 70 per cent more "gold dollars" than before, the Treasury claimed a "profit" of $2,806,000,000. Since the President's power to manipulate the value of the dollar was not renewed in 1943, the weight of the theoretical gold dollar has remained the same to date—but its purchasing power has declined several fold.[31]

No business was more vitally concerned with the prospects of inflation than that of life insurance. Though some company executives seemed to think that "regulated" or "controlled" inflation would help restore the price level and improve business in general, policyholders generally were skeptical. Life insurance agents noted an increasing tendency on the part of prospects and policyholders to question the desirability of purchasing life insurance, the benefits of which would be paid in dollars of uncertain value. Company officers received many letters from worried policyholders and frequently were hard put to frame a satisfactory reply. Even Equitable, which was later to lead the educational campaign against inflation, was reluctant to take a positive stand. Although the inflation bill (the Thomas Amendment) did not indicate how far inflation would go, the President had stated that the object of the Administration was to raise commodity prices only to such an extent that those who had borrowed money would, on the average, be able to repay that money in the same kind of dollar which they borrowed: "We do not seek to let them get such a cheap dollar that they will be able to pay back a great deal less than they borrowed. In other words, we seek to correct a wrong and not to create another wrong in the opposite direction."[32] Treasurer Meredith C.

[31] The Bretton Woods Agreement Act (Public Law 171, 79th Congress, approved July 31, 1945) had the effect of continuing the weight and fineness of the gold dollar in effect July 1, 1944.

[32] In his radio address of May 7, 1933.

Laffey of Equitable thought that the effect of inflation, if accompanied by general stimulation of manufacturing, agricultural, and merchandising activity, might well accrue certain benefits to an institution such as life insurance: "Drastic deflation, as operative in the period immediately behind us, has made it more difficult for mortgagors to meet their interest and tax payments, has caused corporations likewise to have the margin between earnings and bond interest and, or, preferred dividend requirements suffer serious shrinkage, in some cases disappear altogether. Any course of action which can rectify this condition will make more certain the continuance of the current income of financial institutions and will tend to restore to good standing such investment items as may have become non-productive for the time being." The only way in which the individual could circumvent the uncertainty of the purchasing power of the dollar would be through "out and out speculation, with all the hazards always entailed." [33]

General Solicitor Sterling Pierson, who handled many of the replies to policyholders, was apparently impressed by President Roosevelt's statement in regard to inflation and often cited it. As the weeks and months went by, however, the policyholders were not so easily put off. Letters ranged from policyholders who had $1,000 of life insurance to those who had many thousands. Representative of the letters from thinking policyholders was the following, written to the "Office of the President":

The premium on my two insurance policies with your company will be due in a few days. While I have the ready cash to pay this premium, I question the advisability of doing so.

In other words I am thinking of the possibility of an inflation in this country, and the chain of events that would come with it.

If one takes for granted the national debt will never be paid, and inflation of some sort is bound to come, how is it possible for life insurance policyholders to protect themselves against loss of their invested savings, in whole or in part?

What are the insurance companies doing to stabilize their investments to protect as well as possible their clients against loss thru inflation?

I would appreciate very much your unbiased views on this subject, for I anticipate that you have the welfare of your policyholders in mind at all times.

[33] M. C. Laffey, memorandum, "Comments on Inflation," to Sterling Pierson, May 10, 1933. Sterling Pierson files, Equitable Archives.

One large policyholder, an economist for one of the country's leading corporations, after receiving only form letters in reply to his three previous efforts, wrote as follows:

> Notwithstanding my repeated efforts to get from you some idea of what, if anything, insurance companies are doing to help stem the tide toward inflation, I am still left groping in the dark.
>
> I wish, therefore, to write this letter purely from the point of view of a policyholder in your great company. As such I ask definitely what specific steps, if any, have been or are being taken by the Equitable Life Assurance Society to combat the current administrative movement toward debased currency, which, if not checked, may make the principal of life insurance policies largely valueless.
>
> This is a matter which is causing untold concern to great numbers of people in straitened circumstances, particularly old people whose life savings have gone into the building up of a small insurance "estate."
>
> As one of your policyholders, therefore, I ask and believe I am entitled to an unequivocal reply to this letter.

Vice President William J. Graham replied as follows:

> In direct answer to your question, may I say that it is not my opinion that the Equitable Life in rushing to combat the administration's current financial policy would be acting wisely for the country or for the Equitable policyholders. The matter of how best to conserve the policyholders' interest in the monetary situation is receiving alert, open-minded, and continuous attention. We believe the life insurance companies today are the safest institutions in human affairs and we are attempting to conserve and forward this situation by keeping the Equitable at the peak of usefulness and efficiency as we see it in discharge of our duty to all our policyholders and to the national welfare.

Not all inquiries received such an individualized response. The Correspondence Division usually sent a form response which stated that " . . . our contracts have been and will continue to be payable in lawful money of the United States. We are not in a position to estimate for you the value of the benefits which you may expect to derive from the periodical payments provided for in such contracts." [34]

In December 1933, before the final devaluation of the dollar, The

[34] Letters may be found in *ibid.*

Association of Life Insurance Presidents had made a "Statement on the Monetary Problem." (The fifty-seven company members of the Association at this time held about 87 per cent of the total life insurance outstanding in all United States legal reserve life insurance companies.) After pointing out that in times of a depression it was usual for some people to attribute the cause to some defect or deficiency in the currency system and to seek a cure by way of an increase in the currency, the Statement concluded:

> Such proposals, if accepted, or if they become seriously menacing, always create lack of confidence and precipitate trouble and, in some cases, utter chaos. . . . We, therefore, urge that the gold standard be maintained; that our currency be stabilized promptly; and that the people be assured that there will be no experiments with new monetary systems. We are convinced that the maintenance of the gold standard, the prompt stabilization of the currency, and assurance that nothing will be done to impair it, would do more than any other thing to restore confidence, to cause business to go forward, and to promote recovery. This country is still the richest in the world and with great capacity for further creation of wealth. With returning confidence it should resume its course toward an even greater and wider prosperity and well-being.[35]

When an Equitable policyholder wrote that the life insurance companies had fallen down on the job and should do something to protect the policyholders' interests by way of an educational advertising campaign, President Parkinson merely sent a copy of the ALIP resolution and said that since the President of the United States had stated that he was opposed to currency inflation, a campaign such as suggested "would involve assumptions inconsistent with his statement and would also tend to create fears the explicit justification for which could not be exactly demonstrated." [36] Many of the agents understood the problem. An Equitable agent in Kansas City, Missouri, wrote that most of his prospects in business and the professions were reluctant to buy additional insurance "in any considerable amount, or annuities in *any* amount," because of fear of inflation. He hoped that someone at the Home Office would make an "authoritative statement" concerning

[35] *Proceedings of the Twenty-Seventh Annual Convention of The Association of Life Insurance Presidents,* December 7, 1933, pp. 85–86.

[36] Thomas I. Parkinson to Frederick A. Burton, New York City, May 31, 1935. Copy in Sterling Pierson files, Equitable Archives.

further devastating effects of the Administration's financial policy: "The silence of the officials of our great company, and similar companies, about this matter of inflation, is in itself rather disturbing. If you can and will break this silence, you will be doing a very great service to Life Insurance." [37]

In his report to the Board, February 1936, President Parkinson mentioned the letters from the policyholders which insisted that Equitable, or the life insurance companies generally, should undertake the organization of an opposition among policyholders. He said: "In meeting this problem, I would be among the last to concede that the prestige of the Society should be allowed to be drawn upon for the sole purpose of influencing the course of political events. . . ." Only if Government in any way threatened the fulfillment of the promise of life insurance to protect the insured did it become "not alone the prerogative but the duty of those who have assumed the responsibility of protecting the policyholder to lodge a public protest." And a month later, he thought that for life companies to issue formal warnings of the dangers of inflation might readily be misconstrued by the public as a prediction that an extreme rise in prices was inevitable: "Such warnings, as we have recently had occasion to observe, tend to produce the effect which it is hoped we may avoid." [38] These were rather cautious words from the man who was soon to be one of the most outspoken and effective critics of New Deal monetary policies.

CONSERVING THE SOCIETY'S ASSETS

President Thomas I. Parkinson once said that the chief test of management of a life insurance company was its ability to conserve the company's assets, to protect it against loss of principal.[39] The depression years offered an excellent opportunity for application of this principle in the affairs of Equitable.

Since mortgage loans on real estate by 1932 constituted more than one-third of the Society's investments, it was particularly important

[37] Kenneth S. Duncan to Meredith C. Laffey, October 22, 1935. *Ibid.*

[38] Draft of a letter to Charles B. Davis, District Judge, United States District Court, Eastern District of Missouri, March 1936. *Ibid.*

[39] He did not believe that actuarial science—"the technical men"—could be of much help in this important responsibility; with all of its mathematical calculations, it made no provision for the "dead horses" in the investment field. Interview with author, November 30, 1955.

that they be handled wisely.[40] For a better understanding of the residential mortgage problem, it is necessary to go back a few years. In 1923 Equitable's residential investment was largely limited to mortgages under the Home Purchase Plan; these mortgages constituted an investment of about $40,000,000, compared to $4,000,000 in conventional dwelling loans. In order to increase the investment in conventional residential loans, the Society made contracts with correspondents in some of the leading cities of the country. The loans were usually for three or five years and the correspondents were permitted to charge the borrowers what the traffic would bear in the way of commissions for placing the loan.[41] Correspondents also frequently wrote fire insurance and received the commissions therefrom. Loans were guaranteed to the Society for one year and if, for any reason during that year, the Society was not satisfied with either the borrower,

[40] Equitable's admitted assets as of December 31, 1932, were as follows:

Cash on hand or in Bank	$ 47,739,150.39	3.24%
United States Government Bonds	12,022,679.00	.82
State, County and Municipal Bonds	982,350.00	.07
Public Utility Bonds	148,763,988.00	10.11
Industrial and Miscellaneous Bonds	9,319,655.00	.63
Railroad Bonds	242,434,518.00	16.47
Canadian Bonds (Dominion, Province, City, etc.)	7,146,123.00	.49
United Kingdom of Great Britain and Ireland Bonds	85,163.40	.01
Other Foreign Bonds	4,882,051.42	.33
Preferred and Guaranteed Stocks	74,459,784.00	5.06
Common Stocks	2,998,099.39	.20
Real Estate Owned (including Home Office)	38,393,906.42	2.61
First Mortgages on City Properties	328,854,379.47	22.34
First Mortgages on Farms	191,862,496.49	13.03
Policy Loans	305,340,869.37	20.75
Interest and Rents due and accrued	25,428,494.25	1.73
Other Assets	30,983,299.34	2.11
	$1,471,697,006.94	100.00%

In this statement, securities are valued in accordance with the laws of the State of New York and the values prescribed by the National Convention of Insurance Commissioners.

[41] Commissions ran as high as 5 per cent for the original loan and 3 per cent for renewals; in addition, most correspondents received an interest participation of one-half of 1 per cent as a service allowance, for which they serviced the investment for interest, taxes, fire insurance, and maintenance of property.

the security, or the title, the correspondent guaranteed to repurchase the loan. Dwelling loans which came to the Society through the correspondent system were based almost wholly on property value and were not closely checked as to owners' ability to pay: "Amortization in the conventional loan classification was almost unheard of, and if principal reductions were required they were generally meagre. As a result, many homeowners purchased homes when they were barely able to pay first mortgage interest, taxes and second mortgage installments. Equity, in many cases, was as low as 10 per cent and carrying charges were high, involving interest at 6 per cent on the first mortgage and 10 per cent on the second mortgage which, in addition, had to be liquidated over a period of three to five years." [42] Properties were divided into two classes, with one- to six-family residential properties constituting Class I, and apartments, office buildings, stores, and miscellaneous commercial buildings constituting Class II. By the end of 1929, residential investment had increased to $124,500,000, with many of the commitments extending into 1930 and 1931. In addition, $70,000,000 of Home Purchase Loans were outstanding; by mid-1932 these loans had increased to $123,000,000.[43]

The Home Purchase applications were submitted by Equitable agents and the property inspection was handled largely by fee appraisers, few of whom were professional appraisers or mortgage men; they followed rules which specified the types of property acceptable to the Society. Borrowers were required to have a full one-half cash equity over and

42 Vice President John H. Muller, "History of Foreclosed Real Estate," p. 2. This 38-page manuscript, prepared in January 1954 for Senior Vice President Charles W. Dow, covers the history of nonfarm property loans from 1923 to 1947. It contains lists of correspondents, statistical tabulations, rules for management for foreclosed properties, etc., and was based upon records from the Controller's Department and other sources. Muller became Manager of the City Real Estate Department in 1942. The author has made use of this manuscript in the account of nonfarm loans and foreclosures.

43 In November 1931, the Columbus (Ohio) Life Underwriters Association filed a brief against Equitable's Home Purchase Plan with the Superintendent of Insurance. The brief alleged that the Plan violated the Ohio statutes in regard to discrimination and rebates, that the mortgage loan represented an inducement to the applicant to take the insurance, and that under pressure of increased debt, the insured would be likely to let policies of other companies lapse. In July 1932, Superintendent of Insurance Charles T. Warner ruled that requiring a life insurance policy to be taken with a loan and to have the policy assigned as collateral security for the loan was within the rights of the company and did not constitute "giving something of value" in violation of the Ohio law. The complaint was dismissed. Correspondence, briefs, etc., in Sterling Pierson files, Equitable Archives.

above the Society's mortgage and to make monthly payments which included regular amortization. The Home Purchase loans were usually serviced by the Society's agents and cashiers.

Delinquencies in residential mortgage payments began to increase in 1929 and continued at an accelerated rate until 1933, when the peak was reached. By December 31, 1933, 13,882 loans, or 25.5 per cent of all loans in force, were in default for more than 30 days of interest. The peak of foreclosures, however, was not reached until 1934, when 4,214 loans, or 9 per cent of all loans outstanding, were in foreclosure.

In the early years of distress the responsibility for administering relief lay in the hands of Charles J. Martin, Manager of the Mortgage Loan and Real Estate Department.[44] But by mid-1932, when the burden became too heavy, Martin asked President Parkinson for assistance. To handle the situation, the President appointed a committee of Home Office executives which came to be known as the Relief Committee. This committee was to grant leniency whenever it found it was merited; it handled defaults on all loans of less than $40,000; the larger loans were handled directly by the Finance Committee of the Board. At this time there were more than $130,000,000 in mortgages in default of interest for more than three months. Since the Society had curtailed its loans, the organization of the correspondents, whose principal compensation consisted of commissions on new loans, deteriorated. Consequently, it was necessary to recruit experienced personnel and establish a field organization. In some instances Equitable took over the correspondent's organization on a salary basis, and in other instances life insurance agents or correspondents were subsidized in order that they might continue servicing the defaulted investment. Within a few months, Equitable had fieldmen located at various points across the country and key men were brought to the Home Office for briefing and instruction.[45]

[44] By resolution of the Finance Committee adopted November 25, 1930. Martin had previously served as Deputy Comptroller, Assistant Treasurer, and Superintendent of the Home Purchase Department. He became Assistant Manager of the Mortgage Loan and Real Estate Department in 1925 and Manager in 1927. In 1933 his title was changed to Manager, Mortgage Loans, and the following year to Manager, Mortgage Loan Department. In 1936, he was appointed Manager, City Mortgages, and the following year a Second Vice President and placed in charge of the New York City Mortgage Department. In 1942 Martin was placed in charge of Mortgage Loan investments and foreclosed real estate in New York City and the counties of Suffolk, Nassau, and Westchester.

[45] As late as May 1935, President Parkinson decided that the field mortgage

Gateway Center, Pittsburgh

Before redevelopment

An artist's rendering of the finished complex

One of the first problems which confronted the Relief Committee was that of determining whether the borrower really wished to retain ownership of his home; many people had lost faith and wanted to be freed from the responsibilities of property ownership and debt worries —some believed that it was much cheaper to rent. It was the job of the fieldmen to resell these borrowers on the idea of home ownership. Once the fieldmen were convinced, however, that the borrower wished to retain possession and would play fair with the Society, every possible measure was taken to help him. The chief concern was with defaults on interest; not too much attention was paid to defaults for taxes or fire insurance unless the loan was in default for interest. Default on principal was not considered so serious as long as interest payments were maintained, and, besides, numerous states by legislation had prohibited foreclosure for nonpayment of principal.

The Relief Committee devised various forms for the fieldmen's reports. Once the fieldman had determined that the borrower wished to retain possession, he might be given the choice of several options, dependent upon his training, background, and chances for re-employment. If none of these plans was feasible, only then would foreclosure be recommended.[46] One thing the Committee decided against was the reduction of the rate of interest on delinquent loans, nor was defaulted interest capitalized. In some instances, however, it did defer portions of interest for a reasonable period, provided the borrowers appeared able to repay the deferred interest with interest at the end

---

organization needed strengthening. He wrote Manager Charles J. Martin that the examinations of some of the Society's foreclosed properties raised serious questions in his mind as to the inspection and work originally done on applications: "Are the men who passed on these properties for us still in our organization? If so, I think they should be completely detached from any further activity in connection with appraising or accepting mortgage loans." Parkinson to Martin, May 23, 1935. Parkinson files, Equitable Archives.

[46] The plans were as follows:

- "A" Principal payments deferred for a specified period of three to six months; interest and insurance premium (where Home Purchase) payable monthly.
- "B" Insurance discontinued (where Home Purchase), principal and interest payable monthly.
- "C" Interest only payable for a limited period.
- "D" New loan granted for amount of unpaid principal on ten or fifteen year plan.
- "Misc" Assumption of mortgage by second mortgagee, continuing principal and interest payments but without life insurance (where Home Purchase).

of the extension period agreed upon. Some defaulters were carried for a while without any payments at all. In many communities where teachers and other local employees were paid in tax anticipation warrants, Equitable purchased the warrants and used them in payment of real estate taxes. This practice created a great deal of good will for the Society. When foreclosure became necessary, legal counsel sought to temper justice with mercy and to determine and be guided by the attitude of the borrowers and the public as well. As might be expected, foreclosures were much more frequent in the case of conventional residential loans than with the Home Purchase loans; that is, those which were additionally secured by life insurance policies. Between 1927 and 1939, the dollar volume of Home Purchase loans foreclosed was 12.4 per cent of the total, as compared with 21.5 per cent in the dwelling loan category.[47]

The Relief Committee continued to function throughout the 1930's. In general, foreclosures were effected without protest, for many borrowers realized that it was futile to struggle any longer. In some instances, however, borrowers and their attorneys showed extraordinary ingenuity in devising schemes to delay and hinder foreclosure proceedings:

> In this they were aided in their efforts by Congress, State Legislatures, Governors and other officers. Congress amended Bankruptcy laws to provide a refuge from foreclosure courts. State Legislatures passed emergency relief laws and moratoriums staying execution, prohibiting foreclosure sales and giving the courts almost unlimited discretion so that mortgagees and other creditors were practically helpless in enforcing contractual obligations. Governors issued proclamations creating foreclosure holidays. Judges often indulged in dilatory practices and frequently arbitrarily refused to grant decrees or order the entry of judgments. It was a common practice for sheriffs to fail to show up to conduct foreclosure sales. In some sections of the country people used their rights of assembly to congregate around court houses in ugly threatening moods for the purpose of intimidating courts, officers and attorneys.[48]

An example of trouble was that which arose over defaulted mortgages in Sunnyside, Long Island, an early example of "cluster develop-

[47] A tabulated comparison may be found in Muller, "History of Foreclosed Real Estate," p. 12.
[48] *Ibid.*, p. 10.

ment."[49] A local housing corporation had assigned Equitable a senior interest in 263 mortgage loans which represented $1,423,192. When some foreclosures were started in 1935, some of the residents organized a Consolidated Home Owners' Mortgage Committee—"the Strikers' Committee"—which became somewhat obstreperous in its claims. The secretary of this committee, Benjamin Ginsberg, accused Equitable's investigator, Samuel Latour, of carrying on a whispering campaign against the committee and making derogatory remarks about its members.[50] Things came to a climax February 8, 1936, when the Consolidated Home Owners' Mortgage Committee put out the following announcement:

EQUITABLE SWINGS ON JIM GILLEENEY

If the siren blows this week, it will mean the Equitable is using the sheriff to evict the Gilleeneys. The Equitable Life Assurance Company has to date refused any settlement on any Sunnyside mortgage which does not involve payment of every cent of arrears in full; and has refused to make any commitments to reduce future interest, in spite of the public statements to the contrary made by its President, Thomas I. Parkinson. It has demanded its full pound of flesh from Jim and has followed up by serving

[49] See William H. Whyte, *Cluster Development* (American Conservation Association, New York, 1964).

[50] Latour stated that he did not make these remarks, but that some of the residents who were not members of the Strikers' Committee did refer to the committee members as "Reds and Communists who were repudiating their just debts."

Alexander M. Bing of the City Housing Corporation wrote both Mrs. Franklin D. Roosevelt and Governor Herbert H. Lehman, April 11, 1935, and exonerated Equitable from any blame. In the letter to Governor Lehman, he said: "The Sunnyside Mortgage Committee accuses the Equitable Life Assurance Society of commencing wholesale foreclosures at Sunnyside Gardens. The facts are as follows: The Equitable Life Assurance Society took no steps whatever to foreclose any of these mortgages. In certain cases, however, the present mortgage represented 90 per cent of the sales price of the house and the City Housing Corporation assigned to the Equitable Life Assurance Society a senior interest in these mortgages, retaining a junior interest. . . . We have been forced to commence foreclosure on some of the second mortgages. In the case of these 90 per cent participations, it was legally necessary for the owner of the senior interest to join. For this reason, in a few of the foreclosures that have been started, we were compelled to request the Equitable Life Assurance Society to join with us in the foreclosure suit. It is a gross exaggeration to accuse the Equitable of starting wholesale foreclosures as their participation in the suits occurs in only seven cases out of thirty-five foreclosures that we are starting in a community of over five hundred mortgages. I wanted to make this explanation to you in fairness to the Equitable Life Assurance Society and to state that they have been most cooperative with us and through us with home owners." Photostat copy in Parkinson files, Equitable Archives.

a writ of assistance for the eviction. The Gilleeneys cordially invite all Sunnyside to come to tea at their home . . . WHEN THE SIREN BLOWS!

CELEBRATE LINCOLN'S BIRTHDAY AT EQUITABLE LIFE ASSURANCE COMPANY

To protest against this threatened unwarranted eviction and against the general dog-in-the-manger policy of the Equitable Life Assurance Company, Sunnyside will hold a giant demonstration Wednesday morning at the Insurance company's offices on . . . . It will be a fitting way to celebrate the birthday of Abraham Lincoln.

It appears that Mayor Fiorello H. LaGuardia had, through Corporation Counsel Paul Windels, sought an extension of time for Gilleeney. President Parkinson thought that the case deserved "a plain statement of the facts." He wrote the Mayor that not only had Gilleeney failed to make any payments on account of his mortgage for more than a year, but that he had also neglected to pay taxes and water rents. Equitable merely insisted that Gilleeney sign a lease to pay $50 a month for his continued occupancy. Said President Parkinson: "It is not within our discretion to further indulge Gilleeney in the possession and enjoyment of these premises free of any cost. Many of our policyholders and their beneficiaries do not enjoy the opportunity to live in such commodious quarters as those which Gilleeney has occupied at their expense. . . . Surely we cannot be expected to give him what nobody else of my acquaintance is able to get,—free use of comfortable living quarters." When Corporation Counsel Windels found Gilleeney unwilling to sign anything, he wrote President Parkinson that he did not feel justified in requesting any further extension in this case.[51]

Another building project in which Equitable had a substantial investment was that at Radburn, New Jersey, but the foreclosure proceedings connected with these properties did not receive the publicity given those at Sunnyside. In 1937 the Executive Committee of Equitable's Board authorized the readjustment of the obligations of Radburn, Incorporated, and City Housing Corporation under their mortgages to the Society amounting to $1,525,000. It was agreed that interest on the mortgages from August 1, 1934, to January 1, 1937, be

[51] Parkinson to LaGuardia, Febraury 11 and 26, 1936; Windels to Parkinson, February 27, 1936. *Ibid.*

paid at the rate of 4 per cent instead of 6 per cent, and that new purchasers of the repossessed properties were to assume existing first mortgages to the Society. These readjustments, however, did not solve the problem and early in 1942 Equitable instituted foreclosure proceedings on the mortgages of 192 dwellings and two business buildings on which it had, including taxes advanced and overdue interest, an investment of $1,632,315. Foreclosure did not take place, however, and an informal "mortgagee-in-possession" arrangement was worked out under which Equitable operated the properties under a special bank account pending a satisfactory rearrangement with the mortgagor. As of December 31, 1944, the aggregate book value of unpaid principal on 165 parcels in the Radburn development amounted to $1,401,001 and taxes advanced by the Society were $32,581. In May 1945 the Real Estate Committee authorized Equitable to sign a contract with Radburn, Incorporated to provide for the sale of 38 of the one-family houses and the assignment of mortgages on 162 of the properties for a consideration of $1,650,000. By August the terms of the contract had been complied with and Equitable had no further interest in the Radburn development. The total consideration received, including funds resulting from the operation of the Radburn properties, was approximately $2,081,000, and the Society's net profit after all expenses and after interest at 6 per cent on the mortgage indebtedness to August 31, 1945, was approximately $76,000.[52]

During the period of the 1930's Equitable's foreclosures were extensive, even though somewhat below the national average. All told the Society acquired some 14,500 city properties and 8,000 farms. As more properties came into the possession of the Society, the personnel who had previously been concerned with lending mortgage money were confronted with the formidable task of administering a widespread holding of real estate, a task for which they were totally unprepared. Each phase of the problem—the acquisition, the management, and eventual sale of the properties—involved many difficulties.

In 1934 Equitable created a Real Estate Department, headed by Harley Lackey, to handle the urban properties. The Mortgage Loan Department was headed by Charles J. Martin. In February 1935 an executive order established a Home Office department, under the direction of the President, to have jurisdiction over farm loans and real estate. This department was subject to the supervision of the

[52] Real Estate Committee *Minutes*, September 4, 1945. Equitable Archives.

Finance Committee of the Board, and important questions were to be referred to Glenn McHugh, who was Investment Assistant to the President. In February 1936, by executive order, the City Mortgage Department was created and put under the management of McHugh, who by this time was a Second Vice President. This department consisted of the Mortgage Loan Department (Martin) and the Real Estate Department (Lackey).

Glenn McHugh, a native of Wisconsin, received his A.B. degree from the University of Wisconsin in 1916 and his LL.B. degree from Columbia University Law School in 1921. After serving on the Columbia University Legislative Drafting Research Fund, he became Assistant Counsel in the Office of Legislative Counsel of the United States Senate. (Thomas I. Parkinson was Legal Counsel of the United States Senate committees at this time.) In 1926 McHugh became legal assistant on Vice President Parkinson's staff, and in 1933 investment assistant. In May 1933, George N. Peek, Administrator of the Agricultural Adjustment Administration, telephoned President Parkinson that he needed McHugh immediately. Although Equitable could not easily spare McHugh's services, it gave him leave for a year.[53] He returned to Equitable in July 1934 and was appointed Second Vice President in 1936.

Under McHugh's direction the City Mortgage Department made statistical studies of individual cities—population, housing situation, and future prospects. Dr. Raymond Franzen, consulting statistician, and Dr. Watson A. Baumert, Secretary of the Finance Committee of the Board, aided in this work.

The Real Estate Department grew rapidly and by 1937 had approximately sixty Home Office employees. Those who were responsible for repossessed properties were divided into sections for handling repairs, rentals, sales, taxes, and fire insurance. The field organization had grown to about 100 persons, located in 25 offices in the leading cities

[53] George N. Peek to Thomas I. Parkinson, May 31, and Parkinson to Peek, June 6, 1933. July 3, 1934, Peek, the Special Adviser to the President on Foreign Trade, wrote Parkinson as follows: "I have kept my promise to send Mr. McHugh back to you safe and, I hope, sane. In so doing, however, I want you and your directors to know how much I appreciate the help you gave to me in loaning McHugh's services during this hectic period. His help has been of inestimable value, his judgment the best, his loyalty beyond question, and his persistence almost inhuman. His place will be difficult to fill, as you may well imagine." Parkinson files, Equitable Archives.

of the United States.[54] Hundreds of local real estate agents were appointed to arrange for the renting, maintenance, and eventual sale of the foreclosed properties. Standard contract forms were devised, four for the larger buildings in New York City, and four for the miscellaneous properties located throughout the country. These contracts required the real estate agents to rent, to collect rents, to see to the maintenance of properties, and to pay taxes and secure reduction of taxes where possible.[55]

Once the property was assigned to a real estate agent for management, he was required to inspect it and render a report on its conditions, and thereafter to report monthly. General policy of the Society was to govern its repair and decorating expenditures according to income possibilities rather than sales probabilities. Rental rates for the larger properties were established by the Home Office, and in general the making or canceling of leases involving annual rentals of more than $5,000 or terms exceeding five years required specific approval from the Finance or Real Estate Committee.[56] Detailed rules covered expenses of repairs, rentals, fire insurance, and the like. A Repairs Committee was created at a level of authority between that of the Finance or Real Estate Committee and the Repairs Section of the City Real Estate Department; this committee met three times a week and passed upon recommendations for repairs and remodeling which originated in the field. Real estate depreciation written off was subject to the approval of the Finance Committee or the Real Estate Committee, both of which were governed by the provisions of the New York law.[57] Past due taxes and foreclosure expenses were added to the

[54] The cities were: Atlanta; Birmingham; Brooklyn; Buffalo; Boston; Charlotte, N.C.; Columbus; Chicago; Detroit; Elizabeth, N.J.; Indianapolis; Hartford; Huntington, W.Va.; Los Angeles; Memphis; Minneapolis; Newark; New York City; Philadelphia; Pittsburgh; Salt Lake City; San Francisco; Seattle; Stamford, Conn.; and Tampa, Fla.

[55] Commissions under the New York City contracts, which were administered from the Home Office, usually ran from 3 to 5 per cent of gross collections. Under the most commonly used contract for miscellaneous types of properties located throughout the country, commissions were 50 per cent on the first month's rent and 5 per cent thereafter; commissions on leases and sales were according to the rules of the local real estate boards; for the first $500 of repairs, the commission was 10 per cent; more than $500, 5 per cent; for tax reduction, 25 per cent. Muller, "History of Foreclosed Real Estate," p. 18.

[56] The Real Estate Committee of the Board was created by amendment of the By-Laws in 1941 to supervise the Society's investments in real estate and mortgages. It took over these functions from the Finance Committee.

[57] The ratio originally used was 3 per cent of the value of the building. To

cost of acquisition; fire losses, if any, were also included in such costs. A constant study of individual properties by field and Home Office personnel to ascertain what could be done by appropriate expenditures attained excellent results. Certain designated cashiers handled most of the clerical details in the management of properties and thus saved much time for the supervisors.

To handle the accounting work involved in administering the foreclosed properties a Real Estate Accounting Section of more than 100 persons was hastily assembled in the Auditors Department; this section designed accounting forms and established accounting controls. A certain amount of fumbling and trial and error experimentation took place in the beginning but the accounting function eventually became a highly efficient operation. The accounting problems were not confined to the Home Office but extended to the branch offices as well. The majority of the field personnel were untrained in accounting methods relating to real estate management, and were not aware of the many problems involved. Some of the supervisors of the branch offices had been former loan correspondents and were not accustomed to conforming to the pattern of operations of a large corporation. Consequently a team of field auditors was trained to audit the operations of the branch offices and to act as liaison between the Home Office and field. On their first visits to the branch offices these auditors found some highly individualistic and interesting accounting practices which hardly met the Equitable standards.

Results improved with experience. Although operating net income from foreclosed Class I and Class II properties was low during the early 1930's, as organization and economic conditions improved somewhat the results from real estate operations responded accordingly. During the period 1936 to 1945, operating net income (before depreciation) from foreclosed urban properties was slightly more than 2.5 per cent. Although all foreclosed property was for sale from the moment of acquisition, owing to generally depressed conditions in the real estate

---

determine the building value, the practice was to apply to the total cost of acquisition the ratio which the appraised value of the building bore to the total appraised value of the property at the time the mortgage loan was made. In 1944, the Society's practice in depreciating the value of its buildings was revised. The new practice was to write off the value of the building over the remaining useful life of the property on the straight line basis. This required that both the value of the building and the remaining useful life be determined when the property was acquired. Muller, "History of Foreclosed Real Estate," p. 23.

market, sales were not pressed; the Society could afford to wait out the market. Although New York law limited ownership of foreclosed properties to five years, the State Insurance Department was extremely cooperative in granting extensions of time. In June 1937, it became the general policy to dispose first of those properties which were either poor in character or were located in neighborhoods which were deteriorating. So far as possible, cash payment was required for the poorest properties; otherwise, 15 per cent payment was sought, although 10 per cent might be accepted under favorable circumstances. Purchase money mortgages were made available under a variety of plans which produced complete amortization. The term of repayment varied, as did interest rates (usually from 5 to 6 per cent).[58] In some states it was of advantage to dispose of the property by contract sale because redemption laws prevented the quick repossession of a mortgaged property through foreclosure but did permit ready reacquistion of a property sold under a contract sale agreement.[59] The Finance Committee and after 1941, the Real Estate Committee, authorized the President to sell foreclosed properties the book value of which was less than $25,000; sales of properties of greater value were individually submitted to the committee for approval. The Manager of City Real Estate was required to secure the approval of the President for all sales, regardless of size.

Early in 1941, by which time conditions in the real estate markets had improved, Equitable decided to push sales of its foreclosed properties, and a quota system was established for the disposal of some 3,000 properties in Class I. Bulletins describing the program were mailed to agents; advertising expenses were taken care of by the

[58] The most widely used plan involved monthly payments of $10 per $1,000 per month. Interest charged was 5, 5½, or 6 per cent, according to prevailing rates in the different localities. This plan provided for complete repayment at 5 per cent in 130 months, at 5½ per cent in 135 months, and at 6 per cent in 139 months. Since these rates of interest were higher than those which prevailed soon thereafter in general mortgage lending, the Society was able to sell many blocks of these mortgages to other investors.

[59] The states were Illinois, Indiana, Iowa, Kansas, Michigan, Minnesota, Montana, Oregon, Pennsylvania, South Dakota, Utah, Washington, and Wisconsin. Where minimum down payments were made, passage of title through medium of the contract sale was deferred until approximately 20 per cent of the purchase price had been paid in by the original cash payment augmented by the amortizing portion of the monthly payments. In most cases this was brought about in either 24 or 36 payments; after passage of title, the same payments continued under a purchase money mortgage until complete repayment had been made.

Society. Under this program, administered after Lackey's death in November 1941 by John H. Muller, the Society succeeded in disposing of more than 5,000 urban properties within five years.

Equitable learned much from its depression experience with urban mortgage loans. The weakness of the correspondent system, lack of discrimination as to location and quality of property, lack of amortization provisions, failure to reckon with second mortgages, and the absence of personal credit considerations all contributed to a bad situation relative to foreclosures. The absence of a qualified salaried field organization and failure to require assigned life insurance for residential loans were also important factors.[60] The Society was not to repeat these mistakes.

At the end of 1931 Equitable had $197,000,000 in farm mortgages—about 14 per cent of its total investments. Through foreclosure it had acquired 430 farms with a book value of $3,700,000, but these represented less than 2 per cent of its farm loan investment. (For some companies, the foreclosures ran as high as 19 per cent.) By 1933, however, 49 per cent of all Equitable farm loans were in serious default, and during the next three years the Society acquired 5,065 farms.

Defaults on farm mortgages presented special problems. As pointed out by Glenn McHugh, then Investment Assistant to President Parkinson, when there was default in a railroad bond or a preferred steel stock Equitable did not have to undertake the rehabilitating, managing, and disposing of the railroad or steel plant; the chief problem was a Home Office one and concerned bondholders' committees, write-offs, sales, or exchanges. But defaults on farms presented a problem which had to be handled largely in the field. Since the correspondent system had largely broken down Equitable would need substantial field organizations to deal with the delinquencies, tax problems, fire insurance, crop management, and eventual sales.[61]

[60] In the future all residential loans carried the requirement of life insurance, which not only provides for the repayment of the loan upon the death of the breadwinner but, through its cash value, provides the means to carry the borrower over temporary periods of distress. Further, life insurance provides a much better risk from the start because all of the functions of inspection and underwriting which enter into the approval of the insurance in a sense enter into the approval of the loan. Also, the home owner who finances his home with life insurance protection is, in all probability, a more serious-minded and responsible person.

[61] Glenn McHugh memorandum for President Parkinson, February 10, 1933, Parkinson papers, Equitable Archives.

In regard to the weakness of the correspondent loan system Glenn McHugh

One of the troublesome situations which developed as a result of Equitable's reliance upon the mortgage correspondent method of obtaining loans was that which involved Merle H. Collins and his companies. In 1910 Collins organized the Collins Mortgage Company (New Jersey) which during succeeding years served as Equitable's chief farm loan correspondent in the corn belt. In 1928 he organized The Collins Farms Company (also incorporated in New Jersey), which operated from headquarters in Cedar Rapids, Iowa. Collins proposed that this company purchase from Equitable the farms which became in default on mortgages which he had sold to Equitable; these farms were usually purchased for the amount of the Society's loan. Collins Farms also purchased other farms at foreclosure sales and proceeded to combine the properties into units of 1,000 to 1,500 acres as large-scale industrial projects. Collins tore down the fences, limed the soil, bought thousands of dollars' worth of farm machinery, maintained an itinerant machine shop to service the machinery, and rotated the crops. He maintained that corn could be grown at a cost of $11 per acre.[62]

In December 1930 President Parkinson said that Equitable was not in any way interested in The Collins Farms Company but that over a period of eighteen years Equitable had made more than $100,000,000 of loans through the Collins Mortgage Company; he regarded Collins as a man of high character, wide experience, and good judgment, and thought that he was entitled to all the encouragement and support which Equitable could give him.[63] In the summer of 1931 Directors

---

later said: "During the depression, we foreclosed several thousand farms and two or three times as many homes, and also foreclosed practically all of our correspondents, for two reasons: 1) They operated on a cash commission basis and failed to set up reserves so when new business or renewals faded, they asked for a service allowance which didn't seem realistic to our Home Office group; and 2) the contract was really burdensome because they were expected to pay foreclosure costs and to repurchase loans which went bad. Obviously, they couldn't perform—some of them went broke, one or two went to jail, and some went on our payroll as local supervisors primarily handling real estate and delinquent loans." "Policy Aspects of Mortgage Portfolio Management" a paper read before the Life Officers' Investment Seminar at Beliot, Wisconsin, June 28, 1956. Equitable Archives.

62 A feature article in *The Cedar Rapids Sunday Gazette and Republican*, March 30, 1930, described how The Collins Farms Company operated 25,000 acres in Iowa without horses and other livestock.

63 Thomas I. Parkinson to Henry J. Nichols, Vice President of the Shawmut National Bank, Boston, December 3, 1930. Sterling Pierson files, Equitable Archives.

Eugenius H. Outerbridge and John T. Manson went to Iowa and inspected a number of the farms on which there were Equitable loans. Although they found some discrepancies between Collins' records and the Society's records, they reported that Collins' organization appeared to be first class, with many of the unit operators being "husky, intelligent, fine-looking young men, some, if not all of them, of agricultural college training," and that the farms "represented the most up-to-date, scientific management both of the soil and rotations and the methods of cultivation." The directors, after putting the members of the Collins organization "through a sort of 'Third Degree' of questions" decided that the Collins group was a "very able, enthusiastic and optimistic agent of the Society," and concluded that unless there should be a prolonged depression Equitable had nothing to worry about regarding the loans made on the properties inspected.[64]

But by this time the Collins Companies were in trouble. The farms were being run at a loss and Collins Farms owed $85,000 to International Harvester for equipment sold on credit. Collins appealed to Equitable for more assistance and Equitable advanced an additional $400,000 on Collins' representations. Soon thereafter the banking situation in Cedar Rapids became acute and it developed that the Cedar Rapids National Bank had lent practically $1,000,000 to Collins on farm mortgages on the understanding that these mortgages were loans which he had negotiated for sale to Equitable and were merely in transit to Equitable. Upon investigation it was discovered that many of these mortgages were junior to mortgages already on the same properties, and therefore not loans that Equitable would accept. To save the bank, however, Equitable again came to the rescue and agreed to put up an additional $800,000 to relieve the bank of the burden. Despite the additional assistance the Cedar Rapids National Bank was finally forced to consent to its deposit liabilities being taken over by the Merchants National Bank of Cedar Rapids, which assumed the agreements made with Equitable. With all of the help extended the Collins Mortgage Company as of October 3, 1931, still owed $341,000 to the bank. Equitable had canceled the loan correspondent contract with the Mortgage Company but the banks later claimed that President Parkinson had entered into an oral agreement with Collins to the effect that Equitable would, for an indefinite time, finance the acquisition, improvement, and operation of farms acquired by The

[64] The report was signed July 17, 1931, and may be found in *ibid.*

Collins Farms Company. After cancellation of the loan correspondent contract, Equitable opened its own Cedar Rapids office then took over the plant, fixtures, automobiles, and good will of the Mortgage Company and promised to pay a reasonable price for same.

Equitable engaged the law firm of Tinley, Mitchell, Ross and Everest of Council Bluffs, Iowa, as legal counsel and in July 1932 filed foreclosure suits (*Equitable* v. *Buslee-Turner, et al.*) against certain properties of The Collins Farms Company and the Mortgage Company. Both of these companies filed cross petitions asking for an accounting and alleging that $1,562,637 was due them on account of the interest of the Collins Mortgage Company in certain amortized loans, and other items.[65] While this case was still pending Collins Mortgage Company filed suit at law against Equitable for breach of contract and claimed that the Society owed it $1,325,000 on account of cancellation of the loan correspondent contract and the taking over of the company's plant, and for other items. The action (*Collins Mortgage Company* v. *Equitable*) was filed in the District Court of Iowa for Polk County. Equitable counsel succeeded in having this action transferred from the State Court to the United States Court for the Southern District of Iowa and the cause from law to equity.

February 1, 1933, Equitable filed bills of foreclosure in the United States Courts for both the Southern and Northern Districts of Iowa—(*Equitable* v. *Collins Farms Company*). These foreclosures included all of the second mortgages as well as the first mortgages on the same properties, and involved, including interest and advancements, approximately $4,000,000; they affected about 165 farms totaling 30,000 acres. Both Collins Companies and the two banks—Cedar Rapids National Bank and the Merchants National Bank—filed a plea of abatement to stop the foreclosures on the ground that Equitable in assenting to Voting Trust Agreements controlling the two Collins Companies had waived right to foreclose so long as the Voting Trusts were in force; the Voting Trust Agreement was not to expire until 1938. Both of the Collins Companies and the banks insisted that

[65] The suit was filed in the District Court of Iowa for Winnebago County. The counterclaim was based upon the allegation "that the assignment of future interests which was acquired as a condition precedent to the advancement of $810,000 by the Society upon the security of additional mortgages and the purchase of commission mortgages was, in fact, given only as security for the payment of the commission mortgages purchased." Folsom Everest to Sterling Pierson, January 25, 1935. *Ibid.*

Equitable was responsible for The Collins Farms Company which was not acting for itself but as an agent for the Equitable so as to provide a way for the Equitable to escape taking over title to so much real estate in Iowa. International Harvester was an intervenor in this action since it claimed an interest in the assets of Collins Farms because of that company's indebtedness for machinery. International Harvester charged that Equitable was using Collins as a screen behind which to hide poor investments.[66]

In July Equitable counsel concluded that it would be better to require trial of the foreclosure suits before the disposition of the counterclaim in the Buslee-Turner suit and before disposition of the controversy involved in the suit brought by the Collins Mortgage Company against Equitable. Equitable counsel also decided to ask for the appointment of a receiver for the lands involved in the two foreclosure suits. In September all actions except *Equitable* v. *Buslee-Turner,* which remained in the State Court, were referred to Judge F. F. Faville as Master in Chancery for the two United States District Courts. Hearings before Judge Faville ran for several months—until March 7, 1934—and the testimony totaled more than 10,000 pages. Upon their conclusion negotiations were begun to settle all questions out of court, and March 26 a Stipulation was signed by representatives of the Collins Companies and the two banks. The same day Judge Faville appointed a receiver *pendent lite* (Don Preussener).

The chief provisions of the Stipulation, which ran to eighteen legal size pages of typescript, were as follows: The Collins Farms Company agreed to deliver to Equitable special warranty deeds for all land standing in the name of the Company upon which Equitable had mortgages, and to assign to Equitable title to all outstanding leases on said farms, also to release Equitable from all claims which Collins Farms had or might have against the Society. The Collins Mortgage Company agreed to release Equitable from any claims which it might

[66] In a petition in equity in the District Court for Linn County, International Harvester claimed that Equitable owed $160,000 for the farm machinery purchased by Collins. Plaintiff charged that the defendant used the Collins Mortgage Company "as a means to conceal the Equitable's interest and the extent of its defaulted mortgages because of the adverse effect such information might have on the standing of said company and on its sale of life insurance in the state, and particularly because of the publicity which the Equitable had given and continued to give to its alleged conservative loaning policies and the soundness of its investments and the absence of foreclosed lands in its investment portfolio." Copy in *ibid.*

have against the Society and to dismiss all pending legal actions against it. M. H. Collins agreed to similar releases, as did the Merchants National Bank. Equitable agreed to pay the Merchants National Bank $150,000, to release the banks and the Collins Companies from any claims which it might have against them, and to dismiss all of its claims pending in court against the Collins Companies except the foreclosure suits in the Federal or State Courts.

President Parkinson had, by wire, March 22 said that he was prepared to recommend that the Equitable Board of Directors approve the proposed settlement provided that it was approved by all the individuals and companies involved. In June Equitable's Iowa counsel conferred with Alexander and Green and agreed upon certain conditions as requirements for carrying out the Stipulation. Some minor complications resulted when it came to obtaining releases from a few of the minority stockholders and creditors of the two Collins Companies, but they were worked out. Receiver Don Preussener took possession of the properties involved in the litigation August 1, and October 3 the Executive Committee of Equitable's Board authorized the officers of the Society to negotiate a settlement on the basis outlined in letters from Tinley, Mitchell, Ross and Everest. Final papers were signed November 23 and January 9, 1935, arrangements were finally made for Equitable to take possession of the farms. February 6 the Executive Committee authorized payment of the remainder ($80,000) of the fee of Tinley, Mitchell, Ross and Everest, and $8,500 to Special Master F. F. Faville. There remained the work of perfecting the Society's titles to the farms taken over and some titles were still in question as late as 1938.[67]

[67] Glenn Bennett, who had been in charge of the Kansas City office of the Collins Mortgage Company, was a partner with Collins; his compensation in Collins Mortgage Company was an interest participation in the Collins loans. When settlement was made and Equitable took over servicing of these loans, Bennett voluntarily surrendered his interest to Equitable. This so impressed President Parkinson that Bennett was made a Loan Supervisor for Equitable and was, with McHugh, helpful in inducing Nils A. Olsen to join Equitable. He also helped Olsen organize the farm field force.

The above account of the Collins litigation is based largely upon the following documents, all of which are in the Sterling Pierson files, Equitable Archives: 1) a summary of the Collins litigation by Attorney Moncure March of the Mortgage Loan and Real Estate Departments, January 15, 1935; 2) the summaries in letters from Tinley, Mitchell, Ross, and Everest of August 29 and 30, 1934, and January 25, 1935; 3) the Stipulation of March 26, 1934; and 4) the Alexander and Green memorandum of June 29, 1934.

The farms which Equitable took over from the Collins Companies proved to be more of a problem than other farms which the Society had taken over. Most of the buildings were in bad shape, barns had been converted into machine sheds and, since most of the fences had been torn down, the tenants could not keep livestock. The great majority of the tenants were not of the type which Equitable would like to keep on the farms. Consequently protecting the investment in these properties involved greater expenditures than required for other farms which the Society had acquired. In general they were consolidated with and operated as other farms in the different Loan Supervisors' districts.[68]

In June 1934 Congress passed the Frazier-Lemke Farm Bankruptcy Act. Under the provisions of this law, a farmer could petition in bankruptcy that all his property be appraised and that he be allowed to retain possession. If, after appraisal of the farm by a court-appointed appraiser at "its then fair and reasonable value," the creditors agreed, the farm might be sold to the debtor at its appraised value; the farmer was to pay 1 per cent interest on the unpaid balance while purchasing his farm at the appraised value. If the creditor did not agree to the appraisal, the farmer was to be given a stay of five years during which he was to pay "a reasonable rental." This provision for scaling down farm mortgage debts heavily penalized many life insurance companies. President Parkinson urged President Roosevelt to veto the bill as "ineffective as a relief measure for the farmers, unjust beyond reason for honest lenders, institutional and individual, and in the long run, destructive of the farmers' credit for future borrowing." Many life insurance men criticized the Frazier-Lemke Act as a means of robbing Peter to pay Paul; not only would it jeopardize the interests of 65,000,000 life insurance policyholders, but, they pointed out, the insurance companies were generally doing better by the farmer than the law required, for they were frequently furnishing feed, seed, and fertilizer while they left the farmer on the farm to rehabilitate his finances.[69]

[68] There are various memoranda on this subject from A. J. Stanfield, Loan Supervisor in Cedar Rapids, to Second Vice President Nils Olsen in the Farm Mortgage Department files, Equitable Archives.

[69] M. J. Cleary, President of the Northwestern Mutual Life Insurance Company, a heavy holder of farm mortgages, said that the law was legally and morally unsound and would impair the farmers' credit. Reported in *The National Underwriter,* XXXVIII (1934), September 28.

A number of life insurance companies tested the constitutionality of the Frazier-Lemke Act and on May 31, 1935, in the case of *Louisville Joint-Stock Land Bank* v. *Radford*, the Supreme Court of the United States declared the law unconstitutional.[70] Congress then prepared a bill which it thought would meet the Supreme Court's requirements of constitutionality. Among those who testified against this bill was Robert L. Hogg, Associate General Counsel of the Association of Life Insurance Presidents, and later to become a Senior Vice President of Equitable and Vice Chairman of the Board. He and others maintained that this bill also destroyed the right of public sale, while its supporters held that it did not. Friends of the bill sought to make the law permanent. But as passed in August it was limited to expire in March 1949. The new law permitted properties in financial difficulties to be tied up for a period of three years, but the lender was not deprived of any remedial rights except that of immediate foreclosure; he was not compelled to accept compulsory scaling down of the debt, but might demand a sale at auction at the end of the moratorium period if he was not satisfied with the appraised valuation. The constitutionality of the second Frazier-Lemke Act was upheld by the Supreme Court on March 29, 1937, in the case of *Wright* v. *Vinton Branch of the Mountain Trust Bank of Roanoke, Virginia.* The provision for public sale in this law was made meaningless, however, by the Supreme Court in December 1940 in its decision in the case of *Wright* v. *Union Central Life Insurance Company.*[71]

Equitable's foreclosed farm holdings increased steadily throughout the depression until, by the end of 1938, they reached a peak of 6,065 units, comprising more than 1,100,000 acres; these farms represented

[70] 295 U.S. 555. Justice Brandeis in his opinion enumerated five important substantive rights in specific property which had been taken without due process of law. Among them were the right to retain the lien until the indebtedness thereby secured was paid; the right to realize upon the security by judicial public sale; the right to determine when such sales should be held, subject only to the discretion of the court, etc.

Equitable was much interested in this case and the Association of Life Insurance Presidents participated as an *amicus curiae.*

[71] 304 U.S. 502 and 311 U.S. 273. Litigation in this famous case began in April 1934 and lasted until April 1942. For a summary see R. Carlyle Buley, *The American Life Convention*, II, p. 786, note 229. An excellent summary of the Frazier-Lemke Acts is "Shall We Have A Permanent Frazier-Lemke Law?", a paper read by Eli Ferguson before the National Agricultural Credit Committee at Chicago, January 20, 1950. Ferguson was at that time Assistant Manager of Equitable's Farm Mortgage Department. Copy in Equitable Archives.

an investment of $68,000,000. Meanwhile, the Society's farm mortgage portfolio had shrunk to $71,000,000. The foreclosed farms were concentrated largely in seventeen Midwestern and two Southern states; fortunately, few of them were in the dust bowl areas. This concentration simplified management problems, but made liquidation and maintenance of good public relations more difficult.

In April 1935 Glenn McHugh brought in Nils A. Olsen, who had been Chief of the Bureau of Agricultural Economics in the Department of Agriculture, to become Manager of the Farm Investment Department. Olsen, after being graduated from Luther College, Decorah, Iowa, continued his studies in history and economics at the University of Wisconsin and Harvard University, from each of which he received the Master of Arts degree. He served as an instructor in history and economics at Muhlenberg College, as a farm manager, and in 1919 joined the Department of Agriculture as Assistant Agricultural Economist. He was appointed Second Vice President of Equitable in 1936.

In November 1936 Eli Hall Ferguson joined Equitable as Office Manager in the Farm Mortgage Department. Ferguson was born on a cattle ranch in western South Dakota and graduated from high school at Philip. After working on his father's ranch for two years he entered South Dakota State University and was graduated with the B.S. degree in 1932. After another year of ranching he became associated with the First National Bank of Philip as a fieldman. From 1934 to 1936 he held various positions in the Department of Agriculture.

In May 1937 Reynolds I. Nowell became Olsen's chief assistant. Nowell, a native of Utah, received the Bachelor of Science degree from Utah State Agricultural College and the Master of Science degree from the University of Illinois; he also did graduate work at the University of Minnesota. He served as Agricultural Economist for the Federal Farm Board, 1930–32, and for the Department of Agriculture, 1932–34. For the next three years he was Regional Director of the Resettlement Administration in the three lake states of Minnesota, Wisconsin, and Michigan. When Olsen died in 1940, Nowell became Acting Manager of the Farm Mortgage Department, and two months later was appointed Manager. Eli Ferguson became Assistant Manager of the Department in 1943.

Equitable was fortunate in having three men with such excellent qualifications in the field of agriculture and agricultural economics to handle its depression farm problems. First, they made a field survey and decided upon policies which took into consideration not only the Society's obligations to its policyholders, but the effects which they would have upon the tenants on the farms and the communities in which the farms were located. Then the department drew up one-year lease contracts—mostly on the crop-share rental basis; the leases contained a provision for cancellation in the event the farm was sold by a specified date before the new lease-year started. In some of the states there was considerable agitation for longer-term leases for the tenants, but, on the other hand, political pressure was sometimes brought to bear to induce the corporate landowners to sell for the amount of their investment.

The Farm Mortgage Department set up branch offices, and eighty full-time fieldmen trained in agriculture took over the management of the foreclosed farms. These fieldmen selected the best tenants obtainable, and, since many of the farms were in a run-down condition, began a mass rehabilitation program. They insisted upon better crop rotation, and Equitable spent almost $2,000,000 for alfalfa, clover, and other legume and grass seeds; also substantial sums for limestone and fertilizer. The managers carried out a bindweed eradication program in parts of South Dakota, Iowa, and Nebraska, and drilled irrigation wells in the Platte River Valley in Nebraska. For the working season, they hired repair and painting crews which traveled from farm to farm. Lumber, shingles, cement, barbed wire, and paint were purchased in carload lots.[72] Traveling crews applied the paint—specially made to Equitable's specifications—not with brushes, but with spraying machines, in the use of which they were trained in advance.[73] In many of the farm homes the dust storms had filtered the fine silt through the shingles and deposited it, sometimes a foot deep, in the attic; consequently the plaster, if not already down, had to be removed and the ceilings replastered. By 1941 the department had completed 2,860

[72] On one occasion Equitable's desire to save money by buying in large lots worked in reverse. When the Society asked for bids on three carloads of alfalfa seed it found that no dealer in the country could supply anything like an order of that size, and by the time several dealers had obtained enough seed to bid the price had advanced appreciably.

[73] Equitable even made a motion picture to be used in instructing the painters in the use of the spraying machine. The story is told of a farm wife who, when approached by a local painter who offered to paint up her farm buildings at a very reasonable cost, replied: "Oh I wouldn't dare do that for the neighbors would be sure we had been foreclosed."

major repair programs at a cost of more than $3,000,000. The Society also saved money by self-insuring its farm buildings against fire and windstorm damage.

Marketing crop-share rentals of up to $5,000,000 per year constituted another field for the exercise of managerial techniques. The managers worked out a comprehensive system of production, inventory, and sales reports, without which management of the thousands of farms would have been impossible. Small grains were usually sold at harvest, but corn, the leading crop, was frequently stored on the farms to be sold later; delayed sale yielded a net gain of at least $500,000 per year on the crops of the late 1930's. The Society complied wherever feasible with the acreage restriction program of the Agricultural Adjustment Administration and, from 1934 to 1938, received an average of $275,000 per year for so doing.[74]

Although all of Equitable's farms were available for purchase at any time, they were not dumped on the depressed land market of the 1930's. Some farms were sold each year, but it was not until after the coming of World War II that Equitable disposed of the bulk of its properties. Once again, food became important, prices advanced, and farms were in demand. During the period 1941–44, 5,150 farms were returned to individual ownership. Very few of these farms were disposed of by contract sales with the customary small cash payment; on the contrary, the Society insisted on substantial down payments. It was more interested in the property staying sold, even though the price might not be so high. Of all sales made, approximately 23 per cent were for cash and 77 per cent on a credit basis with an average of 30 per cent down payment; the credit sales resulted in new purchase

[74] When President Parkinson read in the newspapers that the Equitable had received $275,000 in one year for crop restriction, he was in favor of publicly denouncing the program and sending the checks back to the U.S. Treasury. He changed his mind, however, when it was pointed out that policyholder suits might result from such action; also that the checks served as only part repayment for Equitable's curtailed income from crops. When the government subsequently put a $10,000 limit on farm benefit payments for corporate owners, Equitable put only its dust-bowl farms under the program. Tenants on other farms might sign up if they wished, but Equitable insisted on getting the landlord's share of crops on the diverted acreage, with the result that most of the tenants figured it would be more profitable to ignore the program and raise crops. The Agricultural Adjustment Administration Administrator for Iowa threatened—early in 1942—to expose Equitable to public view if it did not authorize its tenants to sign up for the crop restriction program without the crop-sharing provision. But in the same mail Manager Nowell received a letter from William S. Knudsen of the U.S. War Production Board directing the Equitable to sell all the corn it had on hand and to urge its tenants to plant and raise as much additional corn as possible in 1942.

money mortgage investments for the Society. A tabulation of 7,294 sales showed that about 40 per cent of the purchasers were tenants, either on Equitable's or other farms; 26 per cent of the purchasers were owners of adjoining land or were other well-to-do farmers. About 26 per cent of the sales were to investors, largely local merchants and professional men. Only a relatively small number of the farms were purchased by former owners.

In December 1939, President Parkinson spoke before the Annual Meeting (in Chicago) of the American Society of Farm Managers and Rural Appraisers. After reviewing conditions in the post-World War I period, he said:

Farmers, like other people . . . are prone to borrow what they can and sometimes more than they should. Lenders sometimes misjudged the real value of farm lands and, in competition to place their money, were too generous in the amounts advanced. In the years following the World War and before the depression, that was very true. Some of you know that as a matter of fact; many of you probably know it as a matter of history. I know it as a matter of experience, and it hurts a little more that way. The appraisers were not careless. They went along with the prevailing atmosphere. These tendencies of lender and borrower, moreover, were supplemented by public policies which promoted inflation and unwise lending.

When the depression struck, farmers and lenders alike were caught in a difficult situation. It was inevitable that foreclosures should bring to the insurance companies a large number of farms and consequent new problems of management. We delayed foreclosure wherever a struggling farmer had a chance to absorb his financial difficulties and get back on his feet. There were, as you know, however, many cases where foreclosure alone could solve a bad situation resulting from excess valuation, over-optimism, and pyramided mortgages and other indebtedness.

As we did not seek to acquire, so we do not desire to retain farm lands. At the same time, our efforts as owners and managers of farms are devoted to improving them, building up their productive capacity and putting them back into the hands of individual owners. In the early days of our experience as farm owners, we devoted most of our effort to the repair, replacement of farm buildings, fences, and drainage systems. In the Equitable alone, our expenditures for these purposes have averaged around a million dollars a year. We annually expend large sums for soil rehabilitation. We have emphasized soil conserving crops and good rotations. On the whole, we believe that the rehabilitation of the farms which we have foreclosed is a constructive contribution to the communities in which these farms are located, and to agriculture as a whole. . . .

On the whole our experience through this depression with farm mortgages, foreclosures and farm management has taught us much without destroying our confidence in farm lands as security for long-term investment. If we apply the lessons which this experience has taught us and, especially, if our appraisers will keep their heads when booms surround them we shall continue to serve the farmers with capital from the funds which our policyholders place in our hands.

President Parkinson was impressed "with the farmer's respect for his obligations as contrasted with the attitude of large corporate owners and their managers toward their obligations. The so-called corporate reorganization statutes have been turned into gentlemanly, dignified cloaks for indefinite postponement and ultimate impairment of corporate debts. We who have the responsibility for the investment of life insurance and similar funds of policyholders and depositors cannot fail to note the attitude of such borrowers, when we come to select our future investments." He then called attention to the fact that when the national Government made a mistake it affected everyone: "Theories take the place of practical common sense based upon facts and measures play up the downtrodden and play down the upstanding with mediocrity the result." As for subsidies: "Subsidies beget subsidies, but they do not provide the means by which to pay these alleged benefits. I think that the farmer's experience and character are such as to make him prefer to build his own land into production and, by co-operation with other farmers, to extend his market for his product, rather than to be dependent upon even the Federal Government for the development of his interests." The speaker then swung into his favorite subject of the government's "easy money policy," short-term financing of the Federal debt, the issuing of tax-exempt bonds, and artificially maintained low interest rates. In conclusion, he pointed out that if "this overgrown and swollen Federal Government" was to be demobilized, it would be up to the individual citizens:

If you do succeed in your own efforts and by the example you set, maybe you can do more to teach and guide government representatives for the benefit of agriculture than they can do to help agriculture. Then, we shall all be free from what has happened to us in the last few years and we shall all have the satisfaction of knowing that in our efforts we have not only been reasonably successful for ourselves and for those whose interests we primarily represent, but that we have also made a real and lasting contribution to the public good.[75]

[75] This talk illustrates not only President Parkinson's breadth of knowledge in many fields but also his ability to speak informally, without a manuscript, and

That Equitable's record in the administration of its foreclosed real estate was outstanding is illustrated by the fact that for the years 1936 to 1945 inclusive, it earned a return of almost 3 per cent on a total cost or investment of about $215,000,000.[76] At the end of 1947, by

---

still produce a polished paper. He usually spoke from notes rather than a manuscript and frequently tried out his forthcoming talk in segments before some of the Equitable staff. But for this important occasion, he asked Nils Olsen to prepare the materials for a speech. Olsen worked conscientiously and prepared what he thought was an excellent paper. But President Parkinson never found time, either on the train, after breakfast the next morning, or at the hotel, to familiarize himself with it. Finally, a few minutes before he was scheduled to talk, he gave the paper a quick going over. Then, speaking "off the cuff," he made his own speech, which was most favorably received. Later published in pamphlet form, it reads as well as it sounded.

In April 1944, Equitable began publication of *Farm Loan News,* a monthly which later was published quarterly. The editor was Forest J. Skogvold.

76 INVESTMENT RATES EARNED ON FORECLOSED REAL ESTATE

1936–1945 Inclusive

	Family (One to Six) Residential	Other City Properties	Total City Properties	Total Farm Properties	Total Foreclosed Properties
Mean Annual Book Value	$35,916,000	$28,105,000	$64,021,000	$46,780,000	$110,801,000
Gross Income	40,803,000	37,602,000	78,405,000	34,892,000	113,297,000
Less Operating & Administrative Expense	33,145,000	28,864,000	62,009,000	22,370,000	84,379,000
Net Operating Income (before depreciation)	7,658,000	8,738,000	16,396,000	12,522,000	28,918,000
Net Profit or Loss, Depreciation & Other adjustments of Book Value	−2,448,000	−3,864,000	−6,312,000	10,386,000	4,074,000
Adjusted Net Income	$5,210,000	$4,874,000	$10,084,000	$22,908,000	$32,992,000
Aggregate Rate of Return	1.451%	1.734%	1.574%	4.897%	2.978%

which time the Society had disposed of the last of its farms and all but four of its dwelling properties, President Parkinson was able to report that, during the preceding nineteen years (1929–47) the Society had recovered the whole amount of its principal investment, the costs of foreclosure, the defaulted mortgage interest, and in addition the sum of $21,020,000, a sum which represented an annual return of 1.39 per cent on the average cost of the foreclosed real estate owned during the period.

* * *

The depression naturally resulted in a large increase in policy loans. From 128,414 in 1928 the number of policy loans increased to 375,641 in 1932, then gradually decreased to 174,512 in 1937. (By 1945 the number had dropped to 30,148.) Although fewer than 5 per cent of the borrowers failed to pay interest on their loans, there was a large incidence of lapses on policies with loans against them. In 1933, for instance, more than 80,000 policyholders with loans discontinued further premium payments on their policies with the result that the loans were deducted from the values of the policies, thus leaving little or no equity with which to continue extended term insurance.[77]

As previously noted, during the depression years banks frequently encouraged policyholders to make loans on their policies and liquidate their bank debts. Another practice which gave the life insurance companies concern was the assignment of policies to the banks as collateral for loans. Since Equitable's interest rate on policy loans was 6 per cent and some of the New York City banks were charging as low as 3 per cent, assignment of policy and borrowing from the bank at the lower rate appeared to be a sensible arrangement. One argument in favor of this practice was that the saving in interest permitted the policyholder to purchase term insurance to cover the amount of the loan and thereby keep fully protected. There were, however, serious objections to the assignment of policies, both from the bank's and the policyholder's viewpoint.[78] Equitable made spot checks on the number

[77] The above figures are based upon a memorandum furnished by Vice President Charles F. Andolsek, Department of Policy Claims, September 10, 1963.

In 1932 policy loans totaled $305,340,869 or about 20.7 per cent of the Society's admitted assets. By 1939 policy loans had fallen to $234,982,704 or 9.8 per cent of admitted assets. Treasurer's Reports for 1935 and 1941, Equitable Archives.

[78] W. H. Bender, a New York Agent of the National Life of Vermont, pointed out that by absolute assignment the policyholder was letting himself in for much

of bank assignments during the years of the late 1930's, and in 1940 sent a form letter to the Society's policyholders in which it made some "observations." The letter called attention to the fact that an absolute assignment might have the effect in some cases of terminating the beneficiary's interest in the policy; also that in the event of death of the insured payment of the balance beyond the loan to the insured's executors might result in administration expenses, inheritance taxes, and possible claims of creditors. As the result of New York law Equitable reduced the interest rate on loans on the Society's new Series 80 policies to 5 per cent, effective January 1, 1939. It then made the same interest reduction on loans on all outstanding policies, effective January 1, 1944. Equitable was the only life insurance company to apply the uniform reduced rate to all policies irrespective of the size of the loans or other considerations. The notice to policyholders who had outstanding policy loans read as follows: "In authorizing this reduction, the Board of Directors reserved the right to revoke this action and from time to time establish other interest rates for its policy loans, not in excess of the rate specified in the policy." [79]

Next to mortgage loans and policy loans, railroad bonds constituted the largest portion of Equitable's assets in 1932—about 16.5 per cent.[80] Important as railroad securities were among institutional investors, they did not escape the effects of the depression. Although a substantial part of Equitable's holdings of railroad securities had been confined to underlying obligations, the decline in earnings of the railroads was so great that defaults on their bonds were numerous. For a time there

---

more trouble and complication than he realized. For instance, if the policyholder died before the loan was repaid, the bank would take over the proceeds and pay to the widow the balance beyond the loan. This would mean wrecking any program of settlement options. *The National Underwriter*, XLII (1938), December 16 (Life Edition).

W. F. Gephart, Vice President of the First National Bank of St. Louis, wrote: "The easy assumption that many bankers have that a loan based on the cash surrender value of a life insurance contract is the highest type of loan is not warranted by the facts." He proceeded to give reasons. "Bank Loans on Life Insurance Policies," *Mid-Continent Banker*, April 1943.

[79] It is worthy of note that following appropriate discussion with the New York Insurance Department and others, the Society, by Board action on September 15, 1966, initiated a program for resuming the contractual 6 per cent policy loan interest rate on those policy series which were affected by this previous voluntary rate reduction. This action was taken as the result of the general rise in interest rates to the highest level since the 1920's.

[80] At the turn of the century, railroad bonds had constituted 38.49 per cent; in 1912, 42 per cent; and in 1919 about 36 per cent.

was doubt as to whether senior obligations would fare much better in the numerous railroad reorganizations than would the junior issues.[81]

During, and for a number of years following the depression, Equitable was confronted on the one hand with the problem of defaults, and on the other with opportunities for successful operations in the market for railroad securities. It succeeded in administering itself out of many weaker issues and building up a portfolio of securities, at attractive yields, in the stronger railroads. Throughout President Parkinson played a very active role, ably assisted by Hunter Holding who joined his staff in 1937.[82]

In 1931, when three important railroads went into receiverships—the Seaboard Air Line, the Florida East Coast and the Wabash—some of Equitable's agency managers inquired as to what would be the effect on Equitable's holdings. Treasurer M. C. Laffey explained that all of them were senior issues and that even in the case of the Wabash, which had gone through reorganization in 1915, the underlying bonds appeared safe. Vice President Albert G. Borden sent Laffey's memorandum to the managers with the statement that "this is further confirmation of the fact that our investments are selected with a view to their capacity for standing up when the going becomes hard." [83] Most of the junior bonds were those of the stronger railroads such as Burlington, Northern Pacific, Great Northern, Rock Island, and Norfolk and Western. In addition to those railroad bonds in default, some others held by Equitable were regarded as being in a critical condition.[84]

Late in 1932, a number of insurance companies (including Equitable), banks, associations, and four universities addressed a statement to the National Transportation Committee which emphasized the importance of the railroad problem and begged the committee to

[81] As of December 29, 1931, junior bonds comprised approximately $25,000,000 of the total of $244,300,000. The figures are taken from a tabulation submitted to President Parkinson December 30 by Treasurer M. C. Laffey, Sterling Pierson files, Equitable Archives.

[82] Holding later became Vice President in charge of railroad securities in the Securities Investment Department. For a sketch of his career see this history, p. 1162, note 90.

[83] Laffey to Second Vice President Albert G. Borden, December 5, 1931; Borden to General Agents and Agency Managers, December 5, 1931. Sterling Pierson files, Equitable Archives.

[84] Among them: Chicago and Eastern Illinois, St. Louis and San Francisco, Mobile and Ohio, and New Orleans and Northeastern.

examine all phases of it and recommend a solution that would allow the railroads to operate on a businesslike basis.[85] Bernard M. Baruch, vice chairman of the committee, asked for written memoranda setting forth each group's views, and the life companies complied immediately.[86] They pointed out the need for immediate action to prevent far-reaching defaults and receiverships, the need for a resurvey of the entire transportation field, and the enactment of measures which, with the return of normal times, would give the railroads an opportunity to earn and retain sufficient income to justify the confidence of conservative investors in their securities. In this connection, they called attention to the fact that the reservoir of life insurance funds was not as widespread a source of new capital for the railroads as it had been in the past, and that the Interstate Commerce Act as amended had failed to produce the degree of financial stability intended. The memorandum recommended a thorough examination of the rate structure, solution of the problem of competition of unregulated carriers, consideration of means to expedite consolidations, relief from taxation used in large part to help subsidize the competition, and relief from state and Federal regulation of working conditions.[87]

In 1935, when the holder of a $200,000 Equitable endowment policy wrote President Parkinson and asked him if it would not be to Equitable's interest to advocate the regulation of all methods of transportation, as the Eastman bill proposed, President Parkinson replied: "We are constantly in touch with the railroad situation and plan to make an appearance at the hearings to be held in Washington on the so-called Eastman bills." [88]

Despite the efforts of the National Transportation Committee the railroad situation failed to improve. Equitable, as owner of railroad securities, became involved in twenty-five receiverships. Some policyholders wanted to know why the Society, as "a large holder of railroad

[85] Members of the committee were Calvin Coolidge, Bernard M. Baruch, Clark Howell, Alexander Legge, and Alfred E. Smith. A copy of this undated three-page statement is in the Sterling Pierson files, Equitable Archives.

[86] Baruch to Thomas I. Parkinson, November 15, 1932. *Ibid.*

[87] Copy in *ibid.*

[88] George Sealy, President, Galveston Wharf Company, to Thomas I. Parkinson, March 13, 1935. *Ibid.*

The bill to provide for government ownership of the railroads was introduced April 15, 1935, by Senator Burton K. Wheeler of Montana. The bill was written by Joseph B. Eastman, Federal Coordinator of Transportation.

bonds," had not been more active in pushing through reorganization of the railroads in receivership; they could not understand what was to be gained by constantly delaying action since the Society, as well as other investors, was losing money. President Parkinson patiently replied to one such inquiry by explaining that reorganizations were not such simple and easy matters as one might suppose; they had been taken out of the hands of the security holders and placed squarely with the Interstate Commerce Commission, and they had to be conducted under "the exceedingly intricate and indefinite provisions" of Section 77 of the Bankruptcy Act. After the railroad filed its petition in bankruptcy, it was not required to file its plan for reorganization until six months had elapsed; then the ICC would hold hearings and in time decide upon the action to be taken. He made it clear that Equitable did "not desire to prolong for a day the period during which we as the owner of underlying railroad bonds have to go without interest on our investments." [89]

Two years later, by which time approximately one-third of the railroad plant of the United States was in bankruptcy, President Parkinson said: "No real progress has been made in reorganization of our bankrupt roads and the restoration to the control of management." He did not think there could be any progress in reorganization until the public policy affecting railroads had been determined, and this included public policy with respect to taxation as well as labor and readjustment of the railroad plant. If success was to attend the formulation of policies looking to the revival of the railroad industry, government, management, and labor would have to face all the facts squarely and honestly and formulate policies accordingly: "Thus far government, management and labor have not worked together for the restoration of adequate earnings and their equitable distribution. Instead of individual and collective responsibility exercised in the general public interest, we have had an excess of self-interest and group-interest. . . . The time has come to face the facts, and where we do not have the facts, to get them. Then we need fewer theories, ambitions and arguments and more application of ordinary common sense." [90]

Regardless of the situation, Equitable refused to be panicked into selling its railroad bonds. President Parkinson and Counsel Sterling

[89] Thomas I. Parkinson to Charles H. Hughes, February 24, 1936. Copy in Sterling Pierson files, Equitable Archives.

[90] Radio address, April 29, 1938. Copy in Parkinson files, Equitable Archives.

Pierson believed that in the numerous reorganizations legal precedent would be followed and that the senior issues would be given prior rights; they even made a study of the past record of one of the influential judges of the United States Supreme Court on such cases. In the end seniority was observed and Equitable came through with only minor amounts of secondary new securities. Of the bonds which did not default, many were noncallable and brought a good return in the low interest era which followed. The results obtained in administering the securities involved in railroad receiverships were well summed up in the following statement: "The Society owned railroad securities (other than equipment obligations) which cost it $62,679,000, in 25 roads which went into receivership since 1930. As of December 31, 1957, the market value of securities held or 'consideration' received for this entire investment was $54,564,000 (87.1% of cost). Earnings on this investment (after full return of cost) gave an average yield of 3.86%." [91] Had the $62,679,000 of securities been sold in 1939 Equitable would have taken a loss of approximately $43,000,000.

In addition to the numerous receiverships there were other factors which tended to depress railroad securities in the late 1930's. In February 1936 the Comptroller of the Currency ruled that commercial banks be prohibited from purchasing securities which he regarded as predominantly speculative. As a result bank examiners put pressure on the banks to liquidate those securities not classified above a certain rating, or to write them down with eventual liquidation in mind. Then in his annual report for 1937 the Superintendent of Banks for New York stated that the "entire problem of railroad securities as investments for savings banks should be reconsidered." And in 1938 the New York legislature removed more than three billion dollars (par value) of railroad bonds from the legal list for savings bank investments. The result of both of these actions was forced sales of railroad securities at reduced market prices. The investment officers of Equitable, however, after careful study decided that there were many opportunities for sound investments in railroad securities, and during the period 1937–42 Equitable increased its railroad bond account by more than $255,000,000. As bond prices rose 1943–46 the railroad bond account was decreased by some $200,000,000. For the period 1938–46 Equitable showed a profit over costs of $24,773,000 while five of the

[91] Hunter Holding, "Railroad Investments," May 1958, p. 31. *Ibid.*

other leading companies showed losses which ran from $3,949,000 to $65,640,000.[92]

* * *

During the 1920's Equitable invested fairly heavily in the bonds of utility companies and these securities constituted approximately 11.5 per cent of its assets in 1930. Despite the effects of the depression and the impact upon investor confidence of a plank in the Democratic platform of 1932 directed toward public ownership and development of hydroelectric projects, top grade utility credits held up relatively well marketwise. The securities of lesser credits, however, fell sharply, and by the time of President Franklin D. Roosevelt's inauguration the yields on so-called second grade utility bonds were nearly two and a half times the yields available on the high grade bonds. Equitable, believing that the underlying securities of many of the operating utility companies had intrinsic values, took advantage of the opportunity. During the period 1935–37 it purchased more than $283,000,000 principal amount, and during the next five years added another $483,000,000 of such securities.[93]

Early in 1935 Equitable began receiving numerous letters—many of them identically worded—from policyholders all over the country asking the Society to take a stand against the Rayburn-Wheeler Bill, which the letter writers claimed was "unjust and . . . has caused a decrease in the value of most utility securities." [94] Sterling Pierson replied that Equitable was studying the bill and suggested that it would be more effective for policyholders to present their views as individuals to their lawmakers. Warner H. Mendel, also of the legal staff, made a long report on the subject and concluded that, despite its propaganda, the Government did not contemplate the destruction of the operating companies or of their ability to earn a fair return; the legislation was a compromise between the Government's policy for immediate rate reductions and the demands of the private utilities to be allowed more

[92] Table in *ibid.*, May 1955, p. 27.

[93] "The Society's spectacular purchases of utility bonds in 1934, 1935 and 1936 has become almost legendary." Thus wrote Joseph M. Bell, Jr., in his "Operations in Public Utility Bonds and Preferred Stocks 1935–1942," p. 4. A copy of this 28-page report plus XIV exhibits and tabulations may be found in Equitable Archives.

[94] The Rayburn-Wheeler Bill became the Public Utility Holding Company Act of 1935. This law increased the power of the Federal Power Commission, and contained the famous "death sentence" provision for holding companies, etc.

time to make the adjustments.[95] When Wendell Willkie, President of The Commonwealth and Southern Corporation, led the attack upon the proposed legislation, Mendel advised President Parkinson not "to permit himself to be quoted on any aspects of the situation, as an expression by him would, no doubt, be magnified and distorted by both sides." Besides: "The dire results predicted by Mr. Willkie should react directly in our interest. The only way sound issues can be obtained to-day at attractive yields is as a result of too hasty dumping. In such a situation, the large investor with an efficient statistical department always profits." [96]

In only one instance did Equitable have a bad experience with its utility bonds, and that was in connection with Associated Gas and Electric Company debenture 5s of 1968, of which Equitable held about $4,773,000 at a "book value" of $4,022,560.[97] Management of Associated Gas, a holding company, had conceived the idea of getting holders of subsidiary company mortgage bonds and preferred stocks to turn them in for the debentures. The inducement, at least for Equitable, was a slightly higher yield and the argument that one big senior security would command a better market. The issue was handled by Harris Forbes and Company, whose prestige in the utility field was well recognized. The Associated Gas and Electric Company, like some of the other complicated holding company setups, not only ran into financial difficulties but also into the Public Utility Holding Company Act of 1935. When the Securities and Exchange Commission refused to approve payment of a dividend from one of Associated Gas' subsidiary companies to the parent company, both companies finally petitioned for reorganization under Chapter X of the Federal Bankruptcy Act. For a time it appeared that Equitable, the largest institutional holder of the debentures, would lose its entire investment. Long and complicated litigation ensued which lasted for ten years. Equitable's interests were handled by William Roberts, Counselor-at-Law, who was one of Equitable's directors. When reorganization plans were finally completed, and upheld by the Supreme Court of the United States in 1945, Equitable came out with common stock of the General

95 Warner H. Mendel, 25-page typescript memorandum to General Solicitor Sterling Pierson, March 20, 1935. Sterling Pierson files, Equitable Archives.

96 Warner H. Mendel to Sterling Pierson, April 22 and August 1, 1935. *Ibid.*

97 The book value in this instance being the value of the debentures which Equitable entered on its books. Equitable had bought the debentures during the 1920's. By 1939–41 this figure had been written down to $620,490.

Public Utilities Company, which carried side features, such as rights, subsidiary stock distributions, and the like. Eventually, the Society got its money back, plus a fair rate of return. Although no permanent loss resulted, this investment caused a minor crisis in Equitable's financial councils somewhat out of proportion to the amount it involved. Treasurer M. C. Laffey believed that the Associated Gas transaction outweighed, in the judgment of some, the many sound investments involving many millions of dollars, which Equitable had made in utility securities.[98]

A large portion (about 45 per cent) of the public utility bonds which Equitable purchased 1935–42 were acquired by way of private placements. The bonds so purchased were largely refundings of existing securities. One advantage of the private placements was that they resulted in a higher effective interest yield than could have been obtained at public offerings; not only did they avoid the usual bankers spread of two or more points, but owing to the fact that frequently companies requiring money could not afford to wait until a public issue could be prepared and sold, good bargains could be had.[99]

Equitable's utility bond portfolio increased nearly threefold during the period 1935–42—from approximately 9 to 20 per cent of assets. In view of the sharp decline in interest rates generally, redemptions or sales were especially heavy and amounted to nearly $350,000,000. During the period of ownership of the securities redeemed or sold, however, the Society derived a substantial return and in addition a profit of $15,453,000. By 1942 the market value of the bonds still held exceeded cost by $17,164,000 and it was estimated that the bonds purchased privately could be valued at $10,000,000 above costs.[100] Most of the so-called second-grade utility bonds which Equitable had acquired in 1934–36 at yields of 5 per cent or more had been refunded by 1943, and many of the larger insurance companies which showed

[98] The Associated Gas and Electric Company investment is covered in a general way in M. C. Laffey's memoir, "A Third of A Century, Plus, with Equitable." A detailed study of this investment was made by the Securities Investment Department in 1963 and was made available for the purposes of this history.

[99] During this period Equitable participated with other institutions in public utility private deals totaling more than $1,000,000,000. It headed (had an equal or greater participation than others) more than $555,000,000 of such business and acquired $343,000,000 of the securities or almost 35 per cent of the total in which it participated. Bell "Operations in Public Utility Bonds and Preferred Stocks, 1935–1942," p. 5–6.

[100] *Ibid.*, p. 3.

Fabian Bachrach

James F. Oates, Jr.
President, 1957–1964
Chairman of the Board, 1958–

no interest in them when yields were 5 to 7 per cent became eager buyers when the yields on the refunding issues were 3 to 4 per cent. So, with respect to its public utility bonds Equitable came out quite well and did better than most of its competitors.

Owing to a dearth of new bond issues, and moratoria and threats of moratoria, not only on farm mortgages but on municipal bonds as well, the life insurance companies invested heavily in United States bonds during the early years of the depression. Equitable's holding of United States Treasury bonds increased from $7,435,000 in 1930 to $439,574,326 in 1937; in addition it held several million dollars in treasury bills and notes. In fact until about 1940 the Society had never failed to subscribe to any of the new Treasury issues. But in 1938, when United States bonds were at a premium and the prospect for continuation of the tax-exempt feature was in doubt, Equitable sold heavily, with the result that the Society's investment in Government obligations was reduced by $149,159,669. As a result of these sales and money derived from other bond redemptions and from insurance operations, Equitable had, in 1939, accumulated a substantial volume of investable funds. So sure was President Parkinson that Government-maintained low interest rates would not continue indefinitely that he decided to keep the Society in a strong liquid position rather than make long-term commitments at low rates of interest. This policy—a form of negative speculation—helped maintain a fair return on investments. By 1940, the Society's combined gross rate of income earned on all stocks and bonds other than United States Government obligations was 3.78 per cent; including Government obligations it was 3.36 per cent.[101]

In addition to its purchase of United States bonds, Equitable, in

101 That Equitable's investment policy was respected by outsiders is indicated by a letter to President Parkinson from H. D. Yates, Deputy Comptroller, Department of Audit and Control of the New York State Government. Yates wanted to know how long the high municipal market would continue, whether the supply of municipal bonds would increase or decrease over the next few years, what rate of interest Equitable expected to average on its investments over the coming decade, whether it preferred short-term, medium, or long maturities, what was the probable course of the bond market, etc., etc. Yates said that the Comptroller of New York had done very well in the "demoralized market during 1932 and 1933," but that conditions had changed: "A high market, with corresponding cheap money and low interest rates, combined with a scarcity of bonds, has brought the State, along with other investors, face to face with a difficult investment problem." Yates to Thomas I. Parkinson, January 28, 1935. Sterling Pierson files, Equitable Archives. What answer, if any, was given, is not known.

November 1933, bought $3,250,000 of City of New York bonds issued for relief of the unemployed.[102]

So strict and uncertain were the requirements of the Securities Act of 1933 that many corporate directors were reluctant to take the risk of security issues, and many contemplated long-term bond issues were postponed. Others, however, were placed directly with the life insurance companies. This was a new type of investment for Equitable and the procedures had to be developed "from absolute scratch." The investment and law men devised techniques and standards for investigation, selection, pricing, restrictive provisions and checking after purchase. Treasurer M. C. Laffey, who, except for the legal work, placed the first of these loans almost single-handed, laid down certain provisions which were new at the time and many of which are still followed.[103] Two practices enabled Equitable to get its share of this kind of loan—courtesy and speed. No potential borrower was ever left dangling in uncertainty for extended periods of time; he was either refused promptly and politely or his request put through with expedition.

In the mid-1930's Equitable began investing in "industrial securities," that is securities which were not government, railroad, or public utility securities.[104] As of December 31, 1934, Equitable had $37,216,000 in such securities representing about a dozen industry groups; the bulk of the investments were in the oil, nonferrous metal, and steel industries. By 1940 the number of industry groups had about doubled and the investment had increased to $254,534,000, which, with $17,-

[102] J. P. Morgan and Company, Committee Agent, Committee of Banks, to President Parkinson, November 6, 1933. *Ibid.* This action was pursuant to an agreement drawn up October 30, 1933, between the City of New York and the Committee of Banks.

[103] One of the first, if not the first, of Equitable's private placements was a $300,000 investment in the Refunding 4s (1960) of a total issue of $2,400,000 of the Madison (Wisconsin) Gas and Electric Company, which was approved by the Finance Committee January 2, 1935. Securities Investment Department files, Equitable Archives.

[104] Nor did the term include bonds of real estate corporations and oil production loans. Investment in this type of securities was made possible by amendment of the Insurance Law of the State of New York in 1928 which recognized investments in unsecured corporate obligations and preferred or guaranteed stocks which qualified under prescribed earnings tests. Richard E. Erway "New York Law Relating to Investments of Life Insurance Companies," pp. 668–69. This pamphlet by Vice President and Associate General Solicitor Richard E. Erway is a reprint of a paper read before the Association of Life Insurance Counsel, May 28, 1962. *Ibid.*

461,000 in stocks, constituted almost 11 per cent of the Society's ledger assets.[105]

Most of these securities were acquired through direct placement, a practice which grew rapidly in the late 1930's and even more rapidly in the ensuing decade. Said President Parkinson:

> The Society's pre-eminent success in this field at times has aroused some criticism on the part of some of our competitors in the insurance and investment banking fields, who would have liked to have bought certain security issues which came to us. First, I would like to emphasize that when I use this expression "came to us," I use it advisedly because it has been our policy ever since we began to participate in this type of financing to refrain from soliciting these loans from prospective borrowers. This platform has been adhered to both as a matter of principle and of practice. Secondly, I should like to emphasize that notwithstanding the Society's success in this field, it always has been and continues to be one which is highly competitive. There are many cases where competitors offer a prospective borrower terms so much better than ours that we lose a prospective deal at a time when it looks as though we are going to get it. Also, there have been many cases in which the Society has started out as the sole or a joint participant in a private financing only to lose the loan through a subsequent refinancing made possible by funds supplied by one of our competitors.[106]

Although Treasurer M. C. Laffey had, for a number of years, handled Equitable's securities investments, President Parkinson, early in the depression, had decided that the base of responsibility should be widened. First, he ordered Laffey to check on all proposed investments with Actuary Robert Henderson and later with Vice President Leon O. Fisher. Then, in February 1933, President Parkinson appointed an Investment Committee to formulate an investment policy for the Society. This committee did not function as he had hoped and later in the year he appointed a smaller committee composed of

105 By 1959 the investment in industrial obligations had risen to $2,484,522,000. Vice President William R. Cowie in his "Report on Industrial Securities 1935–1954" tabulated the investments in various industrial groups for those years. Copy in *ibid.*

106 Report to the Board of Directors for the year ending Dcember 31, 1946, pp. 15–16.

The subject of private placements is briefly covered in William R. Cowie "Direct Placements with Insurance Companies." This 40-page pamphlet is the reprint of Chapter V of Volume VI of *Examination of Insurance Companies* (New York State Department of Insurance, 1955). Copy in Securities Investment Department files, Equitable Archives.

Vice President and Actuary Robert Henderson, Treasurer M. C. Laffey, Manager of Mortgage Loans Charles J. Martin, Assistant Actuary Frank A. Shailer, and General Solicitor Sterling Pierson to meet once or twice a month to consider proposals and recommendations for the Finance Committee of the Board.[107]

This committee, early in 1934, decided that too many of Equitable's funds were deposited in banks at little or no interest and recommended a program of permanent investments "to at least take care of the increase in our available cash." Safety of capital should of course be considered, as well as "reasonable hope that at some time in the future, say within five years from the present time, there will be an opportunity to invest at more normal rates." Long-term investments would only be justified if they yielded higher rates of interest, and "any considerable speculative element should be avoided." A long-term return of 5 per cent would be considered satisfactory, but in view of the current low interest rates, Equitable should be willing to accept 3 per cent on the first five years of any issue provided it could get 5 per cent thereafter. Real estate mortgages should be considered as short-term investments so that, if interest rates rose, the mortgages could be called at maturity or renewed at a higher rate.[108] President Parkinson apparently was not convinced of either the wisdom or feasibility of this program for, as noted above, he continued to "sit on a lot of cash." [109]

In October 1935, Auditor Frank A. Shailer was appointed Vice President and given executive supervision of the Auditor's and the Treasurer's Departments, and in January 1937 he was given control of the Securities Investment Department, to which in February Second

[107] Thomas I. Parkinson, memorandum to Henderson, et al., December 5, 1933. Sterling Pierson files, Equitable Archives; Executive Order No. 710, December 22, 1933, Corporate Records, *ibid.*

[108] Robert Henderson, memorandum to Thomas I. Parkinson, March 20, 1934. Sterling Pierson files, *ibid.*

[109] In March 1934, cash amounted to $66,000,000 and United States Government securities to $107,000,000, a total of $173,000,000 or 12½ per cent of reserves as of December 31, 1933. As of December 31, 1933, the proportion of cash and United States Government issues to admitted assets of the five largest life insurance companies were as follows: Equitable, 9.6 per cent; Mutual, 7.7 per cent; Prudential, 6.7 per cent; New York Life, 6.4 per cent; and Metropolitan, 4.3 per cent. Equitable's loss of income was greater, relatively, than these figures would indicate, because the greater portion of the Society's holdings were in the very short term issues which yielded only fractions of 1 per cent. M. C. Laffey, memorandum to Sterling Pierson, March 13, 1934. *Ibid.*

Vice President Laffey and his staff were transferred.[110] Although Laffey was now second in command of an organization which he had formerly headed, the new arrangement worked satisfactorily. Said Laffey in 1958:

In this situation I had some comfort, for Shailer not only is, and was, an able man, but also kind, gentle, and self effacing. He had no professional knowledge of securities, but unlike many another man in a like situation, he never threw his weight around, nor did he bark out orders about this, that and the other thing. As a matter of fact, for years after he came into the department, I ran things much as I had in the past, and he was quite content to let me do so. I was still doing this after he had picked up enough knowledge to actively control the whole operation had he seen fit to do so. Maybe he felt that I had carried him before he had a grasp of the subject and he would be loyal to me afterwards. Whatever he thought, and he had his share of New England reticence, he was a good friend to me and I can never have anything but the fondest recollections of my association with him.[111]

THE GOLD CLAUSE CASES

For a time in 1934–35, the question of "gold clauses" was a pertinent one. Although the Congressional resolution of June 5, 1933, which invalidated gold clauses in private contracts, did not concern the great majority of Equitable policies, it did concern a few Gold Debenture Bond policies and outstanding mortgages and some of the Society's bondholdings.[112] For instance, in an Equitable mortgage foreclosure

[110] Executive Orders Nos. 723 and 724. In January 1937, Executive Order No. 724 was revoked in so far as it applied to the Auditor's Department and the Auditor ordered to report directly to the President. (Executive Order No. 751.) The following month, Laffey was appointed Second Vice President and his securities investment staff transferred to the Securities Investment Department under the supervision of Vice President Shailer. Auditor and Treasurer were both to report directly to the President. (Executive Order No. 753.) Corporate Records, *ibid.*

Frank A. Shailer, a graduate of Wesleyan University, had joined Equitable, in the Actuary's Department, in 1917. He became Assistant Actuary in 1928 and Auditor in 1933.

[111] Laffey, "A Third of a Century, Plus, with Equitable," pp. 13–14.

[112] For the Gold Debenture Bond policies issued by the Society 1898–1902, see this history, p. 402.

Treasurer M. C. Laffey in May 1932 said that "the Equitable long ago ceased to insist that the mortgages payable to the Society stipulate payment in gold." Memorandum to Thomas I. Parkinson, May 11, 1932. Sterling Pierson files, Equitable Archives.

As of April 1934, Equitable owned more than $23,000,000 of utility, industrial,

case in Ohio in 1934 Judge John R. King of the Court of Common Pleas handed down what was probably one of the first decisions in the country on the gold clause in public and private contracts.

The case of *Equitable* v. *Freda* involved a promissory note for $3,600, payable in gold coin of "present standard," made by Theodore A. and Edna Freda in 1930, payment on which was in default. When Equitable sued for the balance due of $3,598.18, the defendants argued that their promise was nullified by the act of Congress and hence they were not obliged to pay their debt. Judge King, citing a British decision, held that Congress was without authority to cancel the debt owed by the defendants, and ruled that the creditor "under the contract is entitled to have the obligation paid in lawful currency of the United States of America in a sum equal in value to the amount of gold called for in the note." [113] Thus the defendants would have to pay $6,092 to satisfy the $3,598 debt. Senator Carter Glass thought this decision important enough to insert in the *Congressional Record*. He said: "The decision follows the line of the decision of the highest court in Great Britain in maintaining the validity of these gold clauses. It is a matter that is going to concern the American people very much more seriously and to a larger extent than they seem to be concerned about it now." [114]

When a former Equitable policyholder read an Associated Press item on this decision, he wrote President Parkinson that it would be very unfair to force the borrower to pay $100 for every $59 face value of the mortgage:

> Very respectfully, I would urge that your company is making a great mistake if it actually tries to collect on any such basis. The only purpose of the devaluation of the dollar is to enable people who have lost the great share of their capital and/or earning power to pay their debts. All insurance companies must realize this from the difficulties they have had everywhere to realize on their mortgages and the moratoriums they have entered into, more or less voluntarily. They should breathe a sigh of relief for anything that would make the asset side of their balance sheets worth

---

and railroad bonds which bore gold clauses; some of these were not due to mature until 2047. Tabulation in *ibid.*, Closed Files, folder 66.

[113] As reported in the *St. Louis Post-Dispatch* of March 11, 1934, and inserted in the *Congressional Record*, Vol. 78, Part 5, p. 4622 (March 15, 1934).

[114] When General Solicitor Sterling Pierson saw the decision in the *Congressional Record*, he sent Senator Glass a copy of the defendants' demurrer to Equitable's complaint and of Judge King's opinion. Sterling Pierson to Carter Glass, March 27, 1934. Sterling Pierson files, Equitable Archives.

the nominal values written there. They are the last ones who should try to collect in the old gold dollar, because they will pay their own obligations in the new dollar. It always makes a bad impression to play both ends against the middle. Such a procedure on your part would be distinctly anti-social and will make you a great number of enemies. For myself, I certainly would never take out a policy with a company guilty of such a performance.[115]

President Parkinson replied that the question of payment in gold had been brought up, not by Equitable, but as a result of the pleading of the defendants.

Whether or not Equitable collected under Judge King's decision is not known, but in view of the decision of the United States Supreme Court the following year it is doubtful.[116]

Also in 1934 Equitable became involved in litigation over gold bonds of the St. Louis, Iron Mountain and Southern Railway Company which arose out of the proceedings to reorganize the Missouri Pacific Railroad Company. Trustees for $34,548,000 Iron Mountain bonds which matured May 1, 1933, petitioned for payment in gold under the mortgage contract. Equitable's law firm of Alexander and Green presented a brief in support of the validity of the gold clauses.[117] The decision would involve a total of $438,000,000 of Missouri Pacific bonds and if the gold clauses were upheld it was estimated that it would increase the bonded indebtedness to $743,000,000. When the reorganization proceedings came up before Judge Charles B. Faris of the United States District Court, Eastern District of Missouri, the

115 Robert C. Gilles, Ph.D., to Thomas I. Parkinson, April 30, 1934. *Ibid.*

116 The Equitable records in connection with this foreclosure have been destroyed.

117 When Sterling Pierson sent a copy of the brief to John Bassett Moore, Moore said that the courts would be fortunate if they could always be aided by counsel in this way. He reminded Pierson that he had been serving the Government in Washington when the case of *Juilliard* v. *Greenman* was decided. (This case, in 1884—110 U.S. 421—involved the constitutionality of the act of May 31, 1878, which forbade further retirement from circulation of United States legal tender notes issued during the Civil War. The majority opinion by Justice Gray held the act valid and that payment of a debt in Treasury notes was a tender of lawful money. Justice Stephen J. Field delivered a dissenting opinion.) Moore continued: "In the present instance, however, we might well inquire whether any government in the world has ever before undertaken, as the United States did by the joint resolution of June 5, 1933, retrospectively to declare that stipulations in private contracts as to what the buyer was to get for his money were void as against public policy. Such stipulations have been made in all lands from time immemorial, and they have included the specification of what in terms of money the buyer of an obligation should eventually get. I do not believe that any exercise of governmental power mentioned by Mr. Justice Gray went so far as that." Moore to Sterling Pierson, June 7, 1934. Sterling Pierson files, Equitable Archives.

United States Government, through Attorney General Homer S. Cummings and the Reconstruction Finance Corporation, defended the repeal of the gold clause in bond contracts. Judge Faris (June 20, 1934) ruled that the term "payable in gold coin of the present standard of weight and fineness" was a "sonorous and mouth-filling phrase" which might add dignity to a contract but was practically meaningless; upholding these "so-called gold clause contracts would vastly hurt, if not destroy, business, and shake, if not overturn, the entire financial structure of this country." Nor was the borrower required to pay the equivalent in the new currency. Therefore, the trustees were entitled to recover $1,000 for each $1,000 bond in current dollars.[118]

Another case involving gold clauses was that of *Norman* v. *The Baltimore and Ohio Railroad Company*, which was decided by the New York Court of Appeals July 3, 1934. Norman had demanded payment of quarterly interest on a B. & O. bond in gold or its equivalent, but the Court, with Judge Cuthbert W. Pound writing the opinion, ruled that the scope of the money power of Congress was so wide that the Court would not, in the case presented, venture to invalidate its legislation directed to that end. Judge Pound was willing to leave the final decision to the United States Supreme Court.[119]

In regard to this decision of the Court of Appeals, John Bassett Moore wrote: "We have since heard an echo of Judge Faris' views from the Court of Appeals at Albany. This serves to show that our much cherished dependence upon the courts to keep Congressional action within constitutional limits fails in proportion to the magnitude of the exigency." [120]

The question of gold clauses was settled, legally, if not ethically, by decisions handed down by the United States Supreme Court February 18, 1935. In the case of *Norman* v. *The Baltimore and Ohio Railroad Company*, the court upheld the right of Congress to alter private contracts: "Contracts may create rights of property, but when contracts deal with the subject matter which lies within the control of Congress, they have a congenital infirmity." [121] In the case of *John N. Perry* v.

[118] 7 F. Supp. 1.

[119] He said: "In view of the enormous property value at stake and of the possibility that Congress may stamp as legal tender such a vast quantity of paper money as potentially to destroy the value of all past promises to pay in the future, the decision of the Supreme Court of the United States on the question will be fraught with the gravest results." 265 N.Y. 37.

[120] Moore to Sterling Pierson, July 12, 1934. Sterling Pierson files, Equitable Archives.

[121] 294 U.S. 240.

The United States, the Court by unanimous decision held that the action of Congress in invalidating the gold clause in the Government's own gold obligations was unconstitutional. Eight of the justices held that the Government was morally bound to fulfill the stipulations of its obligation, but five of them ruled that since there was no way in which a sovereign power could be sued without its own consent, and the plaintiff could not show actual loss, he could not recover. Said Chief Justice Charles Evans Hughes: "While the Congress is under no duty to provide remedies through the courts, the contractual obligation still exists and, despite infirmities of procedure, remains binding upon the conscience of the sovereign." [122]

Justice James C. McReynolds dissented vigorously from both of the five to four opinions and warned that "the impending legal and moral chaos is appalling."

Dr. Constantine E. McGuire, consulting economist, on whom President Parkinson frequently called for advice, submitted a memorandum on the decisions in the gold clause cases.[123] He thought that the posi-

[122] Chief Justice Hughes did not agree with the Government's argument that when it borrowed money and pledged the credit of the United States, it was free to ignore that pledge and alter the terms of its obligations in case a later Congress found their fulfillment inconvenient. During the argument, he said to the Assistant Solicitor General: "Here we have a bond issued by the United States Government . . . a bond which the Government promised to pay in a certain kind of money. Where do you find any power under the Constitution to alter that bond, or power of Congress to change that promise?" (*The New York Times*, January 11, 1935.) If the Government's argument were accepted, then it followed that the obligation as to the amount to be paid might also be repudiated: "The binding quality of the promise of the United States is of the essence of the credit which is so pledged. Having this power to authorize the issue of definite obligations for the payment of money borrowed, the Congress has not been vested with authority to alter or destroy those obligations. The fact that the United States may not be sued without its consent is a matter of procedure which does not affect the legal and binding character of its contracts. While the Congress is under no duty to provide remedies through the courts, the contractual obligation still exists and, despite infirmities of procedure, remains binding upon the conscience of the sovereign." 294 U.S. 240.

[123] Dr. McGuire, then working with the Treasury Department, had met President Parkinson during World War I when the latter was Major Judge Advocate in the Army and working on the War Risk Insurance Act. He later served with the Institute of Economics (now the Brookings Institution) and as treasurer of the American Historical Association. In 1930 President Parkinson asked him to become economic adviser. As adviser to the President of Equitable, McGuire was called upon to study public policy in a wide variety of fields, to submit reports and opinions upon financial, commercial, and industrial trends, to make recommendations with respect to problems of foreign exchange, and the holdings of Equitable in European public securities, etc. President Parkinson valued McGuire's services highly. McGuire continued to serve as adviser to the President of Equitable until 1955.

tion of the gold clause in obligations of the Federal Government had been left uncertain by the opinions. Four of the justices had held that the Congressional resolution of June 5, 1933, was not a regulation of money but a regulation of contracts, and was unconstitutional in all respects; four had held that it was constitutional in all respects, except in so far as it related to obligations of the Federal Government in the form of bonds. McGuire thought that while the majority opinion of the Court reflected disapproval of the Government's financial policies, it also reflected a disposition in the Court to acquiesce in the substitution—"for the duration of the 'Emergency' "—of public policy, as interpreted by Congress and the Executive, for the provisions of the Constitution. As a result, "the depreciation of the dollar may proceed spasmodically but go far indeed, over the next two or four years." Also, there would likely be a stimulus to speculation in the country as a whole. The memorandum concluded:

> The Constitution conferred upon Congress the power "to coin money, regulate the value thereof, and of foreign coin." That can have meant merely to fix and alter, as necessary, the relation between lawful currency and some stipulated object taken as a measure. The Constitution forbade the States to impair private contracts; its framers can hardly be supposed to have intended to reserve the power expressly to impair contracts to the Federal Government. Private contracts are the foundation of all long-term and short-term operations in economic life. Unless the real substance of the gold clause—namely, the right of contracting parties to measure their respective obligations in an agreed medium—is revived from the suspended animation in which the Supreme Court leaves it, we are headed for the gradual annihilation of private enterprise, and the exaltation of governmental dictatorship in all economic life.[124]

* * *

Although President Parkinson had been cautious in expressing his views on New Deal legislation in the earlier years, by the mid-1930's he became more outspoken. In an address before the Tenth Annual Meeting of the Cotton Textile Institute in October 1935, he spoke of "the error that was made in teaching the people to believe that the Government could do for them something they couldn't do for themselves," in the field of economics and finance, and the dangers of

[124] A copy of this ten-page memorandum, dated February 28, 1935, is in the Sterling Pierson files, Equitable Archives.

overemphasizing security at the expense of free enterprise, which was being "bedeviled" in the process. He said that it was the duty of those who carried the great responsibility of the administration of business interests and the handling of the people's money to take a position on these matters.[125] Apropos of the Federal tax bill of 1935, he said to the New York Chamber of Commerce: "The problem is growing more serious daily, and if the easiest way is to be the way of solution . . . as it has been in the consideration of this pending tax bill, then we are face to face, we who are responsible for the administration and the events of business, with the possibility of resort either through confiscatory taxation, to hitherto unthinkable repudiation or to the easy, indirect, misrepresenting solution through inflation." And early the following year he told the New York representatives of the Society: "The time has come, even from a political point of view, when the wisest thing for those of us who conduct the government, is to put an end to the experiments in currency, whether with gold, silver, or paper —put an end to them in such a way that there can be no further question about it—and put currency on a definite, stable basis." [126] When a policyholder congratulated him on such views he wrote:

> We in the life insurance business cannot avoid emphasizing the importance of sound governmental financing and a sound currency. We have been apostles of thrift; we have sold the idea of insurance protection. Our agents have emphasized life insurance as a service of protection and have aroused in our policyholders the expectation that performance of our contracts will involve not merely the delivery of the dollars called for but provision for the human needs which inspired their purchase of our policies. To the extent that they or their beneficiaries are disappointed, our institution and our personal efforts are a failure. It is not surpising then that the life insurance world—agents in the field and administrators in the Home Office—look with concern upon any tampering with the currency or flirting with inflation. No matter how faithful the administration of our trust, our efforts may be defeated by unsound governmental policies.[127]

The reactions of policyholders to statements such as these were varied. One wrote that he thought the officers of Equitable had been

[125] An address before the Tenth Annual Meeting of the Cotton Textile Institute, Biltmore Hotel, New York, October 23, 1935. Pamphlet copy in Parkinson files, Equitable Archives.

[126] As reported in *The New York Times*, March 3, 1936.

[127] Thomas I. Parkinson to Robert W. Linen, January 15, 1936. Parkinson files, Equitable Archives.

"cowardly neglectful" of the rights of policyholders on the subject of inflation—"as leaders you are beyond contempt." [128] On the other hand, the literary editor of a feature syndicate wrote that since Equitable was being made a branch of the Republican party and "bartering politically with its policyholders' views," he would have to surrender his policy, even though it would mean the loss of a substantial part of his savings: "I would rather depend upon the Government to protect my interests than upon a politically motivated private organization." [129] To all, President Parkinson replied that though the life insurance companies did not regard it as their function to lead the fight against inflation and government spending, the policyholders as individuals could have great influence on the course of public policy. He recurred to this thought in a talk before the New York State Bankers Association:

In my own personal determination of my position as a manager, I am careful to refrain from expressing for my institution my own personal opinions with respect to political or economic questions. I take it that my policyholders did not join my organization in order to give me, as their representative, the power to speak for them in such matters. But I draw the line when the measures involved threaten the capacity of the institution to do that for which they joined it. I take it that those average people—and they are counted by the millions—who are your stockholders, our policyholders, and your depositors, did not put their money into our institutions for us to manage and then expect us to go along with unsound policies which make it impossible for our institutions to do that which alone must have been the inspiration for their joining up with us. Therefore, I do not hesitate to say that all of us, and particularly you who manage the banking business, have a duty, and in a moment I hope to show you an opportunity, to take a real part in the formation of public opinion, public policy, and public measures affecting your business and our business.[130]

[128] President Parkinson replied that since some policyholders were equally critical on the other side, he had tried not to take the Society or its influence into politics or economic questions upon which policyholders might disagree. On the other hand, he had not hesitated "during the past two years to point out the danger of current trends in taxation and public finance. Under the circumstances, I am wondering what else you think we ought to do." Thomas I. Parkinson to W. Cleveland Runyon, Esq., April 20, 1936. *Ibid.*

[129] Henry Montor, Literary Editor, Seven Arts Feature Syndicate, to Thomas I. Parkinson, March 2, 1935. *Ibid.*

[130] "The Democratization of Privilege," an address delivered at the 45th Annual Convention of the New York State Bankers Association, June 27, 1938. Pamphlet copy in *ibid.*

He did not believe that it was enough for managers of life insurance companies and banks merely to be negatively honest in the conduct of their affairs; they were also under obligation to be positively effective for the benefit of their policyholders and stockholders. He insisted that the people have access to and consider the facts:

There is no field in which the facts are more difficult to observe and to interpret than in that of the political sciences, and there is no problem facing the American people today of greater importance than the soundness of our currency and fiscal policies. Do not say that is harping on an old issue! It is as new as it is old! Other problems may be serious, but they do not affect so uniformly all the people. Other problems involve in different ways or at different times different classes of the population, while the results of unsound fiscal and monetary policies affect at once all the people in every section of the country.[131]

From various angles, in speeches before different groups and interviews with the press, President Parkinson tackled the problem of deficit financing, Government-maintained low interest rates, cheap money, and the effects of inflation on the people.[132] As he pointed out, the Federal Government might save a few million dollars on debt interest, but the millions of life insurance policyholders and investors who were taxpayers would lose much more: "There can be no greater threat to the character and economic future of this country than the ceaseless pursuit of fiscal policies which so operate to discourage thrift." He also warned constantly of the increasing powers of the Executive and the President's defiance of Congress and the Supreme Court: "Is that what the American people want? Do they want an Executive with the power to levy taxes without the approval of Congress? Shades of the Boston Tea Party. . . . Do they want an Executive who can spend the public funds without appropriation by Congress?"[133] Perhaps even more basic was the effect of these policies upon the democratiza-

131 "Pursuit of the Facts," an address given at the 48th Annual Dinner of the Controllers Institute of America, New York, October 10, 1939. Pamphlet copy in *ibid.*

132 Many of President Parkinson's addresses were printed in pamphlet form—either as supplements to *Agency Items* or separately—and circulated to Equitable's group patrons, Chambers of Commerce, colleges, railroads, banks, etc.

133 "Congress and Inflation," an address delivered at a meeting of the Chamber of Commerce of the State of New York, October 1, 1942. Pamphlet copy in Parkinson files, Equitable Archives.

tion of the ownership of the American economy and upon the American system of government:

> Now the democratization of privilege and of economic privilege threatens, as I view the situation in our country, to undo what we have done and substitute a mad scramble for something out of the Government's beneficent hand. But that cannot last long. The Government's hand will be empty and however pious-wishing are those who are in control of the Government, however generous-minded they may be toward the downtrodden, there will not be the means, and when that time comes, all that has been gained in the development of the moral fiber of the people, all that has been gained in the distribution among the great mass of the thrifty people of the benefits of business and investment, will have been undone.
>
> No, we don't need democratization of privilege. What we need is the self-discipline of democracy.[134]

President Parkinson called attention to the Reconstruction Finance Corporation's competition with life insurance companies and investment bankers for good railroad loans, and how the Government's gold purchasing policy and short-term debt financing had built up billions of excess reserves in the banking system, which meant that "a very great deal of money is available for lending but nobody wants to borrow because nobody will risk the use of funds in a period of business uncertainty." [135] He advocated repeal of the President's powers over

[134] "The Democratization of Privilege." *Ibid.*

[135] Illustrative of the fact that President Parkinson was seldom intimidated by bureaucrats and officials, even at the Federal level, was his letter to Jesse H. Jones, Secretary of Commerce and former Director of the Reconstruction Finance Corporation. He wrote: "With much respect, personally and officially, and with no desire to develop needless issues particularly at this time, I would like to clear up the facts with respect to that Great Northern refinancing with respect to which you and I have made such contradicting public statements.

"The facts seem simple to me. May I state them? Great Northern wanted $20,000,000. Fairman Dick arranged with the Equitable and others to furnish that $20,000,000 at approximately 3.82%. The R.F.C. had previously offered to lend Great Northern $20,000,000 at 4%. The terms and conditions of the offer made by Fairman Dick on behalf of private investors and the offer made by R.F.C. were substantially the same or equivalent. We expected, under the circumstances, the R.F.C. would withdraw and leave the loan to private investors. R.F.C. did not withdraw but made its loan at 4%. Immediately thereafter R.F.C. sold that loan to Fairman Dick at a profit to R.F.C. of $500,000 and Dick sold the loan to private investors at 3.70% or less yield.

"Now I have interpreted this simple transaction as meaning that R.F.C. made a loan which private investors were ready to make and R.F.C. made a profit at the

currency and credit, the reduction of government expenditures, and creation of a free gold market with circulation of gold coins among the people.[136] Although some other life insurance presidents spoke out in similar vein, President Parkinson's views were the most widely disseminated. These statements concerning the effects of New Deal financial policies caused President Franklin D. Roosevelt, who was running for an unprecedented third term in 1940, to attack the life insurance companies. In a speech at Hartford, Connecticut, on October 30 he said that there were many executives of the insurance companies who were trying to spread fear among the policyholders in every part of the Union and referred to this action as the "most dastardly and the most unpatriotic action of any American I know of." He insinuated that he had saved the insurance companies from insolvency in 1932 and that the reward which the Administration had received was this campaign of fear.[137]

President Parkinson—a life-long Democrat—made no secret of the

---

expense of the stockholders of the Great Northern Railway and of the private investors who finally took the loan off the hands of Fairman Dick to whom R.F.C. had sold it. May I add that the Equitable bought from Fairman Dick at about 3.7% yield nearly $7,000,000 of this loan which, had the original arrangement offered by Fairman Dick gone through, the Equitable would have secured it at not less than 3.82% yield.

"I really would appreciate any statement of the facts of this transaction as you know them which differs from or supplements what I have here stated." Parkinson to Jones, December 5, 1941, *Ibid.*

[136] Address before the Pittsburgh Chamber of Commerce, November 1, 1940. Pamphlet copy in *ibid.*

Occasionally, President Parkinson received spirited criticisms of his policies. For instance, a consulting accountant who had read quotations from Parkinson's speech before the Chicago Association of Commerce wrote "wondering why big business has not yet realized that it cannot influence public opinion in its favor by the time-worn, thread-bare catch words to act as a smoke screen covering up the real issues. . . . Do the lessons of history mean nothing? Must the wealthy always be Bourbons and always suffer the same fate? Why not use some of your intelligence for something more elevating to the general well-being, comfort and culture than the insensate scramble for swollen wealth. That dam is about to break. You may be swept away in the flood of your own wealth." After reminding his correspondent that he did not belong to the wealthy class, President Parkinson replied: 'My concern about and my statements with respect to the questions of public policy on which you differ is based not on my personal interest but on my responsibility for the interests of the policyholders of this institution. Believe it or not, I feel that responsibility, and when public policy makes it difficult for me to do a reasonably good job for those who have committed their affairs to my management, I cannot entirely refrain from placing the blame where I think it belongs." H. E. Biedinger to Thomas I. Parkinson, June 11, and Parkinson to Biedinger, June 17, 1940. *Ibid.*

[137] *The New York Times*, October 31, 1940.

fact that he opposed the re-election of President Roosevelt in 1940. Shortly before the election, he wrote Robert E. Hannegan, chairman of the Democratic Campaign Committee:

> Answering the question whether I believe that President Roosevelt's re-election would injure life insurance policyholders, let me say that I do think Mr. Roosevelt's re-election would be detrimental to all citizens in this country, not as policyholders alone, but also as citizens. This is because I think present public policies, especially fiscal policies, of our Federal Government are detrimental to our citizens and especially those of them who try to provide for themselves through sacrifice, saving and thrift. The Treasury's easy-money policy has brought about a situation in which the man who wishes to save cannot get from his savings that reasonable interest return which constitutes an important part of the incentive to save. There can be no greater threat to the character and economic future of this country than the ceaseless pursuit of fiscal policies which so operate to discourage thrift.[138]

LIFE INSURANCE AND THE TNEC INVESTIGATION

Although in 1936 President Roosevelt had assured a selected group of life insurance company presidents that the Government had no hostility to or desire to compete with, or plan to investigate, the life insurance business, two years later (April 29, 1938) he called for an investigation of the "concentration of economic power" and included life insurance as one of the businesses to be investigated.[139] In June 1938 Congress authorized the creation of the Temporary National Economic Committee, "the duty" of which was "to make a full and

[138] Thomas I. Parkinson to Robert E. Hannegan, St. Louis, Missouri, October 31, 1940. Parkinson files, Equitable Archives.

[139] In an address to the nation April 14, President Roosevelt had asked for closer cooperation between business and the Government. Sixteen prominent business leaders signed a statement and pledged "aid to the full extent of our ability in such efforts as consultation and co-operation." A copy of this statement marked "urgent" was sent to President Parkinson April 26 by Winthrop W. Aldrich. Since Commissioner John W. Haynes of the Securities and Exchange Commission sent a copy of President Roosevelt's acknowledgment of the statement to President Parkinson, one assumes that Parkinson signed the pledge. President Roosevelt in his letter to Haynes asked him to thank the sixteen signers personally and "tell them if they have any specific suggestions, either as a group or individually, which they would like to have reach me, I will be glad to receive them either directly or through you. As you know I am looking for the specific steps which will bring closer co-operation between business and government and which will encourage them to take the initiative and stabilize their industry." John W. Haynes to Thomas I. Parkinson, April 25 and 29, 1938. *Ibid.*

complete study and investigation with respect to the matters referred to in the President's message on monopoly and the concentration of economic power in and financial control over production and distribution of goods and services and to hear and receive evidence thereon with a view of determining, but without limitation, the causes of such concentration and control and their effect upon competition. . . ." The Committee was composed of six members of Congress and six representatives of the administrative departments.[140]

The creation of the TNEC was largely the result of the business "recession" which had begun in the latter half of 1937.[141] Although there were those in the Administration who believed that the program of social, economic, and political reform had been pretty well accomplished and that the time had come to balance the budget, remove legislative blocks, and go easy on policies which would further antagonize business and destroy the confidence of investors, they were in a minority. In July Senator O'Mahoney stated that the investigation

140 Chairman of the Committee, as finally appointed, was Senator Joseph C. O'Mahoney of Wyoming; other Senate members were William H. King of Utah, an anti-New Deal Democrat, and William E. Borah of Idaho, independent Republican of trust-busting fame. The House members were Hatton W. Summers of Texas, chairman of the House Judiciary Committee (who became vice chairman of the TNEC), E. C. Eicher of Iowa, and Brazilla Carroll Reece, Republican, of Tennessee. Thurman W. Arnold represented the Department of Justice; Richard C. Patterson, Jr., represented Commerce; Isadore Lubin, Labor; Herman Oliphant, Treasury; Garland S. Ferguson, Jr., the Federal Trade Commission; and William O. Douglas, the Securities and Exchange Commission (with Jerome Frank as alternate). Leon Henderson, who believed that restricted Government spending and monopolistic price-fixing had been the chief cause of the "recession" of 1937, was made executive secretary of the Committee. Raymond Moley, one of the early New Dealers who had turned against the Administration, said that Henderson's appointment as executive secretary "of an impartial economic survey seemed like nothing so much as the choice of a Salvador Dali to head a museum of art." Moley, "The Great Monopoly Mystery—The Fascinating Story of the TNEC's Neglected Record," *The Saturday Evening Post*, CCXII (1940), March 30.

There were several changes in the personnel of the Committee before it finished its work. Senator Borah and Representative Eicher were replaced, and when Douglas was appointed to the Supreme Court Frank took his place and Henderson became alternate Committee member from the SEC.

141 Perhaps, in the minds of some of the reformers, the recession was an excuse rather than a cause. In July 1937 President Parkinson received a warning from "a confidential Washington source" to the effect that "the next group on the list for a thorough-going investigation will be the insurance companies, particularly a few of the biggest ones." Lewis H. Brown, President of the Johns-Manville Corporation, to Thomas I. Parkinson, July 22, 1937. Parkinson files, Equitable Archives.

was going to be an objective study and that the Committee had no intention of pillorying any industry or group, or pursuing punitive policies. Some weeks later, at the annual convention of the National Advertisers Association, he said that his Committee was merely trying to "find out what is wrong with our economic system" and that businessmen need not be afraid. In October, at a luncheon sponsored by the New York Board of Trade, he said that the Committee was searching for a formula which would curb the "evils of destructive competition" and thereby avoid a planned economy; if there was to be a planned economy, however, "it must be planned by public authority."

Despite Senator O'Mahoney's assurances, editorial writers and columnists of the so-called liberal group played up the possibilities of the investigation. It was to be "1905" all over again. For instance, Drew Pearson and Robert S. Allen in their syndicated column, "Washington Merry-Go-Round," predicted that the Securities and Exchange Commission's investigation of life insurance would be bigger and better in every way than the Armstrong Investigation of 1905–06, and that it would show that the evils exposed by the earlier committee were as rampant as ever: "What the investigators are looking into is the fact that the insurance companies now rival the Federal Government in the amount of money they have to invest and the amount they tax the public. Today insurance has come to be the equivalent of a tax. In fact, probably more people pay tribute to the insurance companies than pay taxes." [142] Most writers of this type agreed that the Securities and Exchange Commission was girding itself for some spectacular tilts with the life insurance giants.

October 6, 1938, President Parkinson spoke before the monthly meeting of the Chamber of Commerce of the State of New York; the title of his talk was "The Monopoly Investigation." He said:

> We thought it might be a head hunting or fishing expedition or that it might be a smoke screen for some other kind of political deviltry. We know that, when that is to be anticipated, we should be on our guard if we would do a good job with the interests that are in our hands. But now we have been assured by spokesmen for the Committee that this is to be a serious and earnest effort to get at the facts. Well, we can not quarrel with that. We may have the feeling that it is a few years late, but certainly it is what we in the business world have thought we ought to have had

[142] Quoted in *The National Underwriter*, XLII (1938), August 5.

from the leaders in government rather than the offhand, half-baked irresponsible theoretical proposals which have been so frequently and speedily put on the statute books without any effort to get at the facts.

He reviewed the antitrust laws and pointed out that the courts had decided that bigness in business was not bad unless it was used for abusive purposes: "*Bigness is bad only when it involves expansion to the point where the whole organization breaks down and fails to function; and that is what is happening in the biggest of all our business institutions, the Federal Government of this country.*" As for the regulation of life insurance, he said that state regulation, despite lack of uniformity and sometimes somewhat annoying effects, had, on the whole, been reasonable and beneficial. He asked what were the real objectives of the investigation. If Federal regulation of life insurance was one of the objectives, then it was perfectly plain that an effort would be made to use that power "to advance the fiscal policies of the Government of the day." Nevertheless, he suggested that businessmen should approach any investigation "with open minds, without prejudice or convictions, with the desire to find the facts and interpret them." He concluded with the following suggestion:

> *That anybody who undertakes to investigate monopoly and restraint of trade in this country today cannot avoid an investigation of current governmental policies.* A stable and just government preserves order, enforces the sanctity of contracts, administers fair and impartial justice, preserves freedom, defends competition and develops conditions which don't even suggest monopoly. On the other hand, a government which is unstable, which gives no assurance of the enforcement of long-term commitments, which does not regard the sanctity of contracts, which changes the currency over which it has control, which increases taxation to a burdensome degree, and especially taxes upon undivided profits, which increases regulation to the point of burdensome interference, including the regulation of wages and working conditions under which management deals with employees—a government which is capricious, irrational and unpredictable, and which boasts of the fact that it is on a 24-hour basis—*that is the government that breeds monopoly. . . . The monopoly that I fear most is the monopoly of government by our Federal organization.*[143]

143 "The Monopoly Investigation," an address by Thomas I. Parkinson, delivered at the monthly meeting of the Chamber of Commerce of the State of New York, October 6, 1938. Pamphlet copy in Parkinson files, Equitable Archives. President Parkinson was a former President of the Chamber.

In an editorial the following day, *The Sun* said: "No finer or more courageous speech on behalf of American business has been made in years." Of the paragraph quoted above, it said: "A fit climax to a valorous speech."

The life insurance part of the investigation was assigned to the Securities and Exchange Commission. Personnel for the task consisted of some two dozen persons, including stenographers, economists, actuaries, and eight or ten fieldmen. Gerhard A. Gesell, twenty-nine-year-old former student of Thurman Arnold and William O. Douglas, was made counsel for the insurance inquiry, and Ernest Howe, who had been brought to Washington by Douglas, was made chief financial adviser. A number of university professors, among them Alvin Hansen and Donald H. Davenport, both of Harvard, were consultants to the Commission. In September the Commission sent six copies of a preliminary questionnaire to each of some 400 legal reserve life insurance companies. Later this questionnaire was followed by another of 112 pages which was sent to 26 of the leading companies. All told, six questionnaires were sent out, totaling 195 pages.[144] The SEC was particularly interested in the investments of the life insurance companies, especially those made by direct placement.

Public hearings on life insurance began February 6, 1939, and lasted for several weeks; they were resumed in late spring and continued through June; further hearings were held in the autumn and during the early weeks of 1940. Manager Charles Burton Robbins and Associate Counsel Ralph H. Kastner represented the American Life Convention, and Manager Vincent P. Whitsitt and Assistant General Counsel Robert L. Hogg of The Association of Life Insurance Presidents were subpoenaed and testified. Early hearings were unspectacular; Senators O'Mahoney and King handled the sessions skillfully and in general endeavored to keep Gesell, who from the company standpoint was the villain of the piece, from providing opportunity for headline butchering of the life insurance companies. The SEC examiners kept banging away at size—the large amount of money the companies had

[144] Naturally, considering the limited personnel and time, the SEC could undertake only a general survey. The New York Insurance Department, for instance, usually used about two dozen investigators and required a year and a half of time to examine the Metropolitan Life Insurance Company alone. Some company officers were more or less irritated by the plethora of questionnaires, the answers to which, in the case of some companies, ran to 1,000 pages. They saw no reason for duplicating information which they maintained was already in the hands of the insurance departments of the various states.

to handle and the apathy of policyholders when it came to voting for management of the large mutuals. At one point, Senator King asked Gesell whether the SEC had a thesis that life insurance should not get any larger or whether it intended to restrict its inquiries to facts. Gesell replied that it was a factual inquiry, but despite this and other assurances, many people believed that the Senator's question had not been answered. When President John A. Stevenson of the Penn Mutual stated that it would not be necessary for his company to get any larger in order to "maintain the integrity of policies now in effect," the statement seemed to impress Henderson and Gesell. It was hard to believe that these experts did not know that this was true of any sound legal reserve life insurance company; perhaps they were impressed because they thought that the statement was a contribution to their thesis.

As their hearings continued, life insurance men began to feel that the TNEC was engaging in another fishing expedition to dig up some "juicy worms out of the dirt piled up by malcontents and hoping that some big fish will jump out of the water to grab the bait, hook, line and sinker." This feeling was not diminished by a statement released to the press February 27 by Senator O'Mahoney in which he reported that during the preceding forty-nine years the premium income of the life insurance companies had been enough to meet all expenditures and that "the investment income of the life insurance companies has been all velvet." It appeared that the Senator either did not understand or was ignoring the fact that reserves had to be built up to meet the ultimate contract payments. Frederick H. Ecker, Chairman of the Board of the Metropolitan Life Insurance Company, explained to the Senator: "These reserves are precisely the same as the deposits that have not been withdrawn from a bank—they are subject to withdrawal at any time in the eventuality of death or other existing rights of policyholders. There is nothing there in the nature of profit or 'velvet'; all such funds are subject to the demand of the policyholder under the terms of his contract. A factual description would be policyholders' funds subject to demand."

After the first round of hearings was over, life insurance men were relieved, but somewhat puzzled as to the next step. Would the SEC recommend legislation to give it control of life insurance investments? Since both O'Mahoney and Douglas had stated that there was no question whatever of the soundness of life insurance as administered by the legal reserve companies, what purpose other than Federal regulation could there be in continuing the investigation?[145] When the hearings were resumed in June, the methods, if not the purposes, of the administrative representatives on the Committee became more clear. Witnesses were seldom permitted to feel at ease—if they talked freely, attempts were made to catch them in loose talk; if they were cautious, it was made to appear that they were holding back. Lubin insinuated that company executives had other than the interests of the policyholders at heart. When company actuaries explained that certain uniformity of rates, surrender values, and options resulted from the general exchange of information rather than from agreements among companies, Henderson appeared disgruntled with the exactness and qualifications of their answers. At the close of one session he said: "Somewhere in these proceedings there will be a direct answer—yes or no. At that point I will buy a drink." Gesell also insisted upon yes or no answers, even though the questions might be somewhat leading in nature. Counsel for witnesses were not permitted to question witnesses before the Committee to bring out the whole truth. The examiners were skilled in the technique of so using words and questions that the over-all implication would be that of "something being somewhat smelly in the state of Denmark." [146] They well knew that, for

[145] Further credence to the idea of Federal regulation was given by publication of an article by Peter R. Nehemkis, Jr., in the March 1939 issue of the *Georgetown University Law Journal.* Nehemkis, a former student of Douglas and Arnold at Yale, was special counsel of the SEC on investment banking. The title of the article was "*Paul* v. *Virginia:* The Need for Re-examination." Nehemkis emphasized that the great investment activities of the life insurance companies had completely changed the scope of the business as conducted at the time of the famous decision of 1869 that insurance was not commerce. He left the impression that the Supreme Court "in the light of the altered significance of the insurance problems" might not follow the earlier precedent.

[146] This method was what Raymond Moley called "the technique of utter confusion"—a second tower of Babel. In June 1939, Arthur Krock of *The New York Times* reported that Stuart Chase, who was a sort of consultant at large, had drawn up a semantics manual so as to enable the government examiners most effectively to use words to change the ideas of the people about debt, spending, and saving. For instance, "thrift" had a high standing in people's minds—was a "thumbs up" word; "hoarding" and "debt," on the other hand, were "thumbs down" words in the public mind. "Thrift" or "saving" should always be referred to as "hoarding," and hence be given a bad connotation; "debt" became "thrift" (government spending is government saving), and hence good. Moley, "The Great Monopoly Mystery—The Fascinating Story of the TNEC's Neglected Record," *The Saturday Evening Post,* CCXII (1940), March 30. See also Arthur Krock, "The Prompters: Stage Managers of TNEC Hearings," *The New York Times,* June 7, 1939; and *Time,* XXXIII (1939), June 19.

At one of the hearings, President Thomas I. Parkinson chided Henderson and

their purposes, more effective than making direct charges of evil was to pick out a situation that could be improved, "exaggerate it, distort its significance, draw misleading inferences, and ignore what those in the business have done to mitigate it or the fact that a great deal of what is complained of is due to circumstances which the business cannot possibly control."

The inquiry jumped from subject to subject without apparent rhyme or reason. Sometimes witnesses were interviewed in private hearings and dismissed without being brought before the Committee. Individual witnesses were referred to as "industries," and when they questioned the accuracy of this statement their demurrers were omitted from the record. Investment policies, mortality tables, pressure sales promotion, lapses, and lobbying were all touched upon. Professor Davenport emphasized the "frustration" which resulted from policy lapses. When the SEC sent out another questionnaire, this time to the state insurance departments, it was referred to as "a streamlined edition of the old-fashioned tanglefoot—that gooey, saccharine and nectareous concoction which became the graveyard of bugs and insects that buzz and bite." [147]

President Parkinson testified before the Committee in October 1939.[148] The questioning was conducted largely by Gesell, with Henderson, Lubin, and others taking part occasionally. The questioners were much interested in the agency system, the cost of training agents, agency turnover, agency campaigns, and what they considered the business of overselling life insurance prospects. They wanted to know

---

Gesell regarding Chase's glossary and manual; they denied its having any influence on their methods of questioning, but the questions themselves seemed to indicate the contrary.

[147] Editorial in *The Insurance Field,* LXVIII (1939), November 17.

[148] *Hearings before the Temporary National Economic Committee, Congress of the United States, Seventy-Sixth Congress,* Part 13, pp. 6505–79.

It had originally been planned that Vice President William J. Graham would testify for Equitable and various members of the Agency Department had prepared material for him to use. All documents were photostated in duplicate and completely indexed; they filled two trunks. Graham was given a thorough briefing in regard to where to find the material on controversial operations, but he was never allowed to testify for at the last minute President Parkinson decided to represent Equitable. Counsel Sterling Pierson, Secretary Alexander McNeill, and Gordon K. Smith, Superintendent of Administration, Agency Department, accompanied Parkinson and rendered what help they could, but he was not as well acquainted with the documents as was Graham. Secretary Gordon K. Smith, interview with the author, February 10, 1964.

why the national banks of the country could not handle the sales of life insurance as well as the insurance companies could. Some of Equitable's sales literature which the Committee had copies of proved slightly embarrassing, and President Parkinson admitted that he did not approve of it. As for the agency sales campaigns, which, according to Gesell, kept the agents "stirred up into a continuous state of emotion," he said that "the agents liked it and expected it." Gesell bore down heavily on Equitable's early lapse rate and President Parkinson admitted that it was high. Counsel tried to get him to admit that the agency system was wasteful and costly on the one hand, and on the other that it was impossible for the average agent to make a living. They showed great interest in the reasons for Equitable's re-entry into Texas and the cost of that step.[149] When the questioners intimated that a life company might be better off if it abandoned aggressive selling practices and conducted itself on a "more intensive basis," President Parkinson said that he would have "no interest in administering that kind of a so-called life insurance company"; he would rather "return to the Government service." He believed that the large life insurance companies would have to continue to grow in order to maintain the soundest policies and render the best services to the country.

When it appeared that the TNEC investigation might be leading toward introduction of legislation for Federal regulation of life insurance, the American Life Convention prepared a pamphlet entitled "Life Insurance Should be Supervised, Regulated and Governed by Law in the States." The pamphlet pointed out the dangers of Federal regulation and stated that centralized control by a single governmental agency would naturally arouse "apprehension of political tampering with the investment of trust funds of the most sacred character. . . . Any proposal for Federal supervision and control would not emanate from policyholders—its source would be purely political—and should one of the principal purposes be to secure indirect but effective domination over the thirty billion dollars held in trust by the companies, its accomplishment would be a calamity." Copies of the pamphlet were sent to member and other companies, all state insurance departments, The Association of Life Insurance Presidents, and The National Association of Life Underwriters. In an accompanying letter, the state vice presidents of the Convention were asked to get in touch with their senators and representatives on the assumption that the majority of

[149] For Equitable's re-entry into Texas, see this history, p. 1099.

them were not "in sympathy with the critical attitude of the Departmental members of the investigation." [150]

In January 1940, two investigators of the SEC appeared at Convention headquarters and asked Manager Robbins to open to them any letters which he had received from members of Congress in regard to the Convention pamphlet. When Robbins refused in no uncertain words, the investigators threatened to get a subpoena from Gesell and seize the letters; Robbins stated that he would go all the way to the Supreme Court, if necessary, to protect his rights. Chicago papers carried the story, insurance periodicals wrote editorials approving of Robbins' action, and members of Congress wrote the SEC and the TNEC asking for an explanation.[151]

The same month a number of executives of life insurance companies met in New York to consider the possibility of getting a statement on behalf of life insurance inserted in the record of the TNEC; they believed that such a statement was necessary to balance what they considered to be numerous misstatements in the record. A committee headed by President Leroy Lincoln of the Metropolitan Life was appointed to draft the statement.[152] The committee met March 7 with

[150] The pamphlet was later revised and filed with the TNEC in May 1940 under the title, "State Supervision of Insurance and the National Association of Insurance Commissioners." The pamphlet carried the signatures of officers of 137 companies, a number of them not members of the American Life Convention. When Manager Charles B. Robbins of the Convention invited President Parkinson to sign, he refused to do so on advice of counsel. This refusal is hard to understand in view of the fact that President Parkinson was strongly opposed to the extension of the Federal power and certainly was not easily intimidated. In regard to state regulation, he had said: "We are, of course, an outstanding exception to the extension of Federal power, but we have become accustomed to regulation by the several states, and while there is a lack of uniformity in it, the fact that the regulators are a little closer to the things they regulate, has always seemed to me to account for the fact that they have been more reasonable and, on the whole, helpful to our business. To me it further illustrates and emphasizes the fact that the greatest thing in our governmental system is local government as to those matters which can be fairly handled locally." Robbins to Parkinson, May 8, and Parkinson to Robbins, May 15, 1940; Parkinson to Lewis H. Brown, President of the Johns-Manville Corporation, August 20, 1937. Parkinson files, Equitable Archives.

[151] *The Chicago Tribune*, January 12, 1940, carried a story of the incident under the heading, "Fight Federal Snooping Into Insurance Mail—SEC Sleuths Balked in Chicago." Representatives of the SEC called upon convention state vice presidents in six states and succeeded in getting some correspondence files, including letters from Congressmen, from three of them.

[152] Other members were E. E. Rhodes, Vice President of the Mutual Benefit Life Insurance Company; M. Albert Linton, President of the Provident Mutual Life Insurance Company; T. A. Phillips, President of the Minnesota Mutual Life;

Senator O'Mahoney, James R. Brackett, then executive secretary of the TNEC, and Leon Henderson, and requested permission to insert a statement in the record. Permission was not given at the time but the committee was told that if it presented a statement it would be turned over to the SEC for examination. It was at this meeting that one of the administrative members of the TNEC unburdened himself of a vehement attack upon the state insurance commissioners as the real culprits in the insurance business. He announced that the Committee was going to ask for another half-million dollars, continue its investigation, and concentrate on the life insurance companies. The following month E. E. Rhodes, chairman of a subcommittee of the Lincoln committee, wrote Senator O'Mahoney and protested against the TNEC's decision not to let the life insurance companies testify. Senator O'Mahoney replied that neither Rhodes nor his committee was speaking for the life insurance business and that it was "an utterly unfair view to write a letter which makes it appear that I, acting for the Committee, have attempted to restrict or restrain you."

As the investigation dragged on through the early months of 1940, syndicated columnists favorable to the Administration, who pretended to have access to "inside" information, began to give previews of the findings of the SEC. Pearson and Allen ("Washington Merry-Go-Round") said that "an explosion was brewing between the TNEC and the big insurance moguls" and that the "insurance tycoons were infuriated by embarrassing disclosures about their business practices." [153] A conspicuous insurance counseling firm, not too highly regarded by the life insurance business, quoted this statement in an advertisement in its endeavor to get policyholders to switch their policies. Ernest Lindley, New Deal defender, in his summary of the TNEC's findings, said that life insurance executives "seemed to quaver that the public would learn things it is entitled to know," and spoke of "pressure being exerted to prevent publication." The *New York Post* and other papers, in a so-called preview of what the coming report would show, spoke of assets "being over-valued hundreds of millions" and that this situation "extended to most of the companies." On the other hand,

---

and Laurence F. Lee, President of the Peninsula Life and of the Occidental Life Insurance Company. The committee's statement was subsequently published as Monograph No. 28-A. It was a commentary on Monograph No. 28, titled *Study of Legal Reserve Life Insurance Companies.*

[153] Drew Pearson and Robert S. Allen, "Washington Merry-Go-Round," January 29, 1940.

when the SEC drew up a lengthy exhibit upon the investments of the twenty-six largest companies for the ten-year period 1929–38, the editor of an insurance periodical wondered whether the TNEC noted that, while the companies were increasing their assets more than $9,000,000,000, the debt of the United States had increased about $21,000,000,000.

Phil S. Hanna of the *Chicago Journal of Commerce* likened these attacks to those made upon the public utilities seven years earlier. He said:

> If there isn't a conspiracy between the left-wing members of the SEC and the high officials of the New Deal to achieve Federal control of the life insurance business, there is certainly a move on behind the scenes which comes so close to conspiracy that a reasonable person cannot distinguish the difference. . . . The plain facts are that a clique of appointed public officials are scheming, with the help of Mr. Roosevelt and by the use of public funds, to injure and embarrass the insurance companies so as to make the public think they ought to be under Federal control.[154]

In June, both Republican and Democratic national conventions went on record in favor of the continuance of state supervision of all insurance. Said the Republican platform: "We condemn the New Deal's attempts to destroy the confidence of our people in private insurance institutions. We favor continuance of regulation of insurance by the several states." The Democratic plank was as follows: "We favor strict supervision of all forms of the insurance business by the several states for the protection of policyholders and the public."

In a speech before the American Life Convention at its annual meeting in October 1940, Senator O'Mahoney positively denied that the TNEC investigation had been inimical to life insurance: "I say it is not true, and I say the record bears me out. Now, let me say here just as explicitly as I can that there is not the slightest evidence to support any one of the three charges I am about to mention. Let me say that no member of the TNEC, no member of any agency connected with TNEC, no member of the TNEC staff, has ever made any report or recommendation (a) that would weaken state supervision of life insurance, (b) that would confiscate any of the life insurance assets, or (c) that would tend to divert the investment of life insurance

[154] *Chicago Journal of Commerce*, February 10, 1940.

funds from sound securities to venture capital." [155] The Senator noted that, though some of the insurance witnesses were probably dissatisfied with the treatment they had received at the hands of the "examining attorney" (of the SEC), the attorney made no recommendations and certainly had no legislative power. Perhaps he was unaware of the fact that Gesell and Howe were then preparing the final report of the SEC, and was overlooking the fact that the SEC could always short-circuit the TNEC because it reported directly to Congress.

December 10 the *New York Post* published an "exclusive" story by a staff correspondent who claimed to have obtained a copy of a summary of the SEC study in which was highlighted the so-called "disclosures" made in the 21 sections of the "monumental report." Among these disclosures were: the big life insurance companies had eliminated real competition by intercompany agreements that cost the public untold millions; many officers and directors juggled the funds of their companies for personal gain; policyholders had virtually no voice in the election of officers and directors; the companies maintained an effective lobby for influencing state and Federal legislation; high-pressure selling with ensuing lapses cost the public millions annually; industrial insurance had failed in its purpose, reaped huge profits, and created serious social problems; the companies through their lobby fought the cheap and popular type of life insurance sold without agents through the mutual savings banks of Massachusetts. The companies were even blamed for their large holdings of United States bonds, which fact indicated their "inability to invest funds to the best advantage," and for "sterilizing the savings funds received and preventing them from flowing into new enterprises for undertakings where the element of venture or risk is present." This was interesting news, if true.

The final report and recommendations of the SEC to the TNEC were presented by Commissioner Sumner T. Pike on February 28, 1941. It was unspectacular. It suggested ten ways in which state supervision could be made more effective, recommended a liberalization of investment laws to permit life insurance companies to invest a small portion of their funds in common stocks, recommended the extension of social service benefits or the like, to the end that industrial insurance would gradually disappear, and considered means of creating Federal

[155] *Proceedings of the American Life Convention* (1940), p. 171. O'Mahoney said that he had just received information to the effect "that out of this room there have gone to Wyoming the charges of life insurance men that the TNEC has been inimical to life insurance."

agencies to cooperate with state insurance departments in the regulation of life insurance. In conclusion, the report stated: "The life insurance business has had a remarkably consistent development and has in most cases fully justified the confidence of its policyholders. In bringing a greater measure of security to millions of policyholders, the life insurance business has performed a useful service which makes its continuance a social necessity. Indeed, there can be no question of the soundness of the basic principles upon which the institution of life insurance is founded. There is no desire on our part to place the Federal government in a position to tamper with insurance investments, to control investment policies, or to interfere in any way with the companies' free exercise of managerial judgment."

Senator O'Mahoney, in commenting on the report, said that he would not favor Federal regulation of insurance companies, "because I believe what the country needs more than anything else is a fundamental cure for the economic trouble and not more Government supervision of what is now being done." He also stated that the final report and recommendations were in no wise to be taken as expressing the sentiments of the TNEC, or even the SEC, but merely the sentiments of Pike and Gesell. As far as he was concerned, "by and large, the insurance companies have come through this study in pretty good shape."

In the *Final Report and Recommendations of the Temporary National Economic Committee* (a document of 783 pages), which dealt with a myriad other matters, 45 pages were devoted to the insurance phase of the investigation; 43 of these were Pike's personal statement.[156]

In regard to the report President Parkinson said that in the eyes of the two members of the SEC the life insurance companies had been guilty of the crime of being conservative in their investment of policyholders' funds: "Life insurance funds were never intended to be risked in new and unproven enterprises. Do the two authors of the SEC

[156] The *Final Report and Recommendations of the Temporary National Economic Committee* was published as *Senate Document* No. 35, 77th Congress, 1st Session. In addition to the hearings and final report, the TNEC published 45 monographs on prices, taxes, industrial concentration, trade associations, savings, antitrust laws, etc., etc. For a summary of the results of the TNEC, see R. Carlyle Buley, *The American Life Convention*, II, pp. 859 ff. See also *Fact and Fancy in the TNEC Monographs*, compiled by John Scoville and Nowell Sargent, published by The National Association of Manufacturers, 1942; and Raymond Moley, "Business in the Woodshed" and "Sharp Shooting at Insurance" in *The Saturday Evening Post*, CCXII (1940), April 6 and 20.

report imagine that the life insurance companies could have come through the depression with the outstanding safety record that they did if they had followed the theories now propounded by these two members of the SEC?" He pointed out that the assets of the life insurance companies were actively at work helping to finance industry, small business, agriculture, home building, railroads, and the needs of the Government in every state of the nation; these companies had invested more than $3,500,000,000 for these purposes in 1940.[157]

Perhaps H. I. Phillips in his column "The Sun Dial" in the New York *Sun* (March 6, 1941) gave about as good a summary of the insurance phase of the investigation as anyone. He did it in eight stanzas of rhyme under the title The SEC Sounds A Warning:

I

If insured, pay attention—
Listen very closely, please!
We've some frightful facts to mention
Just to make you ill at ease:
If your life's insured, mister,
You have confidence in THAT . . .
So the whole darned thing will blister,
Knocking all your faith quite flat.

II

Think of it and shake with terror!
Oh, these bad insurance men
Hate to take a chance on error,
And for daring have no yen!
They are very, very funny—
Just a bunch of timid worms,
Who will not invest YOUR *money,*
Save with old-established firms!

V

They are thrifty with your MONEY,
And with firms most tried and true
They invest it, which is funny;
This no S.E.C. *would do!*
In investments with a rating
They prefer to put YOUR *mon;*

157 Quoted in *The Weekly Underwriter*, CXLIV (1941), March 8.

And they're over-hesitating
Facing companies with none!

VI

They have billions in their coffers,
And they look so big and strong,
It is very plain to scoffers
That there must be something wrong!
They are run by experts wholly,
Men whose interests are wide;
Facts and figures guide 'em solely;
Spendthrift tactics are defied.

VIII

So let's run 'em through the hopper—
At the assets let us scoff;
And let's loudly bellow "Copper!"—
They've the funds to pay you off!
You have put your savings in 'em—
They're the one thing that you trust,
So let's launch a war again 'em—
It's a job that's labeled "MUST."

President Parkinson wrote Phillips the following day:

Cannot refrain from a note of appreciation, flavored with amusement, of your verses in last night's *Sun.* The whole performance would be amusing if it were not so pathetic. For two years the S.E.C. and its smart young men have done as they damn pleased with all of us who have been trying to attend to the affairs of the policyholders, and when last Friday the whole mess was brought by the Acting Chairman of the S.E.C. and dumped by him into the lap of the T.N.E.C. in the long-heralded and mysterious summary of the conclusions and recommendations of the investigation of life insurance, there was not one thing in the summary which could not have been written before the investigation began. Meanwhile it had cost money, a lot of effort, and if I were not a lawyer with some knowledge of the limitations of legal redress of grievances, I would be thinking of trying to recover for the Equitable policyholders what has been expended by management either by direction of this investigation or in its effort to cooperate with it. I don't believe there is any example in the history of the country of such a useless and pretentious so-called investigation.

Now that I have written this, I am sending it to you though I must say I like your treatment of the subject better.[158]

158 President Parkinson to H. I. Phillips, the New York *Sun*, March 7, 1941. Parkinson files, Equitable Archives.

HOME OFFICE AND FIELD

When Equitable assembled the land for its building at 393 Seventh Avenue, it was unable to obtain two or three lots which belonged to George W. Ellis, an attorney; as a result, when the Equitable Building was completed in 1924, there was a 24-story chasm 20 feet wide and 60 feet deep which came to be known as "Ellis Island." The Society later acquired the lot at 148 West Thirty-second Street and then in 1930, after Ellis' death, purchased lots Nos. 150, 152, and 162 from his estate; the purchase price was $355,000. The Insurance Department approved an addition to the existing building, and 18 stories fronting on West Thirty-second Street were constructed; the addition made available about 70,000 square feet of rentable or usable space. Cost of the new construction, exclusive of architect's and contractors' fees, was $950,000. Equitable's tax assessment increased immediately for both land value and improvements, although no similar increase had been made on the land values for the nearby Pennsylvania Railroad station, Pennsylvania Hotel, and Gimbels department store. After Equitable protested, the tax commissioner indicated he would give the Society some relief in connection with the improvement.

In September 1931 heads of departments were instructed to be extremely conservative in recommending salary increases or new appointments and in February 1933 Home Office employees who received less than $5,000 were given graduated salary reductions which amounted to 6 or 7 per cent in the lower brackets and about 10 per cent in the upper brackets; these decreases resulted in a saving of about $400,000.[159] At the same time, salaries of more than $5,000 were decreased in varying amounts which resulted in a saving of about $200,000, and in February 1934 they were reduced still further for a saving of about $100,000. In the case of some of the officers, total reductions amounted to 36 per cent of their previous salaries.[160] Although these salary cuts, particularly in the lower and medium brackets, were probably somewhat less than most employees in industry received, they tended to

[159] There were no reductions for salaries lower than $1,200; from $1,200 to $1,500, the reduction was $90; $1,501 to $2,000—$120; $2,001 to $2,500—$180; $2,501 to $3,000—$240; $3,001 to $3,500—$300; $3,501 to $4,000—$360; $4,001 to $4,500—$420; $4,501 to $5,000—$480. President Parkinson, memorandum for officers, February 27, 1933. *Ibid.*

[160] Assistant Secretary Alexander McNeill to President Parkinson, February 20, 1935. Corporate Records, Equitable Archives.

James F. Oates, Jr., James Hazen Hyde, and Dr. John S. Bonnell outside the Fifth Avenue Presbyterian Church prior to the Centennial

J. Henry Smith, James F. Oates, Jr., and R. Carlyle Buley at the opening of Centennial Week, July 26, 1959

Equitable officers and directors fill the Lithochron. Left to right: Nicholas Kelley, John H. Muller, R. Stewart Kilborne, Grant Keehn, James F. Oates, Jr., Walter Klem

James F. Oates, Jr., and Grant Keehn inspect a unit of Equitable's modern data-processing equipment

reduce morale to some extent. In 1934, some salary restorations were made, mostly in the lower brackets.

The depression was not permitted to dampen Equitable's spirit when it came time for the celebration of the Society's Diamond Jubilee in 1934. A 65-day sales campaign in honor of Secretary William Alexander's 65 years with Equitable began July 1, 1933. By September 5, Alexander's birthday, $183,708,682 of new business had been written. Then began a ten months' sales campaign as a result of which 1,780 agents qualified to attend the Society's 75th anniversary conference in New York, for which the theme was Equitable's motto, "Not for a day but for all time." [161]

At the afternoon session, July 25, the topic was "The Equitable looks back 75 years." Vice President W. W. Klingman presided, and the principal addresses were made by Directors John Lord O'Brian and Gage E. Tarbell. O'Brian, who had had a distinguished record in government service, emphasized the primary virtues of thrift and honesty. He said:

> You know as well as I do, that the honor of a plighted word is the only fundamental basis for society itself. . . .
>
> So in this time of loose talk about us, when the sense of obligation is weakening, those who maintain their austere standards of honor shine out. That is why the record of The Equitable looms up today as it never has before, because here is a great society with over a million partners, with perhaps four or five million people dependent upon its welfare; and it is all based on a mental conception, the conception of a rigid sense of honor, faith in a written contract and faith on the part of the policyholder that its affairs will be administered honestly and conservatively in his behalf.
>
> That idea, that conviction, is the basis of this Society and it is a lesson today to the politicians and the sophists and the demagogues. There it stands, ready now as always to fulfill all its contracts. This Society wanted no legal moratorium on its policy loans. This Society opposed that attitude on the part of the various states. This Society was ready at all times to fulfill its obligations.[162]

Tarbell pointed out the important part played by life insurance in alleviating the distress of millions of people during the depression.

Vice President Leon O. Fisher presided at the morning session

[161] To qualify, an agent was required to pay for a minimum of $110,000 of insurance, representing not less than 15 applications.

[162] Pamphlet copy in Equitable Archives.

July 26. An impressive ceremony started the meeting as the members of the 40-Year, the 45-Year, and the 50-Year Corps of the Equitable Veteran Legion (Home Office and Field) entered the room in a body to the strain of martial airs and, amid hearty applause, filed into specially reserved seats. The color-bearers and Veteran Legion Commander William J. Roddey proceeded to the platform where they saluted President Parkinson and presented the American Flag, the blue and white insignia of the Equitable Veteran Legion, and the Society's emblem, the Equitable Statue Group embroidered in white on a dark blue field.[163] In the spirit of the theme of this session, ". . . and 75 years ahead," President Parkinson spoke on the functions and values of life insurance and the services rendered by the agents. Dr. William Seaman Bainbridge, distinguished physician and surgeon and a Director of the Society, spoke of the importance of the Society's Medical Department and the contributions made by the diagnostic laboratory to mortality savings. Other talks were made by Vice Presidents Klingman, Jones, and Graham and by Secretary William Alexander.

More than 2,700 persons attended the banquet July 26 at the new Waldorf-Astoria. This was said to have been the largest dinner ever served by the hotel up to that time, and also the largest insurance company meeting ever held.[164] President Parkinson presided and again the theme of the meeting was a historical one. Superintendent of Insurance George S. Van Schaick spoke briefly of the services of life insurance during the depression, and stated that in the hectic days of bank closings and moratoria he had leaned very heavily for advice upon the President of Equitable. He did not apologize for his state's moratorium, which limited some of the payments by life insurance companies; he considered it a necessary action which brought "little hardship to those involved, and brought home to people that so far as their life insurance was concerned it was surrounded by every conceivable safeguard to carry it through the greatest panic that could have been imagined that it might have to confront."

163 The members of the 50-Year Corps honored were Secretary Alexander; Gage E. Tarbell; William Henry Brown, New Orleans Cashier; William H. Knowles and Knowles Hyer, Jacksonville, Florida, agents; Henry Hale, General Agent, New York; William B. Rankin, Pittsburgh agent; Michael T. Chernich, Assistant Auditor; James C. Rocquet, formerly Secretary General for Europe; Edwin Van Riper, Assistant Auditor; and Henry Bishop, Edward H. Koniger, Thomas H. Cuming, William J. Slingerland, and James Hassen, of the Reserve Force.

164 *The Eastern Underwriter*, XXXV (1934), August 3.

Director John Bassett Moore made the main speech of the evening—"a brilliant and whimsical speech"—in which he formulated seven commandments for Equitable, one for each day of the week:

First, be provident for the future is always uncertain. Second, on your wedding day take some life insurance. This should be repeated whenever the occasion arises. Third, beware of overspending. The only sure basis of credit, public or private, is a balanced budget. Fourth, do not mortgage the future. It will have ample opportunity to mortgage itself. Fifth, save generously. Your treasurer in Heaven, if any, is not available to those you leave behind. Sixth, invest prudently. Quick profits and total losses tend to flock together. Seven, remember that as an investment life insurance policies in their varied forms combine the best earthly assurance of a tranquil present and a comfortable future.[165]

After the speeches, Secretary William Alexander was presented with sixty-five roses, one for each year of his Equitable service, and responded: "Thank you. I didn't know I was a prima donna, but it's all right." The presentation was made by General Agent E. M. Crutchfield (General Agent, Richmond, Virginia) and Agency Manager Robert M. Ryan (Detroit, Michigan), who represented the general agents and managers of The Old Guard, and Assistant Secretary W. G. Schelker, who had been associated with Alexander for many years. An interested guest at the dinner was former Vice President Henry L. Rosenfeld, who had left Equitable in 1920; he said that "the welcomes were so genuine as to warm the cockles of my heart." [166]

[165] Typescript copy of the proceedings of the 75th Anniversary Conference, p. 154. Equitable Archives.

[166] Rosenfeld later wrote that he had feared that his epitaph was to be that of Keats—"Here lies one whose name was writ in water"—but President Parkinson had eliminated that fear. Rosenfeld (in Paris) to Thomas I. Parkinson, September 8, 1934. Parkinson files, Equitable Archives.

Rosenfeld died in July 1939. After leaving Equitable in 1920, he had served as the United States Manager of two British fire reinsurance companies, then as General Agent in New York City for the Prudential. After four years with the Prudential, Rosenfeld moved to Paris and took over a house in the Passy section, which he filled with rare first editions and paintings; he became well known in the American colony in Paris. He made frequent trips to the United States during which he continued to write a large amount of personal business in the New York financial district. One of his two sons, Henry L., Jr., was killed in action during World War II, and the other, James R., is an agent with the Equitable. At a meeting of Equitable's general agents and managers in New York late in July 1939, William M. Duff, President of The Edward A. Woods Company, and Vice President William J. Graham paid tribute to Rosenfeld's services to Equitable and to life insurance.

One of the interesting events of the week was a showing of a motion picture of the Equitable fire of January 9, 1912. The film, which had been taken by one of the early motion picture news cameramen, had long been in storage and almost forgotten; background material was added and sound effects dubbed in. Another was the formal installation with proper ceremonies of Henry B. Hyde's statue in the arcade of the Home Office building where, as Tarbell said, "it will be found standing so long as the Equitable stands, which is for all time and not for a day." President Parkinson sent four photographs of the statue to James Hazen Hyde in Paris and wrote: "It is appropriate that the Equitable thus pays a tribute to the memory of its Founder, for there are many who have a deep sense of appreciation of his qualities and achievements and of the great contribution he made not only to the progress of the Equitable but as well to the success of the institution of life insurance." Hyde expressed his "deep appreciation and satisfaction." [167]

After the anniversary convention, those agents who had produced $250,000 of new business during the sales campaign were rewarded with a trip to Halifax on the *Berengaria;* the cruise combined business and pleasure, for educational conferences were held on Saturday July 28 and Monday July 30. Gage E. Tarbell and Vice Presidents W. W. Klingman, Frank L. Jones, William J. Graham, and Albert G. Borden conducted the meetings and various agents participated in round-table discussions.

* * *

Numerous changes in the Home Office organization and personnel took place during the mid-1930's. As noted earlier in this chapter, President Parkinson established a Department of Investments in 1933 under the administrative direction of Vice President Leon O. Fisher which, two years later after Fisher's death, was placed under the executive supervision of Auditor Frank A. Shailer, who was made a Vice President at that time. In 1936 supervision of the cashiers' offices in the United States and Canada was transferred from the Auditor's to the Treasurer's Department. The following year when Treasurer M. C. Laffey was appointed Second Vice President, Henry Greaves became Treasurer of the Society, reporting directly to the President. In 1936 the former Mortgage Loan and Real Estate Departments were

[167] Thomas I. Parkinson to James Hazen Hyde, June 12, and Hyde to Parkinson, June 19, 1934. Parkinson files, Equitable Archives.

combined under the title of City Mortgage Department, which was placed under Glenn McHugh who had been appointed Second Vice President. The Underwriting Department, which, with its diagnostic laboratory, had been established in 1930 under Vice President Ray D. Murphy, was divided into three departments in 1936. The purpose was to separate the underwriting function from that of issuance and service with respect to policy contracts. The reorganized Underwriting Department included the Inspection Bureau, Medical Bureau, and Bureau of Lay Underwriters. Group underwriting was transferred from the Group Department to the Department of Underwriting which was placed under Mervyn Davis, who was promoted to a vice presidency. Assistant Secretary Walter G. Schelker was also made a Vice President and given charge of the new Policy Issue and Service Department, which included the Bureau of Issue, the Change Division, and the Policy Forms Division (with the exception of all matters relating to new policy forms, their approval and filing, which were transferred to the Actuary's Department). The Correspondence Division and the Change of Beneficiary Section in the Bureau of Policy Claims were transferred to this department. The other new department, the Claims Department, placed the former Bureau of Claims on an equal footing with the other main divisions of the Home Office. William B. Parsons was appointed Vice President and put in charge.[168] Andrew E. Tuck, an Assistant Secretary since 1919, was also appointed Vice President in 1936. Tuck, a former Deputy Attorney General in New York, had been responsible for relations with the Insurance Departments and trade associations and for the Society's corporate functions. After he became Vice President these responsibilities were gradually taken over by Sterling Pierson of the President's staff. Medical Director Thomas Hawley Rockwell retired in June, although he was retained in an advisory capacity for one year; Dr. Robert M. Daley succeeded to the directorship.[169]

When Assistant Secretary Schelker left the Bureau of Policy Claims

[168] The changes in the Underwriting Department are listed in Vice President Andrew E. Tuck's annual report to President Parkinson for the year 1936. See also Executive Orders Nos. 735, 736, 741, and 746. Corporate Records, Equitable Archives.

[169] June 8, 1936, Dr. Rockwell wrote President Parkinson as follows: "It is a hard thing after forty-six years to give up activity, but I trust to remain loyal to you and to the Society, and to assure you of my keen desire to help at any time. My heart and best wishes must not be questioned, and I shall be glad to aid in any way possible in the name of our motto: 'Not for a day, but for all time.' " Parkinson files, Equitable Archives.

to head the Policy Issue and Service Department, Leo D. Fitzgerald became head of the Legal Reference Division, which remained, for organizational purposes, a part of the Claims Department. Fitzgerald, an honors law graduate of Fordham University, had joined Equitable in 1917 and ten years later became an assistant in the Legal Reference Division.[170] This division handled all of the legal aspects, other than investments, of the Society's business.

In 1936 General Solicitor Sterling Pierson's title was changed to Counsel. Pierson, a native of Tennessee, had been reared in New York and was a graduate of Columbia University and the Columbia University Law School. While in law school he met Vice President Parkinson, who had served as Director of the University's Legislative Drafting Research Fund. Pierson made studies of the old-age pension statutes of Great Britain, Australia, and New Zealand and also was legislative and book review editor of the *Columbia Law Review*. He received his law degree in 1924 and joined Equitable as a legal assistant on President Parkinson's staff the following year. Some years later, after acquiring a wide knowledge of all aspects of the Society's business, he became chief legal adviser to the President and other executives, and the Society's "trouble shooter" on many major problems. He had wide contacts with other companies, insurance departments and trade associations, and a great personal capacity for work. From the early 1930's President Parkinson relied upon Sterling Pierson for many duties, judgments, and decisions over and beyond matters pertaining solely to legal affairs.

After Equitable began the private placement of loans in 1935 it became necessary to have Home Office counsel to handle the legal aspects of these loans and direct the employment of independent counsel and to advise them in regard to the Society's legal requirements and practices. The responsibility for this work was given to Warner H.

[170] As early as 1913 Equitable had a Law Department to handle mortgage matters and real estate investments. This Department was headed by Attorney Moncure March, a graduate of the Columbia University Law School and a former member of the firm of Alexander and Green. Executive Order No. 104, November 24, 1913. Later it was called the Law Division of the Mortgage Loan Department, *The Home Office of The Equitable*, 1934, p. 43. Copies in Equitable Archives.

From about 1915 to 1925 the Secretary's office served as liaison between the Society and its General Counsel, Alexander and Green. Assistant Secretary Schelker handled most of this work and in 1925 the Legal Reference Division was set up. Two years later the Assistant Secretary and his three clerks (John A. Klein, Leo D. Fitzgerald, and Mildred Oats) were transferred to the Bureau of Policy Claims.

Mendel. Mendel, also a native of Tennessee, had received his B.A. degree from Columbia University in 1927 and his LL.B degree from the Columbia Law School in 1930. He served on the University's law faculty until 1933 as research assistant and joined President Parkinson's staff in that year. He was appointed Legal Assistant in 1939 and Assistant Counsel in 1941.

The personnel of the Legal Reference Division grew rapidly as a result of depression problems. Litigation increased from some 700 cases in 1928 to about 2,500 cases in 1935, and the firm of Alexander and Green, Equitable's General Counsel, was not equipped to cope with this volume of work. There was never a clear delineation, official or otherwise, between the work to be performed by the Division and the work to be performed by the attorneys on the President's staff; consequently there was some overlapping of functions and occasional misunderstandings as to who was responsible for what. Although there was no official connection between the Division and Sterling Pierson of the President's staff, there was very close collaboration between Fitzgerald and Pierson on all important matters.[171]

The law firm of Alexander and Green, which had handled the Society's legal business since early in its history, and served as its General Counsel since 1906, resigned as of December 31, 1942; it continued, however, to handle New York City cases already pending until February 1944, at which time cases in suit were transferred to Leo D. Fitzgerald, who, at Sterling Pierson's request, became Attorney of Record in the Society's litigation.[172]

Vice President Leon O. Fisher died in 1935. Upon learning of Fisher's death, Henry L. Rosenfeld wrote President Parkinson from Paris:

To me it is another link with the pleasant recollections of Equitable association, broken. To you I know it must be a keen loss for I know the

[171] "Report on Organization of the Society's Legal Functions," pp. 8–9. This 15-page typescript was probably prepared by Counsel Leo D. Fitzgerald for President Ray D. Murphy in 1953. Copy in *ibid.*

[172] Although Henry M. Alexander and Charles B. Alexander had served at various times as Equitable counsel from 1868, and President Henry B. Hyde had some sort of an arrangement with the firm of Alexander and Green prior to 1894, it appears that the first official recognition of the firm as Equitable's General Counsel dated from January 1, 1906. See President Paul Morton's Memorandum to the Officers and Heads of Departments, December 28, 1905. *Ibid.* For later reorganization of Equitable's Law Department, see this history, p. 1301–1302.

store you set on his co-operation and his loyal service to the Equitable and to you. Paul Morton brought him in, Judge Day valued him highly and he went through successive administrations with fidelity and ability.

So I extend to you and to the Society my sympathy, for despite the impersonality of a great corporation wherein no one individual is irreplaceable, there are individuals, after all, whose going out after years of devotion to the institution, leaves a certain void.[173]

In 1937, Vice President and Actuary Robert Henderson retired after forty years of service with the Society. At a dinner in his honor, President Parkinson paid him a fine tribute. Henderson, a Canadian, was graduated from the University of Toronto in 1891 and was an instructor in mathematics in that institution for some time after graduation. He served five years with the Canadian Insurance Department and joined Equitable's Actuary's Department in 1897. He qualified as a Fellow of the Institute of Actuaries of Great Britain in 1896 and of the Actuarial Society of America in 1902. He became Actuary of the Society in 1911 on the retirement of Joel G. Van Cise. He served as Vice President of the Actuarial Society 1916–17, and as President for two terms, 1922–24. He was the author of several monographs and a member of the Joint Committee which supervised the Medico-Actuarial Mortality Investigation and of the Society's committee which conducted the American-Canadian Mortality Investigation.

Henderson was conservative in his views and Vice President William J. Graham always believed that he had opposed the introduction of group insurance and had never become entirely reconciled to it. On the other hand, Ray D. Murphy, who worked under Henderson for many years and became his successor, said that so far as he was aware Henderson had "never really opposed the introduction of Group life insurance in 1911. He had a very liberal attitude generally regarding the introduction of new coverages. He realized the complexities of group coverage and introduced dividend methods aimed at obtaining satisfactory results and the resulting renewal of such contracts. It was an unplowed field to which he vigorously applied all his skill. He was critical at times of the prediction of results by agency men which current results and methods could not justify. This was typical of his sensitiveness to ethical principles, but was not an indication of op-

[173] Rosenfeld to President Parkinson, October 21, 1935. Copy in Parkinson files, *ibid.*

position generally to the group business."[174] Henderson worked for the improvement of pension funds and served on the committee to advise the Pension Fund Commission of the City of New York; he also acted as actuarial adviser to the Church Pension Fund of the Episcopal Church. He was a member of the American Mathematical Society and the American Philosophical Society, and in 1930 received the degree of Doctor of Science from the University of Toronto. Modest and unassuming, Henderson believed in developing his assistants by giving them complete responsibility for the work trusted to them; he always had the complete respect of his staff.

After Henderson's retirement, Vice President Ray D. Murphy became Vice President and Actuary.

Three new second vice presidents appointed in 1937 were Charles J. Martin, M. C. Laffey, and Vincent S. Welch of the Group Department.[175]

Secretary William Alexander died in March 1937. As late as 1929, when the Secretary was taking a brief vacation at Underledge, Lenox, Massachusetts, he said that he had never felt better or happier; that he was "engaged in getting my head down to a size to fit my hat." When President Parkinson urged him to take plenty of rest, he wrote that as he grew older he regarded his friendships as his most valuable possessions. By 1934, however, he wrote that his heart had become involved with various other impairments, and that he was advised to get away from New York before the winter was over. A year later, he wrote that he had had an attack of "a misery in *medias res*." Some years before his death, the Secretary was suggesting to President Parkinson that he begin an immediate search "for the young man who may measure up to your ideal" to become the next Secretary of the Society.[176]

William Alexander had started his career as a clerk in 1869, became Assistant Secretary in 1871, and had served as Secretary since 1880. Artistic and literary, modest almost to the point of shyness, he had been much more than a Secretary. He had edited various Society magazines, and had written sales literature for the agents, five anniversary histories of the Society, several books on life insurance, and

[174] Ray D. Murphy, memoir on Robert Henderson, February 1, 1961. Copy in *ibid.*

[175] For a sketch of Welch's career, see this history, p. 1196.

[176] Alexander to President Parkinson, October 7, 1928, October 5, 1929, October 3, 1934, and September 6, 1935. Parkinson files, Equitable Archives.

a manuscript memoir, "Early Days of the Equitable." [177] He loved good conversation and liked to play golf; he disliked using the telephone and refused to carry long pencils because they protruded beyond his decorative pocket handkerchief; he was clever with the pencil and at banquets often sketched various persons and accompanied the sketches with impromptu verses. The only one of the Alexanders to remain as an officer after the troubles of 1905, he had been consultant and adviser to six presidents—President Day called him his "Secretary of State"—and his more than two-thirds of a century with Equitable had furnished a continuity to its history such as was furnished by no other officer. In 1929, when he sent a copy of his *Seventieth Anniversary History* to James Hazen Hyde in France, he wrote:

It is merely a fragmentary sketch—much has been left out—but what there is will I hope give no offense.

At the close of our Civil War, those who stayed at home continued to quarrel, while those who had fought soon came together. Billy Yank and Johnny Reb quickly established friendly relations.

You and I once fought on opposite sides in a civil war, each advocating a cause which he thought to be right.

When a certain director tried to seize control by attacking both parties, the two factions united in self-defense, defeating the aim of that director. Then the hatchet was buried as far as I was concerned, and from that day to this I have had only friendly sentiments for those who for a time were in the enemy's ranks.

[177] The brief anniversary histories were for the 50th anniversary (1909), the 60th (1919), the 65th (1924), the 70th (1929), and the 75th (1934). The last of these, entitled *Seventy-Five Years of Progress and Public Service,* contained 35 pages of Equitable history and 52 pages on past presidents, Equitable Home Offices, the great fire, etc. Copies of this history were distributed to those who were qualified to attend the 75th anniversary convention. In 1917 Alexander published his book on *What Life Insurance Is and What It Does.* His most important book, *My Half-Century in Life Insurance,* was published by Harper and Brothers in 1935, less than two years before his death. This book is both an autobiography and a history of the early days of Equitable and the evolution of life insurance. It is charmingly written, as well as instructive. Other books or booklets written by William Alexander were *Life Insurance Simply Explained, How to Sell Assurance, The Art of Insurance Salesmanship, One Hundred Ways of Canvassing for Life Insurance, Income Insurance for Family Protection, The Successful Agent, The Life Insurance Company, Insurance Fables for the Man in the Street,* and *Fables for Life Underwriters.* Although the book used for the Equitable Training Course for agents, copyrighted in 1936 by the Society, does not bear Alexander's name, it was obviously based largely upon his previous writings. It went through six printings by 1939.

I hope this is your attitude also.

In thinking of this episode I am reminded of the fable about the two men who were quarreling over an oyster, when a third person intervened and offered to arbitrate, and then gave one contestant a shell and the other a shell, and ate the oyster. But our experience was different; the director who intervened didn't get the oyster.[178]

Alexander McNeill was elected the eighth Secretary of the Society early in 1938. He came to Equitable in August 1899, as office boy at $3 a week, in the department of Third Vice President George T. Wilson, who was in charge of all the foreign business. In 1919 McNeill was appointed Superintendent of the Foreign Department, and in 1928 Assistant Secretary, with the Foreign Department still under his jurisdiction.

* * *

The depression and other factors led to some changes in Equitable's premium payment requirements and policy offerings. Effective March 17, 1931, the privilege to policyholders of deferring annual premium payments on life and endowment policies by depositing partial payments of at least 5 per cent a month was extended from a maximum of five months to a maximum of eight months beyond the grace period. (This emergency rule, which did not apply to Term or Economic Adjustment policies, was continued until September 1, 1935.) To meet the needs for life insurance during a period of restricted purchasing power, Equitable issued its Economic Adjustment Policy in 1931. This policy, which included all standard features, when originally introduced carried a low initial premium with convenient adjustment options at the end of five years, ten years, and at age sixty. The following year, the high-premium Guaranteed Investment Policy was discontinued since its benefits could be largely replaced by combining other forms. In April 1933, the Life Income Policy was dropped for similar reasons, and the one-year incontestable and suicide clauses, which had been in effect since 1892 and 1886 respectively, were raised to two years. At the same time, the Optional Retirement at Age Sixty-Five Policy was introduced, replacing the Endowment Annuity at Age Sixty-Five Policy, which was discontinued as of November 1, 1933. Disability income benefits were dropped on new insurance after March

178 William Alexander to James Hazen Hyde, October 4, 1929. Parkinson files, Equitable Archives.

5, 1934, but this action did not affect the premium waiver and double indemnity provisions. In March 1934 the Society introduced its new Family Income Policy. Dividends on Equitable policies—which had been increased six different times during the preceding decade—were reduced moderately in 1932 and again in 1933; for Ordinary and Limited Payment Life policies on the 3 per cent reserve basis, the reduction was less than in 1932; on endowment and term policies, and on policies on the 3½ per cent reserve basis, the reduction was somewhat larger. In 1936 Equitable introduced a new optional retirement policy at age sixty.

As a result of low interest rates and the uncertainty of equity investments, annuity sales increased appreciably during the early 1930's. The life companies were reluctant to pass up this business yet hesitated to commit themselves to pay a higher interest rate than they might be able to earn. To meet this situation Equitable introduced, December 1, 1934, a participating annuity with a somewhat lower return guarantee, the policyholder to share in any earnings beyond the minimum guaranteed.

Despite the fact that the life companies did not seem eager to secure the annuity business, they continued to devise new forms in order to secure that business. For instance, in 1927, when Sun Life of Canada announced a new Special Refund Annuity, Penn Mutual followed with a similar contract soon thereafter, and Equitable and Mutual fell in line. This contract was a single premium contract known as the "life annuity with death benefit." [179] President Parkinson became interested in the Sun Life contract when a number of agents requested that such a contract be added to Equitable's offerings. Vice President Frank H. Davis and Secretary Alexander thought that this would be a good idea, but Actuary Robert Henderson, while seeing no technical actuarial reason why Equitable should not issue the contract, pointed out that there was a political factor involved; he was afraid that the prevalence of contracts of this type might cause a revision of the income tax laws which would be damaging to Equitable's regular annuity business.[180]

[179] The Sun Life contract purchase price was $1,050 per unit at all ages up to and including seventy-five; it provided an annuity of $35 per year per unit. No medical examination was required. In the event of death, the policy paid $1,000 per unit plus a proportionate part of the annuity payment for the current year. Annuity payments were increased by a share of the divisible surplus as declared by the company. *The National Underwriter*, LXVII (1927), November 4.

[180] Parkinson memorandum to Henderson, December 24, and Henderson to Parkinson, December 27, 1927. Sterling Pierson files, Equitable Archives.

Nevertheless, Equitable issued its Special Refund Annuity (Form No. 2616), which was approved by the New York Insurance Department in February 1928. Announced to the agency force the following month, the policy was practically the same as the Sun Life contract, and provided a surrender value nearly equal to the amount deposited.[181]

Even before the contract was announced to the agents, the Nebraska Insurance Department disapproved it, ruling that any insurance company issuing such a form would have to be authorized to transact a trust business. And in August the Bureau of Internal Revenue ruled that contracts similar to Equitable's "Special Refund Annuity" were not annuity contracts but merely contracts for the payment of interest or earnings on a certain fund; hence such interest or earnings were immediately taxable income, in contrast to annuity payments, which became taxable income only when their amount exceeded the original consideration. Sterling Pierson maintained that the whole contract was an annuity contract and that payments under it should not be considered taxable until they exceeded the total premium, but in June 1929 the Bureau of Internal Revenue ruled that such contracts actually consisted of two parts—single premium life insurance and a single premium annuity—hence, the annuity payments were not to be taxable until the total payments received exceeded that portion of the premium paying for the annuity, and dividends were not to be taxable until the total dividends exceeded that portion of the premium paying for the life insurance. Then a month later the Vermont Commissioner of Banking and Insurance ruled that the "so-called Life Annuity Policy with Principal Sum Payable at Death" was a banking transaction, and that no insurance company might issue such a policy in Vermont. The New York Insurance Department made a similar decision in December. President Parkinson argued that the policy conformed to the standard policy forms provided under the Armstrong legislation of 1906, but the Attorney General of the state, in April 1931, upheld the Insurance Department's contention that the Special Refund Annuity was not an annuity contract and could not be issued in New York or elsewhere on or after April 20.[182] Meanwhile, the Sun Life, in Feb-

181 Treasurer M. C. Laffey was worried lest a large amount of this type of business on the Society's books might cause a severe drain in time of "panic." Laffey memorandum to President Parkinson, November 5, 1928. *Ibid.*

182 While the status of the Special Refund Annuity was in doubt, Homer Jamison, Equitable Agency Manager at Oklahoma City, sought to secure definite information on the subject. He had in mind selling the Department of the

ruary, withdrew its special refund annuity because of fear of heavy withdrawals on 90 days' notice under these contracts.[183] After the New York Insurance Department extended the deadline, Equitable sold—between April 30 and June 1—$11,495,280 additional Special Refund Annuities. During 1932 and later, various difficulties came up with state tax officials in regard to the outstanding contracts, particularly in Minnesota, Delaware, and Oregon. At the end of 1935, Equitable had 3,530 of the Special Refund Annuity contracts outstanding, for a total of approximately $21,800,000 of investment.[184]

A similar market appeal involved the use of the combination of single premium life insurance at standard rates without physical examination with a life annuity—the two policies to be issued simultaneously. Under this combination the total single consideration for both insurance and annuity was 106 or 110 per cent of the face amount of the insurance issued. The income to the purchaser was from the regular guarantees of the life annuity and such dividends as might be apportioned and taken in cash on the life insurance policy. One of the primary purposes of this plan was to gain an estate tax advantage for an insured who could not qualify for standard insurance.

The "106 per cent combination" was probably first issued by Equitable in 1919, and in July 1922 the combination was restricted to life annuities. In November 1932 the Society ruled that the regular issue age maximum did not apply to combination issues. As a result of an increase in state premium taxes the ratio of total consideration to amount of insurance was increased to 110 per cent. In November 1936 Vice President W. W. Klingman announced to the general agents and agency managers that the plan had been discontinued.[185]

Interior the idea of buying these policies for the Indians. He wrote that "the situation is hot" and that he was "doing everything possible to hold these people in line for Equitable." Jamison to Sterling Pierson, September 30, 1930. *Ibid.*

[183] *New York Post*, February 26, 1931.

[184] In 1940 the Bureau of Internal Revenue revoked the 1929 ruling and held that the "Special Refund Annuity" was not a life insurance or annuity contract within the meaning of the provisions of the Revenue Act of 1938 and the corresponding provisions of prior Revenue Acts, but constituted a contract for the payment of interest or earnings on a certain fund and that the information returns required to be filed by insurance companies showing amounts paid under the contract should show the entire amount of the periodic payments paid.

[185] In 1945 the United States Supreme Court ruled that the proceeds of a single premium life policy issued by Equitable in 1933 under the "106 per cent combination" plan were to be included for estate tax purposes. (*Goldstone, et al v. United States*, 325 U.S. 687). In 1958, however, in *Fidelity-Philadelphia Trust*

The large volume of annuity business issued by Equitable during the depression period, particularly in the 3½ per cent Retirement Annuities available prior to 1935, contributed greatly to the agent's earnings. (See this history, p. 881.) The actuaries were concerned, however, lest the annuity business become too large a proportion of the Society's business.[186] Consequently the agency superintendents were instructed to impress upon the managers and agents the necessity of soliciting life insurance rather than annuities. Vice President W. W. Klingman agreed with the actuaries that 70 per cent of the Society's new business should be from life insurance. He issued rules to the Agency Force, to become effective November 1, 1935, which limited the combined total of single premium life insurance policies and/or single premium retirement and special life annuities issued within any

---

Company v. *Francis R. Smith, Collector of Internal Revenue* (356 U.S. 274) the court ruled that the insurance proceeds were not part of the estate if the insured had irrevocably assigned all rights in the life policies. This decision revived interest in the combination plans and, since other companies were offering them, some Equitable agents thought that Equitable should do so. After careful consideration Equitable decided it was not advisable to promote a plan the sales of which would be motivated largely by current interpretations of the tax laws.

186 The trend in the sales of annuity contracts as contrasted with insurance policies may be noted from the following figures:

Year	Number of Individual Insurance Policies Paid For in Year	Number of Individual Annuity Contracts Paid For in Year
1929	215,847	16,831
1930	221,420	21,799
1931	183,306	33,488
1932	155,061	44,798
1933	129,094	51,200
1934	139,025	76,946
1935	145,287	52,500
1936	137,901	44,844
1937	146,930	33,249
1938	124,704	35,127
1939	107,465	24,913
1940	110,612	9,086

Reserves at End of Year

Year	Individual Life Insurance	Individual Annuities
1929	$ 885,000,000	$ 80,000,000
1939	1,214,000,000	604,000,000

twelve months' period on one person to $50,000; the corresponding total amount effected within five years on existing contracts, including new business, was limited to $100,000. The issuance of single premium endowments with periods shorter than fifteen years was discontinued.[187]

The depression also brought problems in connection with individual disability income insurance. During the 1920's there had been keen competition among the life insurance companies for this type of insurance, usually written as an optional rider benefit on life insurance policies. As a result of inadequate experience, too liberal provisions, and too low premiums it became apparent, even before the depression, that there would be losses. In 1930 the Commissioners of Insurance set up less liberal standard provisions for disability income which were adopted by New York and several other states. The companies then adopted less liberal provisions and raised their premium rates a minimum of 50 per cent. This action did not prove satisfactory, however, and by 1932 most companies ceased offering disability income insurance riders, and those which continued to do so adopted less liberal provisions. Equitable had in early 1930 substantially increased its premium rates and for the first time charged higher premium rates for women. In July it modified the disability clause to conform to the standard provisions promulgated in New York and other states. In November 1931 Equitable abandoned disability income coverage for women, and in January 1932, the year in which most companies ceased issuing disability income, Equitable tightened its provisions by limiting monthly income to $5 per $1,000 of face, by reducing the coverage age from 60 to 55, and by requiring six months of disability for the presumption of permanency. It also began reducing dividends on policies with the disability income provisions dating prior to February 1930.[188]

Like the other companies which issued disability income insurance Equitable suffered sizable losses. Finally, as of March 5, 1934, it discontinued completely issuing this type of benefit. In January 1940 Equitable transferred $61,739,996 to the Disability Fund account to cover the deficit which had been incurred in the fund to December 31,

187 Klingman to the Agency Force of the Society, October 26, 1935. Copy in Sterling Pierson files, Equitable Archives.

188 The legality of distinguishing in dividends between those life insurance policies with disability income benefits and those policies without disability income benefits was tested and sustained in the courts of New York and other states.

1937.[189] A further increase in the annual disability income deductions was introduced in 1941 but the deductions were limited to two-thirds of the dividend that would otherwise have been payable. This increase was not caused by poorer experience during the five-year period 1935–39 used to develop these deductions, but by the fact that the poorer experience of the 1930–35 period had continued with slight improvement.

Despite all the efforts of the New Deal the depression persisted. At the end of 1936 the United States, from the standpoint of recovery, ranked at or near the bottom among the leading nations of the world; billions of dollars of idle capital were still awaiting profitable employment and about 10,000,000 persons were still unemployed. Equitable's new business in 1936 fell to $456,240,864, and in 1938 to $415,980,099, the lowest of any year since 1918, except only 1933. The depression years had been hard ones for the life insurance agents, and many of Equitable's agents thought that the Underwriting Department was being entirely too strict in the selection of risks. One of the Society's older general agents wrote President Parkinson that the agents felt that in case of doubt concerning an application, the decision was always against the applicant and agent: "If this widespread feeling continues much longer, it will disrupt the Equitable's entire field forces without a question of a doubt. Never in my 39 years' experience has the Underwriting Department of the Equitable been so unpopular in the field as at present."[190] Then there was a strong difference of opinion among both agents and officers in regard to the relative merits of the salaried manager system and the old general agency system under which the General Agent paid most of the agency expenses and was compensated largely by the difference between the commissions he received and those he paid to the agents under contract with him.

* * *

The question of the general agency system versus the manager system was brought to the front in 1933 when Edward H. Keating, son of the Society's late general agent in Minnesota, William J. Keating, was given a contract which The General Agency Association con-

189 In recent years part of this transfer was reversed.

190 Thomas B. Sweeney, "Very Personal," to Thomas I. Parkinson, October 21, 1933. Parkinson files, Equitable Archives.

sidered tantamount to discontinuance of the general agency system at the death of the existing general agents. With one exception, no new general agency contracts had been made by Equitable for about twenty-five years. The exception was The Edward A. Woods Company at Pittsburgh, which had been permitted to incorporate (in 1911) and continue as a general agency under its corporate name. Some of the older general agents were interested in securing general agency contracts for their sons, and The General Agency Association wanted a definite decision in regard to Equitable's policy on continuation of the general agency after the death of the incumbent.[191]

When President Parkinson asked Actuary Robert Henderson his opinion in respect to the merits of the two systems, Henderson said that various calculations had been made regarding relative costs and stated his view as follows: "My own idea continues to be that the present general agents' contract is *under average circumstances unduly expensive to the company in comparison with our salaried manager business and that no express or implied promise of its continuance to sons of general agents should be given.*" [192] Some of the officers thought that the older general agents were more inclined to collect the rewards of past investments and efforts than to expand their business. Vice President W. W. Klingman, in charge of agencies, favored the manager system. Secretary William Alexander, however, drawing upon the experience of many years, sought a way out which would "get our

[191] Among the general agents who were trying to get their agencies continued under their sons were Jerome J. Wilson in New York and Thomas B. Sweeney in Wheeling. In April 1934 President Parkinson wrote Wilson, who was seriously ill, that Equitable would continue Wilson's general agency as he had requested. And Wilson put a codicil in his will which provided capital for his son, Horace H. Wilson, to continue the agency. President Parkinson to Jerome J. Wilson, April 23, 1934. Sterling Pierson files, *ibid.* Thomas B. Sweeney had made a partnership agreement with his son John in 1932 and wanted to guarantee the succession in a codicil in his will. After lengthy correspondence with Sterling Pierson, Sweeney wrote: "In my entire forty-three years' history with the Equitable, I have never been confronted with such a condition—and I might say, such anxiety—as has been caused by the, to me, inexplainable delay in getting the approval or disapproval from the Legal Department of a Modification of Contract Letter between my son, John F. Sweeney, and myself." The situation in the Sweeney agency remained unsettled for several years, but in 1938 Thomas B. Sweeney abandoned the idea of incorporating the Wheeling agency and decided to stand on the partnership arrangement. The correspondence between Pierson and Sweeney may be found in *ibid.*

[192] Henderson (at Crown Point, New York) to D. A. Walker, May 27, 1933. Parkinson's memorandum was dated May 24. Parkinson files, *ibid.*

general agents in a good humor again." Although there were not many of them, if they became convinced that they had a real grievance they would "become sour and discontented" and perhaps demoralize the whole agency body. As for the cases of fathers and sons, there were so few of them that they were of trivial financial significance but of vital importance from a sentimental point of view. Equitable could well afford to "let two or three young men inherit their fathers' contracts, and sink or swim if given a fair trial." Lest his recommendation lead to embarrassment, he suggested that President Parkinson give Vice President Klingman the opportunity to make the decision. He could "say something like this to Mr. Klingman":

> In order that we may have the aid of the remaining general agents in maintaining a spirit of loyalty in our entire agency force it is necessary to satisfy these general agents. But, as it is known that you do not believe in doing what they ask, if I take this action it may hurt your reputation and lessen your influence with the agency force. This must not be permitted. Therefore *you* must announce this action as determined upon by *you*.
>
> You can frankly admit that it is well known that you advocate the Agency Manager plan, do not think the general agency system will work satisfactorily in the future, would oppose the revival of that system, but that, after careful consideration, you have come to the conclusion that as we owe so much to our general agents, and as there are so few cases to be dealt with, you have decided to make an exception to the rule which you advocate, and to agree that in any case where a son feels willing and able to take over the agency when his father drops out he will be given the same contract that his father had and will be given the opportunity of making good under that contract.

Such an attitude on Klingman's part would be regarded as generous and candid. "And what would be the result? A temporary and very trifling loss here and there, but an important gain—worth perhaps a great deal of money—in maintaining the loyalty and enthusiasm, and efficient work, of the whole Agency force! The life insurance business is peculiar. Some things are essential that would be inappropriate in other kinds of business. The men who make good agents are, as a rule, high-strung, sensitive, *sentimental*. Therefore, if they are to be serviceable, their sentiment must be appealed to." [193]

The advice of the wise old Secretary was apparently followed, for

193 William Alexander (at Lenox, Massachusetts), confidential penciled note to President Parkinson, August 8, 1933. *Ibid.*

a few weeks later Thomas B. Sweeney wrote that he had found Klingman "very much changed in his attitude toward the general agency system"; Klingman had stated that he was not only prepared to continue the general agency system on the existing or even a better contract basis, but even to appoint a number of salaried managers as general agents the minute that the President and the Actuary thought this course to be the best for Equitable's interests. Sweeney said that when he reported Klingman's decision to the executive committee of The General Agency Association, the committee was at first incredulous, but he had convinced them of Klingman's sincerity, and "the effect was most remarkable." Every man had shown renewed interest and ambition to get behind Klingman the minute he put into operation "the unified system of dual control." [194]

Matters were brought to a head by the resignation of General Agent John M. Riehle (New York City) in December. President Parkinson called a meeting of the officers concerned and they discussed at length acquisition costs, percentage of new organization secured, and the possibility of "opening the door" to the extension of the general agents' form of contract to managers.[195] The officers present all agreed that it would not be to the best interests of the Society to extend the general agency system; they recommended that Equitable continue its practice of the preceding twenty years of refusing to make any new general agents' contracts with the full commission schedule as provided under the existing arrangement.[196] President Parkinson asked for an amplification of the reasons on which the officers' conclusions were based, in order that the recommendations might be more effectively presented to "those members of our Board who, as you know, will not be in-

[194] Thomas B. Sweeney to Gage E. Tarbell; copy enclosed in Sweeney's letter of October 21, 1933, to President Parkinson. Yet Sweeney, January 16, 1934, sent a memorandum of a conversation with Klingman in which he reported that Klingman was as much set against the possibility of appointing new general agents as he ever was. And January 22 Sweeney wrote President Parkinson that Klingman had said in an interview that he had not changed his position since the preceding October; that he still believed the general agency system was the best system for the company. Correspondence in *ibid.*

[195] Present at the meeting were Vice Presidents Klingman, Henderson, and Murphy; Second Vice Presidents Walker and Parsons; General Solicitor Sterling Pierson; and Auditor F. A. Shailer. Vice President Graham was not present at the meeting but expressed agreement with the group's conclusions as outlined in a memorandum.

[196] W. W. Klingman, memorandum to President Parkinson, January 8, 1934. Parkinson files, Equitable Archives.

clined to agree with the conclusions." [197] Furthermore, he wished to explain the action to the executive committee of The General Agency Association.

When President Parkinson met with the executive committee of the Association in January 1934, he presented the reasons which led the officers to their decision, but stated that he would be glad to receive any evidence in rebuttal. As a result, a committee of five general agents was appointed to prepare a "brief" and President Parkinson gave the chairman authorization to secure information from any officer of Equitable or his department.[198]

The committee's "brief," in the form of an eleven-page (legal size) memorandum with attached schedules was ready for President Parkinson by February.[199] It was a rather imposing document. It analyzed costs in considerable detail and sought to prove that if all costs were taken into consideration the general agency system would be more economical; but dollar and cents cost did not represent the whole picture, for total costs should include both "tangibles and intangibles, abstract as well as concrete realities. We believe that such things as *continuity of service, loyalty, permanency,* and many others are a very material part of the Life Insurance business." The committee emphasized that over a period of time the percentage of lapsed policies was lower under the general agents than under the managers. Under the general agents, the Society paid at all times, good and bad, only for what it got. The following paragraph was underscored:

> The element which increases General Agency expense for the Society is good persistency of business; that which decreases costs, the short life of business. On the other hand, in the Managerial System it is just the reverse

197 President Parkinson, memorandum to W. W. Klingman, January 10, 1934. *Ibid.*

198 Appointed to prepare the "brief" were Thomas B. Sweeney and Horace H. Wilson. A subcommittee composed of William M. Duff, Theodore M. Riehle, and Courtenay Barber was appointed to assist in assembling data. The committee asked President Parkinson to assign Sterling Pierson and Frank A. Shailer to act as consultants to assist the committee. President Parkinson did so, but modified his memorandum to provide that no information was to be secured from the various departments unless with the approval and through the cooperation of Pierson and Shailer.

199 The title was "Memorandum for President Parkinson to Demonstrate that it is to the Best Interests of The Equitable Life Assurance Society to Continue and Vitalize the Dual System of General Agencies and Salaried Managers." Copy in Sterling Pierson files, Equitable Archives.

—the element which increases the cost is the short life of business while the long life of business decreases such cost. This furnishes a striking contrast—for, under the General Agency System the Society pays more only when it gets more and pays less when it receives less. Under the Managerial System, it pays less when it gets more and pays more when it receives less in return. This principle is contrary to sound business practice.

The committee believed that this point alone was sufficient to prove the superiority of the general agency system. Further, it questioned the argument that it was wise to grow fast and spend large sums of money which it was impossible for an individual to provide, in the early development of an agency. In comparing turnover between the two systems, it was pointed out that 22 general agents remained with the Society after 25 years but only one salaried manager. No single general agent had left Equitable to go with another company while, since 1922, 14 managers had left the Society to become general agents for other companies. As for turnover of agents, there had been 82 managerial changes since 1921 and "a tremendous turnover of agents of which none of us have much right to boast. Think of it—under our Dual System we have appointed 53,344 new agents in the last ten years and had only 9,502 left on December 31, 1933! What has become of the other 42,842? Is this waste necessary? . . . As a matter of fact, in recent years, the Equitable has probably gained first rank of all Companies as a training ground for other Companies."

In submitting the memorandum, which, incidentally, was signed by members of both the committee and the subcommittee, the members made it clear that they believed that the "weak sister" had no place in Equitable under either system.[200]

The committee's "brief" apparently had its influence. In March President Parkinson authorized the issuance of new general agency contracts to Horace H. Wilson, Theodore M. Riehle, and Edward H. Keating. By May 16, he made his decision on the whole problem, which he said was final.[201] He said that the matter of relative costs had given him the greatest difficulty, for at best the calculations were

[200] President Parkinson said that the committee's report was incomplete because he had discouraged further examination of some of the questions which it had thought material; he thought that further pursuit by the committee would hurt rather than help the situation. Memorandum to W. W. Klingman, May 11, 1934. Parkinson files, *ibid.*

[201] President Parkinson to Secretary William Alexander and to W. W. Klingman, May 16, 1934. *Ibid.*

only an approximation. He did not believe that any difference in favor of the managers was sufficient to outweigh the advantages derived from the general agency system. He concluded, therefore, that Equitable should now be prepared to make new general agency contracts. Whether an existing agency manager should be given a general agency contract, together with the organization which had been built up under his existing contract, was another question requiring further consideration. He suggested that Vice President Klingman announce the decision at the meeting of The General Agency Association at Atlantic City May 18, 1934. This Klingman did, telling the general agents that the dual system of agency management was to be revived and continued. He then proceeded "to electrify all present" by stating that it was his ambition eventually to have as many general agents under contract as he had salaried managers: "He said that the wall which had been for a quarter of a century rising between these two branches would, he hoped, by this announcement be razed to the ground, never to appear again in the Equitable ranks. He further stated that he never believed in halfway measures and that it was his intention to promote the dual system without prejudice to either branch and that he was determined to do all in his power to make the field forces of the Equitable one united, happy and successful family. . . ."[202] The following day President Parkinson said: "I do not like to see the number of our general agents decreasing. Perhaps it is inevitable." He suggested that it was time for The General Agency Association to convert into a "Managerial Association," to be composed of both leading general agents and managers.

At a meeting of The General Agency Association in New York in July 1934, the suggestion was adopted and the Association changed its name to The Old Guard of The Equitable, a name suggested by Secretary William Alexander. Charter members consisted of 22 general agents and 22 salaried managers; the By-Laws limited membership to 25 general agents and 25 salaried managers, but permitted 25 associate memberships. A year later, President Parkinson said: "I depend upon The Old Guard, rather than the new agents, to keep me advised, to be vigilant, to feel the pulse of the owners, the policyholders." (Once again, in 1945, by which time the managers heavily outnumbered the general agents, the organization changed its name to The General

[202] Minutes of The General Agency Association meeting, May 18 and 19, 1934. Corporate Records, *ibid.*

Agents and Managers Association of the Equitable Life Assurance Society of the United States.) When a proposed new general agents' contract was offered to a number of salaried managers, none of them accepted. Gradually, as the older general agents died or retired, they were replaced by agency managers, until by 1959 only nine general agents remained, four of them without subagents.

OLD-AGE BENEFITS

The introduction of "Social Security" legislation in 1935 naturally was of interest to the life insurance companies and to the agents in particular. One of the first life company executives to comment on this subject was President Parkinson. In January he was asked the following question by the *Chicago Journal of Commerce:* "Will the socialization program of the Federal Government be an aid to life insurance generally, group insurance in particular, or will it compete to such an extent as to conflict in any way?" President Parkinson replied in an article which was published in the *Journal* January 16 and was widely copied or summarized in other newspapers and in the insurance periodicals. In his statement, he noted the useful purposes and the limitations of the proposed measures and drew a definite distinction between the unemployable group logically subject to the operations of such measures and the employables who could and should take care of themselves. The old-age relief provisions would take care of the unemployables, which was not a group ordinarily served by life insurance. For the employables, he considered ordinary life insurance a more self-respecting form of relief. He objected to the term "unemployment insurance" as a misnomer, for there was no insurance connected with it. In general, he thought that the Social Security legislation would be an aid to life insurance just as the Federal Government's War Risk Insurance had been in World War I. This statement was published before the introduction of the Wagner bill, which became the basis for the OASI or "Social Security Act," enacted August 14, 1935.

Although the problem of unemployment was a serious one and the "Townsendites" were waging a nation-wide campaign for old-age pensions, the chief impetus for enactment of the Social Security Act of 1935 came from the Roosevelt Administration.[203] Although it was one

[203] "How did we get the Social Security Act of 1935? Mr. Bigge replied that the Administration made the groups think they wanted it. There wasn't any vocal demand, initially from the groups affected. Mr. Cohen said there was no demand

of the most basically important laws enacted in the United States during the present century, it was—and remains—but poorly understood by the average citizen, both as to its provisions and long-term implications. The life insurance companies through their literature and agent training programs provided the public with much information on the benefits and their frequent liberalization, but naturally could not explain to the public the financial basis of the Social Security system.

The initial law provided 1) old-age benefits as a matter of right supported by a payroll tax which later, after expansion, came to be known as the Old-Age, Survivors, and Disability Insurance System (OASDI); 2) a State-Federal unemployment compensation system financed by a payroll tax; and 3) old-age assistance, and aid to dependent children covered by grants-in-aid to the states. Probably the most important part in the minds of most persons was that which provided for old-age retirement benefits. The essential provisions were as follows: 1) A payroll tax of 1 per cent on the first $3,000 of earnings per year was levied against the employee, with a matching amount to be paid by the employer; (Self-employed persons were not included until 1951 with a tax of 2¼ per cent.) 2) A "Trust Fund" was created on the books of the Treasury of the United States to consist of the securities held by the Secretary of the Treasury for the Old-Age Reserve Account. Such amounts of the current taxes as were not required to meet current withdrawals were to be invested in United States Government obligations bearing 3 per cent interest. 3) Any person who had cumulative wage credits of $2,000 and some employment in each of 5 years would, upon reaching the age sixty-five, be entitled to a pension. The maximum amount when the first payment was made in 1940 was $41.20. Under the initial Act, however, no benefit was payable if a person had any earnings from regular employment. Under the 1939 Act, $15 a month of earnings was permitted; successive liberalizations of this retirement or work test have been made. This provision, however, does not apply to individuals who received income from investments. Its purpose is to limit Social Security benefits to those who

and no opposition." *Record of Executive Director's Conference with Bureau of Regional Directors, Washington, D.C., May, 1945*, pp. 417–18, recorded in the Report of Social Security Hearings before a subcommittee of the Committee on Ways and Means, 83rd Congress, first session, 1954. See also Ray M. Peterson "An Appraisal of the Social Security Amendments of 1965" pp. 5–6. This paper was read before the Conference of Actuaries in Public Practice, New Orleans, October 4, 1965. Copy in *ibid.*

have no substantial connection with the labor force. President Franklin D. Roosevelt is reported to have said: "We put those payroll contributions there so as to give the contributors a legal, moral, and political right to collect their pensions and their unemployment benefits. With those taxes in there, no damn politician can ever scrap my social security program." [204]

The principles and provisions of the Social Security legislation of 1935 were debated at the time and continue to be debated. What was its purpose? How was it to be financed? Was the financing plan "actuarially sound" or even "fiscally sound"? Was it "insurance" or primarily welfare legislation? Were the retirement benefits to be based upon "individual equity" or "social adequacy"? What were its political connotations? What would be the ultimate effects upon the individual? Upon the American economy?

The primary purpose of the retirement benefits under OASDI was to provide a modicum of economic security for the individual no longer capable of earning; to establish a "floor of protection" somewhat above the subsistence level below which he could not fall. Although a few informed actuaries from the life insurance business served as technical advisers in the process of enactment of the law they had little influence in the formation of policy. In general those closest to the private insurance business believed that the "full-reserve" system as used by the legal reserve life insurance companies was inappropriate for financing the costs and advocated a "pay-as-you-go" plan. The law as enacted was a blend of "reserve" and "pay as you go," with the latter providing all but a small fraction of the costs. The plan was arrived at "through a pragmatic political process rather than through a theoretical philosophical process." To claim that it was "actuarially sound" would imply that it incorporated the principles used by private insurance and private pension funds, which it did not. On the other hand it might be considered fiscally sound as long as it operated under a plan of financing which would provide income sufficient to meet all benefit costs as they fell due. It would so provide as long as an incoming labor force would be willing to pay the ever-increasing taxes not only for their own retirement benefits but a portion of those for persons ahead of them under the system.

Was "Social Insurance" insurance? On no point has there probably

[204] Arthur M. Schlesinger, Jr., *The Coming of the New Deal* (Boston, 1959), p. 308.

been greater disagreement.[205] In general, advocates of the system, including the Social Security Administration, have sought to identify the Social Security program closely with private insurance. Said one of its advocates: "Social Security is a combination of old-age pensions, disability insurance, and life insurance. It is based on the same principle as private insurance, with variations to accomplish its social purpose and to keep it inexpensive." [206] But it was the "variations" which created the doubts. The promises made under private insurance are based on contractual rights which can be altered only by mutual agreement; OASDI promises are based on statutory rights which may be changed by Congress, which has "the right to alter, amend, or repeal any provision" of the Act. Said the Solicitor General of the United States in argument before the Supreme Court, ". . . social security must be viewed as a welfare instrument to which legal concepts of 'insurance,' 'property,' 'vested rights,' 'annuities,' etc., can be applied only at the risk of a serious distortion of language." [207] And said the Supreme Court of the United States:

> The Social Security system may be accurately described as a form of social insurance, enacted pursuant to Congress' power to "spend money in aid of the 'general welfare,' ". . . . It is apparent that the noncontractual interest of an employee covered by the Act cannot be soundly analogized to that of the holder of an annuity, whose right to benefits is bottomed on his contractual premium payments.[208]

Another important difference between social insurance and voluntary private insurance is that under the latter the principle of individual equity is preserved; that is, there is a direct relationship between contributions and benefits. Under Social Security, however, the concept of "social adequacy" usually makes it impossible to have individual equity, for under this concept many receive benefits far beyond the contributions (taxes) which they make. An early retiree under the Act, having paid in a few hundred dollars, would, if he lived to age seventy-five, receive several thousand dollars in benefits. And with rapidly increasing numbers of other citizens political pressures inevitably demand

[205] See C. Arthur Williams, Jr., " 'Social Insurance'—Proper Terminology?", *The Journal of Insurance*, XXX (1963), March, for discussion of the semantics of the problem.
[206] A. Larson, "Know Your Social Security" (New York, 1959), pp. 3–4.
[207] *Flemming* v. *Nestor*, 363 U.S. 603, Appellant's Brief, p. 68.
[208] *Ibid.*, p. 610.

increasing "social adequacy," or benefits and extension of coverage without proportionate increase in the taxes. Consequently the taxes paid by and with respect to the new entrants under the system must forever be greater than the value of the benefits which they will receive, and the unearned benefits for the older generations constitute a permanent and ever-increasing debt which, in the minds of most persons, constitutes an obligation of the Federal Government just as valid as its bonded debt. Thus the price of "social adequacy" becomes not only perpetual "individual inequity," but a debt which further contributes to the inflation and helps defeat the purpose of the system. "With no reserve fund in sight to reduce the debt, the burden being passed onto future generations is permanent. It is not something that will somehow work itself out or go away; it is not an actuarial fantasy." [209] So, despite numerous increases in both the taxes and the benefits, the retired person was destined to fight a losing battle. At the end of 25 years (1965) the maximum monthly benefit had been raised to $127, or slightly more than three times the original, but, as a result of the declining value of the dollar, the cost of living (including taxes) had risen almost twice as fast.

Director Sterling Morton did not believe that the life insurance companies had made a sustained effort to educate policyholders to the implications of government ownership and government competition. He saw many actuarial faults in the measures and spoke of the unemployment benefits as "bread and circuses." [210] Vice President William J. Graham, in his reply to Morton, said that the action of Equitable had "been more in sympathy with your implied thoughts than . . . the recorded action of the other companies. It is plain, therefore, that we lean to your views rather than to the policy of 'almost complete silence' but we feel that we should fairly state to you the attitude of these other companies seems to be born of the considerations that the policyholders constituted a cross section of the whole population with its often deep-rooted convictions with respect to social and economic

[209] Ray M. Peterson "The Coming Din of Inequity," *The Journal of the American Medical Association*, CLXXVI (1961), April 8. On the Social Security system see the excellent monographs by the same author, who is a Vice President and Associate Actuary of Equitable, as follows: "Misconceptions and Missing Perceptions of our Social Security System (Actuarial Anesthesia)," reprinted from the *Transactions of the Society of Actuaries*, XI (1959), and "How to Preserve Our Social Security System," an address before Fifteenth Anniversary Conference, Council on Employee Benefits, October 27, 1961. Copy in Equitable Archives.

[210] Sterling Morton to Vice President Leon Fisher, September 20, 1935. Sterling Pierson files, *ibid.*

questions." He reminded Morton of the unfortunate experience of some of the companies when they sought to defeat Bryan and "Free Silver" in 1896.[211]

A few years later, however, President Parkinson was more outspoken. He wrote: "It will be for the middle class of this country to determine and to determine in a lasting fashion . . . whether one of its foremost institutions, the collective management of voluntary savings in mutual life insurance companies, is to be given up in return for the bureaucratic idea of a state monopoly, the controls of which must, in the nature of the case, be political with all that this implies as to the handling of compulsory assessments. . . ."[212]

* * *

Early in 1935, Gage E. Tarbell, who in the 1890's and early 1900's had been one of the two most famous agency Vice Presidents in the United States, returned to the Society to render special services in agency affairs. He had resigned in 1907, but had remained a Director of the Society. In recent years he had devoted most of his attention to raising Guernsey cows on his New York farm.[213] Despite his age—he was seventy-nine—much of the old fire remained, and soon Tarbell was addressing agency meetings, relating interesting personal experiences, and inspiring the agents to greater efforts in the sale of life insurance. He died in September 1936, just after addressing an agency meeting at Elkhart Lake, Indiana.

In 1937 Equitable re-entered Texas, from which, together with most of the leading Eastern life insurance companies, it had withdrawn in 1907 as a result of the famous Robertson Law, which required that 75 per cent of the reserves on Texas policies be invested in Texas securities to be kept on deposit in the state.[214] The decision was not a sudden one, for as early as 1927 Vice President Thomas I. Parkinson had considered attending the meeting of the American Life Convention in Dallas and looking over the Texas situation. He said that the possi-

211 W. J. Graham to Sterling Morton, October 16, 1935. *Ibid.*

212 Thomas I. Parkinson, "Compulsory Insurance in the United States," published in *The Insurance Educator* and quoted in *The Weekly Underwriter,* CXLVIII (1943), February 27.

213 Vice President W. W. Klingman and Second Vice President Albert G. Borden had thought that Tarbell could make some regular contributions to the solution of Equitable's agency problems. Borden to Parkinson, March 13; Klingman to Parkinson, September 14 and December 20, 1934; Parkinson to Klingman, January 23, 1935. Parkinson files, Equitable Archives.

214 For the Robertson Law and Equitable's withdrawal, see this history, p. 726.

bility of re-entering Texas had been on his mind for some time.[215] Conditions in Texas had changed during the preceding thirty years; the law had been modified somewhat and numerous investments were available which did not exist at the earlier date, and Equitable's investments in Texas exceeded the requirements of the law. Many Texas policyholders had continued to pay their premiums during the interim, but the Society could render them no services through local agents. Then Equitable had group policies on industrial organizations which had part of their group residing in Texas, and some complicated litigation had arisen as a result of this situation. President Parkinson had Sterling Pierson investigate the procedure of re-entry and Pierson found that it would require $417,845 to meet back taxes, interest, and penalties and thus secure the approval of the state. Although this seemed rather a high price to pay, President Parkinson calculated that the interest earnings on the money not paid in taxes during the thirty-year period more than paid the price of re-entry. Vice President William J. Graham and Merle Gulick were sent to Texas to survey the possibilities. They were well received by the President of the National Association of Life Underwriters, and Jesse Jones, Houston banker and Director of the Reconstruction Finance Corporation, offered the Society office space; officers of the Humble Oil Company also gave encouragement. Equitable received its certificate of authority in March and in September Vice President W. W. Klingman relinquished his duties in charge of the Agency Department and was placed in charge, as General Manager, of the development of Equitable's business in Texas. At the time of this appointment, President Parkinson said: "We are happy to be returning to the State under friendly auspices and good working cooperation with the large number of Texas companies. . . . The selection of Mr. Klingman as state manager brings to Texas the outstanding figure in agency managership." [216] Equitable was

[215] Parkinson had been asked by George T. Wight, secretary and manager of The Association of Life Insurance Presidents, to be chairman of the Association committee which was to attend the annual meeting of the American Life Convention. Parkinson had been told that the Governor of Texas was friendly to the Governor of New York and that Texas was destined to enjoy important industrial and financial development. Parkinson sought Franklin Day's advice in regard to this opportunity. Parkinson to Franklin Day, September 7, 1927. Parkinson files, Equitable Archives.

[216] *The Weekly Underwriter,* CXXXVII (1937), October 2.

Some persons said that President Parkinson wanted to re-enter Texas "to get Klingman out of his hair." President Parkinson said that there was no truth to this

the first of the large New York companies to return to Texas.

Klingman lost no time in completing his Texas organization and appointed four regional managers. Eastern Texas with headquarters at Dallas was placed under his son, Lloyd W. Klingman, who had, since 1930, been Manager of the Salary Savings Division in the Home Office. Southeastern Texas was assigned to Harold J. Rossman as Agency Manager with headquarters at Houston. Rossman had been with Equitable since 1920, first at Chicago and after 1929 in the Home Office as Superintendent of the Southern Agencies and later the New York agencies. Chester W. Klingman, another of W. W. Klingman's sons, who had had both Home Office and field experience, became Manager for western Texas with offices at San Antonio, and southwestern Texas was added to the E. L. Grose agency with headquarters at Phoenix, Arizona.

After Klingman's departure from the Home Office, Vice President William J. Graham, head of the Group Department, was given charge of the Agency Department, and Vincent S. Welch, who had been sales supervisor in the Group Department since 1933, was appointed Second Vice President to assist Graham.

Throughout the depression decade, Equitable backed its sales organization with a national advertising program. In November 1930 it started a sustained advertising campaign in a number of national magazines and a few New York newspapers. Purposes of the campaign were to make the name of Equitable better known; to encourage and support the agency force in their sales efforts; to keep insurance in force; and to secure some new business as a result of the advertising. From the number of coupons received, the Advertising Committee, headed by Vice President Frank L. Jones, concluded that the first year income on business traceable to the advertisements was several times greater than the cost of the advertisements.[217] In general, it was thought that advertisements which featured some form of "selfish interest," such as old-age income, produced the most inquiries. The ads which presented an "appeal to the heart"—such as "Raising Junior," "As the Twig is Bent," and "A Mother's Loving Care"—seemed to have the least appeal. Best results had come from ads in the *Times* and *Tribune* maga-

---

rumor, and that Klingman knew nothing about the Texas arrangement until it was all an accomplished fact. Interview with author, September 2, 1958.

[217] Other members of the Advertising Committee were Secretary William Alexander, Vice President Ray D. Murphy, Second Vice President Albert G. Borden, and Legal Assistant Sterling Pierson.

zine sections and the national weeklies such as *The Saturday Evening Post*, *Time*, and the like.[218] The appropriation for periodical advertising in 1932 was $200,000.

Equitable made its first venture into the field of radio advertising in 1932. Although the Metropolitan Life had sponsored a series of morning exercises as early as 1923, there had been relatively little radio advertising by the life insurance companies; such advertising was still in the experimental stage.[219] Equitable tried a fifteen-minute "one-shot" on the Columbia Broadcasting System in December 1931. But this experiment was designed primarily to give Vice President Klingman a "background" for speaking directly to the agency force. The following year, Equitable set up a series of daily five-minute broadcasts on station WOR for a period of thirteen weeks. These daytime broadcasts were directed particularly toward the women, the principal beneficiaries of life insurance; personal endorsements from some of the leading women in the country were inserted in the talks.

In 1932 Equitable selected Newell, Emmett and Company as its advertising agency. The main criterion on which the decision was made was that the Society's advertising agency should have the ability to grasp the bigness of life insurance and its importance in the nation's economy, as against the merchandising of some commodity. In 1937 the "Advertising Department" in the Secretary's Office was abolished and Arthur H. Reddall became secretary to the Advertising Committee. President Parkinson decided to give the advertising agency more leeway, for he said that in the past Equitable had made the mistake of taking from its agency its initiative and responsibility for the best use of Equitable's funds. In the future, Equitable would give the agency only its general ideas; any criticism of copy would have to be submitted by the whole Advertising Committee, and "we will not be too confident of our capacity to criticize or add to their material." In case of conflict, final decisions were to be made by President Parkin-

218 Arthur H. Reddall, memorandum to Advertising Committee, October 14, 1932; also Reddall, memorandum to President Parkinson, January 25, 1933, which summarized 1932 advertising activities. Sterling Pierson files, Equitable Archives.

219 The first radio program of importance was perhaps that inaugurated by the New York Life in October 1931, when it purchased time from the National Broadcasting Company for a series of half-hour programs on fourteen stations. The programs featured music with short talks by prominent men in public life and ran for fifty-two weeks; the broadcasts covered such points as New York, Boston, Detroit, Chicago, and Jacksonville.

Equitable Home Office
1285 Avenue of the Americas, 1961

son.[220] The following year, the Advertising Committee decided not to accept an advertising program presented by another agency. Among the reasons for this decision were the following: first, the program presented used the word "beloved" as applied to Equitable, which would "seem to be generally not acceptable, and particularly would it be unsuitable under present conditions. The public is critical of corporations because of their size, salaries and methods. We think that the use of the word 'beloved' would likely suggest 'wisecracks' and criticism. . . ." Second, the program proposed stating "boldly a friendly creed of the Equitable man." The Advertising Committee concluded that the professional type of agent about whom such favorable things could be said was in the minority: "We have recommended the agent more or less in all of our advertising in the past, as other companies do, but when we go beyond the point of saying that an agent is desirable and even necessary in American life insurance, we are on dangerous ground. It would be unfortunate if a picture of our agents were presented that over-emphasized their virtues."[221] No doubt the Society's field agents would have been interested in this reason. A study of the results of Equitable's advertising in 1938 as reported by L. M. Clark, Incorporated, an advertising checking service, showed that Equitable's costs in relation to results were second lowest among the four largest life companies.[222]

In February 1940, Equitable created the new position of "Director of Public Relations" and appointed Merle A. Gulick to the position. Gulick was a graduate of Hobart College, where he was a star quarterback on the football team, and received All-America honorable mention in 1928.[223] The coach of that team, Vincent S. Welch, joined Equitable in 1929 and a year later brought Gulick into the Society where he was assigned to the Group Department, of which he became Associate Manager in 1937.

* * *

Equitable's eightieth anniversary and the New York World's Fair coincided in 1939. As a result, the Society received much favorable

220 President Parkinson, memorandum to the Advertising Committee, January 26, 1937. Sterling Pierson files, Equitable Archives.

221 Frank L. Jones, memorandum to President Parkinson, June 9, 1938. *Ibid.*

222 "A Plan for the Equitable 1939 Advertising," prepared by Newell, Emmett and Company, November 3, 1938. *Ibid.*

223 Gulick was elected to the Football Hall of Fame in 1965.

publicity. When Equitable was approached by a representative of Voorhees, Walker, Foley and Smith, architects in general charge of the Fair exhibits, Vice President William J. Graham and his assistant, Louise Ilse, discussed plans for a possible Equitable exhibit. At first, President Parkinson showed no interest in these plans, but changed his mind when the Executive Committee of the Board showed enthusiasm for them.[224] Equitable was fortunate in obtaining a plot of slightly more than half an acre at the approach of the Empire State Bridge, which connected the theme center of the Fair to the amusement area.[225] On this rounded triangle or clover-leaf plot the architects constructed the Garden of Security. At the rounded base of the triangle, and facing the bridge, stood the pedestal which mounted Equitable's symbol, the statue group "Protection"; as the group revolved slowly, floodlights played upon it. A Hammond organ and sound equipment located within the pedestal furnished musical programs. Across the pool, on the other two sides of the triangle and facing Equitable's symbol, was a small amphitheater which seated about 500 persons. The whole was surrounded by lawns and evergreens, and seven fountains added to the effect.

At the official opening of the Garden, April 30, President Parkinson said:

> Life insurance is a very human institution and its greatest by-product is the peace of mind and capacity for human expansion which its protection, symbolized by this reproduction of the Equitable Statuary Group, brings to insured and beneficiaries alike. . . . Security is the goal of all life insurance and cooperation is its method of accomplishment. . . . In the world of tomorrow, security will be not only more important but more effective. As we contemplate the contribution which science and mechanics are prepared to make to the world of tomorrow, we can only add to our admiration the hope and the prayer that there may be like progress in our institutions of political science and economics which deal with human security and human relations.

And again, speaking in the same place to the Equitable agents of the metropolitan area a year later, he emphasized the importance of life

[224] According to Graham, both Frank L. Jones and Ray D. Murphy, members of Equitable's Advertising Committee, saw no reason for the exhibit. Graham Memoir, p. 280. *Ibid.*

[225] Grover Whalen, New York's official city greeter, who was President of the Fair, explained to Graham that *The New York Times* had considered taking this plot and then had changed its mind. *Ibid.*, p. 282.

insurance in furnishing not only security but spiritual qualities which would enable the individual and the nation to survive: "I don't think I overestimate it when I say that our business is the very apostle of thrift, the very teacher of character, the very last fighting ditch of individualism and of freedom."

Equitable personnel took turns attending the Garden which was placed at the disposal of various organizations and group patrons for conventions and open-air gatherings and was also used for a place of rest by Equitable policyholders and Fair visitors. One person who rendered notable services as the Society's representative was the Assistant Superintendent of the Agency Department, David V. Healy, a former steamship purser who had been brought into Equitable by Vice President William J. Graham; he served as host, information bureau, scheduler of events, and public relations man at large. Equitable, through President Parkinson, took membership in the Terrace Club in the amusement area and thus had facilities for entertaining important out-of-town visitors. On one day the State of Delaware took over the Garden—with the du Ponts in large representation on the dais; on another day the New York Southern Society, though not large in numbers, attracted considerable attention when the members displayed the Stars and Bars alongside the Stars and Stripes. Between times, Equitable provided concerts of high school bands, exhibitions by dancing schools, and performances by a jolly group called the "Original Grandma's Night Out Club."

Thousands of people visited the Garden of Security and many times that number viewed it from the Empire State Bridge. The obvious success of the Garden led to its being maintained the following summer under the direction of Director of Public Relations Merle A. Gulick, when it was estimated that about 300,000 persons visited it. The expenditures for the Garden for two years totaled about $180,000, but in proportion to the advertising value they were very moderate.[226] They included, in addition to plot rental, architect's fees, structural work, landscaping, and maintenance, the printing and distribution of a *Guide Book to New York and the World's Fair* and Equitable's pamphlet, "Meet Me at the Garden of Security."

226 There were times, however, when President Parkinson was somewhat perturbed by the costs. When he discovered that Equitable was paying a man $20 a day just to turn the lights on by pressing a button, he was informed that the Fair was conducted in such a way as to maintain good working relations with the labor unions.

July 26, 1939, Equitable's eightieth birthday, was a big day. At 10 A.M. brief exercises were held in the arcade of the Home Office building, and then most of the 1,500 managers and agents who had assembled for the three-day educational conference and some 3,500 Home Office employees boarded special trains for the Fair. On debarkation they were marshaled into parade formation by Second Vice President Vincent S. Welch (a former Army captain) and, led by an honor guard of "Haskell Indians" and a band, marched to the Garden of Security.[227] Henry M. Alexander, chairman of the Equitable Directors' 80th Anniversary Committee, presided and introduced the speakers. Mayor Fiorello H. LaGuardia, Grover Whalen, Vice President William J. Graham, and Patrick J. Dolan, Lord Provost of Glasgow, made talks, and the Saskatoon (Canada) Girl Pipers Band furnished the music.

Approximately 2,000 attended the anniversary dinner, which was held in the Grand Ballroom of the Waldorf-Astoria. The principal after-dinner talk was made by Superintendent of Insurance Louis H. Pink, who said in part:

> The Equitable Society is the same age as the New York Insurance Department. . . . Your Society and the institution generally have come through four depressions and we are, I hope, at last at the end of the fifth, perhaps the most severe of them all. . . . The eighty years of the Equitable have brought not only financial growth and success. . . . You have grown not only in assets and the number of policyholders but, more important, in service to the public and in the confidence and esteem of those who have entrusted their moneys to your hands.

At the 80th Anniversary Educational Conference the official program contained the significant table (quoted in part on next page)[228] depicting Equitable's eighty years of progress and public service.

Significantly, of the total insurance outstanding at the 70th year (1929), $5,403,900,621 was individual life insurance and $1,357,021,904 was group life insurance. The comparable figures of the total approximating $6,750,000,000 at the end of 1938 were $4,750,916,462 individual life insurance and $1,998,261,082 group life insurance. In 1929 new paid-for individual life production was $816,571,837 and in 1938 it amounted to $315, 668, 920. Payments to policyholders and beneficiaries

[227] The Indians were graduates of Haskell Institute, the Government school for Indians at Lawrence, Kansas.

(including dividends) for the year 1929 had reached $152,470,797, and for 1938 had totaled $190,761,068. The increase in assets was thus obviously in considerable part a reflection of Equitable's activity in the annuity business during the decade of the Great Depression.

In 1940, Equitable had an exhibit at San Francisco's Golden Gate Exposition on Treasure Island, San Francisco Bay. Although this exhibit was much less pretentious than that of the New York World's Fair, it received many compliments for its artistry and good taste.

228 Equitable Growth, 1859 to 1939.

Year	Assets December 31	Insurance Reserve and all other Liabilities December 31	Total Insurance Outstanding December 31	Payments to Policyholders Since Organization (Cumulative Basis)
1859	$ 117,102	$ 25,273	$ 1,144,000	$ ....
1884	57,548,716	47,400,758	309,409,171	81,477,006
1909	479,900,419	471,571,675	1,335,347,979	707,377,394
1919	599,423,919	582,300,511	2,270,903,931	1,302,291,678
1929	1,179,391,164	1,122,590,533	6,760,922,525	2,392,210,055
1934	1,657,301,147	1,614,152,090	6,143,158,113	3,401,426,751
1938	2,260,913,149	2,182,101,227	6,749,177,544	4,136,696,205

12

At the End of a Century

All elements of management should be filled with a devotion to the social purposes we serve. The institution and our positions in it should never be diverted to the pursuit of individual gain in contrast to the vigorous pursuit of our social purposes. Only so will the business be free from criticism and avoid harmful and unnecessary restriction. Everyone in high managerial position should be fully persuaded of the high moral purposes to which he has been called. Life insurance is a business which calls for sensitive ethical perceptions as well as adequate ability.—Ray D. Murphy, 1958

Let us not forget that the real aim and end of business, as well as government, is to develop and serve the dignity, welfare and vital importance of the individual human being. . . . Our industry must be continuously conscious of the fundamental social purposes which we must serve painstakingly and effectively if we are to remain free from unnecessary regulatory control, nationalization and socialism.—James F. Oates, Jr., 1958

World War II began in August 1939 with Hitler's attack upon Poland and within a few months most of the nations of Europe were involved. Few people in the United States believed that the safety of their country was threatened, as it had been during World War I. Attitudes changed, however, after Japan's attack on Pearl Harbor in December 1941.

World War II brought an end to the depression. It also brought the expenditure of untold billions of dollars, a huge increase in the already large public debt, more inflation, further centralized controls on the people, and the strengthening of a possible enemy larger and perhaps potentially stronger than the United States. Once again came the necessity for war clauses in policies, loss of personnel, government life insurance for those in military service, bond drives, and investment problems.

Late in 1940, Equitable announced continuance of group insurance to employees and agents, and retention of former positions and seniority rights for those who enlisted or were called for peacetime military service. These arrangements were modified, however, after the United States entered the war late in 1941, and provisions were made for certain allowances and benefits for those who entered military service. Equitable furnished 1,460 men and women to the armed forces; all were assured upon return of positions equal to those which they left. New business for 1941 totaled $449,866,000; there was an increase in the average size of policies and production per agent, and a decrease in acquisition costs, lapse rates, and turnover of agents. These favorable results no doubt derived in part from the improvement in economic conditions as the war in Europe increased demands upon American industry, and in part from an agents' retirement plan adopted during the year and a new agents' contract which placed greater emphasis on renewal commissions. This contract increased total compensation to the agent who stayed with Equitable and who conserved the business written by him. The following year, nonmedical privileges were liberalized in towns with a population of less than 25,000, because of the shortage of physicians.

In August 1941 Equitable began attaching riders to policies issued to persons in the military service or liable for service, and in December appropriate war and aeronautics exclusions riders were attached to all new policies. In the policies with the restrictions, war death claim payments were limited to the return of premiums or the reserve on the policy, whichever was greater. War death claims up to August 1, 1945, most of which arose under policies containing no war restrictions, amounted to about $8,300,000 on 3,397 policyholders, which was only 3.8 per cent of the total death claims in that period. Included in these figures were 282 policies for total death claims of $1,022,000. These policies contained war and aeronautics exclusions under which liability was limited to $76,000.[1] Some beneficiaries were dissatisfied and there was some litigation. In August 1945, the Committee on Insurance authorized the Society's officers to reopen these claims, because "these claims represent a limited number of policyholders who have given their lives for those of our policyholders who were not called upon to make this sacrifice" and "the officers of the Society

[1] Facts taken from memorandum from Vice President Mervyn Davis and W. W. Alderton to the President, August 31, 1945, recommending procedures to reopen claims and make full settlements. Copy in Equitable Archives.

have recommended that in order to maintain equity as between the Society's policyholders as a whole and this limited group, the Society reconsider its action with reference to these claims."[2] Accordingly, all claims on policies containing war restrictions were reopened late in 1945, and the face amounts of the policies were paid.

The Society had consulted the New York Insurance Department before this step was taken, but a few of the life insurance companies with relatively heavier war claims than Equitable protested the action. At the time, President Parkinson said that full payment had been made to the beneficiaries of the servicemen "in the belief that it was in the best interests of the Society and its policyholders and reflected the type of fair treatment which is inherent in the operations of a national life insurance company." He pointed out that the action was in keeping with the precedent set by Equitable at the close of World War I. Commissioner James M. McCormack of Tennessee, former President of the National Association of Insurance Commissioners, commended Equitable for its action and recommended that other companies do likewise.

Although in 1938 Equitable had sold heavily of its holdings in government bonds, the war naturally brought about a change in policy, and most of the funds available for investment were put into United States Government bonds.[3] Whereas in 1940 the Society held $133,119,000 of government bonds, representing 5.3 per cent of its assets, at the end of 1945 government bonds totaled $1,756,667,000, or almost 47 per cent of the assets. With such heavy investments in government bonds, most of which yielded 2 to 2¼ per cent, the Society's net rate of return was reduced to 2.81 per cent—almost 2 per cent less than it had been in the depression year 1932. Said President Parkinson in 1946:

> Public officials who boast of the beneficial effects of low interest rates, brought about deliberately by Government controls of the money market,

[2] Official notice, September 7, 1945, by the Committee on Insurance to Ray D. Murphy, Vice President and Actuary, reporting committee action on August 16, 1945 (two days after the Japanese agreement to surrender), directing officers to recommend plan for settling claims in full. *Ibid.*

[3] Although for many years Equitable had never failed to subscribe to new Treasury issues, it did so late in 1940 when the Treasury offered Defense Notes (4–5 years) at three-fourths of one per cent interest. In connection with this fact, President Parkinson said: "This emphasis on the short term and on extremely easy money is not a contribution to the sound investment of life insurance funds, and, I submit, is not the best policy in the long run for the Federal Treasury." Annual Report to the Board of Directors for 1940.

are failing to recognize the costs that such policies involve, immediately and in the long run. . . . The policy of so-called "cheap money" involves in the long run a great deal more than a current hidden tax upon the thrifty of this country, and therefore, upon your policyholders. It carries with it the threat of eventual shrinkage in the value of the protection for which policyholders have planned their insurance programs. The present benefits of low interest rates are, to say the least, questionable, if the eventual result of the policies which make for low rates is social insecurity. If we are to avoid severe inflation, decisive steps must be taken, and taken now, by attacking the fundamentals of the problem rather than the symptoms of the disease.[4]

As a result of the low yield on investments, Equitable, in January 1944, reduced the interest assumption for single premium life insurance to 2½ per cent with mortality based on the American Experience Table. The reserve or assumed rate for single consideration and group annuities had been reduced to 2½ per cent in November 1940, and in October 1946 the rate for single consideration annuities was reduced to 2¼ per cent. In November 1947 the interest assumption for annual premium life insurance was reduced to 2½ per cent with mortality based on the 1941 Commissioners Standard Ordinary Table, and for single premium life insurance the interest assumption was reduced to 2¼ per cent. The same month, Equitable withdrew its Economic Adjustment, Special Income, Special Protection, and Modified-Two Whole Life policies. The Double Protection to Age 65 and the Modified-Five Whole Life policies were continued. Individual and group annuities and group coverage in the accident and health fields increased rapidly during the war years; in 1945 slightly more than half of the Society's premium income came from other than individual life insurance policies.

Equitable's Home Purchase Plan, which at one time the Society had promoted with great pride, came very near to being a wartime casualty. Although mortgages covered by life policies fared better during the depression than conventional residential loans, relatively few of them were written. In an endeavor to revitalize Home Purchase, the plan was renamed Assured Home Ownership (AHO) in 1939. Still the plan languished and in the early 1940's reached a low ebb. The "technical men" did not like it, the City Mortgage Department opposed it because agents frequently argued in regard to eligibility and valuation of properties, and

[4] Annual Report to the Board of Directors for 1945.

only a few of the agency managers and general agents seemed to be interested.[5] Finally, in January 1944, President Parkinson stated that he would recommend that AHO be dropped if the Agency Department so recommended and if all officers initialed the memorandum. This they did, and President Parkinson had Second Vice President Glenn McHugh make the announcement at the meeting (January 22) of the general agents and managers that Equitable had decided to drop AHO.[6] But a few weeks later, after the "Par for Parkinson" sales campaign, when President Parkinson visited the agencies he found that some of the general agents and managers were more enthusiastic about AHO than had been realized. For example, Kellogg Van Winkle of Los Angeles, who directed one of the Society's largest agencies, protested Equitable's decision in no uncertain words. He emphasized the competitive attractiveness and other features of this plan for the Society's activities in California. J. E. B. Sweeney, longtime general agent at Wheeling, West Virginia, who had been most active in the sale and servicing of AHO loans, and Agency Manager Halsey Wood at Hempstead, Long Island, also expressed their thoughts. When President Parkinson returned to New York "madder than hell," he left Pennsylvania Station, crossed Seventh Avenue to the Home Office, and immediately called a meeting of the investment people of the Society.[7] He said that he had made a mistake, and that he would create a new department, independent of the Mortgage and Agency departments, to promote AHO. He asked the officers to nominate someone to head this department. After several days elapsed without any satisfactory prospects being named, he said that he would select his own. When John H. Muller, who had been Manager of City Real Estate since 1941, came into President Parkinson's office, the latter, without looking

[5] Interview with Thomas I. Parkinson, September 2, 1958; interview with Senior Vice President John H. Muller, September 5, 1962.

Second Vice President Glenn McHugh, who was in charge of the City Mortgage Department, believed that since AHO was a real estate matter it should be handled by his department.

[6] At the end of 1943, Equitable had, excluding purchase money mortgages, less than $32,000,000 invested in residential loans, to fewer than 10,000 borrowers. Second Vice President McHugh thought that the Society might be able to get back into the residential lending field on a volume basis by insuring applicants for loans on homes under a group plan. To make this plan competitive, it would be necessary to change the New York law to permit installment payments to run 20 instead of 10 years. McHugh memorandum to Sterling Pierson, January 24, 1944. Sterling Pierson files, Equitable Archives.

[7] Interview with Thomas I. Parkinson, September 2, 1958.

up from his desk, said: "Are you ready to take the job?" Muller, an engineer by profession, was not certain that he was qualified, but, encouraged by President Parkinson's assurances, he consented.

John H. Muller was a graduate of Stevens Institute, and prior to coming to Equitable had been in the Real Estate Department of the Irving Trust Company. He joined Equitable in 1937 as assistant to Harley Lackey, Manager of City Real Estate. Though Lackey's health was failing, he did not feel that he needed an understudy, so for about three years Muller had few duties. When President Parkinson sought to use Home Office space more efficiently, Muller recovered some 100,000 square feet, which was made available for rent. After that accomplishment, he was put on the President's staff—a group of likely young prospects located in an office close to the President where they were kept under surveillance.[8]

June 16, 1944, Muller was appointed Second Vice President in charge of the "Home Loan and Housing Department." With this department now under one head, the prospects for success improved immediately. Muller, aided by members of his department, spent about two years visiting the agencies and promoting Assured Home Ownership, which was emphasized as an investment operation. It soon became apparent that AHO was a big leader for sales of individual life insurance and helped materially in increasing Equitable's business during the immediate postwar years.

Equitable's success with AHO led the agents of other companies to insist that their companies adopt a similar plan. Some of them did, but usually they did not have the field mortgage organization to enable them to meet Equitable's competition.[9] Certain agents' organizations then sought to handicap Equitable by applying the "anti-inducement" provisions of the insurance laws of the various states. The question came up in Alabama as early as 1926, but the Attorney General gave the opinion that the AHO plan, since it operated without discrimination, did not fall within the inhibition of the state statute. A similar opinion was rendered by the Attorney General of Alabama in 1929, and in 1948 the Superintendent of Insurance came to the same conclu-

[8] The office where these men were located was commonly referred to as Parkinson's "bullpen."

[9] Equitable had never made any attempt to patent the AHO plan. When other companies that wished to adopt it either in whole or in part came to Equitable's Home Office to study AHO, they were furnished with information in regard to its operation and with Equitable's forms.

sion. On the other hand, in West Virginia in 1950 the Attorney General rendered an opinion to the effect that Equitable's AHO plan violated the laws of the state, because the mortgage loan issued in conjunction with a life insurance policy constituted an "inducement" for insurance. This action was taken without notice to the Society, which, however, was later given an opportunity to present evidence in regard to the plan's legality, but the Attorney General did not change his opinion. Equitable then brought action for a judgment in which the Insurance Commissioner, Robert A. Crichton, was named as defendant. The Circuit Court of Kanawha County in October 1951 not only upheld the legality of AHO, but criticized the state administrative officials. The Court pointed out that the provisions of the law had never been considered to apply to life insurance policies, but only to fire insurance policies. The Court continued:

> While the court is not in the least concerned with the motives which may prompt an administrative agency in conducting its affairs, it is quite at a loss to understand the complete "right about face" of the agency here involved in this matter. Certainly there can have been no public agitation or demand for such reversal of a long continued practice which enured greatly to the benefit of a considerable portion of the population of the state, principally people of average or small incomes. Being enabled to obtain such loans upon such beneficial terms, they were thereby furnished an escape from the vicious and usurious talons of building and loan and small loan companies. To sustain defendant's contention would be to strike down a plan and system, advantage of which has been taken by so many of West Virginia home owners without any question by agency or court as to their validity, and for which the court is not conscious of the least murmur of public clamor.[10]

The Supreme Court of Appeals denied the application of the Insurance Commissioner for appeal.

[10] *Equitable* v. *Robert A. Crichton*, as reported in *The Eastern Underwriter*, LII (1951), October 5. The litigation is also summarized in the report of Counsel Leo D. Fitzgerald of Equitable's Law Department to President Thomas I. Parkinson, January 29, 1952. It was said that Judge Julian F. Bouchelle understood the case very well since he had an AHO loan on his home.

The legal history of AHO is summarized in a manuscript history of "Assured Home Ownership Plan of Equitable," prepared by Associate Counsel Leo D. Fitzgerald, December 1950. A copy of this document of 25 legal size typed pages, plus 28 pages of exhibits, may be found in the Law Department files, Equitable Archives.

Then in Ohio the Insurance Department in 1950 asked the Society to discontinue its AHO plan, which the Attorney General of the state had held to be in violation of that section of the Ohio law which prohibited the offering of any loan of money as an inducement for insurance. Equitable filed a petition for declaratory judgment and obtained an injunction restraining the Superintendent of Insurance, Walter Robinson, from taking any steps to revoke the Society's license, pending final determination of the legality of AHO. The following year the defendant's motion to strike the petition was overruled, but the action was not tried until September 1957, at which time Judge Myron B. Gessaman of the Court of Common Pleas of Ohio, Franklin County, held that the Assured Home Ownership Plan as outlined by the evidence did not violate the insurance laws of Ohio and enjoined the defendant (Robinson) from taking any steps or proceedings to compel the plaintiff to discontinue the operation of the plan.[11] The Court of Appeals, Franklin County, dismissed the appeal of the defendant September 1, 1959.

In the meantime a significant change of procedure had been adopted and announced to the Field—Agency and Residential Mortgage Department—in November 1950, by Second Vice President John H. Muller. The announcement read in part: "In order to broaden the service which the Society is rendering to home owners decision has been made to henceforth accept as collateral in connection with Assured Home Ownership loans certain forms of Society policies which are already in force and can be properly utilized as mortgage protection."

Although none of the legal attacks upon AHO was successful, Equitable realized that they were both a disturbing influence in the field of public relations and also a source of annoyance to the various departments and agencies responsible for the supervision of life insurance. Finally, in 1958, believing that the service rendered by the AHO plan was important in the interests of the public, Equitable began study of

[11] 147 N.E. 2d 648. Vice President John H. Muller had explained to the Court that the reason Equitable required its own insurance for an AHO loan was that by so doing the entire operation could be watched with a minimum of labor and expense; the record of payments on the mortgage note and the record of payments on the insurance policy were kept in the Society's offices, whereas, if different security were accepted, Equitable not only would not have a record of payments on the insurance (the security) but would have no control over it. By having both the record and the control of the insurance, the Society's investment was made much more secure.

a supplementary plan. Vice President Muller asked the Residential Mortgage Department to consider the possibility of Equitable's immediately adopting a plan of insured residential mortgages under which the life insurance policies of other companies could be used.[12]

Following further discussions with officers and members of the Executive Committee of the Board a working committee was appointed, regional loan supervisors were consulted as well as members of "The Old Guard," and the details of the plan were worked out largely by Director Manly Fleischmann, Counselor-at-Law; Senior Vice President Grant Keehn; Second Vice President R. O. Brown, head of the Residential Mortgage Department; and Vice Presidents and Counsel Leo D. Fitzgerald and Warner H. Mendel. In January 1959, Agency Vice President Samuel Burgess announced to the agency managers that, although AHO would be continued without any basic changes, a new plan would be made available known as Insured Residential Mortgage. IRM was introduced in March 1959. Under this plan Equitable accepted policies of certain types issued by legal reserve United States or Canadian life insurance companies as the additional security for the mortgage loan.

Shortly thereafter important modifications were initiated in the interest rates charged on residential mortgages. When Senior Vice President Grant Keehn took charge of Investment Operations in October 1958, he noted that, as a result of charging a single rate for the entire country, a significant portion of the Society's funds available for current investment was being placed in residential mortgages in some localities at rates below the going local rates for residential mortgages obtained by competing insurance companies and other mortgage investors. Indeed, the residential mortgage rate was below the rate available in some other areas of investment. Consequently, he recommended that the Society's policy should be changed to meet the residential mortgage rates charged by other mortgage lending institutions. This was done in two steps. First the country was divided into eight zones and in each zone a rate was established from time to time in the light of the going market rate charged by other lenders. Announcement of the zonal interest rates was made June 9, 1959. In addition where necessary the interest rates were adjusted upward to parity with the rates being obtained by other lenders on comparable terms on similar property.

[12] Minutes of meeting, September 23, 1958. Residential Mortgage Department files, Equitable Archives.

Second the zones were discontinued and so-called parity rates were established for each community. Announcement of this change was made February 8, 1960.

Soon it became apparent that the IRM program actually helped to stimulate the continuing growth of Equitable's residential mortgage business and assisted materially in overcoming the previous criticisms of the Society's procedures. The flexible interest rates became effective in June 1959 and new loans for the year totaled $351,000,000, of which $26,000,000 were under IRM. Although a temporary decline in residential mortgage loans resulted in the next two years, Equitable's mortgage field organization, which had been many years in the building, working with the agencies throughout the country was able to reverse the trend. With its fifty-nine offices distributed throughout the United States, and supervisors trained and authorized to render prompt and expert service both to local agents and the borrowers, Equitable was able to hold its position in the field of residential mortgage loans.[13]

At the same time that Equitable came near to abandoning its Assured Home Ownership plan, it was inaugurating a new farm mortgage plan which put the Society into the farm mortgage business in a big way. The germ of the idea came from the Aetna Life Insurance Company, which printed note and mortgage forms and distributed them to local banks in the event that they should decide to sell their mortgages to Aetna; there was no assurance that the banks would so decide, but, if they did, Aetna wanted to be prepared with its own forms. Some of Equitable's Farm Loan Appraisers wanted Equitable to undertake a similar plan. Eli Ferguson, Assistant Manager of the Farm Mortgage Department, thought that Equitable could go a step further and do the whole job by means of a three-way contract between the bank, the farmer, and the insurance company. The result was the Approved Mortgage Plan, under which the bank originated the mortgage—accepted the farmer's application for a five-year loan, and, if it was approved by Equitable, agreed to sell and assign the mortgage to Equitable at the end of two years. Once Equitable approved the mortgage, it entered into an extension agreement with the farmer by which

13 The outstanding residential mortgage investment reached a peak of $1,792,-000,000 in December 1960 (including $64,000,000 of IRM loans), but in 1961 new loans decreased to $169,000,000 from $351,000,000 in 1959 and $219,000,-000 in 1960. The trend was reversed, however, in 1962 and by the end of 1964 the outstanding residential mortgage investment was $1,698,000,000 of which $153,000,000 were IRM loans.

the payments were modified and the term extended in accordance with one of the Society's standard long-term loan plans—10 or 15 years straight, or 20 to 40 years amortized. The bank was responsible for collecting the interest payable during its ownership of the mortgage and for seeing that the taxes were paid; after the mortgage was assigned to Equitable, the bank continued to service the mortgage for a small fee.

The Approved Mortgage Plan gave the farmer a long-term loan at 4 per cent interest—the rate then prevailing—with no application or appraisal fees; under the Prepayment Reserve Plan he was permitted to pay off any amount of the mortgage at any time from farm income. Under this plan extra payments were placed in reserve and interest was stopped on an equivalent amount of the loan, thus enabling the farmer to build up reserves in good years to use on his loan in lean years. The bank obtained a loan highly salable to farmers and a two-year strictly liquid investment at the going mortgage rate at no expense to itself except that of obtaining the application and closing the loan. Some 1,200 banks signed up under the Approved Mortgage Plan, which was first announced in December 1943, and Equitable became the leading insurance company with respect to farm mortgages originating through local banks. Not only did the local banks bring in farm loans, but frequently referred direct loans to Equitable.

The solid reception given this plan by local banks in the corn and wheat country, to which the Equitable had formerly confined its farm loan activity, and the insistent demand by many banks throughout the country, influenced the Equitable to go nation-wide in farm and ranch loans.[14]

* * *

Equitable made a new departure during the war years when it decided to invest in large-scale housing projects, a type of investment which President Day had decided against after World War I.[15] In

[14] The Approved Mortgage Plan was announced and explained in a brochure issued by the Farm Mortgage Department, December 17, 1943. The title was "Your Bank and The Equitable Society Join in Service to Farmers—The Approved Mortgage Plan." Copy in Equitable Archives.

[15] For many years the New York insurance law limited life company investments in real estate to real estate held for the company's own use and occupancy and real estate which it had foreclosed. In 1938 the law was amended to permit the companies to acquire, construct, and operate rental housing projects for persons of low and moderate income. The laws of other states permitted investments in other types of real estate, and in 1946 the New York companies succeeded in getting

January 1942, at a luncheon at the Hotel Bossert, Brooklyn, President Parkinson announced that Equitable would build a large-scale garden-type defense housing project on Clinton Avenue near the United States Navy Yard and the industrial defense plants along the Brooklyn waterfront.[16] The project had been evolved after conferences with Mayor LaGuardia, President of the Tax Board Joseph Lilly, and Comptroller Joseph D. McGoldrick, and received the backing of the leading Brooklyn civic organizations and prominent individuals.[17] Plans called for eleven buildings of 12 to 14 stories each which would provide 1,160 apartments; the buildings were to occupy only one third of the land plot. Architects were Harrison, Fouilhoux and Abramovitz, who had done much of the work on Rockefeller Center.[18] Three buildings were erected before wartime restrictions interfered, four more at the insistence of the Navy, and four buildings were erected immediately after the war, the last of which was ready for occupancy in August 1947. Cost of the eleven buildings was approximately $10,000,000, and by 1950 the investment was yielding about 4½ per cent after allowance of 2 per cent amortization costs.[19] A twelfth building was added and ready for occupancy in February 1955. July 1, 1958, Clinton Hill was sold to Pierpont Associates for $11,500,000.[20]

---

the New York law amended to permit life companies to purchase investment or income-producing real estate up to 3 per cent of their assets.

16 The luncheon was given for President Parkinson by George V. McLaughlin, President of the Brooklyn Trust Company, on behalf of the Brooklyn committee of the Equitable Board of Directors. The other members of the Committee were Edward C. Blum, Chairman of Abraham and Straus, and Edwin P. Maynard, Chairman of Brooklyn Trust. Other prominent persons who attended the luncheon were Mayor Fiorello LaGuardia; Superintendent of Insurance Louis H. Pink; Presiding Justice Edward Lazansky, Appellate Division; and the publishers of the Brooklyn newspapers.

17 Among them, Clifford E. Paige, chairman of the Advisory Committee on Industrial Preparedness of the Brooklyn Chamber of Commerce; Rear Admiral E. J. Marquart, Commandant of the Navy Yard; Henry J. Davenport, President of the Downtown Brooklyn Association; Lewis H. Pounds, of the Civic Council of Brooklyn; Robert Alfred Shaw, President of the Brooklyn Hill Association; Mortimer Steinfels, President of the Brooklyn Real Estate Board; and Charles Pratt, of the Pratt Institute.

18 The landscape architect was Colonel Gilmore D. Clarke; Edwin E. Ashley was the mechanical engineer, and J. DiStasio and Company were the structural consulting engineers. The builders were Starrett Brothers and Eken, Incorporated.

19 President Parkinson's Report to the Board of Directors, February 1952.

20 Total cost of Clinton Hill to the date of sale was $11,097,404.22. This figure had been reduced by depreciation amounting to $2,823,298.48, which made the unrecovered cost $8,274,105.74. Memorandum from Controller Charles B. Lunsford, October 9, 1958. Copy in Equitable Archives.

Encouraged by the amendment to the New York insurance law in 1946 which permitted life insurance companies to invest up to 3 per cent of their assets in income-producing real estate, Equitable embarked upon an even larger building project. This was Fordham Hill, on an eight-acre site on a point of land in the Bronx overlooking the Harlem and Hudson rivers. The site was formerly owned by the Webb Institute of Naval Architecture. Here, around a pear-shaped village green, nine 16-story buildings were spaced symmetrically; they provided 1,118 apartments. Construction was started in March 1947 and completed in the spring of 1950. A modern garage with a capacity of 435 cars was completed about a year later. Fordham Hill was sold to Fordham Hill Associates July 1, 1956, for $15,500,000.[21]

Not one of Equitable's larger investments, but one of its most persistent, complicated, and interesting was that in the Arkansas Valley Sugar Beet and Irrigated Land Company, which it had taken over from The Mercantile Trust Company in the settlement between the Society and the Henry B. Hyde estate.[22] This case is being covered in some detail to indicate the continuous efforts of various Society officers toward working out its complications in an equitable manner for all parties concerned.

Equitable held the bonds and owned the stock of Arkansas Valley, of which Vice President Leon O. Fisher of Equitable was President. Most of the directors were Equitable men. Following the contract of 1905 which Arkansas Valley made with Grant B. Schley—later the Holly Sugar Company—various other agreements were made and abrogated. In 1910 Fisher and Gerald Brown went to Colorado to investigate the prospects for sale of some 27,000 acres in Prowers County, but no sales resulted.

After Leon Fisher's death in 1935, Sterling Pierson, Equitable Counsel, took over the management of the affairs of the Arkansas Valley Company. Troubles continued to pile up. The old Amity Company had sold land and guaranteed water far beyond the amount of water available or the facilities for delivering it. Then came the drought of the mid-1930's, probably the most severe and prolonged in our history. At this time, Pierson decided to mutualize the Amity Canal, but met resistance from a group of water right owners.

[21] Total costs at date of sale had been $17,335,881.49. The depreciation allowance was $2,104,815.39, which made the unrecovered cost $15,231,066.10. *Ibid.*

[22] For the earlier history of the Amity Company and the Arkansas Valley Sugar Beet and Irrigated Land Company, see this history, pp. 498, 729, 937.

As early as 1919 a group of water right owners headed by Henry L. Moran had sued to restrain Arkansas Valley from selling any more water rights, and the District Court of the State of Colorado for the County of Prowers issued an injunction to that effect. In 1926 Arkansas Valley filed a bill of complaint in the United States District Court at Denver against a group of water right owners headed by L. Wirt Markham. In 1928 Judge T. Blake Kennedy referred the case to Special Master Fred Farrar. After seven years (June 24, 1935), Special Master Farrar submitted his report to Judge J. Foster Symes of the District Court.[23] The plaintiff (Arkansas Valley) maintained that there was sufficient water in the system to supply all outstanding contracts and still leave 317 water rights to be used by Arkansas Valley. Defendants claimed that the outstanding water rights exhausted the capacity of the system and left no residue for Arkansas Valley. The contracts and deeds issued to the water right owners over a long period of years varied considerably, and the plaintiff wanted them definitely defined and made to conform with one another by a court decree, thus making possible a plan of mutualization. Special Master Farrar established a standard definition of "water right" to apply to all owners and found that outstanding contracts would leave sufficient water to be used by Arkansas Valley to irrigate 8,931 acres. He laid plans for organization of the corporation to be owned by the water right holders—36,493 shares of stock to be issued, each representing one acre water right, 27,562 shares to be allocated to the outstanding water right holders, the remaining 8,931 shares to be owned by Arkansas Valley. The Court accepted the Master's recommendation and dismissed the injunction issued in 1919.

In 1928 Equitable had decided to buy the Keesee Ranch, of some 2,200 acres which was located upstream on the Arkansas River from both the canals that supplied water to the lands—the Amity and Buffalo Canals; Keesee was important because of its water rights which might be transferred downstream to satisfy possible damages arising from the litigation. Purchase was accomplished by organizing (January 1929) the Keesee Water and Land Company with ten shares of capital stock. Assistant Treasurer Henry Greaves of Equitable was elected President of Keesee in April and in July held four of the ten shares;

[23] The transcript of the testimony consists of five volumes and 2,081 typewritten pages; the exhibits of the plaintiff number 151 and of the defendants 38. The number of defendants varied at different stages of the litigation; all told it appears that there were 505. The records on *The Arkansas Valley Sugar Beet and Irrigated Land Company* v. *L. Wirt Markham, et al.* (not reported) are in the files of the Farm Mortgage Department, Equitable Archives.

three shares were held by Assistant Secretary Walter G. Schelker, and Assistant Secretary McNeill held three shares.[24] Equitable made a $58,773 mortgage loan to Keesee for purchase of the Ranch and water rights, and Arkansas Valley (also Equitable) advanced $10,000 to Keesee Company for rehabilitation and operating expenses.

In 1937, by which time taxes on Arkansas Valley's holdings had accumulated and forfeitures were threatened, a committee of the Equitable Board went to Colorado to decide whether Equitable should not wash its hands of the whole problem. The committee, however, recommended that the taxes be paid. This ultimately turned out to be a wise decision. Arkansas Valley had been in default on interest for many years. In 1941, according to President Parkinson, the Company owned land subject to $3,500,000 of bonds, all of which were owned by Equitable and carried on its books at $880,000. (Equitable also owned all of the stock—$5,000—of the Company.)[25] Speaking of the Arkansas

[24] At the organization meeting at Holly, Colorado, January 7, 1929, each of the following persons subscribed to one share (at $10) of the capital stock: W. S. Partridge, Arkansas Valley manager at Holly; Verna L. Wood; and Henry C. Vidal, Equitable counsel at Denver. Since Partridge had secured an option for the purchase of the Keesee Ranch from the Prowers Ranch and Mercantile Company, he offered to transfer his option and rights in exchange for seven shares of the capital stock of Keesee Water and Land Company, so seven shares were issued to him, thus making a total of ten. A few months later, the original stockholders resigned as directors and officers of the Keesee Company and transferred their stock to Greaves, Schelker, and McNeill. The principal office of the Keesee Company was to be maintained at Holly, with a branch office to be maintained at Equitable's Home Office in New York. Board of Directors' Minute Book, Keesee Water and Land Company, Equitable Archives.

[25] There is considerable confusion and some contradiction among the documents which deal with the Arkansas Valley Company and its finances. According to a report prepared by Robert Kagan for Vice President and General Solicitor Warner H. Mendel in June 1961, Equitable, at that time, owned $1,487,006 par value of Sinking Fund 5's due January 1, 1941, which had been acquired by the Society in 1910 and 1911 at an actual cost of $1,461,520. On the other hand, the books of Arkansas Valley listed the par value of the bonds at $2,164,018, and Equitable for a number of years in Schedule X carried the par value for the outstanding bonds at $2,459,000 instead of the correct figure of $1,487,006, and the cost to the Society for the bonds at $2,433,514, as opposed to the correct figure of $1,461,520. The main reason for the variance in figures lies in the fact that some $971,993 of payments made by Arkansas Valley to Equitable on account of the bonds were not reported as reducing par value or cost, although they were reported as reducing the book value of the bonds. While these payments were supposedly repayments of principal, Arkansas Valley treated them on its books as payments of interest and took an interest deduction for them. Equitable did not treat its receipt of these payments on its tax return as interest income. After default of principal in 1941, Equitable finally charged off the bonds on its annual statement of December 31, 1950, to a book value of $112,290. Just where President Parkin-

Valley situation, President Parkinson said: "It has been a white elephant, to say the least, for a long time. . . ." [26] He was somewhat optimistic, however, in regard to the future prospects, for with the United States Government projecting a big dam in the Arkansas River between Las Animas and Lamar, he thought there would be plenty of water and that some 10,000 acres of the land falling into the irrigable category could be sold at $100 an acre. At any rate, the situation looked good enough to justify Equitable's advancing another $63,000.

Arkansas Valley had leased much of its land to tenants on the crop-share basis, but many of the leases were made merely by oral commitments because, for some reason or other, Sterling Pierson had refused to execute written leases. Arkansas Valley's main man at Holly was W. S. Partridge and the real estate leasing agent was Henry F. Decker.[27] In 1944, when Equitable Auditor Henry T. Fielding "attempted an audit of the books, accounts, and records of the Company at Holly," the situation was found to be something as follows: Arkansas Valley held about 33,254 acres along the Arkansas River just west of the Colorado-Kansas state line in Prowers County; the Keesee Company held approximately 2,170 acres farther up the River in Bent County. Four ditches or canals were supposed to supply this land with water. The Amity Canal, the only one which had a permanent diversion dam, had been mutualized by allotting to the owner of each acre of irrigated land one share of stock; 1,718 shares of treasury stock had not been allocated. The Arkansas Valley Company owned the Buffalo Canal, which, in addition to supplying water to 1,296 acres of land owned by the Company, was obligated to supply water to about 3,223 acres of irrigated land formerly owned by the Company. The diversion dam of this canal, built of logs and old automobile bodies, washed out frequently. The Keesee land was watered by a canal owned by Keesee

---

son got his figure of $3,500,000 of Arkansas Valley bonds is not clear. A copy of the reconstructed ledger statement on the Arkansas Valley bonds is in the Equitable Archives.

[26] In his informal remarks to the Equitable Board of Directors, January 16, 1941.

[27] In December 1943, R. I. Nowell, Manager of Equitable's Farm Mortgage Department, wrote Henry Greaves, President of Keesee Water and Land Company that, upon visiting the Keesee property, he found that "Mr. Decker has made various verbal commitments to prospective Japanese tenants for the rental of land for the crop year 1944." Nowell believed that the rent money was being used to further the costs of new construction. He continued: "I think it would be unwise to interrupt the work at the moment, but new management should be substituted at the earliest possible date." Nowell to Greaves, December 22, 1943. Keesee Water and Land Company, Corporate Records, Equitable Archives.

Land Company. This diversion dam was also a temporary one that required almost constant maintenance. On the land owned by Arkansas Valley, there were about 100 tenants, 60 of whom lived in company-owned farm improvements. Most of these improvements were badly in need of repairs and rehabilitation. Only a part of the land owned by Arkansas Valley was irrigated and under cultivation; other areas could be brought under cultivation provided water were made available. A portion of the land was usable for pasturage but not suitable for irrigation and cultivation. Then there was some land—surplus dry land, seep land, or river-bottom land—which was not suitable for cultivation or irrigation and had no relation to the cultivated land. There had been some talk of oil possibilities but Frank D. Hall, Chief Appraiser, City Mortgage Department, and President of Arkansas Valley, had been unable to find any oil company which was interested in taking leases in Prowers County. The officers of the Company (Hall, Nowell, and Glenn McHugh) recommended to the Board of Directors that they take advantage of the relatively wet years of the early 1940's to sell as much of the surplus dry land as possible and, after rehabilitation of the buildings on farm land under cultivation, market it in orderly fashion. They thought that additional land might be placed under irrigation if the Buffalo Canal were mutualized and a proper dam constructed. The general conclusion of the officers was that the Arkansas Valley Company was an asset well worth salvaging and that the best results could be obtained by a five-year program of management and gradual sale.[28]

By 1945, the debt of the Keesee Land Company to Equitable—including defaulted interest—was $104,378.[29] Keesee then refinanced by giving Equitable a new promissory note in the principal amount of $95,000 and paying $9,378 in cash to the Society.[30] Early the following year, when Vice President Walter G. Schelker retired from Equitable, his three shares of the Keesee stock were transferred to Second Vice

[28] Report of the officers of The Arkansas Valley Sugar Beet and Irrigated Land Company to the Board of Directors, January 5, 1944. Arkansas Valley papers, Equitable Archives.

[29] As follows:

Mortgage principal	$ 58,773.40
Note for defaulted interest	37,074.99
Interest on note 12/31/43—3/1/45	2,162.71
Interest on mortgage 12/31/42—3/1/45	6,367.14
Total indebtedness	$104,378.24

[30] Minute Book, Board of Directors, Keesee Water and Land Company. Entry of March 5, 1945. Equitable Archives.

President R. I. Nowell, who became a Director, as well as Vice President, of the Company.

On March 5, 1946, when President Frank D. Hall rendered his last report to the directors of The Arkansas Valley Sugar Beet and Irrigated Land Company, he stated that during the preceding two years the Company had repaid all Equitable advances, amounting to $187,000; also $70,000 to apply on the Company's bonds, which at this time were carried on the Society's books for annual statement purposes at $500,000, and $15,000 for the common stock of the Keesee Land Company. He reported that a suit to mutualize the Buffalo Canal had been started and said that if the remaining real estate held by the Company could be sold for its estimated recovery value, the affairs of the Company could be liquidated with cash payments to Equitable of $1,000,000. President Hall then resigned, and the same day R. I. Nowell became President of Arkansas Valley. He completed the mutualization of the Buffalo Canal and then, in July 1946, succeeded in getting a release from the Holly Sugar Corporation (successor to the Holly Sugar Company) from any and all claims, demands, and liabilities against Arkansas Valley Company which had arisen or might arise as a result of the contract of February 1905. Unraveling the maze of agreements would have been difficult and expensive, and Holly Corporation never demanded an accounting. In return for the release, Holly Corporation received certain oil and gas leases or rights.[31]

Nowell's next step was to bring about a union of the Keesee Water and Land Company with the Arkansas Valley Company for the purpose of filing a consolidated Federal income tax return. Although Henry Greaves, President of the Keesee Company, was not in favor of seeing Keesee absorbed by Arkansas Valley, this consolidation of assets took place.

In May 1948 the officers of the Keesee Company were authorized to accept an offer of Jake O. and Mary A. Broyles to purchase the real estate owned by the Company. Keesee, in consideration of the release of its note and deed of trust, agreed to convey to Equitable senior participation of an amount equal to the remaining unpaid principal balance of the Equitable loan in a purchase money note and first deed of trust executed by the purchaser in favor of the Company in the principal amount of $100,000, with interest at 4½ per cent; the note was due in 1970. January 3, 1949, the stockholders of Keesee voted

[31] Copy of the agreement is in the Farm Mortgage Department files, Equitable Archives.

to liquidate the Company and distribute its assets to Arkansas Valley. Final liquidation was authorized by the Board November 9. This was the last meeting of the Board.

Despite the fact that President Nowell of Arkansas Valley continued to sell the Company's lands as opportunity offered, and turned operating losses into substantial profits, the Company continued to run an overall loss by reason of accruing interest on defaulted bonds.[32] The Arkansas Valley Board, at a meeting in November 1963, was advised that the Company then had no property, real or personal, except certain mineral reservations in or with respect to land previously sold, and a small amount of cash in banks. The directors proposed that the indebtedness of the Company—$7,096,319 outstanding—be retired in consideration of the transfer to Equitable of an undivided one-half interest in the mineral rights owned by the Company on approximately 1,148 acres of land, and payment of $7,000.[33] The offer was accepted, and the bonds were surrendered for retirement. Arkansas Valley Sugar Beet and Irrigated Land Company maintained its corporate existence until June 15, 1966, when the Secretary of State of New Jersey issued a Certificate of Dissolution. Thus ended the history of a bad loan made by Henry B. Hyde and The Mercantile Trust Company 71 years earlier.

GOVERNMENT AND LIFE INSURANCE

Once again in World War II the United States Government embarked upon a program of life insurance for members of the armed forces. Shortly before the enactment of the draft act, the second Revenue Act of 1940 was amended in conference committee to include provision for National Service Life Insurance.[34] The conferees had not consulted with nongovernment insurance experts but only with officials of the Veterans Administration.[35] NSLI was modeled after, but en-

[32] For 1950, for instance, the net loss was $110,307 and the accumulated deficit $5,836,330; for 1957, the net loss was $108,570 and the accumulated deficit $6,599,017; by 1960 the accumulated deficit was $6,925,101.

[33] Minutes of the Arkansas Valley Board, November 26, 1963. Equitable Archives.

[34] Title VI, Part I, of the second Revenue Act of 1940 (Public Law 801, 76th Congress, approved October 8, 1940). This basic law was subsequently amended by a series of Public Laws, 1941–42, which extended National Service Life Insurance to aviation cadets and other individuals.

[35] "Inquiry into the Operations and Fiscal Cost of the Veterans Administration National Service Life Insurance Program, Seventh Intermediate Report of the Committee on Expenditures in the Executive Departments, July 31, 1950." *House Report* (81 Congress, 2nd Session), No. 2761, p. 6.

tirely separate from, the War Risk Insurance system of World War I.[36] Under the provisions of the act, all persons who served in the military forces after October 8, 1940, were eligible to purchase policies from a minimum of $1,000 to a maximum of $10,000 face value; the United States Government would bear the cost of administration, the excess mortality, disability, and premium waiver costs resulting from the extra hazards of war, certain gratuitous insurance benefits, and the cost of reimbursing the reserve fund for waiving recovery of benefit payments erroneously made when it would be inequitable to require payment. In other words, premium payments—calculated on the American Experience Table and 3 per cent interest (instead of 3½ per cent as in the War Risk Insurance and the United States Government Life Insurance)—were to cover only normal civilian risks. Benefits for death in military service, or as a "result of disease or injury traceable to the extra hazard of the military or naval service," were not to be borne by the National Service Life Insurance fund but by the United States Treasury.[37] Furthermore, the Government paid the death benefit for "extra hazard" only to the extent of the amount of the NSLI policy held; that is, if the serviceman applied for no NSLI policy, there was no death benefit paid to his family by the Treasury.[38] The NSLI plan was "a combination of gratuities and insurance"—"more gratuity than

[36] NSLI was, in fact, the third system of government life insurance to be created by Federal statute. In 1924, after the original War Risk Insurance Act had been amended many times, Congress had created under the World War Veterans' Relief Act (Public Law 242, 68th Congress, enacted June 7, 1924) a a new insurance program known as United States Government Life Insurance (USGLI). Premiums under this program were to be computed on the American Experience Table and 3½ per cent interest and were to be deposited in a special trust fund in the Treasury; the United States was charged with the expenses of administration and the "excess mortality and disability costs resulting from the hazards of war." Under this program, 1,149,304 policies were issued, of which 490,000 were in force and being administered by the Veterans Administration in 1950. *Ibid.*, p. 7. Despite the law of 1924, Congress had from time to time permitted the continuation of term insurance.

The main reason for creating a separate system was that it would be unfair and inequitable to the policyholders who had built up a substantial equity in the USGLI trust fund to permit new entrants to participate in this fund. *Ibid.*, pp. 7–8.

[37] During the war 88 per cent of all deaths in the armed forces of those carrying NSLI were determined to be "extra hazard"; the Government paid not only the face value of the policies held by these individuals, but approximately 19 per cent more than the face value on annuities involving life income settlement options, plus 3 per cent interest on the undistributed principal. *Ibid.*, p. 11.

[38] There were, of course, gratuitous pension benefits payable to eligible dependents which were not based upon the serviceman's having held an NSLI policy.

insurance"—and contained elements of discrimination and inequity which were later to be pointed out.[39] By the end of the war, there was about $135,000,000,000 of NSLI in force.

Despite the fact that National Service Life Insurance was established without consulting the life insurance companies, it was accepted by them with little discussion or criticism. This was in striking contrast to the reception given the War Risk Life Insurance of World War I. Life insurance men no doubt remembered how that insurance had helped popularize life insurance and assumed that the situation would be no different after World War II.

Wartime regulations affected the life insurance companies in many ways. Even before the United States entry into the war, the Wage and Hour Division of the Department of Labor began to apply the provisions of the Federal wage and hour act (the Fair Labor Standards Act of 1938) to life insurance companies, maintaining that they were covered by the "engaged in interstate commerce" clause.[40] Representatives of the life companies pointed out that, as a result of the decision of the United States Supreme Court in 1869 to the effect that insurance was not commerce, the insurance companies operated under state rather than Federal supervision. Nevertheless, the representatives of the American Life Convention, The Association of Life Insurance Presidents, and the Life Office Management Association agreed to prepare a job classification manual for the use of the Wage and Hour Division. After much labor was spent in preparation of this manual, the Wage and Hour Division finally discarded it and in its place substituted an "Interpretative Statement," which it released for publication February 10, 1942. In this statement, the Wage and Hour Division took the position that employees of insurance companies were subject to the Fair Labor Standards Act, and indicated that it

[39] This fact, together with the tremendous cost of NSLI, led Congress in 1950 to a consideration of war risk insurance under which the Government would provide free of charge to the serviceman the war risk policy effective for the duration of his service. This was a plan originally advocated by many leaders in the field of life insurance when government war risk insurance was first considered in 1917. Had it been followed in World War I and World War II, billions of dollars would have been saved the taxpayers.

[40] The Supreme Court, in *United States* v. *F. W. Darby Lumber Company* (February 3, 1941), held that the powers of Congress extended to include those intrastate activities which might affect interstate commerce and that Congress "may choose the means reasonably adapted to the permitted end, even though they involve control of intrastate activities."

expected the companies to set up standards at least equivalent to those required by that act. In the months which followed, numerous letters, releases, forms, and directives, dealing with inside employees, outside employees, maintenance employees, time spent driving employers' automobile, and so forth, flowed from the Wage and Hour Division, which finally fixed July 1, 1942, as the "compliance date." The whole question of wages and hours was still definitely unsettled until it overlapped with the wage and salary stabilization program under the Director of Economic Stabilization (James F. Byrnes) and the National War Labor Board, and the regulations issued by the Office of Emergency Management and the War Manpower Commission. As late as October 1943, at which time the insurance business was contemplating raising the minimum wage to 40 cents per hour—two years before it became compulsory under the law of 1938—life insurance companies were still maintaining that they were not engaged in commerce and hence were not subject to the provisions of the Fair Labor Standards Act.

Although the turning point in the war had been reached by 1943, wartime regulations continued to become more complicated. February 9, President Roosevelt issued an executive order establishing a work week of 48 hours, with overtime rates of pay for hours in excess of the customary work week, which was normally 40 hours. Almost at the same time, bills were introduced in Congress providing for the registration of all persons between the ages of fifteen and fifty and authorizing the President, through the War Manpower Commission, "to provide for the orderly and effective allocation of workers to the particular occupations deemed by the President to be essential for the war effort." There was much discussion, some of it rather fanciful, as to what would be the consequences of "work [in designated war industries] or fight" legislation. For some months life insurance men had been concerned as to whether life insurance would be classified as an "essential" industry. In February, when a committee of the American Life Convention conferred with Chairman Paul V. McNutt of the War Manpower Commission, he gave the impression that life insurance, while not war work, was regarded as an activity essential to the economic welfare and national interest, and would not be classified as nonessential. A joint committee representing the National Association of Life Underwriters, The Association of Life Insurance Presidents, and the American Life Convention sought to have the position of life insurance clarified. But the best these organizations could do was to get the suggestion that persons engaged in occupations not included in the nondeferrable list remain on their jobs until a specific need for a change had been indicated by the War Manpower Commission. As a result of the failure to be classified as an essential industry, life insurance lost heavily of its personnel during the year; because of the uncertainty of their status, many office and field workers who in all probability would not have been disturbed in their jobs took jobs with war industry.

Another uncertainty in the life insurance business was the question of wages and pension trusts as related to wages and income. In October 1942, Congress enacted the anti-inflation law which extended government control over wages.[41] Immediately, by executive order, President Roosevelt created the Office of Economic Stabilization, headed by Fred M. Vinson. Working under or with the Director of Economic Stabilization were the National War Labor Board, the regional war labor boards, and the Wage and Hour Division of the Department of Labor; also the Commissioner of Internal Revenue and the regional salary stabilization units.[42] General orders emanated from the War Labor Board in rapid succession; frequently, by the time schedules and applications had been approved, orders had been amended and the process had to be undertaken all over again.

Somewhat confusing also were the regulations issued by the Commissioner of Internal Revenue pertaining to an employees' trust or annuity plan purchased by employers for their employees. In general, it was ruled that contributions by an employer to an annuity plan or trust constituted salary within the Salary Stabilization regulations insofar as such contributions exceeded 5 per cent of the employee's annual salary. Internal Revenue officials were also interested in making certain that qualified pension plans did not discriminate in favor of those employees and officers whose remuneration exceeded $3,000 per year—the base for Social Security taxes and benefits. Similarly, under informal plans whereby ordinary life or comparable insurance was purchased by an employer for his employees, the 5 per cent of salary restriction also applied to the premium paid and approval was required from the Salary Stabilization Board. Special committees representing the Life Underwriters, the Presidents' Association, and the American Life Convention held numerous conferences with the Treasury

41 This was an amendment to the emergency price control law of January 1942, the administration of which was turned over to the Office of Price Administration (OPA).

42 As in most of the World War II governmental setup, the lines of authority were not very clear.

Department during the year in an attempt to reach a clear understanding of the pension trust regulations. Some businessmen thought these regulations were intended to nullify pension trusts of various companies and integrate them with the government social security program.[43]

All-out mobilization for war did not curtail government plans for further social reforms. In Great Britain the famous Beveridge Plan with its "cradle-to-the-grave" security program had been presented to Parliament late in 1942, and within a few weeks was being widely discussed in the United States. Soon the National Resources Planning Board was recommending that the United States social security program be broadened to include many features of the Beveridge Plan, and that the existing joint Federal-state system be replaced by a wholly Federal system. Later in the year, the Wagner-Dingell bill was introduced in Congress to add health insurance, disability provisions, and the like to the social security laws. Life insurance men viewed these plans with considerable misgiving. For instance, Claris Adams, President of the Ohio State Life Insurance Company, referred to them as "the dangerous habit-forming political drug. If taken in excess, the remedy is more deadly and destructive than the disease." The Insurance Economics Society of Chicago, though not opposed to the extension of the social security program to include groups other than those originally covered, did oppose addition of disability provisions and provisions for hospitalization and medical care. Even Thurman Arnold, former Assistant Attorney General and a member of the Temporary National Economic Committee, positively opposed the recommendations of the social security zealots. In a talk before the Economic Club of New York, he said that for the past ten or twenty years many people had become obsessed by the economics of security. "We have been thinking of stabilizing profits, keeping a fool from losing his money, social security, ironing out depressions, creating a situation where anybody who remains sober and didn't run off with somebody else's wife was assured of a comfortable old age." He was not opposed to any of these things, but believed that if the country became obsessed with the idea of security the same thing would happen to its industrial structure that happened to the French army, which had

[43] Senator Robert A. Taft of Ohio, for instance, said that the regulations of July nullified the employees' pension trusts of many important companies and that they violated the Revenue Act of 1942. Quoted in *The National Underwriter*, XLVII (1943), August 6.

great faith in the Maginot Line. "We must get back to the old economics of opportunity, of taking a chance, which made America great. . . ."[44] The National Association of Life Underwriters, at its annual meeting, gave much time to the discussion of the extension of the social security laws; though no sentiment existed in favor of the Wagner bill, a number of delegates, particularly from the South, feared that if it was openly opposed agents might jeopardize their chance of being brought under the old-age and survivors' insurance provisions of the law. The organization finally adopted a straddling resolution on the subject.

Although advocates of the expanded social security program were rather hazy about costs, it was estimated that the costs would be between 8 and 15 billion dollars a year. Secretary Frances Perkins of the Department of Labor thought that a 10 per cent payroll tax would cover the cost, whereas life insurance men generally estimated it would require twice as much.[45] Dr. Harold G. Moulton, director of The Brookings Institution, speaking of the comprehensive social security recommendations of the National Resources Planning Board, said: "Since this Board is committed to the theory that national prosperity and income are dependent largely upon the government's 'contribution to purchasing power,' through deficit financing, it is deemed unnecessary to give any consideration to the costs." He then pointed out that if the nation should follow the path of permanent deficit spending, disastrous inflation could be avoided only by such widespread regulation and control that it would amount to complete regimentation of economic life.[46]

Despite price and wage controls and increased taxation, the value of the dollar continued to decline and prices to rise; war costs and the mounting public debt saw to that. In August 1943 the life insurance business launched an anti-inflation campaign by way of a series of continued advertisements to be published in 286 daily newspapers with combined circulation of more than 26,000,000.[47] The advertise-

[44] As quoted in *ibid.*, March 5.

[45] Claris Adams thought that it would be nearer 20 per cent, and M. Albert Linton, President of the Provident Mutual Life Insurance Company of Philadelphia, arrived at about the same estimate, that is, one day's work per week.

[46] Harold G. Moulton, *The New Philosophy of Public Debt*, The Brookings Institution (Washington, 1943).

[47] The first of the advertisements appeared in *The New York Times* and the *Tribune* August 16 and 30, and then ran on alternate Mondays until the spring of 1944. Each advertisement stressed "The Personal Postwar World You Want,"

ments, though issued through the Institute of Life Insurance, were labeled "Life Insurance Companies of America," since many companies participated which were not members of the Institute. The advertisements advised the policyholders and citizens of the United States willingly to pay their share of the taxes, buy and hold war bonds, provide for their families' future by carrying an adequate amount of life insurance, reduce their debts and avoid making needless new ones, but only what was absolutely needed, live faithfully by the ration rules, and cooperate with the government price and wage stabilization program. Frank R. Kent, one of the more conservative of the syndicated news commentators, who had criticized the life insurance companies for not acting more aggressively, saw this campaign as an encouraging symptom: "Out of fear, inertia, and lack of cohesion they failed to act against the New Deal economic heresies. But, now, they are going to act—with governmental acquiescence—against inflation. That is very good news indeed, though it has been long delayed." [48]

LIFE INSURANCE BECOMES "COMMERCE"

In 1944, the Supreme Court of the United States overruled the precedents of three quarters of a century and decided that insurance was commerce. The case originated in May 1943 when the Antitrust Division of the Department of Justice obtained an indictment in the District Court of the United States for the Northern District of Georgia, Atlanta Division, against the South-Eastern Underwriters Association, an organization of fire insurance companies, and against 27 of its officers and 198 of its member companies. The defendants were charged with conspiracy to fix and maintain arbitrary and noncompetitive rates and with conspiracy to monopolize trade and commerce in fire insurance in the states affected. The charge was based on the theory that insurance conducted across state lines was interstate commerce. The Government in its brief took the position that *Paul* v. *Virginia* and the subsequent cases should no longer be followed. Since the Government made no distinction between different kinds of insurance, many life insurance men felt certain that all insurance would

---

featured a sample family budget, and ended by urging all policyholders "to join wholeheartedly with all loyal Americans to keep down living costs during these critical war days. . . . Remember that the premiums you pay for your life insurance are also helping to pay for the war—for a large part of them are invested in Government bonds."

[48] Quoted in *The Insurance Field,* LXXII (1943), September 17.

eventually be ruled to be commerce. Many of the state insurance commissioners held the same belief.

In August, Judge E. Marvin Underwood of the District Court at Atlanta upheld the demurrer of the SEUA to the indictment returned previously in the same court. He stated that "if there is to be any overruling of the long line of clear and thoroughly considered decisions of the Supreme Court, acquiesced in for seventy-five years by Congress and administrative agencies, it will have to be done by the Supreme Court itself, or by Congress." In October, it was announced that the Supreme Court would review the case, which Attorney General Francis Biddle had called the most important in a hundred years, and in December the Department of Justice filed its brief with the Supreme Court.

Meanwhile, bills to exempt insurance from the provisions of the antitrust laws had been introduced in both the House of Representatives and the Senate.[49] While the hearings on the states rights bills were being held in Congress, the whole subject of state versus Federal regulation was again widely discussed in the press and in the meetings of the insurance organizations. Senator Harry F. Byrd of Virginia told the National Association of Life Underwriters at Pittsburgh in October that the American free enterprise system could be destroyed in any one of three ways: by exorbitant taxation, by senseless and unnecessary regimentation, or by government competition with private business.[50] And the American Bar Association pointed out the danger of the Federal Government getting a grip on the vast funds invested in life insurance "to support this or that social or economic theory, or even to balance the budget, or to make loans to various pressure groups in exchange for IOU's deposited with the Treasury." The executive committee of the National Association of Insurance Commissioners adopted strong resolutions against encroachment on states' rights by the Federal Government, and promised to stand guard against any Federal legislation which would "usurp the sovereign powers of the several states or weaken the American system of free enterprise." The executive committee of the American Life Convention reaffirmed the 1905 resolution of that body which put it on record as being opposed

[49] In the House of Representatives by Francis E. Walter of Pennsylvania and Clarence E. Hancock of New York; in the Senate by Senators Frederick A. Van Nuys of Indiana and Joseph W. Bailey of North Carolina. All these Congressmen except Hancock were Democrats.

[50] As quoted in *The Insurance Field,* LXXII (1943), October 29.

1860

Equitable Symbols

1871

EQUITABLE

1962

to any interference with state supervision of life insurance and the Convention appointed a committee to work with a similar committee of The Association of Life Insurance Presidents to study the problems involved should the Supreme Court hold life insurance to be commerce.

As the weeks passed, it appeared that both Congress and the Supreme Court were waiting to see what the other was going to do. Finally, June 5, 1944, just a few hours before "D-Day" for the American army in France, the Supreme Court handed down its decision. With seven judges participating, the Court, by a vote of four to three, decided that fire insurance transactions across state lines constituted commerce among the several states and that the Sherman Act of 1890 applied. Thus, by a vote of a minority of the Court, precedents of three quarters of a century were overturned.[51]

Although the SEUA case had arisen in connection with fire insurance, the effect of the decision was to establish Federal jurisdiction over all types of insurance when conducted across state lines. Unlike a few of the other large eastern life insurance companies, Equitable had never favored Federal regulation. Soon after the decision was announced, President Parkinson wrote Commissioner Charles F. J. Harrington of Massachusetts that Equitable would prefer to have the

[51] *The United States* v. *South-Eastern Underwriters Association*, 322 U.S. 533. The majority opinion was written by Justice Black, with Justices Murphy, Douglas, and Rutledge concurring. Chief Justice Stone in a dissenting opinion held that insurance contracts, like other contracts, were not commodities in the eyes of the law, and hence not commerce. To decide otherwise might be the occasion for loosing a flood of litigation and of legislation, state and national: "These considerations might well stay a reversal of long-established doctrine which promises so little of advantage and so much of harm." Justice Frankfurter, in joining with this opinion, had no doubt that the relations of the insurance business to national commerce and finance afforded constitutional authority for appropriate regulation by Congress, but equally without doubt Congress, by enacting the Sherman Act, did not mean to disregard the then accepted conception of the constitutional basis for regulation of the insurance business. He believed the evidence overwhelming that the Sherman Act was inapplicable to insurance transactions. Justice Jackson, in a separate dissent, also saw this same problem: "What role ought the judiciary to play in reversing the trend of history and setting the nation's feet on a new path of policy? . . . The Court now is not following, it is overruling an unequivocal line of authority reaching over many years. We are not sustaining an act of Congress against attack on its constitutionality, we are making unprecedented use of the Act to strike down the constitutional basis of state regulation. . . . The recklessness of such a course is emphasized when we consider that Congress has not one line of legislation deliberately designed to take over Federal responsibility for this important and complicated enterprise."

insurance business continue to be regulated by the state insurance departments, as it had been during all of its history. He thought that it was unfortunate that such an important decision should have been made by only four of the nine justices and that the National Association of Insurance Commissioners might well ask for a rehearing. If the decision was to stand he thought that representatives of all branches of the insurance business should arrange as quickly as possible to cooperate with the NAIC and the leaders in Congress in the endeavor to clear up the confusion.[52] The following year President Parkinson said: "We in the Equitable have long believed that state regulation of the insurance business in the interest of policyholders and the general public has been effective and has permitted the expansion of our business and its services to the general satisfaction and advantage of our policyholders."

The new status of insurance as commerce raised serious doubts as to the validity of many state regulatory laws. To clarify the confused situation, the National Association of Insurance Commissioners, in cooperation with committees representing the various insurance trade organizations, finally in November 1944 proposed Congressional legislation to neutralize the effects of the SEUA decision.[53] Various bills were introduced and amendments made out of which eventually came the McCarran Act (Public Law 15) of the 79th Congress, which was signed by the President on March 9, 1945.[54]

This act, "An Act to Express the Intent of the Congress with Reference to the Regulation of the Business of Insurance," declared "that the continued regulation and taxation by the several States of the busi-

[52] Parkinson to Harrington, June 14, 1944. Sterling Pierson files, Equitable Archives.

[53] The first and second sections of the draft stated that the public interest required continued regulation of insurance by the states, and provided that acts of Congress should not invalidate or supersede state laws unless such acts specifically so provided. The third section declared that the Federal Trade Commission and the Robinson-Patman Anti-Discrimination Acts should not apply to insurance. Section Four provided for a moratorium on the application of the Federal antitrust laws until July 1, 1948, so as to allow time for unhurried consideration of desirable legislation.

[54] An excellent brief summary of the origin and progress of Public Law 15 through Congress, with extracts of pertinent debates, is contained in the Preliminary Report of the Committees of the American Life Convention and the Life Insurance Association of America (formerly The Association of Life Insurance Presidents), which was sent to the Corresponding Officers of member companies July 12, 1945.

ness of insurance is in the public interest, and that silence on the part of Congress shall not be construed to impose any barrier to the regulation or taxation of such business by the several States." Until January 1, 1948, the Sherman Act (except the provisions applying to boycott, coercion, and intimidation), the Clayton Act, and the Federal Trade Commission Act were not to apply to the business of insurance, but after that date they would be applicable to the extent that the insurance business was not regulated by state law; nothing in the act was to be construed so as to affect the application of the National Labor Relations Act, the Fair Labor Standards Act, or the Merchant Marine Act of 1920.

Thus the states were given almost three years to make sure that their legislation was such as to exempt the insurance business from the application of the Federal antitrust laws. Since many of the state legislatures met only every other year, coordinated action on the part of the states would require that no time be lost. In May 1945 the Committee on Federal Legislation of the National Association of Insurance Commissioners met with representatives of nineteen organizations which represented all branches of the insurance business. Out of this meeting came the organization of the All-Industry Committee, to aid in the formulation of a state legislative program to meet the requirements of the McCarran Act. The American Life Convention and the Life Insurance Association of America (formerly the Association of Life Insurance Presidents) pledged their cooperation in this work, the largest task ever undertaken by the insurance business as a whole.

Although the life insurance business was concerned primarily with the adoption by all of the states of the Standard Nonforfeiture and Valuation Laws (see below), its interests were deeply involved in the problems presented by the changed status of insurance in general. All branches of the business were agreed upon certain broad principles: 1) that the Federal Government might now enter and completely occupy the field of insurance supervision; 2) that Federal supervision should be avoided as far as possible; and 3) that Federal supervision could be minimized and state supervision be better preserved through state legislation within the pattern of the McCarran Act.

In 1936 the National Association of Insurance Commissioners had appointed a committee headed by Alfred N. Guertin, Actuary of the New Jersey Insurance Department, to study the need for a new mortality table, and in 1939 appointed a Committee to Study Non-Forfeiture Benefits and Related Matters, the personnel of which was the same as that of the committee which had been working on mortality tables. Out of the work of this committee eventually came the Commissioners 1941 Standard Ordinary Mortality Table and model bills for uniform state legislation on nonforfeiture values, which had the approval of the American Life Convention and the Life Insurance Association of America. By 1945, 34 states had enacted legislation which made policies issued under the new nonforfeiture and valuation laws acceptable; New York, however, had failed for the third successive year to enact the standard laws.

The All-Industry Committee and the National Association of Insurance Commissioners, aided by the two major life company organizations, worked hard to get the legislatures of 44 states which met in regular session in 1947 to meet the requirements of the McCarran Act. Rate regulatory laws, the majority of them based upon the model bills provided, were enacted in 35 states and two territories during the year. Laws relating to fair trade practices were enacted in 15 states and accident and health bills in 17 states. Numerous other laws relating to the All-Industry—National Association of Insurance Commissioners program were also enacted in the various states.[55] At the same time, the life insurance organizations worked hard to get the remaining states to adopt the Standard Valuation and Non-Forfeiture legislation—"the Guertin legislation." New York, which had failed in four previous attempts, finally enacted a somewhat modified bill, and Governor Dewey, in signing it, commented upon the important safeguards now incorporated in the law. New York's action, though long delayed, was welcomed by the life insurance business and used as a talking point to get the other states which had not acted to do so. By the end of the year, Standard Non-Forfeiture Valuation Laws, either mandatory or permissive, were in effect in 47 of the 48 states.

Enactment of the Standard Valuation and Non-Forfeiture Laws was an important accomplishment on the part of the life insurance business. Both the formulation of the model bills and their enactment had

[55] A digest of the All-Industry—NAIC standard bills, together with a listing of enactment by the states, is conveniently presented in "Insurance as Interstate Commerce—the Third Year," issued by the Special Committee of the Section of Insurance Law of the American Bar Association, John V. Bloys, chairman. (In 1946 this committee had issued its summary of "The First Two Years" and the service continued through "The Fourth Year.") One of the most valuable features of this service is the selected bibliography of articles and speeches for the years 1945 to 1947 inclusive, dealing with the subject of insurance as commerce.

been a cooperative job. Within a five-year period, which for most states included only three regular legislative sessions, 39 states had enacted the laws.[56] This fact was all the more remarkable in that the program dealt with a subject in which the public was little interested. There is probably no other instance in American history of comparable results from voluntary state cooperation on a broad legislative program within a similar length of time.

In regard to the McCarran Act and the state legislation to meet its requirements, President Parkinson said: "It must be constantly borne in mind, however, that the Congress may enter the regulatory field at any time so long as insurance continues to be regarded as interstate commerce. It is therefore incumbent upon all elements of the industry to encourage and support every effort to provide an adequate and efficient supervisory system in the various states if regulation by the Congress and Federal bureaus is to be eliminated." [57]

Since premium increases were scheduled to go into effect in many of the states in 1948 simultaneously with the Guertin legislation, some effort was made on the part of the life insurance business to inform the public that the rate increases were caused by falling interest rates rather than by the legislation. As noted earlier Equitable reduced its interest assumption for reserves for annual premium life insurance from 3 to 2½ per cent, effective November 15, 1947, and at the same time adopted the 1941 Commissioners Standard Ordinary Table. Said President Parkinson:

> This step represents an historic transition in our business. The change in interest rate will give us greater assurance that for each kind of new policy our rate of interest earnings will equal or exceed the rate of earnings required to support it. Thus we have greater confidence in our ability to maintain equity between our various classes of policyholders. The change in mortality table, made possible by changes in statutory requirements, will also improve equity in some respects between different classes of policyholders, and should put an end to any public suspicion that the life insurance companies have continued to use an outmoded mortality table because by doing so they were able to make some special profits which would not be available if a more modern table were adopted. This transition is in harmony with the purpose of our Society as a mutual life insur-

[56] There were eight states in which such legislation was not necessary because their insurance laws already conformed to the principles contained in the model bills.

[57] The President's Report to the Board of Directors for 1947.

ance company to operate progressively and equitably in furnishing protection to the public.[58]

* * *

Insurance in force with legal reserve life insurance companies in the United States had increased about 35 per cent during the war years—to $151,762,000,000. But the total savings of the American people had more than doubled. There were 71,000,000 policyholders and the combined assets of the companies were approaching $45,000,000,000. In view of these figures, it is not hard to understand why the life insurance companies were somewhat surprised by the tremendous increase in the purchase of life insurance which came in the immediate postwar years; within eight years the amount of life insurance just about doubled. Between 1946 and 1953 Equitable's insurance in force kept pace—from $10,564,000,000 to $20,457,000,000. Although purchases of life insurance loomed large dollarwise, they did not represent a large increase measured in percentage of national income, nor did the total insurance in force double in purchasing power.[59] As the dollar declined in value, the policyholder had to have more and more life insurance in order to retain the same benefits. Once again, President Parkinson embarked upon an educational campaign to acquaint the people with the causes and effects of inflation. He made scores of talks to life insurance groups, to chambers of commerce, bankers' associations, bar associations, and industrial conferences; the talks were widely reported in the press and many of them were distributed in pamphlet form.[60]

58 *Ibid.*

59 President Parkinson pointed out that the total amount of life insurance in force in the United States at the end of 1947 represented less actual protection than the insurance in force in 1940. "Life Insurance and the Money Supply," p. 14. Copy in Equitable Archives.

60 Among the pamphlets: "Congress and Inflation," an address delivered at the meeting of the Chamber of Commerce of the State of New York, October 1, 1942; "Monetary Manipulation," at the 275th meeting of the National Industrial Conference Board, January 17, 1946; "Dollars and Banks," before the Bond Club of Philadelphia, March 12, 1946; "Financial Facts and Fancies," at a meeting of the New York Society of Security Analysts, March 25, 1946; "Monetizing Debt," before the Savings Banks Association of New Jersey, April 4, 1946; "Too Much Money," before the Chamber of Commerce of the State of New York, March 6, 1947; "Life Insurance and the Money Supply," reprinted from the December 1947 issue of *The Journal of the American Society of Chartered Life Underwriters;* "Business and Government," before the Economic Club of Detroit, September 27, 1948; and "Feeding the Financial Flames," before the Chamber of Commerce of the State of New York, October 7, 1948. Copies in Equitable Archives.

In addition, small circulars on the theme of "Dollars, Prices and You" were mailed to policyholders with their premium notices.

In view of the fact that a life insurance company by its contracts is obligated to pay only in currency of the realm, why should it be so concerned with inflation and depreciation of the dollar? President Parkinson's answer was as follows:

> Although our life insurance contracts . . . call for payment of a specified number of dollars, it does not follow that we should have no interest in doing what we can to preserve the value of those payments. The obligation is implied, and the institution of life insurance should no longer continue its attitude of relative indifference, while the welfare of policyholders is so obviously threatened. All of us, moreover, have a broader interest in this whole problem, for the enduring welfare of our country depends greatly upon thrift and its preservation. . . . While we may prosper for a time under a regime of government spending and cheap money, history is replete with illustrations of the ultimate collapse of such ventures. In all such cases the underlying weakness was the same. Money and wealth were confused. By some twisted mental process more money was taken to mean more wealth. While it is one thing to double the amount of money in the hands of an individual, it is quite another to double the total money supply of a country. In addition to being a medium which facilitates the exchange of goods, a sound money must also be a store of value, for as free men we live for the future and to secure that future, economically speaking, it is essential that we be able to plan for it in terms of a relatively stable value for money—the vehicle of our thrift.[61]

Whence came the inflation?: "Rises in prices are not inflation. Consequent demands for increased wages are not inflation. The inflation is in the debasement of the currency." Persistently, if not patiently, President Parkinson centered his attention on the tremendous increase in the supply of purchasing media which resulted from government debt and deficit financing through the banking system: "I don't care what your money experts or economists say, adulteration of our dollar is the chief cause of the pressure upward on prices. You can't have three or four times the volume of money you had a few years ago and expect each unit of that money to be worth as much in purchasing value as was each unit of the smaller volume." By simple analogies he illustrated the effects of New Deal finance by which, through mere bookkeeping

[61] "Life Insurance and the Money Supply," p. 15.

transactions, the money supply could be increased manyfold. As for the idea that public debt was a public benefit:

> The silliest thing that any human being has ever uttered has been the declaration coming from high places in the last few years, in this country, that the great debt of the Federal Government is a public benefit. How could the American people ever have gone into a state of mind where they would listen for an instant to such nonsense? This debt is a burden on us and our children and our grandchildren. We have, for the last twelve or fifteen years, been spending the savings of our fathers and drawing on the future earnings of our sons and our grandsons, and we cannot get anywhere with that kind of public procedure. . . . We cannot drift along and say that "we owe it to ourselves" or that it will take care of itself. It won't take care of itself but, by the great Jehovah, it will take care of all of us if we do not tackle the job of getting it under control.

To prevent the spiraling of the money supply into some astronomical figure, President Parkinson recommended such old-fashioned steps as balancing the Federal budget and discontinuance of deficit financing. Whatever tax reductions might be made, there should still be sufficient revenue to supply a surplus out of which to reduce the Federal debt. "Then, the Federal Reserve authorities should abandon their insane and fanatical desire for easy money at any price, and establish a fiscal policy which will look to soundness in the future, that is, to put it more plainly, they must stop trying to create funds through banks' purchase of government bonds in any way in order that the supply of funds shall be so great that it will continue to keep the interest rate at a lower and lower point. A low interest rate is not worth the price it costs all the people." Finally, the Treasury should issue long-term bonds with an interest rate sufficient to make them attractive to individual investors and to their savings and life insurance institutions. Such a program would have to be carried out quickly and courageously. It could not be done "by the so-called experts who determined so much of public policy in this country today, or by the jugglers of public policy. . . . The job, if it is to be done, must be done by a Congress of competent, courageous representatives of Americans and we are not going to have that kind of Congress unless we, who represent so large a portion of the population of this country, see to it that that kind of man is promptly elected to the great representative body of this country." [62]

[62] "Monetary Manipulation," pp. 14–15.

In a year-end release to the press in 1947, President Parkinson said that a statement expressing disapproval of the fiscal policies of the United States Government had been approved by the Board of Directors of the Life Insurance Association of America more than a year earlier, but that a committee to which it was referred had "substituted for it a watered-down criticism of inflationary trends." He emphasized that little help in the fight on inflation could be expected from banking circles and that it was the duty of the managers of life insurance institutions to recognize their responsibility in trying to preserve the purchasing value of the dollar in which their contracts were payable.[63] Later in the year he said that for some time there had been an attempt on the part of representatives of the Federal Reserve Board and of the banks to give the impression that the life insurance companies were contributing to the inflation of the money supply: "We in the life insurance business have thought that we were doing just the opposite and had been emphatic in our statements that the money supply has been inflated principally by the operations of the banks." [64] Then, in October, Equitable issued the second in the series entitled "Dollars, Prices and You," which was mailed out with premium notices to the policyholders. This little brochure pointed out that the government and banking monetary policies were the modern substitute for printing paper money: "The resulting adulteration of our dollar reduces its purchasing value just as the addition of 4 quarts of water to 1 quart of milk reduces its food value." The policyholders were advised to protest to their banking officials and congressmen before it was too late: "The value of money is falling; the prices of goods are rising; day by day your savings shrink in value. . . . A free country is as strong as its currency, and a people remain free only so long as their savings and capital are represented by a sound currency. The first step to the disappearance of civil liberties and total regimentation is the dissolution of the national financial structure."

In December 1948, President Parkinson again sought to get the Board of the Life Insurance Association to approve a resolution against inflation, but it was voted down. He said that Equitable would continue to speak out against inflation even when it was necessary to criticize the Treasury Department or the Federal Reserve and that it was unfortunate that some economists and bankers—and top life executives

[63] *The Weekly Underwriter*, CLVIII (1948), January 10.
[64] *Ibid.*, CLIX (1948), August 21.

as well—participated in apologies for inflation and condoned monetary policies which should have been modified or abandoned.[65] He then published a full-page advertisement in *The Weekly Underwriter*, December 25, under the heading, "We Can't Walk Out On 78,000,000 Policyholders!" In this advertisement, he reproduced the text of the resolution which had been turned down by the Board of the LIAA December 8. The key paragraph was as follows:

> The members of the Life Insurance Association of America, noting the continued inflation of our money supply and decreased purchasing value of the dollar, now declare for the guidance of the monetary authorities that the policyholders of our life insurance companies are suffering more detriment as a result of the current monetary policies, particularly the Federal Reserve System's support of the Government bond market than they would be likely to suffer from any decline in the market price of Government bonds if that support were ended.

The resolution also called attention to the fact that while total life insurance in force had increased from $117,000,000,000 in 1940 to approximately $200,000,000,000, the purchasing value of the $200,000,000,000 was, in 1948, approximately $114,000,000,000.

In his open letter to the Board, which accompanied the advertisement, President Parkinson said:

> That you felt it expedient to reject this resolution, on the grounds that it constitutes a criticism of the Government's current monetary policies by the life insurance business, seems to us to be unwarranted timidity contrary to the tenets of good citizenship. In a democracy, the life insurance business, friend and bulwark of the Government in peace or war, has a duty to speak up with sincere and honest criticism whenever opposition is felt. To do less is tantamount to a betrayal of the trust and confidence of 32 million American families who have faith in life insurance.

The writer stated that he would continue to "urge upon every member of the life insurance fraternity and upon the general public, the pressing need for re-examination of our Federal Reserve System's currency and credit policies. Certainly, the ideal way to conduct such an appraisal would be through an impartial monetary commission. We can't walk out on 78,000,000 policyholders!"

[65] *Ibid.*, December 18.

This proclamation was answered by an open letter from Asa V. Call, President of the Pacific Mutual Life Insurance Company, who was then President of the LIAA:

> Your advertisement criticizes the Directors of the Association for their failure to approve such a resolution and by more than inference, suggests that such failure was due to their cowardice and timidity. The members of our Board are men of high integrity. They have an understanding of economic problems. Many of them disagree with you that the maintenance of the government peg on long term government bonds is the principal cause of the inflationary troubles which face us all. . . . The fact that the Board of Directors . . . does not agree with the statements in your resolution is not fairly nor properly a basis for a charge of dull complacency or lack of interest in inflation and its threats. . . . I am sure that no member of the Board yields to you on the matter of his vital interest in the protection of the interest of policyholders. . . .[66]

In calling attention to the problems of inflation, President Parkinson rendered an important service not only to the policyholders of Equitable, but to the people of the United States. His views were approved by many Equitable policyholders, and a news commentator wrote: "I regard your outspoken and courageous analysis of the economic factors as a yardstick with which to measure pussy-footing by some of your colleagues." [67]

* * *

With the possible exception of inflation, no problem in the recent history of life insurance has given the life insurance business more concern than that of Federal income taxation, nor has any problem presented more inherently difficult or complex aspects.

In 1921 Congress, with the support of both the Treasury and the companies, abandoned its policy of taxing life insurance companies in the same way that it taxed other commercial corporations and enacted a law geared to the operations of mutual companies. This was done

[66] *Ibid.*, CLX (1949), January 29.

[67] Merryle Stanley Rukeyser, International News Service economic commentator, to President Parkinson, April 9, 1946. Parkinson files, Equitable Archives. See also editorial by Rukeyser in the *Pittsburgh Sun Telegraph*, March 21, 1946, in which he noted that Presidents Parkinson and Lewis W. Douglas of Mutual, instead of reporting the further decline in interest rates as "good news," were warning their policyholders that inflationary trends were affecting their vital interests.

for the very practical reason that about three-fourths of the business was held by mutual companies. Consequently, the law treated investment income as the only taxable income. Gross income was defined as interest, dividends, and rents, with deductions for tax-free interest, depreciation, and investment expenses. This produced what has been called "net investment income." Allowance was then made for reserve requirements by permitting as a deduction from net investment income an amount equal to 4 per cent of each company's "reserves required by law," regardless of the individual company's own actual reserving rate. The 4 per cent figure was chosen because no company was reserving at a higher rate.

The yield of the 1921 act was disappointing to the Treasury and in 1932 Congress lowered the 4 per cent figure to 3 ¾ per cent. By 1942 this act had not only failed to produce the desired revenue, but had resulted in an inequitable distribution of the tax burden among the companies. In March 1942 the Secretary of the Treasury, Henry Morgenthau, appeared before the Ways and Means Committee of the House and requested more than $7,500,000,000 of new revenue. He cited insurance as an "example of special privilege," called attention to the fact that life insurance received double exemptions, and advocated a tax formula under which the exemptions for interest required to maintain reserves would be reduced from 3 ¾ per cent to 3 ¼ per cent of such reserves. It was expected that this change would bring all life insurance companies in under the tax and about double the total revenue.

The Treasury Department rejected a proposal submitted by the tax committees of the American Life Convention and The Association of Life Insurance Presidents, but finally compromised upon a formula—the "McAndless formula"—which related the reserve requirements of individual companies to a moving percentage determined by figures obtained from all the companies.[68] At that time, the business as a whole required a reserve reduction based on 3 ¼ per cent of reserves. Accordingly, the formula adopted applied the 3 ¼ per cent rate to 65 per cent of the reserve, and the actual reserve interest required to the remaining 35 per cent. The result of this method was a deduction formula frozen as to two-thirds of its effect and one-third based on

[68] Named after Alva John McAndless, President of The Lincoln National Life Insurance Company and of the American Life Convention, who had worked with the tax committee of The Association of Life Insurance Presidents. For the history of the tax laws of 1942 as applied to life insurance, see R. C. Buley, *The American Life Convention*, II, pp. 896–902.

current requirements for the business as a whole. On this basis each year the Secretary of the Treasury was to promulgate a percentage figure which each company was to use in deducting the reserve interest requirements from its net investment income. Thus, the experience of all the companies was involved in the tax of an individual company.[69] This 1942 formula also proved ineffective within the short period of five years, principally because the net rate of interest on invested funds had declined from 3.44 per cent to 2.88 per cent. When the "Secretary's ratio" was released in December 1947, it was obvious that the life insurance companies would require 100 per cent or more of their investment income to meet reserve requirements under the 1942 law and that none of them would have to pay any taxes on their 1947 income.

This situation was satisfactory neither to the Government nor to the companies. It put the life insurance companies in an embarrassing position, for the chances were remote that the people would understand that the companies were not trying to avoid their fair share of the Federal tax burden. All the more so with either uninformed or not entirely candid popular magazines and syndicated columnists speaking of "windfalls" and "fluke in the Revenue Act," and congressmen and the President of the United States speaking of a "tax-free ride" and "quirk" in the law. The impression conveyed was that life insurance, one of the biggest businesses of all, paid no taxes.[70]

[69] August 20, 1942, the Equitable Board of Directors passed a resolution urging Congress to include in the pending revenue legislation three provisions affecting the tax interest of policyholders: the continuance of the $40,000 exemption of life insurance policy proceeds from the Federal estate tax; some reasonable deduction for Federal income tax purposes of premiums paid by policyholders for life insurance; and exemption from the Federal estate tax of life insurance proceeds definitely earmarked by policyholders for the payment of Federal taxes on their estates. This action was communicated to the chairman of the House Committee on Ways and Means, and to the Senate Committee on Finance. While Congress did not adopt these recommendations, it did insert in the Victory Tax Title of the Revenue Act provision for a credit for premiums paid for life insurance. Bills were introduced in both houses in 1943 to permit individuals to deduct from gross income certain amounts paid as life insurance premiums, but they did not pass. Notice of the Board's action was mailed to Equitable policyholders with premium notices from July to September 1943.

Also working for deductions for life insurance premiums was the National Policyholders Committee, headed by Dr. Hugh S. McGill of Chicago. The idea received editorial support from many of the leading newspapers of the country, including *The New York Times*, the *Washington Star*, and the *Atlanta Journal*.

[70] Illustrative of the somewhat unfavorable accounts of the situation was that published in *Time*: "WINDFALL. Life-insurance companies were a little embarrassed

During 1948–49, a congressional committee, the Treasury Department, and the Joint Committee of the Life Insurance Association of America and the American Life Convention worked to develop a new formula. Finally, in October 1949, the Treasury offered the companies a choice between a Treasury formula to apply to 1948 and 1949 business, or a plan presented by the company organizations to apply to business for 1947, 1948, and 1949. Most of the companies approved the latter plan since they believed that it would be equitable to all companies and result in a lower tax base for 1948 with consequent advantages in the years to follow. The bill passed the House of Representatives in January 1950.[71]

Although the two company organizations, the Life Insurance Association and the American Life Convention, approved the bill, President Parkinson opposed it on constitutional grounds. He said: "I know of no instance in which Congress has ever imposed a retroactive tax. . . . It ought to be unconstitutional. It certainly is unreasonable and undesirable. . . . If a life insurance company can be taxed now on the business of 1947, so can automobile companies. So can other industries. American business simply cannot progress and prosper. It must carry on under a constant threat of such retroactive taxation not only in 1950, but in the decades ahead."[72] Although he was criticized in a few instances for purporting to speak for the whole life insurance

---

by one present in their Christmas stockings. By a fluke in the 1942 Revenue Act, the Treasury announced last week, most companies would be exempt from income tax on their 1947 earnings. Secretary of the Treasury John W. Snyder cried: 'The situation calls for the immediate attention of Congress.' In 1942 companies had asked that a percentage of earnings from investments be tax-free, as they were only held in trust for future payments on policies. The Treasury agreed that this was reasonable, and Congress passed a complicated formula to exempt 90 to 91%. When the formula was applied this year, the exemptions worked out to 100.7%. That would mean a windfall of upwards of $34 million. The companies agreed that this was more than they deserved and that Congress should draft a new formula for 1948. They were also willing to work out a retroactive adjustment." *Time*, LI (1948), January 5.

Three things in this account were particularly irritating: 1) the use of the word "fluke" made it appear that somebody had slipped something over Congress in 1942, which was not the case; 2) the protest of the Secretary of the Treasury in regard to the situation—low interest rates—which was created by the Treasury Department; and 3) the last sentence, which was news to the life insurance business.

71 Life company representatives who were in touch with the situation thought it would be unwise to oppose the retroactive tax in the House, for as an alternative the House would probably just double the rates on 1949 business.

72 As quoted in *The Weekly Underwriter*, CLXII (1950), January 14.

business, the executives of many industries and businesses assured President Parkinson of their support of his stand.

When President Parkinson appeared before the Senate Finance Committee in March 1950, he said that life insurance was not nearly so complicated or mysterious as indicated in the hearings and that a fair tax for the future could be decided upon by the technical men of the business in the time taken for the hearings, but "it has not been the technicians, but the tacticians" who had handled the matter; the fight would be carried to the courts and the whole business would become a juicy plum for tax experts. The Committee agreed that retroactive application of the tax was impracticable and its constitutionality "at least debatable." With the retroactive provisions removed, the tax was made to apply only to the business for 1949 and 1950 and became known as the 1950 "stopgap" law. The Senate passed the bill in April. The new law amended the Revenue Act of 1942 as it applied to life insurance taxation so as to eliminate the arbitrary 3 ¼ per cent reserve earning rate in the calculation of the Secretary's ratio and substituted therefor the average rate assumed for the policy reserves of all life insurance companies for the preceding year, treating individual companies' ratios in excess of 100 per cent as 100 per cent. It was estimated that it would produce $42,000,000 of revenue from 1949 income and $70,000,000 from 1950 income.

In May 1950, when more revenue was needed for the Korean War, the provisions of the House bill were again included in the Administration tax bill. Once again, however, the Senate eliminated the retroactive tax provision for the years 1947 and 1948 from the bill, which became law in September as the Revenue Act of 1950. The tax on the life companies was still on the stopgap basis. President Parkinson gave the members of the Senate Finance Committee much credit for their "high sense of public duty in the maintenance of fair and reasonable taxation." In his annual report to the Equitable Board for the year 1950, he said:

> It was not easy to turn the tide against this retroactive income tax after it had enjoyed so much support from the Treasury, the Ways and Means Committee and the House. Indeed, it would not have been possible to save the policyholders and future taxpayers from this very undesirable and unreasonable type of taxation had it not been for the high sense of public duty in the maintenance of fair and reasonable taxation of the Chairman and members of the Senate Finance Committee. To these men [names of

the members of the Committee] are due the thanks of the life insurance companies and their policyholders as well as taxpayers generally, and this seems a fitting place to express it.

We who administer mutual life insurance companies must emphasize the fact that the level premium plan of conducting our business requires us to set aside and accumulate by investment a fund, which we call the policy reserves, out of which we supplement the premiums paid by the policyholder in the later years of life, at which time the premiums alone would be inadequate to cover the current death claims. We have always emphasized the safe custody, careful investment and accumulation of our policy reserves. We cannot fail to keep constantly before public authorities, especially tax authorities, that, if they make demands which interfere with the sufficiency of these reserves, they impair the company's power to perform its obligations to its policyholders and their beneficiaries. That fact was emphasized in the Equitable's resistance to the retroactive tax and, for the same reason, we must in the future insist that any taxation of life insurance funds shall be reasonable and consistent with this major obligation of the companies.[73]

The stopgap act of 1950, with its complicated formula still geared to the Secretary's ratio, satisfied neither the Treasury nor the life insurance companies; what was needed was a simpler law. This was provided by the Revenue Act of 1951, which replaced the Secretary's ratio formula with a flat tax of 6½ per cent on net investment income. The result was a slight increase in the over-all tax take but a tax law which was easily understood. It also contained a relief provision for individual companies which might be having difficulty in meeting their reserve requirements. The 1951 act was extended to cover the years 1952, 1953, and 1954.

Meanwhile the Treasury and the life insurance business were trying to bring forth a new formula. Following very extensive hearings held by the House Committee on Ways and Means, what is known as the

[73] Said *The New York Times*, October 16, 1950: "The life industry's traditional ivory-tower aloofness from controversial economic and political issues of the day is due for a change, it appeared last week. . . . A lesson in the futility of timidity was hammered home to the industry recently by Thomas I. Parkinson, President of the Equitable Life Assurance Society of the United States, who, almost single-handed, won life insurance's fight against retroactive taxation. . . . This unexpected victory by the life insurance industry is one reason for a new willingness to 'come out and mix it' whenever it feels an unjustified attack on life insurance is being made. The nation's insurance policyholders should benefit as a result of Mr. Parkinson's direct approach to the matter." See also *The Insurance Field*, LXXIX (1950), April 14, and the *Insurance Advocate*, LXI (1950), September 30.

Mills Law was enacted in 1955 to replace the cumbersome Secretary's ratio for reserve deduction as well as the flat 6½ per cent tax on net investment income provided in the 1951 stopgap act. The Mills Law provided a flat 85 per cent deduction from net investment income as a "reserve and other policyholder liability deduction." This new law was a substantial improvement over anything previously suggested and eliminated many of the weaknesses in previous laws. Although this new act was intended as a permanent law, the Treasury would accept it only on a stopgap basis. This law was subsequently extended on a year-to-year basis to cover 1956 and 1957 business. The last extension was made about the middle of March 1958 for the 1957 tax year. Congressional leaders voiced opposition to any further extension.

At the time the Senate Finance Committee had under consideration this last extension, the Treasury made a commitment to forward to Congress its recommendations for a new formula. The recommendation was for a regular corporate income tax law modified to meet the peculiarities of the business in which the measure of the tax would be net gain from operations with a deduction of dividends to policyholders. This idea was not new. Two former Secretaries of the Treasury had made the same recommendation. Stemming from the recommendation of the Secretary of the Treasury, at the end of 1958 the Treasury, Congress, and the life insurance industry were still working to create a "permanent" tax formula which would be equitable to both stock and mutual companies, to large and small companies, and which would represent a fair tax burden for life insurance policyholders compared with the tax treatment of other forms of thrift.

In 1958 Equitable incurred Federal income taxes of $42,832,000, state premium taxes of $15,324,000, and real estate taxes of $7,154,000; in addition, it paid OASDI, unemployment, and various other taxes, licenses, and fees.

In all tax deliberations over the years, Equitable has made vigorous pleas for tax equality between insured and trusteed pension plans. The leader in bringing this subject to the attention of the insurance business and Congress was Vice President and Associate Actuary Ray M. Peterson, a nationally recognized expert in the pension field. As a member of the Joint Pension Subcommittee of the Life Insurance Association and the American Life Convention, he succeeded in getting this committee to give some attention to the matter. The subject was discussed at the annual meeting of the LIAA. In 1952 Murphy and Peterson brought the problem before the Joint Committee on Taxation of the

Life Insurance Association, the American Life Convention, and the Life Insurers Conference; and finally, January 1953, three years and four months after Peterson's first recommendation to President Murphy, the Committee included recommendations in its memorandum to the Federal tax authorities. In April 1954, when Peterson was chairman of the Joint Pension Committee of the LIAA and the ALC, his committee again recommended to the Joint Committee on Taxation that tax relief be sought in the pension field. Robert L. Hogg—who had become chairman of this committee the same month he joined Equitable—appeared before a special subcommittee of the Ways and Means Committee in December 1954; the officers of two other companies also appeared as witnesses. In July 1955, the House passed a tax bill which included tax relief for insured pension business.

Despite the fact that the Treasury witnesses did not oppose pension tax relief, the Senate Finance Committee removed the provision from the House bill and the tax bill became law without it. So, after four years of strenuous effort, the advocates of tax relief had to start all over. The problem was again discussed at the annual meeting of the Life Insurance Association in December 1955, and when Congress took up insurance company taxation in 1956 Peterson drafted several alternative bills to give pension tax relief which were considered by the insurance business, but Congress took no action. The following year, when the tax bill was again before Congress, Peterson prepared memoranda for the life insurance companies. President James F. Oates, Jr.—who became President of Equitable June 1, 1957—and Senior Vice President and Actuary Walter Klem lent their efforts to the cause. The year 1958 was critical, since Congress was endeavoring to enact a permanent tax law. Conditions were not favorable, for not only did the Administration want more taxes from industry but the stock and mutual life insurance companies were seriously divided over how the tax burden should be shared. Nevertheless, the advocates of pension tax relief increased their efforts. Senior Vice President Hogg and Vice President Peterson presented statements before the Ways and Means Committee in November and other companies increased their efforts. Even so it did not appear at all certain that a pension relief provision would be included in the House bill. It was, however, and the bill passed the House in February 1959. Once again Equitable took the lead in getting other life companies to present the arguments before the Senate Finance Committee. The bill passed the Senate in June 1959, and, though it was not perfect from the viewpoint of the life insurance companies, it represented a substantial achievement.

Since the provisions of the law, in effect, taxed only the investment income on the surplus associated with "qualified" pension contracts, the tax would be minimized to the extent that such surplus was diminished by strengthening reserves. This change in the law went a long way toward opening the door to fair competition between the banks and insurance companies for group pension business.

Although the Federal legislation of 1959 did much to equalize the tax incidence as between insured and trusteed pension plans, there still remained the problem of state taxation of annuity considerations. At an early period the states enacted premium taxes on life insurance as a means of obtaining money for the support of regulation of the business of insurance. For many years a basic factor which divided the mutual and stock companies was the question of whether the mutual companies would pay taxes on gross premiums or on gross premiums less the dividends refunded to policyholders. In general the mutual companies were successful in getting the taxes based only on premiums received and retained. There was, however, considerable lack of uniformity and precision in defining the premium tax base in the legislation of the various states. Even in recent years such descriptions as the following might be found in the statutes: "gross premiums received in this state," "premiums on insurance," "premiums on business done" and "premiums on policies covering residents of this state." [74]

Since there were no annuity contracts in the early years of life insurance, the taxation of annuity premiums was not a matter of concern, but as both individual and group annuities became available and the public became annuity conscious, the question became an important one, particularly to Equitable which throughout the years had placed more annuity business than any other United States life insurance company. The Society's individual annuities numbered about 4,000 in 1910 but by the end of 1947 the number had increased to 307,894, and during the same period the annual income at maturity under individual annuities in force rose from about $1,500,000 to $136,470,345.[75] The growth of the Society's group annuity business was even more spectacular with the number of certificate holders increasing from 76,140 in 1936 to 1,107,589 by the end of 1961. Annual income at maturity under group annuities in force increased from $6,746,802 to

[74] The trend in recent years has been toward adoption of the residence base.

[75] Historical Record Book, Valuation and Statistical Bureau, Actuary's Department, Equitable Archives. After 1947 there was a gradual decline in the number of individual annuities. At the end of 1961 the number was 202,309 and the annual income in force was $90,772,435. *Ibid.*

$458,078,903 during the same period. Whereas in 1925 only 4½ per cent of the Society's premium receipts consisted of annuity considerations, by 1930 the annuity receipts constituted 11 per cent; in 1935, 32 per cent; in 1940, 34 per cent; in 1945, 40 per cent and in 1950, 41 per cent. In 1956 the total annuity reserves of all United States companies amounted to $14,281,000,000. Of this total Equitable held $3,746,000,000, which meant that it had approximately 25 per cent of the total individual and group annuity business in force.

As early as 1916 the Pennsylvania Supreme Court held that annuity considerations were not taxable as insurance premiums even though the statute applied to "entire amount of premiums of every character and description received from business transacted." And in 1921 the New York Court of Appeals reached the same conclusion in construing a statute that taxed "gross amount of premiums . . . received . . . for business done." [76] So it appeared well established that annuity considerations were not taxable under existing tax statutes and that the social value of annuities would continue to preserve their premium tax-free status. But in the early 1930's a number of states in their need for additional revenue began taxing annuity considerations.

Equitable took a determined stand in opposition to these taxes and urged the Association of Life Insurance Presidents (after 1944 the Life Insurance Association of America) to challenge these proposals on behalf of all member companies. Since most of the member companies of the Association had little or no annuity business, and action by the Association required unanimous approval of its governing board, it was difficult to get united action. Largely as a result of the efforts of Vice President Ray D. Murphy and Counsel Sterling Pierson of Equitable the Association did take action on a case by case basis. Association management of the litigation facilitated the selection of the litigant in each of the numerous test suits which subsequently arose, although Equitable was the litigant in more instances than any other company.[77] From 1937 through 1943 test cases were decided by Appellate Courts of Iowa, Texas, New Hampshire, North Dakota, Arkansas, Wyoming, Mississippi, Missouri, Kansas, and California.[78]

[76] *Commonwealth* v. *Metropolitan Life Insurance Company,* 254 Pa. 510, 98A1072 (1916); *People* v. *Knapp,* 231 N.Y. 630, 132 N.E. 916, aff'g. 198 App. Div. 413, 184 N.Y. 5. 345 (1921).

[77] In California, Kansas, North Dakota, and Wyoming.

[78] *Northwestern Mutual Life Insurance Company* v. *Murphy* 223 Iowa 233, 271 N.W. 899 (1937); *Daniel* v. *Life Insurance Company of Virginia,* 102 S.W.

In most of these cases the issue involved not only the premium tax for the current year but taxes for a number of previous years. Since serious doubt existed as to whether the representative of the state could, without specific statutory authority, make a valid compromise, the choice lay between paying or not paying. The defense was frequently embarrassed during the course of litigation when it found that some companies had actually paid the tax merely because it was small in amount. Of the ten states listed above only in Texas, North Dakota, and Wyoming did the courts hold that annuity considerations were not taxable, but the overall result of the litigation was more favorable than the number of decisions might indicate. In some jurisdictions in addition to contending that annuity considerations were not taxable, in the alternative it was argued that if the court should reach a contrary conclusion, considerations received under deferred annuity contracts during the period of deferment and which were returned before expiration of the deferment period in accordance with contract terms should be deductible as returned premiums. Most of the statutes permitted a deduction for the amount of taxable premiums of amounts returned to policyholders. These deductions would also apply to amounts returned under group retirement plans. In Equitable's case in California (1942), where annuity considerations were held to be taxable, the court recognized the validity of this deduction as return premium, and Kansas did likewise the following year. These decisions were of considerable value when later test cases came up in other jurisdictions. In Arkansas (1939), although the court held that annuity considerations were taxable, it held that such taxes should not be retroactive.

Equitable's firm position in opposition to premium taxes on annuity considerations was not solely the result of its desire to protect the interest of existing policyholders from what it regarded as an improper tax; it also believed that there was a great area of retirement benefit service which could be rendered by life insurance companies. It succeeded in large degree in establishing the social value of an annuity,

---

(2d) 256 (Texas, 1937); *New York Life Insurance Company* v. *Sullivan*, 89 N.H. 21, 192 Atl. 297 (1937); *State* v. *Equitable Life Assurance Soc. of United States*, 68 N.D. 641, 282 N.W. 411 (1938); *State* v. *New York Life Insurance Company*, 198 Ark. 820, 131 S.W. (2d) 639 (1939); *State* v. *Ham*, 54 Wyo. 148, 88 P. (2d) 484 (1939); *State* v. *Mutual Life Insurance Company of New York*, 189 Miss. 830, 196 So. 796 (1940); *State* v. *Lucas*, 348 Mo. 286, 153 S.W. (2d) 10 (1941); *Equitable Life Assurance Soc. of United States* v. *Hobbs*, 154 Kan. 1, 114 P. (2d) 871 (1941); and *Equitable Life Assurance Soc. of United States* v. *Johnson*, 53 Cal. App. (2d) 49, 127 P. (2d) 95 (1942).

and this value was recognized even by the court which rendered adverse holdings as to the taxability of annuity considerations. The result was that in many states such taxes were repealed, while in others they were reduced below the tax rate on life insurance premiums.

NEW FIELDS FOR INVESTMENT

As the group and individual annuity business grew rapidly during the war and immediate postwar years, additional millions of dollars became available for investment, and the Society sought to broaden its investment base. Some interesting investments resulted.

Early in 1950 Equitable embarked upon the largest of its company owned and operated real estate developments—Gateway Center in Pittsburgh. This project was but one phase in the physical rehabilitation of Pittsburgh which had begun some years earlier, and to achieve which many civic and political organizations combined their efforts.[79] The coordinating agency, the Allegheny Conference on Community Development, was activated by Richard King Mellon, President of the Pittsburgh Regional Planning Association in 1943. In May 1945 the Pennsylvania legislature enacted the Urban Redevelopment Law and later in the year the Pittsburgh Regional Planning Association presented to the Allegheny Conference plans for a Point Park project at the forks of the Ohio River. The Conference set up the Point Park Committee, under the chairmanship of Arthur B. Van Buskirk, Vice President, T. Mellon and Sons. A Study Committee was established and in July 1946 it proposed that twenty-three acres of a blighted commercial area lying just east of Point Park be redeveloped through private enterprise. The same month representatives of this Committee met with President Parkinson in the endeavor to enlist his interest in the redevelopment project. It appears that, at this time, the Pittsburgh representatives had in mind a housing project, rather than office buildings, on the area adjoining Point Park.[80] President

[79] For a general survey of Pittsburgh's redevelopment, see "Pittsburgh Rebuilds," *Fortune*, XLV (1952), June.

[80] President Parkinson was already interested in the possibilities of housing developments in Pennsylvania, for in April 1936 he sought an opinion from Mark Willcox, Jr., of the Philadelphia law firm of MacCoy, Brittain, Evans and Lewis as to the legality of Equitable's owning real estate in Pennsylvania for housing. Willcox replied that it appeared that Equitable had no such right for housing developments outside of slum areas. Thomas I. Parkinson to Thomas I. Parkinson, Jr., April 1, 1946, and reply, April 24, 1946. Parkinson files, Equitable Archives.

Parkinson wanted to know—"What about the smoke and floods?" He wished to look into the matter further before making a decision.

In November 1946 the Mayor and Council created the Redevelopment Authority of Pittsburgh—of which Mayor David L. Lawrence became chairman. Early in March 1947 President Parkinson sent Second Vice President John H. Muller of the Home Loan and Housing Department and Sterling Pierson to look over the situation in Pittsburgh. Mayor Lawrence and others escorted the visitors on a motor cavalcade through the city, but Muller was not impressed with the site chosen for Equitable's investment as being a desirable one for a housing project, so plans came to a standstill. Then Robert W. Dowling, Vice President of the construction firm of Starrett Brothers and Eken, suggested that Equitable undertake the construction of office buildings. An aerial photograph was taken of the proposed area, and office buildings superimposed thereon to give some idea of what the project would look like. Later in the month, the Real Estate Committee of the Equitable Board authorized a tentative agreement with the Redevelopment Authority and the purchase of a vital parcel of land in the project area for $150,000. In May the Pennsylvania legislature authorized foreign life insurance companies licensed to transact business within the commonwealth to "acquire, hold, mortgage, lease, and transfer real property," and in July the Supreme Court of Pennsylvania upheld the constitutionality of the Urban Redevelopment Law; in November the Court upheld the constitutionality of the law permitting insurance companies to invest in real estate.[81] In May 1949 certain members of the Real Estate Committee of Equitable's Board and two other directors went to Pittsburgh to survey the proposed project, and the Committee authorized acquisition of the designated real estate at an estimated cost of $10,000,000, the Society to redevelop the area and to negotiate leases with the proposed guaranteeing tenants. After President Parkinson satisfied himself that the flood problem was being taken care of by a series of upriver dams, he recommended that Equitable undertake to erect three office buildings. September 21, 1949, at the annual meeting of the Allegheny Conference, Equitable announced its decision to build Gateway Center, provided Pittsburgh tenants would sign up for long-term leases. After a number of Pitts-

[81] Act No. 92, 1947, P.L. 200, Sec. 341; *Belovsky* v. *Redevelopment Authority of City of Philadelphia et al.*, 54 A.2d 277; *Levis* v. *New York Life Insurance Company*, 55 A.2d 801.

burgh's leading corporations agreed to such leases, Equitable, February 14, 1950, entered into a contract with the Urban Redevelopment Authority for the building of Gateway Center. In May the Allegheny Conference on Community Development sponsored a dinner and program in honor of President Thomas I. Parkinson and Governor James H. Duff. The program listed the highlights of the Point Redevelopment Project—"A Dramatic Story in Civic Achievement, A Major Feature of Pittsburgh's Renaissance."

The site of Gateway Center was a historic one. Here at the junction of the Allegheny and Monongahela Rivers just two centuries earlier the empires of France and England had come together in a struggle for the Ohio, the gateway to the Great West. "Through this river-gate poured the tide of conquest, of trade, and of ideas which made America." Here, as well as at Quebec, was decided whether most of North America would be English or French. At the point of the triangle where the French had built Fort Duquesne in 1753 lay 35 acres which were beginning to be developed as Point State Park. Of the 23 acres—"more or less"—lying immediately to the east, Equitable originally purchased 16.[82] Demolition in the Point Park area began in May 1950 and in November Equitable began construction of the three office buildings. Since the land had been acquired in fee simple, and in part through the exercise of the power of eminent domain, Equitable, under its contract with the Urban Redevelopment Authority, agreed to build on only 25 to 33 per cent of the area, the remainder to be landscaped and available for public use; otherwise, there were no restrictions.

Plans for the buildings were prepared by a Board of Design composed of architects, engineers, and officers of the Society. They provided for buildings, cross-shaped in design, from 20 to 24 stories in height with outer walls of stainless steel panels; also for air-conditioning and fluorescent lighting.

The buildings, which were completed in 1952–53, provided more than a million square feet of office space. Equitable's investment in Gateway Center at the end of 1952 was $40,365,000, and the Society expected that with virtually full occupancy under 20-year leases it would receive a net return of 4 per cent after allowing for 2 per cent amortization annually. Prior to Equitable's signing the contract with the Urban

[82] The seven remaining acres consisted of streets and five properties within the project area. Among the latter were a garage, the Pittsburgh Press Building, and a City Police Station.

Redevelopment Authority eight firms had made commitments to lease 42 per cent of the office space in the three buildings. These sponsoring or "basic tenants" were the Jones and Laughlin Steel Corporation, Westinghouse Electric Corporation, Pittsburgh Plate Glass Company, Peoples Natural Gas Company, National Supply Company, Westinghouse Air Brake Company, Mellon National Bank and Trust Company, and Joseph Horne Company.[83] Even so, renting the office space proved somewhat more difficult than had been anticipated. The Aluminum Company of America and United States Steel had built their own buildings and some prospective lessees failed to become tenants. Among the other tenants of the first three Gateway buildings were Bucyrus-Erie Company, Hercules Powder Company, the Southern Railway System, and Capital Airlines, Incorporated; also the Equitable's Pittsburgh organization, the New York Life Insurance Company, and the Penn Mutual Life Insurance Company.

In undertaking the Gateway Center investment in Pittsburgh's Golden Triangle, Equitable "bit off a large bite." Furnishing mortgage money for such a large enterprise was one thing, but becoming the promoter-entrepreneur-owner was something else. With only three buildings on land adequate for ten or eleven buildings, most of the land was nonproductive. A few of Equitable's directors had their doubts regarding Gateway, and as new directors came on to the Board, some of them, not being familiar with the beginnings of the project, became critical of it and thought it might be well to "give it back to the Indians." Investment-minded directors could appreciate a good bond which started drawing interest immediately after purchase, but did not value so highly a real estate investment which would have to balance out over a period of 25 or 30 years. To reduce the investment somewhat, Equitable in 1954 sold land to the Commonwealth of Pennsylvania for a 16-story State Office Building, and to Bell Telephone Company of Western Pennsylvania for a 12-story branch headquarters building. The Society retained the remainder of the land, with responsibility for taxes, landscaping, and maintenance. Then in 1956 Hilton Hotels Corporation agreed to build a 22-story 800-room hotel on land leased from Equitable, Equitable to furnish the mortgage money—$12,000,000—on a 30-year bond. The hotel was opened late in 1959.[84] In 1957

[83] As of December 31, 1963, seven of these "basic tenants" occupied 68 per cent of the rentable area of the first three Gateway buildings.

[84] Conrad Hilton, who had not yet embarked upon his round-the-world hotel enterprises, had never been to Pittsburgh. But after being entertained by Equitable

Equitable began construction of a three-level underground garage with space for 750 cars. Frank H. Briggs, who had a broad background in real estate management, was brought to the Equitable in 1955 as Second Vice President, to serve under the direction of Vice President John H. Muller in the management of the Pittsburgh complex.

In 1958, with the original three buildings fully rented, Equitable decided to build No. 4 Gateway Center. This building, which was ready for occupancy October 1, 1960, was 22 stories high and had an outer skin of glass with the panes set in slender stainless steel framing. Principal tenant in this building was Crucible Steel Company of America. Equitable's Pittsburgh agency offices also moved into this building from No. 1 Gateway Center. In December 1961 ground was broken for the International Business Machines Building. This 13-story building was the first in which a new structural concept was employed—or rather it was a return to an earlier day when the walls bore the structural load; four giant structural steel trusses constituted the sides of the building and thus supported the whole without interior columns to consume space.[85] The IBM building—sometimes called No. 5 Gateway Center—with its striking exterior of stainless steel and diamond-shaped windows of both clear and opaque glass stands out in marked contrast to the other buildings. It was ready for occupancy in January 1964.

In 1963 Equitable leased land to Tracco Gateway Incorporated, a subsidiary of Tishman Realty and Construction Company, Incorporated, and construction of a 27-story apartment building (Gateway Towers) was begun, on land adjacent to the Pittsburgh-Hilton Hotel. This addition to Gateway Center was financed by an Equitable mortgage and has been operated by the Tracco Company. The building was ready for occupancy in the spring of 1964. The small amount of undeveloped Gateway Center land—possibly enough for one more building—provides welcome parking facilities.

One of Gateway's most impressive features is its park-like appearance. The open spaces cover approximately 70 per cent of the land; on them are beautiful lawns, colorful flower beds, and pin oak, gum, and other trees which color beautifully in the autumn. Separating the three original buildings is the plat on which the bronze and granite "Fountain

---

Director Arthur B. Van Buskirk and shown a view of Pittsburgh by night from the top of the U.S. Steel building, he decided favorably on the hotel project.

[85] Said *Steel Facts*, No. 181 (April 1964): "The world's two tallest buildings planned for lower Manhattan's World Trade Center will employ the steel framing concept first used in the Gateway 5 building in Pittsburgh."

of the Three Rivers" is located; overhead float the United States and Equitable flags. In the spring, this fountain is converted into "the largest Easter basket in the World," and at Christmas time it serves as a pedestal for a large illuminated Christmas tree. During the summer months the fountain area is the locale for lunch-hour band concerts. Equitable Plaza occupies the two-acre area above the underground garage; with its spray pools, scores of trees, and hundreds of shrubs, the plaza has become a sort of focal point for Gateway Center.

A number of lawsuits resulted from, or impinged upon, Equitable's Gateway venture. Representative of the lot were the cases of *Imberman et al.* v. *Alexander et al*, and *Garfield* v. *Equitable Life Assurance Society of the United States et al.*, which will be discussed later in this chapter.[86]

By the end of 1964 Equitable had slightly more than $73,000,000 invested in Gateway Center. Net income after depreciation on the first three buildings was 4.265 per cent and on the second three buildings 5.4 per cent; net income after depreciation on the total investment was 4.834 per cent.[87] Although Gateway was not one of Equitable's high-yielding investments, there were compensating features. As Vice President Muller said: "It [Gateway] has sometimes been described as 'America's Most Ambitious Municipal Face-Lifting Job,' and deserves special credit as the first nonfederal commercial redevelopment project ever carried on in this country." [88] And the *Pittsburgh Press:* "The amazing transformation of the lower downtown district from a beaten-up industrial district into one of the nation's most dramatic examples of urban redevelopment, the far-famed Gateway Center has been an inspiring spectacle. The Equitable Life Assurance Society, the re-developer which made this possible, is to be congratulated on the foresight which brought about this big, brilliant project." [89]

* * *

One of the significant business developments in the life insurance field during 1950 was the inauguration of Equitable's plan for purchasing freight cars and diesel locomotives and leasing them to the railroads. "Purchase and leaseback" was not new to Equitable, but its

86 See this history, pp. 1215–1216, 1227–1232.

87 The figures are taken from the report of Vice President Frank H. Briggs to Senior Vice President John H. Muller, January 15, 1965.

88 John H. Muller, "The Pittsburgh Story—a Renaissance Through Engineering." *Stevens Indicator,* July 1958.

89 The *Pittsburgh Press,* June 24, 1960.

application to rolling stock of railroads was an innovation in the field of life company investments.[90]

About four years earlier, Vice President Glenn McHugh and the real estate men had been discussing a proposed mortgage on Safeway Stores, Incorporated, a chain of supermarkets located mostly on the West Coast. Safeway wanted to sell its stores (real estate and buildings) and then rent them from the owner. Usually under such arrangements, the purchaser would put up one-third of the price and seek mortgage money for the remaining two-thirds; he would pay all the taxes and carrying charges on 4½ per cent mortgage loans, but usually received about 10 per cent on his third of the investment. Someone asked why Equitable could not put up the full purchase price. When McHugh pointed out that the law did not permit this, President Parkinson suggested that it might be possible to get the law changed. When the Life Insurance Association showed no interest, Equitable went to the legislature, where it was successful in securing the amendment to Section 81 of the Insurance Law which permitted life insurance companies to purchase certain classes of income-producing property up to 3 per cent of their assets. The amendment became law in March 1946.

Safeway Stores, however, was not the first sale and leaseback investment to be made by Equitable. Following enactment of the amendment, the Real Estate Committee of the Equitable Board approved purchase of six properties totaling $18,590,000. Among them were the block in Boston occupied by William Filene's Sons, the northeast corner of Fifth Avenue and East Fifty-Sixth Street, New York City, occupied by Bonwit Teller, and Alexander's on Third Avenue, the Bronx, New York. The first sale and leaseback contract executed was that with Sun-Ray Drug Company, Atlantic City, New Jersey, January 6, 1947. During the remainder of 1947, purchase-lease agreements were made with Filene's, Bonwit Teller, American Machine and Foundry Company, Fruehauf Trailer Company, and Westinghouse Electric;

[90] For an excellent introduction to the subject, see Glenn McHugh and Hunter Holding, "Purchase and Leaseback, Another Investment Field for Life Insurance Companies," *The Journal of the American Society of Chartered Life Underwriters*, IX (1954–55). For a sketch of McHugh's career, see this history, p. 1012. Hunter Holding, after graduating from Yale in 1926, had had several years of banking and investment counsel experience. He joined Equitable in 1937 as an investment assistant. In 1944 he was transferred to the Investment Department as Manager of Railroad Securities. He was appointed Second Vice President in 1953, and elected Vice President in 1959.

total investment at the end of the year was $24,716,000.[91] The following year 20 additional properties of Safeway Stores were purchased, 14 in New York City and six in other states. Other purchase and lease agreements were later made with Allied Stores Corporation, Federated Department Stores, Incorporated, Sears Roebuck and Company, Wieboldt Stores, Incorporated, and R. H. Macy and Company. Two Safeway properties were sold by Equitable for $57,835 in 1949 and the remaining 19 in 1954 for $1,668,365 cash, which gave Equitable a small profit in addition to the return on the leases. The lease agreements ran from nine to 50 years, with the majority being in the 25 to 35 year group; rentals ran from 4.65 to 5 per cent for a net yield on the investment of about 4 per cent. Some of the agreements provided for renewals of 10 to 20 years.

The acquisition of investment real estate opened new vistas of investment opportunity beyond the one-tenant net lease acquisitions which had been the normal pattern with Equitable; in addition it offered advantages to owners of multi-tenanted properties under gross leases, who saw an opportunity to sell out for cash with a capital gain. For the purchaser, it offered a higher yield than could be expected by way of the more conventional financing plans, since, if the property was wisely chosen and well leased, the tenant could receive part of the returns available to the entrepreneur. In the case of leasebacks the lessee received full financing and, if the real estate was carried on the books as a fixed asset, could transform this asset into working capital; in addition, there were usually tax advantages.[92] On the other hand, there were various problems which both owner and tenant had to face.[93] Since the owner was engaged in practically 100 per cent financing, and his controls and remedies were limited, it was incumbent upon him to restrict his purchases to those businesses with the very best credit; and for accepting the responsibilities of ownership, he

91 Figures are taken from the annual report of the City Mortgage Department to the President.

92 Where the tax benefit through rental expense is large compared with interest and depreciation allowances, this fact is usually sufficient to make the decision in favor of the sale and lease agreement. Other factors were involved in addition to those mentioned above, such as the favorable effect on a company's stock market position resulting from the elimination of funded debt, and the facility of financing expansion by way of rental payments as compared to stock issues or secured borrowings involving SEC registration and public offering.

93 For these problems, see above mentioned article by Glenn McHugh and Hunter Holding.

should expect a yield at least one per cent higher than attainable from conventional mortgage financing. Most of Equitable's purchase-lease investments in the early years were confined to the retail merchandise field, but later the program was expanded to include shopping centers, office buildings, filling stations, and industrial plants. By 1959 the Society's investments of this type totaled $93,411,000.

Sometime in 1949, Champ Carry, President of Pullman-Standard Car Manufacturing Company, conferred with Associate Counsel Warner H. Mendel and President Parkinson in regard to the possibility of Equitable's financing the purchase of freight cars through a third party, such as a charity organization; Equitable would finance the charity, which would purchase the cars and lease them to the railroads. The pattern had been established by a number of universities and colleges, including Yale and Union College, which were acquiring commercial properties. Mendel asked why it would not be possible for Equitable to handle the purchase and leaseback without bringing a third party into the picture. After he convinced the New York Insurance Department as to the legality of such a plan, the Finance Committee of the Board gave its approval and the plan was announced in March 1950.[94] Equitable then purchased 1,300 freight cars and simultaneously leased them for 15 years to the Atlantic Coast Line Railroad Company.

Under the terms of the lease, the railroad agreed to pay rental on the cars on a per diem basis sufficient to assure a return of the Society's investment by the end of 15 years, with 3 per cent interest for the period. The railroad was given an option to lease the cars for an additional ten-year period at a greatly reduced per diem rental. The

[94] February 9, 1950, Mendel wrote Raymond Harris, Deputy Superintendent of Insurance and Counsel, that "a somewhat unusual investment opportunity has been presented which involves an interpretation of Section 81(4)(b) of the New York Insurance Law." This section permitted life insurance companies to invest in "Equipment trust obligations or certificates which are adequately secured or other adequately secured instruments evidencing an interest in transportation equipment wholly or in part within the United States and a right to receive determined portions of rental, purchase or other fixed obligatory payments for the use or purchase of such transportation equipment."

Mendel explained that Equitable would pay 80 per cent of the purchase price to the car builders in cash and 20 per cent in a form of unsecured contingent obligation payable monthly, with 2 per cent interest on declining balances over a period of five years. The Society's obligation to the car builder was conditioned on the payment of rent by the railroad. Copy in Warner H. Mendel files, Equitable Archives.

railroad assumed the obligation of maintaining the cars, and in the event of loss or destruction the railroad was obligated to pay the Society the balance of the rentals due on such cars, plus their salvage value; at the expiration of the term of the lease, or at any time during the extended lease, the Society might direct the railroad to deliver the cars for its account to properly qualified scrap dealers. The lease provided for the customary remedies on default. In figuring its yield Equitable included the scrap value.

Since all major railroad lines were endeavoring to become completely dieselized, the next step was to extend purchase-lease operations to diesel locomotives. The arrangements for locomotives varied slightly from those applying to freight cars. For the locomotives, Equitable agreed to pay the manufacturer 90 per cent of the cost in cash and the remaining 10 per cent in equal installments over a period of three years. Under the agreement with the railroad, Equitable leased the locomotives for a period of 15 years on a quarterly rental scale; at the end of the 15-year period, the railroad had the option of returning the locomotives to Equitable for scrapping or of continuing to lease them for an additional period up to ten years at a nominal rental. During the period of lease, the lessee was obliged to maintain the locomotives in good order, repair them at its own expense, and carry insurance on them.[95]

By the end of 1950, Equitable had an investment of $24,056,473 in 5,864 freight cars and $14,440,672 in 111 diesel locomotives. In addition, it had signed contracts for an initial investment of $48,675,304 in 11,485 freight cars and $12,452,364 in 96 diesel locomotives, and had authorized other contracts for an investment of $6,870,128 in 1,500 freight cars. The total cost of the equipment acquired or to be acquired was $129,852,500 for 207 diesel locomotives and 18,850 freight cars. By 1958 Equitable had invested more than $200,000,000 in railroad equipment, and some 22,000 freight cars and more than 500

[95] The locomotives were insured by the railroad for their book value, that is, the balance due on the cost of the locomotive plus future rentals discounted to present value. The insurance obligation did not apply to freight cars because the investment in each individual car was relatively small, and at any one time the freight cars would be widely scattered over the United States on many different railroads; in the event of destruction, the line on which the car was destroyed paid the owner. On the other hand, the locomotives cost from $100,000 to $200,000 each and were confined almost exclusively to the lessee's lines, sometimes with four or five of them being used in one train. Thus there was less automatic spreading of the risks in the case of the locomotives.

diesel locomotives were traveling the rails of the country carrying the identification plate on which is inscribed "Equitable Life Assurance Society, Owner and Lessor." By 1963, Equitable's total investment in railroad equipment was $225,986,000, but the maximum total outstanding at any time—$114,421,000—was reached at the end of 1956.

Equitable had not entered into the financing of railroad equipment on the impulse of the moment. A series of studies made in 1948 and 1949 had indicated that the Class I railroads needed about $4,500,000,000 of new diesel locomotives and about $5,500,000,000 of new freight cars in order to cut operating and maintenance costs to a minimum.[96] While population, railroad freight traffic, and demands per capita for railroad freight traffic had increased, the number of freight cars owned by Class I railroads had decreased. Prior to this time, the conventional method of financing the railroads' needs for rolling stock had been the "Equipment Trust," or so-called "Philadelphia Plan"; the Conditional Sale Agreement was also used. These methods did not solve the problem, for the railroads frequently could not afford the 20 per cent cash down payment, nor, with 25-year depreciation rates, could they afford the 15-year installment payments out of net income after taxes. Consequently, the roads tended to limit their equipment purchases to years of good earnings instead of spreading them out more evenly to coincide with their normal replacement needs. The effect upon the equipment manufacturer was "prince and pauper" years, depending upon railroad earnings. Under the purchase-lease plan, the railroads were able to reduce their expenses for maintenance as a result of having the use of relatively new equipment all the time; rental, under the arrangement, was deductible as an expense for tax purposes.

Equitable's announcement of its purchase-lease plan as applied to railroad equipment received considerable publicity. Said *The Journal of Commerce:* "Equitable's Plan Alarms Wall Street." The article indicated that "there was no dancing in Wall Street" because investment bankers were worried lest the plan curtail their business in railroad equipment trust certificates.[97] Some opponents of the plan

[96] Memorandum from Hunter Holding, May 21, 1958, to author.

[97] *The Journal of Commerce,* March 28, 1950.

Ben Merson, in an article in *Collier's,* August 2, 1952, entitled "Insurance Companies: What Do They Do With All That Money?" gave about one column to Equitable and its purchase-lease of real estate, factories, and railroad equipment. The article gave a fair coverage of the subject, but the interesting thing was the brief editorial on the article in the same issue: "We imagine that most of Mr. Merson's

Money for life!

You can't outlive your income with an annuity from Equitable

Retirement can be a great time in your life—if you don't have to worry about your money running out.

With an annuity from Equitable you never have that worry.

You get a regular income every month—without fail—for as long as you live. Even if you live to 100.

That's the beauty of an Equitable annuity. Financial independence with absolute security.

For complete information about annuities that meet your specific needs, call The Man from Equitable. He has the knowledge and experience to help you plan a retirement free of financial worries.

P.S.: It's a fact that more people have come to Equitable for annuities than to any other insurance company in the world.

LIVING INSURANCE...FROM EQUITABLE

THE EQUITABLE LIFE ASSURANCE SOCIETY OF THE UNITED STATES

Home Office: 1285 Avenue of the Americas, New York, N. Y. 10019 ©1964

Advertisement, 1964

argued that it possessed no advantage over the equipment trust, under which up to 100 per cent financing could be arranged. And a spokesman for one of the largest life companies said that his company definitely opposed the plan as presenting a serious threat to railroad credit.[98] On the other hand, many railroad executives favored the plan because under it the insurance company took the risk of obsolescence in the equipment, and most of the equipment manufacturing company officers thought that it had tremendous possibilities.[99]

Highly critical of the plan was Congressman Emanuel Celler of New York who headed the House of Representatives inquiry into monopoly power. While admitting that it appeared to be sound and helpful to the railroad industry, he feared that, if other insurance companies adopted it, the railroads might find themselves in the position of being completely controlled by the life insurance companies. This possibility emphasized the need for a thorough exploration of the ever-growing magnitude of life company assets and the lack of proper and organized state supervision. He said that the life companies which rented cars to railroad companies might find themselves in the anomalous position of coming under the jurisdiction of the Interstate Commerce Commission by the back door. Although he doubted whether the ICC was the proper agency to take over this job, he was convinced of the need for Federal regulation of the insurance companies.[100] The Interstate Commerce Commission in its annual report for 1949–50 said that the Equitable plan presented "questions as to the merits for financing a carrier's equipment requirements" and posed "some serious accounting problems which were now under con-

---

readers will be surprised to learn that insurance companies are the principal sources of money for capital expenditures in this country, and that their investments in the nation's economy are so vast and diverse. We hope that the surprise is a pleasant one. It was for us."

98 *The Journal of Commerce,* June 12, 1950.

99 See also *ibid.,* September 15 and 22, 1950; *The Wall Street Journal,* March 27, 1950; *The New York Times,* March 29, 1950; *Best's Weekly Life Bulletin* (April 3, 1950); *The Eastern Underwriter,* LI (1950), March 31; *The National Underwriter,* LIV (1950), Life edition, March 31; *Business Week,* April 8, 1950; and *The Spectator,* CLVII (1950), May.

100 *The New York Times,* March 29, 1950; *The National Underwriter,* LIV (1950), March 31; and *The Spectator,* CLVII (1950), May. Said *The Spectator:* "So the New Yorker, who has been sniffing about for the slightest excuse to grab the insurance business, tie it hand and foot, and deliver it to Washington bureaucracy, let out a howl of dismay recently at the Equitable announcement. . . . But few Congressmen can see what all the shouting is about."

sideration." The Commission recommended that Congress amend the Interstate Commerce Act so as to make the Commission's approval necessary for contracts under which equipment was leased to the railroads. The report observed that insurance companies, as "persons" furnishing cars to railroads, would be subject to inspection of records by the ICC. No such legislation was enacted.

Within ten years after Equitable's introduction of sale and lease-back, the leasing of all types of equipment became general. The sales of heavy machinery and automobile manufactures were greatly increased by the adoption of leasing.

* * *

For various reasons Equitable did not extend its purchase-lease plan to the financing of airline equipment. It did, however, in 1945, make its first investment in securities of the airline industry when it purchased $10,000,000 (of a $30,000,000 commitment) of Trans World Airlines debentures. This loan pioneered long-term financing of air transportation by financial institutions. Prior to this time no insurance company had purchased any long-term bonds of any air transport company, bank lending had generally been short term and for nominal amounts, and one carrier had issued short-term equipment trust certificates to three institutions. In 1946 Equitable purchased publicly $20,000,000 of American Airlines securities. By 1959 Equitable was also making loans to Eastern Airlines and to Braniff Airways. The Society's investments in airline securities reached a maximum of $279,217,000 by the end of 1964 which amount represented almost 10.3 per cent of its industrial bond portfolio (not including real estate bonds) and about 17.2 per cent of the total funded indebtedness of United States certified trunk airlines (including Pan American). This figure included $99,400,000 of TWA bonds.

Equitable investment association with TWA and its central figure Howard Hughes was an interesting and complicated one. In 1939 Howard Hughes, President and sole owner of the Hughes Tool Company, together with Jack Frye, President of TWA, and Robert Gross, President of Lockheed Aircraft Corporation, conceived the idea of building a four-motor airplane—the Constellation, which they hoped would be superior to the Boeing Model 307 "Stratoliner," and competitive with the Douglas DC-4; TWA was to receive the first models. This association between Hughes and Frye led early in 1940 to the acquisition by the Tool Company of approximately 160,000 shares of

TWA stock from John Hertz, and immediately thereafter to the sale by TWA to the Tool Company of approximately 119,000 shares of common stock for about $1,670,000. The purpose of the stock sale by TWA was to permit that company to purchase from Boeing Aircraft five Model 307 four-motor "Stratoliner" aircraft to be delivered in mid-1940. TWA had been unable to obtain satisfactory financing for this acquisition through normal banking channels. The Tool Company subsequently increased its ownership of TWA common stock from about 21 per cent at the end of 1940 to 46 per cent by the end of 1945. At no time during this period had the Tool Company elected a representative to TWA's Board.

In 1945, following World War II, when the Government relaxed its military orders for Lockheed Constellation aircraft, TWA immediately moved to exercise its right to Constellations for use in its domestic and international service. Equitable then purchased the remaining $20,000,000 of TWA's 1945 debenture issue and an additional $10,-000,000 of a new series—thus making a total of $40,000,000. For 1946, primarily as a result of a 25-day pilot strike in May followed by the grounding by the Civil Aeronautics Board of all Constellation aircraft in July, TWA reported a loss of $14,400,000. During the latter part of that year the Tool Company began taking an increasingly active part in all phases of TWA management, and late in the year indicated dissatisfaction with the management to President Parkinson and other Equitable representatives. Despite the fact that TWA had borrowed $40,000,000 from Equitable, its cash position by the end of 1946 had so deteriorated that it was forced to arrange to borrow an additional $40,000,000 from the Reconstruction Finance Corporation and to cancel orders for several Constellations. By this time TWA management was meeting weekly, almost frantically, in the endeavor to resolve its financial problems. At President Parkinson's request a meeting was held in his office early in January 1947 with Howard Hughes and representatives of the RFC, the CAB, and the Tool Company. Eventually a plan was developed—to be effective at the end of the month—to delay repayments on the Society's loan provided the Tool Company advanced $5,000,000 to TWA by January 31, 1947, and an additional $5,000,000 by May 29, 1947. As a condition TWA, Hughes Tool Company and the Equitable entered into the "Three-Party Agreement" under which the Tool Company's 46 per cent stock ownership of TWA would, in the event either of failure of the Tool Company to lend TWA the $10,000,000 or failure of TWA to meet interest or principal payments on its debt to the Equitable, be placed in a ten-year voting trust. No action under the Three-Party Agreement was ever taken.

President Frye, together with other senior officers, resigned early in 1947 and the Tool Company lent $10,000,000 to TWA. This loan was shortly converted into approximately 1,034,000 shares of TWA stock which increased the Tool Company ownership to about 73 per cent. The Board elected one of its members to the presidency but he resigned in June 1948. At the end of 1947 the National Association of Insurance Commissioners required Equitable to use a market value of 75 per cent of its investment in TWA in its 1947 Annual Statement, and decreased this market value to 60 per cent at the end of 1948. During this period Equitable policyholders and agents continued to write President Parkinson asking for explanations of the Society's position on its TWA investment and questioning the impact of the lower market value on Equitable's dividend apportionments.

In January 1949 Hughes selected Ralph Damon, then President of American Airlines, to be President and Chief Executive Officer of TWA. During Damon's seven years of tenure TWA attained its greatest sustained success in maintaining its competitive position and operating profit margins against other domestic and international United States certified carriers. By late 1954 the Company had re-established its financial standing and Equitable agreed to refinance the loans originally made in 1945 and 1946—which had been reduced to approximately $15,000,000—with a new $40,000,000 secured loan. The $25,000,000 of new money together with Company funds was to be used to purchase 20 modern Model 1049 Constellations. After this purchase TWA would own a fleet of 171 aircraft of which 101 would be Constellations.

President Damon died in January 1956 and TWA again found itself without strong leadership. Meanwhile, in October 1955 Pan American placed orders with Boeing and Douglas for jet airplanes to be delivered starting in December 1958 and December 1959 respectively; American and Eastern prior to the end of 1955 also placed orders for jet aircraft. Finally, in February 1956 the Hughes Tool Company placed an order for eight Boeing jets which it was generally assumed would be for TWA, notwithstanding failure of either of these companies to arrange financing to pay for these aircraft. Although the Company was acquiring jet engines and spare parts and was training ground and flight personnel in jet operations, it owned no jet aircraft, and had no assurance that adequate jet equipment would become available. It was competing domestically (1959–60) and internationally (1960) with a limited number of jets on daily lease from the Hughes Tool Company.

In December 1956 the Tool Company selected and the TWA Board elected Carter Burgess, an Assistant Secretary of Defense, President of the Company. Burgess resigned after twelve months of frustration and no successor was elected until July 1958 when Charles Thomas, former Navy Secretary, was elected President. Thomas resigned after disagreements with Hughes in June 1960. Thus during the period of four and one-half years ending June 30, 1960, TWA was without a President for almost one-third of the time; when it did have a President, he was often unable to communicate with Hughes directly. Only in 1959 was TWA able to compete with its major domestic competitors by maximum utilization of fifteen Boeing jet airplanes leased from the Tool Company; thereafter its competitive position declined drastically through 1961.

Recognizing the importance of TWA to the national air transport industry, the Finance Committee of Equitable's Board in March 1960 authorized the Society to participate in $190,000,000 of senior debt financing of TWA in an amount not to exceed $45,000,000. The proceeds of this loan, together with its own funds and the proceeds from the sale of $100,000,000 of subordinated debt to the Hughes Tool Company were to be used to refinance TWA's outstanding indebtedness and to take over contracts to purchase up to 52 jet airplanes, spare engines and parts involving in the aggregate about $340,000,000, which the Tool Company had previously entered into with Boeing and General Dynamics. This maximum $190,000,000 of senior debt was to be purchased from TWA—$90,000,000 due in four years by the banks, and $100,000,000 maturing in the last five years by insurance companies. In connection with this financing, the Hughes Tool Company and Howard Hughes agreed, under certain circumstances, to place all the TWA stock owned by the Tool Company (approximately 78 per cent) with an agent under an agreement providing for the creation of a voting trust; this agent was to have the power to appoint a majority of the voting Trustees (with the Tool Company appointing the other Trustees). Any change in management considered by the senior debt holders to be materially adverse to their interest, and not corrected in a stipulated time, was deemed to be an actionable default under this proposed Loan Agreement. The legal documents for this borrowing were in their final form in late June 1960 when TWA's President Thomas resigned; this financing therefore was never consummated.

Thereafter the Tool Company sought determinedly from many sources for ways and means both of extricating TWA and the Tool Company from impending disaster; also of enabling TWA to purchase the jet equipment from the Tool Company and the manufacturers without requiring the Tool Campany to place its TWA stock in a voting trust. At one point the lender banks exercised their rights of offset and seized all TWA and Tool Company deposits as partial satisfaction for their defaulted loans. By December 1960 all efforts by the Tool Company to secure the needed financing elsewhere had failed and it was necessary for TWA and the Tool Company once again to negotiate financing with the original groups of banks and insurance companies. So on December 15 arrangements were made to place the 78.2 per cent of TWA stock owned by the Hughes Tool Company into a voting trust controlled by some fifteen banks and the Equitable and the Metropolitan life insurance companies; the voting trust was to terminate December 15, 1970. As a result of this financing, by the end of 1960 Equitable and Metropolitan had purchased from TWA in equal proportions a total of $92,800,000 of senior debt, a group of banks, headed by the Irving Trust, had agreed to purchase $72,200,000 of shorter maturing senior debt ranking *pari passu* with the longer maturities purchased by the insurance companies, and the Hughes Tool Company had purchased $100,000,000 of Subordinated Debentures.

From October 23, 1945, when the Finance Committee first authorized a purchase of TWA securities, through December 31, 1960, Equitable had officially acted upon about ninety separate requests for changes in TWA financing, either through modification of loan covenants or to effect additional purchases of TWA securities. In this fifteen-year period the Society's knowledge of the problems involved in air transportation and air transportation financing was broadened and expanded immeasurably, especially as it applied to TWA.

Early in 1961 following the consummation of the December 1960 financing, most of the Hughes representatives on the TWA Board resigned and were replaced with independent outstanding businessmen selected by the trustees of the voting trust. The trustees, headed by Ernest Breech, former Ford Motor Company Chairman, in April 1961 selected Charles Carpenter Tillinghast, Jr., Vice President of the Bendix Corporation, to be the new President of TWA. The new President, realizing that TWA was far short of the number of jet planes needed to enable it to compete with its chief rivals, almost immediately decided to order 26 Boeing 707s. The new equipment program required about $147,000,000 of senior debt in addition to that included in the 1960 financing. In May Equitable and the Metropolitan each agreed to purchase $53,500,000 of senior debt and the banks to purchase $40,000,000.

In June 1961, TWA sued Hughes, the Tool Company, and Raymond Holliday (its chief financial officer) for $115,000,000 (later increased to $145,000,000) as triple damages for breach of Federal antitrust laws with an additional request that the Tool Company be divested of its stock ownership in TWA. Among other things the suit charged that Hughes had forced the Company to buy planes that did not fit its needs. In February 1962 the Tool Company filed its answer to the TWA suit and a counterclaim naming as defendants not only TWA but also TWA's major creditors and the investment firm of Dillon, Read and Company, Incorporated, together with some of their senior officers.

In 1961 TWA operated at a loss of about $38,700,000, but under the new management its fortunes began to mend. Improved equipment, greater capacity, new terminals, increased efficiency, and increased air travel enabled the Company to handle an increasing share of the air travel market. By the end of 1964 net income increased to more than $37,000,000 and the credit position of TWA had been restored. At this time Equitable owned $99,400,000 of 6 and 6½ per cent obligations which had been acquired during the period December 1960 to December 1964. In February 1965 TWA paid its first cash dividend —25 cents—in 30 years. In March 1965 the United States Supreme Court dismissed the Hughes Tool Company's appeal from a lower court decision which ordered judgement (subject to assessment of damages) in favor of TWA in its antitrust suit against Hughes and dismissed on the merits Hughes' counterclaim against the lending institutions. In May 1966, Hughes sold his 6,584,937 shares of TWA stock (including the 5,221,301 shares assigned under the Voting Trust) for $546,500,000, or about six times his original investment. The proceedings to assess damages in the TWA suit against Hughes were still pending.[101]

* * *

101 The above account of Equitable's investment in TWA was based largely upon material furnished by Equitable's Securities Investment Department. See also *Time*, LXXXVIII (1966), July 22.

One of the most troublesome post-World War II oil and gas loans was that made to Glenn McCarthy. So interesting is the story, so wide was the publicity given it, and so complicated were the steps taken to protect the policyholder's money, that treatment somewhat out of proportion to the amount involved may be justified.

The McCarthy career was one of the more fabulous in a region noted for spectacular careers. McCarthy was the son of an oil field workman and started his plunging early in life. While still in his early twenties, he made some money from a service station and a dry cleaning business. He put his savings into a wildcat oil drilling venture, drilled several dry holes, and then, when both his credit and drilling were about exhausted, hit oil in a big way in the Conroe field some forty miles north of Houston. Other successful discoveries followed and McCarthy came to be known as the "King of the Wildcatters." [102]

The Equitable loans were to the McCarthy Oil and Gas Corporation (incorporated in Delaware in 1945) to which McCarthy had transferred all of his oil and gas properties. So successful had he become by the 1940's that he had built a $700,000 home, acquired a radio station, bought the 22-story Shell Building, built up a string of weekly newspapers, organized an export company, launched a petrochemical company, and was planning the Shamrock Hotel which he intended to make the social center of Houston and thereby direct the city's growth to the south where he had substantial landholdings.[103]

Lending money to the integrated petroleum and gas industry was not a new experience to Equitable, but making oil production loans was. Between 1929 and 1944 the Society had invested some $217,513,000 in the bonds and debentures of natural gas pipeline and integrated oil companies. Fundamentally, the security for these bonds consisted of oil and gas reserves in places either owned or subject to

[102] One of McCarthy's biographers said that he was not typical of early day wildcatters, for his lightning-like decisions were based on a combination of scientific advice, practical information, and a rare intuition for oil probability. He would more properly be called a "field stretcher" than a true wildcatter. See Wallace Davis, *Corduroy Road* (Houston, 1951).

[103] McCarthy Oil and Gas Company had been operated since 1939 as an individual proprietorship. According to *The Houston Press*, April 9, 1952, McCarthy was unable to get credit to landscape the mansion which he had built on a ten-acre estate on Brae's Bayou, so he bought—on credit—the landscape company which had refused to do the job. After he finished the landscaping on his own place, he sold the landscape company at a profit of $1,500.

contract. In the case of production loans Equitable had, therefore, to decide whether it could properly rely upon the reports of independent engineers as to the nature and amount of such reserves which were subject to its liens. After extensive investigation it concluded that it could, and that reliance upon oil and gas as adequate security was not a departure from the Society's previously established policy. In reaching this decision Equitable was guided in part by the opinions of Director Eugene P. Locke, its Texas counsel, and Edward N. Maher, its City Mortgage Department's Southwestern Loan Supervisor. Vice President Meredith C. Laffey did not favor expansion into oil production loans because he believed that there was no adequate expert staff to watch over them, but Vice President McHugh and President Parkinson were satisfied that independent experts could be retained when needed.

In May 1945, Equitable established an Oil Loan Division in its Dallas office, with Ernest Eppenaur, a well-informed oil credit man, in charge of the development of a sound lending program, and in July the City Mortgage Department recommended an oil production loan of $425,000, which was approved by both the Real Estate and Finance Committees of the Equitable Board in November. This loan, which was to run for not more than seven and one-half years at 4½ per cent, was secured by proved oil reserves under a 400-acre oil and gas lease in Crane County, Texas, together with all the equipment owned by the applicants. The loan was granted January 3, 1946.[104]

In the summer of 1945 McCarthy was seeking a loan sufficient to refund his existing indebtedness to the Republic National Bank of Dallas, to provide funds with which to begin construction of the Shamrock Hotel, and to provide him with free funds for exploration and the further development of oil and gas leases which he owned and hoped to obtain under farm-outs. An independent mortgage broker made contact with Maher and Director Locke, and in January 1946 negotiations with McCarthy's representatives culminated in the presentation of a formal application for a loan of $22,000,000, to bear

104 On oil loans prior to 1945, see tabulation made October 1, 1958, by B. Berggren, Investment Statistician. On the oil production loans, see Annual Report of Vice President Glenn McHugh of the City Mortgage Department to the President of Equitable, February 2, 1946. Copies in the Equitable Archives. See also "Statement Submitted by Vice President McHugh . . . at Hearing on Valuation of Oil Production Loans," May 15, 1946, to the National Association of Insurance Commissioners. Copy in Sterling Pierson files, Equitable Archives.

interest at the rate of 3½ per cent per annum. Of this amount, $15,000,000 was to be advanced at once and was to be repaid by fixed, minimum monthly payments to liquidate the loan in 11 years. Of the $15,000,000, all but $3,000,000 was to be applied to the payment of all outstanding indebtedness.[105]

Prior to the formal signing of the McCarthy application, Maher and Locke consulted with Ted Hall, petroleum geologist and engineer, as to the proper procedure for determining the quantity and market value of the McCarthy oil and gas reserves.[106] Since Hall was unable to make the required field examination and field tests, the firm of Knode and Dixon, Houston petroleum engineers, was selected to prepare the field report. After Hall reviewed this report, he estimated, in February 1946, that the market value of the producing and proved, but not producing, oil and gas reserves was approximately $45,000,000. On the strength of this report, Equitable, in April, advanced $15,000,000 and received a 3½ per cent promissory note from the McCarthy Oil and Gas Corporation.[107] In May 1947, a new Hall appraisal indicated a market

[105] At the time of the negotiation of the original application, all of the assets which were to be subjected to the Society's lien were held by McCarthy personally. Prior to the closing of the Society's loan, all producing and nonproducing acreage and interests in mineral leases were assigned by McCarthy to McCarthy Oil and Gas Corporation ("Oil and Gas"), a Delaware corporation. His gasoline plant was assigned to Absorption Plant, Incorporated, a Texas corporation. The pipelines constituting the gathering system for the plant and the delivery lines to purchasers of residue gas were assigned to Jefferson Pipe Line Company, a Texas corporation; and his contracts for the purchase and sale of gas were assigned to Neches Natural Gas Company, a Texas corporation. All these Texas corporations became wholly owned subsidiaries of Oil and Gas. (Report of Associate Counsel Warner H. Mendel to the Special Committee of the Board re McCarthy Oil and Gas Corporation, July 19, 1951.) This 20-page, single-spaced typescript was accompanied by maps which showed the producing acreage and pipeline systems, a summary of dates and amounts of advances, a summary of estimates of the value of the oil and gas reserves, and an organization chart for McCarthy Oil and Gas. Copy in Records of Special Committee of the Board re McCarthy Oil and Gas Corporation. Corporate Records, Equitable Archives.

[106] Hall's appointment was approved by both Director Locke and Director Edward L. Shea, former President of Tidewater Associated Oil Company and then President of The North American Company. Shea said that Hall was so conservative in his estimates that Equitable would probably not make any loan at all.

[107] This promissory note No. 1, as well as all future indebtedness of Oil and Gas to the Society, was secured by the lien of a Deed of Trust dated April 1, 1946, on all of the oil and gas producing and nonproducing properties owned at such date; all of the contracts for the purchase and sale of gas, whether owned by Oil and Gas or any of its subsidiaries; all of the outstanding stock of such subsidiaries; all of the bonds and notes of said subsidiaries owned by Oil and Gas; all of the issued and outstanding stock of Oil and Gas; and a commitment to subject to such lien

value of $61,900,000 for the McCarthy oil and gas holdings; another Hall appraisal of July 1948 raised the figure to $73,500,000. Additional loans by Equitable in 1947, 1948, and 1949 brought the total loans to $51,799,000, but adjusting for amortization the largest amount outstanding at any one time did not exceed $41,600,000.

Meanwhile, McCarthy had embarked upon two very pretentious projects—one the Shamrock Hotel, and the other his chemical plant. In addition, he built a pipeline to Port Neches and started the development of a new oil field. The hotel was originally planned as an apartment hotel surrounded by a shopping center, to be located about three miles south of Houston's business center. This plan was abandoned upon the advice of Equitable and other consultants, and the plan for McCarthy Center was limited to a hotel, garage, and swimming pool. The original estimates fixed the cost at approximately $12,000,000, but when completed in 1949 the total costs exceeded $21,000,000. Of this amount, Equitable advanced $5,000,000 and McCarthy Oil and Gas the remainder. The indebtedness to Oil and Gas was evidenced by a note and bond, both of which were pledged as security for the Society's loan to Oil and Gas. The Hotel was owned by McCarthy Center, Incorporated, a wholly owned subsidiary of Oil and Gas, all of the stock of which was pledged as further security.

The Shamrock Hotel—a green-hued 18-story building with 1,100 air-conditioned rooms—which was intended to be a social and entertainment center as well as a convention headquarters, was opened with elaborate ceremonies March 17, 1949. White doeskin invitations

---

all of the stock and debt of McCarthy Center, Incorporated, in the event that the loan of $5,000,000 from the Society to McCarthy Center, Incorporated, be consummated. In addition to the lien of the Deed of Trust, the Society's indebtedness was secured by an assignment of all the proceeds from the sale of severed minerals and mineral products, and 50 per cent of said proceeds were required to be assigned and paid over to the Second National Bank of Houston as trustee for the Society.

The producing reserves subjected to the Society's lien were located in the Angleton Field, Brazoria County; North Stowell Field in Chambers County; South Stowell Field in Jefferson County; Fannett Area in Jefferson County; Benavides Field in Duval County; West Beaumont Field in Jefferson County; Hardin Field in Liberty County; Coletto Creek Field in Victoria County; Blue Lake Field in Brazoria County; and Hankamer Field in Liberty County.

At this time, McCarthy had contracts to supply oil or gas with du Pont for its Sabine River Plant; with lower Neches Valley Authority; with Houston Oil Company of Texas; with Beaumont Natural Gas Company; with Peoples Gas Company for the purpose of supplying the city of Port Arthur; with Rubber Reserve Company; with Dow Chemical Company; and with Gulf States Utilities Company. Mendel report of July 19, 1951, cited above.

were flown to Latin American cities, 2,500 shamrocks were flown in from Ireland, and McCarthy chartered the Sante Fe's *Super Chief*—at $10,000—to bring in motion picture stars from Hollywood. Crowds milled around the center of activity, sirens screamed, extra policemen tried to keep order, and the searchlights swung their beams across the sky. The mob scenes at the reception would have done credit to Hollywood; some said they resembled the Fort Worth stockyards. The tide of people and champagne was endless. Most of the 2,500 guests dined in the Emerald, Shamrock, and Grecian rooms at $42 a plate, but several hundred were shunted to the Pine Grill at $33 a plate. It was an "incredible and perspiring event"—a party that startled even Texas. The following day, the Southwestern Bell Telephone Company "declared flatly" that the opening of the Shamrock ranked, as an emergency operation, with the Texas City disaster and the Galveston flood.

McCarthy's chemical plant was supposed to remove certain liquid petroleum gases from natural gas and by an oxidation process—the so-called Bloodworth Process—convert them into methanol, which was much in demand as an antifreeze additive.[108] Instead of trying out the process by way of a pilot operation, McCarthy jumped in full depth. The plant, which was estimated to cost less than $4,000,000, actually cost about $8,000,000. After many unsatisfactory experiments and costly changes of equipment, it was finally determined that the plant, as built, could not be operated successfully. It produced little or no methanol.[109] When it became evident to McCarthy and his associates that the cost of their construction program had far exceeded estimates and that they would need more funds, they approached Equitable for an additional loan based on the security of the plants and pipelines. Equitable turned down the loan but the officers of Oil and Gas, with the help of Kuhn, Loeb and Company succeeded in getting the Metropolitan Life (November 1, 1948) to advance $15,000,000 on first mortgage 4 per cent sinking fund bonds.[110] These bonds were secured

108 The process was supposed not seriously to affect the thermal units of the gas, which could be sold as dry gas.

109 Vice President and General Solicitor Warner H. Mendel to author, January 23, 1964.

110 As a preliminary step to the completion of this loan, the complicated relationship between Oil and Gas and its subsidiaries was simplified. Jefferson Pipe Line Company, Neches Natural Gas Company, and McCarthy Chemical Company (which had been formed to take title to the chemical plant) transferred all of their

by a lien on all of the Chemical Company plants and equipment, its pipelines, and the assignment of the interest of the Chemical Company under a contract with Oil and Gas for the purchase of not more than 200,000 MCF of gas per day. Under a Guaranty and Working Capital Agreement, Oil and Gas guaranteed the completion of Absorption Plant No. 2, and the capability of the chemical plant and the two absorption plants to produce and deliver certain quantities of LPG products and residue gas by August 1, 1949. The Agreement further obligated Oil and Gas to pay $175,000 plus operating deficits to the Chemical Company monthly and to supply it with sufficient working capital to operate its facilities at maximum efficiency. The Agreement was intended to provide the Chemical Company with sufficient funds to service the Metropolitan bonds.

Equitable agreed to the terms of the Guaranty and Working Capital Agreement, and the same month (January 1949) made a Loan Agreement with the McCarthy interests by which it agreed to the release of the plants, pipelines, and pledged securities other than the stock and subordinated indebtedness of the Chemical Company in consideration of the payment to the Society of $12,000,000. The same month Equitable advanced or promised to advance $8,000,000 to Oil and Gas. By August the Chemical Company was unable to comply with the terms of the Agreement with Metropolitan, since the Chemical Company was deriving no income from the operation of the chemical plant and the supply of gas coming from Oil and Gas was decreasing rapidly. The Metropolitan bonds went into default. At the very time that the Chemical Company was falling into default on the Metropolitan bonds, and Oil and Gas was applying in excess of 80 per cent of its gross income to the payment of carrying charges on Equitable's loan, McCarthy committed Oil and Gas to a development program for which

assets to Absorption, Incorporated (which held the gasoline plant), and the name of that corporation was changed to McCarthy Chemical Company. McCarthy Oil and Gas continued to own all of the stock of the McCarthy Chemical Company, and agreed to transfer all of the obligations of the constituent corporations to Chemical Company in return for its subordinated note in the amount of $4,000,000. The plan of reorganization likewise anticipated that all contracts for the purchase and sale of gas would be transferred from Oil and Gas to Chemical Company and that a new contract for the sale of gas would be entered into between Oil and Gas and Chemical Company, thus assuring a thruput of sufficient gas to service all of Chemical Company's then existing sales contracts. This reorganization was consummated and the Society agreed thereto in its Loan Agreement with Oil and Gas dated January 12, 1949.

no working capital was available. He made an agreement with Gulf Oil Company for the farm-out and development of the acreage of that company in the vicinity of New Ulm, Austin County, Texas.[111]

June 30, 1949, Ted Hall in his fourth report estimated the market value of McCarthy's producing and proved oil and gas reserves at $58,295,572—down $15,204,428 from his 1948 report—but still apparently enough to assure a safe margin for the total indebtedness to Equitable. By early autumn, however, it was obvious that the McCarthy interests were in trouble. Unanticipated expenditures on the Shamrock Hotel, the failure of the chemical plant to operate successfully, and the unexpected additional costs thereof resulted in a heavy drain on the cash which Oil and Gas had been successful in obtaining from Equitable. At the very time that Oil and Gas should have been curtailing its operational commitments, it had taken on a big obligation under its agreement with Gulf Oil for the development of the New Ulm field. Then not only did the Chemical Company default on both principal and interest payments to Metropolitan, but the principal payment due Equitable September 1, 1949, was deferred; also the April and May installments due in 1950. The first default in principal took place June 1, 1950.

A number of meetings were held during the first three months of 1950 in an effort to evolve a plan out of which sufficient funds could be obtained to pay off current creditors of the Chemical Company, Oil and Gas, and McCarthy Center, Incorporated. Two of McCarthy's important gas customers—du Pont and Gulf States Power—were worried lest their respective supplies be cut off if Metropolitan and Equitable should foreclose. Actually their purchase commitments exceeded McCarthy's ability to supply. Before any readjustments were agreed to in regard to prices for gas, Metropolitan had a survey made of the gas reserves by Ralph Davis, an independent gas engineer. Pending delivery of the Davis report, Oil and Gas continued its expenditures at New Ulm and accumulated unpaid current bills of $2,250,000; creditors were pressing for payment and threatening to file suit. When the Davis report was delivered to Metropolitan in May 1950, it indicated a substantial destruction of Oil and Gas' reserves of gas in the North Stowell field; they were estimated at less than one-third

[111] As the New Ulm acreage was not subject to the Society's deed of trust, Oil and Gas was free to borrow on the security thereof or to sell same. For a period of several months during the latter part of 1949, Oil and Gas attempted to dispose of the New Ulm field to a group of investors headed by Howard Hughes, but the sale failed to materialize.

of the figures presented in the April 1949 Knode and Hall report.[112] Although Hall at first stated that the difference in estimates resulted from use of a different formula in determining recoverable reserves, when he rendered his fifth report in January 1951 he listed 31 well abandonments, which reduced his last preceding valuation by more than $22,000,000. Some of the well abandonments had taken place prior to Hall's April 1949 report; although known to the management of Oil and Gas, they did not show on the company's books and could have been discovered only by a careful field check.

Various factors accounted for the shrinking values of the Oil and Gas reserves. In some instances, especially in the gas wells, they resulted from too rapid production; the gas was removed in such quantities and with such haste that well pressures could not be maintained. In other instances, wells were completed and put on the books when it was doubtful that they were or could be commercial producers. Some of the abandonments were no doubt the result of geological factors that were not anticipated at the time of completion. Then McCarthy blamed the Texas law and production restrictions for greatly reducing his income.[113]

In July 1950 Metropolitan worked out an arrangement with McCarthy whereby it supplied him with funds to meet payment on his current obligations. A new corporation, the New Ulm Corporation, was organized to take over the New Ulm field; all of the stock of this corporation was subscribed by the Chemical Company and pledged as further security for the Metropolitan bonds. Although at the same time Metropolitan obtained certain controls of accounting and management in Oil and Gas, it began to separate the operations of the Chemical Company from those of Oil and Gas. In January 1951 Metropolitan induced Oil and Gas to vote its stock in the Chemical Company for the election of a new board of directors.[114] This board immediately employed Russell M. Riggins of Arthur Young and Company as President of the Chemical Company and the New Ulm Corporation. All management control by McCarthy was terminated, although he was retained as chairman of the board.

While Metropolitan was endeavoring to straighten out its problems with the Chemical Company, officers of Equitable were discussing

[112] Though Equitable did not receive a copy of the Davis report, it was advised of its content.

[113] As quoted in *The New York Times,* May 18, 1950.

[114] By this time Equitable had the right to vote Oil and Gas' holdings of stock in the Chemical Company.

possible remedies in the event that Oil and Gas' difficulties should prove to be more than temporary. Legal counsel was directed to explore the relative advantages of foreclosure as compared to assumption of control through other means. Counsel concluded that Equitable's position could best be protected by avoiding a foreclosure, which would probably result in litigation and resultant waste of substantial assets. The problem thus became one of gradually assuming control of Oil and Gas in such a manner as to avoid the moratorium of a proceeding under Chapter X of the Bankruptcy Act and to avoid as well the risks of being charged with liabilities as a mortgagee in possession.

Equitable outlined its requirements for McCarthy's consideration, August 1950, and the following month he agreed to all of those which did not require Metropolitan's approval. In October, Metropolitan offered to eliminate the contractual controls over certain phases of the operation of Oil and Gas which it had obtained under its agreement with that company in July 1950 if Equitable would relinquish control of the voting stock of the Chemical Company. This Equitable refused to do and held on to its proxy from Oil and Gas, which entitled it to vote the stock of the Chemical Company.

January 10, 1951, by a ninth supplement to the original deed of trust and assignment, Oil and Gas agreed to pay 100 per cent of its gross income—instead of 50 per cent—to Equitable's trustee. Then McCarthy Center, Incorporated, pledged its note in the amount of $16,486,716.72 in evidence of its indebtedness to Oil and Gas; also, a bond in the amount of $175,000.[115] McCarthy Center, Incorporated, executed a deed of trust to secure its pledged note, which deed of trust created a third lien on the hotel property and a first lien on a 14-acre tract adjacent to the Shamrock Hotel and a 400-acre tract in an area some miles south of the hotel.[116] On January 15 McCarthy agreed to the execution of a voting trust agreement under which all of the outstanding stock of McCarthy Oil and Gas Corporation was transferred to voting trustees named by Equitable.[117] A single voting trust certificate covering all of this stock was substituted as collateral for the

[115] The bond was secured by a second mortgage on the hotel property, subject to the Society's first mortgage.

[116] Until January 10, 1951, neither of these unimproved tracts of land had been pledged as security for McCarthy's debts to Equitable.

[117] The trustees were Equitable Secretary Henry G. Wood; Equitable Treasurer Henry Greaves; and Dr. Watson Baumert, Secretary of the Finance Committee of the Equitable Board.

Equitable loans. Under the voting trust agreement, Equitable was given complete control of Oil and Gas for at least ten years.

Three days after the above agreement was made, the Hall report of January 18, 1951, which indicated a decrease of more than one-third in the reserves securing Equitable's loans, became available, and Equitable decided that it could no longer proceed on the basis of theoretical control of McCarthy holdings. A meeting of Oil and Gas stockholders was called for March 1 in Houston and at that meeting the stock of Oil and Gas was voted for a new board of directors consisting of McCarthy, A. G. McNeese, McHugh, Mendel, Maurice Purnell, Maher, and Robert E. Benson.[118] This new board of directors immediately convened and elected McCarthy, Chairman; Mendel, President; Benson, Assistant Treasurer and Assistant to the President; and Henry T. Fielding, formerly a field auditor for the Equitable, to supervise accounts. The new management outlined its initial objectives, among the more important of which were: 1) to obtain complete control of the operations of Oil and Gas and the Shamrock Hotel, while preserving sufficient anonymity to assure McCarthy's cooperation; 2) to obtain reliable data as to producing wells, reserves, cost of production, and geological information on undeveloped leases as the basis for a development program; 3) to institute a system of inventory control and dispose of unnecessary personnel; 4) to systematize accounting methods for better control of Oil and Gas expenditures; and 5) to establish a record for management which would avoid any future claim by McCarthy that the Society or its representatives acted improvidently in disregard of his advice and wishes.

Associate Counsel Warner H. Mendel took control of Oil and Gas March 1, 1951. His first move was to employ Lyle Cashion, a petroleum engineer who had spent twenty years in the drilling and production departments of Gulf Oil Company and, since 1946, had been managing his own company in Mississippi, to assist him. The first task assigned to Cashion was to assemble information on well abandonments, and his second was to test all producing wells and formulate a program for production.[119]

118 McNeese was General Counsel and a Director of the McCarthy companies. Maurice Purnell was a member of the Dallas law firm of Locke, Locke and Purnell, Texas counsel for Equitable. Benson was Assistant Manager of the Public Utilities Division of Equitable's Securities Investment Department. Both McNeese and Benson retired from the Oil and Gas board in June 1951 and were replaced by Ralph Friesner, Treasurer of the McCarthy Oil and Gas Corporation, and Robert Kuns, petroleum engineer employed by Equitable.

119 To assist Cashion, Oil and Gas borrowed Robert Kuns, who had been re-

April 18 the Executive Committee of the Equitable Board of Directors created a Special Committee of the Board to sit on the McCarthy affairs.[120] For a while there was some slight conflict between the views of this Special Committee and Mendel's ideas for the administration of the McCarthy companies. Mendel wished to maintain an organization entirely separate from Equitable for the management of Oil and Gas, without the operating decisions having to be made by Equitable's Board of Directors. He reasoned that control by the Board would place the Society in the position of a receiver with obligations to the stockholders and creditors of McCarthy and an ultimate duty to account.[121] Then some difference of opinion arose between the New York Insurance Department and Equitable in regard to salaries of Mendel and other Equitable personnel who were spending part or most of their time working for McCarthy Oil and Gas. By resolution of the Executive Committee of Equitable's Board (April 4, 1951), these men had been granted temporary leaves of absence without reduction in compensation.[122] In addition, they had drawn pay from McCarthy Oil and Gas Corporation. It was intended that their total compensation would be allocated pro rata with the time spent in New York and Texas. When the Insurance Department questioned this method of compensation, the Society assumed the full burden and the amounts paid by Oil and Gas were returned to it.

Mendel found that handling the McCarthy properties was not a job for an amateur. In addition to keeping track of drilling operations, McCarthy's negotiations with du Pont, disputes with Riggins, land

---

cently employed by Equitable as a petroleum engineer, and hired Milton Cooke, an engineer under part-time retainer to the Texas Railroad Commission, for the purpose of making field tests.

120 The members were Edward L. Shea, chairman; Samuel A. Welldon; Frank R. McCoy; and Nicholas Kelley.

121 Memorandum by Mendel in regard to a meeting with President Parkinson and Vice President McHugh, October 30, 1951. Warner H. Mendel files, Equitable Archives.

122 The men named were Associate Counsel Warner H. Mendel, Assistant Manager Robert E. Benson, and Assistant Auditor Henry T. Fielding.

In a memorandum to Julius Sackman, Chief of the Life Bureau of the New York Insurance Department, Equitable's Secretary Henry G. Wood explained that Mendel had been selected for the job of handling the McCarthy interests because he was known to have been on friendly terms with McCarthy and that Equitable was seeking to avoid some of the trouble which Metropolitan had had with its Manager of the New Ulm Corporation. Copy of memorandum in Records of Special Committee of the Board re McCarthy Oil and Gas Corporation. Corporate Records, *ibid.*

leases, purchasing, and accounting, there were personnel problems. Then there was Glenn McCarthy to manage. Another problem was to keep McCarthy from disposing of his real estate holdings at sacrifice prices. Economies were effected all along the line, and gradually Mendel took over sole management of the Shamrock Hotel as well as Oil and Gas; from 7 A.M. to 6 P.M. he worked on Oil and Gas and from 7 P.M. to 11 P.M. on hotel affairs. In December 1951 McCarthy, after discussion with Mendel, "volunteered" to take a cut in salary; his salary as Chairman of Oil and Gas was cut from $60,000 to $15,000, and as President of McCarthy Center, Incorporated, from $30,000 to $10,000.[123] Mendel suggested that McCarthy, if he flew his plane to New York, might wish to see what kind of offer he could obtain for it. Although McCarthy was reported to have said: "Damn it, I thought you weren't going to mess with the hotel," Mendel found it necessary to do so. Early in 1952 he ordered that publication of *Preview*, the Shamrock magazine which had lost $40,000 in 1951, be discontinued, that some employees be dropped, and advertising expenses be cut: "There seems little justification for continuing to spend $3,000 for the golf professional. I do not imagine anything like that amount of net profit has resulted from having Burke on the payroll." Also, that expenditures such as $14,000 spent on transporting Hollywood stars to the Shamrock's anniversary dinner in 1951 would have to be dispensed with.[124] According to the Manager of the Shamrock, McCarthy threatened to use physical violence upon Mendel, a man of slight stature, if the latter referred to the amount of McCarthy's personal expenditures charged to the hotel. The violence did not ensue, and Mendel told McCarthy that "there were to be no further illusions as to where the final control lay on matters relating to hotel operations." Later McCarthy objected to the cut in expenditure for Fourth of July fireworks; he said the contract had already been let and people who came for many miles to see the fireworks would be greatly let down.

[123] McCarthy to President Parkinson, December 6, and Mendel to Parkinson, December 7, 1951. Warner H. Mendel files. At this time, according to Mendel, McCarthy confirmed that he felt obligated to repay Equitable's loan "whether the source of such repayment was the property subject to our lien, or profits derived from unrelated enterprises."

[124] According to *The Houston Press*, April 8, 1952, McCarthy had paid some of the big name entertainers in the Shamrock's Emerald Room partly in royalties from his New Ulm Corporation, since they preferred long-term investments with depletion allowances to straight salary and huge income tax bites.

He expected 300,000 people and promised to pay the extra cost personally.[125]

All the while Mendel had to be careful to maintain good press relations for, in the minds of some, McCarthy was a local hero and Equitable the big bad absentee Scrooge who was causing all of his troubles. That Mendel succeeded in part is evidenced by some very favorable write-ups in the Houston press. For instance, Steve Booke, business editor of *The Houston Post*, wrote that when Equitable took a good long look at McCarthy's operations, "that look obviously confirmed what Equitable already knew: Glenn McCarthy, wild-catter, plunger, has a characteristic impatience with the thousand and one daily details that make any business tick. . . . Management control and detail, the elixir of life of all business, was conspicuously absent from Mr. McCarthy's day-by-day operations." Equitable and Metropolitan concluded that "with intelligent, careful management and time, they might ultimately be able to show Glenn a big patch of blue sky in what, at present, is a heavy fiscal fog." Somewhat later the same writer wrote of Mendel:

> As Equitable's legal counsel, Mendel, a short man with a keenly intelligent face, has suffered in accounts of the Equitable-McCarthy epic. Occasionally, stories have showed him as a man who feels uncomfortable without a mortgage between his teeth. A man who giggles when the dispossessed old mother sinks neck-deep in snow. . . . Actually, Mendel, a businessman, owns a soul with considerable mileage left in it, has a boundless imagination, readily admits his interest in profit as a necessary spur to business expansion, and harbors a deep social conscience—although he doesn't talk much about it. . . . Capital is this man's tube of paint. He gets tremendous artist's satisfaction out of spreading daubs of dollars on clean land, then standing back to observe the picture of business activity that follows.[126]

At the time Mendel took over control of Oil and Gas, he suggested that McCarthy grant Equitable an option on 20 per cent of the stock of Oil and Gas. A year later he mentioned certain opportunities which Equitable might offer McCarthy if he would agree to a voluntary transfer of his stock.[127] McCarthy's lawyers intimated that he would

[125] McCarthy to Mendel, June 24, 1952. Warner H. Mendel files.

[126] *The Houston Post*, June 25, 1952.

[127] "Briefly outlined, these were to give him the right to buy the mineral properties and equipment for $2 million, subject to a $12½ million Oil Payment,

endeavor, both by publicity and legal steps, to interfere with Equitable's ultimate success in taking over his properties. McCarthy denied that he was responsible for the stories in the Houston papers about his suing Equitable, and still refused to sign over his stock; he saw no reason for it, since Equitable was already in complete control. Mendel informed McCarthy that it might be necessary to sell the hotel or the oil property, and to sell Equitable would have to have ownership as well as control.[128]

There were other reasons why Equitable wanted the McCarthy stock. In the early months of 1952, McCarthy, in the endeavor to recoup his fortunes, had launched several new ventures. He had flown to Cairo, Egypt, and said that he had secured rights to develop millions of acres of oil lands in Egypt which had been abandoned by Standard Oil. Soon after his return, he went to Guatemala City with a large retinue with the hope of getting government concessions which would turn that city into a new world Monte Carlo. He also planned a chain of "little Shamrock Hotels," featuring lavish gambling casinos. More important to Equitable was the announcement in March 1952 that McCarthy, in association with B. V. Christie and Company, Houston investment bankers, was organizing a corporation for oil exploration and production throughout the world. To attract small investors the stock of this company—"Glenn McCarthy, Incorporated" —was to be offered at $2 per share.[129] Organizers of the new company sought assurance from Mendel that he would take no action until the distribution of this stock was completed, but he pointed out that Equitable did not want to take any chance of being associated in the public mind with this new promotion.[130] He issued an "ultimatum" to McCarthy in which he told him that he must devote full time to the companies which he owned and which were under mortgage to Equitable. McCarthy replied that since his advice in regard to the

---

payable out of 80 per cent at 4 per cent; and the right to purchase the Hotel and the unimproved property for $19 million, of which $4 million would be cash and $15 million on mortgage, payable on a 6 per cent constant basis." Mendel memorandum of March 26, 1952. Warner H. Mendel files, Equitable Archives.

128 Mendel memorandum of a telephone conversation with McCarthy, April 7, 1952. *Ibid.*

129 *The Houston Press*, April 7, 1952.

130 When McCarthy filed a registration statement with the Securities and Exchange Commission for his new company June 12, the statement revealed that on April 15 McCarthy still owed Equitable $29,450,000, and that he had paid back $3,211,746 of an original indebtedness of $32,661,746 incurred in 1949. *Ibid.*, June 12, 1952.

operation of Oil and Gas and McCarthy Center was not asked and not taken, he had to organize a new company so as not to remain idle.[131]

In April Mendel wrote President Parkinson that McCarthy's responsibilities to the new company were inconsistent with his prior agreement to devote his efforts to the improvement of Oil and Gas' properties. It was his opinion that no advantage could be derived from seeking the further cooperation of McCarthy; he believed that Equitable should be in a position to negotiate "the best possible deals looking to the sale of the properties subject to the Society's lien, either as a whole or in separate groups"; he did not believe that any purchaser would be interested in paying the maximum prices for these properties if it were necessary for him to have any continued relationship with McCarthy. In view of McCarthy's refusal to make a voluntary assignment of his stock, Mendel was ready to move to the appointment of a receiver pending foreclosure and institute an action in the Federal District Court for the foreclosure of Equitable's lien.[132]

Before any such steps were taken, however, Mendel made one more effort to avoid foreclosure proceedings. May 5 he offered a new plan under which Oil and Gas would apply its McCarthy Center note and its McCarthy Center bond against its debt to Equitable in the amount of $13,000,000. Equitable would consolidate these obligations with its existing obligation and take a new first mortgage bond issue in the amount of $18,500,000, secured by the hotel and the unimproved property. The remaining indebtedness of Oil and Gas would be $15,450,000, and McCarthy would assign his voting trust certificates to the Society so that it would become the complete owner of the Oil

[131] *The Houston Chronicle*, April 7, 1952.

[132] Mendel continued: "As the result of such proceedings, we will obtain title to the indebtedness and stock of McCarthy Chemical Company, and the indebtedness and stock of McCarthy Center, Incorporated, as well as the Voting Trust Certificate evidencing the beneficial interest in the stock of McCarthy Oil and Gas Corporation. In addition, of course, we will also be able to bid in all of the producing and non-producing mineral acreage. I anticipate that there will be a substantial deficiency judgment which will give us a claim on a Note signed by Glenn H. McCarthy maturing in 1960, with 10 years of accumulated interest in the amount of, approximately, $3,000,000, the value of which at this time, is highly questionable. The foregoing procedure will, unquestionably, lead to unfavorable publicity in Texas but I believe that our responsibility to our policyholders at this juncture requires us to ignore such publicity and seek to realize the maximum on our investment." Mendel to President Parkinson, April 17, 1952, Warner H. Mendel files, Equitable Archives.

and Gas properties and the stock and debt of the Chemical Company as well as McCarthy's personal notes. The stock in McCarthy Center would be placed in a voting trust, the trustees to be selected by Equitable. The voting trustees would not have the power to sell the Hotel without the consent of the owner of the voting trust certificates. McCarthy's voting trust certificates, however, would be placed in escrow, to be turned over to Equitable in the event of a default on the bond issue. At the same time, a separate agreement would be made with McCarthy which would eliminate his right to interfere in the management of the hotel, but would give him the continued right to reside at the hotel and to spend a limited amount of money on entertainment in connection with his business.

After further negotiations, Equitable and McCarthy finally came to terms June 3, 1952. By the agreement signed on that date, McCarthy assigned his voting trust certificate covering all stock of McCarthy Oil and Gas Corporation to Equitable. Oil and Gas assigned the $16,486,-716 secured note, and the $175,000 bond and all stock of McCarthy Center, Incorporated, to Equitable for a $14,000,000 reduction of the $29,450,000 debt. The $4,471,821 mortgage debt of McCarthy Center, the $16,486,716 secured note, and the $175,000 bond were then to be assigned to the Center in exchange for $18,472,000 of first mortgage 4 per cent sinking fund bonds maturing July 1, 1977. The stock of the Center, registered in Equitable's name, was to be assigned in blank and placed in escrow to be released to McCarthy if the Center's debt was paid, but it was to be retained by Equitable if there should be a default on the bonds or if McCarthy should violate the agreement to cooperate fully. Equitable was to have full control of the Center, although McCarthy was to remain as President and Director—at no salary, but with a free suite and certain expenses allowed. The debt of $15,450,000 of McCarthy Oil and Gas was to be adjusted to provide for interest at 2 per cent and an approximately nine-year payout at an average of $116,666 per month. Except after default on the bonds, Equitable would not be permitted to sell the hotel and could not lease it until after June 3, 1955; it might, however, turn over the management under a management contract.

In brief, the above-named adjustments reduced the debt of Oil and Gas to Equitable to $15,450,000 and increased the indebtedness of McCarthy Center, Incorporated, to $18,472,000. Equitable became the owner of all of the outstanding stock of Oil and Gas and owner of all the outstanding stock of McCarthy Center, Incorporated, subject to an obligation to turn over the stock of the center to McCarthy on payment of the Center's indebtedness.[133] The terms of the agreement were approved by the Special Committee of Equitable's Board on June 9 and by resolution of the Finance Committee the following day.

Press releases on the agreement went out June 10 with statements from McCarthy and Mendel. McCarthy said: "As the result of extremely cordial relations over the past seven years with Mr. Mendel and other officers of The Equitable, I have been enabled to work out a constructive plan whereby defaults in my obligations have been eliminated so that I can devote full time and effort to the operation of the Shamrock Hotel and to the successful launching of my new company." Mendel's statement was as follows: "The extended efforts of Mr. McCarthy and myself to solve a difficult problem have had gratifying results, all defaults have been eliminated. The Shamrock Hotel will continue to have the benefit of Mr. McCarthy's management and supervision. The Society is in full agreement with Mr. McCarthy's plan to engage through his new company in the exploration for and development of oil and gas properties." The following day, *The New York Times* reported that Equitable and Glenn H. McCarthy "buried the hatchet yesterday."

The Special Committee of the Board reported (August 20, 1952) to the Board of Directors of Equitable the results of the June 3 agreement and stated that the actions taken by the Society's management in handling the McCarthy properties "were constructive and designed to improve the Society's position." The Special Committee was then discharged.

Although a settlement had been reached, problems still remained. Mendel's functions and responsibilities in his three capacities as chief executive of the two McCarthy companies, as an officer of the Society charged with the duty of supervising its investments in the two companies, and as counsel to the Society to advise on legal problems were not too clearly defined. For instance, a resolution adopted by the Finance Committee of Equitable's Board, September 16, 1952, defined the area in which drilling operations could be carried on and permitted withdrawal of $150,000 per month from the Society's trust account

[133] The terms of the agreement are taken from the Agenda attached to the minutes of the meeting of the Special Committee of the Board re McCarthy Oil and Gas Corporation, June 9, 1952, and Resolution No. 201–52 of the Finance Committee, minutes of June 10, 1952, meeting. Corporate Records, Equitable Archives.

for operations, but no similar resolution was adopted in connection with the operation of the Shamrock Hotel. Another complication arose from the fact that though McCarthy Oil and Gas (Equitable) owned all the stock of Texas Gas Corporation (formerly McCarthy Chemical Company), the first mortgage on that company was owned by Metropolitan Life. Since there had been a principal default on this mortgage, Metropolitan had established a claim to penalty interest. Oil and Gas gave its proxy annually and permitted Metropolitan to name its Board of Directors and Mendel was a member of that Board. He was not satisfied with what he considered the wasteful manner in which Texas Gas was being operated; he thought it was jeopardizing Oil and Gas' equity.[134] For a while it appeared that Metropolitan might purchase Equitable's equity in Texas Gas Corporation, but negotiations failed to lead to an agreement.

As for the Shamrock Hotel, Equitable realized that it could be managed better by someone experienced in the operation of hotels. Consequently, on May 18, 1954, the Finance Committee of Equitable's Board consented to a modification of the McCarthy Center's indenture so as to reclassify the bonds into three series as follows: $13,108,000 of Series A, $2,500,000 of Series B, and $2,500,000 of Series C. The 10,000 shares of stock of McCarthy Center, Incorporated, and the $5,000,000 of Series B and C bonds were exchanged for 5,000,000 of Hilton Hotels Corporation debentures bearing 4 per cent and due July 1, 1977, Equitable continued to hold the $13,108,000 Series A mortgage bonds. Hilton Hotels Corporation received a fifteen-year management contract from McCarthy Center, Incorporated, by which it agreed to operate the Shamrock Hotel on a fee basis. McCarthy was given the right to regain all the stock of McCarthy Center, Incorporated, owner of the hotel and 530 acres of nearby land, by paying off that corporation's debt. About a year later, however, Hilton Hotels bought out McCarthy's rights to regain the hotel for $625,000.[135]

Since Equitable had no desire to remain in the oil business, it had tried, as early as December 1951, to interest various companies in the purchase of the McCarthy oil properties. Among the possible purchasers whom Mendel approached were Cities Service Oil Company, Lion Oil Company, and Gulf Oil. During 1952 Equitable continued

[134] Memorandum, Mendel to Senior Vice President Charles W. Dow, April 23, 1953. Warner H. Mendel files, Equitable Archives.
[135] *The Houston Press,* May 2, 1955.

its search for a purchaser, but without success, and during the next four years explored the possibilities of sale to Metropolitan Life; Nelson Hunt of Dallas; Wymore Oil Company of Corpus Christi; Lanston Industries, Incorporated; Ventures, Incorporated; and Governor Allan Shivers and Transcontinental Oil Corporation. Finally, in 1957, Equitable found a purchaser.

May 21, 1957, the Finance Committee of the Equitable Board authorized Mendel to bring about the dissolution and liquidation of McCarthy Oil and Gas and to dispose of all its "real property and appurtenant personalty."[136] July 3 a plan of liquidation was agreed to by which McCarthy Oil and Gas transferred its property, real and personal, to Equitable effective September 1, 1957. The property received consisted of warehouse land and buildings, $300,000; leasehold, mineral, and other interests, $6,587,000; and cash $142,801. The value of the property received was applied as a credit against the McCarthy Oil and Gas Corporation 2 per cent promissory note owned by Equitable and evidencing indebtedness in the principal amount of $7,029,-801. September 6 Equitable sold the properties it had acquired to Houston Natural Gas Corporation and Houston Natural Gas Production Company, a wholly owned subsidiary. Houston Natural Gas gave Equitable its promissory note for $1,000,000 at 4 per cent due September 1, 1958, and an indenture for a reserved production payment in the amount of $5,587,000; also $300,000 in cash.[137]

Thus Equitable was out of the oil business so far as the McCarthy properties were concerned. In the seven and a half years during which Mendel and his team had been operating these properties, the debt of almost $16,000,000 had been cut in half, and the sale to Houston Natural Gas practically took care of the remainder. So, as Mendel said, "Equitable came out all right."

* * *

In 1952 Equitable expanded its lending program to include loans on tree farms, or forestry loans. It became interested in this field

[136] At this time, McCarthy Oil and Gas Corporation was indebted to Equitable in the amount of $8,238,871.30 and was liable in addition for the payment of $316,557.33 of interest accrued since September 1, 1955, and $1,228,305 of postponed penalty interest unpaid on refunded notes previously held by the Society. Minutes of Finance Committee, May 21, 1957. Corporate Records, Equitable Archives.

[137] *Ibid.*, October 8, 1957.

largely as a result of the recommendation of Dr. Porter L. Gaddis, who had been head of the Appraisal Division of the Farm Credit Administration from its organization until he joined the Society in 1944 as an Assistant Manager of the Farm Mortgage Department.[138] For many years Gaddis had watched the operations of the Federal Land Bank of Columbia, South Carolina, in making loans on farms with substantial values in timber. In June 1952, Richard E. Huff of Mars Hill, North Carolina, was employed to assist in formulating a program and to serve as reviewing forest appraiser. Huff, a forestry graduate of North Carolina State College, had been in the lumber business and served as appraiser for the Federal Land Bank.[139] Eli Ferguson, Assistant Manager of the Farm Mortgage Department, acquainted himself with the problems and techniques of forest appraisal and developed methods for applying the principles of financial analysis to timber growing and to timber-owning firms. In September Vice President R. I. Nowell announced that Equitable had closed one tree farm loan and was negotiating others.[140] The announcement went to agency managers, general agents, farm loan supervisors, and appraisers. In the beginning, lending operations were restricted to eastern Texas, eastern Oklahoma, through the Gulf and adjoining states, and the southeastern coastal states. Briefly, the plan was as follows: 1) minimum amount of loan was $25,000, no maximum; 2) terms were up to 30 years at 5 per cent interest; 3) loans were to be limited to 25 to 33 per cent of the current market value of the security; 4) the loans were protected by

138 Gaddis, a native of Nebraska, was a graduate of Greenville College in Illinois. He later attended the University of Illinois and the University of Nebraska, where he specialized in agronomy. He served as a professor at the University of Nebraska and as appraiser for the Lincoln Joint Stock Land Bank. In 1930 he was appointed Assistant Chief Reviewing Appraiser of the Federal Farm Loan Board, predecessor of the Farm Credit Administration. While working for the United States Government, he continued his studies at the American University, from which he received his Ph.D degree in Economics.

139 Early in 1958 Huff was appointed Manager of Timber Loans, a new position in Equitable's Farm Mortgage Department.

140 By 1962 forest appraisers were located in North Carolina, Louisiana, Florida, and Oregon.

The importance of timber loans was well set forth in an article in the March 1954 Equitable *Farm Loan News*. In this article, Dr. J. V. Hofmann, former dean of the School of Forestry, North Carolina State College, and manager of the 80,000-acre model forest of the North Carolina Forestry Foundation, Incorporated, said: "I believe timber and timber land loans will supply a definite need and be an important movement in a national conservation program and I commend The Equitable Life Assurance Society of the United States for the active part taken in this pioneering field." Farm Mortgage Department files, Equitable Archives.

first lien on fee simple title of the timber land; and 5) repayment on an amortized basis with usual prepayment on interest dates up to 20 per cent of loan in any one year without reinvestment charge; other prepayment privileges subject to individual negotiation.

A question arose as to whether tree farms could be classed as improved property under the New York insurance law. Counsel Mendel and his staff decided that managed timber lands of the type visualized as security for tree farm loans were improved rural property within the meaning of the law. A more serious problem was the question of fire hazard. The New York Insurance Department in its triennial examination of Equitable as of December 31, 1953, "recommended that the Society re-examine its investment policy with respect to such loans."[141] Huff and Ferguson made a thorough study of fire damage resulting from various fires, the experience of certain pulp and lumber companies, insurance costs, methods of determining the volume of timber on the land offered as security, and the methods used in controlling and accounting for cutting of timber. While the report was being prepared, a widely publicized fire near Waycross, Georgia, seemed from newspaper and television reports to confirm the contentions of the Insurance Department examiners. Several officers and particularly some directors were worried. It appeared that the new venture in financing ownership of standing timber was to be short-lived. In order to observe the effects of the Waycross fire at first hand, Ferguson and Huff flew to Georgia and were in the fire area while embers were still smouldering. Their interviews with local experts convinced them that they had not misjudged the effect of fire on southern pine. As a result of the study, the following conclusions (supported by a large number of color slides) were submitted to the Real Estate Committee of the Board: 1) much southern pine of all ages remained alive after an extensive fire; very severe fires killed only a small percentage of the timber of merchantable size; 2) southern pine trees of merchantable size that were killed by a severe fire could be salvaged for sawtimber, poles, piling, posts, or pulpwood; 3) assuming that a fire was so severe and extensive as to deaden all of the timber, large and small, the value of the land and of the timber that could be salvaged would be more than sufficient to pay off any

[141] "Report on Examination of the Equitable Life Assurance Society of the United States" (December 16, 1954), p. 36. It was said that the preliminary draft of this report forbade Equitable to make timber loans.

loan which Equitable would make; and 4) fire insurance covering standing timber was not available at costs commensurate with the risks.[142] The report pointed out the importance of selecting favorable locations for the tracts to be financed, the division of typical properties into several noncontiguous tracts, and the attitudes of the communities toward the landowners.[143] Within two years, Equitable had made a total of approximately $3,500,000 of loans on growing timber, mostly in the South Atlantic states. During ensuing years, timber loans were made in the tall timber country of the Far West, and by the end of 1963 some 108 loans for a total of $38,300,000 were on the Society's books. These loans constituted about 6 per cent of the Society's farm loan investments.

HOME OFFICE—CHANGING PERSONNEL

After Vice President W. W. Klingman took charge of the Texas operations of Equitable in 1937, Vice President William J. Graham was put in charge of the Agency as well as the Group Department. Klingman retired from active service in 1946 and was elected to Equitable's Board of Directors in 1949. He had accomplished an important task in re-establishing Equitable in Texas. Not only had he built up a strong agency organization; he had also cooperated in the development of an effective mortgage investment organization. All this required a certain amount of diplomacy as well as sales and managerial ability. As President Parkinson said at the time of Klingman's retirement: "A large number of companies had developed there after the mutuals had withdrawn and their welcome to us was formal. They could not be enthusiastic about a vigorous representation of the Equitable in Texas. Klingman did accomplish it and he did give us a vigorous representation in Texas and maintained increasingly good relations with mostly stock companies which had grown up in

142 The reasons for this were as follows: 1) lack of demand by timber land owners for insurance against a risk which they deemed negligible; 2) resultant lack of sufficient knowledge of the subject by fire insurance companies; 3) the complexity of any sound rating structure; 4) the cost of underwriting an individual risk; and 5) the extreme difficulty in determining the amount of loss, if any.

143 For instance, when some of the southern states required the cattle raisers to fence their livestock, the cattlemen resented being shut off from the grazing on land owned by the pulp companies and sometimes set fires in retaliation. Also, grazing was improved by burning the underbrush. This long-standing practice of burning timberlands each year was responsible for the fine stands of pine timber in much of the South; otherwise the inferior hardwoods would have crowded out the pine, which is largely fire-resistant.

Texas. . . . Klingman has handled that situation as no one else could have done." [144]

In 1929 Graham had brought in Vincent S. Welch as Resident Supervisor in the Group Department. Welch, after being graduated from the University of Pennsylvania, where he played on the football team, had served as a captain in World War I, then for a number of years was football coach and director of athletics at Hobart College, Geneva, New York. While coaching football, he also served as Secretary of the Geneva Chamber of Commerce. In 1933 Welch was appointed Sales Supervisor of the Group Department; in 1937 he became Second Vice President and for two years supervised the Equitable agencies in the central and western sections of the country from headquarters in Chicago. At the time of this appointment, President Parkinson wrote:

I remember very well that you starred as a lineman, and I realize that since you have joined the Society's staff, you have been used largely to carry the ball. The reason I have great faith in you is partly explainable in football terms. Two qualities stand out in my mind, which, even as I express my appreciation of them, I emphatically recommend them to you for the future. In the first place, your performance when entrusted with the ball is only exceeded by your co-operation when someone else has it. That is a quality which is much needed and as much demanded by intelligent business executives as by football coaches. Again, you give yourself to your assignment and its performance without regard at the moment to the impression which you are making on the side lines or the benches. This devotion to performance is another quality which we need in the business world as much as on the football field.[145]

After thanking President Parkinson for his confidence, Welch replied:

My entire life since leaving college has been wholly and entirely devoted to teamwork and leading men. First, coaching football; then as a Captain of Infantry during the war; later as Secretary of the Chamber of Commerce and finally as Manager of the Group Department. I told the Managers in Chicago that I did not know how to accomplish any goal working alone. My background and training over the past twenty-one years have made

[144] Remarks at Executive Committee and Board meetings, October 16–17, 1946. Parkinson files, Equitable Archives.

[145] Thomas I. Parkinson to Vincent S. Welch, August 18, 1937. *Ibid.*

cooperation, teamwork, self-sacrifice, will power, loyalty, determination, a fighting spirit and instant, willing obedience to authority all second nature to me. Your letter is an inspiration to me. I read between the lines a challenge. I accept it and will play my position from an institutional standpoint always.[146]

"Deac" Welch kept his promise and in 1943 was appointed Vice President in charge of the Group Department. A star salesman in his own right, he also developed almost as many outstanding insurance representatives for Equitable as he did football stars at Hobart College. He knew how to "pep them up," and group sales continued to expand. In 1946 both Agency and Group Departments were placed under Welch's executive supervision. In 1950 he was appointed Executive Vice President. A most successful and promising career was cut short by death August 3, 1951. Many letters and telegrams from Equitable representatives throughout the United States testified to Equitable's loss.

When in 1946 Deac Welch was placed in charge of all sales operations, both Agency and Group, Merle A. Gulick, who had recently returned to President Parkinson's staff following distinguished service during World War II, was made General Manager of the Group Department and was elected Vice President of that department in 1950. The years of the war and immediately thereafter had given real impetus to the growth of all phases of Group Insurance and to the complexity of the various programs which employers and/or their employees utilized for providing these benefits. It soon became apparent that a larger salaried field organization would be necessary to carry forward the growth in sales and service of these lines of business. Vice President Gulick and his associates were faced with difficult problems both in the recruitment and training of personnel for these posts and in the reorganization of the field operations in the Group Department.

During the early years of the development of Group Insurance under the direction of Vice President William J. Graham most agencies had given one or more agents the title of "Group Supervisor." They were compensated entirely from overriders on the Group business written in their particular territories. It was now necessary to phase out this arrangement and finally to terminate the remaining special agreements

146 Welch to President Parkinson, August 24, 1937. *Ibid.*

in order to accommodate the requirements for compensation of the technically trained salaried field staff which was being organized for carrying forward the sale and service of Group Insurance.

In December 1951 Alvin B. Dalager was appointed Vice President and in February 1952 Agency Vice President. Dalager had joined Equitable as a part-time representative in Austin, Minnesota, in 1916. At that time he was assistant cashier of the Austin National Bank and, although he rose to the vice presidency of that institution, his success in life insurance sales led him to sign a full-time contract with the Klingman agency at St. Paul. He became Field Assistant, Unit Manager, and, when W. W. Klingman was called to the Home Office in 1928, Acting Manager of the Klingman agency. In 1930 Dalager became Agency Manager at Wilmington, Delaware, and eight years later came to the Home Office as a Second Vice President in the Agency Department. His promotions reflected his capabilities in managerial positions as well as in personal production.

After serving one year as Agency Vice President, Dalager was appointed Senior Vice President (March 1953) and in this capacity was given general supervision of the sales and service activities and organization of the field force, the Agency Department, the Group Department, and the Residential Mortgage Department. Within the next two years, all previous sales records in Equitable's history were broken, and Equitable's insurance in force rose from $20,457,000,000 at the end of 1953 to $24,572,000,000 in 1955.

Vice President and Counsel Sterling Pierson died in May 1949 at the age of forty-seven. It was said that his heart condition had been made more critical by the tremendous work load which he assigned himself. Not only did many duties devolve upon Pierson in Equitable, but he fell heir to many assignments from outside. As stated in the memorial resolution from the Association of Life Insurance Counsel:

> Sterling Pierson's best known contributions to the life insurance industry were in connection with his work on committees, often in the capacity of chairman, and special assignments. Such committee work and assignments ranged over a wide field, including the standard valuation and nonforfeiture laws, problems surrounding the original New York abandoned funds statute, and the effects upon life insurance companies of the South-Eastern Underwriters Association case. But in addition he frequently and generously gave of his time on a host of less known but important problems which affected the industry. He was a standing member of the Joint Legislative Committee

BRANIFF
AIRWAYS

Policyholder Dollars at Work

of the ALC and the LIAA and served as chairman of a number of its subcommittees. He became a member of The Association of Life Insurance Counsel in 1927 and delivered a paper on the Federal Revenue Act at our meeting the following year. Many will also recall the scholarly paper on Mutuality and Trusteeship which he read before us here just eight years ago. He leaves an inspiring record of service and of high intelligence combined with modesty and humility. . . .

Sterling Pierson combined in his personality a mixture of exceptional legal ability, unusual powers of perception, wisdom, and selflessness which won the trust and respect of all with whom he came in contact. President Parkinson had come to depend upon Pierson very heavily and thought of him as being the logical selection as the next President of Equitable.

Rising rapidly to a position of importance and influence in Equitable after the death of Sterling Pierson was Raymond H. Weins. Weins, a native of Wisconsin, had attended high school in Racine and the University of Wisconsin Extension Center at Milwaukee. He completed a three-year course in accounting and business adminstration at the Alexander Hamilton Institute in 1917. He became a major in the Signal Corps in World War I and served as an aide to Major General George O. Squier, Ph.D., Chief Signal Officer of the United States Army. After the war, he served as an assistant to John Barton Payne, Chairman of the United States Shipping Board, and in 1934–35 as Manager of the Credit Department of the Export-Import Bank of Washington, D.C.[147] In 1937 Second Vice President Glenn McHugh brought Weins into Equitable's City Mortgage Department and two years later he was appointed Administrative Assistant to President Parkinson. His advancement during the next few years was rapid; he was given charge of the Personnel Department early in 1942, he became Controller in 1945, a Vice President in 1948, and Executive Vice President in February 1951.[148]

In February 1951, after the retirement of Secretary Alexander McNeill, who had been with Equitable fifty-one years, Henry G. Wood

[147] The Export-Import Bank, created in 1934, was headed by George N. Peek, with whom Second Vice President Glenn McHugh had worked in 1933–34 when Peek was Administrator of the Agricultural Adjustment Administration.

[148] The positions held were as follows: 1940, in charge of simplifying and coordinating management reports and Controller of Expenditures; 1941, Chairman of Committee on Research; 1942, in charge of the Planning Division and Personnel Department; 1945, in charge of Home Office Administration Department.

was elected Secretary of the Society. Wood was a native of Maine and, after being graduated from Bowdoin College, attended the University of Maine Law School for a year. He served in the Canadian Army in World War I, received his law degree from Columbia University in 1924, and spent a year studying French law at the University of Paris Law School. While at Columbia, he worked with the Legislative Drafting Research Fund and in 1926 joined the office of Legislative Counsel of the United States Senate; in 1936 he became head of that office. Wood helped draft the Tariff Act of 1930, various financial measures including the one which created the Reconstruction Finance Corporation, also the Social Security legislation and the Selective Service Act of 1940. He came to Equitable late in 1943 as Investment Assistant on the President's staff, and two years later became Special Assistant to the President. He was appointed Second Vice President in 1950 and elected Secretary of the Society in February 1951 and a Director in 1952.

Important changes took place in Equitable's Medical Department, both in personnel and scope of activities, during the 1940's and 1950's. Although Equitable had, over the years, a number of competent, even distinguished, Medical Directors and Associate Directors, all of them were essentially clinicians. They prepared manuals for the Society's examiners, some of them contributed articles to the medical journals, and several were honored with the presidency of the Association of Life Insurance Medical Directors, but they had neither the time nor the resources to make original contributions to the sum total of medical knowledge.[149] Dr. Robert M. Daley, who had come to Equitable in 1900 and became Medical Director in 1936, retired in 1947. The Medical Department was then separated into two parts: Dr. Edgar W. Beckwith, who had been with Equitable since 1916, was promoted to Medical Director, Underwriting; and Dr. Harry E. Ungerleider, who had joined Equitable in 1926 as a medical examiner in Philadelphia, was promoted to Medical Director, Research. When the Research Division was created, President Parkinson, seeking to develop young men to think and engage in original work in all fields affecting life insurance, told Dr. Ungerleider to "do something."[150]

149 Equitable Medical Directors who were presidents of the Association of Life Insurance Medical Directors were: Dr. Franklin C. Wells in 1915; Dr. Robert M. Daley in 1925; and Dr. Harry E. Ungerleider in 1949.

150 President Parkinson's interest in medical research had developed gradually over the years. In 1929 Irénée du Pont, Vice Chairman of the Board of E. I.

Within a short time, the work of the Research Division came to be known nationally. Dr. Ungerleider and his associates engaged in research in many fields ranging from urinalysis to arteriosclerosis. In 1949 Dr. Richard S. Gubner and Dr. Ungerleider published an article, "Arteriosclerosis—A Statement of the Problem," in *The American Journal of Medicine.*[151] Ultimately, 75,000 copies of this article were distributed by Equitable to colleges, hospitals, and physicians. By this time the Division of Medical Research was receiving recognition from the American Medical Association, hospitals, and medical schools. Scores of articles were published by members of the Division.[152]

Among significant contributions were several committee reports of the American Heart Association in which Drs. Ungerleider and Gubner figured prominently. These included an American Heart Association monograph on "Examination of the Heart," a committee report on "Ballistocardiography," and a study on "The Factor of Error in Blood Pressure Readings." The last helped greatly to bring about standardization and uniformity of blood pressure measurements; the recommended methods were approved by the medical associations of England, Canada, and the United States.[153] Dr. Ungerleider also was among the first to contend that medical expenses were insurable. With the

---

du Pont de Nemours Company and a Director of Equitable, spoke before The Association of Life Insurance Presidents on "Vision in Industry and Business." He emphasized the importance of research: "One-eighth of one per cent of your trust fund would finance the greatest research organization the world has ever applied." (*Proceedings of the Twenty-Third Annual Convention of The Association of Life Insurance Presidents,* New York, New York, December 12 and 13, 1929, p. 21.) At this time President Parkinson was a member of the Executive Committee of the ALIP. Then in 1938 Dr. Thomas S. Gates, President of the University of Pennsylvania, spoke to the Association on "Education, Insurance, and Research." He said: "Even a fraction of one per cent on the business of each company, a fraction such as many industries think nothing of applying to group advertising alone, would provide a sizable fund for research." (*Proceedings* . . . 1938, p. 25.)

151 *The American Journal of Medicine,* VI (1949), January.

152 During the years 1934 to 1959, Dr. Ungerleider published more than sixty articles, chapters, and books. Most of these were written in collaboration with Dr. Richard S. Gubner or other associates. They appeared in such journals as *American Journal of Medicine, American Heart Journal, Journal of the American Medical Association, Radiology, American Journal of Public Health, American Journal of Roentgenology, Journal of Clinical Investigation,* and in the *Transactions* or *Proceedings* of the Association of Life Insurance Medical Directors, the American Heart Association, the Inter-American Cardiological Congress, and the Medical Section of the American Life Convention. Several of the papers were read before various international scientific or medical congresses.

153 *American Heart Journal,* XVI (1938), October.

aid of Dr. Henry Steinhaus, research assistant on the President's Staff, Vice President Weins, and the Personnel Department, a two-year study was carried out on Home Office employees which proved that such insurance was feasible, and a modest plan was adopted for their medical expense coverage.

The problem of basing underwriting practice upon actuarial studies was well stated later by Dr. Gubner:

> A relative stability in health and disease—which allowed actuaries to draw on mortality experience of the previous generation in the formulation of reasonable inferences as to the present and future—existed in the early years of this century. This stability no longer exists; it is now difficult or impossible to observe the natural course of disease.
>
> Sometimes the truth of this has burst on us quite suddenly, as with the advent of antibiotics—which caused enormous change in the mortality of infectious diseases. All the carefully-based underwriting practices in pulmonary tuberculosis became thoroughly obsolete with the introduction of streptomycin and isoniazid. We were left only with clinical anticipation as a guide to underwriting experience.

Similarly, he noted the changes in mortality experience resulting from new treatments of diabetes (insulin), and hypertension:

> Diabetes has been a fruitful example of the value of *enlightened* experimental underwriting based on good clinical insight and anticipation. . . . The underwriting situation with regard to congenital heart disease has also undergone great change—with the advent of by-pass open heart surgery. Today we are all underwriting many types of congenital heart disease on the basis of reasonable anticipation as a guide to experience. But even with the massive experience now available to us, our guidance still is one of clinical anticipation, and the prospects of statistically valid mortality investigations—for any of the many congenital heart lesions, operative or inoperative—is remote. Coronary heart disease is another area where, like hypertension, it may become increasingly necessary for us to rely on anticipation rather than on actuarial analysis of mortality experience—as new clinical developments dictate.[154]

In 1950 Drs. Ungerleider and Gubner published a book entitled *Roentgenology of the Heart and Great Vessels*, which had first ap-

[154] Dr. Richard S. Gubner, "Medical Experience as a Parameter of Experience," a paper read before the 51st Annual Meeting of the Medical Section of the American Life Convention, June 24, 1963. Summary in *ALC Newsletter*, No. 685 (July 8, 1963).

peared as a section of the Encyclopedia, *Diagnosis and Treatment of Cardiovascular Diseases.* The preface was written by President Parkinson. The book came to be known as "The Equitable Bluebook on Roentgenology," and was widely used as a text in medical colleges. An abbreviated edition was published in 1953, which was a reprint of the chapter Drs. Ungerleider and Gubner had contributed to the text, "The Chest and The Heart" (edited by J. A. Myers and W. McKinlay), with a printing of 100,000 copies by C. C. Thomas Company.

Largely as the result of the studies of the Medical Department, Equitable in July 1951 issued its In-Hospital Major Expense Policy (Series 92) to provide coverage against the costs of so-called "catastrophic" illnesses. This policy, written for either individual or family coverage, provided insurance against the various types of medical expense which arose during periods of hospital confinement. It included two new features—the deductible and the coinsurance provisions which were to become popular in various forms of health insurance in subsequent years. These plans as originally offered by the Society provided either $10 or $15 as the daily room and board benefit limit with comparable maximum benefits for each hospital confinement of $2,500 and $5,000 respectively. Either scale of these benefits was made available with the $100, the $300, or the $500 "deductible"—the applicant being free to choose whichever would best fit his needs and premium budget. In December 1953 this In-Hospital Major Expense program was replaced by a single form known as the Major Medical Expense Policy (Series 95). This policy provided a simple program for covering major medical expenses both within and outside the hospital; the deductible amount was $500 and the benefit for any one accident or sickness was $7,500. Originally the policy was renewable to age 65 and later the option was granted for continuance of coverage beyond age 65 with appropriate limitations. Although commercial (cancellable) in form, the policy stated that renewal would not be refused by reason of deterioration of health. Soon "major medical" was being featured by most life insurance companies.[155]

In 1951 the Medical Department was again reorganized under the supervision of Executive Vice President Mervyn Davis, head of the Underwriting Department. Dr. Beckwith was appointed Medical Direc-

155 For further modernization of Major Medical insurance in 1962, see this history, p. 1311. At that time Agency Vice President Coy G. Eklund said: "The Equitable, as many of you know, was the first major life insurance company to make individual major medical expense coverage available on a nationwide basis." Letter to The Equitable Field Force August 11, 1962. Equitable Archives.

tor and Dr. Ungerleider became Director of the new department of Medical Research. Two years later, with the general reorganization of Equitable's Home Office, Dr. Norvin C. Kiefer was appointed Chief Medical Director and the Medical Department was divided into four bureaus as follows: Medical Selection (Dr. Whitman M. Reynolds); Medical Research (Dr. Ungerleider); Employees' Health (Dr. Thomas H. Deely); and Public Health (Howard Ennes, M.P.H.).

Dr. Kiefer, a native of Ohio, received his M.D. degree from the University of Michigan School of Medicine and his M.P.H. (Master of Public Health) degree from Johns Hopkins University. After fourteen years of private practice, he entered the United States Public Health Service in 1945, serving first in the Tuberculosis Division and later in the Office of the Surgeon General. He then served in various capacities in the Office of Civil Defense Planning, the National Security Resources Board, and the Federal Civil Defense Administration. He is a member of, and has served in an official or advisory capacity in many medical and professional organizations and is a Diplomate of the American Board of Preventive Medicine.

The purpose of the 1953 reorganization was to develop a coordinated and integrated medical program. The pre-existing "Medical Department," which had dealt largely with underwriting, became the Bureau of Medical Selection with Dr. Whitman M. Reynolds as head. The medical research activities and laboratory services became the Bureau of Medical Research (Dr. Ungerleider), and the health services for personnel were transferred to the Medical Department as the Bureau of Employees' Health (Dr. Thomas H. Deely). A new Bureau of Public Health was established under Howard Ennes, M.P.H. Under the new arrangement, more administrative authority was centered in the Office of the Chief Medical Director.

Research activities continued, with some of the important projects being carried on in collaboration with Kings County Hospital, the St. Francis Cardiac Hospital, and the Department of Biological Chemistry at Harvard Medical School. Among the studies undertaken were those on biochemical factors predisposing to atherosclerosis and coronary artery disease, and diagnostic and prognostic studies in electrocardiography, matters of considerable importance to medical underwriting. A new drug, "Equilite," was developed and tested for the treatment of tuberculosis by Dr. Gubner in collaboration with Drs. René Dubos and Cynthia Pierce of the Rockefeller Institute for Medical Research. After experimental studies at the Rockefeller Institute and at the

Sterling-Winthrop Research Institute, it was tested clinically at the Seaview Hospital in New York. A report was presented at the American Medical Association annual meeting of this work. Dr. Frank R. N. Gurd, who was in charge of the Chemical Laboratory at Equitable, made a study of blood lipids and their relationship to coronary artery disease. Dr. Richard S. Gubner, Associate Director of the Bureau of Medical Research, was appointed Clinical Professor of Medicine at State University of New York College of Medicine, Downtown Medical Center. Drs. Ungerleider and Gubner edited the book, *Life Insurance and Medicine: The Prognosis and Underwriting of Disease*. The editors contributed several chapters on heart diseases, high blood pressure, and kidney disorders. The book was published in 1958.

The Medical Department underwent further reorganization in 1959 when the bureaus were reduced to three, as follows: the Bureau of Insurance Medicine, under Medical Director Whitman M. Reynolds, M.D.; the Bureau of Public Health, under Director Howard Ennes, M.P.H.; and the Bureau of Medical Services, under Medical Director Thomas H. Alphin, M.D. The Diagnostic Services Division (Medical Director Richard S. Gubner, M.D.), the Medical Claims Consultation Division (Medical Director William J. McNamara, M.D.), and the Employees' Health Center (Medical Director Thomas H. Deely, M.D.) were placed under the Bureau of Medical Services.[156] Under the new arrangement, medical research functions of the department were to be carried on by the appropriate bureaus or divisions under the guidance of their medical directors and the general supervision of the Chief Medical Director. Dr. Harry E. Ungerleider, formerly Medical Director of Research, retired as of June 30, 1959.

A NEW ADMINISTRATION AND THE REORGANIZATION OF EQUITABLE

October 16, 1947, the Board of Directors of Equitable paid tribute to President Parkinson on the completion of twenty years of service as President. The distinguished lawyer and Equitable Director Joseph Perkins Chamberlain said of him:

> He was always a pioneer, a true representative in this era of the Americans who pushed our frontier to the Pacific. . . . He regarded his coming to the Equitable as continuing his public service, and he has applied to

[156] Executive Order No. 59–19 (June 1, 1959).

his work here his pioneering spirit and his trained powers of persuasion and of cooperation. It may be said of him that you do not work for Parkinson, you work with him. . . . His constructive thinking has been evidenced by extension of the Society's coverages to meet new needs of policyholders, thus giving recognition to the social obligations which a great mutual insurance society such as ours must have. . . .

Let me also comment on his quality of modesty. It is the modesty of an executive proud of his share in the work of his organization, glad to give recognition to the contribution which each one has made, and rejoicing in the achievement in which he shares with them.[157]

Director John Lord O'Brian, who was unable to attend the meeting, wrote as follows:

While the statistics summing up your amazing record speak for themselves, to me the more important fact is that during your entire presidency, including an unparalleled depression, the problems presented by the great war and a hostile Congressional investigation, never at any time was any criticism or dissatisfaction expressed by those who knew your work. This is indeed an astonishing record, and I congratulate you with all my heart.[158]

Four days later, the officers of the Society gave President Parkinson a testimonial dinner at the Union League Club. Many letters of congratulation came in from agents, directors, Home Office personnel, and friends.[159]

Again in October 1952, directors and officers of Equitable gave President Parkinson a dinner, this time in celebration of his 25th anniversary. The principal after-dinner talk was made by Director Douglas Southall Freeman, Richmond editor and internationally known biographer-historian.[160] Since Freeman had considerable experience in portraying American personalities and was a skilled literary artist, his remarks are worth quoting at some length. After relating the changes

[157] As read to the Board by Chamberlain. Minutes of the Board of Directors. Corporate Records, Equitable Archives.

[158] O'Brian to President Parkinson, October 16, 1947. Parkinson files, *ibid.*

[159] Said Gordon K. Smith, Superintendent, Agency Department, and later Secretary of the Society: "I am sure that, when the history of life insurance is written, your administration will rank foremost among the leaders of all companies." And General Agent Theodore M. Riehle: "All of us who are worth a 'damn,' would like to leave a touch of immortality behind us and certainly as long as America lives, you have done so." Parkinson files, Equitable Archives.

[160] Author of *Robert E. Lee*, 4 volumes (1934–35); *Lee's Lieutenants*, 3 volumes (1942–44); and *George Washington*, 4 volumes (1948–51); etc.

in the United States since 1927 and portraying the great growth in the field of life insurance, he said:

Life insurance in this country gloriously demonstrates the ancestral ability of Americans to be self-dependent when they are not pampered by political subvention or shackled by restrictive law. Every developing economic need of our people they have shown they can provide by their voluntary association, their adaptability and their thrift. Security for old age, financial provision for sickness and invalidism, their own "endowed scholarships" for the education of their children, capital for sons who adventure in private business, dowries for daughters, annuities for widows, assured home-ownership—all these Americans have established for themselves through their own mutual insurance companies without the expenditure of one dollar of government funds. The achievement of this in a generation that has been lulled with the siren song of personal security at the expense of someone else, is today's noblest assertion of the individual American's desire and ability, if left alone, to be the master of his destiny, however wide the changes in social structure may be. We do not flatter you, Sir, but merely recall facts of demonstrable record when we say that no man has done more to organize this rally of self-respect and self-dependence than have you. The deepest faith of your soul is in thrift, in individual effort, in the ambition that leads a man to sacrifice today for a larger life tomorrow. You have made these your highest goals because you believe in them and in the reward the quest of them brings to honest men.

The qualities you have displayed in your dedicated service to the American people make us profoundly grateful to Judge Day and to the directors who perceived in 1927 that you possessed unique equipment for the presidency. Every endowment of mind and spirit, the daily discipline of personal life and administrative duty, each expression of your interest in your fellow men—all these have yielded increasing return to the members of our Society. If the rate of interest on their assets has fallen in spite of you, the level of a different type of interest in their welfare has mounted because of you and your like-minded associates.

This sense of duty has been displayed along with a singular sense of values. You have not hesitated to seek expert service and to pay for it; you have not been "penny wise and pound foolish"; but your almost intuitive appreciation of the issues that will be decisive, your instant perception of the ground where the battle must be waged, always has led you to labor longest where the planning was hardest, the execution most complex and the gain or loss the largest. We instance, as typical and transcendent, your valiant struggle for honest money, your greatest if, as yet, your unrewarded contribution to the national economy.

So integrated is your character, Sir, that even in paying tribute to your extraordinary sense of values, we are spared the task of trying to determine the special attributes that explain your career. We need not attempt to say in what fortunate combination your penetration, your clear reason, your integrity, your logic, your fabulous memory, your energy and your courage are cast. For the weal of this Society, this generation and this nation, the "good stars met in your horoscope." It is enough for us to say, it is our pride to say, that you have done what you have because you have been unflinchingly, unswervingly, yourself.[161]

In his report to the Board of Directors for the year 1951, President Parkinson noted that Equitable's Federal taxes under the new tax formula (see this history, p. 1150) had been $11,350,000, or an increase of $5,100,000 over the preceding year. This tax was equal to more than one-fifth of the dividends which the Society was paying to its ordinary life policyholders. Then, in addition to state and local taxes, Equitable had paid $79,000 to cover its statutory assessment for the expenses of conducting the New York Insurance Department, and $165,000 for its triennial examination, still incomplete by representatives of the New York Insurance Department and those of other state departments. He called attention to the handicap under which life insurance companies still labored in furnishing contracts in the pension fiield where their investment earnings were taxed while the investment earnings of trusts set up for pension purposes were tax exempt. Under the new rules laid down by the National Association of Insurance

[161] Copy in Parkinson files, Equitable Archives. One thousand copies of Freeman's address were sent to a selected list of managers, district managers, and others. A folder in the Parkinson files contains press releases, congratulatory letters and telegrams, and President Parkinson's replies to some of them. Frank Farrell, writing in the *World-Telegram and Sun*, October 20, 1952, said that President Parkinson had celebrated his 25th anniversary in his office on that day and claimed that the best way to stay young on any job was to plant dahlias and watch them grow.

Soon after the dinner Clarence Axman, editor and publisher of *The Eastern Underwriter*, wrote President Parkinson and asked him to be sure to "tip him off" on any news in regard to who would succeed him as President. According to Axman, Parkinson had told the group at the dinner that he realized there had been some discussion as to who was to fill his shoes, but that his shoes "were tightly laced" and that he expected to be with the Society for some time to come. He hoped, however, that his successor would be someone from inside the organization. Axman continued: "Of course, we did not print that. But if I get trimmed on the story of your retirement when that day arrives . . . I shall feel greatly humiliated and will certainly lose a lot of prestige in my own office where it is known the big play I have given the Equitable over the years." President Parkinson assured Axman that when there was news, he would make sure that he got it. Axman to Parkinson, November 4, 1952, and Parkinson to Axman, November 13, 1952. Parkinson files, Equitable Archives.

Commissioners, the Society's annual statement showed a net return on its assets of 3.06 per cent before Federal income taxes, and 2.87 per cent after.[162] One encouraging development, however, was the fact that during the year the Federal Reserve System was permitted to unpeg the market on government bonds. As President Parkinson said:

For nearly twenty years we have had to invest our funds under the severe handicap of inordinately low and artificially determined interest rates resulting from the Government's monetary policies. This condition over a period of such length resulted in the refunding of practically all the previously acquired, higher yielding items, except some non-callable rail bonds, and in establishing the Society's portfolio of security investment at those low prevailing rates. But with the unpegging of the United States Government bond market early in the year, the available rates of return on new investment improved considerably, thus permitting institutions to start the slow process of rebuilding their investment returns to a level appreciably nearer the interest rates we assumed when we fixed the premiums on policies issued in earlier years.

In his report for the year 1952, his last, President Parkinson stated that the foreign business of the Society, once an important part of its total business, had, except for a small volume of business in Canada and Great Britain, been completely liquidated: "Thus an interesting, though sometimes troublesome, chapter in the Society's history is now approaching its close." He questioned the wisdom of the NAIC requirements for a security valuation reserve, believing that such matters should be left to the discretion of management, and hoped that the requirements of the New York law on expense limitations would be modified.[163] He ended his report with some remarks on his favorite subject, investments:

162 Under the new rule depreciation on transportation equipment and real estate was to be deducted from investment earnings to determine the net rate of return.

163 Under the rules of the NAIC, each life insurance company was required to establish and carry as a liability a valuation reserve of 1 per cent of the admitted value of amortizable bonds and 20 per cent of the admitted value of non-amortizable bonds and stock. This reserve was to be accumulated by annual charges of one-twentieth of the above-named amounts plus 100 per cent of net capital gains or less 50 per cent of net capital losses each year. This liability item appeared for the first time in Equitable's annual statement for 1951 and amounted to $1,400,000. At the end of 1952 Equitable's security valuation reserve totaled $30,600,000. Had it not been for this reserve requirement, Equitable's surplus, at the end of the year, would have been listed at $425,800,000 instead of $395,-200,000.

In regard to expense limitations, the New York law of 1906 had been interpreted

The past two decades have been difficult ones for the investment of life insurance funds. The marked influence which governmental action has had on investment problems, and the unpredictable character of such action, has required investment officers to keep alert to changing conditions and the alterations of investment opportunities so brought about. A life insurance operation requires prompt investment of idle money in a form which secures principal and yields a reasonable return. At the same time one must attempt to look ahead and exercise a seasoned judgment, concerning influences which may affect the future. Some of the old, comfortable landmarks are not present. We must, therefore, be alive to new forms of investment which will serve our policyholders well and also will be consistent with the public interest. This we have tried to do, and judging by the results of the Society's financial affairs, we think we are entitled to feel that our obligations have been fully met.

In 1953 President Parkinson was in his seventy-second year and past the normal retirement age for officers of the Society. For a number of years he had thought of Vice President and Counsel Sterling Pierson as his "carefully chosen and trained prospective successor," but after Pierson's death in 1949 he had indicated no choice of a successor. By Executive Order August 19, 1952, he had created a Committee on Organization composed of officers of the Society, which was assigned the duty of reviewing all aspects of the Society's Home Office organization and making any recommendations to the President which it believed were warranted.[164] The next day the Executive Committee of the Board appointed a subcommittee also entitled "Committee on Organization." Chairman of this committee was Douglas Southall Freeman; other members were Directors J. Reuben Clark, Jr., Francis B. Davis, Jr., Nicholas Kelley, Russell B. Lowe, and John Lord O'Brian.

The Officers' Committee held a number of meetings, frequently without its chairman being present. It considered not only personnel

---

to include as "acquisition expense" many incidental agency expenses such as the cost of group insurance and pension benefits that Equitable and many other companies provided for their agents. A committee of life company representatives was preparing an amendment which would enable the companies to give more adequate recognition to the services of agents. The law was modified in 1954.

[164] The members of the committee were Executive Vice President Raymond H. Weins, chairman; Vice President Charles W. Dow, vice chairman; Vice President Walter Klem; Vice President R. I. Nowell; Second Vice President Clarence B. Metzger; and Assistant Treasurer Harold A. Spiller. Secretary Henry G. Wood served as secretary of the committee.

problems but the space problem in the Home Office as well.[165] Some positive differences of opinion arose between members of the Committee and its chairman in regard to whose function it was to handle the space situation. In the discussion which followed the Committee was instructed to continue its deliberations under the chairmanship of Vice President Dow. The Committee eventually decided that Equitable should rent outside space for the four investment departments pending selection of a site and construction of a new Home Office building.

The Directors' Committee on Organization also held a number of meetings and various rumors circulated as to who would be its choice for the presidency of Equitable. Here again some persons in touch with the situation believed that the chairman of this Committee considered himself eminently eligible for the position and that he would use his influence to bring in a man who would soon be eligible for retirement in order to hold the position open for himself. The Committee finally decided to ask President Parkinson to become Chairman of the Board and, although it had been generally understood that Executive Vice President and Actuary Murphy was not to be considered for the presidency, Freeman came to him one day and said: "The hand of the Lawd is about to descend upon you." Murphy asked whether he, as President, would have full executive power or would such power remain with the Chairman of the Board. He was assured that he would have full power. So on February 19, 1953, Murphy was elected President of Equitable, with the understanding that one of his chief duties would be to find a new President.[166]

Ray Dickinson Murphy, Equitable's seventh President, was born in Springfield, Massachusetts, February 28, 1887; he was a direct descendant of William Bradford of Plymouth Colony. At Harvard College he majored in mathematics, was elected to Phi Beta Kappa, and received his A.B. degree in 1908. After graduation he became a clerk in the actuarial department of the Massachusetts Mutual Life Insurance Company at Springfield where, in addition to his actuarial duties,

[165] During the depression years Equitable had leased considerable space in the Home Office building to outside tenants, but by the 1950's it was badly in need of this space.

[166] Ray D. Murphy, interview with author, December 27, 1960.

At the executive session following the Executive Committee meeting of February 18, 1953, the Committee on Organization asked to be discharged at the close of the annual meeting, February 19, 1953. The request was approved.

he played second base on the company's baseball team. In 1910, at the age of twenty-three, he became Actuary of the Hartford Life Insurance Company. He joined Equitable as Assistant Actuary in 1913, became Associate Actuary six years later, and was appointed Second Vice President and Associate Actuary in 1923, Vice President in 1930, and Vice President and Actuary in 1936. He was elected a Director in 1947 and appointed Executive Vice President and Actuary in 1950.

President Murphy had been a Fellow of the Actuarial Society of America (now the Society of Actuaries) for a number of years; he served on many of the Society's committees and was President in 1938–39. Among the many contributions which he made in the field of actuarial science, perhaps his pioneering studies in Major Medical Expense Insurance were the most important.[167] He was chairman of the Actuarial Advisory Committee to the Veterans Administration and served as a Director and a member of the Executive Committee of the Life Insurance Medical Research Fund. In 1949–50 he served as chairman of the Special Committee on Compulsory Health Insurance of the Life Insurance Association of America and represented both that organization and the American Life Convention before Congressional hearings on bills to provide temporary disability benefits and comprehensive compulsory health insurance under the Social Security system. Though primarily an actuary, President Murphy had had broad experience as an underwriter—he was Vice President in charge of the Underwriting Department (1930–36)—and varied and intimate contact with the field forces. "His whole technical background has been closely related to the life and daily routine of the field agent."[168] More than most actuaries, President Murphy was aware of the public relations aspects of the life insurance business; he was sensitive to public restlessness and demands for sounder public relations. Consequently, he was one of the founders of the Institute of Life Insurance. General Agent Horace H. Wilson, who had worked with Murphy for years, well described his breadth of interest:

[167] Murphy had read papers before the leading life insurance company organizations and actuarial and medical societies. A number of his articles were published in the *Transactions of the American Society of Actuaries*. In 1953 he spoke to the American Life Convention on the "Impact of Economic and Social Forces on Life Insurance in the United States"; and the following year read a paper on "Government's Role in Providing Economic Security" at the annual meeting of the National Industrial Conference Board.

[168] General Agent Horace H. Wilson to Clarence Axman of *The Eastern Underwriter*, April 17, 1953. Copy in Equitable Archives.

In the course of his experience he has attended literally hundreds of meetings and other sessions, formal and informal, with agents and managers, dealing with such field problems as compensation and contract provisions, acquisition costs as they affect the daily operations of an agent and an agency, underwriting and reinsurance, devising new life insurance and accident and health contracts to meet changing trends and new public needs. As an actuary he was steeped in the practical as well as the scientific aspects and impacts of these problems, and through the years he "had his nose to the grindstone" of reality so that he learned early to temper and modify purely scientific and mathematical conclusions in the fires of public reaction, merchandising necessity and the human welfare of agents' problems. He has been a scientist whose part was not merely laboratory work but testing and trying in the field as well. Certainly he has been no starry-eyed theorist. He has worked shoulder to shoulder with field men to help them solve the daily problems of life insurance men at work. It was no accident that his awareness of field requirements and public necessity produced the individual major medical expense protection. He turned his technical background to the service of the agency organization and to the solution of pressing national problems, for his roots are in the solid ground of basic human needs. So often he has been able to crystallize and articulate in practical, salable, sound form many changes which we in the field have needed to the advantage of all parties at interest. He has had almost prescient foresight in his ability to separate that which will be truly helpful from a long-range viewpoint from that which is merely expedient and a response to momentary clamor.[169]

Modest, approachable, and with a smiling twinkle in his eyes, the new President of Equitable had many friends. He was interested in art, music, and community affairs, and served as a trustee or officer in numerous charitable, religious, and educational organizations.

* * *

Now culminated a series of events which became magnified beyond all proportion to their importance and were, for a time, to be a major disturbing influence in the affairs of Equitable.

As early as 1948, the *United States Investor* had published a series of articles severely critical of President Parkinson's views on inflation and accusing the life insurance business of being stricken with "Parkinson's Disease."[170] Parkinson's views in regard to what constituted

[169] *Ibid.*

[170] October 16, 1948: "Life Insurance Flirting with Federal Regulation of Investment Practice"; November 6: "Life Insurance Fraternity Stricken With

sound currency were characterized as being "as dangerous as hammering dynamite." The articles also attacked the practice of life insurance companies making loans by private placement, and blamed these companies for heavy sales of government bonds, "thus abetting the inflationary spiral through multiple credit expansion." In November 1951 Superintendent of Insurance Alfred J. Bohlinger completed his report on the regular triennial examination of Equitable for the period ending December 31, 1950, but the report was not released at this time. Then, January 30, 1952, appeared the first of a series of articles in the *New York Journal-American* written by Leslie Gould, financial editor. The first of these articles was titled, "State Investigating Equitable Life Rule—Sift Deals and Fees to Kin." It dealt largely with the revelation that President Thomas I. Parkinson, beginning in 1948, had placed a substantial amount of Equitable's advertising through an agency headed by his son, Courtney V. Parkinson. An article the following day concentrated the attack on legal fees paid to lawyers on the Equitable Board and to the firm of Milbank, Tweed, Hope and Hadley, in which another son, Thomas I. Parkinson, Jr., was a partner. Succeeding articles highlighted Equitable's real estate projects (Clinton Hill, Fordham Hill, and Gateway Center) and charged favoritism in the awarding of the building contracts; they also called attention to an alleged conflict of interest on the part of some directors of the Society and charged mishandling of the McCarthy oil loans.[171] It appeared that these very critical articles were based upon a preview of Superintendent Bohlinger's unreleased report, and they were published with a flavor of sensationalism in the *Journal-American* and other Hearst newspapers.[172] Later the Associated Press released an article

---

'Parkinson's Disease' "; November 13: "We Answer a Letter From Parkinson of the Equitable Life"; January 29, 1949: "Why the Life Insurance Industry Rejected Parkinson's Resolution."

[171] Titles of the second and subsequent articles were as follows: January 31, "Equitable Life Legal Fees Examined in State Probe—Attorneys on Board"; February 1, "Equitable Building Projects Probed"; February 4, "Sift Equitable Handling of McCarthy Oil Loans"; and February 5, "Changes Recommended in Life Insurance Study."

[172] The revelation of the contents of Superintendent Bohlinger's report one year and nine months before the report was released intrigued the newspapermen. According to *The Eastern Underwriter* of November 6, 1953, the New York Insurance Department disclaimed responsibility for the leak and said that it had not been able to ascertain where Gould had got a copy. When the report came into the hands of the press October 29, 1953, the newspapermen found in the back part of it a page or two of items which conveniently summarized the

which said that architects and builders for Equitable's real estate projects had been selected without competitive bidding.

January 31, 1952, the day after Gould's first article appeared, process was served upon Equitable in two actions brought in the Supreme Court of the State of New York by policyholders, naming as defendants directors and officers of the Society.[173] Soon thereafter seven more actions were begun in the Supreme Court by other policyholders and four similar actions were started in the United States District Court for the Southern District of New York. The actions were of the type referred to in law as stockholders' derivative actions—brought in the name of a corporation, usually against directors, seeking a money judgment on the basis that the corporation suffered loss because of fraudulent or negligent acts of the directors. Generally speaking, the wrongful acts claimed in these actions were the payment of excessive and duplicative legal fees to Directors William Roberts and Robert J. Dodds, the payment of excessive amounts to directors for travel and other expenses, the payment of excessive construction fees to Starrett Brothers and Eken in connection with Gateway Center and Fordham Hill, the making of improvident loans to the Glenn McCarthy interests, the placing of Equitable's advertising through C. V. Parkinson Associates, Incorporated, and the publication of press releases through Continental Press Syndicate.

In April Justice William C. Hecht of the New York Supreme Court consented to a consolidation of the nine pending actions, which thereafter were known as *Imberman et al.* v. *Alexander et al.* The actions in the Federal court were stayed pending decision on the actions in the New York Court. Before Equitable was served with the complaint in the consolidated action, counsel for both sides entered into a stipulation discontinuing the action as to the officers of the Society. The complaint in the consolidated action was served July 24, and the

---

critical portions of the report. When reporters asked Superintendent Bohlinger whether he was trying to force President Parkinson out, he intimated that they could draw their own conclusions. *Ibid.*

[173] The defendant directors were Nicholas Kelley, Thomas I. Parkinson, Samuel A. Welldon, Henry G. Wood, and Samuel R. Walker. They were represented by the law firm of Davis, Polk, Wardwell, Sunderland and Kiendl. Defendant officers were Joseph R. Boldt, William M. Donohue, Charles W. Dow, Glenn McHugh, John H. Muller, William J. November, R. I. Nowell, and Frank A. Shailer. The officers were represented by the firm of Milbank, Tweed, Hope and Hadley. Later actions added the name of Director Henry M. Alexander and others to the list of defendants.

defendants filed answers. Before trial, plaintiffs, by stipulation, started an examination of the various defendants. Among those examined were Thomas I. Parkinson, C. V. Parkinson, Robert Dowling, and Samuel Walker. The case was placed on the Special Term trial calendar in October 1952 but was never brought to trial and was adjourned by successive stipulations until January 1956 when the Calendar Justice, on his own motion, marked the case off the calendar. The rules provided that if a case was marked off the trial calendar and not restored within one year it would be deemed abandoned and dismissed. (For the restoration of this case to the calendar and its final disposition, see this history, p. 1226.)

In June 1953 Thomas I. Parkinson had advised the Equitable Board that, at the completion of his term as Chairman of the Board (February 1954), he would sever his official connection with the Society, both as Chairman and as a Director; he had also informed the Superintendent of Insurance of this decision. On October 28 Superintendent Bohlinger issued a statement to the press announcing that his report on Equitable had been filed and coupled this statement with an announcement to the effect that Parkinson had declared his intention to resign.[174] This was an unprecedented act and seemed to contain implications beyond that which was expressed in Parkinson's statement. In a press conference following the release, Bohlinger summarized the main points in his report and said that the Equitable knew that he was going to announce Parkinson's retirement; when asked whether he had been instrumental in having Parkinson resign, he said: "I discussed it with them (Equitable)." [175]

On October 29 a dozen or more reporters called Equitable, some of them several times, and wanted to know whether the Society had any release in reply to Bohlinger's statement of the preceding day. President Murphy then issued a statement in which he pointed out that

[174] Equitable did not receive a copy of Bohlinger's release and first learned of it the following day at 9:40 A.M. when Arthur Merins of the Associated Press called Leslie R. Shope, Equitable's Advertising Manager. At 10:15 A.M. Shope reached Carl Pierson, Publicity Director of the New York State Insurance Department, on the telephone and Pierson read the second part of Bohlinger's release, as follows: "Mr. Bohlinger also announced that Thomas I. Parkinson, Chairman of the Board of Directors and a Director of the Society, had informed his Executive Committee of his decision to resign at the meeting of the Board on February 18, 1954."

[175] From summary notes on the conference taken by C. J. Guterl of Equitable's Advertising Department. Equitable Archives.

the more important items brought up in Bohlinger's report had been fully discussed in the Society's Annual Report for 1951, and that "as long ago as last June Mr. Parkinson informed the Board of Directors of the Society of his intention to relinquish all official connection with the Society at the end of his present term as Chairman which expires on February 18, 1954." He regarded the most important point in Bohlinger's report to be that stated in the "Summary and Conclusion" as follows: "The examination of the Equitable Life Assurance Society of the United States indicates that it is in sound financial condition."

The next day, October 30, Thomas I. Parkinson issued the following statement to the press:

> I am not ill and I will not resign. I am undergoing an eye operation for which arrangements were made several weeks ago. I am proud of all my record with The Equitable and of The Equitable's growth under my direction, including its contribution to public welfare.
>
> I have not resigned and I will not resign. The Superintendent of Insurance earlier this year threatened proceedings against the directors of The Equitable to induce my retirement. Now, however, his report discloses no illegal act has been committed. My continued association with The Equitable will therefore be determined by its Board of Directors.
>
> Neither the Superintendent nor any other state official is being considered for the vacancy which my ultimate retirement might create.[176]

Later the same day, Superintendent Bohlinger told the press that he had read Parkinson's statement and had requested President Murphy to convene a special meeting of the Board of Directors for Wednesday morning, November 4, to consider the matter.[177]

Since Chairman of the Board Thomas I. Parkinson was keeping his date with the eye surgeons, President Murphy presided and stated the purpose of the meeting. He then introduced Superintendent Bohlinger, who spoke at length and stated his position in detail. First, he said that the Department had, in June 1951, called the Equitable Board's

[176] Copy in Equitable Archives. When newspapermen checked with Shope on this release, they were informed that the only release sent out by Equitable's Advertising Department was that issued by President Murphy.

[177] October 30 *The Wall Street Journal* telegraphed President Murphy at his home and informed him that the *Journal* was polling the entire Board of Directors in regard to their stand on the Parkinson question. Some of the replies, which revealed little, were published in the *Journal* November 2. The directors also received a number of telegrams from policyholders and others.

attention to the fact that President Parkinson had turned over a "substantial volume of advertising" to his son, Courtney V. Parkinson, "a man of most tender years who had had little experience in advertising matters." When a member of the Board questioned the propriety of this act (May 1950), President Parkinson replied in a memorandum which Bohlinger said he believed had been given to the Board "for the purpose of making a deliberate misrepresentation." The Superintendent then took up the payment of legal fees to members of the Board and the construction contracts, which he said had been "angled to one builder" and without competitive bidding. He claimed that he had got no satisfaction from President Parkinson on these matters, and so had taken them up with the Executive Committee of the Equitable Board, which soon thereafter terminated the advertising contracts and resolved that no contracts in excess of $50,000 could be awarded except by the Board. He considered these actions an admission that there had been "improprieties here." Consequently, since his examiners were not trained as lawyers, he had asked Judge William Mertens, Jr., to conduct a supplementary investigation. He said that Mertens' report had not only buttressed the report of the Department's examiners, but had brought up another matter, namely, that President Parkinson had begun to send a substantial amount of legal business to the firm of Milbank, Tweed, Hope and Hadley just after his son had joined that firm. Furthermore, the Mertens report pointed out that "there was a breach of Mr. Parkinson's fiduciary obligation to your Board in connection with the Gateway Center project and concluded . . . by recommending that I, as Superintendent of Insurance, institute proceedings under the provisions of the insurance law for Mr. Parkinson's removal as an officer and director on the ground set forth in the statute, namely, untrustworthiness and dishonesty."

At this point Theodore Kiendl, counsel for the Society, stated, "I do not think you mean 'dishonesty.'" Bohlinger replied, "Untrustworthiness, I stand corrected." When asked whether he was going to make the Mertens report available, he replied that the directors were at liberty to see it, but that he did not think that it should be filed, because if it were, "limitless harm could come to the Society and its policyholders." He said that he had shown a copy to Parkinson in May and that Kiendl had pointed out that Parkinson's face might be saved by an announcement on his part that he would retire at the expiration of his term as Chairman of the Board. Bohlinger said that he "saw no reason to delight if the man made this decision, and step on his neck when he was down," so he went along with it as a graceful exit. When asked to agree to Parkinson's remaining on the Board, he said that he could not and would not go along with such an arrangement; if the Board did not agree with him he had no choice but to proceed under the statute for Parkinson's removal. He said that he had taken Parkinson's letter of June 3, 1953, expressing his intention to retire, in good faith and would await Parkinson's public announcement, "but upon a condition that should circumstances dictate I would announce it." Following a discussion of the semantics of "retire" and "resign," Bohlinger said that they were synonymous and both signified ending a relationship. He stated: "What had been agreed to in a sense is borne out by the statement of your present president, Mr. Murphy, that Mr. Parkinson had notified your Board of his intention to retire. I held a press conference . . . and I made an observation in connection with Mr. Parkinson's stepping down that he had been ill and wanted to retire." Then came Parkinson's statement that he would not resign: "At that point, the fat was in the fire. . . . Had I known that Mr. Parkinson would change his position in any manner I would have started proceedings for his removal last June. . . . I cannot compel him to undo what he has done or do what he said he would do; I am left with only one alternative. I say that we have to take the bull by the horns and make the decision for Mr. Parkinson. . . . This matter must be brought to a termination immediately. If it is not, I must proceed with a statutory hearing for his removal. I have the citation, as we call it, all ready. I cannot temporize with this, gentlemen."[178]

Reactions to Superintendent Bohlinger's presentation of his case were positive and varied. Some of the directors believed that he was exceeding his powers and playing politics; others believed that President Parkinson had made mistakes not in the best interests of the Society. While the Superintendent waited in an adjoining room for the Board's action, the debate continued for several hours. Finally, by a majority vote, the Board expressed its willingness to undertake, by resolution, the responsibility for seeing that Parkinson's promise to retire as Chairman and Director on February 18, 1954, be carried out. To implement this resolution, the Board presented an amendment to the Society's By-Laws which would authorize the removal of any director for cause.[179] It then resolved that whereas on June 3, 1953,

[178] The above summary of Superintendent Bohlinger's long talk is taken from a stenographic report of the special meeting. Copy in Equitable Archives.

[179] The existing By-Laws authorized the removal of any officer of the Society but this provision did not apply to directors.

Thomas I. Parkinson had advised the Executive Committee that he intended to retire and stated this intention to the Superintendent of Insurance, the Board would assume full responsibility for carrying out this arrangement. The proper officers of the Society "were authorized and directed" to take the necessary steps to implement and carry out the purpose of this resolution. When this was accomplished, the meeting ended; it had lasted twelve hours. November 5, President Ray D. Murphy released a statement summarizing the Board's action.

Thus retired from Equitable the man who had recovered the Vereinsbank deposit from Germany, directed the liquidation of the Society's foreign business, won the Russian Cases, guided the Society through the great depression, made many profitable investments for it, and led the opposition against retroactive taxation. Perhaps more important than any of these things was the campaign he had waged on behalf of the policyholders of the country against New Deal financial policies which had resulted in inflation and the ensuing depreciation of the value of their policies. Thomas I. Parkinson had been chief executive officer of Equitable for more than twenty-five years. During that period, Equitable had again been brought to a position of pre-eminence among the life insurance companies of the world; its insurance in force had increased from $5,469,715,564 to $21,101,606,385, and its assets were almost seven times as great as they had been at the beginning of the period. In Parkinson's mind, however, mere size was not the basic standard for judging an executive's success in the management of a life insurance company. The most important thing that management could do was to provide against loss of principal. As he said: "Management is not a trusteeship legally, it is not a trusteeship ethically, but it is a trusteeship 'poetically.'" [180] Judged upon this criterion, Thomas I. Parkinson earned his place among the small group of top-flight life insurance company executives in the nation's history. Said *The Eastern Underwriter:* "Often controversial, not always in harmony with attitudes of other companies, a man of courage who has not been reluctant to swing punches when he considers his attitude in the best public interest, a strong individualist, his record is that of one of the most successful executives in the business." [181]

Parkinson's retirement under these circumstances had serious repercussions. Not only was the Board divided on the question as to

[180] Thomas I. Parkinson, interview with author, November 30, 1955.
[181] *The Eastern Underwriter*, LIV (1953), November 6.

whether the proper action had been taken, but so were officers, Home Office personnel, and the field forces. Not since 1905 had Equitable received such unfavorable publicity at the hands of certain newspapers. Many persons regarded the whole affair not only as unfortunate, but also unnecessary. Why then did it happen? Various factors were involved, both internal and external, some having to do with management policies, and some personal; there were also important political connotations.

All of the recommendations made by the examiners of the Insurance Department had been complied with long before the Superintendent's pronunciamento of October 28.[182] Why then the unusual procedure? Said *The Insurance Index* in an article entitled "Bohlinger Victorious?" "Since Mr. Parkinson had already indicated an intention to retire, it is clear that Superintendent Bohlinger's actions must have been motivated by issues outside the sphere of normal official responsibility and that indignation and animosity were important to their design." [183] The editor of the *Insurance Advocate* wrote: "Having known the New York Superintendents who served during the past 40 years, it seems difficult to understand why the present holder of that high office is unmindful of the traditions his predecessors have handed down.

182 Members of the Executive Committee of the Board had conferred with Superintendent Bohlinger August 15 and September 4, 1951, relative to certain matters presented to him by the Department's examiners. As a result of the first conference the advertising contract with C. V. Parkinson Associates, Incorporated, was terminated, and resolutions were adopted to the effect that no person related by blood, marriage, or adoption to any director, officer, or manager of the Society be employed by the Society or be a party to any contract with the Society without approval of the Executive Committee or other appropriate committee of the Board. November 14, 1951, the Executive Committee held a special meeting in Superintendent Bohlinger's office. It was at this meeting that Julius Sackman, Chief of the Life Bureau, in the absence of Mr. Bohlinger due to illness, announced that the Superintendent had appointed Judge Mertens as special counsel to aid in the investigation of Equitable. President Parkinson said there could be no objection to this procedure, and the Committee resolved that the officers of the Society should cooperate with the Insurance Department and its special counsel and should report to the Executive Committee. Minutes of Executive Committee. Corporate Records. In December President Parkinson appointed Counsel Leo D. Fitzgerald of Equitable's Legal Department to work with Judge Mertens in the examination of Equitable. Parkinson wrote Mertens December 21: "I think that will facilitate your work and co-ordinate our contribution to it. . . . I shall, of course, be glad to respond to any call that you may want to make to my office." Parkinson files, Equitable Archives.

183 *The Insurance Index,* XV (1953), December. The article was written by James E. Dunne, publisher of the *Index* and of *Dunne's International Insurance Reports,* Louisville, Kentucky.

And for fear that I have been misjudging his actions, I have devoted most of the past two weeks to a canvass of opinion, only to discover that almost every insurance man I have consulted is alike shocked by Mr. Bohlinger's course of action in the Equitable case." After publishing this editorial, the *Advocate* received numerous letters of endorsement.[184]

One of the most severe criticisms of Bohlinger's actions came from the pen of a fellow commissioner. John J. Holmes, State Auditor and Commissioner of Insurance for Montana, accused the New York Commissioner of having a very exaggerated idea of his own importance. Then in regard to the advertising contracts Holmes wrote:

> Since when did Government assume to dictate where and how private industry should conduct its private affairs, so long as the practice is not detrimental to the affairs of the public which may be dealing with the private industry? Is it possible that "the political powers" in Albany who appointed you . . . had selected advertising firms through which "big business," domiciled in New York, should place their advertising? . . . No, Mr. Superintendent, I cannot condone your actions in this matter. I believe it to be the duty of state insurance supervisors to protect the insuring public, and interfere with internal company operations only where such operations are detrimental to the good of the public.[185]

There still remained, however, the question of nepotism—Parkinson's Achilles' heel. When Superintendent Bohlinger was asked whether there had been any misapplication of funds in placing nearly one million dollars in advertising over a three-year period with the agency in which Parkinson's son was interested, his reply was, "No." Said *The Spectator*: "While this is nepotism, it is neither unmoral, un-

[184] The *Insurance Advocate*, LXIV (1953), November 14 and 28.

[185] John J. Holmes to Alfred J. Bohlinger, November 17, 1953. Copy in Equitable Archives.

January 14, 1954, Thomas I. Parkinson wrote Commissioner Holmes as follows: "I would always be in favor of the power to investigate as a basis for legislative or administrative action in the interest of the public welfare. I never objected to any phase of the examination of the Equitable or of my own participation in its administration. Some of the questions were a little annoying but, after all, I preferred to have them asked so that I might answer, rather than have a doubt remain in the examiner's mind. What I do object to in this particular instance, and would object to in any other instance, is the one-sidedness of the inquiry, the failure to provide an opportunity to present our side of some of the actions involved, and the use that was made of tentative findings." Copy in Parkinson files, Equitable Archives.

ethical, nor, in this particular case, was it unprofitable to the company." [186] But nepotism is a word which has unfavorable connotations in the mind of the public, and there were those among the members of the Board who did not think that Equitable should have to face that issue. The *New York World-Telegram and Sun* said: "Can it be they as directors of this life insurance organization had no alternative but to bend to the will of this state official? Is this state official so powerful he can require directors of the third largest life insurance organization in the country to do his bidding? Or, to hide their own shortcomings, were they willing to sacrifice a fellow director and the man who probably was most responsible for their selection as directors?" [187]

Although Parkinson, as President, had been largely responsible for the selection of most of the members of the Board, it was never unanimously "his Board." Director George V. McLaughlin had strongly opposed Equitable's Gateway Center project, and other directors were skeptical. Parkinson believed that some of the directors were working behind the scenes with the newspaper reporters and with the construction companies which did not get the Gateway contracts.[188] Then there were friendly directors who no doubt felt that President Parkinson had not exercised good judgment in acting on certain matters without first consulting the Board. There also seemed to be some feeling that he had erred in concentrating too much executive power in his own hands. On this subject the *New York Journal-American* had this to say: ". . . his biggest mistake was allowing himself to become an autocrat and not to take kindly to negative advice." [189] Some persons thought that the Board's greatest mistake was in temporizing; that Parkinson should have been eased out in February 1953, then when Superintendent Bohlinger's report came out it would have been "water over the dam." The Board in its endeavor to spare Parkinson's feelings had been too sentimental: "That's sentiment gone rancid; it is sentimentality." [190]

As for the political aspects of the case, there had been much speculation as to whether Superintendent Bohlinger was maneuvering for the

186 *The Spectator*, CLXI (1953), December.
187 *New York World-Telegram and Sun*, November 6, 1953.
188 Thomas I. Parkinson, interview with author, September 2, 1958.
189 Leslie Gould in the *Journal-American*, November 4, 1953.
190 See interviews reported in article in the *Washington Post*, November 4, 1953, over the by-line of J. A. Livingston.

presidency of Equitable. Some thought that he was not working for himself but for Governor Thomas E. Dewey. As early as April 5, 1952, a signed article in *The Daily Mirror* stated that "a top administrative berth with Equitable Life is still open to the Governor." Then, after the special meeting of the Board, speculation became rife. November 6 Leslie Gould noted that several political figures had been named as possibilities for the Equitable presidency, including Governor Dewey and Superintendent Bohlinger, and *The Wall Street Journal* mentioned the same names but stated that both the Governor and Bohlinger had denied their candidacies.[191] A week later, Dorothy Kilgallen in the "Voice of Broadway" stated that Governor Dewey could have the $100,000-a-year job at Equitable Life if he merely dropped a hat, and Earl Wilson in his column said: "Equitable Life Directors chose Alfred Bohlinger, Superintendent of Insurance, for President, and would elevate Ray Murphy to board chairman." [192] Walter Winchell in his column, "On Broadway," said that Equitable would like to replace Parkinson with either Dewey or Truman. Even more interesting was the account in the Yonkers *New York Record* of Lieutenant Governor Wicks' threat to blow the Senate session wide open with the charge that Superintendent Bohlinger had, at Dewey's request, demanded that Parkinson be liquidated in order to make way for Dewey to take over his post at an annual salary of $100,000.[193]

Almost two weeks after the special meeting of the Board, Parkinson wrote each director as follows:

A misunderstanding of fact, which seems to me vital, has come to my attention and I take the only presently available means of communicating with you promptly.

[191] *New York Journal-American* and *The Wall Street Journal,* November 6, 1953.

[192] Dorothy Kilgallen, "Voice of Broadway," *New York Journal-American,* November 12 and 18, 1953; Earl Wilson, "It Happened Last Night," *New York Post,* November 17, 1953.

[193] Winchell, "On Broadway," various papers, November 21 and 26, 1953; the Yonkers *New York Record,* November 15, 1953.

According to Parkinson, Governor Dewey was not eager to run for re-election in 1950. When some sentiment developed for an Eisenhower candidacy, Parkinson told the General that if he wanted to run for the Presidency in 1952, it would be better that he not run for governor. Incidentally, Parkinson and Thomas J. Watson, President of International Business Machines Corporation—both trustees of Columbia University—had been influential in getting General Eisenhower elected to the presidency of Columbia. Thomas I. Parkinson, interview with author, September 2, 1958.

At the time of the recent special meeting of the Board, I understand representations were made to the effect that I knew, or had reason to know, that the Superintendent of Insurance had determined to announce my retirement unless I did so myself.

Such was not the fact. I had intended to announce my retirement at our Managers' meeting in January and I had no reason to believe that demand was being made on me for an earlier announcement. Mr. Kiendl told me that the Superintendent wanted to include my statement of June in the triennial report and that he, Mr. Kiendl, objected, and, in his last word to me on the subject, he said he would vigorously protest its inclusion. This confirmed my understanding that the statement was not to be used in connection with the triennial report.

If demand had been made on me for announcement of my retirement, I would not have hesitated to make the same statement publicly as I made to the Board in June.

It was the Superintendent, not I, who violated the understanding of June.[194]

In reply, a number of directors expressed their disapproval of the actions of the Board and their faith in Parkinson. Said one prominent director: "It seemed to me that it was a trial without giving the defendant an opportunity to testify. I was unhappy at the kind of decision that the Board felt necessary to make, although you must know that we labored long and hard to try to protect you as well as the good name of Equitable. . . . On the other hand, many of my acquaintances who are intelligent people recognized, and have so stated to me, that the action of the Insurance Superintendent was a sort of persecution." Wrote another:

It was with the greatest possible reluctance that the directors finally adopted the resolution. Some of us tried time and time again to retain our original wording in the resolution, but were met with formidable opposition on the part of the adversary. . . . In the final analysis there seemed

[194] Letter dated November 17, 1953. Copy in Parkinson files, Equitable Archives.

December 16, 1953, Parkinson, in reply to a letter from James E. Dunne, publisher of *Dunne's International Insurance Reports*, said: ". . . my recent experiences disclose to me two important and, I think, unfortunate, probabilities in the life insurance industry. First, there is the matter of political bullying of officers and directors whose efforts do not receive any real support from policyholders who have been well served. Second, I think the operations in this and other cases of our State Insurance Department have advanced the cause of those who favor substitution of Federal regulation." Copy in *ibid.*

no alternative, but to vote for the resolution. The other course would have thrown the Society into the turmoil of litigation, accounts of which would have been widely publicized, and which would have taken a toll on your health and strength, and torn down considerably the institution you labored for thirty years with might and main to build up.[195]

Director Sterling Morton, Chairman of the Board of Morton Salt Company, summarized the distressing events of 1953 very judiciously:

Remembrance of my father's part in selecting you to head the Equitable adds to my disappointment in not being present at this farewell party. I share his faith in you and, as at the special meeting, am ready to affirm it. At the same time, as I said at another meeting, we all make mistakes at times. Those have in no way changed my feelings toward you nor dimmed in any way my appreciation, as a policyholder as well as director, of the wonderful things you have done for the Society.[196]

* * *

Although many of the bitter feelings resulting from the decisions made in 1953 became somewhat mellowed with the passage of time, some of the legal actions instigated were to remain unsettled for years.

First, to return to the Imberman case: after this case was stricken off the court calendar in 1956, the plaintiffs, in April 1958, moved to restore it to the calendar. Despite the fact that more than a year had elapsed since it had been marked off, Justice Thomas A. Aurelio granted the motion.[197] The case came to trial in the Supreme Court before Justice Henry Epstein in November. At the opening of the trial, the Court dismissed all of the causes of action except those relating to advertising placed through Courtney V. Parkinson Associates, Incorporated. Justice Epstein rendered his opinion January 15, 1959. After noting that the combined Equitable policies held by the nine plaintiffs totaled only about $10,000, or less than one six-hundred-thousandth of the assets of the Society, Justice Epstein reviewed the charge that the advertising contracts awarded to Courtney V. Parkinson represented a waste of Equitable's assets. He could find no proof of excessive charges, nor was he impressed with the fact that young

195 Copies in *ibid.*

196 Sterling Morton to Thomas I. Parkinson, February 9, 1954. *Ibid.* Morton, in Santa Barbara, because of his doctor's orders was unable to attend the farewell dinner for Parkinson held February 17.

197 12 Misc. 2d 630.

Parkinson was not a college graduate and hence not qualified to handle such an advertising program. He said that the plaintiffs had failed to make out a case to show that these contracts represented a "property" advantage to Thomas I. Parkinson:

> Not the slightest proof is offered, nor can any inference be drawn, that Thomas I. Parkinson either had a financial interest in or derived any profit from his son's services. The charges that defendant Equitable's President sought to have "Equitable subsidize his son" finds no support in the record. . . . One fact remains outstanding—the commisions earned by young Parkinson and his company, almost all paid by the advertising media, newspapers and magazines, were at customary rates and did not cost the Equitable one cent more than if placed through any other agency. Nor is there any basis for a conclusion that such expenditures were excessive, duplicatory or unnecessary or that the material so used was, either in content or format, inferior to top standards.

The complaint was dismissed.[198]

In March 1959 all counsel stipulated that the final judgment of the state court was *res adjudicata* as to all issues in the four Federal court cases. April 8 Judge Edmund L. Palmieri of the United States District Court of the Southern District of New York signed an order dismissing the actions.

Even more lengthy in its history than the Imberman case was the Garfield case. Actually, the "Garfield case" involved three separate litigations spanning a period of almost thirteen years. On November 9, 1953, five days after the special meeting of the Equitable Board with Superintendent Bohlinger, Gustave B. Garfield, a policyholder, commenced a mandamus proceeding in the Supreme Court, New York County, in which he sought to force the Superintendent of Insurance and the Attorney General, as his legal representative, to bring an action against the directors and officers of Equitable for improper acts. Failing in this, in 1956, he commenced a derivative action in the same court against the corporation and twenty-two of its directors. Eventually this action was dismissed after trial and the dismissal was affirmed on appeal by the Appellate Division of the Supreme Court.[199] In May 1965, and while his appeal in the derivative action was pending, Garfield started a third suit in which he sought to recover his

[198] 16 Misc. 2d 330.
[199] 24 A.D. 2d 840.

attorney's fees and expenses and it ended in June 1966 with the affirmance of the dismissal of the complaint by the New York Court of Appeals.[200]

In the mandamus proceeding, many of the charges were the same as those presented in the Imberman action, but an important addition was the claim that Equitable's investment in Gateway Center was illegal because it was in excess of the investment limit set forth under the New York Insurance Law.[201] Garfield criticized the Imberman action on the ground that the plaintiffs had not attempted initially to secure redress from the Insurance Department and on the further ground that Imberman merely charged improper business judgment, while Garfield's action was based on the sounder ground of illegal and *ultra vires* acts.

Equitable became a party to the Garfield proceeding when it was granted permission to intervene. The application for hearing was opposed by the Attorney General's office and by Counsel Leo D. Fitzgerald of Equitable. The Superintendent of Insurance and the Attorney General asserted that there was no basis for the maintenance of an action for waste against Equitable and there was no reason to believe that such an action could be successfully maintained. On these bases, the public officials refused to institute the action. The application was denied by Justice Ernest Hammer in September 1954, and was affirmed in February 1956 on Garfield's appeal to the Appellate Division.[202]

When Garfield intervened with the commencement of the man-

[200] 17 N.Y. 2d 841.

[201] N.Y. Ins. Law 81.7 (h). Garfield maintained that the original three office buildings of Gateway Center constituted one parcel of real estate because they were constructed on contiguous lots in one ownership.

[202] 1 A.D. 2d 820.

The Equitable also contended that a policyholder of a mutual life insurance company, such as Garfield, unlike a stockholder, did not have the right to sue on behalf of the corporation. In his decision Justice Hammer sustained the Equitable's contentions. The Appellate Division however, specifically refused to rule upon the question. Immediately after the commencement of the derivative action, Equitable moved to dismiss that complaint on the policyholder's lack of capacity to sue. Justice James B. M. McNally ruled that a policyholder had such a right, concluding that there appeared to be no public policy to be served by refusing to equate a policyholder with a stockholder (164 N.Y.S. 2d 819). No appeal was taken and throughout the litigation no further contention along these lines was made by defendants. Thus, the question of the policyholder's capacity to sue was denied in one lower court decision and affirmed in another without a ruling by an appellate court in either case.

damus proceeding in 1953, Equitable, in accordance with its contract with the Urban Redevelopment Authority (see this history, p. 1158) had in June 1950 undertaken the redevelopment of a twenty-three-acre blighted area located in the golden triangle of Pittsburgh. The construction contract was awarded to Starrett Brothers and Eken on a cost plus fixed fee basis. In accordance with plans and estimates drawn in 1950, the construction of the original three office buildings was completed in 1953. At this time, tenants were in the process of moving in. There were unoccupied areas and leases were being negotiated. Studies and plans for further development were being made. The three buildings occupied about six of the twenty-three acres. The remaining land was cleared and was converted temporarily to parking areas.

In March 1956 Garfield instituted the derivative action against the Equitable and its directors.[203] Garfield charged that the investment was illegal. He complained that the cost plus fixed fee contract with the construction company was improvident, that favoritism was shown in the choice of the contractor, that there was self-dealing on the part of the directors and the directors were negligent in permitting the cost of construction to go beyond what had been estimated in 1950. There followed a series of motions by defendants to dismiss the complaint and three amended complaints. His charges of illegality were dismissed in May 1957 by Justice Harold A. Stevens, and his attempts to reassert the same charge in subsequent complaints, despite the admonition of the courts, were frustrated. From July 3, 1956, to July 13, 1960, the complaint and three amended complaints were reviewed by the court with the result that the case, when it was reached for trial in June 1964 on the fourth amended complaint, involved charges of improvidence based on the increased costs of the original three buildings.[204] These increased costs had derived from a number of changes made in the original plans; the buildings had been increased in size,

[203] The summons and complaint in the action was served on Chairman of the Board Ray D. Murphy on March 29, 1956. President Charles W. Dow, Senior Vice President Walter Klem, and Vice Chairman of the Board Robert L. Hogg were served April 16, 1956. Later service was made on eighteen additional individual defendants (directors).

[204] 164 N.Y.S. 2d 819, Justice McNally's decision; 7 Misc. 2d 419, Justice Steven's decision; 184 N.Y.S. 2d 755, Justice Aurelio's decision; 182 N.Y.S. 2d 626, Justice Markewich's decision; 9 App. Div. 2d 887, decision of the Appellate Division affirming and modifying Justice Markewich's decision; N.Y.L.J., April 20, 1960, Justice Aurelio's decision; and 205 N.Y.S. 2d 758, Justice Greenberg's decision.

their exterior changed from masonry to stainless steel, a television studio had been added to one building and a parking garage and restaurant in the basement of another. Garfield complained that these increased costs were in no way compensated for by increased income. He claimed that Equitable's directors were negligent in this respect and should restore to Equitable the amount of the excess costs, several millions of dollars. With regard to the remaining land in the project, plaintiff contended at various times that these parcels should not have been purchased, the purchase was illegal, that having been purchased they should have been sold immediately, that the directors had opportunities to sell and that they delayed unduly in making plans for an underground garage to take the place of the open parking areas.

The directors contended that the record of the planning, construction, and earnings of the original three buildings justified the undertaking. They took the position that because of the magnitude of the project, its costs could not be confined to original estimates made some years before and that its success or failure could not be judged on the income produced in its initial stages, but that from the nature of the project a certain time would elapse between the undertaking of the project and its ultimate development. The directors also contended that in the proper exercise of business judgment it was for them to say when and how the property should be further developed and that the pace of development would, of necessity, be geared to the needs of the City of Pittsburgh. Defendants showed that, in accordance with plans for expansion made in 1953, portions were sold in 1954 to the State of Pennsylvania for its Western State Office Building and to the Bell Telephone Company for the erection of an office building. As demand for space increased, further expansion of the project was undertaken. The construction of the underground garage was started in 1957 as was the construction of the fourth office building. In 1956 the land lease for the Pittsburgh Hilton Hotel was made and a similar lease for the apartment house was entered in 1962. In 1961, the Equitable made plans for construction of the I.B.M. building. Over this period of time the project became a financial success as well as a pioneer project in privately financed urban redevelopment.

The case was tried and argued before Justice Samuel C. Coleman of the Supreme Court, New York County, during the summer of 1964, and in December the Judge rendered his decision which completely exonerated the defendants and dismissed the complaint. In his opinion,

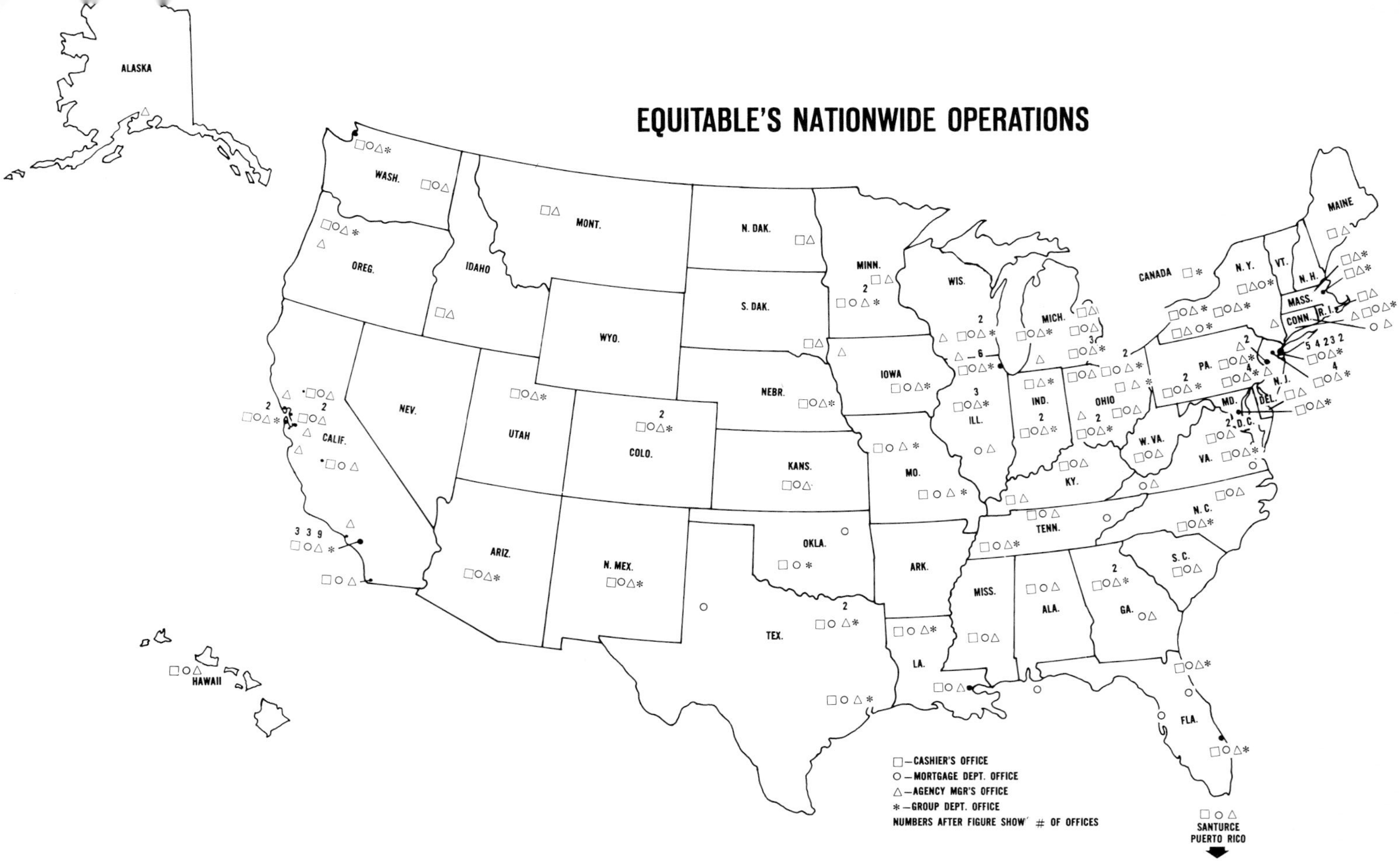

Field Offices, 1964

he stated: "No one of the contentions made by the plaintiff whether in the original pleadings or as now presented, has any validity." He quoted with apparent approval the following passage from the 1954 report of the New York Insurance Department:

> In reviewing all that the Society has accomplished to date it is fair to say that the Gateway Center project seems assured of success. The Society undertook a pioneering step in revitalizing a portion of a city that had outlived its economic usefulness and by thoughtful planning and aggressive promotion has developed what appears to be a successful investment.

In conclusion he said:

> The plaintiff may say that I have been indulging in mathematical rationalization. Perhaps so. The plaintiff's entire argument proceeds upon the basis of formulas unrelated to the actual events, formulas which I believe to be erroneous when applied to the circumstances confronting the directors. Directors should direct, but I see nothing in the record of this case to call for the conclusion that the directors, in undertaking the additional expenses that the plaintiff complains of and in retaining the parking lots, were guilty of negligence or of wrongdoing. The complaint is dismissed.[205]

Garfield's appeal from the decision of the trial court was affirmed by the Appellate Division of the Supreme Court in October 1965.[206]

In May 1965 and while his appeal from the trial court's judgment was pending, he at first moved in that action for an award of plaintiff's counsel fees and disbursements. This application was denied by Justice Amsterdam who said: "The applicants have not demonstrated adequately that the action brought on behalf of the Corporation 'was successful, in whole or in part, or [that] anything was received by the plaintiff or plaintiffs or a claimant or claimants as the result of a judgment, compromise or settlement of an action or claim.'" The court added that the denial of the application was without prejudice to Garfield's right to institute a plenary action for his expenses if he was so advised. Thereupon in May 1965 he brought a separate action to recover from Equitable his attorney's fees and disbursements. Immediately Garfield served a notice to examine before trial all of the

205 N.Y.L.J. December 29, 1964.
206 24 A.D. 2d 840.

directors who were named in the prior proceedings. The corporation moved to dismiss the complaint, which was denied.[207] Equitable appealed from the denial of its motion and its appeal was argued in September, 1965, immediately following the argument of Garfield's appeal from the decision in the derivative action. The appellate court reversed the decision of the lower court and dismissed the complaint.[208] Garfield did not appeal from the affirmance of the decision in the derivative action but appealed to the Court of Appeals from the dismissal of his complaint in the action for attorney's fees and expenses.

The basis for Garfield's claim was that, by means of his actions, he established the right of a policyholder to sue in a derivative action in behalf of a mutual insurance company. In this respect, the Appellate Division stated that it was not clear that such a right had been established but that even if it had been, it resulted in no benefit to the corporation. The second benefit Garfield claimed as a basis for recovery was that his litigations had provided the impetus for the successful development of the project. On this point, the court noted Garfield's vacillation and substantial position shift from his initial claims and concluded that there was no evidence to support Garfield's contentions that his actions supplied the impetus which resulted in the financial success that the Gateway project became. The Court of Appeals dismissed Garfield's action for counsel fees and expenses.[209] Thus ended thirteen years of unnecessary litigation from which neither the Society nor the plaintiff gained anything. Plaintiff persisted in his efforts when at the outset he was admonished by the courts, the Superintendent of Insurance, and the Attorney General that there was no basis for maintenance of an action for waste, that there was no reason to believe that an action for waste could be successfully maintained, and that there was no basis in fact for the allegations and charges set forth in his complaints.

* * *

When Ray D. Murphy became President in February 1953, he considered his most important immediate task to be the reorganization of the administration of the Society. As a result of his long observation of Equitable affairs, he had developed certain convictions which guided his actions. It was not his nature to adopt an autocratic attitude; he

207 N.Y.L.J., July 13, 1965.
208 24 A.D. 2d 74.
209 17 N.Y. 2d 841.

believed in sharing responsibility. He thought that closer coordination could be achieved by putting the responsibility for directing related parts of the Society's operations upon a few senior officers; that only by being given such responsibilities could men be developed to fill the top positions. He also realized that there were certain shortcomings in the existing staff and that, no matter how unpleasant it might be to make replacements, duty should not be shirked, particularly when the incumbents were already beyond retirement age and it would be better to replace them by younger men. The reorganization begun in 1953 was not to be a final and completed thing; rather, it was to be a continuing process, an evolving program which was to extend over a number of years.

As a result of the reorganization program begun in 1953, several of the older vice presidents retired, and three senior vice presidents were appointed.[210] Among the retiring vice presidents was Henry Greaves, who had come to Equitable as an office boy in 1894, served as Assistant Treasurer, Treasurer, and Vice President. His career of fifty-nine years of active service was one of the longest in Equitable's history; he had known all of Equitable's presidents except the first, William C. Alexander. Over the years, he had handled many millions of dollars in securities.[211] Other officers who retired were Mervyn Davis, Executive Vice President, Underwriting Department, and Joseph R. Boldt, Vice President, Claims Department. Executive Vice President Raymond H. Weins ceased to be an active officer of the Society September 30, 1953, and Vice President Frank L. Jones, who had been in charge of Public Relations and Advertising since 1933, died in December 1953.

The title of Senior Vice President was new to Equitable; there had been first, second, third, and fourth vice presidents, agency vice presidents, and executive vice presidents, but no senior vice presidents. The three new positions were filled as follows:

All sales operations were placed under Senior Vice President Alvin B. Dalager, who had been in the Home Office since 1938 and Agency Vice President since 1952.[212]

Senior Vice President and Actuary Walter Klem, who had been with

210 By Executive Order, February 16, 1953.

211 In January 1964, Greaves was honored at a luncheon given by the Board of Directors on his 70th Equitable anniversary. For a brief sketch of Greaves' Equitable career, together with some charming reminiscences, see "The Proud Boy: 70 Years Later," in *Equinews*, VIII (February 1964).

212 For a sketch of Dalager's career, see this history, p. 1198.

the Society since 1947, was made head of the Actuary's Department and also given general supervision of all departments engaged in insurance operations, namely, Claims, Controller's (except audit functions), Medical, Policy Issue and Service, and Underwriting; he also became Chairman of the Rules and Regulations Committee and of the Committee on Co-ordination of Machine Procedures, and (later in the year) was given the general supervision of the Home Office Administration Department. Senior Vice President Klem began his insurance career as an office boy in the Actuary's Department of the Mutual Life Insurance Company in 1918 at the age of fourteen. Home study, night school classes, and Columbia University extension courses enabled him to qualify as a Fellow of the Actuarial Society of America at the age of twenty-three. In 1926 he was appointed Actuarial Assistant at the Mutual Life and three years later was promoted to Assistant Actuary; in 1941 he became Associate Actuary. During his years at Mutual, Klem taught actuarial mathematics to intercompany classes and lectured for the Insurance Society of New York. He was elected Secretary of the Actuarial Society of America in 1939 and held that office—with a three-year war interruption—until 1949, when he was elected Vice President. During the 1930's he was a member of the International Congresses of Actuaries which met at Stockholm and Paris, and became a United States member of the Council of Direction for the International Congresses of Actuaries. Klem joined Equitable as Second Vice President and Associate Actuary in July 1947 and in 1951 was appointed Vice President and Associate Actuary. The same year that he became Senior Vice President, Klem was appointed by President Eisenhower to a three-man board to assist the Department of Defense in formulating and administering a system to provide survivorship options in the pensions of retired servicemen. The following year he was elected President of the Society of Actuaries, which had been formed as the result of a merger of the Actuarial Society of America and the American Institute of Actuaries in 1949.

All investment operations were placed under the general supervision of Senior Vice President Charles W. Dow. These included the City Mortgage Department, City Real Estate Department, Farm Mortgage Department, Securities Investment Department, Treasurer's Department, and Counsel-Investment.[213]

Henry G. Wood, Secretary of the Society, resigned as Director in April 1953 and as Secretary in December. His successor was Gordon K.

[213] For a sketch of Dow's career, see this history, p. 1245.

Smith, CLU, who was elected Secretary of the Society December 17. After being graduated from Colgate University with Phi Beta Kappa honors, Smith enrolled in Equitable's Cashier's Training Course at Spokane, Washington. He served as Assistant Cashier at Spokane and Denver, and as Cashier at Providence, Rhode Island, and Syracuse, New York. While at Syracuse, he earned the Chartered Life Underwriter designation. He came to Equitable's Home Office in 1931 to handle the conservation work in the Agency Department. Six years later, he was appointed Superintendent of the Agency Department—a new position—to organize and coordinate all administrative functions of the Department. In this position, Smith introduced the idea of measuring agents' production solely by first year commissions.[214] Prior to this time agents' production had been measured by three factors—volume of business, premiums, and number of policies written—a rather complicated process. The new Superintendent, together with Assistant Superintendent John E. Hartigan, who handled research and statistical data for the Department, got the idea from two small Canadian companies. Both men believed that the single-factor measurement would not only be simpler and much less expensive to handle, but also more reliable. They prevailed upon Agency Vice President William J. Graham to try the new plan on an experimental basis for six months. It worked, and not only did Equitable adopt and retain the plan, but many other United States companies subsequently adopted it.

In 1947 at the Lake Louise Conference of leading agents, a session was devoted to "life insurance for estate planning, business insurance, and related subjects." After hearing the talks, President Parkinson observed that the speakers were not too well informed on the subject. He discussed the problem with members of the General Agents and Managers Association who agreed that an Advanced Underwriting Service would be a good thing for Equitable. A committee of this association recommended that a new division be established in the Agency Department to be called the Agency Special Services Division for the purpose of supplying information to the field for the assistance of agents in these specific areas.[215] Vice President Welch recommended

214 Commissions were weighted double for trainee agents who operated under an apprentice agent's contract which provided a salary plus one-half the usual scale of commissions.

215 Members of the Committee were Warren V. Woody (Chicago); Lee Wandling (Milwaukee); Horace H. Wilson (New York City); A. R. Cassidy (Jacksonville, Florida); Martin I. Scott (Los Angeles); and Simon D. Weissman

that Gordon K. Smith be designated to organize and head this division with the title of Director of Agency Special Services. He stated that Smith was well prepared for this assignment and it was pointed out that he had organized, about three years previously, the Equitable Chartered Life Underwriters Association and was serving as its Executive Secretary and administrative head. Thus this new facility came into existence August 1, 1948.

The need for such a division was emphasized by the passage of the Federal Estate Tax Law of 1948 which introduced a marital deduction applicable to married people in those states which did not have community property laws. In his letter to agency managers and general agents, Smith pointed out that it was practically impossible to set up a planned insurance estate independently of a person's general or non-insurance estate and emphasized that a well-planned estate was the responsibility of both the client's insurance agent and his lawyer. In each case the client was required to have the cooperation of his lawyer and for their assistance the Special Services staff designed forms for different types of agreements and issued numerous bulletins on tax and estate problems.[216] After Gordon K. Smith became Secretary of the Society, Eugene D. Badgley took over the directorship of Special Services. (In 1962 the name of the Division was changed from Agency Special Services to Advanced Underwriting Service.)

The new Secretary of Equitable inherited the normal duties of the position; he was Secretary to the Board of Directors and all of its committees—except the Finance and Real Estate Committees—and custodian of the Society's corporate records other than those of the Finance and Real Estate Committees; he planned the Board and committee meetings, handled correspondence in many fields, and administered the Society's contribution program to education, research, community services, and other worthy causes. He continued to serve as Executive Secretary and administrative head of Equitable's Chartered Life Underwriters Association. Then, in addition, he was given the assignment of supervising Equitable's history project, which in-

---

(Boston). A copy of the Committee report, as well as Welch's recommendation, may be found in Equitable Archives.

[216] Sample titles of bulletins: "Cooperation Between the Life Underwriter and the Attorney in the Field of Estate Planning" (December 1948), "Optional Modes of Settlement with Buy and Sell Agreements" (November 1959), "Insurance for Estate Settlement Charges" (December 1958), "Gifts of Insurance to Children" (January 1951), "Employee Benefits Plan for the Small Employer" (March 1960), "Split Dollar Plan" (March 1956), "Individual Major Medical Expense Insurance Purchased by Employer" (May 1957), etc.

volved the making of an inventory of the historical materials available in the Society's Archives as well as furnishing secretarial help and taking care of the many details connected with the writing of both the Hundredth Anniversary and the comprehensive histories of Equitable. This was a logical choice, for the Secretary's Office, more than any other, maintained knowledge of the historical continuity of the Society.

In August 1944 the Equitable Board appointed Mrs. Grace W. Jordis Assistant Secretary of the Society, the first woman officer in the company's history. She had joined the Equitable as a stenographer in 1921 and had subsequently served as secretary to officers in various areas of the Society's operations. As Assistant Secretary she was given authority to act in an official capacity in the absence of the Secretary or during his inability to act. Beginning in 1945 Mrs. Jordis served as secretary of the Insurance Committee of the Board and was responsible, under the Secretary, for maintaining the Society's corporate records. She also participated in formulating Equitable's policy with respect to corporate contributions, and spent considerable time and assumed large responsibility in the administration of the program in recent years. It is a point of historical interest that Helen B. Taylor, secretary to Sterling Pierson (and later secretary to President Murphy and staff assistant to Chairman Oates), became Assistant Secretary in June 1945 and Mrs. Margaret D. Eggleston, an attorney in the Agency Department, was appointed to this office in February 1950.

In June 1953 Edward A. Robie was appointed to the new position of Personnel Director (effective September 15); he was to report directly to the President. Robie, a native of Ontario, Canada, had received his secondary education at Phillips Andover Academy and Westminster School, London. He received his B.A. degree at the School of Public and International Affairs, Princeton University, where he was elected to Phi Beta Kappa. He had a broad experience background in research in industrial relations, in labor relations, and from his service as legislative assistant to United States Senator H. Alexander Smith of New Jersey. Just prior to joining Equitable he was in charge of personnel development work at the Lee Paper Company, Vicksburg, Michigan. Soon the practices in Equitable's personnel management were to be brought abreast of the latest and best developments in that field.[217]

[217] Equitable had no separate Personnel Department until 1939. The evolution of the Department was somewhat as follows: in 1919 the existing "Bureau of Employment" became the "Bureau of Employment and Service" and included the

In April 1954 Robert L. Hogg was appointed Senior Vice President and Advisory Counsel. Hogg was a graduate of West Virginia University, from which he received the LL.B. degree in 1916. He served in the United States Army from 1917 to 1919 and then resumed the practice of law at Point Pleasant. As a member of the West Virginia Senate, 1924–28, he served as chairman of the Committee on Taxation and Finance. He represented the Fourth West Virginia District in Congress, 1930–33, and from 1935 to 1944 served as Assistant General Counsel and Associate General Counsel for The Association of Life Insurance Presidents. In 1944 he became Manager and General Counsel of the American Life Convention and two years later Executive Vice President and General Counsel, which position he held when he joined Equitable. As Counsel for the two leading life insurance company associations, Hogg had served on numerous committees and represented the life insurance companies in Washington. No one was more familiar with legislative and tax problems as they affected the business of life insurance than Equitable's new Senior Vice President and Advisory Counsel. Two days after joining Equitable, he accepted the chairmanship of the Joint Committee on Federal Income Taxation of Life Insurance Companies of the American Life Convention, the Life Insurance Association of America, and the Life Insurers Conference.

In August 1955, when Senior Vice President Alvin B. Dalager retired, Joseph L. Beesley, CLU, who had been Field Vice President since 1953, was appointed Senior Vice President in charge of all sales operations. Beesley, who was born at Alert, Indiana, was a Phi Beta Kappa

---

Files Division, Employment and Welfare Division, Phonograph Division, Building Division, and Mail Division. Two years later, the Service Bureau, including the above-mentioned divisions (except for Employment and Welfare), was placed in the Secretary's Department, under the supervision of Assistant Secretary Andrew E. Tuck, whose brother Charles H. Tuck became Personnel Officer, with general supervision over the Bureau of Employment. In 1926 the administration of personnel was placed under Second Vice President Leon O. Fisher, but in 1936 it was transferred to the newly created Department of Home Office Administration under Vice President Andrew E. Tuck. This department also included Emergency Hospital, Rest Camp and Reserve Force, Purchase and Supply, Files (including Storage), Phonograph, Mail, Telephone, and Statutory Requirements. In 1939 the Personnel Department was created and the personnel activities previously administered by the Department of Home Office Administration were transferred to it. It was placed under the supervision of Assistant Secretary James F. Fleming. In 1942, when Fleming became ill, the Personnel Department was placed under the direction of Raymond H. Weins, Controller of Expenditures, where it remained until Weins severed his connections with the Society in 1953.

graduate of DePauw University in 1926. Soon after graduation he was accepted for Equitable's Cashier's Training Course. For eighteen years he held Cashier's assignments in Denver, Phoenix, Syracuse, New York, and Chicago. He earned the Chartered Life Underwriter designation in 1932. In 1945 he became Manager of Equitable's Syracuse agency and from that position moved to the field vice presidency in charge of the New York Metropolitan Department.

Also in August 1955 Melville P. Dickenson, Agency Manager at Philadelphia, was appointed Assistant to the President; in February of the following year he was appointed Senior Vice President, with general supervision of public relations and of the Advertising and Press Relations Department. Dickenson had attended Wyoming Seminary in Kingston, Pennsylvania, and then entered Princeton University, where in his senior year he was elected captain of the undefeated and untied 1922 football team known as the "Team of Destiny." After graduation from Princeton he had begun his insurance career as an agent for the New York Life Insurance Company. Later he served as head of the Group Department of the Prudential Insurance Company. In 1929 he joined the banking firm of Eastman Dillon and Company and from 1931 to 1935 was also a member of the New York Stock Exchange. He joined Equitable's Philadelphia office as an agent in 1937 and two years later became Agency Manager. As Manager in Philadelphia, Dickenson not only built up a large agency but aided many Philadelphia corporations in setting up pension and group insurance programs for their employees.

President Murphy summarized the purposes of his reorganization as follows:

> Observation of large and successful American enterprises has seemed to teach two lessons, first, the high value of competent specialization and, second, the necessity for an adequate conception, especially by the higher management staff, of the whole enterprise, its purposes and the interrelations of its parts. In considering important questions of policy, caution must be exercised to avoid changes in one direction which will produce unanticipated detriments in another direction. Or, to put the point another way, it is the good of the whole which must be the concern of top management, bringing to all questions a balanced point of view. Belief in the validity of such principles, coupled with a conviction that responsibility furnishes the main source of individual growth, has led to such changes in organization as I have been making over the past two years. The

results I believe have been beneficial to the healthy growth of the Society and increased confidence in the future.[218]

During the three years of President Murphy's administration, Equitable had witnessed a number of changes and improvements. In 1953 the Society completed the funding of all past service reserves under its previously adopted pension plans for employees and agents in the amount of $4,544,000. Two years later all welfare and pension plans were reviewed and a number of changes made to provide more comprehensive coverage and greater uniformity of treatment. An important change was the introduction of health insurance for retired employees and older agents who qualified.[219]

Studies begun two years earlier by the Methods Research Group operating under the supervision of Senior Vice President and Actuary Walter Klem began to bear fruit in 1954 with improved methods in premium billing and accounting, in the disbursement of the large volume of annuity payments, and in the transformation of group insurance records and procedures. Soon, intricate electronic procedures were applied to the calculation of policy dividends.

Important changes were also taking place in the field of underwriting. In December 1953 Equitable announced a far-reaching change in its Ordinary insurance program, to become effective January 1, 1954. The result was a general reduction in premium rates for individual policies and for the optional policy coverages through which an insured might have his premiums waived in the event of total disability or be given additional protection against death by accident. In August 1954 Equitable introduced its Adjustable Whole Life Policy, which immediately proved popular. This policy, available in amounts of $10,000 or more, was issued with low gross premiums and low net cost but contained provisions whereby the policyholder, at a later period in life, could elect to have his policy become paid up or mature as an endowment at a date specified in the policy, without losing the financial benefit of the special basis of issue. This policy met the needs of the policyholder who in early years required the maximum amount of low

[218] In his report to the Board of Directors for the year 1954.

[219] The plan used both a "deductible amount" and a "coinsurance factor" of the general nature found in Major Medical insurance. It was offered at a charge to the retired employee and older agent of about 40 per cent of the expected cost, and was well received, with more than 92 per cent of all who were eligible subscribing thereto.

premium permanent protection but in later years either wanted to pay up his insurance during his remaining working years or have it mature as an endowment. Several new retirement contracts were introduced, and after extensive research a new mortality basis was adopted for all forms of annuities which reflected recent experience and allowed for a future downward trend. Premium income on group insurance in 1953 reached the unprecedented total of $504,679,700, and the amount of group insurance in force rose to $11,046,000,000. The following year Equitable joined some 160 other companies in providing group insurance for more than 1,750,000 Federal government employees under a plan which had been worked out through intercompany reinsurance arrangements. Equitable's share of the whole was approximately 6 per cent.

The Society's group annuity business, initiated in 1927, enjoyed a moderate growth during the 1930's. Several large group-writing companies began writing group annuities during that period and employer interest in private pensions was stimulated in part by the enactment of the Social Security legislation. At the end of 1940 Equitable had 174 group annuity contracts in force which covered 193,000 lives with premium income of $28,000,000 for the year.

The early 1940's was the Golden Age for the Society's group annuity business. As a result of low interest rates available on new investments several large life insurance companies actually or virtually ceased writing group annuities, but Equitable's officers decided that this service should continue to be made available to the business community. Under conditions of high profits, high taxes, tight employment, and a wage-salary freeze, pension programs became attractive to employers; they could be paid for with tax-exempt dollars. Because of low investment returns and improving mortality, the insurance companies remaining in the group annuity business increased the premium rates. Since Equitable increased its rates (effective January 1, 1947) a year or two later than the other companies, its group annuity business increased rapidly. As a result, the Society at the end of 1945 had 473 contracts in force covering 440,000 lives with premium income of $99,000,000—or three and one-half times the income for 1940.

Troubles began, however, as the banks became more active in the pension field. As interest rates improved, insurance companies turned again to the pension business but the banks and independent consultants had moved into the vacuum that existed in the early 1940's. Not only did the banks offer effective competition for new business, but they began to take away the clients already on the books of the insurance companies. The Equitable lost its first contract to a bank in 1946 and by the end of 1950 had lost eighteen cases. Some of these lost group annuity plans were those of large New York banks covered by Equitable group annuity contracts; others were contracts which were discontinued in the Society and were rewritten by leading banks in New York and elsewhere. In 1949 by the Inland Steel decision pensions were declared to be a subject of collective bargaining. Consequently many bargained plans were adopted and, although Equitable adapted its Deposit Administration contract to the new type of bargained plans, the banks got most of the business.

In order to help conserve business, explain the "mysteries" of the group annuity dividend formula, the need for increase in group annuity rates and in general to improve communication with group annuity clients, Equitable inaugurated a series of forums to be conducted by the Society's pension experts in a number of the leading cities of the United States. These forums, which were held in 1949, 1953, and 1955, were unique in the life insurance business. Representatives of group annuity clients were invited to one-day programs of prepared talks by Equitable officers, and the talks were followed by a period of informal exchange of ideas and response to questions. Seven of these forums were held in 1949, 12 in eleven cities in 1953 and 13 in eleven cities in 1955. The 1949 and 1953 forums were conducted by representatives of the Group and Actuary's Departments; in the 1955 forum they were joined by representatives of the Securities Investment Department.

The 1953 forums presented a project which had a marked impact on the pension business throughout the United States. Under the direction of Vice President and Associate Actuary Ray M. Peterson, a new mortality table was developed for pension purposes. By action of the Society of Actuaries this table became officially known as the Group Annuity Table for 1951 With Projection (GA-1951 Table), and was published in the *Transactions of the Society of Actuaries* in June 1952. With certain adaptations it came to be generally used by both insurance companies and consulting actuaries for group annuity rates and pension valuations; it was made a minimum valuation standard for group annuities in all states and was widely used in Canada.

Although group annuity premium income continued to increase in the early 1950's—reaching $277,000,000 in 1955—it started to decline thereafter as business continued to be lost to bank trustees. Insurance companies were still laboring under the distressing handicaps of the Federal income tax, the average portfolio method of allocating investment income as interest rates on new money were rising, and the inability to provide equity investments. These handicaps were largely overcome by the Federal tax legislation of 1959 and the Society's adoption of the investment year method and the establishing of separate accounts for qualified pension plans.[220] As a result the Society's group annuity business entered another period of growth.

In 1954 Equitable's new investments exceeded a billion dollars for the first time; this was an average of about $22,000,000 per week. The net rate of investment income on all assets increased to 3.15 per cent after Federal taxes. Assets of the Society rose to a new high of $7,560,000,000 and the Society distributed $544,000,000 in benefits, more than two-thirds of which sum was paid to living policyholders. The following year assets rose to $8,047,000,000, and at the end of the year investments in mortgage loans represented 27.7 per cent of the Society's investments, as compared with 17.4 in 1950. One of the Society's new investments was the Equitable Building in San Francisco, which was officially opened in December 1955. This 25-story office building, located at the intersection of Montgomery and Sutter Streets, was the tallest on the West Coast and had been built at a cost of $12,300,000. It was the first earthquake-resistant building to be constructed in San Francisco under the city's rigid 1948 "Earthquake Code" and was intended not only as a profitable investment but as an asset in the Society's public relations on the West Coast.

In December 1954 President Murphy was elected President of the Life Insurance Association of America, the first President of Equitable to be so honored.

In June 1955 the Executive Committee of Equitable's Board of Directors authorized President Murphy to appoint a Committee on Organization. To head this subcommittee of the Executive Committee, President Murphy appointed Dr. Fordyce B. St. John, distinguished New York physician and surgeon. Other members of the Committee on Organization were Francis B. Davis, Jr., Director, United States Rubber Company; Charles R. Hook, Chairman, Armco Steel Corporation; Nicholas Kelley, Counselor-at-Law, New York; and Russell B.

220 See this history, p. 1314.

Lowe, textile manufacturer, Fitchburg, Massachusetts.[221] A tentative "frame of reference" was prepared and Dr. St. John, while on vacation in Vermont, gave it his careful attention. He visualized the objectives of the Committee as having a wide scope; not only would it give consideration to the immediate and practical problems and solutions, but to present and future trends in the development of life insurance, the broad field of public relations, and the possibility of governmental interference. What should be Equitable's responsibility to educational institutions and to the health of the public, and what was its responsibility in the general scheme of the national economy? Had Equitable within its organization men with broad understanding of these things and with the ability to lead?: "To my mind the vital consideration this organization committee faces is men. Men of vision, stature, and character as well as effectiveness. . . . You have a group of men as directors outstanding in many fields, and the ones interested, realizing their responsibility, feel as I do that the Equitable has the potentiality to become the leader in this great industry, not necessarily in number of policies and in dollars, both of basic importance, but in its responsibility as a great institution of service in our democracy as well." [222]

The Committee held a number of meetings and interviewed the senior vice presidents of the Society, as well as several directors who were not members of the Committee. It submitted a report containing six major recommendations to President Murphy, January 16, 1956; the report was approved by the Executive Committee of the Board two days later. It recommended that the senior officers of the Society consist of Chairman of the Board, Vice Chairman of the Board, and President. For these positions the names of Ray D. Murphy, Robert L. Hogg, and Charles W. Dow were presented. The Chairman of the Board, in addition to presiding at meetings of the Board and being an ex officio member of all standing committees, would be responsible for seeing that the general policies of the Society were carried out in accordance with the By-Laws and the decisions of the Board. More specifically, he would be prepared to act with respect to developments

[221] Alternate members were James B. Black, Chairman, Pacific Gas and Electric Company; John Lord O'Brian, internationally known Counselor-at-Law; Edward L. Shea, President, Ethyl Corporation; and Arthur B. Van Buskirk, Vice President and Governor, T. Mellon and Sons. Because of the importance of the work to be undertaken by this Committee, the members and the alternates acted as one unit.

[222] Dr. St. John (at Woodstock, Vermont) to Ray D. Murphy, July 31, 1955. Equitable Archives.

in insurance practices in relation to social needs and governmental policies, to handle relations with governmental officials and with other life insurance companies and associations, and to supervise the Law Department-Insurance and the work of the Secretary of the Society.[223] Some of these duties were delegated to the Vice Chairman.

The Vice Chairman of the Board would have authority to act with respect to national and state tax policies affecting the Society, responsibility for handling legislative problems and relationships with government officials, and supervision of the Law Department-Insurance. The President, under the general direction of the Chairman of the Board, would be responsible for the operation of the Investment Departments (including the Law Department-Investments) the Home Office and branch office buildings, and all departments concerned with insurance administration and with sales. Any special resolutions concerning general policy which the President might wish to recommend to the Board would first be presented to the Chairman of the Board for his approval. The responsibilities of the Senior Vice President and Actuary were also outlined and personnel changes in the Actuary's Department indicated. Organization charts were included in the report for each of the major departments. Changes in the By-Laws were proposed dealing with the composition of important standing committees of the Board, namely, the Finance Committee, the Real Estate Committee, the Agency Committee, and the Insurance Committee.

Following the recommendations of the Committee on Organization, the Board of Directors, February 16, 1956, elected President Ray D. Murphy Chairman of the Board; Senior Vice President Robert L. Hogg Vice Chairman of the Board; and Senior Vice President Charles W. Dow President. As Chairman of the Board, Murphy was to retain chief executive authority.

Charles W. Dow, a native of Iowa, received his Bachelor of Science degree in Mechanical Engineering at Iowa State College in 1929. Soon

[223] The Committee proposed a change in the By-Laws as follows:

Section 3.2—line 3: "The Executive Committee shall act as a Nominating Committee in recommending to the Board of Directors nominations for the filling of vacancies on the Board of Directors and nominations for membership in the standing committees of the Board of Directors."

Other changes resulted in the Committee on Retirement and Employees' Insurance being renamed the Welfare Committee, and the sections which dealt with Limits of Risk, Overdue Interest, and the Medical Department being eliminated. A section was added providing for the payment of directors' fees and the indemnification of directors, officers, and employees of the Society.

after graduation he signed up as a "cadet engineer" with the Public Service Company of Denver, which at the time was an affiliate of Cities Service Company. In this position, Dow helped dig ditches, install gas ranges, climb poles, and build generating stations. After this apprenticeship, he was transferred to the office of the Cities Service Company in New York, where he became a budget engineer. In this capacity he learned much about the country's raw material resources and how they are processed; he also became acquainted with the financing and valuation of public utilities. He resigned from Cities Service and in 1935 on the recommendation of Treasurer Meredith C. Laffey was appointed Security Analyst for Equitable. He became Manager, Industrial Securities, in 1943, Second Vice President in 1949, Vice President in 1951, and Senior Vice President in 1953. In 1954 he was elected a Director to fill a vacancy in the second class caused by the death of Douglas Southall Freeman.

The year 1955 had been a busy one for President Murphy. In addition to his normal duties as President of Equitable and the extra work involved in the Society's reorganization, he had accepted the responsibilities of the presidency of the Life Insurance Association of America. At this time the Association was working on a number of things which affected the business of life insurance; among them were the development of a new and equitable tax formula for life insurance companies, research on the regulation of union welfare plans, cooperation with other trade associations in solving problems involved in variable annuities, and continued observation and appropriate action on all legislative fronts of concern to life insurance.

In January 1956, while the Committee on Organization was considering Charles W. Dow for the presidency, it also considered possibilities for his replacement as Senior Vice President in charge of investments. After discussing this matter with certain members of the Finance and Real Estate Committees of the Board and two senior officers of the Society, the Committee agreed that an outstanding person, "a man of experience and stature in the financial world; one who has a comprehensive knowledge of our national economy; one who understands fiscal and monetary policies," be selected for the position.[224]

[224] In the words of Director Arthur B. Van Buskirk, the person selected should have the following qualifications:

"He should be a man of experience and stature in the financial world; one who

After Dow became President, he was reluctant to give up his work as chief investment officer. Matters finally came to a head when he went to Chairman Murphy and asked to be made Chief Executive Officer so that he would have the authority to organize the Financial Department according to his own plans. Chairman Murphy said that such a decision would have to be made by the Committee on Organization. The Committee backed Murphy and by December 20, 1956, President Dow was aware of the fact that he would not be re-elected. There followed a series of interviews between Dow and members of the Executive Committee of the Board after which, on January 2, 1957, the Executive Committee, sitting as a Nominating Committee, resolved that it would not renominate Dow for President of Equitable. When informed of this action, President Dow submitted his resignation January 14 and asked that his name not be considered for either the presidency or as a Director at the annual meeting of the Board February 21. The resignation was accepted January 17 and Dow was granted a leave of absence from his duties as President until the effective date of his resignation, February 21. The Board then requested Chairman Murphy to assume the duties of both the Chairman and President, and he agreed to do so; it expressed its appreciation of Dow's service with Equitable in the following words: "In the many years of service which Mr. Dow has rendered to the Society, we have found him to be a devoted and effective fellow worker. His abilities and energy won for him recognition as an employee, officer and director. He is recognized as an authority in the field of finance and investment. He leaves us with our good wishes for his continued success in the years ahead." [225]

A press release of January 18 stated that "Mr. Dow's resignation was

---

has a comprehensive knowledge of our national economy; one who understands fiscal and monetary policies, and who has a working familiarity with the relationships between these policies and money rates, the bond market, and security values generally; one who knows firsthand the prime industries of the country and the key corporations in them; one whose judgment we would trust in an appraisal of these corporations and of their managements; one who can deal with people, and who in negotiating loans for Equitable would instill confidence in the borrower, and perhaps lead him to think of Equitable for his insurance as well as his financial needs; one who would be sought out by the heads of industry to advise them respecting their toughest financial problems; and finally, one who would have the stature necessary to become President, Vice Chairman, or, indeed, Chairman of Equitable at some future time." Memorandum No. 10. Committee on Organization, January 19, 1956. Corporate Records, Equitable Archives.

[225] Minutes of the Board of Directors. Corporate Records.

due to differences of opinion with the Board on matters of organization structure which have been under discussion for some weeks."

A few days after the announcement of President Dow's resignation, Leslie Gould announced in his column in the *Journal-American* that Equitable was "looking for a top executive officer." He mentioned various possibilities, and *The Eastern Underwriter* said that Gould, in the "role of a self-appointed adviser to the Society," might possibly be considering himself as a dark horse candidate for the position.[226]

The Equitable Board authorized severance pay of one year's salary for President Dow and, since it desired no repetition of the publicity given to the Society's affairs in 1953, the New York Insurance Department was advised of its action. Director Manly Fleischmann, who had drawn up the settlement terms, reported the action to Superintendent Leffert Holz, who gave his approval.[227]

The Committee on Organization headed by Dr. Fordyce B. St. John, which had been appointed in June 1955, was discharged with thanks in February 1957, and an Organization Committee (a special Committee of the Board, not a subcommittee of the Executive Committee) was appointed to consider a new President for Equitable. This Committee was composed of the following directors: Dr. St. John, Chairman; Malcolm P. Aldrich, President of The Commonwealth Fund; Manly Fleischmann, Counselor-at-Law; Henry T. Heald, President of The Ford Foundation; and Richard H. Mansfield, Vice President of Rockefeller Center, Incorporated.[228]

The Committee, after due deliberation, decided that the man they wanted was already a member of the Equitable Board—James F. Oates, Jr.; the only question was whether he would accept the position. When Oates was invited into President Murphy's office and informed of the Committee's decision, the offer of the presidency of Equitable came as a complete surprise to him. The task of persuading him to accept was assigned to President Murphy and Director Henry T.

[226] *The New York Journal-American*, January 24, 1957; *The Eastern Underwriter*, LVIII (1957), February 1.

[227] Director Manly Fleischmann, interview with author, January 22, 1964. Other directors who conferred with Superintendent Holz were Messrs. O'Brian, Welldon, Heald, Aldrich, and Hogg.

[228] Alternate members were: James B. Black, Chairman, Pacific Gas and Electric Company; Charles R. Hook, Chairman, Armco Steel Corporation; Robert E. Blum, Vice President and Secretary, Abraham and Straus; and Harold H. Helm, Chairman, Chemical Corn Exchange Bank.

Heald.[229] After further discussion of the problems involved, Oates accepted the offer, and on April 1, 1957, the Board elected him President and Chief Executive Officer of Equitable. It also announced that Ray D. Murphy had agreed to remain as Chairman of the Board until the next annual meeting.

James F. Oates, Jr., was born at Evanston, Illinois, in 1899 and educated in the public schools of that city. He grew up with an insurance background, for his father, James F. Oates, was, for thirty years, a general agent for the Northwestern Mutual Life Insurance Company. Oates graduated from Phillips Exeter Academy in 1917, and in 1918 was commissioned as Second Lieutenant of Infantry and served at Camp Hancock, Georgia, 1918–19. He received his B.A. degree from Princeton in 1921 and his J.D. degree from Northwestern University Law School in 1924. For twenty-four years Oates practiced law in Chicago and in 1946–47 served as President of the Chicago Bar Association. During World War II he was legal adviser to the Chicago Ordnance District and worked with the Ordnance Department in Washington. In 1948, at which time he was a partner in the law firm of Sidley, Austin, Burgess, and Harper, Oates was elected Chairman of the Board and Chief Executive Officer of The Peoples Gas Light and Coke Company of Chicago. At the time that he was elected President of Equitable, he was also a director of The First National Bank of Chicago, the International Harvester Company, the Great Northern Railway Company, and Miehle-Goss-Dexter, Incorporated, machinery manufacturers.

The new President of Equitable was a large man with an expansive personality; he possessed an impressive speaking voice and had an incisive mind. Said Frederic W. Ecker, Chairman of the Board of the Metropolitan Life Insurance Company: "He is truly a man of parts—eminent lawyer, soldier, head of one of the great life insurance companies of the country, college and university Trustee, tennis player, sportsman, and, perhaps equally important, an expert fisherman. I must add that he is in fact 'The Compleat Angler,' having fished,

229 One of Oates' enthusiastic sponsors was Director Henry T. Heald, who, in the 1940's as President of the Illinois Institute of Technology and the Institute of Gas Technology, had worked closely with Oates, then Chairman of The Peoples Gas Light and Coke Company of Chicago. He doubted, however, that Oates would be interested in the presidency of Equitable. Other directors believed that Oates might be persuaded. Interview with Ray D. Murphy, December 28, 1960, and Manly Fleischmann, January 22, 1964.

particularly for trout, in this country and in Canada, South America, Europe, and even in New Zealand." [230] Already familiar with the operations of the Society, President Oates took over his new duties June 1 with a minimum of adjustment. He had the confidence and wholehearted support of both the directors and officers of the Society.

The reorganization which had been started under President Murphy in 1953 was completed with minor changes in 1958. The four large functional divisions of the Society became: 1) Insurance Operations, under Senior Vice President and Chief Actuary Walter Klem (elected a director in 1954); 2) Sales Operations, under Senior Vice President Joseph L. Beesley; 3) Investment Operations, under Senior Vice President Grant Keehn (elected a director in 1958), former Executive Vice President of The First National City Bank of New York; and 4) Public Relations and Personnel, under Senior Vice President Melville P. Dickenson.[231] Within each of these broad divisions, the vice presidents, second vice presidents, and other officers—Controller (Charles B. Lunsford), Treasurer (Richard D. Kernan), and Chief Medical Director (Norvin C. Kiefer)—headed the two dozen subdivisions and departments. Lines of authority descended directly from the President through the senior vice presidents to these other officers. Outside the four major divisions and also responsible directly to the President were the Vice Chairman (Robert L. Hogg); the Secretary (Gordon K. Smith); Vice President and Economist (Reynolds I. Nowell); and Vice President John H. Muller, who was responsible for maintenance of all the Society's office buildings and the construction of the new Home Office building.

When Ray D. Murphy resumed the presidency following President Dow's resignation he created a new staff position—that of Vice President and Executive Assistant. For this important post he selected Vice President and Associate Actuary J. Henry Smith. Smith had originally joined the Equitable Group Department in 1930 immediately after graduation from the University of Delaware. Following Group Department experience at Equitable and with another company he was appointed Assistant Superintendent of the Society's Group Insurance Actuarial Bureau in 1942 and had advanced successively to Vice President and Associate Actuary by 1953. During these and subsequent

[230] Introduction of President Oates at New York, December 3, 1959, on the occasion of Oates' address to The Newcomen Society in North America.

[231] For a sketch of Grant Keehn's career, see this history, p. 1339.

years he was active in the various life insurance organizations and in 1952–53 was chairman of the Joint Group Insurance Committee of the Life Insurance Association and the American Life Convention. He assisted in the organization of the Health Insurance Association of America in 1956 and served as its President in 1957–58. J. Henry Smith served with Ray D. Murphy and James F. Oates, Jr., in this executive staff position until February of 1958 when he was elected Underwriting Vice President. (In 1965 he was elected a Director and in 1967 President of Equitable.)

In addition to the primary organization structure, and playing an important part in the administration of the Society, were the fifteen Office Committees. Members of these Committees were selected from the various departments concerned, and the Committees served to coordinate the administrative activities. Responsible to the President were the Salary Committee, E. A. Robie, Chairman; the Committee on Complaints, Leo D. Fitzgerald, Chairman; the Employee Health Policy Committee, Dr. N. C. Kiefer, Chairman; the Committee on Rules and Regulations, Walter Klem, Chairman; the Officers' Committee for the Home Office Building, John H. Muller, Chairman; the Committee on Welfare Benefits, J. Henry Smith, Chairman; and the Public Relations Committee, Melville P. Dickenson, Chairman. Subcommittees of the Committee on Rules and Regulations and responsible to Senior Vice President Walter Klem were the Committee on Ordinary Commission Rules under Policy Changes, Replacements, and Reinstatements, Leo D. Fitzgerald, Chairman; and the Committee to Administer Group Commission Rules under Policy Changes, Replacements, and Reinstatements, Charles B. Lunsford, Chairman. Also responsible to Senior Vice President and Chief Actuary Walter Klem were the following: Ordinary Underwriting Policy Committee, J. Henry Smith, Chairman; Group Underwriting Policy Committee, W. W. Mincks, Chairman; Group Annuity Underwriting Policy Committee, Ray M. Peterson, Chairman; Policy Committee for Individual and Family Major Medical Expense Insurances, M. D. Miller, Chairman; and Office Committee on Policy Claims—"Senior Group," C. F. Andolsek, Chairman. The organization chart for 1958 defined the functions of these various committees.[232]

[232] In July 1955 Equitable began preparing Organization Charts for the directors. The following year these Charts were more generally distributed. They comprise 30 or 40 pages which chart the various departments and define the functions of the departments and office committees. A new set of Charts is

Not a part of the formal structural organization, but playing an important part in the management of Equitable was the General Policy Committee, which came into being in July 1957 when President Oates called a meeting of the senior officers of the Society.[233] At this meeting the group considered methods of improving the Society's internal communications and increasing the public's awareness of its value to society and the contributions which it was making to the public welfare. From this beginning the General Policy Committee evolved as a part of the management machinery. It expanded in size as new departments were created which reported directly to the President or Chief Executive Officer. Other officers were called into meetings of the General Policy Committee when subjects directly involving their departments were being discussed. The Committee also initiated the practice of holding quarterly meetings of all the officers of the Society. As defined by President Oates, the functions of the General Policy Committee were as follows: "The Committee's role is advisory; it does not make decisions. Its chief function is to provide a forum for discussion of important matters affecting the Society, in order to assist the President (and other Senior Officers within their areas of responsibility) in making decisions."

* * *

Equitable celebrated its 95th Anniversary with a three-day conference July 26–28, 1954. Headquarters for the conference was the Waldorf-Astoria Hotel, although six other of New York's leading hotels were also used to house the 1,346 qualified agents and 1,574 other guests.[234] Monday, July 26, Equitable's birthday, the general business session was devoted to talks on "Insurance Affairs" by Senior Vice President and Actuary Walter Klem; "Legislative Affairs" by Robert L. Hogg, Senior Vice President and Advisory Counsel; "Investment Affairs" by Charles W. Dow, Senior Vice President; and "Agency

---

compiled each year after the annual meeting of the Board and brought up to date by replacement pages at various times during the year.

233 Present at this meeting were Senior Vice Presidents Walter Klem, Joseph L. Beesley, and Melville Dickenson; Vice President and Executive Assistant J. Henry Smith, and the Society's Public Relations Consultant T. J. Ross. Senior Vice President Robert L. Hogg was unable to attend the initial meeting of this committee.

234 Forty-five years earlier, in 1909, Equitable had held its Jubilee Convention in the old Waldorf-Astoria Hotel.

Affairs" by Alvin B. Dalager, Senior Vice President. Director Charles W. Kellogg, Chairman of the Agency Committee of the Equitable Board, made the closing address of the morning session. The afternoon session was devoted to panel discussions of Special Services, Assured Home Ownership, Pension Trusts, Major Medical, and Salary Savings.

At seven o'clock in the evening some 3,400 guests assembled for Equitable's 95th Anniversary banquet. Not only did the guests fill the Grand Ballroom, which accommodated 120 tables, but seven additional foyers, balconies, and rooms were required to take care of the remaining 560 tables. President Murphy presided and reviewed the history of Equitable, pointing out some of the lessons which could be learned from that history. Director J. Reuben Clark, Jr., spoke on the humanitarian services rendered by the life insurance agent, and the Society's senior Director, John Lord O'Brian, "the last of the Victorians," delivered an impressive address in which he emphasized the spirit of kindness, cooperation, and helpfulness which had permeated the American people. He pointed out the impact of the social and economic revolution through which the country had recently passed and the problems it faced as a result of a chaotic world situation in which the war of ideas would likely continue for an indefinite length of time. He held much hope for the future, however, for he saw "in the history and evolution of American life insurance a great stabilizing influence which has its foundations far below the surface in that great underlying web of human relationships that are so definitely a characteristic of the American civilization." He said further:

> The degree to which life insurance companies like the Equitable have contributed to the economic growth and the economic stability of this country is an immeasurable influence. The diversification of the investments, the willingness to experiment prudently in new fields of investments, all have contributed a web of strength below the surface. But that is not what chiefly interests me. What interests me chiefly . . . are the human relationships that grow up in an organization like this—the sense of common understanding that we don't have to talk about, the sense of toleration, the willingness to help. That is the great underlying characteristic and out of that grows both the strength of this great society and the strongest confirmation of our hopes for the future. Because if the American people hold to the development further of that sense of personal obligation, personal responsibility, then, as freemen, I venture to say we need not fear the future too much, because no artificial creations of government, no evolution of new ideologies

of conduct . . . can stand against the will of the people who have that basic characteristic.[235]

The general Business session Tuesday morning, July 27, dealt with "Markets for the Future" and "The Career Underwriters of the Equitable." Four papers were read on each of these subjects. A luncheon at noon marked the 20th anniversary meeting of the Group Millionaires Club. The afternoon sessions were devoted largely to the subject of business insurance under the sponsorship of the Equitable CLU Association. Wednesday was Home Office Day and many of the delegates renewed their contacts and discussed their problems with Home Office personnel.

During the conference Equitable had published, in addition to the various programs, the *Equitable Conference Daily*, which reported the meetings and summarized some of the more important papers.

EQUITABLE IN OPERATION

People frequently ask, "How is it possible to manage a business or corporation as big as Equitable?" It is a good question and one which is not easily answered, for the administrative and investment activities required to meet the obligations and provide the services to some 11,000,000 policy and certificate holders constitute a large, complicated, and interesting operation. As President Oates said in 1959: "Frequently, during the course of the past two and one-half years, I have had occasion to envy Henry Baldwin Hyde. He fixed the premiums, wrote and sold the policies, paid and received the commissions, issued the policies, conducted the underwriting, kept the records, paid the bills, invested the proceeds, investigated the claims, determined the dividends, and made the payments to the beneficiaries. He cooperated with himself 'real good'!"[236] But management of a modern corporation requires cooperation on the part of many individuals.

By its Charter of May 2, 1859, the corporate powers of Equitable were vested in a Board of Directors, to be exercised by them and by such officers and agents as they might appoint. The 52 directors were elected by the stockholders—one-fourth of them each year—and the

[235] If the speaker spoke from a manuscript, it was not obvious. There are, however, tape recordings of the talks made by both Directors Clark and O'Brian in the Equitable Archives.

[236] "For All Time," an address delivered before The Newcomen Society in North America, December 3, 1959.

Charter provided that a majority of them should be citizens of the State of New York. No important changes affecting directors were made until 1906 when Article IV of the Charter was amended to provide that 28 of the directors were to be policyholders elected by the policyholders, and 24 were to be either stockholders or policyholders elected by stockholders. In August 1918 the mutualization plan was adopted by the stockholders, and to comply with Section 94 of the Insurance Law the provision that "a majority of the directors of the company shall be policyholders elected by the policyholders" was dropped.[237] In April 1927, two years after mutualization was completed, Article III of the original Charter which dealt with capitalization was omitted, and Article IV which dealt with the Board of Directors became Article III. As provided in the New York law, it required "a majority of officers and directors" to be citizens and residents of the State of New York but provided for reductions in the number of directors to 36, divided into three classes, one class to be elected each year for a term of three years.[238]

An important change affecting officers and Board membership was made in January 1940, when an "Amended Charter" was adopted by the Board. In accordance with a modification in the law, Article III was changed to eliminate the "citizens and residents" restriction as to officers and to require that no fewer than three of the directors be residents of New York and a majority be citizens and residents of New York or of adjoining states.[239]

By-Laws in effect on December 31, 1964, provided that the Board of Directors "may at any regular or special meeting" elect from among their number a Chairman of the Board and a Vice Chairman of the Board, and at the annual meeting "elect from among their number a president," who was to hold office until the next annual meeting and until the election of his successor; the Board also determined from

[237] Sec. 94 added to the Insurance Law of 1892 by Laws of 1906, Chap. 326, Sec. 30; amended by Laws of 1907, Chap. 623, Sec. 2; incorporated in Laws of 1909, Chap. 33; became Sec. 198 by Laws of 1939, Chap. 882. Sec. 56 (2), Laws of 1939, provided that "the directors of every such corporation . . . shall be elected at the annual meetings of the members, and all except four of the directors . . . must be members of the corporation, or officers of member corporations." "Members" in the case of a mutual life insurance company means "policyholders." "Member corporations" has been generally construed as group insurance clients.

[238] Sec. 71-a(1) added to the Insurance Law of 1909 by Chap. 659, Sec. 3, Laws of 1922, effective April 13, 1922.

[239] Sec. 48-5(2), Laws of 1939.

time to time whether the Chairman of the Board or the President should be the Chief Executive Officer of the Society. At the annual meeting it also elected a Secretary. The Chief Executive Officer had the duty of nominating "for consideration and election by the Board of Directors such Vice Presidents and other officers as may be deemed necessary for the conduct of the business of the Society."[240]

A principal function of the Nominating Committee, which was composed of the thirteen "outside" directors who were members of the Executive Committee together with designated officer directors (the Chairman and the President), was to submit nominations to fill vacancies on the Board. In March 1953 the Nominating Committee appointed a subcommittee of five directors to recommend from among individuals suggested for consideration as candidates those having specified qualifications. (In 1961 the functions of the subcommittee were assumed by the Organization Committee of the Board.) Names were proposed by Board members, officers, and others. In selecting new candidates, the Board endeavored to maintain an effective balance among the professions and businesses, as well as a wide geographic distribution. In order to maintain continuity of representation, candidates were frequently selected from the same profession, field, or area as that of the retiring director.[241]

In 1958 the Board adopted a rule which provided that no person should be nominated for election to a term on the Board for the first time, or be nominated for re-election to a term if he should have passed his seventieth birthday by the date such term commenced. As a result of this automatic age retirement rule, 20 of the 36 members of the Board as of December 31, 1964, were elected after James F. Oates, Jr., took office as President and Chief Executive Officer June 1, 1957.

[240] By Equitable's original Charter, Article V gave the directors the power to enact By-Laws, Rules, and Regulations for the management of the affairs of the Company not inconsistent with the Charter or the constitution and laws of the State of New York. This section remained unchanged by the amended Charter of 1940.

No copy of Equitable's first By-Laws adopted in 1859 is available. The revised By-Laws of October 1861 provided for four "stated" meetings of the Board per year—January, April, July, and October. It was not until June 1905 that the By-Laws provided for holding the "stated" meetings of the Board monthly.

[241] In March 1959 the Nominating Committee suggested that in the future, when directors were notified of vacancies and the names of suggested candidates were requested, the President (who at that time also served as Chairman and Chief Executive Officer) mention any special qualifications desired, including geographical location and principal business affiliation or profession.

In February 1961 the Nominating Committee adopted the following procedure for filling vacancies on the Board. First, the Chairman notified all directors of vacancies on the Board and requested suggestions for replacements. He then called a meeting of the Organization Committee to report on replies received from directors and to select a candidate and an alternate for each vacancy. The Chairman reported the names of selected candidates to the Nominating Committee and that committee either approved the recommendations of the Organization Committee or agreed upon other candidates. The candidates selected by the Nominating Committee were then reported to all directors, and if no objections were received within thirty days, the Chairman approached the candidates to determine their availability. Once the availability of candidates was determined, a meeting of the Nominating Committee was called to take formal action. In the case of the Administration Ticket, this meeting was held not later than the Wednesday before the April Board meeting. The names of the candidates were then presented to the Board for election, if they were to fill vacancies on the Board, or for nomination, if they were to fill vacancies on the Administration Ticket to be voted upon by the policyholders in the December following.

The New York Insurance Law (Sec. 198) requires that nominations for the Administration Ticket be made at least seven months before the annual election of directors, which under the Society's Charter takes place on the first Wednesday in December of each year. Notices of the election are published in newspapers in major cities throughout the country and also sent to policyholders by way of their premium notices. Ordinarily relatively few policyholders vote, but if they are dissatisfied with the Administration Ticket they can have the right under the provisions of the Insurance Law to nominate an Independent Ticket at least five months before the election. Since the mutualization of Equitable, this right has never been exercised.

Equitable, throughout its history, has taken pride in the caliber of its Board of Directors, and at no time has it been more justified in this attitude than in recent decades. It is impossible to mention by name the many distinguished individuals who have contributed their time and talents to the administration of Equitable's affairs, but a few names may serve as representative.[242]

There have been such outstanding personalities as J. Reuben Clark, Jr., an Apostle in the Church of Jesus Christ of Latter-day

[242] See Appendix for a list of directors.

Saints, who served seven Presidents of the United States in high office or on special missions; John Bassett Moore, "the high priest of international law"; John Lord O'Brian, legislator, Federal Government administrator, and a practitioner before the Supreme Court of the United States for more than fifty years; and John Clark Knox, who served as Judge of the United States District Court for the Southern District of New York from 1918 to 1955. Each of these men served on the Board for many years.

Equitable's Board of Directors is a working Board. It is a remarkable fact that men, busy with tremendous responsibilities in their own professions or businesses and with no financial interest in the Society other than as policyholders, give so unstintingly—with small compensation—of their time and knowledge.[243] Perhaps it is the semi-public nature of the business and a sense of trusteeship which leads to this result.

The Board meets regularly once a month—on the third Thursday—and special meetings may be called at any time by the Chairman of the Board, the President, or five directors. Much of the work of the Board, however, is done in the meetings of its committees, which report their actions and recommendations to the Board. As of December 31, 1964, there were seven standing committees, as follows: 1) the Executive Committee, consisting of 13 non-officer directors, including the Chairman of the Agency Committee, the Chairman of the Insurance Committee, and four officer directors; 2) the Finance Committee, consisting of ten directors, of whom two are officer directors; 3) the Real Estate Committee, eight directors, of whom two are officer directors; 4) the Agency Committee, 11 directors, of whom four are officer directors; 5) the Insurance Committee, 13 directors, of whom three are officer directors; 6) the Public Relations Committee, 14 directors, of whom four are officer directors; and 7) the Nominating Committee, consisting of the 13 non-officer directors serving on the Executive Committee and two officer directors. The members of the standing committees are designated by the Board at the annual meeting, which is held in February. A 1964 amendment to the New York Business Corporation Law and a change in the Society's By-Laws to conform, eliminated ex officio members and provided that alternate directors could be named to serve in place of absent directors.

In early 1963, pursuant to the provisions of the New York State

[243] As of December 31, 1964, the directors received $100 plus expenses for each Board or committee meeting attended.

Defense Emergency Act, Emergency By-Laws were adopted to become operative only during an acute emergency, as determined pursuant to declaration by the Superintendent of Insurance under a provision in The Emergency Act. The provisions of these By-Laws deal with such matters as notice of meetings, quorums, acting directors, and who shall be Chief Executive Officer during an acute emergency.

The Executive Committee meets twice a month—on the day before the Board meeting and two weeks prior thereto; special meetings may be called at any time by the Chairman of the Board, the President, or five members of the Committee. The Agency and Insurance Committees meet regularly once a month. The Finance and Real Estate Committees hold regular meetings as specified by resolution (usually twice a month), and the Public Relations Committee meets at the call of the Chief Executive Officer of the Society. The Nominating Committee holds such meetings as may be called by the Chairman of the Board, the President, or five members of the Committee.

Special committees may be designated by the Board of Directors from time to time to undertake specific assignments. Both standing and special committees may appoint subcommittees of their members. Thus, with seven standing committees and a varying number of special committees and subcommittees, a director frequently finds himself a member of two or more. In addition to the director members, a number of officers of the Society, representing the areas of operations covered by the various committees, attend the committee meetings. About a dozen officers of the Society also attend the Board meetings.

An interesting custom was inaugurated in 1957 as a result of a suggestion by one of the directors to President Oates that it might be a good idea for the directors to have a dinner the evening before the monthly meeting. President Oates immediately adopted the idea and decided that the main event of the dinner would be a talk by one of the directors on his particular calling in life or any other subject which he might choose. The talks were limited to forty-five minutes and the dinners had a nine o'clock curfew. These dinners, which are often attended by one-half to two-thirds of the directors, have done much to give the members of the Board something more than a formal acquaintance with one another.

* * *

As Henry B. Hyde realized a century earlier, a life insurance company, to be successful, must offer to the people insurance which meets their economic and social needs. And as society becomes more complex, it is incumbent upon life insurance companies to furnish policies and benefits which are more sharply differentiated in order to meet the needs of the various classes within that society. In other words, in addition to a well-established portfolio of general purpose plans and benefits, the life company must continue to adapt and combine individual elements of coverage to meet special needs. Equitable never forgot this fact and at the end of a century was still maintaining a position of leadership in the development of insurance and annuity coverages even though it was faced with competition from more than 1,300 life insurance companies.[244] Twice within a five-year period Equitable made major changes in its insurance program, involving long periods of research, planning, and detailed preparation. Although these labors involved many departments of the Society—legal, medical, underwriting, and agency—the chief burden fell upon the Actuary's Department.

When Equitable announced its "Series 95" program in December 1953—to go into effect January 1, 1954—many months of labor lay behind the announcement. Vital to the new "Ordinary Insurance and Annuity Program" was the construction of a mortality table suitable

[244] Since Equitable's important underwriting developments during recent years have been mentioned at various points in the text of this history, a brief summary follows:

In the 1930's the Society offered its policy on juvenile lives and also the Family Income and Retirement Income policies. Pension Trust services were first provided in 1936. In 1940 Equitable was one of the early companies to remove extra premiums for passenger travel on regularly scheduled airlines without any restriction as to travel destination. In the latter part of 1947, with the adoption of the 1941 Commissioners Standard Ordinary mortality table, the Society's entire ordinary insurance portfolio was recast as to both rates and policy forms. Major Medical Expense policies to meet "medical catastrophes" were issued in 1951. The same year the Society agreed to accept for insurance substandard risks, in some cases up to 500 per cent of standard mortality.

Equitable group coverages, which had previously been confined to group life insurance, accidental death and dismemberment, and weekly indemnity benefits, were also developed extensively in the 1930's and subsequent years. Hospital expense benefits were first issued in 1934, credit life insurance in 1935, and surgical expense benefits in 1937. The 1940's saw the addition to the group portfolio of group permanent life insurance, medical expense benefits, weekly indemnity insurance to fit the requirements of certain state laws, and life insurance for dependents. Group Major Medical, or "catastrophe" medical expense insurance, was developed in 1950, individual policies for conversion of group health insurance in 1954, insurance for groups of fewer than 25 employees in 1955, and long-term disability insurance with a waiting period in 1958.

for the annuity contracts and the life income settlement options of the projected new series. The result was a Life Income Mortality Table based on an analysis of intercompany experience but adapted to the Society's own experience and requirements.

This new table represented an original and ingenious answer to the serious practical questions raised by a pattern of mortality which not only depended on the annuitant's age and sex, in accordance with earlier understanding of the subject, but also displayed a decreasing trend from year to year at each age. Such a trend, now well established, was too important to ignore; at the same time, it was difficult to take into account without introducing major complexities into the eventual contract structure. The prime importance of the Society's work in developing the new table lay in the resulting ability to develop new settlement options and annuity rates in line with the latest mortality experience without the drawbacks of over-complication.[245]

In addition, many special studies were made on such subjects as interest rates, expense levels, premium rates, agency compensation, medical expense, and the changing pattern of the national economy. Approximately a half million new premium, settlement option, dividend, and other figures were needed which were obtained largely by the use of modern, high-speed computing machinery. Not only did fifty-three new policy forms have to be prepared and printed, but many new application forms, riders, and rubber-stamp endorsements had to be devised. The contracts and related forms had to be filed with the insurance departments of the various states—a total of more than 4,000 individual filings. Six new rate books with more than 1,000 pages of tables had to be printed for distribution with the announcement of the new program.

Again, in December 1958, Equitable announced a new program of policies and of liberalization of far-reaching importance. The most significant feature of the new "Series 100" program was the adoption of a "cheaper by the dozen" principle of grading premiums by size of policy for *all plans* of individual insurance. The complicated actuarial structure was developed by Vice President and Actuary William J. November and members of his staff under the general supervision of Senior Vice President and Chief Actuary Walter Klem. For policies with face amounts of $10,000 or more, higher cash values in the early

245 "Series 95 Program," *Agency Items* (July 26, 1954).

policy years were provided; lower premiums on all plans of life insurance for women in policies of $10,000 and over were also included in this Series 100 Program. Another attractive feature was an elective provision, for which a nominal extra premium was charged, whereby the insured was given the right to purchase additional permanent form insurance of moderate amounts at stated future intervals and regardless of his physical condition or other underwriting considerations.

Not quite ready on Equitable's 100th birthday but announced at that time, to be effective in November, was the Assured Life Income Policy. Under this policy the normal form of benefit at the insured's death consisted of a monthly income of predetermined amount payable for the lifetime of the beneficiary (provided the original beneficiary was still alive). This policy was designed primarily to provide protection for a wife. Sold in units each of which provided $10 of monthly income to the beneficiary up to her age sixty-two, and $5 thereafter, the ALI policy was based on the use of $1,000 of permanent life insurance for each unit, and supplemental term insurance. It contained the cash and other nonforfeiture values corresponding to the permanent insurance.

The importance of Equitable's policy modernization program was indicated by the fact that during 1959 more than 70 per cent of ordinary life insurance sold was on policies introduced in the previous five-year period.

Notwithstanding all these innovations and improvements, Equitable was not content to rest upon its past accomplishments. Already it was considering plans for the future. As Underwriting Vice President J. Henry Smith said in 1959:

> The list of liberalizations and extensions of underwriting practices—in occupational ratings, aviation coverages, dozens of medical impairments—is too long to spell out here. It's a remarkable record of progressive improvement in keeping with the best traditions of American business. And now we have that astounding concept of guaranteed insurability, the Option to Purchase Additional Insurance!
>
> What more is left? Has underwriting actually gone about as far as it can go? Perhaps this question is a little like asking whether the high jump record will ever reach an absolute maximum. . . . Who knows what lengths our athletes will reach tomorrow! So it is with underwriting. Exactly when and how the next improvements will come it is hazardous to say, but certainly they will come.[246]

[246] J. Henry Smith, "What's Ahead in Underwriting?" *Agency Items*, (July 26, 1959).

Equitable Chicago Building, 1965

Possible future developments in the underwriting field were well outlined by Senior Vice President and Actuary Walter Klem in a paper entitled "A Ten Year Look Ahead at Coverages of Life Insurance Companies" in December 1955.[247] In this stimulating survey, the author considered the possibility of further liberalization in the underwriting of ordinary insurance risks, premiums graded according to size of the policy, further use of the monthly premium plan for ordinary business, further development of major medical insurance, the possibility of integration of total and permanent disability benefits with retirement benefits, and the provision for pension plans which would make the life company the principal source of service in this field. In regard to pension plans the author said:

> Our business as a whole is built upon the two great economic risks involving human life contingencies, the risk of early death and the risk of outliving one's financial resources. The first of these is declining, and the second increasing. The need for insurance protection during the working years does not diminish, but its cost goes down with decreasing mortality rates. On the other hand, both the need for an assurance of continued income during later years and the cost of purchasing that assurance are becoming greater. So long as we continue, as an industry, to furnish the same over-all services as we have in the past, these trends should result in adding greater proportionate weight to the part of our operations concerned with post-retirement benefits.

To bring its policies to the people Equitable had, in 1959, some 9,000 agents organized under 122 agency managerships—plus five general agents with subagents, and four without—which were grouped into six departments or geographic districts.[248] At the head of each department was a Field Vice President who rode circuit on the agency managerships in his district and reported to Agency Vice President Samuel A. Burgess through a Vice President located in the Home Office.

The new agent received his preliminary training (Agency Induction

[247] Before a symposium December 15, 1955, at the 49th Annual Meeting of the Life Insurance Association of America. Copy in Equitable Archives.

[248] The geographic divisions were as follows: Northeastern, New York Metropolitan, North Central, Southern, South Central, and Western.

An agency managership was established in Hawaii in 1958. A branch managership was set up in Alaska in 1960 and a managership established in 1966. A Unit Manager was placed in Puerto Rico in 1959 to be responsible to the Agency Manager in Miami; then in 1964 Puerto Rico was given an Agency Manager.

Plan) largely from the unit manager—of whom there were more than 600—and by way of instruction material from the Home Office covering practically every phase of life insurance. Equitable, which conducted the first training school for prospective agents (1902), now maintains a continuous training program both by way of direct instruction and by correspondence. By 1959, a dozen courses were presented which ran from basic instruction through career sales training to advanced work in business insurance and estate planning; there were also correspondence courses for those who wished to prepare for the examination to qualify as Chartered Life Underwriters. In 1959 more than 260 separate courses were given for agents and managers; 4,153 students were enrolled in instructor-conducted courses and 4,426 in the correspondence courses. The training program was under the direction of Vice President Clarence B. Metzger, CLU.

Each Agency Manager held an annual three-day educational conference for his qualified agents. At these meetings one or more Home Office or outside speakers would participate in the program as well as the agents, who read papers and engaged in panel discussions. Late afternoon and evening hours were usually reserved for sports and social affairs. Other meetings of managers, supervisors, and agents were held both in the field and at the Home Office as a part of a general program for keeping the agents fully informed as to the services available to Equitable policyholders.

Membership in the production clubs for Equitable agents—for example, the $500,000 Club, the Equitable Million Club—was determined by the production credits earned during a calendar year.[249] Periodically, sales campaigns were waged in honor of some Equitable officer or some important occasion, and competition became keen not only among the individual agents but among the agency managers and the six departments. In addition, recognition (membership in the Group Millionaires' Club) was given to agents whose production of

[249] The clubs, in the late 1950's were: the $100,000 Club; the $150,000 Club; the $200,000 Club; the $250,000 Club; the $300,000 Club; the $400,000 Club; the $500,000 Club; the $600,000 Club; the $700,000 Club; the $750,000 Club; the $800,000 Club; the $900,000 Club; the Equitable Million Club; the Equitable Two Million Club; the Equitable Three Million Club; and the Equitable Four Million Club. The unit for production club qualification was $1,200 of first year commissions paid for each $100,000 of club designation. To maintain equity in these production credits for club purposes certain weighting formulae were used, as for example for beginner agents operating under the 12th edition salary and commission contract.

group life and other group protection equaled $1,000,000 in volume in a given year. GMC had its own organization and in 1958 established an educational fund for college scholarships to be awarded to children of Equitable agents and employees.

As with an army, the agency forces at the front required supporting personnel. There were many "Men Behind the Man from Equitable."

In addition to the agency forces, there were several other field organizations. The Inspection Bureau gathered information on the applicant for insurance over and beyond that revealed in the application and by the medical examination—his need for, and ability to pay for, the insurance, as well as possible occupational hazards and other pertinent facts. In more than 300 locations throughout the country there were key correspondents, and a correspondent inspector in every town in the United States with a population of 200 or more. Some three dozen salaried inspectors and a score of district and assistant inspectors completed the organization. The Inspection Bureau provided several hundred thousand individual reports annually. There were also approximately 12,000 practicing physicians authorized to examine applicants.

The Group Department (in the 1950's headed by Vice President Merle A. Gulick) maintained eight field departments, each headed by a manager; within each department were divisions headed by divisional managers. Both departmental and divisional employees assisted the local agent in preparing group proposals and accompanying him at times on interviews with the prospects. In the late 1950's there were about 400 salaried field personnel in the Group Department.

At the same time, the Salary Savings Division had twenty-one field supervisors, who assisted agents locally in placing Salary Savings plans with business and industrial firms.

The Residential Mortgage Department had sixty full-time supervisors distributed over the country. The large volume of Assured Home Ownership written in recent years is ample evidence of the cooperation between the agents of the Society who initiate this business and the regional representatives of the investment operations. The Society also blanketed the country with an extensive farm mortgage organization which operated through ten branch office supervisors and about 100 appraisers.[250]

250 The regional offices were located at Chicago, Dallas, Denver, Des Moines, Kansas City, Memphis, Newark, Raleigh, San Francisco, and Spokane.

There were more than eighty cashiers' offices in the United States—and one in Montreal—with about 2,000 salaried employees. The cashier's office is the principal point of contact between the Society and many of its policyholders; it is in fact a miniature Home Office—Equitable's method of decentralization to insure prompt service to its policyholders. The cashier keeps the accounts and with proper authorization pays all agency expenses. He reviews applications and calculates and pays some agents' commissions. He is the fiscal agent in the city, maintains the local bank accounts and makes collections of premiums, policy loan and mortgage payments, and other moneys due. He keeps records of policies, services these policies, pays out dividends, loan disbursements, mortgage advances, and—as authorized by the Home Office—death claims, surrender payments, and large policy loans. An increasing number of group casualty claims are processed and paid by cashiers each year.

In view of the importance of the cashier's work, Equitable initiated an administrative training course in 1920. Selected college graduates take the training courses in cashier's offices, and clerical employees are encouraged to study for and take the tests of the training courses while working at their regular duties. Many of the executives of Equitable came into the Society by way of this training program.

Maintaining liaison between field and Home Office were several other groups of salaried employees. Fifteen field auditors, some of whom were graduates of the administrative training course, and some certified public accountants, covered the country to make sure that Equitable's system of internal control was properly administered. These auditors reported periodically to the Home Office to confer with representatives of various departments. The specialists in the Pension Trust Division not only provided sales aids to the agents for retirement pension and profit-sharing plans by way of literature, but also conducted seminars and conferences. The Agency Department's research staff kept the agents and agency executives informed of changes in the life insurance market, on the competitive situation faced by Equitable agents, and, with the aid of the Actuary's Department, devised new methods to help the agent meet the competition. If the agent or manager was confronted with problems too complicated for his experience, he could call directly upon Agency Special Services in the Home Office (established in 1948) where twenty full-time consultants were available for expert counsel.

The Sales Promotion Division provided sales aids and promotional materials for agents and other sales personnel. Specialists in marketing and advertising, writers, artists, and public relations men devised the materials to make the agent's work easier. The products of their labors was integrated with a continuous national advertising program. To head up these activities, Charles R. Corcoran, a native of Manhattan, joined the Society in 1946. Corcoran had had previous experience in direct sales and sales management, and with an advertising agency which handled the account of a major New England life insurance company, as well as direct mail promotional services for a number of companies.

From 1945 to 1952 Equitable sponsored a weekly radio program, "This Is Your FBI," which was based upon actual incidents taken from records of the Federal Bureau of Investigation. In 1955 the Society inaugurated a series of display advertisements in leading magazines on the theme of "Living Insurance": "Living Insurance means benefits to the living. Benefits for you while you live. If you die, benefits for those who live after you." Since in recent years more than 70 per cent of all life insurance benefits have been paid to living policyholders this theme was particularly well chosen. The advertisements, accompanied by changing captions and illustrative photographs selected from thousands of entries, had wide appeal. Many thousands of requests came in for reprints and the advertisements won several national awards. In January 1959 Equitable extended its advertising media to include television with the co-sponsoring, once a week, of "Douglas Edwards with the News." October brought the first of the "Our American Heritage" series of six shows. American Heritage Publishing Company, Incorporated, the National Broadcasting Company, Milberg Enterprises, Incorporated, and Foote, Cone and Belding, the Society's advertising agency, collaborated to produce the shows. Promotional material was mailed to some 8,000 libraries, history teachers, and historical societies. The six shows featured the lives of Thomas Jefferson, Eli Whitney, John Charles Fremont, Ulysses S. Grant, Oliver Wendell Holmes, and Andrew Carnegie.

In the Home Office at 393 Seventh Avenue—and the seven overflow buildings—there were, in 1959, approximately 7,000 employees. (In addition to the Home Office Equitable owned and maintained buildings for its own use in Albany, Atlanta, Brooklyn, Chicago, Fresno, Los Angeles, Milwaukee, Richmond, and San Francisco.) The Society's buildings, as well as offices rented in 456 cities, were under the supervision of the Home Office Building Department (Vice President John H. Muller) which had about 600 employees, about a quarter of whom operated in the field. Although the Home Office force had grown rapidly it had in no wise grown in proportion to the Society's business; while the insurance in force more than doubled during the 1950's, Home Office personnel increased by only about 35 per cent.

Handling the business in the Home Office required personnel with varied talents and skills; there were messenger boys and engineers, typists and artists, guards and electricians, photographers and doctors, librarians, lawyers, editors, actuaries, accountants, economists, and many others. The largest department was the Policy Issue and Service Department, but not far behind in number of employees were the Claims, Actuary's, and Controller's departments.

Since 1953 the Personnel Department had been enlarged and various functions added to emphasize the importance of maintaining high employee morale, establishing adequate internal communications, and providing greater opportunity for advancement and growth of the individual. The Department included the following principal Divisions: Activities and Services, Benefits, Education and Training, Employment, Research and Planning, Salary Administration, and Suggestion. Between 1954 and the end of 1958 a major job evaluation project for virtually all non-officer salaried positions in the Society was completed. This project resulted in the establishment of twenty-two grades, or work levels, which represented increasing degrees of responsibility. From the time of his election in 1957, President Oates gave added emphasis to the performance-reward concept of the merit system. This concept was the underlying principle upon which the salary ranges included in the graded system were established; it became the supervisor's responsibility to evaluate performance and recommend merit increases which fairly recognized the differences in employee performance.

In 1956 Equitable's Employees' Health Center installed a periodic checkup plan covering some 1,500 persons in the Home Office. Home Office and salaried field employees age forty-five or more—later reduced to forty—were eligible for these periodic health examinations. Examinations were voluntary and the results a matter of confidence between the examiner and the employee.

In 1958, to help counteract the incidence of inflation, the Society's Retirement Plan was revised to provide increased pensions for both active employees and those already retired; employee contributions were reduced, earlier eligibility provided, and more liberal early retirement benefits and increased disability allowances established.

In 1958 a new and important program in the field of supervisory training, methods improvement, and cost control, known as the Methods and Production Analysis Program, was instituted under the sponsorship of the recently established Methods Research Department. This program was planned to lead to the establishment of production standards for supervisors in measuring and controlling the problems of their particular organizations. Apart from the technical results of such a program, it was expected to broaden the perspective of supervisory personnel and increase their understanding of the supervisory processes. To head the Methods Research Department the Equitable found within its organization David H. Harris—born in New York and educated in England—who had begun his career with the Society in 1946 in the Actuary's Department. As this program progressed, Harris and his associates familiarized themselves with the great challenge of Electronic Data Processing equipment and soon Equitable was blazing new trails in this important field.

In addition to the administrative training course mentioned previously, various other educational programs were continuously in operation to enable the employee to increase his knowledge and usefulness. There were courses in effective reading, effective writing, effective speaking, typing, stenography, and keypunching. Young mathematicians could, by way of the Actuarial Trainee Course, prepare for the examinations given by the Society of Actuaries which, if passed, qualified them as Associates or Fellows of that Society. The School of Insurance, conducted by the Insurance Society of New York, provided courses on the various aspects of life insurance. A number of these courses prepared students for the examinations of the Life Office Management Association Institute which, if passed, qualified the student for a Fellowship in the Institute. Tuition and examination fees were refunded by Equitable upon satisfactory completion of the courses or passing of the examinations. Other courses administered by the Health Insurance Association of America prepared for the annual examinations qualifying the student for a certificate from the Association. To encourage employees to undertake or complete college careers, Equitable's Education and Training Division of the Personnel Department announced in 1957 the Tuition Refund Plan. Under this plan, which included employees in the field as well as the Home Office, 50 per cent of the tuition in any approved course in an accredited college or university was refunded at the time of enrollment and the remainder on completion of the course. During the first year of operation there were almost five hundred enrollments under the Tuition Refund Plan. A similar plan for CLU candidates had been introduced in 1945 by the Equitable CLU Association.

Mechanization of office methods which began with the typewriter and Elizur Wright's arithmeter in the early 1880's developed at an accelerating pace in the 1950's. Electric calculating machines were used as early as 1920, and in 1955, when such machines became available, Equitable added an IBM 650 electronic data processing machine. Two years later a giant IBM 705 was installed, the first to be delivered in New York City. This machine, which required a fifty-ton air-conditioning plant, was soon put to work computing premiums due, dividends payable, and interest owed on policy loans, and printing the notices at the rate of 3,600 per hour. Within a year or two, it was also used to compute renewal commissions on ordinary insurance. Since several million calculations are made annually and notices sent to policyholders, the saving in time and labor is important, as is also the virtual elimination of error. Although machines such as this are beyond the comprehension of the lay mind, they do not think; some mind has to prepare the data for them. Much advance planning was necessary before this machine could be used to advantage. Then further to utilize its possibilities, the Methods Research Department was created. This department worked closely with the Ordinary Insurance Administration and Group Insurance Administration Departments. Very soon the 705 was being utilized twenty hours per day, six days per week. It is interesting to note that installation of the electronic equipment, although it eliminated a tremendous amount of routine work, did not result in the discharge of a single employee nor the reduction of a single individual's salary owing to reassignment of duties.[251]

Similar mechanical improvements were made in communications, not only within the Home Office, but between the Home Office and field. In 1958 an 83 B1 Automatic Selective Teletype System was installed. Messages from Underwriting, Policy Issue, Group, Residential Mortgage, and other departments coming into the message center could be relayed by direct private line to the leading cashiers' offices east of the Mississippi. In 1959 the network was extended to the West Coast. Through this system questions and answers could be exchanged directly and immediately.

Important operations which were not mechanized at this time were the processing of applications and the sending out of the policies.

[251] For the addition of other electronic calculators, see this history, p. 1303.

As the applications and abstracts came into the receiving desk of Policy Issue and Service—sometimes during a sales campaign at the rate of more than 3,000 per day—they went into the indexing section where a control was established and a temporary index card made. Then on an endless belt the applications went to the Underwriting Department (until April 1962 under Vice President William E. Walsh) where they were sorted according to size of policies. The bulk of the applications for amounts of $10,000 or less was handled by special production underwriters. Applications for larger amounts or those which were questioned for any reason were referred to experienced underwriters, and about 15 per cent of all cases were reviewed by the medical directors. There are different kinds of underwriters for different kinds of insurance: Life and Health, Individual and Group. The underwriter has been described as the "man in the middle"; his job is to grade and classify applications for life insurance. His greatest responsibility "is not only to protect the Society but to do a service to the sales force. . . . The underwriter's decisions are really a part of the product we sell." [252] Although it is possible that some of the underwriter's work may be mechanized in the future, there will always be the need for flexible human judgment based upon experience.

Once approved by the underwriters, the application returned on the endless belt to Policy Issue and Service where information on it was translated into numerical codes and converted into a number of punched cards which were sent to the 705. From these cards the machine prepared various records, and printed, on what was eventually to be a page of the finished policy, the names of the insured and beneficiary, and the premium structure pertaining to the contract. This policy page was then sent back to Policy Issue and Service which assembled the completed policy from loose preprinted pages, including the appropriate nonforfeiture values, inserted the photostats of the application in the policy, arranged the policies geographically, and mailed them to the cashiers' offices throughout the country.

Since 1950, as a precautionary measure against loss or destruction,

[252] The underwriter's work has been described as follows: "To an actuary, I guess I'm kind of a policeman. I've got to keep a tight rein on things. I've got to be awfully careful when it comes to deciding if an applicant qualifies for Equitable insurance. To an agent, I'm an ogre, a necessary evil, a guy who sits at a desk in the Home Office and says no. To Equitable's management, I'm the guy who can't be too tough or too easy—a fellow who has to make the right decision every time. I'd guess you'd call me—and the men like me—the man in the middle." Pete Olson, "My Job, Underwriter," *Equinews* (September 1964).

vital policy, corporate, and other records have been microfilmed periodically and stored at a location outside of New York City.

The publishing activities of the Home Office constituted a sizable business. Tons of manuals, sales literature, health and hobby pamphlets, educational brochures, rate books, calendars, instructions, and forms were published annually. The Supply Division, housed in three buildings in lower Manhattan's warehouse district, shipped more than 100 freight cartons and 1,500 parcel post packages per day. One publication, the Society's annual statement to the New York Insurance Department, was a document some 12 by 18 inches of more than 200 pages, weighing about four pounds. In addition to these publications, Equitable issued several magazines. Oldest of these was *Agency Items*, a small-sized magazine, which began publication in 1907; in the late 1950's it was a biweekly publication with a circulation of approximately 15,300. In January 1962 *Agency Items* became a weekly and was issued in small newspaper format, and later in the year *Equitable Leaders*, a bimonthly magazine, made its appearance; in 1963 the title of this magazine was changed to *Equitable National Leaders* and the following year to *Equitable National Leaders Magazine. Leadership News*, a newspaper-type publication of the Advertising and Publications Department, was issued monthly during the Centennial Campaign and daily during Centennial Week. *Equinews*—one of the most attractive and informative of house organs—began publication in December 1956.[253] This large-sized, well-illustrated monthly magazine covered all phases of Equitable's activities and was sent to some 14,000 Equitable employees throughout the country. *Farm Loan News*, a small-sized magazine published by the Farm Mortgage Department made its first appearance in April 1944 and was issued monthly until 1958 when it became bimonthly; in 1959 this periodical became a quarterly.

The scope and functions of Equitable's public relations were broadened in 1956 when they were placed under the direction of Senior Vice President Melville P. Dickenson. Public relations of an institution the size and nature of Equitable constitute a basically im-

[253] For the Society's earlier magazines, *Our Mutual Friend, The Protector, The Equitable Gazette, The Equitable Record*, and *The Equitable News*, see this history, Index. From the demise of *The Equitable Record* in 1905 until 1956, Equitable had no general magazine. For some of the minor and short-lived publications such as *The Tattler, The Equitable Public Bulletin, The Interoffice Chronicle*, etc., see *Equinews* (December 1956).

portant part of the Society's work and involve much more than if it were an organization engaged in manufacturing and selling material things. Not only do they require maintenance of free and dependable communications between administrators and employees, between the employees and the policyholders, but also sound relations with other insurance organizations, public officials, and the general public. The Society's code says: "It is imperative to place the public welfare first in reaching business decisions."

Equitable was largely instrumental in organizing The Association of Life Insurance Presidents in 1906 (since 1944 the Life Insurance Association of America) and became a member of the American Life Convention, the other general life company organization, in 1945. In 1939 the Society participated in the organization of the Institute of Life Insurance and the President of Equitable served on its first Board of Directors. It is also a member of the Health Insurance Association of America, the Life Insurance Agency Management Association, the Life Office Management Association, the Canadian Life Insurance Officers Association, and dozens of other organizations—economic, scientific, and professional. Many of the Society's personnel naturally participate in the activities of their own professional organizations, such as medical, law, actuarial, and agency associations. In 1940 President Parkinson served as chairman of the committee composed of representatives of the American Life Convention, the Institute of Life Insurance, and The Association of Life Insurance Presidents which brought into being the S. S. Huebner Foundation for Insurance Education. Equitable, together with more than a hundred other companies, has continued to support this foundation, which has done much to promote the teaching and study of insurance in the colleges of the United States and Canada.

For a number of years the Society has contributed financially to selected organizations and institutions which engage in research projects in the fields of community services, medicine, public health, business, and economics. Equitable was one of the original contributors (1945) to the Life Insurance Medical Research Fund for research in the field of cardiovascular diseases, and since 1951 has supported the National Fund for Medical Education which was established to "encourage the development and advancement of constantly improving standards of medical education." It also contributes to the American Cancer Society, the American Heart Association, and various other social and welfare activities.

In 1954, under the direction of Dr. Norvin C. Kiefer, Equitable instituted its own Public Health Program, a principal part of which was the preparation and distribution of a series of booklets based on the theme "Assurance of a Fuller Life," which dealt with health subjects with particular reference to the family.

In 1955 a plan for the support of higher education was inaugurated under which grants were awarded to selected privately supported accredited colleges and universities with strong liberal arts programs for the purpose of improving faculty salaries. Subsequently, grants were made on an unrestricted basis.

The occasion of the 100th Anniversary was deemed not only fitting but indeed a most appropriate time for Equitable to make a substantial contribution to the public welfare. A committee, known as the National Awards Committee, consisting of three directors, three officers, three agency managers, and three representative and experienced policyholders was invited to consider the matter. After months of study and deliberation, the Committee came forth with a proposal to fulfill the requirements as expressed by President Oates when he stated that the 100th Anniversary would be "a time for an expression of faith in the future, and for rededication to the high public service opportunities for which the Society was founded." Accordingly, a grant was made to the National Academy of Sciences in Washington, D.C., for the construction of an addition to its building, to be known as "The Equitable Life Assurance Society Hall of the Life Sciences," to house the medical research organizations of the Academy and its Research Council.

Since Equitable's investments have been treated elsewhere, suffice it to say at this point that keeping more than $9,000,000,000 of assets at work required constant study and activity on the part of economists, security analysts, and real estate and farm mortgage specialists. These men not only had to have knowledge of past experience in many fields, but sufficient imagination to make educated guesses as to the future. So, by way of stocks and bonds, mortgages, or purchase and lease, Equitable used the billions ultimately destined for the policyholders' benefits to finance all phases of the American economy; oil and steel, transportation and office buildings, housing projects, homes and hospitals, factories, dams and power plants, garages, shopping centers, farms, mines, and colleges. Every three years, the New York Insurance Department in connection with its thorough examination of Equitable operations must count and check the bonds and stocks in the subterranean vaults—amounting, in 1959, to almost $6,000,000,000. It requires some thirty examiners and an equal number of Equitable watchers and checkers two and a half days to complete the task. Needless to say, everything must come out even—to the cent.

As the Home Office at 393 Seventh Avenue became too small to accommodate the personnel, Equitable began to make plans for a new Home Office building.[254] In March 1954 Senior Vice President Charles W. Dow, after making preliminary studies of the Home Office space problem, recommended to President Murphy that a Committee of the Board be appointed to consult with officers of the Society and formulate a program for meeting the long-term Home Office requirements. Such a committee was appointed in June and in late November it recommended "construction of a new Principal Office Building" and that Equitable promptly initiate a program to acquire an appropriate site for such a building.[255] On December 1 Dow, in a detailed memorandum, advised President Murphy that, since it was difficult to determine the Society's requirements for the next 40 or 50 years, a Home Office program be planned for two stages of development—the first to take care of needs for the next 15 years, and the second to accommodate future needs. Ultimate expansion would call for some 2,600,000 square feet of office space, requiring a site of 180,000 to 200,000 square feet. Officers of the Society had examined some 13 possible sites, five of which they considered "particularly worthy of consideration," and made studies of the residential distribution of Home Office personnel and the transportation patterns used by them. Since the majority of the employees came from Queens, Brooklyn, and Long Island, it was finally decided that a midtown location would be desirable. So Dow recommended that the Real Estate Committee of the Board approve purchase of a land area of some 183,000 square feet on part of the blocks east and west of the Avenue of the Americas (formerly Sixth Avenue) between Fifty-first and Fifty-second Streets and in close proximity to Rockefeller Center. This the Committee did December 7. Individual lots were to be purchased pursuant to Section 81-7(h) of

[254] President Parkinson at one time even thought of renting all of 393 Seventh Avenue and moving back to 120 Broadway. Amortization payments on the mortgage held by Equitable on 120 Broadway had begun to default in May 1941, at which time the Equitable Office Building Corporation petitioned for reorganization. For the history of the various steps by which Equitable finally acquired the fee to the property at 120 Broadway, see this history, p. 1278, note 260.

[255] Members of the committee were Nicholas Kelley, Chairman; Robert E. Blum; Richard H. Mansfield; and Ray D. Murphy, ex officio.

the New York insurance law with a view to their retention as income-producing real estate if the site could not be completely assembled; once the site had been substantially assembled, application would be made to the Insurance Department for approval of the acquisition of the site under Section 81-7(a) as the location for the Society's Home Office.[256]

Equitable succeeded in acquiring all of the lots on the east side of the Avenue except that occupied by a prominent restaurant owner who wanted a high price for his land at 51 West Fifty-first Street plus the promise of a fully equipped restaurant in the proposed Equitable building. After prolonged negotiations, the parties arrived at an agreement. On the west side of the Avenue ("Manhattan West"), Equitable had difficulty in getting possession of the lot occupied by the Geneva Club, a headwaiters' club, but finally succeeded in doing so. On this side of the block were also a number of cheap entertainment houses and other "centers of culture" the owners of which were not so reluctant to sell.

After the land was pretty well assembled, Equitable decided to utilize the land on the west side of the Avenue as a site for the Home Office building to meet existing needs and to make arrangements for the construction of an office building on the east side of the Avenue in which, as the need arose, additional space might be made available. Consequently, in May 1956, Equitable entered into a contract to lease "Manhattan East" to Galbreath-Ruffin Corporation, builders, and to finance 90 per cent of the cost of the building to be erected thereon.[257] Meanwhile, in February, Equitable had decided to request the approval of the Insurance Department for the transfer of "Manhattan

[256] Although Equitable had made no formal application to the Insurance Department for approval of the purchase of the lots, Counsels Leo D. Fitzgerald and Warner H. Mendel had a meeting, December 14, with Deputy Superintendent Adelbert G. Straub, Jr. A memorandum was drawn up and signed by the three men which, in effect, agreed that Equitable's purchase of lots be treated as a confidential matter. Straub showed the memorandum to Superintendent Bohlinger, who had no objections to Straub's signing the document on behalf of the Department. The reason given for the need of such confidential treatment was that public knowledge of the Society's plans would, in all probability, make it prohibitive to assemble the site at realistic prices. The signed memorandum is in Corporate Records, Equitable Archives.

[257] After fifteen years, Equitable was to have refusal of all space available upon termination of leases. At this time it did not own title to one parcel in "Manhattan East" (51 West Fifty-first Street) which was subject to a long-term leasehold.

West" from the classification of investment real estate to real estate to be used for its Home Office building. It submitted a formal application in July, but the Insurance Department pointed out that acquisition of the east tract as well as the west tract involved a relatively large expenditure for Home Office purposes—to say nothing of the cost of the building—and questioned whether land purchased for investment could be approved for a Home Office site.[258] Equitable then withdrew the application (October 1956).

After Galbreath-Ruffin failed to comply fully with the terms of the agreement to erect an office building on "Manhattan East," Equitable, August 31, 1957, canceled the agreement and three days later petitioned the Insurance Department for approval of "Manhattan West" for the Home Office site, with the understanding that it would place "Manhattan East" on the market for sale or lease at its fair value; if the land was leased, Equitable would have no part in financing any buildings erected thereon.[259] The cost of the Society's building, including architects' fees, was not to exceed $50,000,000. The petition was approved September 12, subject to submission of detailed plans, the construction contract, and cost figures.

In January 1958 the real estate development firm of Webb and Knapp, Incorporated, offered a proposal to pay approximately $13,-200,000 for "Manhattan East" by selling to Equitable the underlying fee of 120 Broadway. After some negotiating, Equitable, on September 8, signed simultaneous transactions with Webb and Knapp, Incorporated, and a subsidiary, Subill Realty Corporation. As a result of these

[258] The Insurance Department noted that Equitable, in regard to certain lots, had paid "amounts in excess of their reasonable market value as separate parcels," but also recognized the fact that in bringing together a large number of smaller parcels it was not unusual to find owners who refused to sell at a reasonable price, and that Equitable, not being a public agency, could not resort to condemnation proceedings to avoid paying excessive prices for real estate it wished to acquire. *Report on Examination of the Equitable Life Assurance Society of the United States by the Insurance Department of the State of New York,* December 31, 1956.

Another matter which concerned the Insurance Department was the amount of money Equitable was investing in one spot—not only in "Manhattan East" and "Manhattan West," but also in a large mortgage on the Time-Life Building at Fiftieth Street and Avenue of the Americas.

[259] The Insurance Department had calculated that the land on the east side of the Avenue (including 51 West Fifty-first Street) would, by the end of 1957, have cost Equitable $13,100,510, and, if leased as a parking lot as Equitable at one time contemplated, would yield less than one per cent. *Ibid.*

agreements, Equitable acquired the fee to 120 Broadway at a price of $15,625,000, subject to a mortgage held by the John Hancock Mutual Life Insurance Company with a balance of $9,003,784 at 4 per cent, with a final payment due November 1, 1974.[260] The fee was purchased subject to a lease to 120 Broadway Associates at a net annual rental of $850,000 until July 31, 1976, with options for renewals. On the same day (September 8) Equitable sold "Manhattan East" for $13,-625,000 in cash, subject to two existing leases. So once again Equitable became the owner of the historic site which it had occupied from 1870 to 1924.

While the negotiations with Webb and Knapp were under way, the Real Estate Committee of the Equitable Board had, February 18, 1958, authorized the Society—subject to the approval of the Insurance Department—to enter into a contract with the Turner Construction Company to build the Home Office building and June 17 approved its erection at a guaranteed maximum price estimate of $56,000,000. Architects for the new building were Skidmore, Owings and Merrill, and the building contract was let on preliminary plans. The Insurance Department was finally persuaded to raise its earlier maximum cost to

260 In brief, the steps which made possible this transaction were as follows: After the Equitable Office Building Corporation defaulted on the amortization payment on the mortgage held by Equitable in 1941, the company was reorganized by way of Federal court action in December 1947. Under the plan approved, the $15,583,865 mortgage held by Equitable was reduced to $14,750,000 and assigned to the John Hancock Mutual Life Insurance Company with modifications. Holders of the debentures of the Equitable Office Building Corporation were paid in cash and holders of the company's no par common stock received one share of new stock (par value $1) for each five shares of the old stock and warrants to purchase 1⅕ shares of new stock at $3 for each share of old stock held. The warrants expired December 24, 1947. In May 1954 Webb and Knapp, Incorporated, offered to purchase the stock of the Equitable Office Building Corporation on the basis of $5 cash and $7 Webb and Knapp, Incorporated, debenture 5s of 1974 for each share. By January 1955 Webb and Knapp held 1,172,002 of the 1,229,659.6 shares outstanding. In 1955 the property interest in 120 Broadway was divided into fee and leasehold. The leasehold was sold to 120 Broadway Associates, a partnership consisting of Lawrence H. Wien, Henry W. Klein, Alvin S. Lane, Alvin Silverman, and Fred Linden as equal partners. The price totaled $16,750,000 ($10,000,000 cash and $6,750,000 leasehold mortgage, term nine years). Equitable was paid $13,625,000 for its parcel of land on the east side of the avenue, and the purchase price for the fee of 120 Broadway was $15,625,000, including a mortgage of $9,003,784 with interest at 4 per cent held by the John Hancock Mutual Life Insurance Company. This fee acquisition was subject to a lease to 120 Broadway Associates at a rental of $850,000 net per annum running to July 31, 1976, with renewal options at the same rent to run to July 31, 2954. The Society's book value of the fee as of September 30, 1964, was $3,825,060.13.

$58,000,000, which it did August 4, 1958.[261] The original plans called for 42 working floors and at one time it appeared that the cost would run at least $10,000,000 more than the maximum authorized by the Insurance Department. But by cutting off four floors and making other changes, Equitable's experts working together with the architects brought the cost within the allotted limit.

The building was designed with a tower of 42 floors (38 working floors) facing the Avenue between Fifty-first and Fifty-second streets, and a 15-floor section to the rear. One half of the exterior skin was to be of anodized aluminum and structural glass and the other half window glass; floor space was to total 1,715,000 square feet. It was said that the new Equitable Home Office would be the largest building ever designed for occupancy by a single private owner. Thirty-four automatic passenger elevators, four service elevators, and escalators to the second floor and the first basement floor were provided to take care of the 7,400 employee traffic. Automatic conveyors were designed to move documents and other material from department to department. The air-conditioning system had a capacity of 1,250,000 cubic feet of air per minute. The restaurant on the second floor seated some 1,400 persons and provided both waiter and cafeteria service to a total of 5,000 persons daily. Comfortable lounges adjoined the cafeteria. On the first sub-surface floor facilities were provided for shops, with a passageway or arcade leading through to the Time-Life building on the south side of Fifty-first Street and thence to the subway. Thirty-eight feet below the lobby and resting on bedrock was the electrically welded water-tight steel security vault which weighed 155 tons; it was encased in walls, floor, and ceiling of 28-inch thick steel reinforced concrete.

Since the exterior of the new building was metal and glass, there was no cornerstone in which to place documents and other mementos. Instead, a "Lithochron" was designed for this purpose, consisting of an eight-foot column in which many-faceted pieces of clear plastic had been joined. Balanced on the tips of two converging pyramids of plastic was a stainless steel cylinder inscribed with quotations from the four Equitable presidents who were in office at the end of each quarter century of the Society's history. The quotations were as follows:

261 Superintendent of Insurance Julius S. Wikler in a letter attached to the minutes of the Real Estate Committee meeting of August 5. Corporate Records, Equitable Archives.

The man of one idea, whose course is marked by enthusiasm, is a power in the world. All leaders, both in great and small affairs, have been men capable of inspiring enthusiasm in their followers.

Henry B. Hyde

A life insurance company is a beneficent institution, protecting the widow and the orphan, and making provision for the aged and infirm; but it distributes nothing in the way of charity. It is a business enterprise pure and simple, cultivating thrift, self-reliance and independence.

Paul Morton

We are engaged in an enterprise, the very essence of which is co-operation, and which exists not for gain but for service. To us are entrusted the savings of countless individuals who look to us to fulfill their self-imposed obligation to provide for those who come after them.

Thomas I. Parkinson

Man is a sacred personality. He, the individual, is the important unit in life. Thus, the real aim and end of all endeavor should be to develop and serve the dignity, welfare and vital importance of the individual human being.

James F. Oates, Jr.

Monday, August 11, 1958, a power shovel began scooping a hole on the building site, and Vice Chairman Robert L. Hogg, Vice President John H. Muller, and representatives of Skidmore, Owings and Merrill and the Turner Construction Company took part in the groundbreaking ceremony.

* * *

Equitable's 100th Anniversary Convention was the most elaborate and impressive in its history. Planning began about three years ahead of the date and the Coliseum was reserved for the occasion, but when it appeared that the Coliseum's facilities would not be adequate to handle the large crowds the scene was shifted to Madison Square Garden.

The theme of the Centennial program was "For All Time."

On Equitable's birthday, Sunday, July 26, 1959, opening ceremonies were held in a tent on a parking lot on the east side of the Avenue of the Americas. Across the Avenue nine floors of the steel skeleton of the new Home Office building faced the crowd. Vice President John H. Muller presided and delivered the opening address. New York's

Mayor, Robert F. Wagner, joined with President Oates in dedicating the "Lithochron," which was to be installed in the lobby of the new Home Office building.[262] Said President Oates: "This is a proud moment. The Equitable today inaugurates the observance of one hundred years of service through the adaptation of the great principle of life insurance to the continuing and growing needs of millions of people."

Monday, July 27, was "Equitable Day." Some 15,000 people, employees, field delegates, and guests converged upon Madison Square Garden where usherettes, dressed in the costumes of an earlier day, directed them to their seats. After the trooping of the colors by a Boy Scout group and the invocation, President Oates delivered the principal Centennial address. He said:

> Now that we are serving an institution one hundred years old—we have come of age. We are, indeed, required to think beyond ourselves, if we are to think effectively of ourselves. . . . Mankind is at the crossroads of civilization. The people must choose between the "road to serfdom" and the "road to freedom." *The time for decision is upon us.* . . . Our Society recognizes man as an end in himself and not as a mere instrument in an economic-political complex. Totalitarianism degrades man; we, on the other hand, believe that man is a sacred personality, that he, the individual, is the important unit in life and that the real aim and end of all government and of all business is to develop and serve the dignity, welfare and vital importance of the individual human being.

He reminded his audience that confidence in the dollar would be necessary if the nation was to carry its struggle with totalitarianism to a successful conclusion; should the purchasing power of the dollar continue to decline, it "could destroy completely our incentive to save and to lend money. Should that incentive be destroyed, our economy would collapse around us like a pack of cards. . . . We must, therefore, continue to do all in our power to fight inflation in whatever form it appears."

Senior Vice President Melville P. Dickenson, who was the chairman

[262] Among the items placed in the steel cylinder for posterity to view were a copy of *The Equitable* 1859–1959, by R. Carlyle Buley; the annual report of President Oates for 1958; current editions of *Equinews*, *Agency Items*, and *Farm Loan News;* current Equitable policy forms and rate books; a photograph of the unveiling ceremony of the "Lithochron"; a typical housewife's shopping list; and copies of New York City newspapers of July 26, 1959.

of the program, spoke on the subject of employee education; and Superintendent Thomas Thacher of the New York Insurance Department told the audience that free enterprise, cooperating "with government regulation in the public interest," had produced the world's leading economy: "Equitable achieved its present position because, like many others, it exercised private initiative in an effort to meet the needs of the market place and to develop better protection against the hazards of illness, old age and death for millions of American citizens."

Maurice E. Ogborn, Joint Actuary of the "Old Equitable" of London, a special guest of Equitable of the United States, noted the tremendous growth of the younger company and presented President Oates with a beautifully framed set of British and American stamps current in 1859 as a Centennial gift from his company.

After the intermission, the curtain went up on "A Century of Song," led and produced by Ed Herlihy, television's "Man from Equitable." There followed numbers by the Equitable Choral Club, prominent opera singers and television entertainers, and the "Buffalo Bills," famous male quartet from the popular show, "The Music Man." The entertainment ended with dancing by the Butleroff Dancers and a rendition of "76 Trombones" by 76 youngsters ranging in age from six to fourteen years and in height from about 40 inches to five and one-half feet. This last number was a fitting finale to a thrilling musical program.

Monday evening more than 3,000 persons attended the Equitable Veteran Legion Centennial Year Dinner, served in five ballrooms at the Waldorf-Astoria Hotel. Field Vice President Edwin R. Jeter presided in the Grand Ballroom, which featured the Society's towering Centennial birthday cake; and Senior Vice President Walter Klem presided in the Empire Room. Other members dined on the Starlight Roof where Senior Vice President Melville P. Dickenson was chairman, in the West Ballroom where Senior Vice President Grant Keehn presided, and in the Sert Room, in charge of Senior Vice President Joseph L. Beesley. President Oates talked briefly to each group.

The afternoon of Equitable Day was devoted to a physical fitness show in Madison Square Garden. The *Sports Illustrated*-sponsored program presented nationally known stars in archery, golf, tennis, baseball, football, boxing, and other sports. Bonnie Prudden led her pupils through floor gymnastics; Dick Mayer, former United States Open golf champion, demonstrated iron shots; Don Budge and Vic Seixas played a tennis doubles match with Bill Talbert and Dick

Savitt; and professional basketball players demonstrated their techniques. But it was Ann Marston, eleven-times national archery champion, who stole the show with what many concluded was an impossible performance. Gertrude Ederle, the first woman to swim the English Channel, received a trophy, and Jack Dempsey, former heavyweight boxing champion of the world, was on hand to greet all and sundry.

The program for Tuesday, July 28, was sponsored by the American Life Convention, the Life Insurance Association of America, and the Institute of Life Insurance. Holgar J. Johnson, President of the Institute, presided, and the leading speakers centered their comments around the theme of "The Economic and Social Contributions of Life Insurance to the Nation." This symposium constituted the most solid part of the week's program.

The Rev. Dr. John S. Bonnell emphasized the altruistic aspects of life insurance and stated his belief that there was "more conscious dedication to high moral and spiritual ends in life insurance than in any other phase of business life in the nation." Dr. Detlev W. Bronk, President of the Rockefeller Institute and of the National Academy of Sciences, after complimenting Equitable on its million dollar Centennial gift to the Academy, pointed out that life insurance made an important contribution toward preserving man's creative spirit: "The gravest threat to our nation's survival would be the decadent loss of our ancestral pioneers' creative, adventurous spirit. One of the greatest social contributions of life insurance is, I think, encouragement of that spirit. Bold adventurers in new undertakings are fortified by the assurance that the risks they take will be shared by many others."

Dr. Neil H. Jacoby, Dean of the Graduate School of Business Administration, University of California at Los Angeles, noted the importance of the business of life insurance as "a defender of the dollar." Offering as it did benefits payable in dollars long in the future, no other business was more interested in fighting inflation: "Small wonder that, of all business groups, the life insurance industry has been the strongest critic of inflationary policies. By their words and their deeds its executives have aroused people to the wastes of inflation." As for the future, he believed that life insurance would continue to "foster progress, undergird our freedoms, and elevate our sense of responsibility for a sound dollar as effectively as it has in the century of progress we celebrate today." Mrs. Ivy Baker Priest, Treasurer of the United States, also sounded a warning against the dangers of inflation: "The life insurance industry, the Government and all others concerned with the future of America have a common interest in halting this impairment of confidence in the nation's currency." Complacency in the face of "imprudent spending and . . . other measures that threaten the stability of the dollar could in time destroy the basis of both our economic growth and our national security."

President Frederick R. Kappel of the American Telephone and Telegraph Company called attention to one aspect of life insurance which was little understood by the public or even by the policyholders, namely the stake every policyholder has in the success of our whole enterprise system; that it was the investment of the policy reserves in all phases of the economy which justified the faith the policyholder put in his policy: "As I understand it, 124 million Americans hold life policies. The more we can bring home to them that the strength of their policies and the strength of private enterprise are two sides of the same thing, the better they will understand the need for a political climate that fosters and encourages enterprise, and the wiser will be their judgments—and their votes."

Perhaps the highlight of the Anniversary celebration for the women of Equitable was the fashion show in the Grand Ballroom of the Waldorf on Tuesday afternoon. This show was produced with the co-operation of the International Silk Association and was fashion's "Salute to Silk" and Equitable's salute to the women.

Wednesday, July 29, was Progress Day. Agency Vice President Samuel A. Burgess presided and introduced the speakers, who talked of "The Years Ahead." Senior Vice President Joseph L. Beesley reviewed Equitable's sales accomplishments and presented the challenge to the agency forces for the decade ahead. Group Vice President Merle A. Gulick warned that the life insurance business must find a way to provide the benefits which the public wants or the government would attempt to do the job, and Senior Vice President and Actuary Walter Klem said that he and his associates were prepared to see that Equitable did not fail to offer the required needs. President Oates ended the formal program with an inspirational talk to the field forces. He said:

We have in The Equitable a noble heritage. We humbly accept from our predecessors, in a sense of stewardship and as a trust, the eminent position to which they have brought this Society. We have our dedication to each other, our sense of mutual confidence, understanding and trust which these meetings here in New York during our Centennial observance have served to clarify and cement in lasting permanence. We have our growing record of performance and our determination to grow and not to wither on the vine and die. We have our solemn determination to examine the needs and requirements of the American public for security and protection in order that we can, perchance, discover original and heretofore unrecognized opportunities for service with the vehicle of life insurance.

During the four days of the Centennial convention escorted tours through the Home Office at 393 Seventh Avenue gave more than 1,000 delegates opportunity to see the headquarters of their business in operation. Some 59 different groups took advantage of these tours, which included everything from the Policy Issue and Service Department to the Society's vault; special exhibits depicted the history of Equitable. In addition to the major programs conducted in Madison Square Garden there were numerous departmental meetings, conferences, and luncheons. Perhaps as valuable as all of the prepared programs was the opportunity offered to the delegates to talk shop, exchange information, and renew friendships.

The 100th Anniversary Convention carried sentimental as well as social significance. Delegates and guests realized that it marked a milestone in the history of Equitable and, while they were reflecting upon the past, they were preparing for the future.[263]

* * *

A note of solemnity was added to the Sunday dedicatory program July 26 when the Rev. Sidney Lanier of St. Thomas Episcopal Church announced to the audience that James Hazen Hyde, the son of Equitable's founder, had died that morning exactly one hundred years from the day in 1859 when his father, Henry B. Hyde, established the Society; he was eighty-three years of age. Those who were familiar with the history of Equitable realized that one of the last personal links with its beginning had been broken.

In December 1905, when James Hazen Hyde went to Paris "for a rest," he did not realize that the "rest" would last thirty-five years. France had been, since his early years, a second home, and for a generation he became an expatriate and one of the better known members of the American colony in Paris. He took a town house at 18 Rue

[263] The 100th Anniversary convention was well covered both in text and illustrations by the Centennial issues of *Agency Items, Equinews,* and *Leadership News.*

Adolphe-Yvon and purchased a suburban estate at 7 Rue de L'Ermitage, Versailles, part of which had belonged to the estate of Madame de Pompadour, one of the mistresses of Louis XV.

In 1913 Hyde married the widow of Count Louis de Gontaut-Biron; she was the former Martha Leishman of Pittsburgh, whose father, John G. Leishman, had been United States Ambassador to Turkey, Italy, and Germany. To this union was born Henry B. Hyde on October 31, 1915. Hyde and his first wife were divorced in 1918, and in 1930 he married the ex-wife of Count Manfred Matuschka, a former officer in the Kaiser's bodyguard. Countess Matuschka, before her marriage, had been Ella Walker of Detroit. This marriage ended in divorce in 1932, and the same year Hyde married Mme. André Thome, whose husband, a member of the House of Deputies, had been killed at the Battle of Verdun; her maiden name was Marthe Dervaux.

Hyde had more than a casual interest in the theater, art, and history; he made it a point to know people of importance in government and international affairs. He knew most of the Presidents and Prime Ministers of France, former President Porfirio Diaz of Mexico, former King Alphonso XIII of Spain, Hjalmar Schacht, later to be Hitler's Minister of Finance, and Konrad Adenauer, later to be Chancellor of West Germany. He contributed liberally to museums, historical restorations, and organizations which promoted Franco-American friendship.[264] Though a member of numerous societies in three

[264] For Hyde's work in establishing the Alliance Française in the United States and the exchange professorships, see this history, pp. 523–525, 528.

Two of the honors which Hyde prized especially were the Grand Cross of the Legion of Honor and election to membership in the Académie des Sciences Morales et Politiques. He was also elected (in 1927) one of the six Honorary Life Fellows of the Royal Society of Arts. This honor came in recognition of the generous support which he gave to the Fund for the Preservation of Ancient Cottages. (See obituary in the *Journal of the Royal Society of Arts,* September 1959.)

About 1907 one of Hyde's friends, a member of the Académie, asked him if he would like to gamble with 100,000 francs. The result was that Hyde contributed to the raising of a large number of Greek sculptures and bronzes from the remains of an ancient ship which had been discovered submerged off the coast of Tunisia. The sculptures and bronzes are exhibited in the Mahdia Rooms of the Bardo Museum. Letter of M. Mohamed Yacoub, Directeur of the Bardo Museum to Dorothea L. Havighorst, August 2, 1965, Equitable Archives. See also A. Merlin and L. Poinssot *Cratères et Candélabres de Marbre trouvés en mer près de Mahdia,* published by the Direction des Antiquités et Arts of the French Protectorate in 1930.

countries and honored with chairmanships, directorships, degrees, certificates, and medals, Hyde always maintained that he was never so much interested in titles as in men of culture.[265]

During World War I Hyde turned his town house into a hospital at his own expense. He became a captain and aide to Henry Pomeroy Davison, Chairman of the War Council of the American Red Cross. When General Ferdinand Foch insisted that the United States troops be brigaded into the French army, Hyde called upon Foch in the Invalides and told him that President Wilson would not overrule General Pershing, who insisted that the United States troops be organized into their own army and fight under their own commanders. Foch yielded and Pershing had his way.[266] When the large and unwieldy United States delegation arrived for the Versailles Peace Conference, Hyde, who had a large automobile as well as his house in Versailles, rendered useful service making arrangements and running errands for Edward Mandell House, whom he had known since House's Texas days.

The German occupation of Paris in June 1940 did not seriously inconvenience Hyde. Being largely a vegetarian, he did not find himself on short rations. (He did not use tea, coffee, or tobacco and disliked whiskey; he did like good wines.) Nevertheless, with his beloved Paris no longer the same, he returned to New York March 10, 1941, and settled in a suite in the Savoy Plaza Hotel where he was attended by a butler-valet and a French-speaking secretary-librarian.[267] The Germans took over his art collection, but later returned it; and, although he placed most of his paintings in storage, he surrounded himself in

265 Interview with author, May 7, 1955.

266 Hyde considered this one of his important services to his country. Interview with author, December 6, 1955.

267 Except for this accident of history, it probably would not have been possible for the historian to get access to the Hyde papers (see introduction and bibliographical note) which James Hazen Hyde had placed with Baker Library, Harvard Graduate School of Business Administration, in 1929 under a fifty-year seal. Even so, Hyde was hesitant about opening these documents until he (and his legal counsel) were satisfied that the author would give both his father and himself a "fair" treatment. Hyde did not live to read the Equitable 100th Anniversary history, but had read (or had read to him) the manuscript chapters, which he pronounced "excellent." He did, however, ask the author to delete the reference to the New York-Philadelphia coaching trip of 1901 and mention of the fact that his father had, in the midst of preparations for his sister Mary's expensive wedding, reminded the Cashier of Equitable that both Caleb's and Mary's weekly allowances were overdue. (See this history, p. 311.) For the Anniversary history, the author did this.

his suite with choice books, furniture, tapestries, and clocks which represented both sentimental and historical values of a day gone by.

Marthe Dervaux Hyde remained in Paris to continue her charitable and educational work with French children until 1944 when she came to New York and took up residence in the Carlton House; she died in 1948. For a number of years after his return Hyde continued his interest in art, education, and history and engaged in many private and anonymous charities.[268] Almost daily he stepped into his black and green brougham and took a drive through Central Park.[269] He deposited his voluminous journal, or diary, of his French years with The New-York Historical Society with the restriction that it not be made available to historians, until after his death.[270] In April 1955, after he became interested in the Equitable history, Hyde was invited by President Murphy to a luncheon in the Home Office at 393 Seventh Avenue. This was the first time he had visited Equitable since the distressing events of 1905.

In his later years Hyde became quite feeble, but his memory, especially for social and personal affairs, remained clear. His eyes, which had always been weak, failed rapidly and he was able to read little. But his graciousness and fine manners remained to the end. He continued to spend his summers at Saratoga Springs, the traditional summering place of his family. On the morning of July 26, 1959, President Oates received the following telegram from Henry B. Hyde: "Father died peacefully early this anniversary morning." It would seem that James Hazen Hyde had, by sheer will power, lived to the date of the 100th Anniversary of the company which his father had founded. Funeral services, July 29, were conducted by the Rev. John S. Bonnell of the Fifth Avenue Presbyterian Church, the church of which Henry B. Hyde was a member when he decided to start a life insurance company. The theme of the sermon was the story of "The Prodigal Son," one

[268] For instance, he had a "talking Bible" prepared as a gift for a blind minister.

[269] See photographic reproduction in the New York *Journal-American*, February 21, 1943.

[270] These diaries comprise 93 "volumes" and cover the years 1920–40. They are "scrapbooks" as well as diaries and contain hundreds of clippings, programs, and obituaries of politicians and persons prominent in the social and entertainment world. Hyde told the author in an interview May 7, 1956, that he had destroyed a journal of his trip to Germany in the early 1920's and the last volume of his Paris diary, the latter because he feared that, if revealed, it might possibly do harm to some of his French friends who more or less accepted the German occupation.

of James Hazen Hyde's favorities.[271] A number of Equitable officers attended the services.

Thus the lives of two men—father and son—spanned the first century of Equitable.

A CENTURY OF SECURITY

During the last two decades of its first century, Equitable maintained a remarkable growth.[272] At the end of 1939 Individual Life Insurance in force was $4,741,575,000, but ten years later the figure reached $7,381,542,000 and by the end of 1959 had grown to $14,580,-051,000. Group Life Insurance in force registered even larger relative gains—from $2,194,641,000 in 1939 to $6,698,578,000 in 1949 and $19,773,631,000 at the end of 1959. In 1959 new paid-for Individual Life Insurance was $1,785,766,000 as compared to $278,091,000 in 1939 and $664,801,000 in 1949. At the end of its first century Equitable had more than 2,500,000 policyholders (who were its sole owners); more than 8,000,000 group insurance and annuity certificate holders; total premium income of $1,099,801,000; $34,353,682,000 of insurance in force; and assets of $9,663,974,000.

This was an impressive record, but such figures by no means tell the whole story. What part had the Society played in the lives of millions of policyholders and beneficiaries all over the world? One can only conclude that its influence was beneficent and that its work contributed much to the total of human security and happiness. And the labors of thousands of individuals were necessary to achieve that result. As Elizur Wright said almost a century ago: "Forethought and mutuality of effort to provide most effectually against future contingencies is

271 Some of the newspapers in their notices of Hyde's death republished some of the stories about Hyde which they had published in 1905—his having 100 suits and a French valet while at Harvard, sending his valet ahead with his black rugs and draperies so he would be comfortable at a house party, etc., etc.

272

Year Ending December 31	Admitted Assets	Total Premium Income All Lines	Total Insurance In Force	Dividends and Benefit Payments to Policyowners and Beneficiaries
1939	$2,401,892,000	$ 281,050,000	$ 6,936,216,000	$197,448,000
1944	3,507,983,000	420,342,000	8,897,754,000	227,462,000
1949	5,255,608,000	600,600,000	14,080,120,000	334,668,000
1954	7,560,708,000	886,223,000	22,322,457,000	544,487,000
1959	9,663,974,000	1,099,801,000	34,353,682,000	850,555,000

not a spontaneous growth of the human soil. It is a matter of special cultivation, the result only of some sort of missionary labor, notwithstanding its manifest coincidence with the highest interests of all concerned."

A century, though a long period in the life of an individual, is but a short period in the life of an institution, of a nation. Nevertheless, it was a far time from that little one-room Home Office to the giant modern skyscraper, from the goose-quill pen to the modern electronic calculator. But other and perhaps more significant changes had taken place. Had Henry B. Hyde returned to Equitable at the end of a century he would no doubt have been impressed by its great size and by the mechanics of modern science—certainly he would have been interested in planning the details of the new Home Office building—but possibly another thing might have impressed him more: while the general price level had risen by several hundred per cent and taxes by thousands of per cent, the premium on an Ordinary Life Policy at age thirty-five, after remaining at substantially the same level for 95 years, was now at a lower level for policies of $5,000 and more. This fact was the result largely of the advances in medical science, with which actuarial science kept pace. But the mortality experience is but one of the foundations of life insurance, and benefits derived from increased life expectancy can be jeopardized if the sound principles followed by actuarial science are not also applied to the economic and political institutions upon which life insurance depends and which ultimately determine the value of the benefits paid.

The institution of life insurance is more than a fiduciary relationship based upon the law of averages, and life insurance companies are more than just quasi trustees responsible for meeting the obligation of long-term contracts—some of which may extend for a century into the future. They, as well as schools, a free press, and other agencies bear a responsibility for educating the people to the fact that basic ethical principles are in the end most conducive to their welfare and happiness; that no business can money-wise be more honest than the government under which it operates; that the efficacy of life insurance itself is ultimately dependent upon man keeping his promises to himself. There has been no greater paradox in our history than the fact that in recent years while people have been turning to life insurance for security in overwhelming numbers they have, at the same time, been approving fiscal policies on the part of their government (themselves) which constitute a powerful influence tending to vitiate and nullify that security. This dilemma presents the people with an intelligence test of no mean validity—one which, if failed, may result in loss of much more than so many purchasing units.

In 1956 Chairman Murphy said:

> Inflation works like a cruel and cynical tax that strikes hardest the patriotic and thrifty who have accumulated government bonds, savings accounts, pensions, life insurance and annuities. Inflation destroys part of the benefits to the aged, provided through our social security laws. Some people through good fortune or speculation are enriched, while others suffer dreadful hardships. Our objectives of social welfare can become an ironic jest. The inequity of the process shatters faith in our political institutions. When therefore we use our best influence for a stable dollar we are working in behalf of the public interest. Let there be no doubt about that.[273]

That Equitable has not been unaware of its responsibilities in this respect is manifested by point two in its Public Relations Policy: "It shall be the continuing purpose of all concerned with public relations to support with vigor those economic and political conditions under which The Equitable will be best assured of the freedom of opportunity necessary to bring effectively, extensively, and economically its insurance services to the American people." And said President James F. Oates, Jr., late in 1958:

> Now is the time to face up to the very essence of our democracy and to show the world that we *do* have the courage to govern ourselves wisely; that we *do* have a proper sense of values and are ready to decide what needs we shall give up to make other needs more secure; that we *do* possess capable reasoning powers and have the wit to think our problems through to an effective solution; and that we *do* have the self-discipline, ability, and courage to stand by our values and see our policies through whatever the personal cost.
>
> Now is the time to destroy some of the illusions we have acquired, to destroy the belief that easy money which encourages excessive debt is sound, to destroy the illusion "that we can get more out of our economy than we put in." Instead we must develop higher levels of economic citizenship and still higher levels of public and private responsibility. We must display the moral stamina necessary to place long-run interests of our nation ahead of individual personal desires.
>
> If we can all recognize even mild inflation for what it is—a symptom

[273] Address, "A Stable Price Level," at the Annual Meeting of the National Association of Life Underwriters, Washington, D.C., September 26, 1956. Copy in Equitable Archives.

of failure—failure on our part to govern ourselves wisely, if we can all recognize that for the community as a whole there is no hedge against inflation, and, finally, if we can all recognize "the price paid to avoid any inflation is much less than the price exacted by further inflation"—then, and only then, shall we have laid the groundwork for a successful anti-inflation campaign.[274]

* * *

In 1885, at the end of Equitable's first quarter of a century, Henry B. Hyde said:

> There are some here today who will undoubtedly survive the next twenty-five years, and meet to read the history of the first half century of the Equitable. Let us hope that the results of the twenty-five years upon which we have just entered will be satisfactory as those presented to you now, and that the Officers and Directors then in charge of the institution will be men wisely chosen, whose fidelity and skill will be commensurate with the great trust committed to their care. . . . Without claiming that life assurance is a benevolent institution, I know of no other that is, in reality, of greater benefit.[275]

Hyde's hope became a reality and may well be extended into the second century with the expectation that it will be as well realized as in the first.

In 1926 at the end of fifty-seven years of service the historically minded Secretary of Equitable, William Alexander, expressed his thoughts under the heading of "Yesterday, Today and Forever." He said:

> I should like to be here on the Equitable's One Hundredth Birthday when presumably the history of the Equitable's First Century will be written by some competent historian having accurate knowledge of all the facts. Such a story will be as interesting as the history of a great nation, and the record of the achievements of its Presidents and others who have aided in its building, will be as interesting as the achievements of the rulers of a nation.

Though no historian could have "knowledge of all the facts," it is possible that William Alexander was right both in his faith and in his prophecy.

[274] Address before the New York Chamber of Commerce, December 4, 1958. Copy in *ibid.*

[275] Report to the Directors, 1885.

13

Equitable Embarks Upon Its Second Century 1960-1964

The challenges and changes of the "Soaring 60's" will find Equitable prepared to be a strong and imaginative ally to the American people in their continuing search for greater economic security.—James F. Oates, Jr., January 1960

As Equitable embarked upon its second century, changes and new developments came rapidly; only the more significant will be outlined in this chapter.

Equitable began its planning for the "Soaring 60's" some time before they arrived. Although formal long-range planning at the corporate level was a relatively new development in American business, President Oates and other senior officers of the Society were aware of the need for more systematic methods of forecasting money flow, allocating resources, and measuring financial results, as well as determining the qualifications and characteristics of future personnel necessary to meet the requirements of the plan. The need for this type of planning was emphasized by two groups working independently, which eventually presented similar recommendations to the senior officers of the Society.

As early as 1956 Chairman of the Board Ray D. Murphy had requested Vice President Reynolds I. Nowell to head up research. Nowell thought that this work would better be left in the hands of the line departments. Dean Donald K. David of the Harvard Graduate School of Business Administration had pointed out to Chairman Murphy that the life insurance companies were falling behind in the field of research upon which management decision could be based. As a result of further conversations with Dean David Equitable decided, in the spring of 1958, to commission a group of six members of the faculty of the Harvard University Graduate School of Business Administration to make a study of the uses of basic research in long distance planning for the Society. The group was headed by Dr. John Desmond Glover,

Professor of Business Administration. As Professor Glover explained, basic research was different from operating research, which "is designed to be useful in current operations." Basic research would include "efforts to keep abreast of and to understand the underlying and fundamental trends in the American technology, economy, and society; and efforts to perceive the new opportunities and needs that these trends may present for underwriting, investment, and selling." The study commission would endeavor to determine what areas of basic research the Society should engage in; what kinds of talent it should use; what steps it should take to establish the work of reassessment of objectives on a continuing basis; and what changes in company policy, organization, and management might help it respond effectively to changing opportunities and needs in the economy.

The study group submitted its "Report on Innovation" in May 1959. Among its recommendations were: 1) a more specific and more concrete statement of Equitable's corporate objectives and policies; 2) addition of two assistants in the Investment Department to collect and analyze "data of significance for longer-term decisions," and to investigate "new investment outlets and instruments"; 3) systematic research in the field of marketing so as to enable the Society "to anticipate changes and hence program, in advance, shifts in emphasis"; 4) further research to discover better ways of agent selection and training; 5) addition of a statistical officer to the President's staff to establish and maintain a "control panel" for the benefit of senior officers and directors, and to coordinate the budget with existing policies; 6) creation of a secretariat to organize "top level staff services to the President"; and 7) creation of a research and development department under a Senior Vice President to engage "in basic research into the security and savings needs of the different categories of the population" with the objective of providing "substantially new approaches . . . to the needs of the American consumer."

The second group was an interim committee of officers under the chairmanship of Vice President John H. Muller which was appointed in July 1959 to study and recommend a method of analyzing Home Office and Field expenses in order to establish control procedures and reduce, where possible, the costs of operations.[1] This committee, after some months of work, recommended the establishment of a "cost analysis and planning" unit which would report to the chief executive

[1] Other members of the committee were Vice Presidents J. Henry Smith, Harold J. Rossman, Edward A. Robie, and Eli Ferguson.

CHART—APRIL 1965

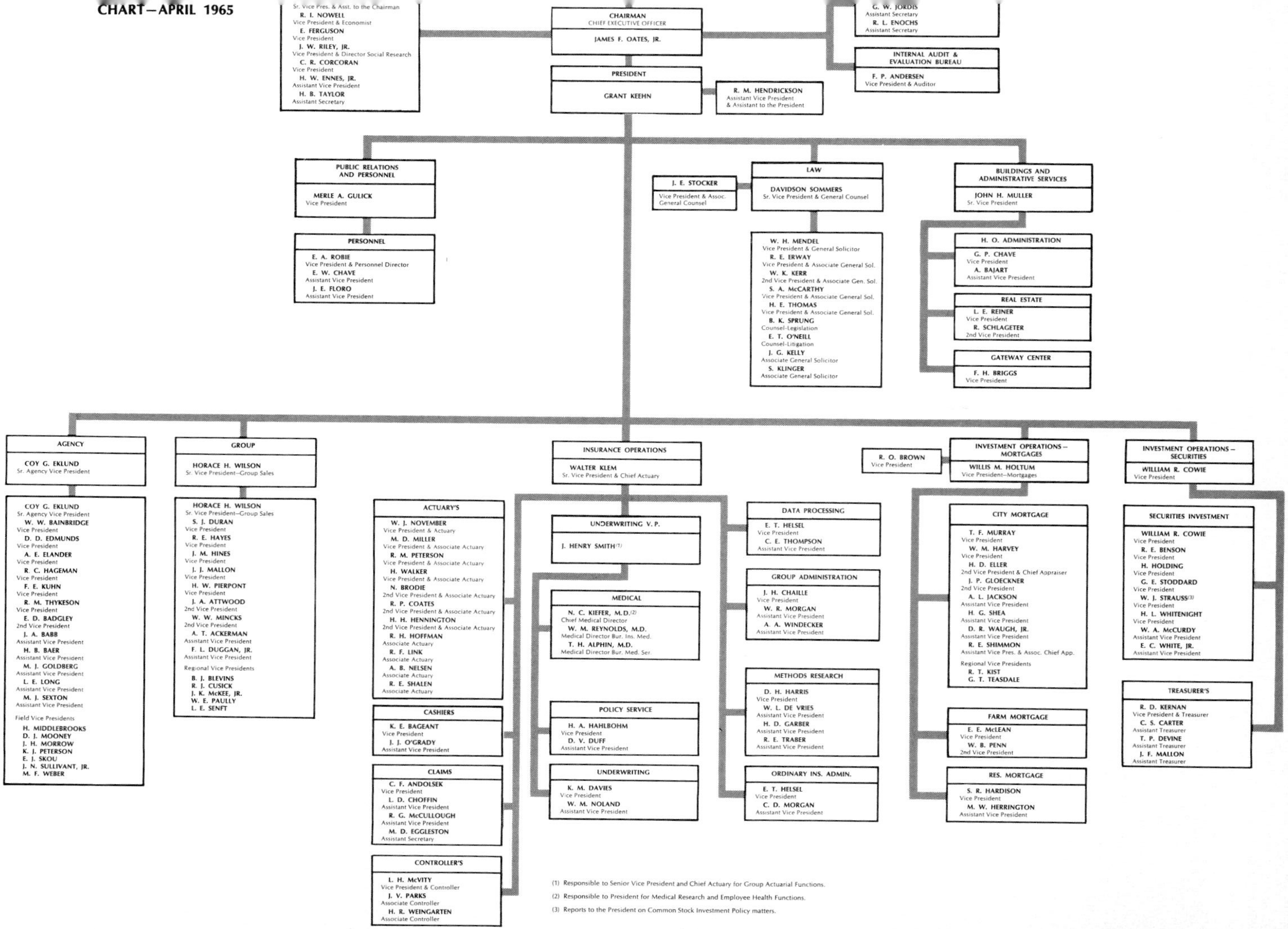

(1) Responsible to Senior Vice President and Chief Actuary for Group Actuarial Functions.

(2) Responsible to President for Medical Research and Employee Health Functions.

(3) Reports to the President on Common Stock Investment Policy matters.

and stated that "there should be some kind of long-range forecasting, department-by-department, coordinated and combined by this unit to indicate where the Society as a whole is going; what its year-by-year expenses of operation could and should be; and what the excess of receipts over disbursements are likely to be." At the time this committee made its recommendations it had not seen the report of the Harvard study group.

A special officers' committee and a subcommittee of the Organization Committee of the Board made a study of the Harvard Report and submitted eleven pages of "Recommendations and Conclusions" to the General Policy Committee and the full Organization Committee of the Board. At a joint meeting of these two committees, November 23, 1959, favorable consideration and approval was given to the basic recommendation of the Report which related to specialized research. From these "Recommendations and Conclusions" it became apparent that many of the things recommended in the Harvard Report had already been undertaken by the Society on the recommendation of its officers, or could better be handled in another way. For instance, the work of the officers' committee on cost analysis and budget planning and control had, by this time, covered more thoroughly the subject of long-distance planning. As for a "secretariat" and a "personal assistant," President Oates had inaugurated the rotating administrative assistant practice more than a year earlier.[2]

Two of the recommendations of the Harvard Report, however, were carried out, one of them almost immediately, namely that the Society develop a program of research focusing on the changing pattern of the security needs of the people. In June 1960, Dr. John W. Riley, Chairman of the Sociology Department at Rutgers University, was appointed Director of Social Research. Dr. Riley was a graduate of Bowdoin College and received his M.A. and Ph.D. degrees from Harvard University. After teaching at Marietta, Wellesley, and Douglass Colleges, he joined the faculty of Rutgers University in 1937. During World War II he served in the Office of War Information, the Psychological Warfare Division of the Army, and the Far Eastern Research Group of the Air Force. The chief function of the new office would be the investigation of population changes, changes in family life, the security needs of the American people—and the relation of

[2] The recommendations of the Harvard study group and the conclusions of the Equitable committees may be found in Harvard Report "Recommendations and Conclusions," a typescript copy of eleven pages. Equitable Archives.

these things to the institution of life insurance. Some of the studies would be conducted in Equitable, others in collaboration with various universities. Said President Oates: "This innovation in The Equitable —indeed in the life insurance industry as a whole—arises from our desire to study scientifically the security needs of all Americans. . . . It is conceivable to us that social scientists today may carry the same potential for the development of the future as the physical scientists did half a century ago. We feel it is The Equitable's obligation to underwrite objective studies in these new areas." [3]

The other recommendation, to the effect that Equitable enlarge and state more specifically its corporate objectives so as to "provide a general set of criteria against which all proposals . . . can be measured when decisions need to be made and action taken . . ." required more time to develop. As a result of the work of the officers' committee (the Muller Committee) a Cost Analysis and Planning Unit under the direction of Vice President Eli Ferguson was established in January 1960 as a part of the President's Staff. The creation of this Unit was a step toward long-range planning. Before these plans could be formulated it was necessary to prepare a statement which would define the basic purposes of the Society. After a series of meetings with department heads and their immediate associates, President Oates and the senior officers met at Princeton, New Jersey, in December 1960, and drafted a statement which was titled "The Fundamental Purpose, Business Objectives and Implicit Goals of The Equitable Life Assurance Society of the United States." The statement was distributed to Directors and officers December 31. Said President Oates:

> All of us who participated in the preparation of this statement clearly recognize that this is but the first step in charting our course for the future. To have specific meaning and to become a better guide to plan and to work by, this statement will be implemented by the determination of more specific goals in each area of our operations and by the establishment of criteria developed for measuring our effectiveness in attaining these goals. To this task we are now applying ourselves.[4]

[3] Dr. Riley edited the May 1963 number of *The American Behavioral Scientist* which was devoted to articles on those aspects of society and human behavior relating most closely to the institution of life insurance. The twenty articles centered on "Population—the Basic Social Environment"; "Family—the Basic Social Institution"; and "Death—the Basic Human Uncertainty."

[4] Report of the President to the Board of Directors for the Year Ended December 31, 1960. For the statement of fundamental purposes, see this history, pp. 1346–1347.

The task of coordinating and reducing the long-range plans to print was assigned to Vice President Eli Ferguson, head of the Cost Analysis and Planning Unit. For general guidance the following questions were posed: Where is Equitable now? Where is it going? And how is it going to get there? Various officers supplied data on such subjects as business organization, corporate citizenship, research and development, sales, investments, administrative personnel, office space, and cost control. One of the first pieces of information sought was the outlook for the nation's economy, for a major goal to be kept in mind was that the Society's growth should at least be proportionate to the growth of the nation's population and productivity.

The result was a large loose-leaf book entitled "The President's Long-Range Plans." Major sections of this book deal with policy statements and decisions, description of existing situations and specific long-range objectives, and plans for the future. Each section (with its distinctive color-coded pages) covers its subject matter in only a general way; the detailed plans remain in the hands of department heads and other officers. The distance into the future on which the planning is projected is determined by the time needed to make basic decisions: national productivity estimates are made for a decade ahead; agent recruiting and training estimates for ten years; and for most other subjects, two to five years. The President's Book (since February 1964 The Chairman's Book) is never "finished"; it is a flexible, ever-changing thing, devised to give the Chairman, at all times, up-to-date information on each of the Society's far-reaching operations and "outlines in a general way Equitable's hopes, aspirations, and goals, and the basic philosophy by which they will be attained." After the Chairman agrees to the policy interpretation, changes in plan or projections, releases are provided for the loose-leaf books of each senior officer and department head.

THE BIG MOVE

Though 1960 was not a "boom year," Equitable agents, 9,385 of them, sold $2,967,807,000 of life insurance.[5] Payments to policyholders and beneficiaries rose to $899,629,000, an increase of 5.8 per cent over 1959. Total life insurance in force established a new record of $37,032,916,000 and the Society's assets climbed to $10,039,070,000. During the year investments totaled $738,000,000 and the yield on all assets rose

[5] Of which individual life represented $1,730,046,000 and group life insurance $1,237,761,000.

to 3.95 per cent before taxes; this rate had not been exceeded in the preceding 28 years.

Meanwhile, all Equitable personnel were eagerly looking forward to the big move to the new Home Office. It may be recalled that ground was broken for the 42-story building in August 1958, and that the steel work had reached upward through nine floors by the day of Equitable's 100th Anniversary, July 26, 1959. While the steel work was going up, the builders, Turner Construction Company, had erected a two-story mock-up of the actual building on a 40 by 50 foot plot on West Fifty-second Street just to the rear of the main building. This building, known as X-Building, was designed to test the relative merits of various construction materials and techniques. In it were tested floor coverings, walls, ceilings, venetian blinds, types of desks, doorknobs, heating, lighting, air conditioning, acoustic properties, and color schemes; also the type of exterior covering or "skin" for the building.[6] Although this experimental building which was later torn down cost $175,000, it was estimated that it saved several times its cost.

Construction proceeded without serious interruption until September 1959, when a huge derrick lifted a large steel girder into place on the fifteenth level. It was the last piece of the 17,000-ton supply stock-piled before the steel strike had begun July 15. Work did not cease, however, and some 700 workers representing ten construction trades poured concrete floors, installed the metal and glass outer skin, and put in the complicated labyrinth of plumbing, air conditioning ducts, and electric conduits for the first 15 stories. Steel construction resumed in December, and April 20, 1960, while several hundred newspapermen and guests watched from the fifteenth floor, President Oates pressed a button which sent the last beam—painted white for the occasion—to the top of the tower. As it was bolted into place, the workmen doffed their safety helmets and the flags of the United States and

[6] Even the color of the glass was tested for best appearance. Eventually chosen after months of testing was a combination of anodized aluminum and black glass. Before a final decision was made on any material or method, the Real Estate Committee of the Board of Directors, the Officers' Committee and the Home Office Building Department considered costs, appearance, and maintenance. Members of the Officers' Home Office Building Committee were: Senior Vice President John H. Muller; Vice President and General Solicitor, Warner H. Mendel; Vice Presidents Glenn McHugh, Harold J. Rossman, Ogden Johnson, David H. Harris, DeSaussure D. Edmunds, and George P. Chave; and Second Vice President Laurence E. Reiner. Robert Schlageter served as Secretary of the Committee.

Equitable were raised. This completed the "topping out" ceremonies.[7]

By August the outer covering of the building was in place and workmen were busy on every floor. Then came a strike of the elevator and maintenance workers, but about 500 men continued to work on the completion of the interiors of the first 15 stories. After this strike ended in December no further major interruptions occurred.

Moving to the new Home Office was a much larger operation than Equitable's move in 1924 from 120 Broadway to 393 Seventh Avenue.[8] Plans started months ahead of time and as of January 1961 the tentative date for the beginning of the move was set for the first weekend in August. Departments and equipment to be moved were divided into five "clusters," detailed schedule charts were prepared, and about 75,000 items were coded and tagged with 10 different colors and several symbols, so that each would reach its designated place.

About 1,400 Home Office employees worked through Friday, August 18, at 393 Seventh Avenue and reported for work the following Monday, August 21, at 1285 Avenue of the Americas. During the interval 360 van loads of furniture and equipment had moved the 22 blocks and "Cluster A" was in its new home.[9] The same thing happened on four succeeding weekends. The moving operation was handled by the Weissberger Moving and Storage Company, Incorporated, the same company that had moved Equitable in 1924. Three separate moving crews worked from 6 P.M. to midnight on Mondays, Tuesdays, Thursdays, and Fridays, and from 8 A.M. until midnight Saturdays. The moving operation was complicated by the fact that the equipment moved came not only from 393 Seventh Avenue, but from six other buildings, and the arrival schedule had to be synchronized with the installation of new furnishings being delivered from the manufacturers. Once a unit was on the dolly, it stayed on wheels until it was placed in the new building. Special dollies and handling were required for the heavy but delicate electronic data processing machines, the moving of which was supervised by representatives of the manufacturers.[10] Not

[7] A good description of the building of 1285 Avenue of the Americas may be found in "Headquarters for a Colossus," *Real Estate Forum*, January 1961. See also *Equinews*, March-April 1961.

[8] See this history, p. 941.

[9] Cluster A included six departments: Actuary's, Controller's, Claims, Treasurer's, Cashiers', and Medical; also the Communications Division of Home Office Administration and others.

[10] Among the pieces moved in about 1,800 van loads were 6,626 desks, 7,159 legal and letter-size files, 2,303 card files, 1,722 card file sections, 3,000 transfer

publicly scheduled was the moving of almost six billion dollars' worth of securities to the Society's vaults in the new building; this job was handled by five armored trucks of the United States Trucking Corporation and took place Sunday morning, September 3.

While the big move was in progress, a shuttle service of station wagons and messengers maintained communications, and a tie-in telephone service made internal dialing possible between the new building and the various other buildings involved. By September 18, 1961, the 7,200 Home Office employees were settled in their new offices, the first time they had been housed in one building for many years. There had been a minimum interruption in the routine work while the move was in progress. A familiar landmark in the new Home Office was the statue of Henry B. Hyde. When it took its place just inside the lobby at the corner of the Avenue of the Americas and Fifty-second Street, it served as a reminder of the fact that though Home Offices might change, there was a continuity in the spirit of Equitable.

Sunday, September 24, was formal dedication day. A thousand guests gathered in the lobby and plaza area of the Fifty-first Street side of the building. The United States and Equitable flags were raised, Senior Vice President John H. Muller welcomed the group, and the Society's Choral Club sang. President Oates paid tribute to "the unstinted effective work . . . done by hundreds of individual human beings," which had, as if by magic, created the building—"a bright symbol of our high future"; and Mayor Robert F. Wagner again welcomed Equitable as one of the city's "very great corporate citizens." Twenty specially trained young ladies—all Equitable personnel and dressed in identical ensembles of Equitable blue—made their debut as guides for tours of the building.

CHANGES IN ADMINISTRATIVE PERSONNEL

Numerous changes were made in Equitable's administrative staff 1952–62. Vice President Glenn McHugh who, since 1936, had been head of the City Mortgage Department, retired June 1, 1960, after more than thirty-three years of service with the Society.[11] During his career as head of the City Mortgage Department, the Department's

---

files, 1,500 tables, 500 supply cabinets, 525 business machines, 625 documentary file sections, and an unrecorded number of chairs.

[11] For McHugh's earlier work in connection with farm mortgages during the depression period, see this history, p. 1016.

investments grew from $78,000,000 or about 4 per cent of the Society's assets, to $1,800,000,000 or almost 19 per cent of its assets. At a retirement dinner in McHugh's honor, President Oates said:

> He obtained his department's substantial growth by pioneering in loans on theaters, shopping centers, truck terminals and parking garages; on baseball parks, hospitals, manufacturing plants and distribution warehouses; on merchandise marts, post offices, and many other types of property. Before his time, insurance companies tended to limit investment classifications to office buildings, apartments and stores. His pioneering extended to methods as well as to properties, so that under his leadership, credit was utilized to supplement the basic security of the real estate.[12]

Vice Chairman of the Board Robert L. Hogg who had been Senior Vice President and Advisory Counsel 1954–56, retired December 31, 1959. In November 1959, Davidson Sommers was elected to the newly created position of Senior Vice President and General Counsel to take office February 1, 1960. Sommers, a native of Minnesota, received his law degree from the Harvard Law School in 1930 and after practicing law in New York City for several years became Assistant Corporation Counsel of the City of New York. He served as Lieutenant Colonel in the Army Air Force in World War II and in 1945 became Special Assistant to the Secretary of War. The following year he joined the Legal Department of the World Bank, was promoted to General Counsel in 1949 and became Vice President in 1956. During the next two years he also served as General Counsel of the International Finance Corporation, an affiliate of the World Bank

Vice President and Counsel Leo D. Fitzgerald, who headed the Law Department-Insurance, died suddenly January 29, 1960, and after his death, the two divisions of the Society's legal work (Law Department-Insurance, Law Department-Investments) were combined into one

[12] One of the larger loans handled by McHugh was negotiated in 1954. A telephone call from Conrad Hilton conveyed the information that the famous hotel operator was preparing to acquire the entire Statler chain of ten hotels and would need approximately $50,000,000 of long-term financing. He had approached Equitable because he thought that it was the only mortgage-loan organization able to appraise the properties and put through the loan in the brief time allotted to close the deal. Equitable's experienced field men immediately began to work. The Home Office staff expedited the loan papers, Investment Department officers considered the details and the Real Estate Committee of the Board gave its approval. This loan made hotel as well as financial history.

law department under a single administrative head, Vice President and General Solicitor Warner H. Mendel.

In September 1961, sales operations were reorganized into two major areas—the Agency Department and the Group Department—each under the direction of a Senior Vice President who reported to the chief executive. Senior Vice President Joseph L. Beesley was given the title of Senior Vice President and Assistant to the President. In this capacity he was designated to represent the President in all assigned areas and to act in a senior staff capacity without line responsibility. At the same time Agency Vice President Samuel A. Burgess was advanced to Senior Agency Vice President. Burgess, a native of Kingstree, South Carolina, was a graduate of Davidson College; he had joined Equitable by way of the Cashier's Training Course at Cleveland in 1921. After serving as assistant cashier, office manager, and district manager in several of the Society's offices, he became Agency Manager at Louisville in 1936 and in 1937 Agency Manager in Jacksonville for the state of Florida. Burgess came to the Home Office in 1945 as a Second Vice President and was promoted to Vice President in 1952. On the retirement of Alvin B. Dalager in 1955 he became Agency Vice President.

Succeeding to the position of Agency Vice President was Coy G. Eklund, formerly Vice President and Assistant to the President. Eklund began his life insurance career in 1938 while still a student at Michigan State University. After graduation in 1939, he became a full-time life underwriter in Lansing, Michigan. During World War II he served in Europe and advanced from Second Lieutenant to Lieutenant Colonel on the staff of General George S. Patton, Jr. After the war he returned to Equitable as Assistant Manager of the Detroit agency. He became Manager of the agency in 1947 and built it into one of the Society's leading agencies. He was transferred to the Home Office as Vice President and Assistant to the President in 1959.

Horace H. Wilson, who had been elected Vice President-Group Sales in 1959, was appointed Senior Vice President-Group Sales. Wilson was the son of Jerome J. Wilson, one of Equitable's leading general agents, who had been associated with the Society for almost a half-century. He joined his father's agency in New York City in 1917 at the age of twelve; he "swept the floor, cleaned the baskets, filed papers, chased lapsed policies, and dug up leads for the agents." He sold his first policy about the age of fourteen and then after graduation from Princeton at the age of twenty he became a full-time member of the agency. He made his first important sale in the Flatiron Building where there were signs saying that soliciting was not allowed, by evading the elevator operators. He became head of the Wilson Agency in 1935. During the next few years two other Equitable agencies were merged with the Wilson agency. Horace Wilson taught life insurance at New York University and served in World War II as a Lieutenant Colonel.[13]

The above-named changes became effective September 1, 1961. On that date Senior Vice President Melville P. Dickenson, who had been in charge of Public Relations since February 1956, retired to resume personal sales production with the W. T. Walsh Agency in Philadelphia. He continued, however, to serve as consultant to President Oates on public relations and personnel affairs until the end of the year. Merle A. Gulick, who had been Vice President-Public Relations and Personnel since 1960, assumed Dickenson's responsibilities as head of the Department.[14]

Vice President William E. Walsh, Underwriting Department, retired May 1, 1962, after almost forty-one years of service with Equitable. From Assistant to the Superintendent of the Inspection Bureau (1921) he had advanced to Superintendent of the Bureau, Superintendent in the Underwriting Department, Second Vice President (1949), and Vice President (1952). He was a member of numerous insurance organizations and a past President of the Home Office Life Underwriters Association. Walsh was highly regarded by agents and managers alike not only for his competence and fairness as an underwriter but also for his availability to attend agency and other meetings throughout the country.

Assistant Vice President Karl M. Davies succeeded Walsh as Vice President, Underwriting. Davies, a Harvard graduate, had joined Equitable in 1940. After five years of military service he headed the Policy Forms Bureau, served on the staff of Senior Vice President and Chief Actuary Walter Klem, was appointed Manager of Underwriting in 1958, and Assistant Vice President in 1961.

ELECTRONIC DATA PROCESSING

Certainly one of the most important developments of the late 1950's and early 1960's was the effect of electronic data processing (EDP) upon the organization as well as the operation of Equitable. After the installation of the first 650 machine in 1955, the use of data

[13] For the reorganization of the Group Department, see this history, p. 893.
[14] For sketches of the early careers of Dickenson and Gulick, see this history, pp. 1239, 1103.

processing machines expanded rapidly. The Ordinary Insurance Administration Department, organized early in 1956, recognized the potential impact of EDP and, since it was the largest user at that time, was given the responsibility for operating the EDP equipment for the Society.[15] After the installation of the second 705 machine, the Group Insurance Administration Department (established in 1958) became the Group Administration Department (January 1960); the new department was given the responsibility for improving group annuity procedures and adapting them to EDPM systems. As Second Vice President Joseph H. Chaille, who headed GAD, explained it: "There is a great job ahead to use the speed and economy of EDPM for Group annuity business as well as Group insurance. GAD's responsibility in this area is purely administrative—compiling and keeping accurate records and statistics, and deriving data from this material for the use of other departments." The new department was composed of the former Group Insurance Administration Department plus approximately 400 persons from the Actuary's and Controller's Departments who were responsible for administration of the Society's group annuity contracts. The personnel of GAD totaled approximately 1,100 persons.[16]

In 1961 Equitable installed its third 705 machine and three small "satellite" computers (IBM type 1401) to replace certain peripheral components of the 705 system. It also experimented with other type machines for possible use in new developments. At the same time it began research on a system which soon came to be known as "Cashiers' Automatic Processing System" (CAPS) under the direction of Vice President Harris. As this system developed, Equitable in 1962 installed a new "second generation" computer (IBM type 7080) which was fully compatible with the 705 machines, and discontinued use of two of the 705's; it also installed a fourth 1401. The following year with the installation of the second 7080 and a fifth 1401 the use of the last 705 was discontinued. In 1964 a third 7080 and other electronic equipment were added. In general the Society's policy was to plan and work in terms of available equipment rather than wait for the next equipment development which was just "around the corner." The question was not "can it be used?" but "how can it best be used?"

[15] For the first use of small electronic data processing machines in 1955 and the creation of Methods Research and the Ordinary Insurance Administration Departments, see this history, p. 1270.

[16] The organization and functions of the Group Administration Department are described in *Equinews*, February 1960.

The development of Cashiers' Automatic Processing System was begun in 1963 after more than two years of research and planning. At that time Equitable maintained two complete individual policy files, one in the field for up-to-date records necessary for over-the-counter handling of policyholders' inquiries and processing current transactions, and one in the Home Office as a basic record amenable to processing by EDP for premiums, dividends, commissions, valuation, and statistics. The problem was, how could the two be combined without sacrificing the prompt, over-the-counter services in the agency offices. The solution decided upon was to put all the individual policy records into one large computer-controlled file in the Home Office, this file to consist of magnetic discs, operating on a "random-access" basis in such a way as to make any individual record accessible to the computer in a fraction of a second. The computer would also control a central communications unit which would be connected by a wire communications network to terminal sets in each of the Society's Cashiers' offices. As described by Senior Vice President and Chief Actuary Walter Klem:

> As a whole, this system of files, computer, communications facilities, and terminal sets will provide what is generally known as an "on-line, random access" processing. CAPS will make it possible to eliminate local policy records except—and the exception will probably prove to be only a temporary one—for an alphabetical index, in each office, of the policyholders assigned to that office for service. Designated personnel in the field offices will enter inquiries, requests for policy disbursements such as surrenders, loans or dividend credit withdrawals, address and similar changes, claims data, and so on, through their terminal sets. The same sets will transmit premium collections. Answering time for information requests will almost always be under five minutes.[17]

CAPS was "an immense undertaking." The designing of the system was a more complex project than any which Equitable had undertaken before, both in terms of new technical accomplishments and in scope of operation. It affected the operations not only of the Cashiers' Department but also of Policy Service, Ordinary Insurance Administration, Residential Mortgage, Actuary's, Controller's, Claims, and Home Office Administration. At various points in the development of the

[17] Walter Klem, "New Directions in EDP," a paper read at the Annual Meeting of the Life Insurance Association of America, December 9, 1964.

specifications other departments such as Law and the Internal Audit and Evaluation Bureau were consulted to review the plans. More than five hundred separate jobs were involved in the CAPS project, most of them interrelated; special kinds of programing techniques were required and a large-scale training program became necessary. It was estimated that five years would be required to complete the implementation of the system.

CAPS, however, was only one important application of EDP. By early 1964 EDP was in operation in the following fields or departments: Individual Insurance and Annuities; Group Insurance; Group Annuities; Personnel, Accounting and General Operations; and New York 65.[18] The following table shows the use of EDP in 1964 and projected use:

IN OPERATION 1964	UNDER DEVELOPMENT
Individual Insurance and Annuities	
Issue and New Business Administration	Valuation
Basic Policy Data File Maintenance	Payment of Deferred First Year Commissions
Billing and Collection Accounting	AHO Administration
Dividend Calculation and Accounting	"CAPS"
Payment of Renewal Commissions	"System-Matic" Record Maintenance
Security Review Program	Health Insurance Record Maintenance
Agency New Business Reports	Annuity and Supplementary Contract Payments
Actuarial Research and Developmental Work	
Rate Books	
Group Insurance	
Basic Policy Data File Maintenance	Billing
Collection Accounting	Maintenance of Records of Individual Lives (Home Office Accounting)
Dividend Calculation	

[18] For New York 65, see this history, p. 1319.

IN OPERATION 1964	UNDER DEVELOPMENT
Group Insurance	
Commission Processing (In Part)	Commission Processing (Full)
Maintenance of Experience Records and Preparation of Underwriting Reports	
Proposal Calculations for Health Care and Disability Coverages	
Actuarial Research and Developmental Work	
Claims Audit Selection	
Group Annuities	
Dividend Calculation	Employee Data File Maintenance—Deferred Annuity Contracts
Actuarial Research and Developmental Work	Benefit Calculation—Deferred Annuity Contracts
Commission Processing (In Part)	Proposals and Actuarial Valuation—Deposit Administration Contracts
	Retired Life Annuity Payments
	Commission Processing (Full)
Personnel, Accounting, and General Operations	
Agency Production Credit Reports	Payroll
Agency Force Simulation	Maintenance of Personnel Records (Full)
Expense Analysis (In Part)	Expense Accounting (Full)
Maintenance of Personnel Records (In Part)	Payment of Managerial Compensation
Payroll Tax Calculations	
Home Office Supply Inventory	
Payroll Changes Analysis	
MPA Staffing Analysis	
Economists' Time Series Analysis	

IN OPERATION 1964	UNDER DEVELOPMENT
New York 65	
Issue of Certificates	
Basic Certificate Data File Maintenance	
Billing and Collection Accounting	
Payment of Commissions	
Processing of Claims	
Preparation of Operating Reports	

All EDP operations were handled in a single data-processing center which, though administratively a part of the Ordinary Insurance Administration Department, acted as a service bureau for the Society as a whole.[19] Planning and development work became the responsibility of the Methods Research Department—another service operation for the whole organization. Even so the "customers" for these services—the departments which use EDP in their work—have needed to learn a great deal about the nature, if not the technicalities, of the system. As Senior Vice President Walter Klem pointed out:

> Those who have been directly concerned with the transition from clerical operations to EDP systems have learned—sometimes the hard way—that to get the job done properly without an immense amount of careful advance planning is practically impossible. They have learned that "playing it by ear" won't work in this situation, and hence have found substitutes for that time-honored way of doing things—and they have found that the substitutes often have something quite worth carrying over into other contexts. In many ways they have had to think more broadly: to plan over longer time spans, to assess effects over wider spans of function and organization, to think in terms of people-machine interaction instead of concentrating on personnel or on machinery as essentially separate responsibilities.[20]

[19] In April 1965 a separate Data Processing Department was created to operate all machines. The new department, headed by Vice President Earl Helsel, began operations with almost 300 personnel and more than 200 pieces of electronic data processing and electronic accounting equipment. For description of the new department see *Equinews*, May 1965.

[20] Walter Klem, "Changes in Management and the Management of Change," a paper read at the Annual Conference of the Life Officers Management Association, September 30, 1964.

Although in the early stages of the development of EDP emphasis was placed largely upon its "cost displacement" uses in those areas of insurance administration which involve heavy clerical expense, it soon became apparent that the system had important implications in the whole field of decision-making and management.[21] Again to quote Senior Vice President Klem:

> Considerations growing out of computer installations—but not limited to computer-oriented work—have led to greater recognition of the importance of "production" management as an important activity in its own right. The clerical functions of a life insurance company often grew up as the adjunct of professional, technical, sales or other specialist activities, with their management a secondary concern of people whose primary interest lay in their own fields of specialty. Machine developments have required a unified perspective in looking at the "production" functions—and have shown that, with or without machines, the man responsible for, say, getting out premium notices has more in common with the man whose job is, say, to pay group commissions than either has with the actuary, the accounting officer or the sales specialist. . . .
>
> The "system" concept sees, for example, one process in the agent's taking of an application for new business, his submitting it to his local office, its handling there and in the administrative, underwriting and perhaps medical functions at the home office, the writing of the policy, its return to the field for delivery, its establishment in force through collection and reporting of the first premium, and the preparation of all the records to be needed subsequently for its maintenance. This way of analyzing the company's over-all operation is certainly no more significant than the other, perhaps more familiar concepts; but it does add to our understanding, and improve our grasp, as managers, of the total environment.[22]

Naturally, the adoption of a computer-based system tends to concentrate responsibility in management "and its pyramid shape tends

[21] As the author makes clear in the above-mentioned paper, when a life insurance company applies automation to its office files, etc., it is actually automating its production line: "Our 'office work' is not a supporting function backing up the factory as in the case of the typical manufacturing industry—our office *is* the factory, engaged in writing policies, computing dividends, sending out premium notices, and so on. It is on these functions that we spend by far the largest part of our administrative expense dollar, and hence it is natural that we looked to these functions first when automation began to seem a possibility for our kind of work."

It was understood from the beginning that no employee in Equitable would lose his job as a result of automation. Unreplaced turnover and reduction in the number of new persons employed made maintenance of this policy possible.

[22] *Ibid.*

to become a good deal narrower and sharper." To make sure that the "hardware" not outrun the "software" it becomes necessary for the organization to develop and make more use of people of superior intellectual qualifications. Hence it creates additional problems in management training.

FURTHER INNOVATIONS AND MODIFICATIONS

Although more than 70 per cent of the ordinary insurance sold by Equitable in 1959 was written on policies introduced in the preceding five years, the process of liberalization and innovation continued. On January 1, 1960, rates on single premium insurance policies and single premium deferred annuity contracts were reduced. Then in November lower rates became effective for single consideration immediate Life, Refund, and Joint and Survivor Annuities. With this change Equitable resumed the sale of annuities on a nonparticipating basis, a practice which it had discontinued in 1934. In March 1960 a Fifth Dividend Option was made available under most forms of permanent individual life insurance issued for more than $5,000. Under this provision the annual dividend could be used to purchase one-year term insurance in an amount equal to the guaranteed cash value of the policy at the end of the following policy year. Various ways were incorporated in this provision for the utilization of any balance of such cash dividend in the given year. In later years if the cash dividend was not sufficient to purchase the addition equal to the cash value then a lesser amount of term addition was purchased. This provision was particularly attractive for many of the insurance situations encountered by the agents in the sale of individual life insurance in substantial amounts for business needs.[23] Also during the year the limits for standard insurance were substantially increased in all age ranges, and raised for substandard risks in all categories. The maximum amount of insurance available without medical examination in the 5 to 25 age group was raised from $15,000 to $25,000; and for the first time in its history, Equitable began to accept term insurance policies in amounts up to $15,000 without medical examination at ages 15 to 30.

After months of research by a committee appointed by President Oates—Vice President Clarence B. Metzger, Chairman—Equitable

23 The other traditional options are: taking dividends in cash; applying them to premiums; taking them as paid-up additions; or leaving them at interest.

re-entered the Disability Income field on January 1, 1961, using the individual policy approach rather than by the use of a rider on the policies. A bread range of policies was designed with varying durations of benefits and waiting periods from onset of total disability to the date income begins. These new policies made available guaranteed income of from $100 to $500 per month in event of disability within the definition of the policy provisions. A unique special optional feature of increased income similar to the Family Income feature on life insurance was introduced with this new portfolio. Robert W. McCabe, Director, Individual Health Insurance, and Robert S. Schoonmaker, Jr., who had broad experience in the Health Insurance field, were brought into the Equitable organization to take the lead roles in the Agency and Underwriting Departments respectively. They were the only specialists brought into the Society to promote this new line of business and enlisted their assistants from the existing personnel. Special extensive training programs were promptly initiated for both the agents throughout the country and for Home Office and Field employees who would be involved in the administration of this business.

August 1, 1962, Equitable revised its Major Medical Expense Policy which expired at age 65, to its Lifetime Major Medical Expense Policy. This policy was guaranteed renewable, regardless of the number of claims made, as long as the insured continued to pay his premiums. The maximum benefits ran from $10,000 to $20,000. The deductible amounts were as low as $250 or as high as $1,000, depending on the income and the preference of the applicant; the coinsurance feature was retained at the 25 per cent figure. The policy also contained a relatively new (at that time in individual policies) provision for coordinating the benefits under the policy with the policyholder's other medical expense coverages, both Group and Individual. This feature was in response to a growing acceptance of the principle that duplication of benefits led inevitably and naturally to abuses of Health Insurance, and was not only impractical from the standpoint of appropriate risk bearing but that it was also socially wrong. To the satisfaction of, and somewhat surprisingly in the opinion of a number of the Society's officers who participated in the decision to offer a Major Medical Expense Policy with this feature, the philosophy of the coordination of benefits provision was well accepted by the agents and their prospects.

February 1, 1963, well in advance of the date specified by law,

Equitable began operating under the Commissioners 1958 Standard Ordinary Mortality Table which necessitated the revaluation of its whole line of policies.[24] Many departments were involved in the change: Actuary's, Law, Agency, Advertising, Press Relations and Publications, Methods Research, Claims, Cashiers', Policy Service, Ordinary Insurance Administration, Underwriting, and Home Office Administration.

The new policies were appropriately labeled Series 104—after the 104th year of the Society's operations. Major changes were: 1) The Ordinary Life Policy, for many years the backbone of Equitable sales, was discontinued, and in its place was issued the Adjustable Whole Life Policy, which for the first time was made available in amounts of less than $10,000. 2) The 20-Year Term Insurance Policy was replaced by a "Term to Age 65" policy. 3) A new Pension Plan Insurance Policy specially adapted to pension trust and profit-sharing purposes, replaced the Retirement Plan Insurance Policy for such purposes. 4) The right to convert from term to permanent insurance was liberalized for the Family Protection and Planned Security Policies, and also for the Family Income and Increased Protection riders. 5) The graded premium system was extended upward to recognize policies of $25,000 and more as a separate class with premium rates 50 cents less per $1,000 than on $10,000 policies. Policy forms for the new policies were reduced in size and simplified in wording, and for the first time the cash and reduced paid-up values were completed by EDP equipment at the time of issue and shown in the policy for the actual face amount of the policy, rather than per $1,000 as previously shown.

Series 104 was a modernizing and streamlining of Equitable's insurance offerings. The new policies helped to keep Equitable abreast of the best and put it into a stronger competitive position with reference to deferred annuities, life income settlement options, large-amount policies, and term insurance.

But in modern life insurance, as in aviation, new ideas are on the

[24] As early as 1956 the American Life Convention and the Life Insurance Association of America had called the attention of the National Association of Insurance Commissioners to the fact that the Commissioners Standard Ordinary table of 1941 was largely outdated; improvements in medicine, public hygiene, and the introduction of new antibiotics had added several years to the average life. After two years of labor the Society of Actuaries, an Industry Advisory Committee and the NAIC produced the 1958 table which was based largely upon the 1950–54 experience of fifteen large life insurance companies. It was adopted by the NAIC in 1958 and ratified by the last of the fifty states in 1962; the companies were given until January 1, 1966, for adoption.

"drawing boards" by the time the latest models are on the market. While the agents were beginning to market Series 104, the Actuary's and Agency Departments were already planning improvements. Within two years after the Series 104 revisions, Sales Folio '65 was announced which included: 1) Extensions of the graded premium principle to policies of $50,000 and over. 2) A new Executive Security Policy—$25,000 minimum—with higher gross premiums than the Executive Policy and correspondingly higher initial cash values and paid-up insurance amounts. 3) A new Double Protector Policy—minimum $10,000—with high initial protection in relation to premium; the protection remains level to age 65, then is reduced in five steps to half the original amount at age 69; the premium remains level throughout the life of the policy. 4) A new Husband-Wife Retirement Annuity—an Equitable exclusive. 5) A new Joint and Survivor Immediate Annuity which allows a larger income to both annuitants while living by decreasing income to the survivor. And 6) A revised Five-Year Renewable Term policy—renewable to age 70 and convertible to permanent insurance up to age 65. In addition, by the use of multiple units of Family Income protection and by several different combinations of term insurance with a basic permanent form policy, other attractive provisions to help the agents meet the needs of their prospects and the competition in the market place were announced. These changes were accompanied by a reduction in gross premium rates for Equitable's entire line of level term insurance policies. The maximum age for Adjustable Whole Life, Executive, and Single Premium Whole Life policies was raised to 75.

Equitable celebrated its fiftieth anniversary of the introduction of group insurance June 1, 1961. During the half century it had paid a total of $3,610,000,000 in benefits to the insured employees and their families. January 1, 1962, it introduced the Circle E Compact Group Insurance Plan, for groups of 10 to 24 employees, which offered flexible benefits in a "packaged" program. The Circle E policy offered basic life, health, and weekly indemnity coverages in fourteen different combinations. The provisions of the Circle E policy were liberalized late in 1962 by removing the pre-existing conditions limitation from all health insurance with the exception of Major Medical Expense coverage, and raising the age definition of dependents to provide for coverage of full-time students to age 23.[25] Both these changes were

[25] Also for cases involving transfer of Circle E where the prior carrier does not provide maternity-obstetrical benefits, Equitable modified the Circle E deferment

effected without any increase in premium rates. The success of Circle E led to the development of the Diamond E group policy for 1965, designed for groups of 25 to 200 members. This policy was designed to fill the gap between Circle E and regular group insurance, but was not the only type of group program offered to groups of this size, whereas the Circle E was the only group plan in its size class. Under each of these programs the experience of package plans was pooled for the purpose of determining such dividends as might be earned, and then the ultimate cost to the group patrons of the Circle E or Diamond E program. The benefits were similar and the package principle the same.

The "Self-Employed Individuals Tax Retirement Act of 1962" (the Smathers-Keogh Act) which enabled self-employed persons to establish retirement plans with tax-deductible contributions broadened the pension market for life insurance companies. Under this law a self-employed person, provided he also covered permanent employees, if any, could contribute up to 10 per cent of his earned income or $2,500, whichever was the lesser sum, and deduct one-half of the amount from his taxable income on the Federal Income Tax Return.

To meet the needs of an estimated 7,000,000 persons who might qualify under the Smathers-Keogh Act, Equitable offered a Pension Plan Endowment and an Adjustable Premium Annuity. The latter was to be used in all annuity plans, or for participants who did not qualify for insurance in plans using the Pension Plan Endowment policy.

A development of considerable importance to group annuity contractholders was Equitable's adoption in 1962 of the "investment year method" and the establishing of "separate accounts" for allocation of funds paid to the insurer to provide fixed guaranteed annuities under qualified pension plans. The background of this development was as follows:

As early as November 1957 Associate Actuary Howard H. Hennington proposed that the Society recognize the rate of return on new investments in allocating investment income for dividend distribution purposes under group annuity contracts. Then in October 1958 President Oates in an address made before the Law Club of Chicago on "Private Pension Plans" outlined the competitive difficulties which

---

period by allowing credit for the time the person was insured for such benefits under the prior carriers plan. This change made possible a continuity of coverage for employees becoming insured under Circle E plans.

the insurance companies were having in the pension business. At that time these were 1) the discriminatory Federal income tax; 2) the inability of the companies to provide substantial investment of pension funds in common stocks; and 3) the disadvantage, at a time of rising interest rates, of the traditional method of crediting average investment portfolio rates of return on pension funds. As noted earlier, the Federal income tax handicap was substantially removed by the Federal tax legislation of 1959.

In regard to the common stock problem, President Oates referred to the activity of the John Hancock Mutual Life Insurance Company in the endeavor to secure "separate account" legislation in Massachusetts, and of the Prudential Insurance Company to obtain "variable annuity" legislation in New Jersey on a separate account basis. Legislation of this type was enacted in 1959 in New Jersey and Connecticut, and in 1960 in Massachusetts. This legislation spurred efforts to secure similar legislation in New York and other states.

About the same time, some insurance companies, including the Aetna Life Insurance Company, the Bankers Life Company, and the Prudential Insurance Company were changing the method of allocating investment income of the general account in connection with their group annuity business in order to recognize the interest return on new investments—a method of allocation that has become known as the "investment year" or "new money" method.

During the summer of 1959, after an unsuccessful attempt to obtain legislation conferring limited trust powers on insurance companies for pension purposes, an ad hoc committee of Equitable officers, at the direction of President Oates, studied the alternatives of a "separate account" (segregated account) approach, similar to that provided in the Connecticut and Massachusetts laws, and the "trust powers" approach. Drafts of amendments of the law were prepared for each approach and the Committee recommended that the "first legislative moves should encompass both bills with the expectation that we will later settle on the more likely one." The Equitable arranged an informal conference with other life insurance companies. Superintendent of Insurance Thomas Thacher suggested that the Equitable develop its plans and take them to the department for discussion later in the year.

Because of the separate account laws of other states, the New York Insurance Department was receiving from out-of-state companies important and challenging questions as to operations in New York. In 1961, a Subcommittee on Segregated Funding of the American

Life Convention-Life Insurance Association of America Joint Legislative Committee was appointed to consider (a) Federal income tax matters affecting all forms of separate accounts including variable annuity accounts, and (b) support of legislation in all states permitting segregated accounting for pension and profit-sharing plans. These activities stimulated the New York Joint Legislative Committee (the "Condon Committee") to hold hearings in October 1961 on a number of subjects including segregated account legislation. President Oates was the principal insurance company spokesman on October 25, 1961. He made a very impressive case for the need of appropriate legislation that would provide separate investment facilities for pension plans. His effective presentation gave the project a much-needed impetus. After referring to Connecticut law he said:

> We at the Equitable favor similar legislation in New York. In essence, it permits life insurance companies to have separate accounts in which an employer's payments under a qualified pension plan may be accumulated, free of mandatory investment restrictions and reflecting the investment experience of the assets in such accounts, but with the provision that the annuities for employees when they retire shall be guaranteed and fully supported by investments of the type traditional in the life insurance industry. Under our proposal, the risk of market fluctuation of equities occurs only during the accumulation period and is on the employer.[26]

A number of other life insurance companies' witnesses, but not all, supported the proposal.

Superintendent of Insurance Thomas Thacher also appeared as a witness. While he was sympathetic with the objectives of the proposed legislation, he had a number of questions which needed resolving. He said that as soon as the Insurance Department was satisfied that public interest would be protected it would in the near future be submitting recommendations for legislation along the proposed lines to the governor's office. He submitted a list of twenty questions to Equitable which supplied answers.

The Variable Annuities and Pension Plan Funding Subcommittee of the National Association of Insurance Commissioners, on December 4, 1961, resolved that "this Subcommittee present to the June meeting of the Association a statement of recommended principles to be observed with respect to variable annuities and segregated accounts in

[26] As reported in *The Eastern Underwriter*, LXII (1961), November 6.

the field of pension funding, as a preliminary to the drafting of model legislation in this field."

Representatives of New York insurance companies worked with Superintendent Thacher to develop a separate accounts bill. Separate account legislation was finally enacted in the 1962 session of the Legislature as Section 227 of the New York Insurance Law and became effective November 1, 1962.

Another important problem remained, that is, exemption from the requirements of the Investment Company Act of 1940 and the Securities Act of 1933. Here again the Equitable played a leading role in working with the Securities and Exchange Commission. Discussions were continued through the summer of 1962. After publication of a proposed Rule 3c-3 on October 31, 1962, exempting from the requirements of the Investment Company Act of 1940 certain segregated account group annuity contracts, the rule became effective January 7, 1963. Then, effective on August 1, 1963 the SEC announced adoption of Rule 156 exempting from the requirements of the Securities Act of 1933 transactions with respect to certain segregated account group annuity contracts.

On April 8, 1962, the Equitable received approval of its separate account group annuity contract forms from the New York Insurance Department. Equitable officers then proceeded to make plans to offer such contracts by November 1, 1962, the effective date of Section 227.

Then with reference to the third problem area of crediting interest to group annuity funds, on April 14, 1961, Superintendent Thacher published a Proposed Amendment of Regulation 33 and announced a hearing for May 11, 1961. After reviewing recommendations presented at the hearing for modification of the proposed regulation, Superintendent Thacher promulgated a new Regulation 33 on June 29, 1961, which accommodated the operation of the "investment year" method by lines of business and within a line of business. On October 20, 1961, Vice President and Actuary William November submitted to Superintendent Thacher a detailed method of operation, as required by the new Regulation 33, that the Equitable wished to adopt starting in 1962. After furnishing additional information as requested by the Insurance Department, Assistant Superintendent Julius Sackman notified the Equitable of the Department's approval on February 5, 1962. Then, on March 16, 1962, the Equitable announced to its group annuity contractholders the adoption of the investment year method of allocating investment income for group annuity contracts. Thus was removed the third major obstacle the Equitable found in competing for group annuity business with both the banks and other insurance companies.

Prior to authorization of the investment year method, group annuity funds were credited for dividend purposes each year with the uniform average earnings rate determined on the basis of the total earnings of the Society's entire investment portfolio. Since the portfolio included many investments made during the period of low interest rates, funds made available through new insurance contracts were at a disadvantage. Under the investment year method, the earnings rate on new investments is identified each calendar year, and funds made available for new investments each year receive the earnings rate for that year. The new method provides a higher order of equity in the allocation of investment income among the various lines of annuity business, as well as among different group annuity contracts.[27]

Under the law of 1962 a separate account could be established only for group annuity contracts covering at least twenty-five employees, and only the employer's contribution could be allocated to a separate account. Although the assets of a separate account were owned by Equitable, income, gains, and losses from the assets in a separate account were credited or charged to that account without regard to other income, gains, or losses of Equitable. Two kinds of separate accounts were offered: 1) a pooled separate account in which the funds of a number of contractholders would be commingled; and 2) an individual separate account. The first was made available for new contractholders, providing the total employer contribution to Equitable was at least $200,000 each year. The second could be established for an individual contractholder provided the amounts allocated to the separate account would be at least $1,000,000 in the first year with the prospect of being at least $5,000,000 in the first five years. The quantitative restrictions which apply to common stock investments for regular insurance operations do not apply to the separate accounts, and as much as 100 per cent of the employer's contribution may be invested in common stock.[28] Although no specific standards could be set up for all

[27] Under the investment year method Equitable's net group annuity new money rate applicable in 1963 to money made available for new investments in 1963 was 5.17 per cent; for 1964 it was 5.219 per cent. These rates applied to "qualified" pension plans and were net after investment expenses and Federal income taxes.

[28] The existing qualitative restrictions on common stock investments were continued for separate accounts except for the "basket" provision, which permits the

cases, Equitable's initial policy in general, pending an accumulation of experience, was that for new cases approximately 50 per cent of the current contribution would be an appropriate maximum allocation to investment in equities.

During the years following World War II considerable interest developed in regard to health care for the aged. Insurance companies including Equitable modified their group policies in many cases to permit the conversion to individual hospitalization of the group health insurance coverage after retirement or made available continuing benefits for retirees in these situations. In fact New York State enacted legislation (to go in effect January 1, 1961) which made it mandatory to give the conversion right to a group certificate holder for this hospitalization coverage upon discontinuance as an insured employee. The emphasis on this social need, however, was a continuing matter of concern to the companies and to the public.

In March 1962, the New York legislature authorized a nonprofit, low-cost health insurance program for residents of the state 65 years of age or older, which came to be known as "New York 65." [29] Equitable and six other companies organized the New York 65 Health Association which established headquarters in Equitable's Home Office.[30] Vice President and Associate Actuary Morton D. Miller of Equitable was elected President of the Association, and the administration of the new program was placed in the hands of Equitable's Vice President Joseph H. Chaille. New York 65 provided a basic health plan and a major medical plan—both insured without medical examination. The basic plan paid benefits up to thirty-one days for hospitalization, doctors' fees, and convalescent nursing home charges. The major medical plan supplemented the basic and paid up to $3,600 for each confinement and in addition lifetime benefits up to $10,000 for doctors' bills and many other medical expenses. Benefits were subject to reduction if the insured had benefits under other hospital or medical

---

purchase of nonqualifying investments up to 10 per cent of the total assets held for the separate account, whereas only 2 per cent of such investments are permitted for the general portfolio.

[29] Health care insurance for older state residents was first established by Connecticut in 1961, and Equitable participated in the program.

[30] The other companies were Fidelity and Casualty Company of New York, Guardian Life, Metropolitan Life, New York Life, Security Mutual, and Union Labor Life. By the end of 1964, forty-nine companies were members of the Association.

plans. Cost of the basic insurance was originally fixed for a two-year period at $8 or $10 per month per person—depending on choice of benefits—and for the major medical $9 per person. Either spouse was eligible if the other was 65 and enrolled under the plan; open enrollment was restricted to certain periods, the first of which was October 15 to November 15, 1962.

By the end of 1964, 122,000 persons had been insured under New York 65 and $26,173,000 in benefits paid to 46,200. Claim payments and operating expenses, however, had exceeded premium income and the operating deficit had mounted to more than $3,000,000. The original premiums had been established with no precedents and limited statistical data, and the first two years of New York 65 had coincided with a period of rapidly rising hospital and medical costs. Consequently, the Association, late in 1964, filed a request with the New York Insurance Department for permission to increase the premiums on the basic insurance to $12 per month and on the major medical to $11. This change became effective February 1, 1965. At this time forty-seven companies were members of the Association and sharing the risk.

Massachusetts 65 was launched about the same time as New York 65 and Equitable was one of the first out-of-state companies to join. Texas 65 was established in 1963 and Western 65 was organized in California the same year. In 1964 Virginia-North Carolina 65 and Ohio 65 were opened for enrollment. In all of these states Equitable participated and lent its assistance. Agents of all companies assisted in the enrollment of eligible participants largely as a public service, since the enrollment fees were nominal.

In its development of health insurance coverages Equitable recognized the importance of the cooperation of the medical profession. It used not only its own resources but worked closely with the Health Insurance Council, the Health Insurance Association of America, and other organizations in joint educational and promotional activities with the suppliers of health care. Especially noteworthy was the establishment of the medical society review committee mechanism to provide an objective professional forum for the discussion of questions arising between doctors and third party insurers. These committees were formed directly by local or state medical societies, usually with the cooperation of the Health Insurance Council. Representatives for Equitable also engaged in liaison activities with medical specialty groups such as the American Dental Association, the American Society of Reconstructive and Plastic Surgeons, the American Psychological

Association, the American Society of Podiatrists, the American Osteopathic Association, and others.

Equitable's extensive group insurance programs presented substantial problems in claims cost management and hence travel by an Equitable physician to group patrons' locations in all parts of the United States was necessary so that an on-the-spot appraisal could be made not only as to the exact causal nature of an unusual claim cost, but of the health care situation as a whole as it pertains to that locality. To take care of this service Equitable in 1961 created the Bureau of Medical Services headed by Dr. T. H. Alphin as Medical Director. By 1964 the Bureau Director was spending about half of his time in the field and traveling some 60,000 miles per year; more than fifty of the Society's largest group clients had availed themselves of the Bureau's services. In addition to emphasizing control of claim costs, the Bureau encouraged a better mutual understanding of the role of the health insurer and of the role and responsibilities of both the individual and institutional purveyors of health care. Not only were local professional organizations of physicians, dentists, and pharmacists alerted to their responsibilities, but local group management was encouraged to interest itself in, and become a part of community health care organizations such as hospital boards.

Early in 1964 steps were taken further to define the responsibilities of the Agency and Group Departments as earlier established in September 1961. The Group Department was given the responsibility and authority to service existing group cases of all sizes, including the responsibility and authority to conserve and retain cases, and the right to negotiate and arrange for enlargement or extension of coverage with the same policyholder in the same or other group fields. Further, the Group Department was authorized to sell group insurance and annuities to new names where no agent was representing the Society with respect to that case. To protect an agent in a new name case, it was agreed that before members of the Department engaged in direct solicitation, every reasonable effort would be made to ascertain whether any agent had an active contact on such a case. The Group Department was also given the function of setting group sales objectives, but these objectives as they related to agents' production would be subject to review by the Agency Department. The Group Department was authorized to continue to provide a program of training for agents and to release specialized group information to certain group producing agents such as Group Millionaires. General Group information to managers, however, continued to be released through the Agency Department. The Group Department was to deal directly with managers or agents on all matters of appeal and inquiry, including underwriting and commissions questions, which directly affected the Group business.

THE SUPERIOR SALES FORCE

During the period 1958–61 Equitable's sales of life insurance had leveled off somewhat. Agency Vice President Coy G. Eklund attributed this result primarily to the fact that "manpower development had stalemated, both quantitatively and qualitatively." To remedy this situation Equitable embarked upon a program of building "the Superior Sales Force of the entire life insurance industry," to be composed of full-time Equitable agents. Instead of emphasis upon production per se the emphasis would be placed upon manpower development with the expectation of achieving "Production Growth through Manpower Development with Expense Control." The central theme was the success of the individual agent.

One of the first steps towards implementing the new program was the establishing of a "manpower format." The sales force was divided into two groups: 1) Trainees—those agents in their year of appointment and during their next three full calendar years of service with the Society, and 2) the Experienced Sales Force—those who had completed more than three full calendar years, plus the appointment year. The Trainees were subdivided into four groups—those in their year of appointment, and those in their first, second, and third full years. The Experienced Sales Force was subdivided into "Actives"—those under age 65, and "Retired"—those 65 and over.

Then came the important step of completely revising the managerial compensation arrangements for both Agency Managers and District Managers. Since a major emphasis was to be upon the selection and development of the new agent, higher overriders were given on the business of successful Trainee Agents. An innovation among life insurance companies was the introduction of a factor that remunerated for production growth in relation to expenses incurred. This factor was designed to compensate the Agency Manager for his agency's contribution to the overall growth of the Society; in this compensation formula appropriate weight was given to a satisfactory expense and persistency performance of the agency.

To serve as a guide to the selection of agents, Equitable made a study of the experience of some 32,000 of its agents who signed contracts between 1945–60, and developed a probability chart as the basis for assigning a numerical value to a prospective agent in order to assess aggregate probabilities of success. This tool, the "Relative Development Potential" (RDP), made it possible to rate a prospective agent on three items—age, education, and previous occupation—and to rate the recruitment results of an Agency on the basis of its average RDP.[31]

Since the highest percentage of "dropouts" among agents occurred during the early years when it remained to be seen whether or not they could produce at a rate to insure a reasonable livelihood in later years, special care was taken to provide adequate compensation during the training period. Practically all new agents were given a salary plus one-half regular first year commissions for the first two years. The extra cost was regarded as an investment in quality manpower, the returns from which would be realized not only immediately, but in the years to come. The standard by which performance of the new agent was measured—and compensated for—was "Honor Club" membership, achieved by an average of at least $300 per month in first year commissions. Beyond this point managerial compensation, evaluation of agency performance, benefit plans, and agency educational conference requirements all reflected the distinction between the agent who was performing satisfactorily and the one who was not. Under a "spacing requirement," a district manager was required to bring each new trainee up to a minimum standard of production before he could add another to his district.

Once the new agent became a member of the Experienced Sales Force, he had the advantage of programs devised by the newly created "Career Advancement Division" which promoted activities in CLU and LUTC and provided special training for advanced underwriting. This included, among a variety of services, estate planning with a

[31] On the problem of agent dropout the life insurance business had compiled statistical studies and had developed a variety of selection tests. Equitable participated in these studies and like other companies made studies of its own experience. For a number of years Equitable had been using the Steward inventory—a series of tests on personality traits and background factors—in its agent recruitment. The Harvard Report for Equitable released in May 1959 had also commented that "the situation presents a real challenge to see if better ways of agent selection, training, and supervision might not be discovered by further research." Accordingly, under the direction of Coy G. Eklund, newly elected Vice President and Assistant to the President, this broad study was undertaken by the Bureau of Applied Social Research at Columbia University using their EDP equipment and research facilities. From this study Eklund, Dr. Riley, and staff associates developed the new selection guide for agents.

knowledge of tax questions, the marital deduction, community property, and the broad range of business life insurance needs. The agent was encouraged to advance to membership in the Leaders Corps, the National Leaders Corps, the President's Council, and the Million Dollar Round Table, all honors based on higher sales performance.[32] An effective Communications, Recognition, Information, and Motivation Program was formulated to maintain a close relationship between the Home Office and the sales force.

One of the annoying problems of this period which confronted the old line life companies was the practice of some of the newly formed companies of trying to obtain the services of established agents or "surplus" business from such agents with tempting offers of stock options, directorships, and profit-sharing benefits. Though relatively few Equitable agents were attracted by these offers, nevertheless two of the regulations which accompanied the building of the Superior Sales Force dealt with "prior rights" and "conflict of interest." Under the first it was emphasized that the agent was expected to give Equitable first option on new business and to obtain approval if for any reason the business had to be placed with another company. The conflict of interest regulation was aimed at restricting the activities of Equitable agents insofar as their possible affiliation with other life insurance companies was concerned, in terms of investment, ownership, or management.

The success of the new program was apparent almost immediately. During its first year of operation (1962) first year premiums on all three individual lines of business—life, health, and annuity—increased 16.9 per cent, although overall changes, including the policy of hiring no new part-time agents, had reduced the sales force by more than 500. First year commissions on all lines of business increased almost 6 per cent, and the number of agents who made the National Leaders Corps increased by one-third. Productivity of the active Experienced Sales Force increased 13 per cent, while that of the "Class of 1962"—the first to be recruited under the new plan—increased 23 per cent.[33] By

[32] Qualification requirements were as follows: Leaders Corps—$6,000 production credits (roughly first year paid commissions); National Leaders Corps—$12,000 or more in production credits; President's Council—$18,000 or more in production credits. Later the name of the President's Council was changed to Chairman's Council and the President's Club was established for those NLC qualifiers who had at least $12,000 in production credits for each of the two preceding calendar years. See *Agency Items,* October 17, 1966.

[33] See chart in *Equinews,* March 1963.

the end of 1964 the "Class of 1962" showed a per capita production increase of 27.9 per cent over the record of the previous class.[34] Long-range planning for the Agency Sales Force projected an increase in total production credits for agents at a compound rate of 9.8 per cent over the ten-year period ending December 31, 1974.

Vice President Clarence B. Metzger, who had been head of the Manpower Division of the Agency Department, retired October 1, 1963. Metzger had begun his insurance career as a sales specialist with the Edward A. Woods Agency in Pittsburgh in 1924, and helped Woods in the preparation of some of his books on life insurance. He became superintendent of training for the Agency, served as Agency Manager at Buffalo, and in 1940 was appointed Assistant Treasurer in charge of the Cashiers' Division. Six years later he was made Director of Agency Training and in this position modernized and improved the Society's training program—first inaugurated in 1902—to its position of pre-eminence. As a result Equitable lost many of its "graduates" to other companies, but "C.B." took the broad view: "It is in our self-interest that we do all we can to help the entire industry set up good training programs for agents. Nothing would more effectively stop proselyting." [35]

On Metzger's retirement Vice President DeSaussure D. Edmunds became head of the Division which was renamed Manpower Development Division. Edmunds began his career with Equitable in the Cashier's Training Course in Cincinnati in 1925. He served at Nashville, Minneapolis, and Jacksonville as Assistant Cashier, as agent and District Manager in the Carolinas, as Agency Manager for the State of Alabama, and as Field Vice President. He came to the Home Office as a Second Vice President in 1957, became Vice President in charge of the Southern, South Central, and Western Divisions in 1959, and head of the Marketing Division of the Agency Department when it was formed in 1961.

Senior Agency Vice President Samuel A. Burgess retired December 1, 1963, and Agency Vice President Coy G. Eklund became Senior Agency Vice President February 20, 1964.

Group coverages for agents were broadened to keep pace with the development of the sales force. A comprehensive Disability Income Plan for Honor Club agents was added January 1, 1963, and a year later additional improvements were made. In July 1964 a new Sup-

[34] *National Leaders,* March-April 1965.
[35] For a sketch of Metzger's career see *Equinews,* September 1963.

plementary Group Life Insurance plan based upon service fees paid from the second to the tenth policy years was put into effect. Also the maximum amount of group life insurance for agents was raised from $75,000 to $100,000. In certain instances an agent selling substantial amounts of group insurance or individual health insurance involving service fees not vested at death could qualify for a maximum of $125,000. As a member of the Committee on Benefit Plans, Vice President A. E. Elander of the Agency Department had given a great deal of study and attention to keeping the various phases of the Agents Benefit Program on a parity with the similar program for salaried personnel both in the field and in the Home Office.

PERSONNEL

Equitable's salary costs for full-time salaried employees for 1960 reached a new high in excess of $63,000,000. In addition the Society contributed another $9,000,000 for the employees' Group benefit programs which included Group Life Insurance, various health and medical insurance coverages, and retirement benefits. In May 1960 the Manpower Development Unit was set up in the Personnel Department to carry out the central manpower planning function and coordinate the operations of the Employment and Education and Training Divisions of the Personnel Department. This unit worked with all departments in analyzing job requirements and engaged in a study of development programs. Not only did Equitable conduct its own salary surveys, but it also participated in Federal, state, and local salary surveys. The major objective was to insure the Society a body of qualified personnel capable of developing their top capacities and of deserving promotion for more demanding jobs. In general the ability to promote from within was the desired policy.

Equitable's employment policies were definitely outlined in 1958 when President Oates introduced "A Code to Work By." This code announced that it was the Society's policy not only to maintain fair pay and encourage individual development, but to "attract, select, place, and promote employees, based on their qualifications for work requirements, without discrimination." [36] In 1961 President John F. Kennedy initiated a plan for equal employment opportunity and

[36] The code of ten points was printed in *Equinews*, May 1958, in the employee handbook, "You and the Equitable," in the Personnel Management Information Release Manual in 1963, and in other Society publications.

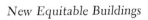

New Equitable Buildings

Atlanta

San Francisco

Los Angeles

placed it under the direction of Vice President Lyndon B. Johnson. Equitable, as one of the leading employers not involved in government contract work, was invited to become acquainted with this program. Although under its "Code to Work By" Equitable was substantially complying with the provisions of the program, it did not formally join until 1964 when President Johnson's Committee on Equal Employment Opportunity presented its "Plan for Progress." Equitable needed to make no serious modifications in its employment policy; it merely made more specific the policies already being followed. Equitable's "Plan for Progress," as announced in June 1964, stated that selection, compensation, training, and promotion of all personnel would be based upon job skill, job performance, training, and education "without discrimination because of race, creed, color, or national origin, and without setting quotas for selection of members of particular religious or racial groups." Home Office and local field office managers were required to report annually their observations covering the employment, by job category, of members of four minority groups—American Indians, Negroes, Orientals, and Spanish Americans. As Chairman Oates said, Equitable's Plan for Progress was "not a panacea but a working, developing policy. As such, from time to time, it will call for interpretation and redirection."

To round out its training program Equitable in 1961 established its Management Training Program. Although the Cashier's Training Course, begun in 1920—and after World War II renamed the Administrative Training Course—had been highly successful, the need became apparent for another training course aimed primarily at supplying potentially high management personnel in the Home Office.[37] The low turnover of personnel during and after the depression years and the low rate of employment of new college graduates had resulted in a shortage of personnel sufficient to meet future needs at the higher management levels. Thus after studies made by the Personnel Department and the consulting firm of McKinsey and Company, Incorporated,

[37] For earlier mention of the Cashier's Training Course, see this history, p. 1266. From the inception of the Cashier's Training Course to the end of 1964, 876 students completed the program. Of these graduates, 27 were officers of the Society, 52 were cashiers, 56 were assistant cashiers, 78 were supervisors, and 143 were Home Office employees in management positions. There were also 97 of the graduates in management positions in other Field offices of the Society. These were in addition to the retired and deceased graduates of the course. A number of trainees, after becoming grounded in life insurance fundamentals and Equitable procedures, transferred to the Agency force.

Equitable, in 1960, inaugurated the Management Training Program to supplement the Administrative Training and Actuarial Programs.

The new program was designed to increase the effectiveness of the Society's recruiting at the college and graduate level and to provide more competitive salaries for accelerated on-the-job training and development aimed at filling well-defined key positions at the beginning level of management five or six years after employment. The program is administered by the Personnel Department, but the candidates are assigned to the various departments of the Society for training. A typical trainee spends a year or two on assignments in the department to which he is assigned, and attends numerous seminars conducted by officers of each of the Society's operating departments. Trainees are also given temporary assignments in other departments such as Cashiers', Group Field offices, and the CAPS project. This training program gives the trainees a broad acquaintanceship with the operations of Equitable, and it is expected that an increasing proportion of the promotions to the beginning levels of management will be made from its graduates.

PUBLIC RELATIONS AND PUBLIC AFFAIRS

In 1958, following intensive, studious consideration by Public Relations Committees representing both the directors and officers, an Equitable Public Relations Policy statement was drawn up and published in pamphlet form over President Oates' signature. It stated that the Equitable's public relations activities shall be so conducted as to earn and retain friends for the Society by accurately and simply interpreting the high purposes and objectives of the Society and communicating that interpretation to all interested groups. In discussions with officers leading to adoption of this policy, President Oates emphasized the view "that it is exceedingly important that the Equitable develop to the full an awareness on the part of the general public of the Equitable's value to society and of its current contributions to the public good." He visualized "a continuing vigorous communications effort, honestly founded on superior performance and sound principles."

One of the immediate results of the policy announcement was an expansion of the publicity and press relations staff; greater efforts were made to capitalize on the news potential of Equitable sales, investment, research and insurance operations. An improved program of regular communications to policyowners through attractive annual reports and premium notice enclosures was inaugurated. Other activities involving relations with various publics were given new attention, including opinion research studies, film production and distribution, and printed institutional materials. Increased appropriations for national advertising and the new directions taken in theme and media are also covered in this history.

But public relations has other dimensions, too. As was emphasized in Equitable's statement of fundamental purposes, a great mutual life insurance company, in addition to supplying protection against financial hazards, should keep in mind those "inherent, deeper and less tangible purposes." It should, as a public service institution and a corporate citizen, feel its responsibility to aid in the promotion of the welfare not only of its policyholders but of the citizens of the community and the nation. It could do this through public service programs, by contributions to educational, civic and charitable organizations, and by participating, through the efforts of individual officers, employees, and agents, in public service activities.

To encourage voluntary and constructive participation by personnel in the Field and in the Home Office, Equitable, in 1962, established its Office of Community Services and Health Education as a part of the President's Staff. The Office was headed by Howard Ennes, M.P.H., and placed under the general supervision of Senior Vice President and Assistant to the President Joseph L. Beesley with Chief Medical Director Norvin C. Kiefer as medical advisor.[38] The new facility was intended to provide professional and experienced guidance to employees and agents who voluntarily interested themselves in community affairs. Its interests ranged over a great variety of topics from accidents, allergy, and alcoholism, to family life, health education, urban planning, and youth activities. The Office keeps in contact with health agencies, service clubs, religious organizations, educational institutions, labor organizations, trade associations, and the like. It furnishes information, plans programs, and suggests methods. It maintains a Basic Service Library of nontechnical publications and motion pictures, files of professional and technical journals, organizational reports, and unpublished data collected from professional relationships and participation in meetings. Equitable employees and agents throughout the

[38] Executive Order 62-6.
After the Equitable administrative reorganization in 1964, Community Services and Health Education remained as a part of the staff of James F. Oates, Jr., who became Chairman of the Board and Chief Executive Officer.

country are thus encouraged to participate in community service work and have taken advantage of the Library's material and staff consultation available from the office.

The same year the Society cooperated with President John F. Kennedy's Council on Youth Fitness by producing a motion picture for television and community use. The thirty-minute film which was designed to motivate parents and others in improving the physical fitness program in the nation's schools, was produced after consultation with Charles (Bud) Wilkinson, nationally known football coach and athletic director at the University of Oklahoma. Wilkinson was at the time Special Consultant on Youth Fitness for the Council. The film was made available through both Equitable and the President's Council and was widely distributed by way of audio-visual libraries throughout the nation. Given wide acclaim by educators, health personnel, and physical education specialists, the film received the Chris Award from the Tenth Annual Columbus Ohio Film Festival, and Honorable Mention at the San Francisco International Film Festival.[39]

In 1964 Equitable appropriated $754,850 for contributions, which were listed under three categories. Community Services, such as contributions to American Red Cross, Greater New York Fund, and United Appeals Outside New York City, received $375,650 or about 50 per cent of the contributions. A total of $280,500 was contributed as aid to Higher Education, with the largest portion of this sum going to liberal arts colleges, 135 of which received $1,000 each and ten $5,000 each. Other items included $50,000 for the National Fund for Medical Education, $15,000 for medical scholarships, $7,500 for the College of Insurance (Insurance Society of New York), and $10,000 for the United Negro College Fund, the first contribution for which was made in 1946. The contributions for higher education constituted 37½ per cent of the total. The remaining 12½ per cent went to health, safety, and medical research, and included donations to such organizations as American Heart Association, the American Cancer Society, and the National Association for Mental Health. Allotments were also made to the Lincoln Center for the Performing Arts, Incorporated, the New

[39] Other films produced and distributed publicly by Equitable as part of its public relations program included "For All Time," which dramatized the company's first 100 years of service and was issued in connection with the Centennial celebration in 1959; "The Owl and Fred Jones," a cartoon on improving health habits; and "Ever New, New York," developed in connection with construction of Equitable's new Home Office building.

York Public Library, and the Educational Broadcasting Corporation.[40]

In addition to the $753,500 actually disbursed for contributions Equitable appropriated $851,319 for membership dues (and assessments) in some 70 organizations and associations in the field of life insurance, general business and the like. The largest of these items was $411,643 for the Institute of Life Insurance and its Cooperative Advertising Program; $186,469 for membership in the Life Insurance Association of America; $94,816 for the Life Insurance Medical Research Fund, and $37,225 for the Health Insurance Association of America.[41]

As adopted by the Board of Directors in November 1964 the budget for contributions and memberships for 1965 was fixed at $1,666,852.

In July 1963 Equitable set up its Program for Citizenship. President Oates' announcement to all employees and agents read in part:

> It is the policy of the Equitable to encourage its employees to exercise their rights and carry out their responsibilities as citizens; to vote, to become informed on politics, economics and government, and to participate in the affairs of their government and of the political party of their choice at community, county, State and Federal levels to the extent that their individual situations permit. This policy is founded on the belief that our American form of government can best be preserved and strengthened through the broad participation of an enlightened citizenry in its processes.
>
> It is understood and fully accepted that the opinion of an employee on a given issue may differ from that of the Society.

In addition, the Society's Public Relations Policy states that "All Equitable men and women will be encouraged, whenever the discharge of

[40] In 1962, when the Equitable's Contributions Policy was comprehensively reviewed, a formula was devised and adopted under which the total budget for contributions, as recommended by the Public Relations Committee of the Board of Directors and approved by the Board, could not exceed a limit equal to .034 per cent of a contributions base defined as the sum of 1) the total premium income of the second year preceding the budget year, and 2) one-tenth of the admitted assets of the Society at the end of the second year preceding the budget year. A new formula for placing a limit on the amount which can be budgeted for contributions was adopted in 1966 to apply to 1967 and thereafter. This provides that the budget shall not exceed a Contributions Limit resulting from .00625 per cent of Admitted Assets as of December 31, 1965, plus .003125 per cent of the increase in Admitted Assets after that date.

[41] Other items of $5,000 or more: American Life Convention $14,200; American College of Life Underwriters $12,846; National Safety Council $10,660; National Industrial Conference Board $7,500; Chamber of Commerce of the United States $7,500; Life Insurance Agency Management Association $7,270; S. S. Huebner Foundation $6,714; Associates of Harvard Business School $5,000; and Greater New York Safety Council $5,000.

their duties to the Society permits, to serve their local communities and the Nation through acceptance of responsibilities in charitable, religious, educational, and governmental organizations."

As later expanded and developed, the Program established guide lines and specific goals. It emphasized that being informed on issues was not enough; the citizen would also have to act. Hence it was recommended that Equitable employees not only register and vote but also participate by way of personal investment of time and by contributions. The central goal of the Program for Citizenship, which was nonpartisan in the fullest sense, was to encourage and support effective voluntary citizenship participation. Responsibility for the administration of the Program was given to the Office of Community Services and Health Education which set up an Advisory Council to consult and communicate with Equitable personnel.

On completion of the Equitable Life Assurance Society Hall of the Life Sciences (Washington, D.C.) in April 1962, the Society formally presented the wing to the National Academy of Sciences. Dr. Fordyce B. St. John, former Equitable Director and Chairman of its National Awards Committee, presented a ceremonial key to Dr. Detlev W. Bronk, President of the Academy. The occasion was the annual spring meeting of the National Academy. The Hall was dedicated at a luncheon June 27. President John F. Kennedy sent a congratulatory message and President Oates said: "It was quite natural that we should find in the National Academy a most fitting and appropriate object of our primary interest which, as a life insurance company, obviously lies in the area of the conquest of disease, the improvement in health and the prolongation of life." [42]

In July 1962 Equitable's Board of Directors approved the Society's participation in the New York World's Fair of 1964–65. So for a second time Equitable arranged its exhibit, this time a pavilion the main feature of which was a large "Demograph," a scientifically accurate mechanism for recording the country's population growth, state by state. On a 45-foot map of the United States the machine recorded births, deaths, and immigration and emigration figures by pulsating lights in four colors. Overhead an immense counter kept a running tally of the country's total population as it increased by one every

[42] It may be recalled that Equitable made the donation to build the Hall as a part of its Centennial Program in 1959. See this history, p. 1274.

twelve seconds. The map also portrayed such population data as density, rate of growth, and sex distribution. The Demograph was the idea of Dr. John W. Riley, Vice President and Director of Social Research. Along the sides of the pavilion auxiliary exhibits provided banks of telephones on which fairgoers could dial or push-button their own states and receive specific local population information, as well as information on the Equitable's role in their state's economy.

Despite the rain, unfinished exhibits, and civil rights demonstrations, the Fair opened April 22, 1964, with some 90,000 visitors in attendance. Although Equitable had a little mechanical trouble with the map, the Demograph blazened forth with the population figure of 191,509,464. (When the Fair opened for the second year on April 21, 1965, the figure was 194,205,102.) Equitable's exhibit was not as pretentious or expensive as many others, but it attracted much interest and attention. Approximately 1,500,000 persons visited the Equitable Pavilion during the first year that the Fair was open. As President Oates said, the population explosion is "the most significant social, human and economic fact in the world today. Everyone is interested in it, and it is part of our trust to call it to the attention of the 70 million people who will be coming to this Fair. Our exhibit, so closely related to our business, is a clear demonstration of the relevance of life insurance to the certainty of death, as well as the growing market for protection. Every man, woman and child who goes to this Fair and sees the Equitable exhibit will remember it as long as he lives." [43]

In 1959 the Advertising, Publications and Press Relations Department of Equitable decided that the Society's symbol or trademark needed a new look. It seemed that Equitable's classical statue group, "Protection," which had been the Society's symbol for ninety years, was outdated and old-fashioned, and was not doing its part in "building a company image." A survey of 200 persons by the Society's advertising agency indicated that though one person out of three who saw the symbol associated it with protection, only one out of thirteen associated it with the name Equitable, even after they were told that it represented a life insurance company. A study of corporate symbols fixed four desirable characteristics: memorability, recognition, appropriateness, and uniqueness. It appeared that Equitable was handicapped not only by a symbol which was too complex, but by the fact that it did

[43] For a description of Equitable's exhibit, see *Equinews,* July 1963, May 1964, and March 1965.

not carry the Society's name which was "a long, ponderous, even formidable cognomen." And because a number of people found difficulty in pronouncing "Equitable" some thought was even given to changing the name. But changing the name of the Society would be a break with tradition.

Ideas in regard to a new symbol were presented by Equitable artists, by the Society's advertising agency, and by outside artists and sculptors. Many designs were discarded because they were no improvement over the old symbol, "and many lost the Society's traditions, still of infinite value." Those planning the new symbol found that there was a sense of loyalty to the old symbol which permeated the field forces as well as the Home Office: "It seems more than a business loyalty, subject to change if another, drastically different symbol would be more productive. It borders on an affection. This attitude would not be reflected by our newcomers. But it seems true of the hard core of longer-term workers. This fact, alone, would not militate against radical change were there cogent reasons for such a step. It does support moderation." [44]

The proposed elements of the new symbol were finally turned over to two designers, Fred Ludekens and Eugene Ettenberg, who worked independently of each other. From designs submitted by these two men evolved the Equitable symbol which is used in two slightly different versions. It portrays a sturdy female figure holding the outline of a shield; bisecting the figure is the single word "Equitable." The new symbol, "a wedding of the old with the new," is supposed to represent "protection, strength, power," and give "greater name identification and more meaningful exposure." [45]

NATIONAL LEADERSHIP IN THOUGHT

Since the business of life insurance relates to many phases of American life, the President of a large life insurance company is called upon to make numerous talks outside the company. So it has been with President Oates, who has made scores of talks before various associations and organizations—legal, economic, educational, and religious.

[44] Charles R. Corcoran, "Search For a Sign," p. 46. This 60-page mimeographed booklet which was made available in September 1961, carries in addition to the text, reproductions of many corporate symbols, as well as the artists' models which portray the evolution of the new Equitable symbol. See also *Equinews*, December 1962.

[45] *Ibid.*, pp. 42 and 54.

These talks have ranged in subject from pension plans to inflation, the responsibility of citizenship, and the philosophy of business management; they have been widely reported in the public press.[46]

Despite the variety of subjects and diversity of audiences, a central core of thought permeated these talks. It centered around the importance of the individual human being, the advantages of the free enterprise system, and the danger of the ever-encroaching powers of government. In his talk on "Philosophies of Business Management" President Oates said:

> The real aim and end of business and government is to develop and serve the dignity, welfare and vital importance of the individual human being. This cannot be accomplished alone by the supply of more and more material goods. Each employee needs recognition, respect, and the sincere interest of his business supervisors. He must have more than a passing opportunity to earn a livelihood; he must be provided with a reasonable framework for a life. A man needs more than food, shelter, and clothing; he needs an environment in which he can realize a substantial percentage of his dream. In the final analysis a corporation is no more than a composite of all of the people who work for it. . . . I believe that if the American economy is to survive and our people are to prefer enlightened capitalism to the nationalization of industry, we must act consistently with our belief in the individual man and our belief in individual freedom (as guaranteed by the Constitution) and effectively implement our principles where they count—that is in the daily lives of the American working men and women.

And in regard to the free enterprise system:

[46] A representative list of talks and where delivered: "Philosophies of Business Management," Chicago Bar Association, June 19, 1958; "Private Pension Plans," The Law Club, Chicago, Illinois, October 10, 1958; "Inflation: What Can Businessmen Do About It," New York Chamber of Commerce, December 4, 1958; "For All Time," The Newcomen Society in North America, December 3, 1959; "Thinking Through Some Of Our Social Legislation," Los Angeles Rotary Club, September 30, 1960; "The Responsibility of Citizenship," The Citizens Budget Commission, New York, January 11, 1961; "Morality in Our Lives," The Church of the Redeemer, Baltimore, Maryland, March 21, 1961; "The Role of Government," Iowa Bankers Association, Des Moines, October 31, 1961; "Federal Taxation: Reduction and Reform," The New Jersey Association of Real Estate Boards, Atlantic City, December 6, 1962; "How Can We Improve Our Unfavorable International Balance of Payments?" The Economic Club of Detroit, October 30, 1963; "Public Policy and Unemployment," 34th National Business Conference Harvard Business School Association, Boston, June 6, 1964, and "The Believability of the Bible," American Bible Society, New York City, May 13, 1965.

The freedom of individual initiative embraces many freedoms. Among them are the freedom to employ one's person or wealth in any line of production one cares to enter; the freedom to buy, sell, or enter contracts; and the freedom to save, invest and acquire private property. Capitalism assumes that individuals are rational and informed (and, believe me, by and large they *are*) and that they will use their freedom of initiative to pursue their self-interest to their best economic advantage. Capitalism assumes further that individuals will direct their efforts to perform that work in which they can be most productive and for which there is the greatest demand. It assumes free mobility of labor and investible funds from one type of employment to another or from one area to another. It also assumes that individuals will spend, save or invest their income so as to obtain the greatest possible satisfaction. The freedom of individual initiative finds an important economic expression in creative managerial initiative.

The dominant force sparking initiative under the capitalistic structure is the right to acquire and own privately the means of production. In our society, for example, most of the wealth is owned and controlled by individuals either directly or indirectly through corporate equities. Within limits the owner can use that property, sell it, or give it to others as he sees fit.

As for the effect of government upon the free enterprise system:

I am against Governmentally imposed restrictions on our ability to finance, produce, price and market the fruits of our labor anywhere in the Free World. I believe that Government activities and intervention should be kept to a minimum; and that this minimum be assigned, whenever it is practical to do so, to that level of Government operation which is closest to the citizen.[47]

As noted earlier President Oates pointed out the results and fundamental dangers of inflation: [48]

By permitting the dollar to erode in value, we are striking at the very concept of individual freedom. The freedom to save—an important freedom in our quest for security—is continually being thwarted by rising prices. Inflation is irreparably damaging to the millions who are living on pensions, to the millions who are building up pension rights, to the millions who

47 "The Role of Government," Des Moines, Iowa, October 31, 1961. Copy in Equitable Archives.

48 See this history, p. 1291, for a previous quote.

look toward life insurance for protection, and to the millions on fixed incomes of various kinds. . . . Inflation is a cruel capital levy, imposing, as it does, a penalty on thrift. To deliberately create it is on the same moral plane as the repudiation by Russia of its so-called "citizens" bonds.[49]

Inflation also has injurious economic effects. Under the impact of inflation, the quality of managerial decisions is lowered and more speculative steps are induced. The desire to beat anticipated price increases leads to overspeculation and premature expansion of plants and inventories. Excess capacity develops and results eventually in unemployment of plant and men. Inflation, instead of aiding economic growth and stability—as some would have us believe—actually operates to undermine them.[50]

He also saw the need to clarify public understanding as to the nature of the Social Security program, while at the same time recognizing that social insurance does have a place in our American society:

Most people, for example, believe social security to be similar to private voluntary insurance and consider the taxes they pay as equivalent to premiums for benefits bought and paid for. They have been led to believe that their contributions along with a similar amount that is paid by their employer is being held in an earmarked fund which will be ready and waiting for them upon the day of their retirement. Official literature published by the Government tends to support and nurture this erroneous impression.[51]

He pointed out that the analogy to private voluntary insurance was very misleading and cited the decision of the United States Supreme Court in *Flemming* v. *Nestor* to the effect that the "noncontractual interest of an employee covered by the Act cannot be soundly analogized to that of the holder of an annuity whose right to benefits are bottomed on his contractual premium payments." [52] He continued:

The present generation of oldsters is getting a handsome subsidy. . . . We, in no sense, begrudge them this benefit. We only say that it should be understood for what it is. . . . We not only are taxing present workers

49 "Philosophies of Business Management," Chicago, June 19, 1958. Copy in Equitable Archives.

50 "The Role of Government."

51 "Thinking Through Some Of Our Social Legislation," Los Angeles, September 30, 1960. Pamphlet in Equitable Archives.

52 *Flemming* v. *Nestor*. 363 U.S. 603.

to support the oldsters, but we are also creating liabilities for our children and grandchildren to struggle with.[53]

President Oates did not confine his efforts toward better citizenship to speech making. He participated in numerous major civic, philanthropic, religious, and educational endeavors, as well as in leadership in the business, educational, and insurance communities. For example, he served as Chairman of the Institute of Life Insurance in 1964, on the Task Force on Economic Growth and Opportunity of the United States Chamber of Commerce, and upon Presidential Commissions which studied youth employment and the problems of heart disease, cancer, and stroke.[54]

Other officers of Equitable also participated in various fields of corporate and individual citizenship. For example, Senior Vice President Grant Keehn served as a member of the Board of Trustees of the New York Public Library and as Chairman of the Board of Trustees of Hamilton College. Senior Vice President Joseph L. Beesley was a member and Treasurer of the National Commission on Community Health Services, and two-term member of the Board of Trustees of De Pauw University; Senior Agency Vice President Coy G. Eklund was a Trustee of the National Foundation (for Infantile Paralysis) and the Salk Institute; Assistant Vice President Howard Ennes served as President of the International Union for Health Education; Vice President Merle A. Gulick served as President of the National Council on Alcoholism and as Chairman of the Board of Trustees of Hobart and William Smith Colleges; and Dr. Norvin C. Kiefer was a leader in the field of occupational medicine and an active participant in the work of the National Safety Council.

GRANT KEEHN ELECTED PRESIDENT

Former President Ray D. Murphy died in February 1964. Said *Equinews:* "He will be remembered most as a man who changed things—his specialty, his industry, his company. Others may remember him for his modest, approachable manner, or for the ever-present twinkle in his eye. Yet it was upon the organization of The Equitable that he made his most lasting imprint."

[53] "Thinking Through Some Of Our Social Legislation."

[54] President Oates had served on the Board of Trustees of Princeton University since 1954 and was General Chairman of its Fund Raising Program, 1959–62. In 1966 he became Chairman of the Executive Committee of the Board.

Organizational changes in the Society's internal administration advanced another step in February 1964, when the Board of Directors elected Grant Keehn as tenth President of Equitable. James F. Oates, Jr., was re-elected Chairman and Chief Executive Officer; he had held all three titles since 1957.

Grant Keehn was born in Kenilworth, Illinois, in 1900. He attended New Trier High School, Kenilworth, and Hamilton College, where he was elected to Phi Beta Kappa and received a Bachelor of Arts degree in 1921; he received a Master of Business Administration degree from the Harvard Graduate School of Business Administration in 1923. For the next eight years he served with the investment firm of Goldman, Sachs and Company, of which he became a partner in 1931. He was Vice President of the Kelsey-Hayes Wheel Company of Detroit, and an officer and director of Equity Corporation for several years. In 1939 Keehn organized his own investment firm, Grant Keehn and Company, a member of the New York Stock Exchange. From 1942 to 1945 he served as major and colonel in the United States Army and upon discharge joined the First National Bank of the City of New York as a Vice President; he became Executive Vice President in 1950. In 1955 when the First National Bank merged with the National City Bank, Keehn became the Executive Vice President of the First National City Bank of New York. He resigned from that position to join Equitable October 20, 1958, as Senior Vice President and was elected a member of the Board of Directors. In addition to being a Director of Equitable, President Keehn is a Director of a number of other corporations, Chairman of the Board of Trustees at Hamilton College, and a Trustee and the Treasurer of the New York Public Library. Although he and Chairman Oates grew up within a few miles of each other, they did not become well acquainted until the late 1940's when both were serving as directors of the Great Northern Railway.

Though President Keehn's experience had been largely in the field of finance, his contacts in industry and public affairs gave him a broad knowledge of the problems to be faced in the management of a large life insurance company. As the *New York Journal-American* said: "Few men achieve success in more than one field, but Grant Keehn has carved a niche in three important areas of business and finance." Tall, athletic, and youthful appearing, the new President had many outside interests, among them golf, the Boys' Clubs of America, and his Alma Mater, Hamilton College. With James F. Oates as Chairman and

Grant Keehn as President, Equitable was given an able and experienced leadership team with the prospect that it would continue in office for a number of years.

Other management changes were as follows: Vice President William R. Cowie assumed general supervision of the Securities Investment and the Treasurer's Departments; Vice President Willis M. Holtum assumed general supervision of the City Mortgage, Farm Mortgage, and Residential Mortgage Departments; and Vice President Thomas F. Murray was designated to succeed Vice President Holtum as officer in charge of the City Mortgage Department. Leonard H. McVity, former Second Vice President and Associate Controller, was elected Vice President and Controller to succeed Charles B. Lunsford, who died in January 1964 after a brief illness. Second Vice President Frederick P. Andersen was named Second Vice President and Auditor, and he and the Internal Audit and Evaluation Bureau (organized in July 1960 in charge of Andersen under the Controller) were transferred to the Staff of the Chairman.

AT THE END OF ONE HUNDRED AND FIVE YEARS

As of December 31, 1964, Equitable had a total of $46,366,803,000 of life insurance in force, of which $27,633,818,000 was group insurance and $18,732,985,000 was individual life insurance. It had more than 12,000,000 policy and certificate holders. During the year it had sold $2,146,298,000 of individual life insurance and $1,220,374,000 of group insurance.[55] General expenses, including commissions to agents, amounted to $188,549,000. The Society set aside $41,723,000 for Federal income taxes on 1964 operations, and paid $1,183,509,000 in dividends and benefit payments to policyholders and beneficiaries. Surplus was increased to $615,258,000 and admitted assets of the Society were $11,731,361,000. (During the one hundred five and a half years the Society had paid $17,903,930,000 in benefits to its policyholders or their beneficiaries.)

The Society ranked third among the leading life insurance companies of the United States in total life insurance in force, in total assets, and in group life insurance in force. It led all other companies in total annuities in force (individual and group), and had more than two

[55] Equitable first achieved sales of $1,000,000,000 of individual life insurance in 1953 when it was 94 years old. Eleven years later (1964) individual life sales totaled more than $2,146,000,000.

and one-half times the amount of individual annuities held by any other company.[56]

In 1964 the volume of new investments made by Equitable rose to the level of $1,148,000,000; the average gross yield from these investments was approximately 5.5 per cent. Of the total of $11,480,206,000 of cash and invested assets at year's end, 47.6 per cent was in bonds, 40.9 per cent in mortgage loans, and the remainder in stocks (preferred and common), real estate, policy loans, and transportation equipment.[57] Recent years witnessed a trend from home and farm financing toward greater emphasis upon loans in the commercial field, with the largest amount of financing being for apartments, office buildings, shopping centers, and industrial structures.

A new development in the field of real estate ownership was the condominium, which provides for individual ownership of apartments in multi-unit housing and of parts of commercial buildings.[58] President Oates encountered condominium on a trip to Puerto Rico in 1961 and foresaw its potentialities in fostering home ownership in urban centers and at the same time opening a new field for Equitable's residential mortgage lending. Vice President and General Solicitor Warner H. Mendel and Second Vice President and Associate General Solicitor William K. Kerr provided much of the impetus for the popularization of this type of ownership and its implementation through state legislation.

Two changes in the New York Insurance Law in 1964 enabled the Society to compete more effectively with out-of-state insurance companies and other financial institutions for desirable investments. First, the limitation on the proportion of total admitted assets permitted to be invested in conventional mortgage loans—that is, loans not insured by the Federal Housing Administration or guaranteed by the Veteran's

[56] "Ten Largest U.S. Life Insurance Companies—Indices of Relative Size." This study issued by the Actuary's Department in April 1965 contains 24 charts which show the general scope of insurance activities of the ten United States life insurance companies with the largest amount of assets. See also *The Unique Manual and National Underwriter Life Reports* (Cincinnati, 1965).

[57] Industrial bonds constituted 23.8 per cent of the total investment; public utility bonds 9.8 per cent; railroad bonds 5.7 per cent. Of the mortgage loans, city mortgages constituted 20.9 per cent; residential loans 14.8 per cent; and farm mortgage loans 5.2 per cent.

These figures do not include the funds invested in separate accounts.

[58] The National Housing Act was amended in 1961 to permit Federal insurance of mortgage loans on condominium apartments, and within three years most of the states had enacted legislation recognizing condominium ownership.

Administration—was raised from 40 to 50 per cent. Second, the amount permitted to be loaned on a conventional mortgage was increased from 66⅔ to 75 per cent of appraised value, subject to certain conditions.

Relatively new to Equitable was the development of a common stock program. Although the New York legislature in 1951 authorized New York life insurance companies to invest up to 3 per cent of admitted assets or one-third of surplus—whichever was the smaller figure—in common stocks (changed in 1957 to 5 per cent of assets or one-half of surplus), Equitable showed no immediate interest in embarking upon a common stock purchase program.[59] At the end of 1956 its investment in common stocks was $19,005,535 (market value), or only two-tenths of one per cent of admitted assets. In general the Society, as a matter of policy, had been striving for greater immediate yield on fixed income securities. Post World War II developments, however, brought about a modification of this policy. Vastly increased industrial production, rising corporate and personal income, and "creeping inflation" centered the attention not only of individuals but institutional investors more and more upon common stocks. Also there was the fact that various other administrators of pension funds had a wide latitude in the selection of investments.

Soon after President Oates took office he ordered a study made by the Securities Investment Department. The result was a report (September 1957) which, after analyzing the pros and cons of the subject and the respective yields on stocks and bonds during the preceding twenty-nine years, recommended that the Securities Investment Department select a theoretical portfolio of stocks and study the results. Phantom "books" were opened on a balance of $30,000,000 which was invested in equal thirds in railroad securities, public utility securities, and industrials. These imaginary investments were carefully followed through stock splits, stock dividends and regular cash dividends in the endeavor to derive reliable measures of the actual returns realizable in equity investment. The results revealed a high order of investment judgment but failed to be impressive enough to convince the Society to embark upon a major stock purchase program.

After Grant Keehn joined the Society as Senior Vice President, the question of common stocks was again reviewed, but the inquiry proceeded along a different course: assuming that investment in common

59 For the Armstrong legislation which prohibited purchase of common stocks, see this history, p. 703.

stocks were adopted as a policy, what kind of a program should be considered and what should be the method of operation? After consulting with other life insurance companies which had had more experience in dealing in equities, Second Vice President Robert E. Benson outlined a program (February 1959) which set down the parameters within which it might operate.[60] A list of companies was prepared, arranged by industry group, the stocks of which would meet the qualitative standards proposed for equity investment. A formal program for the acquisition of common stocks in amounts annually to reach the statutory limit in ten years was presented to the Finance Committee of the Board. The Finance Committee in August 1959 authorized the purchase of $21,000,000 of common stocks for the remainder of the year. As initially suggested and closely followed over the next several months, purchases were made broadly through the list on a dollar averaging basis. As experience was studied it became evident that all stocks were not equally attractive at the same time and that more flexibility in selection was desirable, so the Finance Committee gave its approval for exercise of greater discretion to the managers of the program.

The establishing of separate accounts for qualified pension plans (see this history, p. 1314), afforded prospects of considerably enlarged equity investment activities and necessitated close liaison between the Investment, the Actuary's, and the Group Departments. Consequently a separate Common Stock Division was created in the Securities Investment Department. On January 1, 1964, Wilbur J. Strauss joined the Society as Vice President to head the new division.

By the end of 1964 Equitable had a total of $214,351,000 invested in common stocks with a market value of $278,282,000 at that date.[61] Although this investment constituted only 2.4 per cent of the Society's invested assets, it is proving to be an interesting and important part of its financial operations.

Equitable's real estate investment at the end of 1964 totaled $345,-831,000 (admitted value) or 3 per cent of its investment portfolio.

60 The companies which shared their experience with Equitable were the College Retirement Equities Fund of the Teachers Insurance and Annuity Association; the New York Life Insurance Company; and the Prudential Insurance Company of America.

61 This figure does not include purchases for separate accounts, but does include the so-called nonprogram stocks. In addition to the common stocks, Equitable had an investment of $198,105,711 in preferred and guaranteed stocks.

Largest items, of course, were Gateway Center and the new Home Office building at 1285 Avenue of the Americas. The Society owned seven other office buildings which were located in Albany, Atlanta, Brooklyn, Fresno, Milwaukee, Richmond, and San Francisco.[62] The former Home Office building at 393 Seventh Avenue, completely modernized in 1963, was 98 per cent rented as of December 31, 1964, and producing a 7.6 per cent investment return after depreciation. The leading tenant was Montgomery Ward and Company and the building was renamed "The Montgomery Ward Building."

On May 16, 1961, the Real Estate Committee of the Board authorized construction of the Equitable Building in Chicago. On May 17 the Executive Committee of the Board concurred in this resolution, and it was reported to the Board May 18. The site chosen was on the east side of Michigan Avenue just north of the Chicago River. The land had been acquired by Colonel Robert McCormick of *The Chicago Tribune* and lay just south of the Tribune Tower. The deed to the land was conveyed by the Tribune Company to Equitable January 8, 1963. The Tribune retained the property extending from the Tribune Tower across the former block of Hubbard Street to the north edge of E. North Water Street.

Like Gateway Center, this too was a historic site. Past this spot Louis Joliet and Father Jacques Marquette paddled in 1673, the first white men to navigate the inland waterway, and LaSalle followed a few years later. The Haitian-born Indian fur trader, Jean Baptiste Point du Sable, built a cabin there in 1779 which was purchased in 1804 by John Kinzie, an employee of the American Fur Company, who was considered to be Chicago's first settler. Across the river stood Fort Dearborn, the garrison of which was massacred in the War of 1812. And in 1847 Cyrus Hall McCormick, inventor of the reaper which bore his name, located his Chicago factory on this site.

The 35-story building of aluminum, granite, and glass, designed by Skidmore, Owings and Merrill, was set in the rear center of a landscaped plaza of about 130,000 square feet. Ground was broken in June 1963 and the topping-out ceremony took place in July 1964, at which time both the United States flag and a replica of the Fort Dearborn

[62] The Los Angeles building was sold at a substantial profit in 1964, and early in 1966 Equitable announced that it would build a new southern California headquarters in Los Angeles—a 32-story tower on Wilshire Boulevard. The building was scheduled for completion in 1968. The Fresno building was sold in June 1965.

garrison flag were raised.[63] The ceremony was attended by Chairman Oates, President Keehn, Director William H. Avery, and other officers of Equitable.

The building was dedicated June 23, 1965, with impressive ceremonies. The day's activities began in the forenoon under threatening skies, when more than 1,000 persons assembled in Pioneer Court to listen to talks by Chairman Oates; Senior Vice President John H. Muller; J. Howard Wood, President of the Tribune Company; Mayor Richard J. Daley; and Directors Arthur B. Van Buskirk and William H. Avery. While "Welcome" signs flashed from neighboring buildings the water in the white marble fountain was turned on, and a time capsule, sealed until the year 2,000, was placed in a stone monument erected in Pioneer Court. Across the base of the fountain in bronze letters were the names of twenty-five of Chicago's distinguished citizens.[64] The planning and cost of Pioneer Court were shared by the Tribune Company and Equitable. The *Tribune's* television station, WGN-TV, saluted Pioneer Court with a half-hour television special and President Wood said, "This is a great day for Chicago."

These ceremonies were followed by a luncheon for Equitable officers, directors, leading agents, and other key personnel in Chicago at the Chicago-Sheraton Hotel. Later at a dinner in the Palmer House for more than four hundred of Chicago's leading citizens, Chairman Oates spoke of Pioneer Court and the significance of the new building for Chicago and the Equitable. Assisted by Senior Vice President Muller, who translated, he welcomed the guests in Potawatomi Indian language as the first settlers at the historic site might have been greeted. He then introduced Adlai Stevenson, United States Representative to the United Nations, with reminiscences of their early days as law partners. Ambassador Stevenson responded affectionately and made a stirring defense of the United Nations, probably one of the last speeches he made before his untimely death on July 14.

Equitable's Chicago building stands in good company; among its

[63] One of the building techniques that attracted considerable attention was the use of forty old railroad tank cars as forms for foundation caissons. "Sidewalk superintendents" were supplied with piped music which some used for dancing. The topping out beam was displayed on Michigan Avenue and autographed by many persons before it was elevated into position. Chairman Oates phoned the Equitable Demograph at the New York World's Fair and the population figure for July 6 was inscribed on the beam.

[64] The names were selected by Paul M. Angle, Director of the Chicago Historical Society.

neighbors are the Wrigley Building, the Chicago-Sheraton Hotel, the turreted Tribune Tower, and the circular Marina City—the world's tallest apartment building. Beneath its windows pass ocean-going vessels, bound for the ports of the world. With its Pioneer Court the Equitable building became one of Chicago's leading landmarks; it contributed importantly to the realization of the dream of forward-looking Chicagoans who foresaw the development of the city's Magnificent Mile. At the time of the dedication about 90 per cent of the 742,000 square feet of rentable space was already rented. Equitable occupied the first seven floors, and fittingly enough, the leading tenant, which took twelve floors, was the International Harvester Company.

Even before the completion of the Chicago building, Equitable announced plans for a new 32-story office building in Atlanta. Equitable's first building in Atlanta, built in 1892, was an eight-story fireproof structure. Then in 1952 it built a four-story brick building on West Peachtree Street. The projected building will add nearly 700,000 square feet of office space to downtown Atlanta, and Equitable plans to occupy about 10 per cent of the building. This building will also have a plaza which will feature a pool, fountains, and blooming peach trees.

As a result of higher yields on both new money invested and reinvestment of money accumulating from maturing securities, Equitable's total investment earnings before Federal income taxes rose to 4.46 per cent in 1964.

FUNDAMENTAL PURPOSES AND GOALS

The Fundamental Purpose, Business Objectives, and Implicit Goals of the Equitable were stated in December 1960. The fundamental purpose of the Society "is to provide on a scientifically sound, demonstrably fair, and economically attractive basis, mutual insurance protection against financial hazards which people encounter because of disability and uncertainty as to length of life." Its business objectives are to sell sound life and health insurance, to conserve the insurance in force, and to invest the reserve funds productively and for the benefit of the American economy. The Society recognizes that its officers are actually professional managers who, since they have no equity ownership, must find part of their compensation "in a sense of satisfaction springing from growing service to the public and honest, respected, substantial operating achievements." In insurance operations it is committed to engage in research both basic and applied, and be willing to embrace progressive change and be prepared to innovate: "We must employ, consistently and fearlessly, the developed principles of actuarial science to assure absolute and unquestioned fulfillment of financial and legal responsibilities and restrictions. Our policies must have a quality which induces and deserves pride and confidence." The Equitable must be "a good and respected corporate citizen and the public must be aware that it deserves such a stature." Its operations must be economical, consequently it "must design, maintain and regularly refine workable procedures to analyze and control costs through Society-wide centralized staff operations, conducted by respected experts." And since the financial interests of the policyholders are dependent in no small measure upon the financial yields brought by the investment of policyholders' funds, "there is no higher responsibility than the stewardship of this vast reservoir of wealth entrusted to our care. Security, with optimum returns available under current conditions, constitutes the goal."

The statement of Fundamental Purpose, Business Objectives, and Implicit Goals ended with the following conclusion:

> Thoughtful men are daily confronted with the gnawing concern as to their individual contribution to the furtherance of the American ideal. Doubts creep in and question whether America has a purpose. We are blessed since we can believe in the high human and economic importance of a mutual life insurance company operating today in America. No one of us, in all probability, can make a greater contribution to the fulfillment of the American ideal and to the demonstration that America has a noble purpose than by the daily performance of our jobs; by the advancement, development and improvement of the Equitable. But this is true only if we mightily resolve individually to fulfill the best that is in each of us and to see that the performance of our daily jobs meets the highest of standards. If this statement of objectives is to be most helpful in fulfilling our future mission, or in resolving uncertainties and doubts, it probably will from time to time require refinement and improvement. It can only be successfully implemented, however, by joint effort and when sincerely agreed upon and thereafter steadfastly supported and observed with pride and loyalty. We must know, understand and believe in our common goals and objectives if we are to succeed in their attainment.

In their report to Equitable's Board of Directors February 18, 1965, Chairman Oates and President Keehn said in regard to the Society's goals:

We will seek to accomplish these goals by developing a better understanding of the insurance needs of our fellow Americans and of the nature of our business. We will attempt to make the most of our manifold strengths and resources through uncompromising allegiance to principle, by systematic planning, by encouraging and expecting innovation and improvement in products and processes, and by concentrating on what is important.

It has been wisely observed that mediocrity can be comfortable. But we choose to serve the goal of excellence with humility. This is most difficult and will continue to require work and worry. Yet no other course is conceivable or acceptable.

* * *

Long gone are the days of the tontine wars, of the battles between Mutual and Equitable in which they aired their differences through a controlled press; "when every officer and every agent carried a knife, and each company was at war with all its competitors." Gone too are the days when the large life companies could use their assets for purposes not germane to the business of life insurance, and when control of Equitable was a rich prize to be struggled for by capitalists and banking groups. Today life insurance is regulated in detail by fifty states, the District of Columbia, and, in part, by the Government of the United States. No other business, not even that of the government, lives so exposed to the public eye. There is still plenty of competition —most of it healthful—which challenges the skills of the agent and the resourcefulness of the Home Office as to all coverages. Today competition also exists between life insurance as a voluntary cooperative effort in private hands and the government programs conceived for broad social purposes.

In the dim far past man, after some thousands of years of life, learned to use primitive tools and fire, and thereby established a great advantage over the other animals. In time he learned to girdle the globe with supersonic flight, to penetrate into outer space and to release forces which might be used either for his own benefit or destruction. Yet these accomplishments pale in significance in comparison with others such as the development of conscience and the creation of the family, "that one supreme human relationship . . . the source out of which man's highest qualities have grown up to transform the world. As historical fact, it is to family life that we owe the greatest debt which the mind of man can conceive. The echoes of our own past for immemorial ages bid us unmistakably to venerate, to cherish, and to preserve a relationship to which the life of man owes this supreme debt." [65]

The mortality experience of man constitutes much of his history: "It is seen through charred remains and crushed ruins, surviving human strife. Earliest the fight for existence, then the fight for security of life, then the struggle for individual and collective freedom. The skeleton in the wilderness, the mounds on the battlefield, the places of the mighty and the hovels of the humble, all proclaim the story." [66] And the history of the Western World has been that of a long struggle by which man emerged from slavery under some form of absolutism to serfdom, from serfdom to freedom and greater abundance. But apathy and selfishness can lead to a reversal, or rather a completion of the cycle, and many portions of the earth's people have taken that path. If self-government ("democracy") and freedom are to survive in our country, they can only survive as a result of the application not only of intelligence but of moral courage on the part of the great majority. As Henry B. Hyde said in 1889: "Truth, as expressed in correct business principles, is a fixed quantity, eternal in its character and not susceptible to change. Those institutions which, for ephemeral advantage, depart from such principles, are sure to pay the penalty in the end." [67] And the responsibility rests with the individual as well as the group. Once again to quote two of the men who have helped direct the destinies of Equitable in recent years: said President James F. Oates, Jr., in 1957: "I believe that man is a sacred personality—that he, the individual, is the important unit in life and the indispensable ingredient of business. . . ." And President Thomas I. Parkinson in 1943: "The members of the middle class have been the builders of civilization and the makers of free governments. They have been men and women of energy, experience and initiative. They have faced risks and have overcome them. They have not been dependent on the government of the day and they have not looked to the representatives of government for help."

In a free society life insurance is a materialization of the doctrine of

[65] James Henry Brested, *The Dawn of Conscience* (New York, 1934), p. 411.

[66] John R. McFee, "The Mortality Experience," *National Underwriter*, XXII (1918), May 16. McFee was at this time manager of agents in Chicago for The Penn Mutual Life Insurance Company.

[67] Henry B. Hyde, Circular to the Managers, December 1889. Equitable Archives.

duty; it is a part of the ethical code as practiced by civilized man. It is the manifestation of a philosophy which in its breadth of acceptance has created in the United States above all other countries "an aristocracy built upon merit and worth and composed of those who have met their moral and social obligations . . . an admirable and noble class." [68] And, social and political institutions permitting, American life insurance companies will continue, long into the future, to extend to Americans the privilege of belonging to that aristocracy. For as the Actuary Emory McClintock said: "A life company is not successful unless it is able to go on successfully throughout all time."

No doubt it was with this thought in mind that Equitable almost a century ago selected as its motto, "NOT FOR A DAY BUT FOR ALL TIME."

[68] Byron K. Elliott, Vice President John Hancock Mutual Life Insurance Company, in *Insurance Field,* LXVI (1937), December 17.

APPENDICES

CHARTER
of the
Equitable Life Assurance Society of the United States

(Adopted May 2, 1859)

DECLARATION

WE, THE UNDERSIGNED, do hereby declare and express our intentions to associate and form an Incorporated Company, for the purpose of making insurance upon the lives of individuals, and every insurance appertaining thereto or connected therewith; and to grant, purchase or dispose of annuities, pursuant to the provisions of the act entitled "An Act to provide for the incorporation of Life and Health Insurance Companies, and in relation to Agencies of such Companies, passed June 24, 1853," and amendments thereto. And the subscribers do further declare that the following is a copy of the Charter proposed to be by them adopted:

CHARTER

ARTICLE 1

This Corporation shall be called and named "THE EQUITABLE LIFE ASSURANCE SOCIETY OF THE UNITED STATES." The principal office for the transaction of business shall be located in the City of New York.

ARTICLE 2

The business of this Company shall be to make insurances upon the lives of individuals, and every insurance appertaining thereto or connected therewith; and to grant, purchase or dispose of annuities, as set forth in the act aforesaid, passed June 24, 1853, and amendments thereto. And this Company shall possess and enjoy all the powers, privileges and franchises granted to, and shall be subject to all the regulations, restrictions and obligations imposed upon incorporations organized and existing under the said act of the Legislature of the State of New York, passed June 24, 1853, and any amendments thereof.

ARTICLE 3

The capital of said Company shall be ONE HUNDRED THOUSAND DOLLARS in cash, divided into ONE THOUSAND SHARES of ONE HUNDRED DOLLARS each; which shall be personal property, transferable only on the books of the Company, in conformity with its By-Laws. The holders of the said Capital Stock may receive a semi-annual dividend on the stock so held by them, not to exceed three and one-half per cent of the same, such dividends to be paid at the times, and in the manner designated by the Directors of said Company. The earnings and receipts of said Company, over and above the dividends, losses and expenses, shall be accumulated.

ARTICLE 4

The corporate powers of said Company shall be vested in a BOARD OF DIRECTORS, and shall be exercised by them, and by such officers and agents as they may appoint, and from time to time empower.

The Board of Directors shall consist of FIFTY-TWO persons, a majority of whom shall be citizens of the State of New York, each of whom shall be a proprietor of at least five shares of the said Capital Stock.

The Board of Directors may, previous to any annual election, and after giving notice at the previous meeting of the Board, provide for diminishing the number of the Directors to not less than TWENTY-FOUR, in which case one-fourth of the total number, as thus diminished, shall be elected annually, in the same manner as hereinafter provided, in regard to the fifty-two Directors above named; and the same powers and authority shall vest in said Board of Directors, thus diminished, as were previously exercised by the former Board of Directors.

The following-named persons shall constitute the first Board of Directors, who shall hold office until their successors are appointed:

William C. Alexander,
William Walker,
Henry Young,
Irad Hawley,
James Low,
James M. Beebe,
Henry A. Hurlbut,
Thomas A. Biddle,
Benjamin E. Bates,
John T. Moore,
Thomas U. Smith,
William Whitewright, Jr.,
William G. Lambert,
Wilmot Williams,
Peter McMartin,
George H. Stuart,
James Lenox Kennedy,
John Slade,
Henry J. Gardner,
Henry H. Hyde,
E. Spencer Miller,
Solomon R. Spaulding,
Dudley S. Gregory,
Stephen H. Phillips,
John Auchincloss,
James M. Halsted,
Henry S. Terbell,
Thomas S. Young,
Bennington F. Randolph,
Wayman Crow,
Geo. Talbot Olyphant,
Alexander Young,
Samuel Frothingham, Jr.,
Thomas A. Cummins,
Henry B. Hyde,
Francis B. Cooley,
H. D. Newcomb,
Henry G. Marquand,
Moses A. Hoppock,
George D. Morgan,
H. V. Butler,
Ezra C. Read,
Dwight Townsend,
Henry M. Alexander,
William T. Blodgett,
Benjamin F. Manierre,
E. J. Hawley,
Alanson Trask,
Edward W. Lambert,
Daniel D. Lord,
Robert Bliss,
Henry Day.

In case either or any of the above-named persons shall decline to serve, or prove to be ineligible, the vacancy or vacancies may be filled by the remaining Directors.

The first Board of Directors shall, immediately after the organization of the Company, divide themselves by lot, into four classes of thirteen each. The term of the first class shall expire at the end of ONE YEAR from December 31, 1859; that of the second at the end of TWO YEARS from that time; that of the third at the end of THREE YEARS from that time; and that of the fourth class at the end of FOUR YEARS from that time; and so on, successively, in each and every subsequent year.

One-fourth of the Board of Directors shall hereafter be elected annually, as provided in the following section, and shall hold office for four years, or until their successors are chosen; but any Director shall be re-eligible for election. Vacancies occurring in the intervals of elections, by death or resignation, may be filled by the Board in the manner set forth in the By-Laws.

The annual election of Directors shall be held on the first Wednesday in the month of December, at the principal office of the Company, in the City of New York, and of which fourteen days' previous notice shall be given, in two of the daily papers of said city. The Directors shall be chosen by ballot, and a plurality of votes shall elect. The Board of Directors shall appoint three Inspectors of Election, who shall be life policyholders in the Company; and the President may supply any vacancies occasioned by the omission of any Inspector to serve. In case of failure to elect on that day, the remaining Directors, whose terms of office do not then expire, shall have power to fill the said vacancies.

In the election of Directors, every stockholder in the Company shall be entitled to one vote for every share of stock held by him, and such vote may be given in person or by proxy. At any time hereafter, the Board of Directors, after giving notice at the two previous stated meetings, may, by a vote of three-fourths of all the Directors, provide that each life policyholder, who shall be insured in not less than FIVE THOUSAND DOLLARS, shall be entitled to one vote at the annual election of Directors, but such vote shall be given personally, and not by proxy.

The Board of Directors shall have power to declare, by By-Law, what number of Directors, not less than SEVEN, shall constitute a quorum for the transaction of business.

ARTICLE 5

After each annual election, the Board of Directors shall elect annually from among their number a PRESIDENT, and may, at their option, also elect a VICE-PRESIDENT. The Board of Directors may also appoint at any time a President and Vice-President to act temporarily, when said officers are absent, interested or unable to act. The Board shall also appoint a SECRETARY, and such other officers as they may deem requisite, and who shall hold office during the pleasure of the Board of Directors.

The Directors shall have power to enact By-Laws, Rules and Regulations for the government of the officers and agents, and for the management of the affairs of the Company, not inconsistent with this Charter, or with the Constitution and Laws of this State; and such By-Laws, Rules and Regulations may be amended or repealed by them at pleasure.

The Directors may determine the rates of premium, and the amounts to be insured on any one life, and the terms of such insurances, and shall have power to purchase, for the benefit of the Company, any policy of insurance, dividends or other obligations issued by the Company.

ARTICLE 6

The Insurance business of the Company shall be conducted upon the MUTUAL PLAN.

All premiums shall be payable in cash. In case any policyholder shall omit to pay any premium due from him to the Company, or violate any other condition of the Policy of Insurance, the Board of Directors may forfeit his policy, and apply all previous payments to the benefit of the Company.

The officers of the Company, within sixty days from the expiration of the first five years from December 31st, 1859, and within the first sixty days of every subsequent period of five years, shall cause a balance to be struck of the affairs of the Company, which shall exhibit its assets and liabilities, both present and contingent, and also the net surplus, after deducting a sufficient amount to cover all outstanding risks and other obligations. Each policyholder shall be credited with an equitable share of the said surplus. Such equitable share, after being ascertained, shall be applied to the purchase of an additional amount of insurance (payable at death or with the policy itself), expressing the reversionary value of such equitable share at such interest as the Directors may designate; or if any policyholder so direct, such equitable share of surplus shall be applied to the purchase of an annuity, at such rate of interest as the Directors shall designate, to be applied in the reduction of his or her future premiums. In case of death, the amount standing to the credit of the party insured at the last preceding striking of balance as aforesaid, shall be paid over to the person entitled to receive the same; and the proportion of surplus equitably belonging to him or her, at the next subsequent striking of balance, shall also be paid, when the same shall have been ascertained and declared.

In case of the death of any party insured prior to passing any period for striking of balance, as aforesaid, the Board of Directors may provide what (if any) share of such surplus shall be paid to such person.

The officers of the Company, within the first thirty days after the expiration of five years from the thirty-first day of December, 1859, shall cause a general balance statement of the affairs of the Company to be made, which shall be open to the inspection of any policyholder for sixty days during the usual hours of business. Said statement shall show the amounts received during the preceding five years for premiums, interest and annuities, and also the amounts paid during the same time for losses, expenses and otherwise, and the balance remaining in the treasury, together with the manner in which the same is invested.

ARTICLE 7

The fiscal year of the Company shall commence on the FIRST DAY OF JANUARY, and terminate on the THIRTY-FIRST DAY OF DECEMBER, in each year.

ARTICLE 8

William Walker, Henry A. Hurlbut, James Low, Thomas A. Cummins, Peter McMartin and Henry G. Marquand shall be Commissioners to open Books for Subscription to the Capital Stock, at such times and places as shall be proper, and to keep the same open until the said sum of one hundred thousand dollars shall be subscribed in full.

IN WITNESS WHEREOF, we, the subscribing corporators, have hereunto subscribed our names, this second day of May, one thousand eight hundred and fifty-nine.

William C. Alexander,
Wm. Walker,
Henry Young,
Irad Hawley,
James Low,
Jas. M. Beebe,
Henry A. Hurlbut,
Thomas A. Biddle,
Benj. E. Bates,
John T. Moore,
Thos. U. Smith,
W. Whitewright, Jr.,
Wm. G. Lambert,
Wilmot Williams,
P. McMartin,
George H. Stuart,
John Slade,
Henry J. Gardner,
Henry H. Hyde,
E. Spencer Miller,
S. R. Spaulding,
D. S. Gregory,
Stephen H. Phillips,
John Auchincloss,
J. M. Halsted,
H. S. Terbell,
T. S. Young,
Bennington F. Randolph,
Geo. Talbot Olyphant,
S. Frothingham, Jr.,
Henry B. Hyde,
Thomas A. Cummins,
Henry G. Marquand,
Moses A. Hoppock,
Geo. D. Morgan,
H. V. Butler,
Dwight Townsend,
Henry M. Alexander,
William T. Blodgett,
Benj. F. Manierre,
E. J. Hawley,
Alanson Trask,
Edward W. Lambert,
Daniel D. Lord,
Robert Bliss,
Henry Day.

CITY AND COUNTY OF NEW YORK, SS:

Henry B. Hyde, of said city, being duly sworn, says that he was present at the signature of the foregoing Declaration and Charter by the above-named William C. Alexander, William Walker, Henry A. Hurlbut, Henry G. Marquand, Daniel D. Lord, Thomas A. Cummins, Thomas U. Smith, Henry Day, Moses A. Hoppock, William G. Lambert, H. S. Terbell, J. M. Halsted, Robert Bliss, Edward W. Lambert, James Low, Dwight Townsend, H. V. Butler, George Talbot Olyphant, Wilmot Williams, E. J. Hawley, Benjamin F. Manierre, William T. Blodgett, Henry M. Alexander, John Auchincloss, John Slade, P. McMartin, W. Whitewright, Jr., George D. Morgan, E. Spencer Miller, George H. Stuart, Benjamin E. Bates, Alanson Trask, Thomas A. Biddle, T. S. Young, James M. Beebe, S. Frothingham, Jr., Henry J. Gardner, Stephen H. Phillips, S. R. Spaulding, Henry H. Hyde, John T. Moore and Henry Young, and saw them sign the same.

And that the above-named Bennington F. Randolph, D. S. Gregory and Irad Hawley acknowledged to him that they signed the same, and that the above are their signatures.

HENRY B. HYDE

Sworn before me, this ninth day of May, A.D. 1859; and the said Henry B. Hyde acknowledged to me that he subscribed the same.

THOS. L. THORNELL,
Commissioner of Deeds.

STATE OF NEW YORK
Attorney-General's Office,

Albany, May 10, 1859.

I do hereby certify that I have examined the annexed Charter of the Equitable Life Assurance Society of the United States, and that I find it to be made in accordance with the requirements of the act entitled "An act to provide for the Incorporation of Life and Health Insurance Companies, and in Relation to Agencies of such Companies," passed June 24, 1853, and amendments thereto, and not inconsistent with the Constitution or Laws of this State, and of the United States.

LYMAN TREMAIN,
Attorney-General.

TO HON. S. E. CHURCH,
Comptroller.

CERTIFICATE OF AUTHORITY

STATE OF NEW YORK

Comptroller's Office,

Albany, July 25, 1859.

WHEREAS, the Equitable Life Assurance Society of the United States, located in the City of New York, having complied with all the provisions of Chapter 463 of the Laws of 1853, providing for the incorporation of Life and Health Insurance Companies, and having deposited with the Comptroller of the State of New York, One Hundred Thousand Dollars of United States five per cent Stocks, in pursuance of the law aforesaid:

Now, THEREFORE, I, Sanford E. Church, Comptroller of the State of New York, do hereby certify that the said Company has complied with the said law, and deposited with me the amount of securities required by law, they are duly authorized, on filing this and the other papers herewith attached, in the County Clerk's Office of the City and County of New York, to commence the business of Insurance as provided in their said Charter.

IN WITNESS WHEREOF, I have hereunto subscribed my name and caused the seal of my office to be affixed, the day and year aforesaid.

P. PHELPS,
Deputy Comptroller.

AMENDMENTS

(*Adopted June 20, 1906*)

ARTICLE 4

* * * * *

The Board of Directors shall consist of fifty-two persons, a majority of whom shall be citizens and residents of the State of New York.

* * * * *

At the regular annual election of the company in December, 1906, there shall be elected by the policyholders twenty-eight directors, all of whom shall be policyholders of the company. Such directors shall be so elected in four classes of seven directors each, the terms of such classes to begin on the first day of January, 1907, and to expire respectively in one, two, three and four years. At every subsequent annual election of the company seven policyholders shall be elected by the policyholders to serve as directors for a term of four years to succeed the seven directors, elected by the policyholders, of the class whose term expires on the next ensuing thirty-first day of December.

* * * * *

In case the number of the directors of the company shall hereafter be reduced, a majority of the reduced number shall at all times be policyholders elected directly by the policyholders pursuant to the provisions hereof.

* * * * *

AMENDMENTS

(*Adopted April 14, 1927*)

(Former Article 3, which referred to the One Hundred Thousand Dollars of Capital Stock became obsolete with the mutualization of the Equitable in 1925 and was omitted.)

ARTICLE 3

* * * * *

Except as hereinabove set forth, the number of Directors shall be thirty-six, and the Board of Directors, with the approval of the Superintendent of Insurance, may at any time, by vote of a majority of the Board, further reduce the number of Directors to not less than twenty-four by providing for the election at every annual election thereafter held of not less than eight Directors to succeed all Directors whose terms expire on the thirty-first day of December next ensuing after the date of each such election.

* * * * *

ARTICLE 4

* * * * *

In the election of Directors every policyholder in the Company whose insurance shall be in force and shall have been in force for at least one year prior thereto, shall be entitled to vote for all Directors, without other qualification, as provided in Section 94 of the Insurance Law of the State of New York, and such vote may be given in person or by proxy.

* * * * *

EQUITABLE DIRECTORS—1859–1966

The Directors are listed in 25-year periods. If a Director's term ran over into another period he is listed only once. An asterisk (*) identifies Equitable Officer-Directors.

Original Board

George T. Adee, 1859–1884
Henry M. Alexander, 1859–1899
*William C. Alexander, 1859–1874
John Auchincloss, 1859–1876
Benjamin E. Bates, 1859–1878
James M. Beebe, 1859–1861, 1863–1875
Thomas A. Biddle, 1859–1888
Robert Bliss, 1859–1888
William T. Blodgett, 1859–1875
Henry V. Butler (No. 1), 1859–1872
Francis B. Cooley, 1859–1867
Wayman Crow, 1859–1877
Thomas A. Cummins, 1859–1882
Henry Day, 1859–1893
Jose F. de Navarro, 1859–1909
Samuel Frothingham, Jr., 1859–1861
Henry J. Gardner, 1859–1866
Dudley S. Gregory, 1859–1874
James M. Halsted, 1859–1888
E. Judson Hawley, 1859–1875
Irad Hawley, 1859–1865
Moses A. Hoppock, 1859–1872
Henry A. Hurlbut, 1859–1897
*Henry B. Hyde, 1859–1899
Henry H. Hyde, 1859–1873
James L. Kennedy, 1859–1864
*Edward W. Lambert, 1859–1904
William G. Lambert, 1859–1882
Daniel D. Lord, 1859–1893
James Low, 1859–1878
Benjamin F. Manierre, 1859–1860
Henry G. Marquand, 1859–1902
Peter McMartin, 1859–1873
E. Spencer Miller, 1859–1862
John T. Moore, 1859–1876
George D. Morgan, 1859–1884
George T. Olyphant, 1859–1866
Stephen H. Phillips, 1859–1893
Bennington F. Randolph, 1859–1890
John Slade, 1859–1873
Thomas U. Smith, 1859–1874
Solomon R. Spaulding, 1859–1863
George H. Stuart, 1859–1890
Henry S. Terbell, 1859–1898
Dwight Townsend, 1859–1872
Alanson Trask, 1859–1902
William Walker, 1859–1886
William Whitewright, Jr., 1859–1886
Wilmot Williams, 1859–1863
Alexander Young, 1859–1864
Henry Young, 1859–1874
Thomas S. Young, 1859–1902

Between 1860 and 1884

*James W. Alexander, 1872–1905
*William Alexander, 1878–1905, 1917–1937
Oliver Ames, 1883–1895
Cornelius N. Bliss, 1884–1905
William M. Bliss, 1879–1893
*Samuel Borrowe, 1877–1896
Henry V. Butler (No. 2), 1877–1884
George W. Carleton, 1877–1901
E. Boudinot Colt, 1877–1900
William F. Coolbaugh, 1876–1877
Theodore Cuyler, 1862–1876
T. DeWitt Cuyler, 1876–1922
George DeF. L. Day, 1883–1893
Chauncey M. Depew, 1877–1905
John J. Donaldson, 1867–1878
Horace J. Fairchild, 1884–1900

Cyrus W. Field, 1873–1877
Simeon Fitch, 1873–1877
Eustace C. Fitz, 1883–1895
*Louis Fitzgerald, 1878–1905
William H. Fogg, 1874–1884
Samuel G. Goodrich, 1880–1883
Ulysses S. Grant, 1882–1884
Ashbel Green, 1868–1885
Parker Handy, 1873–1888
Marcellus Hartley, 1884–1902
Samuel Holmes, 1861–1881
L. C. Hopkins, 1865–1868
Alexander P. Irvin, 1874–1883
John D. Jones, 1875–1895
George G. Kellogg, 1868–1883
Eugene Kelly, 1884–1894
William B. Kendall, 1884–1898
Robert L. Kennedy, 1865–1887
Charles G. Landon, 1879–1893
George C. Magoun, 1884–1893
Robert L. Maitland, 1864–1866
Charles J. Martin, 1860–1879
John J. McCook, 1873–1911
Gustav G. Pohl, 1883–1892
Horace Porter, 1872–1897
*Edward W. Scott, 1883–1895
Joseph Seligman, 1875–1880
John Sloane, 1866–1905
Daniel H. Smith, 1874–1877
Henry F. Spaulding, 1875–1881
John A. Stewart, 1861–1905
Samuel W. Torrey, 1864–1884
George B. Upton, 1872–1874
Anthony Van Bergen, 1883–1900
Theodore Weston, 1875–1883
William A. Wheelock, 1877–1905
Benjamin Williamson, 1867–1892
Henry R. Wolcott, 1881–1896

Between 1885 and 1909

Waldo Adams, 1889–1892
John J. Albright, 1905–1906
Charles B. Alexander, 1885–1927
Henry Martyn Alexander, 1898–1906, 1935–1951
John Jacob Astor, 1898–1905
William H. Baldwin, Jr., 1900–1905
John N. Beach, 1906–1924
August Belmont, 1892–1905
C. Ledyard Blair, 1899–1906
Emanuel W. Bloomingdale, 1905–1915
Abraham Brittin, 1906–1932
Joseph Bryan, 1905–1907
Alexander J. Cassatt, 1899–1905
T. Jefferson Coolidge, 1897–1905
*William A. Day, 1907–1928
Henry W. DeForest, 1909–1916
Henry C. Deming, 1902–1905
Alfonso de Navarro, 1908–1926
Marcellus Hartley Dodge, 1902–1905, 1940–1954
James H. Dunham, 1888–1901
Thomas T. Eckert, 1896–1906
James B. Forgan, 1902–1924
Henry C. Frick, 1901–1905
Thomas A. Gillespie, 1906–1926
Robert Goelet, 1909–1918
George J. Gould, 1893–1906
Henry C. Haarstick, 1899–1907
Edward H. Harriman, 1901–1905
D-Cady Herrick, 1905–1906
James J. Hill, 1902–1905
Marvin Hughitt, 1893–1905
Alexander C. Humphreys, 1905–1927
*James H. Hyde, 1895–1907
Melville E. Ingalls, 1891–1905
Samuel M. Inman, 1895–1906
Brayton Ives, 1893–1905
Bradish Johnson, 1902–1918
*Thomas D. Jordan, 1892–1906
John D. Kernan, 1905–1922
Alvin W. Krech, 1904–1911
Ernest B. Kruttschnitt, 1905–1906
Robert T. Lincoln, 1897–1905
Charles E. Littlefield, 1905–1915
Daniel Lord, 1893–1899
Joseph T. Low, 1887–1905
John T. Manson, 1906–1944
Robert Mather, 1908–1911
*John A. McCall, 1888–1892
Willis F. McCook, 1905–1923
*William H. McIntyre, 1900–1907
James McMahon, 1905–1913

Between 1885 and 1909 (*cont.*)

D. O. Mills, 1898–1905
David H. Moffat, 1895–1911
Edward DeV. Morrell, 1907–1917
Joy Morton, 1908–1934
Levi P. Morton, 1886–1918
*Paul Morton, 1905–1911
Ludwig Nissen, 1907–1919
Daniel R. Noyes, 1888–1897
Eugenius H. Outerbridge, 1906–1932
William E. Paine, 1906–1925
*George W. Phillips, 1893–1898
Wallace L. Pierce, 1905–1920
Tom Randolph, 1905–1918
William C. Redfield, 1905–1913
*Sidney D. Ripley, 1892–1905
Edwin W. Robertson, 1905–1928
Ferdinand W. Roebling, 1905–1908
Jacob H. Schiff, 1893–1905
Jacob G. Schmidlapp, 1905–1919
John E. Searles, 1895–1901
Charles S. Smith, 1886–1905
Valentine P. Snyder, 1900–1934
Thomas Spratt, 1905–1928
*George H. Squire, 1898–1905
Louis Stern, 1905
J. Edward Swanstrom, 1905–1911
*Gage E. Tarbell, 1894–1936
Eben B. Thomas, 1905–1919
Frank Thomson, 1893–1899
Daniel A. Tompkins, 1905–1914
William A. Tower, 1896–1904
Alfred G. Vanderbilt, 1901–1905
William C. Van Horne, 1893–1915
Alfred Van Santvoord, 1895–1901
George F. Vietor, 1905–1910
William Whitman, 1905–1913
*George T. Wilson, 1899–1919
*H. Rogers Winthrop, 1904–1906
Frank S. Witherbee, 1905–1917
Charles Wurts, 1867–1869
Charles H. Zehnder, 1905–1927

Between 1910 and 1934

Rufus L. Allen, 1925–1931
William Seaman Bainbridge, 1924–1947
Charles D. Barney, 1911–1941
Edward C. Blum, 1922–1945
George C. Boldt, 1911–1916
Ralph Budd, 1933–1943, 1948–1955
Joseph P. Chamberlain, 1923–1951
J. Reuben Clark, Jr., 1933–1958
George Clinton, 1917–1934
John D. Crimmins, 1911–1917
Edgar M. Cullen, 1916–1922
Bertram Cutler, 1924–1951
*Frank H. Davis, 1926–1928
Victor J. Dowling, 1915–1929, 1931–1932
Irénée du Pont, 1928–1931
Samuel M. Felton, 1911–1930
William W. Finley, 1911–1913
*Leon O. Fisher, 1923–1928, 1934–1935
Arthur A. Fowler, 1923–1934
Martin H. Glynn, 1918–1924
Frederick H. Goff, 1920–1923
Edward F. Goltra, 1922–1928
John F. Harris, 1917–1941
*Alfred R. Horr, 1919–1922
George S. Hovey, 1920–1927
Herbert P. Howell, 1919–1929
George L. Ingraham, 1916–1922
Frederick P. Keppel, 1926–1943
Francis K. Kernan, 1923–1944
Milas Lasater, 1924–1929
Elisha Lee, 1929–1933
Edgar J. Levey, 1911–1912
Sam A. Lewisohn, 1928–1951
Arthur H. Lowe, 1913–1932
Russell B. Lowe, 1933–1958
*John B. Lunger, 1912–1919
Richard C. Maclaurin, 1915–1920
Frank W. Matteson, 1915–1929
Edwin P. Maynard, 1918–1949
Allan McCulloh, 1918–1932
George V. McLaughlin, 1927–1963

William H. Miner, 1929–1930
John Bassett Moore, 1924–1947
Henry Morgenthau, 1915–1921
George Welwood Murray, 1934–1943
Charles D. Norton, 1911–1923
John Lord O'Brian, 1926–1958
Alton B. Parker, 1911–1926
*Thomas I. Parkinson, 1922–1954
Leonard Peckitt, 1918–1948
John J. Pelley, 1932–1946
Evans S. Pillsbury, 1915–1928
Horace D. Pillsbury, 1929–1940
Samuel Rea, 1911–1929
Norman B. Ream, 1911–1915
Owen J. Roberts, 1926–1930
William Roberts, 1923–1952
Douglas Robinson, 1911–1913
William J. Roddey, 1926–1939
Joseph B. Shea, 1924–1930
William Skinner, 1911–1947
Jesse Slingluff, 1922–1952
Thomas W. Slocum, 1913–1924
Frederick Strauss, 1915–1924
George Carroll Todd, 1924–1947
John T. Underwood, 1918–1937
John H. Walbridge, 1917–1939
Edmund Walker, 1915–1924
*John V. E. Westfall, 1919–1926
Frank O. Wetmore, 1924–1927
Richard H. Williams, 1911–1923
Daniel G. Wing, 1920–1921

Between 1935 and 1959

Malcolm P. Aldrich, 1956–
William H. Avery, 1959–
Raymond N. Ball, 1949–1951
Arlie R. Barnes, 1952–1965
James B. Black, 1940–1965
Robert E. Blum, 1948–
H. Beach Carpenter, 1947–1955
Walker L. Cisler, 1958–
Francis B. Davis, Jr., 1938–1959
Harry A. deButts, 1952–
Robert J. Dodds, 1936–1953
*Charles W. Dow, 1954–1957
Franklin Spencer Edmonds, 1941–1945
John C. B. Ehringhaus, 1939–1949
Manly Fleischmann, 1953–
Douglas S. Freeman, 1943–1953
*William J. Graham, 1937–1958
Henry T. Heald, 1952–
Maurice Heckscher, 1957–
Harold H. Helm, 1953–
Robert C. Hill, 1936–1947
*Robert L. Hogg, 1955–
Charles R. Hook, 1941–1959
J. Erik Jonsson, 1958–
*Grant Keehn, 1958–
William A. Keleher, 1946–1961
Nicholas Kelley, 1949–1961
Charles W. Kellogg, 1944–1959
R. Stewart Kilborne, 1947–
*Walter Klem, 1954–
*William W. Klingman, 1949–1957
John Clark Knox, 1948–1960
Richard W. Lawrence, 1938–1948
Harold B. Lee, 1958–
Elmer L. Lindseth, 1954–
Eugene P. Locke, 1943–1946
Augustus C. Long, 1958–
Richard H. Mansfield, 1952–1958
Dean Mathey, 1953–1966
Frank R. McCoy, 1944–1954
J. Raburn Monroe, 1959–1961
Sterling Morton, 1941–1961
*Ray D. Murphy, 1947–1962
*James F. Oates, Jr., 1955–
Seward Prosser, 1935–1940
David Rockefeller, 1959–1965
Fordyce B. St. John, 1948–1960
Edward L. Shea, 1944–1963
John A. Sibley, 1953–1963
James M. Symes, 1950
Stanley F. Teele, 1958–1966
Arthur B. Van Buskirk, 1951–
Samuel R. Walker, 1949–
Samuel A. Welldon, 1945–1960
*Henry G. Wood, 1951–1953
Philip Young, 1951–1953

After 1959

J. Leland Atwood, 1966–
Eugene R. Black, 1963–
Roger M. Blough, 1964–
Charles W. Buek, 1966–
David R. Calhoun, Jr., 1961–
*Coy G. Eklund, 1965–
James B. Fisk, 1962–
Robert F. Goheen, 1960–
Robert F. Loeb, 1960–1966
Neil H. McElroy, 1962–
J. Irwin Miller, 1962–
Milton C. Mumford, 1961–
Stuart T. Saunders, 1963–
*J. Henry Smith, 1965–
*Davidson Sommers, 1960–
*Horace H. Wilson, 1965–
Francis C. Wood, 1966–

Officers

All those who have held the office of Chairman of the Board, Vice Chairman of the Board, President, and Secretary since the organization of the Equitable in 1859 are shown below.

CHAIRMEN OF THE BOARD

Paul Morton, 1905
William A. Day, 1927–1928
Thomas I. Parkinson, 1953–1954
Ray D. Murphy, 1956–1958
James F. Oates, Jr., 1958–

VICE CHAIRMEN OF THE BOARD

Robert L. Hogg, 1956–1959
Grant Keehn, 1967–

PRESIDENTS

William C. Alexander, 1859–1874
Henry B. Hyde, 1874–1899

PRESIDENTS (*cont.*)

James W. Alexander, 1899–1905
Paul Morton, 1905–1911
William A. Day, 1911–1927
Thomas I. Parkinson, 1927–1953
Ray D. Murphy, 1953–1956, 1957
Charles W. Dow, 1956–1957
James F. Oates, Jr., 1957–1964
Grant Keehn, 1964–1967
J. Henry Smith, 1967–

SECRETARIES

Edward P. Williams, 1859–1860
Edmund C. Fisher, 1860–1861
Joseph W. Paine, 1861
George W. Phillips, 1863–1866
James W. Alexander, 1866–1871
Samuel Borrowe, 1871–1880
William Alexander, 1880–1937
Alexander McNeill, 1938–1951
Henry G. Wood, 1951–1953
Gordon K. Smith, 1953–1966
Rodney L. Enochs, 1966–

EQUITABLE OFFICERS—*December 31, 1964*

James F. Oates, Jr. *Chairman of the Board and Chief Executive Officer*
Grant Keehn *President*
Gordon K. Smith *Secretary*
Walter Klem *Senior Vice President and Chief Actuary*
Davidson Sommers *Senior Vice President and General Counsel*
Joseph L. Beesley *Senior Vice President and Assistant to the Chairman*
John H. Muller *Senior Vice President*
Horace H. Wilson *Senior Vice President-Group Sales*
Coy G. Eklund *Senior Agency Vice President*
Merle A. Gulick *Vice President-Public Relations and Personnel*
J. Henry Smith *Underwriting Vice President*
William J. November *Vice President and Actuary*
Warner H. Mendel *Vice President and General Solicitor*
Willis M. Holtum *Vice President-Mortgages*
Charles F. Andolsek *Vice President*
Kenneth E. Bageant *Vice President*
Robert E. Benson *Vice President*
Frank H. Briggs *Vice President*
R. O. Brown *Vice President*
Joseph H. Chaille *Vice President*
George P. Chave *Vice President*
Charles R. Corcoran *Vice President*
William R. Cowie *Vice President*
Karl M. Davies *Vice President*
S. Jerold Duran *Vice President*
D. D. Edmunds *Vice President*
A. E. Elander *Vice President*
Richard E. Erway *Vice President and Associate General Solicitor*
Eli Ferguson *Vice President*
Richard C. Hageman *Vice President*
David H. Harris *Vice President*
Walter M. Harvey, Jr. *Vice President*
Robert E. Hayes *Vice President*
Earl T. Helsel *Vice President*
John M. Hines *Vice President*
Hunter Holding *Vice President*
Richard D. Kernan *Vice President and Treasurer*
Frank E. Kuhn *Vice President*
John J. Mallon *Vice President*
Elgin E. McLean *Vice President*
Leonard H. McVity, *Vice President and Controller*
Morton D. Miller *Vice President and Associate Actuary*
Thomas F. Murray *Vice President*

R. I. Nowell *Vice President and Economist*
Ray M. Peterson *Vice President and Associate Actuary*
Howard W. Pierpont *Vice President*
Laurence E. Reiner *Vice President*
John W. Riley, Jr. *Vice President and Director of Social Research*
Edward A. Robie *Vice President and Personnel Director*
Harold J. Rossman *Vice President*
Harry W. Rothrock *Vice President*
George E. Stoddard *Vice President*
Wilbur J. Strauss *Vice President*
Ralph M. Thykeson *Vice President*
Harry Walker *Vice President and Associate Actuary*
Hudson L. Whitenight *Vice President*
Dr. Norvin C. Kiefer *Chief Medical Director*
Hugh Middlebrooks *Field Vice President-Agency Affairs*
Donald J. Mooney *Field Vice President-Agency Affairs*
Joseph H. Morrow *Field Vice President-Agency Affairs*
Karl J. Peterson *Field Vice President-Agency Affairs*
Edward J. Skou *Field Vice President-Agency Affairs*
John N. Sullivant, Jr. *Field Vice President-Agency Affairs*
Milton F. Weber *Field Vice President-Agency Affairs*
Frederick P. Andersen *Second Vice President and Auditor*
James A. Attwood *Second Vice President*
Eugene D. Badgley *Second Vice President*
William W. Bainbridge *Second Vice President*
Norman Brodie *Second Vice President and Associate Actuary*
Robert P. Coates *Second Vice President and Associate Actuary*
Hubert D. Eller *Second Vice President and Chief Appraiser*
John P. Gloeckner *Second Vice President*
Howard H. Hennington *Second Vice President and Associate Actuary*
William K. Kerr *Second Vice President and Associate General Solicitor*
Robert F. Link *Second Vice President and Associate Actuary*
Stuart A. McCarthy *Second Vice President and Associate General Solicitor*
W. Walter Mincks *Second Vice President*
Robert Schlageter *Second Vice President*
Jule E. Stocker *Second Vice President and Associate General Solicitor*
Howard E. Thomas *Second Vice President and Associate General Solicitor*
Bernard K. Sprung *Counsel-Legislation*
Eugene T. O'Neill *Counsel-Litigation*
A. Tusten Ackerman *Assistant Vice President*
Arthur Bajart *Assistant Vice President*
Edward W. Chave *Assistant Vice President*
Leon D. Choffin *Assistant Vice President*
W. L. DeVries *Assistant Vice President*
Jack E. Floro *Assistant Vice President*
Harry D. Garber *Assistant Vice President*
Milton J. Goldberg *Assistant Vice President*
Henry A. Hahlbohm *Assistant Vice President*

Max W. Herrington *Assistant Vice President*
Andrew L. Jackson *Assistant Vice President*
Leroy E. Long *Assistant Vice President*
William A. McCurdy *Assistant Vice President*
William R. Morgan *Assistant Vice President*
William M. Noland, *Assistant Vice President*
James J. O'Grady *Assistant Vice President*
W. B. Penn *Assistant Vice President*
H. Gregory Shea *Assistant Vice President*
Carl E. Thompson *Assistant Vice President*
Ralph E. Traber *Assistant Vice President*
Donald R. Waugh, Jr. *Assistant Vice President*
Edward C. White, Jr. *Assistant Vice President*
Arthur A. Windecker *Assistant Vice President*
Boyd J. Blevins *Regional Vice President-Group Affairs*
Robert J. Cusick *Regional Vice President-Group Affairs*
John K. McKee, Jr. *Regional Vice President-Group Affairs*
Walter E. Paully *Regional Vice President-Group Affairs*
Lawrence E. Senft *Regional Vice President-Group Affairs*
Richard H. Hoffman *Associate Actuary*
Alvin B. Nelsen *Associate Actuary*
Robert E. Shalen *Associate Actuary*
Howard B. Baer *Associate Controller*
Joseph G. Kelly *Associate General Solicitor*
Solomon Klinger *Associate General Solicitor*
Dr. Whitman M. Reynolds *Medical Director, Bureau of Insurance Medicine*
Dr. Thomas H. Alphin *Medical Director, Bureau of Medical Services*
Raymond G. McCullough *Director of Underwriting*
Margaret D. Eggleston *Assistant Secretary*
Grace W. Jordis *Assistant Secretary*
Helen B. Taylor *Assistant Secretary*
Conway S. Carter *Assistant Treasurer*
Lester T. Demarest *Assistant Treasurer*
John F. Mallon *Assistant Treasurer*

THE EQUITABLE—*105 Years of Growth and Progress*

1859—Equitable founded by Henry B. Hyde in March, began operations July 26.
1862—Conditional receipts originated, protecting policyowner and company if policy is being issued as applied for.
1864—Assets passed $1,000,000.
1865—First five-year dividend paid to policyowners.
1867—Annual Dividends authorized.
1868—Insurance in force passed $100,000,000.
1870—First Home Office building (120 Broadway) completed.
1874—Henry B. Hyde elected President on death of William C. Alexander.
1878—Payments to policyholders and beneficiaries totaled $5,000,000 in a single year.
1879—Three-year Incontestable Clause originated.
1881—Practice of paying death claims immediately pioneered; first Joint and Survivor Annuity placed on market.
1883—Assets passed $50,000,000; Life Annuity introduced.
1886—Full freedom of residence and travel granted; Two-year Incontestable Clause introduced.
1888—Insurance in force passed $500,000,000.
1894—Right to change beneficiary introduced.
1895—100,000th policy issued; assets reached $200,000,000.
1896—Cash surrender values and policy loans introduced.
1899—Henry B. Hyde dies in office; James W. Alexander elected President.
1900—Insurance in force $1,000,000,000; assets $300,000,000; automatic surrender values and extended term insurance introduced; Policy No. 1,000,000 issued.
1902—Training school for agents originated.
1905—Grover Cleveland appointed Chairman of Trustees empowered to vote controlling interest in Equitable stock in interests of policyowners; Convertible Policy introduced; Paul Morton elected President.
1907—Optional Modes of Settlement inaugurated.
1911—Group Life Insurance originated; refund and cash refund annuities introduced; Home Purchase Plan announced; William A. Day elected President.
1912—Equitable Building (120 Broadway) destroyed by fire; first Disability Waiver Clause introduced.
1915—New Equitable Building (120 Broadway) opened.
1916—Total payments to policyowners and beneficiaries since founding reached $1,000,000,000.
1917—Additional Indemnity Clause introduced.
1920—Group Accident and Health insurance announced.
1922—Insurance in force passed $3,000,000,000; Accidental Death and Dismemberment added to group coverages.
1924—Home Office building at 393 Seventh Avenue completed.

1925—Mutualization of Equitable completed and all stock retired.
1926—Non-Medical insurance offered; Salary Allotment introduced.
1927—Group Annuities introduced; Thomas I. Parkinson elected President.
1934—Family Income Policy introduced in individual line and hospitalization announced for group coverages.
1943—Insurance in force passed $8,000,000,000; assets $3,000,000,000.
1944—Assured Home Ownership (stemming from Home Purchase Plan) modernized and reintroduced.
1945—Full payment made on claims on policies of those killed in war.
1950—Equitable's Gateway Center in Pittsburgh begun.
1951—Individual In-Hospital Major Medical Expense insurance originated.
1952—Group Major Medical insurance introduced.
1953—Insurance in force passed $20,000,000,000; assets passed $7,000,-000,000; Ray D. Murphy elected President.
1954—Adjustable Whole Life Policy offered; "Living Insurance" advertising theme.
1957—James F. Oates, Jr., elected President; first electronic data processing machinery installed; 1,000th Group Major Medical plan installed; System-Matic (preauthorized check) Premium plan introduced.
1958—Principle of grading premiums by policy size adopted.
1959—100th Anniversary; more than $34,000,000,000 insurance in force.
1960—The Fundamental Purpose, Business Objectives, and Implicit Goals of The Equitable Life Assurance Society authored by James F. Oates, Jr.
1961—Home Office moved to 1285 Avenue of the Americas.
1963—Cashiers' Automatic Processing System (CAPS) planned.
1964—James F. Oates, Jr., re-elected Chairman of the Board and Chief Executive Officer; Grant Keehn elected President; $46,000,000,000 Life Insurance in force; assets in excess of $11,000,000,000.

A CODE TO WORK BY

1.—To recognize and respect the dignity and individuality of each employee and to treat him courteously and considerately.
2.—To attract, select, place, and promote employees, based on their qualifications for work requirements, without discrimination.
3.—To maintain fair and consistent standards of performance, objectively reflecting these standards in decisions concerning the promotion, compensation, and retention of each employee.
4.—To use the ability of each employee as fully as possible by work assignments in line with individual interest, aptitude, and experience and by recognition of constructive ideas and suggestions.
5.—To encourage individual growth and development both for improvement of present performance and for promotion.
6.—To maintain fair pay by considering job requirements, prevailing salaries for similar work in other organizations, and job performance.
7.—To maintain a benefit program that provides each employee with the opportunity to protect himself against the major economic uncertainties of life.
8.—To maintain working conditions conducive to health, comfort, and efficiency.
9.—To give clear information to each employee about job duties, job performance, and to the greatest extent practicable, the Society's policies and activities that affect him.
10.—To emphasize continuously the interdependence of the individual employees, the units, and the departments of the Society.

BIBLIOGRAPHICAL NOTE

Since the hundreds of special works, monographs, magazine and newspaper articles, pamphlets, company publications, and the like have been identified in the footnotes which accompany the text, and the majority of them listed in the index, no attempt is made to catalogue them here. Rather this bibliographical note is intended as a general introduction to the more important materials used in the preparation of the history. A more detailed bibliography on the development of life insurance and the history of life insurance in the United States may be found in the author's *The American Life Convention—A Study in the History of Life Insurance* (2 volumes, Appleton-Century-Crofts, New York, 1953).

MANUSCRIPT MATERIALS OUTSIDE THE EQUITABLE ARCHIVES

THE HYDE PAPERS—Most important to the history of Equitable during its first forty-five years were the Hyde papers, which were deposited at Baker Library, Harvard Graduate School of Business Administration, by James Hazen Hyde in 1929 and not to be opened for historical purposes until 1979. These papers begin with the letters of Henry H. Hyde in 1838 and end with the letters and other documents of James Hazen Hyde in 1905. The Henry H. Hyde letters to various members of his family, but mostly to his son Henry B., and letters from Henry B. to his father covering the period 1838 through 1869 are in a separate folder. The papers of Henry B. Hyde covering the period from 1870 to 1899 are contained in some 66 "volumes" or cases numbered under various alphabetical and numerical labels. The "A" series which runs from 1 to 39 is chronological, but the various other alphabetical series are arranged partially topical and partially miscellaneous, and consequently overlap the chronological series. The "volumes" are mostly letterpress copies bound in letterpress books of 500 to 1,000 pages each.[1] As should be obvious from the text of the history, the papers of Henry B. Hyde cover not only the history of Equitable in all of its phases, but family affairs and other business interests. Then the papers of James H. Hyde—some twenty-odd feet of file space—cover the period on through 1905. Among them are reports of committee meetings,

[1] *For the information of students and researchers whose labors have never taken them into letterpress copies: The pages in a letterpress book are of very thin tissue paper. Outgoing letters or other documents were placed under these sheets, and at the end of the day the book was put in a letterpress, the big wheel at the top screwed down, and copies of the documents were transferred to pages of the book. Until about the middle 1880's, the copies of the Hyde papers were in the script of various hands, but the bulk of those after that date were of typed letters, memoranda, etc. One advantage of the letterpress filing system over the modern loose-leaf filing system is that all the copies were preserved; that is, documents could not be removed or lost without a numbered page showing up missing.*

conferences, and tabulations on financial affairs, particularly on the troublesome events of 1905, not available elsewhere. At the time this history was begun no one connected with Equitable was aware of the existence of the Hyde papers; presumably they had been lost in the great Equitable fire of 1912. Fortunately, however, they were not in the Equitable Building but in Henry B. Hyde's home or uptown office at 9 East Fortieth Street and thus came into the possession of his son James Hazen Hyde who made them available to the author in 1955.

OTHER MANUSCRIPT COLLECTIONS—The Elizur Wright papers—also deposited in the Baker Library, Harvard University—contain correspondence and other items relating to the history of Equitable. The Elizur Wright Scrapbooks are in the Library of Congress. The Charles Evans Hughes papers in the Library of Congress were particularly valuable for the period of the New York Legislative Investigation of 1905. Among the Hughes papers are 33 scrapbooks (Volumes 195–228) of newspaper clippings for 1905 from papers all over the United States; the major newspapers have separate volumes. Also used were the Levi Morton papers in the New York Public Library, the Dwight Morrow papers in the Robert Frost Library, Amherst College, and the Elihu Root papers in the Library of Congress. The manuscript "The National Bank of Commerce in New York, A Retrospect—1839–1919," author unknown, was made available by C. C. Lescher, assistant manager public relations, of the Morgan Guaranty Trust Company. It contains important material on finances, particularly for the Civil War period, the depression of the mid-1880's and the period of World War I.

THE EQUITABLE ARCHIVES

MANUSCRIPT MATERIALS—Included under the listing of "Equitable Archives" are all documents in possession of the Society wherever filed or stored. The corporate records are in the Secretary's office; other documents are in the Library, the Law Library, the Law Department, the Treasurer's Department, the Actuary's Department, the Agency Department, etc. Many cases of documents are in storage in a building other than the Home Office. During the writing of the history, a number of documents came into the possession of the office of the "History Project." Most important of these were the documents which came in from Equitable's Paris building in 1955—the Paris office files. Among these papers were one or more bundles from the following countries: Austria, France, Belgium, Germany, Great Britain, Hungary, Italy, Portugal, Russia, Servia, Spain, and Switzerland. Also among these papers were the reports and correspondence of James C. Rocquet, Secretary General for Europe. Without these documents the history of Equitable's foreign business would have been quite sketchy. Other accessions included the three large scrapbooks on the period 1866 to 1915 which were compiled by Fred H. Fenning and others in the Policy Writing Department, and presented to the Society in 1941 by Jules E. DuBarry. These books were particularly valuable in giving a picture of Home Office affairs. Other materials which came to the history office were the collections of letters of Vice President Henry L. Rosenfeld donated by his son, James R. Rosenfeld, and the family letters of President Paul Morton which were supplied by his grandson, James Hopkins Smith, Jr.

Among the named collections of manuscript materials in Equitable Archives are the papers of William A. Day—ten letterpress volumes January 1912 to May 1928; the papers of Thomas I. Parkinson (1920–53) and the Sterling Pierson files (1925–49). (The papers of Paul Morton, 1905–11, were destroyed in the fire of 1912 as were those of E. H. Harriman.) In addition to these collections are thousands of letters, reports, memoranda, statistical tables and the like scattered through the various departments. Many of these documents were inventoried and described in three loose-leaf volumes prepared by Dr. Thomas P. Martin, Consulting Archivist. Former Vice President and Director William J. Graham prepared a memoir of several hundred pages which deals largely with Equitable's introduction and development of Group Insurance, and Alexis Wiren compiled a "two-volume" manuscript record on the same subject. The manuscript entitled "Early Days of the Equitable," written by Secretary William Alexander in 1918, furnished a number of leads on the early history of the Society. A manuscript bound in seven volumes titled "Information Gathered by Waller Holladay," covers the period from 1859 to 1894. Of this manuscript Secretary William Alexander said: "Probably of no great value unless it contains facts otherwise not saved from the fire." Holladay, an employee in the Home Office, was interested in statistics and comparisons and he did have access to much material which was destroyed in the fire. The Letter Book of Alexander Munkittrick, Equitable's first agent in Great Britain, covers the period from November 1869 to March 1871 and constitutes a unique record of the problems involved in Equitable's entry into a foreign country. The manuscript prepared by Assistant Actuary Joel G. Van Cise in December 1895 titled "History of the Deferred Dividend Policy Issued by the Equitable Life Assurance Society," fortunately escaped the fire of 1912 and aided materially in straightening out the complicated history of the tontine policies. The minutes of "The Old Guard" (the General Agents' and Managers' Association) were given to the Society in 1944 by The Old Guard. They cover the period 1905 to date.

CORPORATE RECORDS—The minutes of the meetings of the Equitable Board of Directors prior to 1912 were destroyed in the fire of January 1912 but were reconstructed in part from collateral sources. The minutes of the Board and of its important committees since January 1912 are preserved among the corporate records in the Secretary's Department as are the reports of the President to the Board. The annual reports of the Society to the Insurance Department of the state of New York date from 1859 and are available in the Equitable Archives from 1867, as are the triennial reports on the examinations of the Society by the Department. The annual reports of the Society and the triennial reports on the examination of the Society are also available in the Archives of the Insurance Department.

EQUITABLE PUBLICATIONS—The *Proceedings at the Convention to Commemorate the Fortieth Anniversary* was published in book form in 1899, and *Henry Baldwin Hyde—A Biographical Sketch* was published in 1901.

The latter in the preface states: "This book is not a biography; it is merely a gathering together of reminiscences which might otherwise be lost. Not until a detailed history of the first forty years of the Equitable Society has been written can the story of the life of its founder be adequately told." Among the reminiscences included in this volume were those of a number of the early employees of Equitable and some of the early agents. In 1909 Equitable published its first history, *The Equitable Society's First Half-Century*. This 125-page booklet which appeared under the name of President Paul Morton was written by Secretary William Alexander, as were the *A Brief History of the Equitable Society* (1929) and *Seventy-Five Years of Progress and Public Service* (1934). In 1916 Equitable published *The Home Office of the Equitable*, a 144-page book, which described the various departments and included photographs of contemporary personnel. The 400-page *Equitable-Hyde Settlement—Reports and Settlement Papers* was published in May 1910.

Equitable has at one time or another published a number of company magazines. The first, *Our Mutual Friend*, was published in 1867. The only surviving volume is in the New York Public Library. *The Protector* was published monthly from February 1871 to March 1872, and *The Equitable Gazette* ran from August 1881 to December 1886. *The Equitable Record*, a monthly magazine, was first issued in August 1887 and continued to December 1899. The New Series of the *Record* was issued as a quarterly from 1900 to 1905. The *Equitable Home Office News* was published from March to December 1919, and *Equinews*, a monthly magazine for Home Office and field employees, began publication December 1956 and continues to date. *The Human Factor*—a magazine for policyholders—was published from September 1911 to July 1915. Among the numerous magazines intended primarily for agents were *The Equitable News* (January 1900 to July 1909), and *Agency Items* (monthly) which has had a continuous existence since 1907 under the following titles: *Items for Agents* (October 1907–December 1910); *Agency Items* (January 1911–May 1930); *Equitable Agency Items* (May 1930–January 1946); *Equitable Items* (January 1946–January 1954); *Equitable Agency Items* (January 1954–January 1962). In January 1962 *Agency Items* became a weekly and was issued in newspaper format, in which form it continues to date. *Equitable Leaders*, a bi-monthly publication, was first issued in July 1962; in January 1963 the title was changed to *Equitable National Leaders*, and in March 1964 to *Equitable National Leaders Magazine*. Periodicals of limited life were *The Tattler*—"the first employees' magazine"—(1914–16); *The Equitable Public Bulletin*—"for the Members, the Public and the Press"—(1917); *The Interoffice Chronicle*—"the first nationwide employee magazine"—(1920–22); *The Equitable Spirit*—"official organ of the Equitable Veteran Legion"—(1933–39); and *The Listening Post*—which was mailed to employees in the armed forces during World War II. For the foreign business Equitable published *El Tesoro Del Hogar* (1880); *Der Amerikanische Hausfreund* (1883); *Le Messager de L'Equitable* (1883); *Revista Peninsular* (1886) and *O Thesouro Do Lar* (1894). More or less complete files of all these periodicals, except *Our Mutual Friend*, are in the Equitable Archives.

The most valuable for purposes of the history were those of *The Equitable Gazette* and *The Equitable Record.*

Over the years Equitable has published scores of pamphlets—tontine pamphlets, sales booklets, instructions to agents, booklets to policyholders, reports of investigations, presidential addresses and the like. So far as the author knows, no complete listing of these pamphlets has ever been attempted.

THE INSURANCE PRESS

Next to the materials listed above, most valuable for the purposes of this history, particularly for the first half century of Equitable, were the insurance periodicals. These journals contained much material not available elsewhere—speeches made, statistical tables, extracts and articles from the foreign insurance press, interviews, biographical sketches, life company advertisements, debates by way of letters, personal reminiscences, reports of meetings and the activities of the various state insurance departments.

Most useful of the early insurance periodicals was *The Insurance Monitor* which began publication in March 1853. The following year it was published under the title of *The Insurance Monitor and Commercial Register* and in 1855, *The Insurance Monitor and Wall Street Review.* Editor and proprietor until 1868 was Thomas Jones, Jr. In 1869 after C. C. Hine became the proprietor and editor, the title again became *The Insurance Monitor.* C. C. Hine was not only a student of life insurance and life insurance history, but had a broad knowledge of economics and politics. As a result of his close friendship with Henry B. Hyde, he had a more intimate knowledge of Equitable's affairs than any other insurance editor. Upon Hine's death in 1897, Walter S. Nichols, an honors graduate of Princeton who joined the *Monitor* staff in 1869, became the editor. Nichols who had training in mathematics and law compiled and published in 1877 *The Insurance Blue Book,* a very useful compendium of insurance facts and history. The *Monitor* later moved to Chicago where it continues to date as the *American Insurance Digest and Insurance Monitor.*

The Wall Street Underwriter and General Joint Stock Register began publication in 1859. Editor and proprietor was Joseph B. Ecclesine. In 1868 the title was changed to *The New York Underwriter and General Joint Stock Register,* in January 1879 to *The New York Underwriter,* and a year later to *The Weekly Underwriter.* In 1880 *The Weekly Underwriter* claimed the largest circulation of any insurance periodical. Editors were A. D. Brigham and H. R. Hayden. Fairly complete files of the *Monitor* and *The New York Underwriter* are in the Equitable Archives. *The Spectator* began publication in January 1868 as a monthly magazine, later became a weekly but in 1942 reverted to a monthly publication and continues to date. Stephen English's controversial *Insurance Times* (1868) though not of the same high reputation as the better insurance journals, contained interesting material on the inter-company wars of the 1870's. Charles C. Bombaugh, of the *Baltimore Underwriter* was another editor with whom Henry B. Hyde maintained close relations, and scattered issues of his journal have been used.

Three insurance periodicals, each founded in 1899, rose to the front rank in the present century. The *Insurance Field* (Louisville) was edited for a number of years by Young E. Allison, historian, musician, and author. A complete file of the *Insurance Field* is in the office at Louisville. The *Ohio Underwriter* was begun at Cincinnati in 1897 and two years later the title was changed to *The Western Underwriter,* which moved its editorial offices to Chicago. In 1917 this journal became *The National Underwriter.* Charles Merritt Cartwright headed the editorial department from 1899 to 1948. The fiftieth anniversary number issued in 1947 in itself constitutes a good review of the history of life insurance in the United States. *The Eastern Underwriter,* first published in 1899, was for many years edited by Clarence Axman whose knowledge of insurance and its history was encyclopedic. In addition to running the files of *The National Underwriter* and *The Eastern Underwriter,* the author was fortunate to have had a number of interviews with editors Cartwright and Axman. (Incidentally, the present *Western Underwriter* of San Francisco, started in 1886 as the *Pacific Underwriter,* has no connection with *The National Underwriter.*)

Best known among the newspapers for its insurance news was the *New York Journal of Commerce* which added an insurance column in the 1870's, and which later, with Sumner Ballard as insurance editor, built its insurance department into an important part of the paper. *The Wall Street Journal,* the *Chicago Inter Ocean,* and the *Chicago Journal of Commerce* also carried life insurance news.

INVESTIGATIONS OF LIFE INSURANCE

The chief document on the New York Investigation of 1877 is *The Condition of the Life Insurance Companies of the State of New York. Revised Tabulated Edition of the Official Stenographer's Notes of the Investigation by the Assembly Committee* (W. S. Manning, publisher, Albany, New York, 1877). For the New York legislative investigation of 1905 the indispensable document is the official report issued in ten volumes: *Testimony Taken Before The Joint Committee of The Senate and Assembly of The State of New York To Investigate and Examine into the Business and Affairs of Life Insurance Companies Doing Business in The State of New York* (seven volumes); *Exhibits Accompanying the Testimony . . .* (two volumes); and *Report of The Joint Committee . . .* (Brandow Printing Company, Albany, N.Y., 1905). For other materials on the Armstrong Investigation, see Chapter VII of this history, footnote 258. The Wisconsin investigation of 1907 is covered in the *Report of the Joint Committee of the Senate and Assembly on the Affairs of Life Insurance Companies* (Madison, Wisconsin, 1907). For the New Jersey investigation: *Testimony Taken before the Select Committee of the Senate of New Jersey April 1906 to Inquire into the Business of Life Insurance Companies Doing Business in New Jersey* (four volumes, Trenton, 1906–07). The TNEC investigation of 1939 may be followed in the *Hearings before the Temporary National Economic Committee, Congress of the United States, Seventy-Sixth Congress* (Senate Document), and the *Final Report and Recommendations of the Temporary National Economic Committee* (Senate Document No.

35, Seventy-Seventh Congress, 1st Session). See also references in Chapter XI, footnote 156.

MISCELLANEOUS SOURCES

The court reports, particularly for the State of New York, and reports of the New York Insurance Department are obvious sources. Also important were the *Proceedings of the National Convention of Insurance Commissioners* (since 1935 the National Association of Insurance Commissioners) which date from 1871, and deal with all phases of life insurance. The *Transactions of the Actuarial Society of America* date from 1889, and the *Record of the American Institute of Actuaries* from 1909. Upon the merger of these societies in 1949 was begun publication of the *Society of Actuaries Transactions.* The *Proceedings of The Association of Life Insurance Presidents* (since 1944 the Life Insurance Association of America), which date from 1907, contain many valuable papers, studies, reports and statistical compilations. The *Journal of the American Association of University Teachers of Insurance,* dating from 1933 (in 1957 changed to *The Journal of Insurance*) contains many useful articles and studies. Since 1946 the Institute of Life Insurance has been issuing, among other publications, the annual *Life Insurance Fact Book.*

INTERVIEWS

To supplement the documents the author spent many hours in interviews with persons who helped make the history of Equitable. For a listing of the most important of these interviews, see Acknowledgments at the front of Volume I.

Index